THE RELIGIOUS EXPERIENCE

FOURTH EDITION

Ninian Smart

MACMILLAN PUBLISHING COMPANY
NEW YORK

COLLIER MACMILLAN CANADA, INC.
TORONTO

MAXWELL MACMILLAN INTERNATIONAL
NEW YORK   OXFORD   SINGAPORE   SYDNEY

Editor: Helen McInnis
Production Supervisor: George Carr
Production Manager: Aliza Greenblatt
Cover Designer: Jane Edelstein
Cover art: Reginald Wickham
Photo Researcher: Barbara Schultz-PAR/NYC, Inc.

This book was set by Maryland Composition, and printed and bound by Book Press.
The cover was printed by Lehigh Press.

Macmillan Publishing Company
866 Third Avenue, New York, New York 10022

Collier Macmillan Canada, Inc.
1200 Eglinton Avenue East, Suite 200
Don Mills, Ontario, M3C 3N1

Library of Congress Cataloging-in-Publication Data

Smart, Ninian, 1927–
    The religious experience / Ninian Smart.—4th ed.
      p. cm.
    Rev. ed. of: The religious experience of mankind. c1984.
    Includes bibliographical references and index.
    ISBN 0-02-412735-3
    1. Religions. 2. Religion. 3. Experience (Religion) I. Smart,
Ninan, 1927–   Religious experience of mankind. II. Title.
    BL80.2.S6 1991
    291—dc20
                                        90-39370
                                        CIP

Printing: 1 2 3 4 5 6 7   Year: 1 2 3 4 5 6 7

PRE

PREFACE

THIS BOOK is a history of religious experience. To approach that experience in its many manifestations, it is necessary to know something of the nature of religion. For that reason I have begun the book with an account of the main aspects of religion and the chief kinds of faith found in world history.

Since Marxism and Humanism rival religion in certain respects, I have drawn them into this portrait of religions, and I have also finished with some observations on the present state and future of religion. But the bulk of what I have written is about the major world religions.

I have attempted to tell the story without entering unduly into technicalities, so that I hope that the reader will have no difficulty in following it. But suggestions for further and supplementary reading are included as an aid to students in colleges and universities.

This edition has involved a fair amount of rearrangement and rewriting. I have absorbed the bulk of the chapter on Native American and Pacific religions into other parts of the book; I have added a chapter on North American religion; I have entirely rewritten the chapters on the humanist experience and the contemporary religious experience. In all this I have incorporated an account of the recent vicissitudes of orthodox Marxism in Eastern Europe, the Soviet Union, and elsewhere. I have made sundry smaller revisions elsewhere. In various ways, therefore, I have had the opportunity to revise and update the material. Basically it remains a treatment of the religions by traditions (rather than regionally).

I am indebted to Sara Duke, Brian Wilson, and Helen McInnis for helping me to see this edition through the press.

NINIAN SMART

CONTENTS

CONTENTS ix

THE RELIGIOUS EXPERIENCE

Chapter 1

RELIGION AND HUMAN

EXPERIENCE

THROUGHOUT HISTORY and beyond in the dark recesses of the human race's earliest cultures, religion has been a vital and pervasive feature of human life. To understand human history and human life it is necessary to understand religion, and in the contemporary world one must understand other nations' ideologies and faiths in order to grasp the meaning of life as seen from perspectives often very different from our own.

But religion is not something that one can see. It is true that there are temples, ceremonies, religious art. These can be seen, but their significance needs to be approached through the inner life of those who use these externals. Consider the ceremony of baptizing a baby. How can we understand it, save by knowing what the idea of baptism means to Christians and by knowing the hopes and feelings of those who participate in the occasion? We must see the way in which the externals and inner meanings of religion are fused together. This is why the history of religions must be more than the chronicling of events: it must be an attempt to enter into the meanings of those events. So it is not enough for us to survey the course which the religious history of human-kind has taken: we must also penetrate into the hearts and minds of those who have been involved in that history.

Religion is a doubly rich and complex phenomenon. Not only has it the complexity indicated by this need to hold together its outer and inner aspects, but it also has existed and exists in a variety of forms of faith. There are many religions to be discovered in the world. The study of these is a fascinating and stimulating task, for not only is this variety a testimony to the richness of the religious sense and imagination of mankind, and often—though by no means always—to the nobility of the human spirit, but also it gives rise to some profoundly important questions about the truth of religion.

But just as it would be unwise to make claims about the nature and scope of science without understanding something of the present state of the sciences, together with their methodology and history, so it would not be helpful to speculate about religious truth without a proper knowledge of the facts and feelings of religion. The aim, then, of this book is to try to convey these facts in relation to the experiences which religions attempt to express. The intention is to describe, rather than to pass judgment, on the phenomena of religion. The intention is not to speak on behalf of one faith or to argue for the truth of one or all religions or of none. Our first need is to understand. The result, I hope, will be that the reader will be in a better position to judge wisely about religious truth.

The description of religion and its history could be said in one sense to be a scientific undertaking, for it is necessary to look at the facts dispassionately and objectively. Of course, as we have already partly seen, it would be foolish to think that being "objective" means that we only look at temples, churches, and outer behavior. We must penetrate beyond what is publicly observable. How could we give a proper account of Paul's career without referring to his shattering experience on the Damascus Road? This experience was not observable by others, though Paul's outer behavior was. But though there may be difficulties in our appreciating fully the content and quality of prophetic, mystical, and other forms of religious experience, there is a sense in which we can deal with them objectively. That is, we can describe these inner events and meanings without prejudice and with sympathetic understanding. The study of religions is a science, then, that requires a sensitive and artistic heart.

But just because religion has a profound impact on people's beliefs and emotions, religious people often find it hard to be objective and dispassionate about the faiths of other folk. Agnostics too, who may have broken away rather violently from religion, often have difficulty being objective about it. It is sometimes said that religion entails commitment and that without belief there cannot be real understanding of a faith; and it is sometimes therefore inferred that it is impossible to appreciate a faith to which one is not committed.

This conclusion is a dangerous exaggeration. It is an exaggeration for, as a matter of fact, a great deal of sensitive work in the comparative study of religion has been done in the last hundred years—and this implies that some people are capable of understanding other people's faiths. Moreover, dialogue between adherents of different religions has been growing in this century. Admittedly, there has been some bad and prejudiced work done by scholars in this area, but it is absurd to hold that religious commitment must blind a person to the virtues of faiths other than his own. Furthermore, this is a dangerous thesis since it is liable to make people feel that there is no need to make a sympathetic effort to try to understand other religions.

The range of our survey must indeed be great, both in space and time.

Each of the great religions is like a growing organism. It is necessary not only to see how the different parts of a faith like Christianity or Buddhism stand in relation to one another: it is necessary also to understand the life of a faith from the time of its inception. We cannot understand Christianity without knowing the circumstances of its birth two thousand years ago.

In this sense, the study of religions has to have an historical component. But history also shows that some religions have declined or disappeared, and some of these have been too important for them to be neglected in an account of the religious experience of mankind. Thus Zoroastrianism, though only now practiced by a small number of people—nearly all of them Indian Parsees—was at one time a powerful and flourishing faith; and one indeed that rested on profound intuitions about the nature of good and evil.

It will also be of some importance to discover something about the origins of religion in prehistory, though the relative paucity of archeological remains and the absence of written records mean that any conclusions are bound to be tentative. Some have attempted to explain prehistoric religion by reference to what goes on among technologically primitive peoples today. The assumption is that folk who live today, or until very recently, at a Stone Age level will display some of the religious characteristics of Stone Age men. It is therefore convenient to treat the religions of non-literate peoples together, whether they be prehistoric or contemporary.

Naturally most folk will be chiefly interested in the great living faiths— the "world religions" as they are sometimes called: Christianity, Judaism, Islam, Buddhism, Hinduism, and Confucianism. Taoism in China, Shintoism in Japan, the Jain and Sikh religions in India, together with certain modern offshoots from Christianity in the West, such as the Latter Day Saints, are also important. But though some of these faiths, and especially Christianity, Buddhism, and Hinduism, continue to have hundreds of millions of adherents, new forces are competing with them for men's allegiance.

In western countries, there has been a considerable growth in agnosticism in the last hundred years, and this could be said to have its focus in an ethic which centers on human welfare, while rejecting the supernatural. In brief, it proposes Humanism as an alternative to Christianity. During the same period, a new metaphysical creed has had startling political successes—Marxism. In eastern countries as well as in the West from which it had its origin, Marxism proposes itself as a rival to traditional religion.

These two new movements fulfill many of the roles played by religion. This is especially true of Marxism: it has a set of doctrines to explain the whole of reality, it has a policy for realizing a future "heaven on earth," it has grown its own form of public ceremonial, and so on. It would therefore be wrong to describe the religious experience of mankind without trying to understand these new rivals to religion. But both Marxism and Humanism, though they are a bit like religions, are explicitly opposed to religions. Marxism in practice has often persecuted the religious. This raises a problem about the definition of religion. If we look at the social and intellectual roles played by Marxism—its attempt to provide a new social ethic and a vision of reality as a whole—there are grounds for counting it as a new religion. If, on the other hand, we look at its rejection of the supernatural, its lack of concern with the invisible world, its repudiation of revelation and of mystical experience, then we shall be inclined to say that it is not a religion. For are not some or all of these things found in Christianity, Buddhism, and other systems which we call "religions"?

THE DIMENSIONS OF RELIGION

The problem arises because there are different aspects or, as I shall call them, *dimensions* of religion. Whether we include Marxism as a religion depends on which dimension we regard as crucial for our definition. It will therefore be useful to analyze these various dimensions.

The Ritual Dimension

If we were asked the use or purpose of such buildings as temples and churches, we would not be far wrong in saying that they are used for ritual or ceremonial purposes. Religion tends in part to express itself through such rituals: through worship, prayers, offerings, and the like. We may call this the *ritual* dimension of religion. About this, some important comments need to be made.

First, when we think of ritual we often think of something very formal and elaborate, like a High Mass or the Liturgy of the Eastern Orthodox Church. But it is worth remarking that even the simplest form of religious service involves ritual, in the sense of some form of outer behavior (such as closing one's eyes in prayer) coordinated to an inner intention to make contact with, or to participate in, the invisible world. I am not concerned here with those who deny the existence of such an "invisible world," however interpreted, whether as God's presence, as nirvana, as a sacred energy pervading nature. Whether or not such an invisible world exists, it forms an aspect of the world seen from the point of view of those who participate in religion. It is believed in. As was said earlier, it is not here our task to pass judgment on the truth or otherwise of religious conceptions. First, then, even the simplest service involves ritual.

Second, since ritual involves both an inner and an outer aspect it is always possible that the latter will come to dominate the former. Ritual then degenerates into a mechanical or conventional process. If people go through the motions of religious observance without accompanying it with the intentions and sentiments which give it human meaning, ritual is merely an empty shell. This is the reason why some religious activities are condemned as "ritualistic." But it would be wrong to conclude that because ritualism in this bad sense exists, therefore ritual is an unimportant or degenerate aspect of religion.

It should not be forgotten that there are secular rituals which we all use, and these can form an integral part of personal and social relationships. Greeting someone with a "Good morning," saying goodbye, saluting the flag— all these in differing ways are secular rituals. Very often in society they are integrated with religious rituals, as when men say "God be with you," which is more than taking leave of someone: it is invoking a blessing upon the other person.

Third, it will prove convenient to extend the meaning of "ritual" beyond its reference to the forms of worship, sacrifice, etc., directed toward God or the gods.

It happens that a crucial part is played in India and elsewhere by yoga and analogous techniques of self-training. The ultimate aim of such methods is the attainment of higher states of consciousness, through which the adept has experience of release from worldly existence, of nirvana, of ultimate reality (the interpretation partly depends on the system of doctrines against which the adept tests his experience). Thus the essence of such religion is contemplative or mystical. Sometimes, it is pursued without reference to God or the gods— for example, in Buddhism, where the rituals of a religion of worship and sacrifice are regarded as largely irrelevant to the pursuit of nirvana. Nevertheless, the techniques of self-training have an analogy to ritual: the adept performs various physical and mental exercises through which he hopes to concentrate the mind on the transcendent, invisible world, or to withdraw his senses from their usual immersion in the flow of empirical experiences. This aspect of religion, then, we shall include in our definition of the ritual dimension. It can be classified as pragmatic (aimed at the attainment of certain experiences) in distinction from sacred ritual (directed toward a holy being, such as God). Sometimes the two forms of ritual are combined, as in Christian mysticism, for the Christian mystic both worships God *and* trains her mind toward contemplation.

The meaning of ritual cannot be understood without reference to the environment of belief in which it is performed. Thus prayer in most ritual is directed toward a divine being. Very often, legends about the gods are used to explain the features of a ceremony or festival; and often the important events of human life, such as birth, marriage, death, are invested with a sacred significance by relating them to the divine world.

All this can happen before a religion has any theology or formal system of doctrines. Theology is an attempt to introduce organization and intellectual power into what is found in less explicit form in the deposit of revelation or traditional mythology of a religion. The collection of myths, images, and stories through which the invisible world is symbolized can suitably be called the *mythological* dimension of religion.

The Mythological Dimension

Some important comments need to be made about this mythological dimension. First, in accordance with modern usage in theology and in the comparative study of religion, the terms "myth," "mythological," etc., are *not* used to mean that the content is false. Perhaps in ordinary English to say "It's a myth" is just a way of saying "It's false." But the use of the term *myth* in relation to religious phenomena is quite neutral as to the truth or falsity of the story enshrined in the myth. In origin, the term "myth" means "story," and in calling something a story we are not thereby saying that it is true or false. We are just reporting on what has been said. Similarly, here we are concerned with reporting on what is believed.

Second, it is convenient to use the term to include not merely stories about God (for instance the story of the creation in Genesis), about the gods (for instance in Homer's *Iliad*), etc., but also the historical events of religious significance in a tradition. For example, the Passover ritual in Judaism reenacts a highly important event that once occurred to the children of Israel; their delivery from bondage in Egypt. The historical event functions as a myth. Thus we shall include stories relating to significant historical events under the head of the mythological dimension—again without prejudice to whether the stories accurately describe what actually occurred in history.

The Doctrinal Dimension

Third, it is not always easy to differentiate the mythological and the symbolic from what is stated in theology. Doctrines are an attempt to give system, clarity, and intellectual power to what is revealed through the mythological and symbolic language of religious faith and ritual. Naturally, theology must make use of the symbols and myths. For example, when the Christian theologian has to describe the meaning of the Incarnation, he must necessarily make use of Biblical language and history. Thus the dividing line between the mythological and what I shall call the *doctrinal* dimension is not easy to draw. Yet there is clearly a distinction between Aquinas's treatment of creation at the philosophical level and the colorful story of creation in Genesis. The distinction is important, because the world religions owe some of their living power to their success in presenting a total picture of reality, through a coherent system of doctrines.

The Ethical Dimension

Throughout history we find that religions usually incorporate a code of ethics. Ethics concern the behavior of the individual and, to some extent, the code of ethics of the dominant religion controls the community. Quite obviously, men do not always live up to the standards they profess. And sometimes the standards which are inculcated by the dominant faith in a particular society may not be believed by all sections of that society.

Even so, there is no doubt that religions have been influential in molding the ethical attitudes of the societies they are part of. It is important, however, to distinguish between the moral teaching incorporated in the doctrines and mythology of a religion, and the social facts concerning those who adhere to the faith in question. For instance, Christianity teaches "Love thy neighbor as thyself." As a matter of sociological fact, quite a lot of people in so-called Christian countries, where Christianity is the official, or dominant religion, fail to come anywhere near this ideal. The man who goes to church is not necessarily loving; nor is the man who goes to a Buddhist temple necessarily compassionate. Consequently, we must distinguish between the ethical teachings of a faith, which we shall discuss as the *ethical* dimension of religion, and the actual sociological effects and circumstances of a religion.

Pertinent to this point is the consideration that most religions are institutionalized. This is most obvious in technologically primitive societies, where the priest, soothsayer, or magician is closely integrated into the social structure. Religion is not just a personal matter here: it is part of the life of the community. It is built into the institutions of daily life. But even in sophisticated communities where a line is drawn between religious and secular concerns, as in contemporary America, churches exist as institutions to be reckoned with. They are part of the "establishment." In areas where there is active or latent persecution of religious faith, as in the Soviet Union, there are still organizations for continuing religious activities.

The Social Dimension

Religions are not just systems of *belief*: they are also organizations, or parts of organizations. They have a communal and social significance. This social shape of a religion is, of course, to some extent determined by the religious and ethical ideals and practices that it harbors. Conversely, it often happens that the religious and ethical ideals are adapted to existing social conditions and attitudes. For example, Japanese fishermen reconcile the Buddhist injunction against taking life (even animal or fish life) to their activity as fishermen. The Christian's dedication to brotherly love or his attitude to war may be determined more by patriotism and a national crisis than by the Gospel. Thus, it is important to distinguish between the ethical dimension of religion and the *social* dimension. The latter is the mode in which the religion in question is institutionalized, whereby, through its institutions and teachings, it affects the community in which it finds itself. The doctrinal, mythological, and ethical dimensions express a religion's claims about the nature of the invisible world and its aims about how men's lives ought to be shaped: the social dimension indicates the way in which men's lives are in fact shaped by these claims and the way in which religious institutions operate.

It is, incidentally, clear that the ongoing patterns of ritual are an important element in the institutionalization of religion. For example, if it is believed that certain ceremonies and sacraments can only be properly performed by a priest, then the religious institution will be partly determined by the need to maintain and protect a professional priesthood.

The Experiential Dimension

The dimensions we have so far discussed would indeed be hard to account for were it not for the dimension with which this book is centrally concerned: that of experience, the *experiential* dimension. Although men may hope to have contact with, and participate in, the invisible world through ritual, personal religion normally involves the hope of, or realization of, experience of that world. The Buddhist monk hopes for nirvana, and this includes the contemplative experience of peace and of insight into the transcendent. The Christian who prays to God believes normally that God answers prayer—and this not just "externally" in bringing about certain states of affairs, such as a cure for illness, but more importantly "internally" in the personal relationship that flowers between the man who prays and his Maker. The prayerful Christian believes that God does speak to men in an intimate way and that the individual can and does have an inner experience of God. Hence, personal religion necessarily involves what we have called the experiential dimension.

The factor of religious experience is even more crucial when we consider the events and the human lives from which the great religions have stemmed. The Buddha achieved Enlightenment as he sat in meditation beneath the Bo-Tree. As a consequence of his shattering mystical experience, he believed that he had the secret of the cure for the suffering and dissatisfactions of life in this world. We have records of the inaugural visions of some prophets of the Hebrew Bible, of the experiences that told them something profoundly important about God and that spurred them on to teach men in his name. It was through such experiences that Mohammad began to preach the unity of Allah—a preaching that had an explosive impact upon the world from Central Asia to Spain. One cannot read the Upanishads, the source of so much of Hindu doctrine, without feeling the experience on which their teachings are founded. The most striking passage in the *Bhagavadgita,* perhaps the greatest religious document of Hinduism, is that in which the Lord reveals himself in terrifying splendor to Arjuna. Arjuna is overwhelmed by awe and filled with utter devotion. We have already remarked on the seminal importance of St. Paul's similar experience on the Damascus Road.

The words of Jesus Christ reveal his sense of intimate closeness to the Father; there is little doubt that this rested upon highly significant personal experiences. These and other examples can be given of the crucial part played by religious experience in the genesis of the great faiths.

For this reason, it is unrealistic to treat Marxism as a religion: though it possesses doctrines, symbols, a moral code, and even sometimes rituals, it denies the possibility of an experience of the invisible world. Neither relationship to a personal God nor the hope of an experience of salvation or nirvana can be significant for the Marxist. Likewise Humanism, because it fixes its sights on this-worldly aims, is essentially non-religious. Nevertheless, it is necessary for us to examine the impact of these faiths upon the contemporary world. But the main emphasis will be upon the inner side—what religions mean in personal experience, and how they have been molded by such experience.

There is a special difficulty, however, in undertaking a description of a religious experience. We have to rely upon the testimony of those who have the experience, and their reports must be conveyed to us either by telling or writing. Sometimes accounts of prophetic or mystical experience of important religious leaders have been preserved by oral tradition through many generations before being written down. But for the most part, the individual religious experiences that have influenced large segments of mankind occurred in cultures that knew the art of writing.

This means that the experience occurred in the context of the existing religions which already had a doctrinal dimension. This raises a problem for us in our attempt to understand the unique religious experience of the prophets or founders of religions, for their experiences are likely to be interpreted in the light of existing doctrines, as well as clothed in the mythological and symbolic forms of the age. There is less difficulty when we consider the "lesser" figures of the religions—not the founders, but those saints and visionaries who come after. They interpret their experiences in terms of received doctrines and mythologies.

For these reasons, it is not easy to know about a given report which of the elements in it are based, so to say, purely on the experience itself, and which are due to doctrinal and mythological interpretation. To some extent the problem can be overcome by comparing the reports of men of different cultures—such as India and the West—which had virtually no contact during the periods crucial for the formation and elaboration of the dominant religious beliefs.

Moreover, it is worth noting that there is an *interplay* between experience and doctrine. Thus, though the Buddha, for example, took over elements from the thought-forms of his own age, he was genuinely a creative teacher, who introduced new elements and transmuted the old. The prophets of the Hebrew Bible fashioned a genuinely original ethical monotheism from an existent belief in Yahweh. The changes they made in the ethnically centered teachings they inherited can be understood, to some degree, in terms of the impact of the personal religious experiences that were revelatory for these men. Thus experience and doctrinal interpretation have a dialectical relationship. The latter colors the former, but the former also shapes the latter. This book will attempt to exhibit this dialectic at work.

This dialectical interplay also helps us to understand some of the features of personal religion at a humbler level. The Christian, for example, is taught certain doctrines and mythological symbols by his parents. He learns to call God "Our Father"; he is instructed to believe that the world is created by God and sustained by God. These ideas will at first simply be "theoretical" as far as the young Christian is concerned, on a par with other non-observable theories he learns about the world, such as that the earth goes round the sun. But suppose he progresses to a deeper understanding of the Christian faith through a particular personal experience, or through his response to the ritual and ethical demands of the religion. Then he will come to see that in some mysterious way God is a person with whom he can have contact; God is not just like the sun, to be thought of speculatively, or to be looked at. Personally, then, he discovers that he can worship and pray to God. In short, "I believe in God the Father Almighty, Maker of Heaven and Earth" will come to have a new meaning for him. In a sense, he will now believe something other than what he first believed. In this way, the interplay between doctrine and experiences is fundamental to personal religion.

EXPERIENCE AND REVELATION

The crucial importance here assigned to religious experience might encounter the following criticism. Surely, it will be said, the truth of religion is discovered through revelation. For instance, Christian revelation is to be found in the words of the scriptures, which are themselves guaranteed by God. Is not an analysis in terms of the experiential dimension untrue to the actual beliefs of Christians?

This objection is an important one, and the discussion of it will serve to clarify further what we mean by experience, doctrine, and mythology. The first point to make is that we are not here primarily concerned to say anything directly about the truth of religion. It may well be that such a profound and widespread phenomenon in human history and culture will strike us as conveying truth. But this is a philosophical and doctrinal question we are not here called upon to decide. We must first describe the facts about man's religious experience scientifically. Using this approach we need only say this: the idea that God's revelation is to be located in the words of scripture is a doctrine believed by many people; the theory of revelation is part of the doctrinal dimension of Christianity.

Second, whatever we may say about the inerrancy of scripture, there is no doubt that the Bible describes some religous experiences and historical events of great mythological and doctrinal significance. The Bible is not itself an experience or an historical event: but it tells us about these things. Consequently, it is important to approach Biblical religion by considering what the words of the Bible are about.

This is one reason why some modern Christian theologians tend to speak of revelation as "non-propositional." What they mean is that revelation is God's self-disclosure in human experience and in history, as recorded by the Bible. It is God revealing himself in the history of the Jews, in the experience of the prophets, and in the person of Christ. The historical events, the religious experiences, Jesus—these are not statements: they are what the statements of the Bible are about. They are not propositions: they are what Biblical propositions refer to. Nevertheless, a scientific or descriptive account of Jewish and early Christian religion such as is described and expressed in the Old and New Testaments cannot avoid some judgment about the inerrancy of scripture, and about its manner of composition. Fortunately, however, the approach here adopted will not be valueless, even from the point of view of those who hold a very different position regarding the inerrancy and inspiration of the Bible. This is so for two reasons.

First, there is little doubt from any point of view that the Bible gives us the essential information we need for describing the experiences and teachings of the key figures in the narrative, although with regard to Christ there are certain special difficulties, both religious and historical, in understanding the precise nature of his inner life in relation to the Father.

Second, in the whole field of human knowledge, whether in the liberal arts or the sciences, there is always a margin of disagreement between expert scholars. But very often knowledge advances precisely because of this. It is out of the dialogue and argument that new insights are won. Consequently even though I have little doubt that there will be some disagreement over the facts of religion as here presented, the presentation is a fair one, I trust: even those who because of doctrinal commitment to the Bible will wish to qualify or supplement the account should be enabled to see something of the approach which many Biblical experts and theologians have adopted during this century.

Finally, it is worth pointing out that many Hindus regard their scriptural revelation as verbally inerrant, and that the vast majority of Muslims regard the Qur'an in this way. It is thus reasonable to treat all the world's scriptures in the same way, and to try to penetrate to the spirit and significance of what they say, rather than to rest content with an acceptance of the letter of these writings. But throughout it must be remembered that the content of scriptures represents (whatever factual accuracy) an important aspect of the doctrinal and mythological dimensions of the religions in question.

The foregoing may be summed up by saying that here revelation will be treated as "non-propositional." It is clear that when God reveals himself to a prophet, this involves some kind of experience on the part of the latter: God must reveal himself through a person's human experience. Thus it is possible to approach revelation from the human standpoint, by considering what it means to the recipients and how they interpret it. However, for some faiths, and notably for Judaism and Christianity, revelation does not occur merely through the inner experiences of individuals: it also occurs "externally" through historical events such as the crossing of the Red (or Reed) Sea, and the Crucifixion of Jesus. Clearly these are events occurring within human experience. Indeed, they must be so if they are correctly described as "histori-cal" events. For what we mean by history, in its primary sense, is the complex and ongoing interplay of events occurring through the agency of human beings, or occurring to, and in relation to, human beings.

Caesar's crossing of the Rubicon is part of history because Caesar, and his enemies, were human beings. The eruption of a crater on Mars is not counted as part of history, unless perchance it affects an astronaut, or upsets an astrologer. Consequently, when we say that something is revealed in his-tory, it must be within human experience. Further, it makes no sense in any case to say "This has been revealed," without knowing to whom. But does not this mean that all revelation falls within what we have called the "experiential dimension" of religion?

This question is well worth asking, for it points to an ambiguity in the word "experience" which ought to be cleared up. Hitherto, when we have talked of religious experience, we have been referring to a specific range of experiences which are religiously important, such as St. Paul's on the Damas-cus Road, or a pious person's inner recognition of an answer to his prayers. But in speaking of the experiential dimension of religion, we do not want to refer to all the experiences that a religious person might have. For example, St. Paul perhaps rode down the Damascus Road in a chariot: his perception of the chariot and the horse was an experience. But such a perception could not properly be called "religious experience," unless for some special reason the sight of the chariot suddenly revealed something fundamental about God's nature. A religious experience involves some kind of "perception" of the *invisible* world, or involves a perception that some visible person or thing is a manifestation of the invisible world. The ordinary person in Jerusalem who simply saw Jesus walk by was not having a religious experience, but the disciples who saw him transfigured on the mountain *did* have such an experience: the Transfiguration was precisely the manifestation in Jesus' person of the glory of the invisible world.

If the Transfiguration story describes the way an historical person was, on a particular occasion, invested with depth through the experiential dimension of religious faith, the Crucifixion is an example of the way in which an historical event is given depth through the doctrinal and mythological dimensions. Jesus' death on the Cross is seen by the Christian tradition not just as the execution of a person who proved inconvenient and dangerous to the authorities. It is also seen as part of a divine drama that has cosmic significance. Mythologically, it is the defeat of Satan and the restoration of the link between man and God that was severed by the Fall. The event is given further depth by the attempts to express a consistent and meaningful doctrine of the Atonement. It is often not easy to draw a clear line between the mythological and the doctrinal dimensions of religion, but the former is typically more colorful, symbolic, picturesque, and story-like. Myths are stories, and they bring out something concerning the invisible world. This is the case for treating significant historical events as part of the mythological dimension. The Crucifixion story is a true story about the death of a religious leader: but it is also a story that is seen to be part of a divine drama. The visible story illuminates the invisible one, and conversely.

Thus we can count both *historical* myths (that is to say, stories concerning the invisible world which have an anchorage in history) and *non-historical* myths (those that have no such anchorage) as aspects of the mythological dimension.

MYTH AND THE UNCONSCIOUS

There is one further aspect of the mythological dimension which needs to be mentioned here. Earlier we saw that there is an interplay between the experiential and the mythological and doctrinal dimensions. The conscious experiences which men have had of the invisible world both shape and are shaped by the mythology and doctrine of the cultures in which the experiences occur. But as well as what goes on consciously in man's mind, there are the processes of the "unconscious." There is no need at this point to judge whether particular theories of the unconscious, such as are employed in depth psychology, are correct; nor do we need to enter into a philosophical discussion of whether it is strictly necessary or accurate to speak about a realm of the unconscious. What is undeniable is that certain characteristic patterns of mental activity and symbolism occur that have depths of meaning not always obvious to the consciousness of the individual in whom they occur. An investigation of these can sometimes be illuminating. They can throw light on certain aspects of mythology. There is, as it were, a frontier between the kingdom of dreams and the kingdom of myths. Consequently an investigation of the experiential dimension by no means exhausts the range of the psychology of religion. The psychologist of religion needs to consider the ways in which the mythological dimension is sometimes shaped by these "unconscious" factors. But once "psychology" is mentioned we must take note of a danger. It is easy to jump to the conclusion that because a psychological explanation is offered for a phenomenon, therefore the phenomenon—such as a myth—cannot, so to say, speak the truth about the invisible world. This conclusion is too facile. For instance, a physiologist may be able to explain the workings of the eye, the brain, and the central nervous system, when a perception takes place. In this sense, he "explains" the perception. But this does not at all show that the perception is true or false. The physiologist simply wants to explain the normal process of sight perception. Normally, what we think we perceive we do in fact perceive: most perceptions "tell the truth," so to say. Now this is not by itself a *conclusive* argument against those who wish to "explain away" religion in psychological terms. But it is enough to show that rather complex philosophical issues are raised, which, of course, bear on the whole question of the truth of religion. But we have remarked earlier that we are not primarily concerned here with these philosophical issues. Rather, we wish to delineate the whole history of the religious experience of mankind: we must describe and analyze the facts of religion before we can wisely judge about its truth.

RELIGION AS AN ORGANISM

To sum up our account so far of what religion is: it is a six-dimensional organism, typically containing doctrines, myths, ethical teachings, rituals, and social institutions, and animated by religious experiences of various kinds. To understand the key ideas of religion, such as God and nirvana, one has to understand the pattern of religious life directed toward these goals. God is the focus of worship and praise; nirvana is found by treading the Noble Eightfold Path, culminating in contemplation.

Indeed, one can say something even stronger than this. God is to be *defined* in relation to worship. To say "My God, my God" is to acknowledge that he deserves my loyalty and praise. God and gods are essentially the foci of men's worship and ritual activities. So, when, by a metaphor, we say that a man makes a god of his stomach, we do not mean that he makes a Creator or First Cause of his stomach: but that he "worships" his stomach—eating is his greatest object of loyalty and reverence. To say that there is a God is therefore different from saying that there is a Creator or First Cause. God may be Creator: but primarily he is the object of worship. Thus the understanding of ideas about God requires close attention to their milieu in men's religious life. And the rituals people direct toward God and the gods need in turn to be understood by reference to their inner side, and thus ultimately by reference to a man's religious experience.

This general account of religion which we have given depends on comparing religions as we find them in the world. Comparisons, though, need to be handled carefully. For we are not confronted in fact by some monolithic object, namely religion. We are confronted by *religions*. And each religion has its own style, its own inner dynamic, its own special meanings, its uniqueness. Each religion is an organism, and has to be understood in terms of the interrelation of its different parts. Thus though there are resemblances between religions or between parts of religions, these must not be seen too crudely.

For example, it is correct to say that some religions are monotheistic. They each worship a single God. But the conception of God can vary subtly. For instance, though Islam and Christianity both draw upon the Old Testament heritage, and though Allah has many characteristics of the Christian God, such as being Creator, judge, merciful, providential, nevertheless even the points of resemblance are affected by the rest of the milieu. Thus the Christian idea of the Creator is affected by the fact that creation is not just seen in relation to Genesis but also in relation to the opening verses of John. Belief in Christ seen as the Logos affects belief in God and affects one's view of creation.

It is like a picture. A particular element, such as a patch of yellow, may occur in two different pictures. One can point to the resemblance. Yet the meaning of one patch of yellow can still be very different from the meaning of the other. What it means, how it looks—these depend on what other patches of color surround it. Likewise, elements in a religious organism are affected by the other elements present.

So although we are inevitably drawn to compare religions in order to make sense of the patterns of religious experience found in the history of men's faiths, we also have to recognize that each religion must also be seen essentially in its own terms, from within, as it were. This means that we have to have a sense of the multiplicity of human religious life, as well as for its points of unity and contact. We are not only concerned with religion: we are concerned also with religions. And we have to see them in the perspective of the world's history.

Let us therefore look at this history and the ways in which the multiplicity of religions has developed. A quick summary of the history of religions can provide perspective for viewing the various manifestations of the human spirit discussed in subsequent chapters.

A BIRD'S-EYE VIEW OF HISTORIC RELIGIONS

How religion started we cannot tell for certain. Some theories will be discussed in the next chapter. There is ample evidence that religious rites were practiced in early prehistoric times and it may well be that the sense of the sacred has been part of man's experience from the very beginning. It is notable that before the emergence of the human species proper (*homo sapiens*), Neanderthal Man—some 150,000 years ago—practiced the ritual interment of the dead. This seems to point to a belief in an afterlife of some kind and to belief in an "invisible" world.

A dramatic turning point in man's history occurred between 4000 and 3000 B.C. in the Middle East, with the beginnings of urban civilization. In the latter part of the fourth millennium B.C., a settled agricultural life in the more fertile areas of Egypt and Mesopotamia provided the resources for the establishment of cities, which in turn allowed not only centralization of civil and religious administration, but also the growth of elaborate temple cults and of an organized priesthood. The discovery of writing had by then created a profound change in human life. Written words gradually came to replace memory as the source of tradition, and provided a creative means of expressing man's religious heritage. Egypt and Mesopotamia become centers of civilization, and further east, in the Indus Valley, in northwest India, and in China, there developed important cultures.

It is no accident, perhaps, that from these three areas—the Middle East, India, and China—the three great sources of the world religions evolved. It is curious, in this connection, that between a three-hundred-year span, 800 to 500 B.C., the great religious traditions of the world crystallized. In Palestine there occurred the decisive emergence of a monotheistic faith through the work of the Hebrew prophets; the Judaism they developed became the foundation upon which both Christianity and Islam were later built. In India this was the period of the composition of the most important of the Upanishads—the writings that form part of the sacred scriptures of Hinduism. The Upanishads contain germinally the ideas later elaborated in the various theologies that remain to this day the forms under which the Hindu sees the world about him.

During the same three hundred years, unorthodox teachers in India challenged the tradition of the Aryans who had invaded India during the second millennium B.C. and whose beliefs, rituals, and social structure had long dominated north India. Two of these unorthodox teachers have lived in the memory of religious people until today: Mahavira, the *"jina"* or "Conqueror," who restored an archaic tradition of religious belief, and whose teachings are handed down today in the faith known as Jainism; and the Buddha, the "Enlightened One."

Both lived in the sixth century B.C. Though Jainism has diminished to less than two million people at the last census—there are only a handful of Jains outside India—Buddhism has been the most successful missionary religion, at least statistically, that the world has seen. Buddhism spread to Ceylon, Burma, and Southeast Asia—where it is of the so-called "Lesser Vehicle" variety—and it also penetrated into China, Tibet, Mongolia, Korea, and Japan—where it is predominantly the so-called "Greater Vehicle" variety. It is no exaggeration to say that the whole of the East Asian continental mass has been permeated or influenced by Buddhism, with the exception of Siberia. In brief, Buddhism has become a major world force: Jainism has remained, with ups and downs, a religion of the Indian subcontinent. Admittedly, by about 1100 A.D. Buddhism was virtually finished in its homeland; but like Christianity, which also did not survive strongly in its place of origin, Buddhism spread far and wide. There are currently Buddhist missions in Europe and the United States; nor are they without success.

While Zoroastrianism and Judaism developed in the Middle East (which was later the cradle of Christianity and, in the seventh century A.D., Islam), and while Hinduism and Buddhism developed in India, largely in the crucial period between 800 and 500 B.C., there were similarly important events in China. Confucius, who lived approximately from 551 to 479 B.C. (the Buddha lived from 563 to 483 B.C. or later), reformed, clarified, and systematized the earlier traditions of China into a coherent social and religious system. The Confucian ethic has remained until this day a powerful factor in Chinese culture, both at home and overseas. A legendary contemporary (many scholars dispute his existence and date) Lao Tzu, whose more mystical and contemplative teachings are summed up in the *Tao-te Ching* (*The Classic of the Tao and its Power*), was the source of a religion which has also had profound influence upon Chinese life. Though Taoism may now be in a state of deep decline, it not only was a powerful cultural and spiritual force, but it also had an effect on Buddhism when that religion came to evangelize China. Zen Buddhism is indeed the Japanese form of a movement which represents a blend between Taoist and Buddhist ideas and contemplative techniques.

In China three religions were dominant through most of the period from the second century A.D. until modern times—Confucianism, Taoism, and Buddhism. In Japan, through the cultural influence of China, Confucianism and Buddhism came to permeate Japanese life. But the indigenous faith, Shinto (the Way of the Gods), survived the intrusion. Although Shinto was used by militarists in the period preceding and during World War II to promote nationalism, this was in effect a distortion of its values, and certainly it continues to be important in Japanese life.

Let us now make a few further observations on the development of religions in the Western and Middle Eastern world. Some time about the sixth century B.C. or earlier, the prophet Zoroaster was preaching an ethical monotheism based on the principle that there is a cosmic struggle between the supreme Good Spirit (Ahura Mazda) and the Evil Spirit (Angra Mainyu). In so doing, Zoroaster, or more correctly, Zarathustra, transcended the existing polytheistic faith which was closely related to that of the Aryans who invaded India. Further west, the Hebrew people became the first of all the Semitic peoples occupying the area from Egypt to Mesopotamia to attain a true monotheism. (Akhenaten in Egypt, during the twelfth century B.C., had attempted to elevate Aten to solitary and exclusive godhood over the various gods of a complex polytheism, but the attempt was unsuccessful and after his death the traditional rituals were restored.) Jewish monotheism might not have achieved an important place in the ancient world had it not been transformed through the life of Christ and the subsequent spread of Christianity through most of the Middle East and Graeco-Roman world. In all probability, Jewish monotheism would otherwise have remained the faith of a minor, though widely dispersed, nation within the structure of the Roman Empire.

Christianity had spectacular success in converting Europe, North Africa, and the Middle East, and by the fourth century A.D. became the official religion of the Empire. Thereafter, its onward course was checkered. Over a period of centuries, the Eastern Church, centered in Byzantium, and the Western Church, headed by the Pope in Rome, grew apart. In the seventh century A.D., the teachings of Muhammad began to spread explosively beyond his Arabian homeland, and in fifty years Islam was the dominant faith of North Africa, a large part of Spain, nearly all the Middle East, and parts of Central Asia. From the eleventh century, it penetrated into India, and in the fifteenth, finally destroyed the Byzantine Empire, thereby gaining an entrance into eastern Europe. In the early part of the sixteenth century, Luther sparked off the Reformation, so that Christendom split into three main segments—Roman Catholic, Protestant, and Eastern Orthodox. This division has continued to the present time, though there are now powerful forces at work to bring about reunion.

Christianity lost many adherents through the impact of Islam in the Middle Ages. In the Renaissance, though internal divisions hampered it, a new era of expansion opened up for Christendom with the navigational successes of the sea-going nations of Europe. The discoveries of the New World and of the sea-route to India and beyond gave Christian missionaries amazing opportunities. Moreover, the settlements in North America, Australia, and New Zealand by European people, and the conquest of Latin America, naturally meant that Christian culture was to dominate these areas. Though missions had some success in Asia, the population on the whole remained loyal to the long-established traditional faiths.

During the last two centuries, both Hinduism and Buddhism have gone through a revival. Such a revival can be partly put down to the rediscovery of the past among peoples long dominated by European powers, who now desired to reform and clarify their heritage as part of the incipient struggle for freedom and independence.

Modern Humanism and Marxism

In the West, there has been in modern times a diminution in Christian belief. This has two main causes—the growth of religious scepticism among the educated classes and the Industrial Revolution, which forced people into cities and into new types of work and life and which destroyed traditional social patterns. In England, as in some other places, the majority of workers became alienated from the churches. Religious scepticism partly stemmed from the rationalism of the late eighteenth century: in addition to these philosophical roots, there were causes of disbelief of a rather different character. They issued from the collision between scientific enquiry—and above all the theory of evolution—and a literalistic interpretation of the Bible. There was thus an incompatibility between science and one type of Christian theology, which happened at the time to be influential.

Two non-Christian reactions were generated by the problems of nineteenth-century industrialism and discussions of the relations between science and religion. On the one hand, there was the liberal reform movement, expressed by such figures as John Stuart Mill. This type of thinking issued in Humanism, which fragmented into a number of varieties. On the other hand, as against liberalism, which was dedicated to the freedom of the individual and *laissez-faire* economics, Marx gave powerful shape to socialist ideas. Marxism, through the organization of the Communist Party, ultimately, if rather unexpectedly, was a factor in the Russian Revolution of 1917. Since then, of course, it has become the official philosophy of a number of other countries—though it is notable that where revolutions have occurred "independently" (that is, not through territorial conquest by the Soviet army) differing interpretations of Marxism have been put forward: thus in Yugoslavia and China there were interpretations of Marxism not fully in accord with the Marxism of the U.S.S.R.

Newer Religions

Roughly, the great religions have stemmed from three sources—the Middle East, India, and China—giving rise to three groups of faiths: the Semitic group—Judaism, Christianity, and Islam; the Indian group—Hinduism, Buddhism, and Jainism; the Sino-Japanese group—Confucianism, Taoism, and Shinto. The interplay between religions of different groups have produced some new religious movements. Thus the Sikh religion originated as an attempt to combine the best of both Hinduism and Islam. More recently, the Ramakrishna Mission and the Sri Aurobindo Ashram, both within the main structure of Hinduism, offer different modes of synthesizing Eastern and Western religion and metaphysics. From within Islam, the Baha'i movement, dating from the last century, is in effect another reforming religion. Earlier in China, Buddhism intermingled with Confucianism and Taoism, and one result was Ch'an, or Zen, Buddhism. In Japan, there was also a syncretistic Buddhism, incorporating Buddhist and Shinto ideas and practices. And in various parts of the world, new cults have arisen as a result of the impact of Christianity on tribal religions weakened by foreign conquest and modern technology. Thus where religions come into contact, there is a tendency toward syncretism. Often this leads to the creation of a third religion, claiming to be inclusive, but in fact separated from the traditional faiths it is supposed to include.

In addition to such synthesizing movements, there has been a growth during the last hundred years or so of new religions having an historical relationship to Christianity but not belonging to orthodox Christendom. Notable among these have been the Church of the Latter Day Saints, the Jehovah's Witnesses, and Christian Science. In the 1960s and onward, new religious movements, sometimes referred to as cults, have spread in western countries.

The Religions in Dialogue

Our bird's-eye view of the religions of the world must finally recognize that although some of the great faiths have come into contact with one another in the past, it is only in comparatively recent times that they all belong to a single world, as it were. In the past there have been numerous national histories: now with modern means of transportation and communication there is a single world history. Moreover, only in the last hundred years has the patient work of many scholars made available the sacred writings of the world. Now most of the chief texts have been translated and edited. Thus only recently has it become possible for a genuine dialogue between religions to take place. Hitherto, although Westerners, for instance, knew quite a lot about the externals of Hinduism, they were largely ignorant of the doctrinal and mythological dimensions of that faith. There was much misunderstanding. We can well imagine how hard it would be for an Indian who knew nothing of the Bible to have a correct view of Christianity simply on the basis of observing Christian behavior or Christian rituals. So we must not underestimate the dramatic change that has come over the religious scene in the last eighty years and more: now for the first time in human history it is possible for members of the various religions, East or West, to speak to one another in an informed and sympathetic manner. One result may be to stimulate a growth of the syncretism referred to above. But whatever may be felt about this aspect of the matter, it is surely a cause for rejoicing that now at last men of different faiths have the opportunity for mutual comprehension. Ignorance was never a virtue.

The shape of the religious past—the confluence of a number of separate streams into a single river of history today—dictates the order of our survey of religions. Clearly, we must start at the beginning, with an attempt to penetrate the secrets of prehistoric religion. It is convenient to move on from there to look at the traditional religions of relatively small-scale societies and in particular those of Africa. Next the three main streams of the major religious traditions must be independently discussed. Since Chinese religion became so permeated by Buddhism, and since Buddhism originated in the Indian subcontinent, Indian religion must be described before that of China. For various reasons it is convenient also to treat India before we turn to the rise of Jewish monotheism and its Christian consequences. The early history of Christianity sets the stage for the explosive history of Islam. From there we shall turn back to the West to observe the later developments of the Christian tradition. Finally, we shall review the state of religions today and attempt to forecast some of the consequences of the present division between the traditional faiths and the Marxist and Humanist movements.

The vast and fascinatingly rich panorama of humanity's religious experience must strike any observer, whether or not she is personally committed to a religious faith, as a central feature in the geography of human behavior. Many of our deepest feelings are expressed here, and religion is a record of the visions by which people have interpreted the cosmic reality in which they are immersed. No one can understand mankind without understanding the faiths of humanity. Sometimes naive, sometimes penetratingly noble, sometimes crude, sometimes subtle, sometimes cruel, sometimes suffused by an overpowering gentleness and love, sometimes world-affirming, sometimes negating the world, sometimes inward-looking, sometimes universalistic and missionary-minded, sometimes shallow, and often profound—religion has permeated human life since obscure and early times. As an experience, what has it meant? We shall now begin to see.

SMALL-SCALE RELIGIONS

Chapter 2

PREHISTORIC AND PRIMAL

RELIGIONS

IT HAS SOMETIMES been thought that one could penetrate to the earliest forms of human religion by considering what goes on in contemporary small-scale societies that are technologically "primitive." The last term is perhaps unfortunate, since it suggests that contemporary tribal religions are crude and unsophisticated. This is far from being the case. Nevertheless, there are, or have been in the recent past, tribal societies that depend upon food-gathering and other primitive techniques to maintain life. Since their mode of life corresponds to that of prehistoric man, it is not unnatural to try to divine what went on in prehistoric times by reading into them the experience of contemporary "primitives." This is one reason for treating the two types of religion together. There is another reason too.

Historical religions, in the ancient Near East, China, India, etc., are historical because there are written records of them. That there are written records is a partial consequence of the invention of writing. Because literate cultures tend to prize intellectual knowledge, the historical religions generally have a more developed doctrinal dimension than is the case in tribal and preliterate religions.

This is one reason why modern folk, and Westerners especially, who tend to regard religions in terms of doctrines, find it easy to equate the non-doctrinal faiths of remote antiquity with those of contemporary tribal societies. This attitude, though misleading in certain respects, is not entirely without reason. The word "faiths" used in the previous sentence is significant. For many folk, a faith is a system of belief to which one may or may not become committed. Yet for prehistoric humans, and for contemporary counterparts, religion is part of the fabric of ordinary existence, of custom rather than of conscious choice.

It is impossible to discuss the religion of the earliest humans except in terms of speculative theories. Evidence of religion from prehistoric times is so slight that there cannot be as yet, and perhaps there never will be, any definitive account of the origins of the religious sentiment among mankind. Estimates of such evidence as there is very often depend upon prior evaluations of the status and nature of man—for instance, evolutionary theory has suggested to some students of religion that there is a sequence of stages in religion, from lower to higher. It is probable that the ultimate origins of human religion will never be clearly known. Nevertheless, we can gain some insights by considering the various major theories, and to understand these, we must have a picture of the world of preliterate peoples in the present and recent past.[1]

THE PRIMAL WORLD

Both primal and prehistoric peoples have lived chiefly by food-gathering rather than by food production—that is, by organized agriculture. Hunting, fishing, and the gathering of wild fruits have given people their food since the earliest times. Prehistoric people did not begin to domesticate animals or to practice agriculture until fairly recently in the Neolithic Age, between 10,000 and 3000 B.C. Thus the ability to regulate the food supply occurs long after the time from which we date the existence of *homo sapiens* or "true men," about a hundred thousand years ago (the "near men," Australopithecines, may have existed as long as a million years ago and recent finds in Africa push the dates even further back). There still exist in the world today groups of people who live at a pre-Neolithic level as non-agrarian food-gatherers: among such groups are the Kalahari bushmen and the Australian aboriginals. We can speculate that their life-patterns must be something like the life led by early humans during the major part of prehistory. But though today's technologically primitive cultures are reminiscent of prehistoric man technologically, we must remember that the modern small-scaler has a culture that undoubtedly evolved and changed during the immense span of time since Neanderthals lived. Because of the lack of written records and the paucity of archeological evidence, we can know almost nothing about this. Further, the modern hunting cultures have, in the last few centuries, come into contact with cultures more advanced technologically, and these have begun to change their whole style of life. The Eskimos, for instance, now receive education in reading and writing: they are learning modern skills and are deserting their traditional occupations of fishing and hunting.

[1] In the ensuing discussion I use the term "primal" in place of the unsatisfactory word "primitive." The main characteristic of primal societies is that they are relatively small-scale and, until lately, technologically underdeveloped, tend to have a close religious relationship to the natural environment.

In the following pages we shall pick out some typical features of the primal world-picture. Naturally, it is necessary to be selective, for hundreds of different cultures are represented here under the blanket title of "primal," and they vary considerably. The hard and cruel life of the Australian aboriginal contrasts with the more peaceful and settled existence of the South Pacific islanders, who supplement their fishing with the produce of gardens; the complex cultures of the American Indians contrast with the jungle life of the central African pygmy; the cold white environment of the Eskimo contrasts with the tropical landscape inhabited by the Amazonians; the Ainus of Japan and the people of Tierra del Fuego live in very different surroundings from those of the Nuer in the South Sudan or the Andaman Islanders in the Bay of Bengal. Nevertheless, and perhaps surprisingly, there are certain recurrent patterns which can be perceived in these varying cultures—evidence of the universality of religious and magical ideas within the history of humankind.

MANA

Primal peoples conceive of themselves as surrounded by a myriad of unseen forces. These forces range from impersonal power which anthropologists, borrowing a South Sea Island expression, call *mana*, to spirits and gods, including, in many such cultures, a supreme High God. Their world is alive, populated, shot through with the unseen. But it would be wrong to think that this sort of religious and magical view of reality makes any sharp distinction between the spiritual and the material aspects of the universe. These are inextricably interwoven into a single but complex fabric.

Mana is a hidden or secret force which operates silently and invisibly in things and persons that are in some way especially powerful, impressive, or socially important. *Mana* is somewhat analogous to the idea an ignorant person has of electricity—powerful and unseen, capable of doing much for his benefit, yet capable too of destroying him. As a person, or a speech, can be said to be "electrifying" in impact, so *mana* is ascribed to people and events of a striking nature. It resides in the tribal chieftain, in animals, plants, and rocks of a significant kind. It can be transferred from a person to an object: an arrow can be endowed with it.

Mana is a conception that floats between the spiritual and the magical. Within limits, *mana* can be manipulated for the use of men, and in primal society a technology of magical practices develops around such manipulation. The sacred, magical force represented by *mana* can be used both in a positive and negative way. Things endowed with *mana*, like the hunter's arrows, can be made effective in the pursuit of what men desire. Also, the use of *mana*-endowed objects, like amulets, enables one to ward off the dangerous assaults of maleficent powers and spirits. Insofar as *mana* can be manipulated, it is related to magic rather than to religion. Thus some scholars have believed that religion originated in magic. One need not agree with their conclusion to admit that in primal societies, and indeed even in the "higher" religions, magic and religion are mixed together.

There are two ways to understand this. First, religion in tribal societies is simply part of the culture of these societies. A member of such a society can no more choose to be religious or not than he can choose, say, to be an Algonquin or not. There is no division between the sacred and the secular, between religion and the rest of life, such as western men make today (as though religion were just a "personal" affair—a matter for private life, not relevant to professional and social life). Religion is mixed with everything else in primal people's existence. It is mingled with their whole way of mastering their environment and with their techniques of survival. Since magical manipulation of unseen forces is also part of their survival technology, magic is necessarily bound up with their religion.

Another way of understanding why magic and religion shade into one another in primal religion is that *mana* itself, as an unseen force, carries implications that closely relate to the intuition of the holy. Rudolf Otto, the German historian and philosopher of religion, in his *Idea Of The Holy* (published in 1917 in Germany), pointed to the importance in religion of what we called the "numinous" experience—the feeling of awe, dread, mystery, and fascination men experience when confronted with what is holy, uncanny, or supernatural. Otto considered the numinous, a word he derived from the Latin *numen* meaning "spirit"—the *numina* dwelt in sacred groves and other places with a sacred significance—to be the fundamental element in religious experience. The numinous experience he describes in various aspects; it may

> at times come sweeping like a gentle tide, pervading the mind with a tranquil mood of deepest worship. It may pass over into a more set and lasting attitude of the soul, continuing, as it were, thrillingly vibrant and resonant. . . . It may burst into sudden eruption up from the depths of the soul with spasms and convulsions, or lead to the strangest excitements. . . . It has its wild and demonic forms and can sink to an almost grisly horror and shuddering. It has its crude, barbaric antecedents, and early manifestations, and again it may be developed into something beautiful and pure and glorious. It may become the hushed, trembling, and speechless humility of the creature in the presence of—whom or what? In the presence of that which is a *mystery* inexpressible and above all creatures.[2]

[2] 2nd edition, translated by John W. Harvey (New York, 1950), pp. 12–13.

The numinous is, then, an experience of unseen presences that can range from the uncanny to the sublime and holy. The unseen forces surrounding primal people can be personal or impersonal. Some scholars have tried to make an impersonal dynamism the basis of primal religion—dynamism is the belief in impersonal, supernatural power that can exist in anything. Others have considered animism to be central—animism is belief in particular, more personalized, spirits that inhere in natural objects, such as trees or hearth fires. However one need not insist upon either one view to the exclusion of the other. *Mana* may operate in a fluid, dynamic way, or it may be a personal property of human or supernatural beings. Indeed, just as religious feeling normally involves a spectrum from magical fears and hopes to lofty adoration and self-surrender, so the primal world-picture includes a whole range of forces, from impersonal dynamic energies to the gods, and sometimes to a supreme God.

This range of forces can be illustrated by looking at the religious concepts of one particular group, the Australian Aborigines.

THE AUSTRALIAN ABORIGINAL EXPERIENCE

Australia is a haunting and devastatingly hot land, where nonetheless life goes on in its own ingenious ways, and even the deserts conceal a thousand opportunities for life for the hunter and gatherer. In these varied and often harsh surroundings the Aborigines have fashioned a style of life. The land became a series of tracts to be navigated, and the Aborigines developed a keen sense of the powerladen places lying along the various routes to be taken. Their religion reflects the bounds between society and the sacred forces lying around them.

Two aspects of Aboriginal religion have attracted widespread attention by scholars in the history of religions—totemism and the concept of the Dream Time. The latter has had a particularly strong effect on the thinking of Mircea Eliade, who sees the idea of a primordial time before real time as being characteristic of archaic thought throughout the world. Perhaps it is unwise to try to find a single universal characteristic in modern Aboriginal religion, even as it existed before it was touched by the whites. But there is a special force in the Aboriginal myth, as we shall see. The inhabitants of Australia fashioned a complex religio-social system which has its own characteristic message.

Totemism is a system whereby a given section within a tribal group is specially associated with a given animal species or other aspect of nature. The system is often elaborated so that there are also special individual totemic relations to particular phenomena or geographical features. The pervasive classifications of society are, as it were, read into the classifications of nature, and vice versa. The membership of a totemic group carries with it prohibitions, for example against eating members of one's own totemic species, or regarding who one might marry (e.g., outside one's section and age group). Totemism thus produced in Australian Aboriginal society (until its modern modifications under the disintegrating impact of white culture) a complicated interweaving and cross-classification in society and in the world. It is a particular variety of that ritual and social relationship to a spirit-driven environment which is characteristic of many hunting and gathering peoples.

In addition, prevalent among Aborigines is the institution of cult lodges which are each associated with a particular portion of myth, and so with the hero or place that the myth especially concerns. There is a whole network of secret lore divided not merely within a given tribe but between tribes. Often the sacred place which is the focus of a myth is in some other tribe's traditional territory. The sacred places are interconnected by a whole web of sacred paths, which reflect the routes taken by the original heroes. These heroes are celebrated in secret rites, during which members of the tribe are dressed appropriately and carrying the relevant cult symbols. In this way the events of Dream Time are projected into the here and now, and recreated. The knowledge of the old lore is not common property, but resides in the totemic lodges. Indeed in an important sense the particular mythic deposit by which you live by is not a matter of choice but is determined by your spiritual heritage. But it is your property in one sense; you belong to it, and it belongs to you. This constitutes then a complex system of mythic distribution, within an overall social framework.

This sense of a special religious destiny is connected with the consequences of the Dream Time belief. Thus, the conception of an individual is rooted in Dream Time by the idea of a *djarin* or life-essence which brings about his begetting. It is linked to a being in the Dream Time and therefore with the geographical and other associations which are projected from the Then to the Now. The Dream Time is a network of various primordial events beginning with the creation or shaping of this world, which serves as the stage upon which the first feats of the culture heroes are enacted in our imagination.

The myths and rituals are in principle secret and sacred to the relevant lodge or totemic clan that controls the performances and recitation of their stories. Thus the handing on of myth occurs within a context of initiatory knowledge. Because such lore belongs to a group it can even be exchanged with some other myth—as if religion were a collection of pieces of property.

In practice, males have a virtual monopoly of the sacred lore. Nevertheless, the female element is by no means subordinate in many myths of the Creative Era, or Dream Time. In one major cycle of stories, the primary creators of the human race are the Djannggawul, Fertility Sisters and daughters of the Sun (also conceived as female) who, together with their brother, fashioned the first humans, suitable animals and plants, and holy places for them to live in. There is even a motif in some Aboriginal thinking that men stole the original sacred rituals from the primordial female creators. This implies a protest against the latter-day spiritual situation of women in traditional Aboriginal society.

Dream Time is not just an indeterminate time of First Things. Interestingly, it connects with the destiny of each individual through the notion of the *djarin*. This is characteristic of Australian religion, and has distant affinities to the concept of karma in Indian religion. *Djarin* gives the individual, already tightly integrated into a kinship group, another means of classifying himself, and connecting his life in the here and now to the particularities of heroic life and other prototypes. The person is tied to the sacred dramas which supply an underlying pattern for the world about him—a world consisting of water holes, desert grubs, eucalyptus groves, red mountains, and rivers and valleys shimmering with heat, flies, and strange echoes in high summer.

There has been little in the way of new prophecy to interpret and reorganize Aboriginal life in the face of the crushing white presence. The whole system of the old life is breaking up. Sometimes the Aborigine is saved by the Mission station; sometimes he looks back with powerful nostalgia on a way of life that has little apparent future. A number of Aboriginal peoples have come to think that we face the imminent end of the world, some great final catastrophe. However, a new Aboriginal consciousness is also emerging, like the pan-Indian movement in the United States. Perhaps one day it will create a new synthesis. After all, modern nationalism partially incorporates totemism by stressing social connection to territory and the beauties of one's own country. Perhaps a new Australian consciousness is possible once the Aborigines have a deeper political lien upon the territories that once were theirs without question.

THE HIGH GOD

The idea of a supreme High God is quite widely held by small-scale peoples. In most, if not all, of the indigenous cultures of Africa there is belief in a supreme Spirit ruling over or informing the lesser spirits and gods. He governs natural forces, dwells on high, is inexplicable, creates souls, men, and all things. The lower spirits and deities are more familiar and intimate, yet for many Africans such a God exists and is not altogether neglected in worship and prayer.

Thus, ruling over the world which teems with divinities and sacred forces, there is—high above in the sky, but not *of* the sky—some kind of supreme Being. Among many primal peoples outside Africa a similar belief is attested.

This has led some scholars, notably Father Wilhelm Schmidt (in *The Origin of The Idea of God*, first published in 1912), to postulate a primordial monotheism at the dawn of human existence, a monotheism later overlaid by polytheistic beliefs and yet preserved in recognizable form in the religions of primal peoples. This is a reversal of the usual position of those who have been influenced by evolutionary theory, who tend to equate "later" religion with "higher" religion, and who regard monotheism as the highest development of all. The evolutionary theory implies, then, that polytheism preceded monotheism, and probably had even more rudimentary antecedents, in animism and dynamism. In any event, it is a striking fact that many primal cultures have a belief in some sort of High God, even though there very often is no specific ritual directed toward such a Being.

The relative absence of ritual for the High God has puzzled scholarly observers of religions. On the one hand, there is the evidence of belief in such a supreme Being: and on the other, there is the paucity of ritual observance. How does one reconcile this evidence?

It is a common belief in different parts of Africa that God has, as it were, "gone away." He is terribly remote from the ordinary concerns of human beings. Consequently rituals do not much concern him. A possible reason for belief in the absence of God is that men worshiped him in increasingly exalted terms, until at last he was conceived as existing way beyond the firmament— too glorious to be contaminated and implicated with earthly affairs. Nevertheless, among the tribal religions of Africa it is often believed that the great Spirit is the First Cause, the Creator of the world; and there are expressions of yearning for communion with him through prayer. Yet he is not represented in images, as are many of the other spirits (save in at least one place in Dahomey in West Africa), and there are very few temples and priests devoted to his cultus.

The existence of such conceptions among folk as far apart as the inhabitants of Tierra del Fuego and the Arctic is a significant indication that primal religion is not simply concerned with everyday transactions with the spirit world, but possesses sophisticated ideas about the beginning and creation of the world, and about a supreme architect of the world.

The perception of the numinous, we have seen, issues in belief in impersonal *mana* at the lower end of the sacred hierarchy, and in belief in a High God at the top end. *Mana* has also a special relevance to the social dimension of primal cultures. Certain people and certain actions are regarded as sacred. Chiefs and medicine men are regarded as sacred by virtue of the *mana* residing in them, which is indicated by their power and magical control. Certain acts are sacred: others are so potent and dangerous that they are to be avoided: they are *tabu*.

TABU

Tabu, or taboo, is a Polynesian expression which has come to be used by anthropologists to describe an intricate social phenomenon. Both persons and acts are *tabu* when they are so full of sacred force that a profane person must keep his proper distance. The ordinary folk in a Polynesian tribe must treat the chief with propriety and reserve, and keep their distance. Similarly, in India, the lower-caste person, or outcaste, must avoid coming close to the Brahmin. Sacred objects must be handled by sacred persons, such as priests, and should not be handled by profane folk on pain of dangerous effects. But not only are sacred things and persons *tabu:* there are also people and things which are essentially impure, and these are also *tabu* and must be avoided, or dealt with circumspectly. Usually anything involving blood is *tabu:* a woman during her period of menstruation is *tabu*, as is a newborn baby. A warrior on the eve of battle is *tabu;* a dying person and a corpse are *tabu.*

Tabu arrangements are meshed into the whole social structure of primal groups. Clearly a chieftain is sacred not solely for religious reasons: his social and political position is given protection and sanction by *tabu* arrangements. These can become extraordinarily complex. Often what is permissible for one group or clan within a society is not permissible for another.

TOTEMISM

Similar to *tabu* restrictions on the social life of a tribe are the rules pertaining to totemism. *Totem* was an Algonquin word, but as with *tabu* and *mana,* it has been taken by anthropologists for use in a wider context. Totemism is rooted in the primal people's sense of deep kinship with creatures or things other than human. A tribe may feel itself especially allied to one particular animal, like the bear, or the wolf, or snake. A plant frequently is regarded as a totem object, and occasionally, a stone or a river or a celestial body. So intimate is the relationship, the totem object is usually regarded as the great ancestor of the clan, and is honored with greatest courtesy, reverence, and ceremony. Totemism is an important feature in the life of Australian aboriginals, and has been widely observed elsewhere. Some scholars have used it as a key concept in explaining the origin and growth of religion.

Totemism has a social dimension and a ritual dimension. The social side of a clan's totemism is evidenced in certain attitudes to blood kinship and in rules about marriage and descent. Among the Australian aboriginals, marriage must be exogamous—that is, a partner must be taken from outside the totem group. On the ritual side, it is forbidden for members of a clan to kill or to eat the particular animal or plant the clan is related to, except on special ritual occasions. (There is nothing wrong with eating the totem animal of another clan.) Where the food supply is poor, as in the Australian bush, these arrangements have a sort of economic function: by preserving a species from pursuit by all members of a tribe, the danger of over-hunting leading to its extinction is reduced. Totemism thus coordinates ritual, social custom, and the gathering of the food supply.

ANCESTOR VENERATION

The solidarity of the clan is also promoted by honoring the ancestral heroes of the past. Ancestors are generally assumed to be interested in some way in the continuance of the line, so the gift of offerings to them is a means of promoting the fertility both of human beings and of their environment. It is common among primal folk to leave some personal effects and offerings with their dead, partly to help the deceased person in his next stage of existence, and partly because a person's *mana* is not limited to his body, but permeates his possessions as well. There is a strong sense of the continued presence of the dead, and it is a common belief that mediums can be possessed by departed ancestors.

The spirits of the dead are treated with a certain affectionate awe, though this can be mingled with dread and fear if the dead person had been wrongly killed or for some other reason is thought to seek vengeance on the living. Like the gods, even the good ones, the dead can be capricious. In fact, one can generalize this remark to apply to the whole spirit world around primal peoples. Nature is capricious; and life is filled with fears of doing something disastrous. The spirits are a source of strength, but they are also causes of anxiety.

SHAMANS

Many people believe there can be contact with the dead through mediums. This phenomenon is a feature of much primal religion. Other than priests, who have a defined ritual function, and medicine men, who have a special professional position in tribal society, there are those who, often because of special traits of temperament, have a gift for ecstasy through which they mediate the commands and personalities of the spirit world. They are the shamans, and shamanism—a word deriving from the Siberian word *shaman*— is a widespread feature of northern religions in Siberia, Greenland, and among the North American Eskimos. The person who becomes a shaman may have undergone some vision in early life, and is capable thereafter of inducing ecstasy. Often a potential shaman will develop his gift by disciplining himself in austere practices and lonely meditation. Shamanism is not confined to the northern peoples: it has close analogies in tropical Africa. In West Africa it is not uncommon for novices who have shown some special spiritual or spiritualistic aptitude to undergo long months of training in cult-houses, secluded from the world. Ultimately they emerge as personalities transformed, bearing new names, and imbued with authority to speak of the spirit-world from which they have, as it were, returned.

Among the Nuer in the southern Sudan there are many instances of ecstatic prophecy, which compare in certain ways to early prophecy in the Bible.

But such possession by God, or by ancestral spirits, or by some particular god, is different in character from the so-called possession by evil spirits which bring sickness and death upon a person. The two forms of possession are clearly distinct in tribal society: the latter situation is one which needs treatment by a qualified medicine man or witch doctor. (This last term is misleading, in view of the European notion of witchcraft—African witch doctors are not, by and large, evil sorcerers, but practitioners of a sort of traditional and often psychologically effective medicine.)

In *African Ideas of God,* edited by Edwin Smith (Edinburgh House Press, 1950), there appears the following scheme to outline the beliefs of many primal peoples: the shape of their view of the world, including its important invisible aspect, can be represented by a triangle. At the top comes a High God or Creator Spirit. Along one side are arranged the lesser gods, divinities, spirits; along the other, the ancestral spirits. And along the base of the triangle lies the range of magical beliefs and practices which folk add to common sense in order to cope with their environment. Sometimes one side of the triangle will loom large, sometimes another. As a rough approximation to the situation of many small-scale peoples, the picture is useful.

PATTERNS OF MYTH

There is a vast body of mythological stories through which primal peoples seek to interpret the world and themselves. These range from creation legends to explain how the earth came into existence, to stories which explain features of daily ritual.

In his analysis of African mythology in *The Primal Vision*,[3] John Taylor has shown that there are certain recurrent patterns in the numerous myths of culturally independent peoples in tropical Africa. An important form of myth is that which seeks to explain why God is so remote—for, as we have seen, there is a widespread conviction that though the Great Spirit exists, he no longer much concerns himself with human affairs. One version of the story is that the sky, where God dwells, was once much nearer. So near was it that the sky could be touched. But one day some women took bits of the sky to cook in the soup, and God became angry and retired to his present distance.

Such a myth. though naive, rests upon an intuition that is central to the numinous experience of a holy Being, especially when connected with moral feeling. God as a holy Being stands over against man; his exalted nature is symbolized by his distance. This distance is felt to be linked with men's incapacity for perfection. So strongly does the African feel the distance that he

[3] Philadelphia: Fortress Press, 1964.

turns to lesser and more familiar spirits to help him with his daily concerns and worries.

Among many peoples there are similar myths about the anger of God. There are various versions of the idea that men were destined for immortality but lost their immunity to death because they made God angry, through mischance or some evil act.

Many peoples, as far apart as the Eskimos, Central Americans, and Oceanians have myths of a great flood. The complexity of the mythological tradition of primal peoples has by no means been fully explored; the scholar finds it difficult even to suggest the richness and strangeness of the many myths in any kind of summary. Suffice it to say that among primal peoples there has developed a tendency to interpret experience in terms of stories: the stories express an intuitive apprehension of the sacred world, and also exhibit something of the surrealistic quality of dreams. The symbolism of such myths requires considerable investigation and a detailed sympathy for and understanding of the cultural heritage of those who believe and retell them.

Today the world of tribal and primal religion is beginning to crumble under the impact of modern technology and social change. The African who moves into the city gradually loses his concern for ancestors, and the hunting rituals of the Ainu and the Eskimo begin to disappear when new forms of settled, agricultural life are opened to them, or imposed upon them. The American Indian religions have changed as a result of the decimation of the tribes and the impact of their heavy defeats at the hands of the white man. Later, we shall see that the reaction of tribal religions to these puzzling, often tragic events has given rise to new cults, which sometimes incorporate Christian elements, and which attempt to recreate traditional values in a new context or to combat social diseases which have flowed from the overwhelming and indiscriminate influx of the West.

PREHISTORIC BELIEFS

So far we have been discussing general features of primal religion. Now let us turn to man's prehistoric beliefs, insofar as these can be inferred from rather inadequate archeological remains. Perhaps an examination of the prehistoric evidence will enable us to evaluate the various theories of the origin of religion.

Homo sapiens is a branch of the family of hominids who may have first appeared on the earth some 600,000 years ago or earlier, and is possibly in line of direct succession from Neanderthal man, who flourished around 100,000 to 50,000 years back (though Neanderthal man may well be a separate offshoot from the stem from which *homo sapiens* has sprung).

It is impossible to say, in regard to the earliest hominids, whether they had any religious apprehension or ritual. However there is archeological evidence that some Neanderthal communities practiced interment of their dead, and this quite possibly had a ritual and mythological significance. At one site the remains of adults and children have been found with flint implements placed near their hands. Elsewhere there is evidence of the cult of skulls. At Monte Circeo in Italy, a skull surrounded by a ring of stones was unearthed, and in Bavaria a collection of skulls was discovered that had been immersed in red ochre (a color used at a later period in cave paintings).

Thus even before the emergence of *homo sapiens* proper, there is evidence of religious belief, though it would be hazardous to attempt to reconstruct its nature.

In the late Paleolithic era, after the beginnings of the human race as we know it today, archeological evidence of ritual practices become more extensive. There are many remains of burial sites, often splashed with red ochre: this we will consider in a moment. First, however, let us turn to the most spectacular archeological discoveries of this period, which dated from about 50,000 to 10,000 B.C.; that of the prehistoric paintings which decorate the walls of certain caves in France and Spain, and which are found as far east as the Ural mountains.

These amazing paintings have high artistic value, but it would probably be wrong to suppose that artistry was the main impulse of their creators. Their chief function was no doubt magical. Some of these pictures portray, with extraordinary realism, deer, bison, horses, rhinoceros, and other animals—mostly animals important as sources of food. For instance in the caves at Altamira, in Spain, there is a painting of a bison most magnificent in execution. The paintings quite probably had to do with hunting ritual, especially as many of these beasts have lances and arrows planted in their sides. It would seem that here is evidence of sympathetic magic: by drawing the animals successfully hunted, they would in fact be successfully hunted—possibly this was the rationale of this tremendous art.

More important, however, for the student of religion are certain details of these paintings. Here and there within the paintings there are found figures that appear to be human beings disguised as animals. The most spectacular of these is the so-called "Dancing Sorcerer" in the cave of the Trois Frères at Ariège. There has been some dispute among scholars about the interpretation of this detail of the painting, and about the sketches and reproductions of it first given to the world at large. Apparently the figure is of a sorcerer, who has a more or less human face but who has wolf ears, the claws of a lion, the tail of a horse, and the antlers of a stag. Also, his eyes have an owlish aspect. Some scholars think this figure represents a priest whose attire symbolizes the bond between the hunter and his supply of living food and whose ritual in some way promotes the increase of the quarry.

Naturally, the discovery of the Dancing Sorcerer has raised questions as to whether totemism was a feature of paleolithic society. As there is no evidence of the social dimension of the society which produced these paintings, however, one can say no more than that totemism is suggested by this figure but not at all proved by it. Other interpretations might be placed upon the figure of the Dancing Sorcerer.

Freud's Totem and Taboo

It is appropriate here to mention a very widely known theory about the totemic origins of religion. It is that of Sigmund Freud, and was expressed principally in his *Totem and Taboo,* published in 1912–1913 (the English translation appeared in 1918). Freud attempted to combine a psychoanalytical approach to religion with a current theory of totemism. According to this theory, the sacrifice of an animal, which is a very widespread phenomenon and occurs in all sort of cultures, originates from a totemic feast, in which the solidarity of the clan with its totem animal is affirmed and expressed. Since also there is associated with totemism a typical social arrangement, namely that of exogamy, Freud wished to give a psychological explanation of the relation between sacrifice and marriage outside of the clan.

To do so, he adopted a speculative account of the earliest form of human society—he proposed that originally humans banded together in small hordes, consisting of a male, a number of females who were his wives, and the offspring of this polygamous arrangement. According to Freud's psychoanalytical theory, a male child early in life has sexual desires toward his mother, and consequently has ambivalent feelings about his father. Though the father is protective, so that the child to this extent loves him, the child is also jealous of his father because of his relationship to the mother. This hatred of the father gave Freud the idea that the first group of human offspring banded together to kill the father. After the murder, they ate him in a ritual meal thereby taking into themselves the substance of the father's hated power. Yet the guilt occasioned by this act induced them to forbid to themselves the possible fruits of the father's removal. A ban was put upon incest and upon marriage within the clan, and a symbolic animal sacrifice was substituted for the ritual killing of a human being. The animal sacrificed was, however, normally *tabu* to members of the clan. Hence the social arrangements of totemism. Furthermore, God as a father figure is regarded by Freud as a projection, and represents the physical, human father who is both respected and rejected.

Needless to say, Freud's theory is extremely speculative. There is no evidence of the primeval murder he postulates. It is not confirmed, and could never be confirmed, that men in the earliest times banded together in polygamous groups. Totemism is not a universal phenomenon among primal peoples. Sacrifices are not plausibly interpreted as totemic, and the offerings of first-fruits do not involve a sacral communion. In brief, as a theory of the genesis of religion, Freud's account is hardly credible.

Nevertheless, the notion of the Oedipus complex is an extremely important one, and can in certain circumstances illuminate the relationship between an individual and God conceived as a father figure. But the fact that men may have ambivalent and guilty attitudes toward God because of certain psychological events in their early childhood does not entail that such psychological forces explain men's belief in, and experience of, God.

Consider a parallel case. Some religions conceive of God as King or Lord or Emperor, and transfer the kind of obedience the earthly king demands to the heavenly one. Quite obviously, the ritual language here has been affected by the political and social arrangement typical of the time or location wherein the religion developed. Nowadays, of course, there are few kings and emperors. In England, for instance, the monarchy is constitutional and politically powerless. Thus the epithets "Lord" and "King" do not convey to people today what the "kingship" of Christ meant to those living in apostolic times. But we need not suppose that because certain attitudes to God may have been affected by political and social facts (that may be now obsolete), they originate from or depend upon the latter.

Paleolithic Art

To return to prehistoric paintings. The painting of the Dancing Sorcerer and other pictures which depict human figures either possessed of animal attributes or wearing animal masks present us with a puzzle that the numerous and often splendid paintings of animals do not. It is fairly clear that hunting magic was an important motive for the animal drawings. But it can scarcely be supposed that the human figures dressed up as animals are themselves the objects of the chase. It is true that there are indications that war magic was practiced, but the Dancing Sorcerer and other such figures are probably not part of this phenomenon. It is quite possible that here we have represented a genuinely mythological personage, a dancing god who is lord of the beasts. If this is so, it would be an indication that Paleolithic man was concerned with much more than the magical technology which helped him to gain his sustenance, and that tales of God and the gods formed part of the fabric of his culture.

It is worth noting too that the reason why it took so long for these cave paintings to be discovered in modern times was that they are nearly all in places to which access has been difficult, concealed, and sometimes dangerous. In the depths of the mountains and in the bowels of the earth, early people somehow contrived these remarkable paintings and statues, using the weak light of primitive lamps. The inaccessibility of the cave paintings is an added sign of their sacred significance, though we cannot guess at the forms of ritual which may have been used there. Nor can we know what early people experienced of the divine figures (if they were such) which they symbolized in painting.

Another interesting feature of Paleolithic art is that attention is confined to men and animals, or to mythological figures compounded out of men and animals. We cannot tell, on the basis of these pictures, what men's attitudes were to the natural world around them—the rivers, mountains, sun, moon, plants, and trees. However, it is possible that there was a cult of a great Mother, associated with the earth and with fertility—a goddess who was destined to loom large in the religious world of the ancient Mediterranean and Near East, and whose power was closely connected with vegetation. The evidence, however, of such a cult is ambiguous.

What we do have from Paleolithic times is a numerous collection of stone figurines or statuettes, representing nude women with large breasts and bodies, sometimes indicating pregnancy. The sexual organs are often accentuated, so that there is a fair presumption that in some way the statuettes were concerned with the mystery of reproduction and birth. Among the paintings in one cave in Cogul, Spain, it is possible to make out a group of nine women, wearing skirts, and a tenth figure may represent a phallic male. In this case, the picture would represent some kind of fertility ritual directed toward a male deity.

By and large, however, it is the female role in human fertility that was emphasized by early folk, so far as can be seen. Whether it is right to conclude that the exaggeratedly female (and larged faceless) figurines represented a mother goddess is an open question; but in view of the fact that such a deity was found in the earliest times in the ancient world to which we have more direct historical access, and that such beliefs are not created overnight, it would be not unreasonable to ascribe some such cult to early prehistoric people.

Paleolithic Burial Remains

If the beginning of life is a mystery, so its termination. We have already seen that even Neanderthal man practiced some kind of funeral ritual. Three features of Paleolithic burial customs are especially significant.

First, at a number of sites red ochre was sprinkled on the corpses. There is little doubt that for prehistoric man, as for Australian aboriginals today, this powder symbolized blood and hence life. Its frequent use suggests that early

1. *Rock painting from Zimbabwe, Southern Africa, showing a tradition of killing the king as a sacrifice, releasing his spiritual energies. The figure at the top represents the spirit released from the sacrifice. The ritual stretches to include ancestral figures beyond the wavy lines in the other world, on the lower right. (Courtesy of the Frobenius-Institut, Frankfurt am Main.)*

2. *Indus civilization figurine.*
(Courtesy of the Museum of
Fine Arts, Boston.)

3. *Egyptian bird deity (ca.*
4000–35000 B.C.). (Courtesy of
The Brooklyn Museum,
Museum Collection Fund.)

4. *Great bathing tank at Mohenjo-daro, Pakistan. (Courtesy of Information Division, Pakistan*
Mission to the U.N.)

5. *The volcanic crater of Kilauea in Hawaii is one of those points where gods reveal themselves: fearfully here the fire god role is evident. (Courtesy of The Bishop Museum, Hawaii.)*

6. *Dancers of the Dogon people in Mali in ceremonial dress. (Courtesy of the United Nations.)*

7. *Boyo Ancestor Figure, Africa.*
(Courtesy of The Metropolitan
Museum of Art, The Michael C.
Rockefeller Memorial Collection,
Gift of Nelson A. Rockefeller,
1978.)

8. *Senufo Rhythm Pounder, Ivory*
Coast. (Courtesy of The
Metropolitan Museum of Art, The
Michael C. Rockefeller Memorial
Collection, Gift of Nelson A.
Rockefeller, 1978.)

men desired to bring about, or to depict, the continued life of those who had died.

Second, in some graves there are necklaces, implements, and other offerings interred with the skeleton, and this again indicates that the dead were believed to live on in some way. Or, it may have been thought that the *mana* of the deceased person extended to his possessions which were, so to say, an extension of himself, and which therefore must be buried.

Third, some corpses have been found bent into a huddled-up position before interment. This means that the dead must have been trussed up quickly after death, for otherwise *rigor mortis* would prevent this operation. It may be that the position, which corresponds to that of a child in the womb, symbolizes a continuance of existence through being born again, into this world or another. Alternatively, and perhaps more probably, it may be that the trussing was a means of securing the corpse, so that it could not move around to trouble the living. Either explanation suggests that early men had both respect for and fear of the departed. This is consistent with contemporary evidence from tribal religions.

Elsewhere, separate human skulls have been discovered, and sometimes· these have been fashioned into cups. The latter phenomenon has suggestive parallels among contemporary primal religions: it may well be that early man, like his descendants of a much later period, believed that through drinking from the skull of a notable person—a mighty warrior or formidable foe—one could acquire the substance of his power. The cult of skulls extended beyond the human: bear skulls have been found at a site in Switzerland, and they are oriented in one direction. It is quite possible that these were an offering to a deity—a further clue to early man's belief in God or gods.

The funerary cult of prehistoric people shows that there was some sort of belief in an afterlife. In view of oldest beliefs in different parts of the world since the earliest historical times, it is possible to hazard the guess that similar beliefs extend quite far back into prehistory. For example, the cult of ancestors, found in China and elsewhere in the earliest period known to us, may have been found among the prehistoric peoples with whom we are now dealing. The care lavished on some of the interments is suggestive of such an interpretation.

It may be too that some idea of reincarnation motivated our ancient forebears, though there is no direct evidence of this, except possibly trussing up the dead as a preparation for rebirth. But in any event it would be rash to suppose that a single set of beliefs about the dead was held by all the farflung groups of prehistory whose remains have come down to us.

We can only make inferences about the various dimensions of prehistoric religion, and already we have speculated about the ritual of early man. Can we say anything about his ethical insights? Again, we can do no more than make a rather shaky inference from what is found among preliterate folk in the contemporary world.

First, primal societies tend to be "closed" societies—that is, they are ruled essentially by customs and tabus. No small-scale groups have approximated a stage of development comparable to that of ancient Athens, where all sorts of ethical rules were called into question and examined in a rational and critical manner. Doubtless this was also true of prehistoric folk. Moreover, in tribal religion it often occurs that "mankind" is identified with the particular tribe, so that people outside the tribal relationship are not necessarily accorded the same rights and privileges due a member of the group. If prehistoric men indulged in head-hunting, as the skull evidence cited earlier might lead us to suppose, then it is possible that there were mutually warring groups, and that social obligation was strictly tribal and confined in character. And if the evidence of prehistoric totemism is valid, then we can be fairly sure that social custom was elaborate and governed by a host of tabus.

Second, if we assume that there genuinely was belief in a High God, which admittedly is debatable, we could infer that he was somehow connected with early people's understanding of moral behavior. For a contemporary example of this connection, consider the Andaman Islanders in the Bay of Bengal who believe that the supreme Spirit built a bridge from this world to the next world, and that the rainbow is the bridge. They imagine the next world to be a place where the virtuous prosper and where there is no birth or death. Their belief in immortality is linked to ethical prescriptions for this world: thus the idea of God as judge of men's moral behavior is implicit in their religion. Whether such a developed view of the relation between the good life and the afterlife was characteristic of prehistoric man is hard to say; it is worth remembering throughout this discussion that the modern primal religion and culture may have changed and developed quite a lot over the last few thousand years. Closed societies are not necessarily static ones.

THEORIES ABOUT THE GENESIS OF RELIGION

Let us now turn attention to other theories of the genesis of religion. We have already discussed Freud's theory of totemic origin. How do other theories stand up to the evidence?

After Charles Darwin published *The Origin of Species* in 1859, scholars and anthropologists began to apply the notion of evolution to religion. They envisaged a series of stages of religious development culminating in whatever was taken to be the highest form of faith—usually monotheism was so conceived.

E. B. Tylor

The anthropologist E. B. Tylor, in his book *Primitive Culture* (published in 1871), advanced the theory that the beginnings of religion lie in animism—the belief that there are spirits that can exist independently of material things, but which inform them. According to the theory, primal people formed their notion of the soul from their own experience of dreams, where people appear in a mysterious and immaterial fashion; from their experience of death, where seemingly the lifeforce departs from the body; from visions and ecstasy, where one is temporarily transported (so it seems) out of one's body. Having got the notion of a soul distinct from the body, primal people then projected the idea of the soul on to the animals and things which they perceived in their environment. The development of ancestor worship, according to Tylor's theory, gave people the idea that departed spirits could exist permanently in a bodiless state, and could take possession of living people at will. This belief then generated belief in spirits whose activities explained natural events and phenomena—gods who ruled the rain, the sky, fire, and so on. This transition to polytheism is ultimately followed by a further transition to monotheism, where the powers of the many gods are now ascribed to a single deity.

Other evolutionary theories which give a picture of people's religious development have different points of departure: Herbert Spencer, the English philosopher, thought that ancestor worship was the first stage; Sir James Frazer viewed magic as the original manifestation. But we can take Tylor's theory as the most detailed and typical of the evolutionary theories.

One feature of the evolutionary theories is that they make primal folk very logical in their approach to religious belief. They are supposed to operate according to a kind of natural theology, in which they first infer the existence of a soul, then infer that natural objects also have souls, and then connect up different phenomena, such as rain, or fire, in order to ascribe them to a single deity working behind and through them. The theory also presupposes that a sharp distinction between spirit and matter can be drawn in primal thinking. But we have seen in contemporary preliterate cultures that the personal and impersonal shade off into one another and that the visible and the invisible are inextricably interwoven. Moreover, the use of red ochre in primitive burials to symbolize blood and life suggests that prehistoric men did not think simply in terms of an invisible and immaterial soul-force.

However, it is perfectly true that the earliest human remains indicate a cult of the dead, while the cave paintings which hint at mythological beliefs about divine beings must be dated later; and this is consistent with the view that ancestor worship precedes polytheism. But the evidence is not at all conclusive, simply because it is more likely that modern archeologists will find much more evidence of interment than of other features of religious belief—skulls and bones survive a long, long time, while the language and thoughts of the earliest men are lost forever.

Father Wilhelm Schmidt

We have seen that one writer, Father Wilhelm Schmidt, has argued strongly for a very different, and non-evolutionary, sequence—namely, that first there was belief in a single High God and that this primitive monotheism came to be overlaid by animistic, polytheistic, and other elements. Certainly, the evidence from contemporary primal religions is not very favorable to Tylor's theory, though it is equally inconclusive in regard to Schmidt's monotheism postulated on the basis that belief in a High God is so widespread among primitives.

If there was indeed belief in a High God among prehistoric men, it is probable that there were legends concerning the origin of the world or of the human race. Such myths, as we have seen, are typical of preliterate folk of the present era. Perhaps as man learned to fashion statuettes and statues of animals out of clay and to create the masterly paintings which are found in the caves of Lascaux and elsewhere, he conceived the idea that a great God had similarly fashioned the world. If so, there might have been in prehistoric thought a foretaste of the famous Egyptian, Jewish, and other narratives of the creation. But about this, as about so many things concerned with human origins, we shall probably never be in a position to know.

Sir James Frazer

In regard to the origin of religion, it is useful to mention again the theory discussed earlier, that religion grows out of magic. In the second edition of his famous *The Golden Bough,* published in 1900, Sir James Frazer made a distinction between magic and religion which can be stated briefly as follows. On the one hand, man believes that the world is in some degree governed by personal beings, or by one personal Being; it is possible to secure the help and favor of such deities by sacrifice, prayer, and other religious works. The substance of the religious belief, then, is that men have some kind of relationship to personal gods. On the other hand, there are impersonal forces at work in nature. Man, in the absence of a scientific technology, seeks to control these and bend them to his own purposes by the use of magic. Thus magic has relations with the impersonal, and is the forerunner of science. Nevertheless, on evolutionary grounds, Frazer placed magic before religion in time, as the first phase of men's mental development. The crude simplicities of magic are somehow at a "lower" intellectual level than belief in personal gods, and being lower they ought (according to the evolutionary thought then fashionable) to have come earlier.

Man, finding that magic does not after all help him deal effectively with his environment, turned to a religious conception of the world and sought to find security through ritual rather than through magic. In this way, according to Frazer's theory, religion develops out of a prior phase of magic.

The Experience of a Holy Environment

We have seen that magic and religion shade into one another in primal society, and indeed in so-called "advanced" religions there are often magical elements woven into the fabric of traditional belief. Frazer was quite right to point to such a connection between religious dynamism and magical technology. However, it is a crude over-simplification to think that religious rites, attitudes, and beliefs were "thought up" to take the place of a magic that had proven itself relatively bankrupt. As with Tylor's animistic theory, there is too much rationalism in the Frazer idea. If indeed early men were strongly empirical and experimental in their approach to magic, then they would surely also have recognized that prayers to the rain god were no more reliable than magic as a means of producing rain.

Moreover, Frazer's theory neglects the perception of the numinous to which we referred earlier. Religion, and man's relationship to deities, are not simply means to certain ends. They are not simply instruments whereby men promote the solidarity of the tribe and the security and fertility of the food supply. It is true that these last concerns are quite obviously of the greatest importance to people struggling in a difficult environment, and it would be surprising if these concerns did not appear in a fairly central way in religious rituals and beliefs. But also men have seen the world as transfused with significances of a different order.

For the primal person, as indeed for many folk who have a strong religious sense, the world is not just a beautiful or ugly place, a difficult or easy habitat, a place for living in: they have also seen it as an awe-inspiring, sacred, holy environment, in which the forces of the unseen shine through the visible environment and in which terror and love, hate and favor, the ghostly and the demonic, the spirit-world and the shining glory of deities are perceptible to the inward eye. It is a world of strangeness, it is uncanny, but it is also familiar and peopled with beings not totally dissimilar from ourselves. In brief, the world provides the material for religious experience as well as for ordinary perception and technological manipulation. It is thus useless to attempt to derive religious beliefs and practices from magic or from social needs. These things color religion, but they do not fully account for it.

Two further points about magic are worth making. First, though magic and religion have coexisted through a great part of the religious history of mankind, magic has tended to transform itself and to become science. Thus alchemy, which had many magical elements, became transformed into scientific chemistry, and astrology was replaced by astronomy. This suggests that the two realms of human endeavor are quite distinct and that religion can finally divorce itself from magical practices.

Second, we have more than once referred to magic as a kind of primitive technology. But it should not be supposed that a culture in which magical ideas and techniques flourish is thoroughly incompetent in dealing with the environment. The common sense of primal people and their capacity to fashion and to use tools is in constant evidence in the primal tribes of today; doubtless the same was true of early prehistoric men. The bushmen of the Kalahari, for instance, display the greatest sagacity, patience, and ingenuity in hunting giraffes—first tracking the quarry, then weakening it with poisoned arrows, and trailing the slowly failing animal until it can be finally dispatched with safety. The Pacific islanders cultivate their gardens with great acumen even if they also use magical spells. The painters of Lascaux and the other caves had acquired a high order of artistic expertise even if their motives for painting were of a magical nature. It is not to be thought, then, that the use of magic is supposed to replace native intelligence or skill. Primal folks' capacity to deal with the environment and their magical attitudes are not separate areas of their consciousness. There is a continuum between knowing how to fashion a flint implement and knowing what spell or incantation to utter.

The Myth of the Golden Age

One final consideration about the earliest religious experience. Throughout time, people have believed a number of myths about their primeval ancestors. One of the most persistent ideas is that there was once, at the beginning of time, a Golden Age when man lived in peace and innocence, that something happened to destroy this blissful existence, and that ever since man has lived in misery and suffering. The myth of the Noble Savage depends on such a conception.

Perhaps the most familiar of all the Golden Age stories is that found in the Genesis account of Adam and Eve in the Garden of Eden. Does such a story shed any light on the real experience of early men? Certainly Father Schmidt's thesis that there was an original monotheism—though his theory is unproven and open to many objections—would point to a sense in which the Eden myth might be considered "true." Also the notion that people were once upon a time in right relationship with the world and with God, but now no longer are, reflects a common religious experience, and expresses symbolically the sentiment that people remain disobedient to a God who has mysteriously become remote—as in the African legends we described earlier.

The seventeenth-century English philosopher, Thomas Hobbes, held a view of man's earliest antecedents exactly opposite the Golden Age theory or the Noble Savage idea. He believed the life of early man was nasty, brutish, and short.

With more scientific, though still meager, evidence at our disposal, we can say that neither the Noble Savage nor the savage brute picture of early man is close to the mark. Early men were a prey to disease and calamity; their implements were not always adequate for the tasks of food-gathering necessary for their sustenance; their shelters were rudimentary; their wars were cruel and bitter. But at the same time they were certainly not brutes and life was not short for all. Their religious and magical artistry was at times superb, reflecting a world transfused with the glowing, harsh poetry of the numinous. Just as there are values to be discovered in the (to the Westerner) superficially unattractive life of primal peoples, so there must have been great values and satisfactions, and obviously there were extraordinary achievements, in the life of Paleolithic societies.

But we shall never know, on purely scientific and historical grounds, what the emergence of human consciousness was really like. The evidence is gone forever.

Neither can we know how people first experienced the holy. It may have been that humans, becoming aware of themselves through the power of speech and in discovering their capacity to change the world, however slightly, also felt a sense of rupture from the natural world about them—an alienation from the cosmos of which they formed a part. The paintings and carvings of animals testify in a vivid way to the manner in which men conceived themselves as having a close affinity to the animal world; but also men must have become aware, perhaps painfully, that mankind is different, that we men are not merely immersed in nature, like the bison bindly lumbering across the plain, but are also reflective and mysteriously set apart. Here was a rupture with the innocence of unselfconsciousness, an alienation resulting from the emergence of a self-aware humanity.

The prehistoric age, then, so far as we can tell from the scanty remains, was neither golden nor brutish. The religion, or religions, was, or were, perhaps a good deal more sophisticated and penetrating than archeology allows us to say. Perhaps from earliest time there has been a mixture of attitudes among people and a complicated fabric of beliefs incorporating elements which are singled out in the different theories. It well may be that *mana*, magic, personal spirits, a High God, and so forth have figured in our religion since the beginning of human consciousness and culture.

That this religion was directed toward the crucial themes of birth, death, and survival—this we know. That neat theories about the pattern of religious evolution are hazardous—this we know too.

RELIGIONS OF AFRICA

Chapter 3

THE AFRICAN EXPERIENCE

THE HUMAN GEOGRAPHY OF AFRICA

THE CONTINENT of Africa is both the origin and the receiver of a large number of cultures. Some Westerners tend to think of it as new, only discovered lately, as if Africa had not as long a history as any other great continent. Indeed it may have the longest, for perhaps man had his prime origin in East Africa, in the Olduvai Gorge and elsewhere. The main difficulty in piecing together African history is the absence of enough written records, for many of her cultures were not literate until recent times; and though oral tradition is often relatively good, it does not take us back reliably more than a century or two.

But let us look first at the human geography of the continent, which can be carved up into several bands. Across the north are the countries of the Maghreb and the Islamic world as far as Egypt—a world built upon the ruins and elements of a preceding classical and then Christian civilization. Once this was the granary for Europe; it is now somewhat dry, but it does produce grapes and fruits and that new treasure of the soil, oil. To the south is the next band, a set of increasingly desert-like areas, from the Sahara eastward to the Sudan (which is refreshed, however, by the Nile) and southward to Lake Chad, survivor of what was once the center of a well-watered region—the Sahara once abounded with game. It was fertile, too, in religious symbolism, for the ancient hunters of 8000 B.C. and onward began to shape their ritual rock paintings, reminiscent of those of prehistoric France. To the east lie mountainous and cryptic Ethiopia, so often the focus of men's later hopes of an African destiny, and the dry regions along the torrid Red Sea. The next band that we can place across Africa ranges from the tropical parts of the west down toward the less rainy, but still promising, lands of East Africa below Somalia—rich in game and backed by the sultry forests of the Congo and Central Africa. And next there is the rather arid, but sporadically mountainous, region of South Africa, productive of grapes, grain, gold, and diamonds in different areas—the latest area of conquest by the blacks and about the earliest by the whites. Offshore to the east lies Madagascar, the westernmost achievement of the Polynesians, who settled there after long voyages from the Pacific and the fringes of the Indian Ocean.

The old center of gravity for black Africans was to the northwest, in our second band. From there it seems they spread in varying ways into Central and finally South Africa. From Chad they spread outward, under pressure from the drying ecology of the Sahara, no longer so productive of the food of animals to hunt. To this day there are African peoples who subsist primarily on hunting, but with the impact of the West and of the colonial condition and later post-colonial independence such economies, like that of the Kalahari bushmen, have been increasingly open to cash economy and other changes. There is scarcely now a people in the world which has not been affected deeply by cultural contact. But perhaps the two most important ways of life in Africa have been the settled agriculture of tropical West Africa, stretching south into Zaire, and the pastoral existence of the peoples of the east, such as the Masai and the Dinka. Largely, however, it is a question of emphasis—a people majors in food-growing and minors in domestic animals, or majors in cattle and goats and minors in crops.

Black Africa is, of course, a rich mosaic of cultures and types of folk, from the Pygmies of the rain forest to the kingdoms of Benin and West Africa and the partly nomadic Somalis of the east. The vast variety of racial and cultural types has been augmented by various incursions and influences—the spread of Egyptian values south along the Nile in ancient times, the powerful spread of Islam along the northern band, and subsequently by trade routes across the Sahara into West Africa and by sea along the east coast to Zanzibar and beyond, and then the great European and Christian incursions, mainly from the sea. The Portuguese and Spaniards pioneered the route down the west coast; the Dutch settled at the Cape; the British began the most decisive carve-up of Africa in the colonialist period; followed by the French, powerful from Dakar to Chad; the Belgians in the Congo; the Germans in Tanganyika and the southwest; the Portuguese consolidating their more ancient gains; and the Italians, late in Somalia and even later in Ethiopia, invading to keep up with the new imperial image of the Fascist ideology.

Basically Africa came under Western rule in the late nineteenth century—the period of the Ashanti wars, the Zulu wars, the building of railroads north from the Cape in the style of Rhodes' dream, the dispute between the Afrikaaners and the more arrogant British, the occupation of Madagascar by the French, and so forth. This imposed a new order upon Africa and generated a new way of dividing it, not so much by the geographical bands described earlier, but more by traditions of colonial administration. Thus the modern states of Africa are with few exceptions based upon the rather arbitrary and sometimes careless frontiers of colonial divisions evolved from the nineteenth-century experience. In addition it should be noted that some areas became increasingly white, notably Zimbabwe and of course South Africa, expanding their white population to dominate the blacks and importing quite a number of Indians and other folk to run some services. Thus the nineteenth century determined the present shape of Africa.

From a religious perspective, Africa is a mixture of indigenous sub-Saharan cults, Christianity, and Islam. The traditional religions are innumerable and varied. Even Islam has undergone some transformations in Africa, for instance in Somalia. Christianity came in pluralistically, for the style and intentions of missions were varied. But in addition a host of new religious movements, mostly bearing some kind of Christian imprint (if only because they represent responses to the alien values of the West), has sprung forth from the indigenous soils. They represent a mediation between older societies, often small-scale, and the impressive power of European culture and technology.

This frontier between white and older black values is alive with creative and extravagant new movements. It represents one of the most significant new developments in world culture and echoes similar responses along cultural frontiers —one thinks of the T'ai P'ing Rebellion in China, the Ghost Dance and Peyotism of American Indians, the Cao Dai Sect in Vietnam, and so on. Of all this there will be more in the final chapter, where we shall try to discern some of the emerging patterns of the religious future.

One other factor in fairly recent history needs mentioning. The slave trade reached deep into Africa, as far as the Nile, and involved great dislocations of tribal life in some areas. It also profited from and to some extent stimulated warfare, so that the European powers looked beyond the fires and miseries of interethnic warfare to greater conquest. The slave trade exported suffering, but also African values, to the New World—to Brazil, the Caribbean, and above all America. If for the most part the African slaves became rather Christianized, they nevertheless represented a new dimension in African consciousness and contributed to the reassertion of African values on the continent itself, with some moves toward liberation and new forms of Christianity coming from the New World to the old black world.

Because black African religion is such an incredible mosaic, it is not easy to describe historically: it is many histories. Perhaps the best method is to look at certain concrete situations, having analyzed some of the major themes in traditional African religion. Since the new religious sects springing up alongside and inside Christianity are important, I shall choose an example of one such and hope also to look at all of them thematically. Regarding Islam I shall say less, for there is a separate chapter devoted to that faith. But the main treatment must be of indigenous black religions of that area from the Sahara into South Africa and from the west to the east.

As for the main themes, they, too, are necessarily highly selective, but it seems reasonable to pick out the ideas of God and lesser spirits, ancestors, rites of passage, special experiences, and such activities as divination and so-called magic.

(The distinctions among religion, magic, and common sense are hard to make: if a man crosses himself as a plane takes off, it is for him a religious act; but it also reassures him as being perhaps effective and so may verge on the magical; while he is not doing anything to endanger the flight, and that is common sense.)

THE HIGH GOD AND OTHER SPIRITS

As we have already noted, the High God is a common theme in small-scale societies of relatively primitive technology. The earlier assumption in the Victorian West that because men evolved one might expect "primitive" folk to be animists or perhaps polytheists, rather than having achieved the "higher" state of monotheism or even (according to some a still "higher" state) atheism, has rather little basis in the evidence. Most societies are more complex than such easy categories. In fact many religions in Africa involve belief in a supreme God, though typically there are lesser beings consulted and worshipped by ordinary folk— beings such as spirits and ancestors. It is indeed a common theme that the High God withdraws from contact with men, either because they have offended him or more simply because their daily concerns are too unimportant. There is a Mende myth that the first man and woman used to ask God frequently for things, which he generously provided. But when they began to pester him he moved to heaven to get away. Before he left, however, he made an agreement with them, leaving them a fowl as a sign of the pact; they on their part were to refrain from having an evil disposition toward each other. If, however, they did do evil, they were to call God and he would come and reclaim the fowl. In brief, God was available for the expiation of evil. He had not deserted us.

The exalted nature of God is part of the explanation for the need to have contact with lesser, more immediate spirits. (We shall come later to a description of some of these.) It also is connected with the idea of the "fall" of man, for in many of the myths man offends the High God and by consequence the gulf between God and man is deepened. Thus among the Chagga it is related that in the beginning God used to visit the first couple every morning and evening and would look after their welfare. He provided them with yams, bananas, and potatoes. But he forbade them to eat a certain special sort of yam. A stranger came to visit the first man and tricked him into eating the forbidden food. Straightaway sickness broke out in the family. But God promised the first man that when he got old he would shed his body and be rejuvenated, like a snake shedding its skin—but he had to do it in secret. Unhappily, when the time came the man's granddaughter was coming back from fetching water and saw him when he was only halfway through the process. So he died, and this was how death came into the world. There are many variants of this theme illustrating ways in which traditional African beliefs have an affinity to the story of the Garden of Eden (this being one of the many reasons for the grip which the Old Testament ha.. upon African Christianity).

Generally speaking God is seen as creator, and even though he may be figured as being distant, many African religions see him also as near. This paradox simply means that he is both exalted and at the same time present everywhere—a dual conception found in the theistic religions.

But as we have noted, the affairs of everyday life drive men toward lesser spirits and forces. Among the Nupe in Nigeria, for example, there are various forces implicit in phenomena and ritual actions. Thus one solution is to look upon the lesser spiritual beings as forces rather than as gods. But by contrast it is not unusual to think of the forces as highly personal, and sometimes indeed they are figured as fragments or projections of the higher divine reality. Sometimes the multiplicity of gods and spirits is the product of a certain hospitality to outside influences, where new gods or spirits have been given a place in the pantheon and in the life of ritual or worship (for it must not be forgotten, especially in the African context, that religion is not primarily about beliefs, but rather about the cults practiced by, and the experiences of, people).

Belief in gods and spirits is of course fairly typical of agricultural communities, and therefore the most developed hierarchies of gods tend to occur in the third band of Africa described earlier. Many of the rites concern fertility in one way or another, including the making of rain. But more intimately African cults often concentrate dramatically upon rites of passage—since, for example, the initiation ceremonies in many tribes are important for the continuation and prosperity of the community. Later we shall examine instances of these things in their practical setting.

So first there is usually a God, who is creator and largely sustainer of the world; and then there are lesser sacred forces and minor gods. These deities attract cults, though the High God because of his remoteness very often gets little overt attention.

THE CULT OF ANCESTORS

Frequently in descriptions of Africa and elsewhere (say China) there is talk of ancestor worship. This is a typically Western way of misinterpreting other folk's experience. In Africa ancestors are not seen as gods, and they are therefore, strictly speaking, not worshipped. It is more proper to think of the relationship between man and his ancestors in terms of communion. The African, within the framework of his traditional faith, is often more concerned with communication than worship. Still, the numinous character of the ancestors imparts a certain reverence, and the act of pouring libations (for instance) to them adds a dimension of feeling to the religious system.

The feeling for the ancestors is well put in a poem quoted by John Taylor

ision (a book in which the author paves the way for a dialogue
ans and the spokesmen of the African tradition or traditions).
s:

Those who are dead are never gone:
  They are there in the thickening shadow.
  The dead are not under the earth:
  They are in the tree that rustles,
  They are in the wood that groans,
  They are in the water that runs,
  They are in the water that sleeps,
  They are in the hut, they are in the crowd:
  The dead are not dead.

Those who are dead are never gone,
  They are in the breast of the woman,
  They are in the child who is wailing,
  And in the firebrand that flames,
  The dead are not under the earth:
  They are in the fire that is dying,
  They are in the grasses that weep,
  They are in the whimpering rocks,
  They are in the forest, they are in the house.

The dead are not dead.

The ancestors represent a kind of continuity between past, present, and future. They concern the future because they have to do with the ongoing life of the ethnic group. Their prestige in the past arises from the fact that age traditionally generates respect, and they are necessarily older than the old. The rather opposite view of contemporary Western culture creates tensions in areas where Westernized elites are in effect an integral part of the family, clan, or ethnic group and are rather interestingly divided into two sorts in some East African thinking as follows. The dead, so long as they are remembered personally, still have a rather full life—they are what Joseph Mbiti has called the "living dead." Older ancestors no longer personally recalled, though real, have a vague and hence impersonal existence.

The ancestors belong to the wider population of spirits, in mountains and copses and caves and rivers and lakes—for African religions tend to place man emphatically in a communion or living-together with the natural world around him. Often natural features are the dwelling place also of God when he descends to earth—for example, Mount Kenya is a kind of "Olympus" for the Gikuyu, as we shall see.

The fact that death is a kind of social promotion for the living dead means that funeral rites are indeed rites of passage from one human state to another. Most frequently corpses are buried, very often within the tribal compound near the dead person's hut. Thus too, when a village moves the dead may be taken to the new site. But though the dead are ever-present, they are also sometimes believed to migrate upward to live close to God in the sky.

THE RITUAL DIMENSION

In many parts of Africa initiation rites play an important role. Common in East Africa is the practice of circumcision for boys, clitoridectomy for girls. The significance of this is that the children are thereby prepared for a new adult sexuality, which is important not merely for the pleasure and company of later marriage, but also and more significantly for the cementing of family and other social alliances and as a symbol of fertility beyond human reproduction. The whole matter has generated controversy because white missionaries were strongly critical, especially of female initiation. However, they also largely failed to see the wider web of meaning surrounding the rite. Consequently, some of the new breakaway Christian movements in Africa have provided justification for the older traditions. In particular, African polygamy is regarded as vital in the incoming religions, so it is no surprise that here Islam has had a more forceful message than Christianity.

These issues are in modern times strong and challenging. The reason is that in a certain sense Africa is modernizing. At the same time it needs to come to terms with the traditions that give life to the various peoples. The new religious movements are an experiment, or rather a series of experiments, in crossing the divide between comfortable and meaningful ethnic traditions on one hand and the new technological, modern Christianity complex, on the other hand, which has its African components and which heralds necessary changes in the society and in the mind. Further, the transactions across the "white frontier," where the diverse cultures of black Africa have met the dominating influences and pressures of the white man, have been complicated by the colonial pose and hence the ideology of black inferiority which has been so early and so unfortunately built into the European (and American) mind.

In the new movements, as to an important extent in the older ethnic circumstances, the person who has experienced God or the Spirit or some supernatural being has charismatic opportunities. New religions often arise from new prophets. But the experience of prophecy can be found often in pre-Christian and non-Christian religions. The phenomenon of possession is widely known in Africa: the question is, possession by whom? Here a variety of interpretations is offered, as with mystics and prophets the world over. The fact that experience of the divine is regarded as important is a factor in the growth of charismatic and pentecostalist movements in Africa. The perception of the numinous is strong in African religion, and it is supplemented by instances of possession by supernatural beings, including ancestors. Such powers fade into those of a different type of person in the African context, variously called (e.g., "witch doctor," "medicine man," and so forth) and yet miscalled. These people are specialists in rituals and other activities that are reckoned to have actual or empirical effects. One of the most important of these effects is rain.

The rainmaking rituals are various. But let us describe one in outline—from the ceremonial of the Gikuyu in Kenya. The ritual, after certain preliminaries, centers on the sacred tree. A procession goes around it in the auspicious (clockwise) direction, and milk and fermented honey-beer are sprinkled onto the base of the trunk. On the eighth day of the celebrations the people, facing the sacred Mount Kenya, sacrifice a lamb by strangling. Its meat is roasted and part of it is offered to God. After various. other events, a procession wends its way home with a small portion of the lamb for planting to promote fertility. After all of this, it is hoped, there will be a deluge.

This of course is a communal ritual: the rain is for the whole group, and the customs of the group dictate the form and occasion of the rite. But there is also much individual concern in African religions for good and evil; and corresponding to this there are specialists in various mysterious arts. Sometimes such magical sorcery is directed toward bringing disaster upon personal or family enemies; and conversely those attacked may employ defensive magic, such as specially made amulets and charms. Also important in much of Africa is the use of specialists in traditional medicine (and now, as in a number of other cultures, both traditional and Western medicine may be used side by side).

These then are some of the features of traditional African religions. It need hardly be stressed that such religions were closely integrated into the whole social life of the group. The individualism of much Protestant Christianity and the reflection in Africa of European divisions between church and state have necessarily posed problems in a rapidly changing continent. Fortunately in recent decades it has been possible for Africans to rediscover and reevaluate their religious heritage and to restore a sense of the nobilities of their past (despite those blemishes so eagerly seized upon by the arrogance of Europe). Meanwhile new religions are on the march, as we shall shortly see.

Facing Mount Kenya

The first instance of a particular African religion I shall describe is that of the Gikuyu, often called the Kikuyu in English. Their religion and life is well described by the great Kenyan leader Jomo Kenyatta in his classic *Facing Mount Kenya*—classic because it is an early description by an anthropologically trained African conveying the structure and values of his own society. As the title of the book indicates, the Gikuyu live in the region by Mount Kenya and indeed are the dominant ethnic group in Kenya. To face the mountain is important religiously, for it is the resting place of God, the focal point for the Gikuyu people.

Religion centers upon belief in Ngai, the Supreme Being, and on communion with ancestors. It occurs within a hierarchical social framework—hierarchical largely by the system of age-groups. Thus very strong bonds are formed between young people of the same age, while superior age is a mark of increased authority. Thus the people are divided vertically into family groups and clans, horizontally into age-groups—it is not a hierarchy of caste. The initiation and other rituals cement the age-groups together. Everyone surviving into old age will—if he does not exclude himself by wrong conduct—play a part in decision making. As we have seen, the ancestors are part of this general scheme. In a number of important rituals it is the elders, women, and children who participate, rather than the actively procreating husbands.

There are a number of myths to explain the social order. Some concern the primordial man, Gikuyu, ancestor of the present people of that name, who was assigned land by God in his aspect as Divider of the Universe. God built a mysterious high mountain, Mount Kere-nyaga, which was to be his resting place whenever he came to inspect men's deeds. He took Gikuyu up the numinous mountain and showed the land of the Gikuyu spread out before them. At the center was a clump of sacred fig trees. This was to be the sacred center of the people's rites. (More generally throughout Gikuyuland such trees are venerated as sacred, though many have been cut down by the Europeans in the course of settlement.) God finally promised that whenever Gikuyu had need he should sacrifice, facing Mount Kenya, and the Lord would come to his aid.

Gikuyu made his way to the sacred spot and to his delighted astonishment found there a beautiful woman, Moombi, whom he espoused. They had nine daughters, but not a son, until nine young men appeared miraculously under the prototypal sacred fig tree after a sacrifice. The account is a means of explaining the nine traditional clans of the Gikuyu and also points to a matriarchal system. However, the myth goes on to describe how the system was overthrown when the women became tyrannical and the men successfully rebelled. The myth may allude to some historical change in Gikuyu society, but at any rate it is designed to show the origins of its modern shape.

The ritual dimension of the Gikuyu religion is partly determined by natural rhythms, as with the rites performed at seed time and harvest, and partly by recurrent needs. Gikuyu society is also highly conscious of the divine and spiritual hierarchy. Thus if a man falls sick (and generally the need to pray arises at times of crisis, for in tranquil and happy circumstances it is assumed that God is pleased with men's conduct), first ordinary treatment is tried, including what might be classified as magic but from another point of view is simply traditional medicine. Then it may be necessary to consult the ancestors. Even if they are not displeased, the sick person may not recover, in which case the elder of the family may institute a sacrifice to Ngai, supported invisibly by the family members. This reflects on the one hand the social cohesiveness of Gikuyu ritual and on the other the prevalent feeling in Africa that the High God should not be unduly bothered. The very fact that the whole family unites both visibly and invisibly in the supplication and sacrifice is a sign of the seriousness with which the affair is regarded.

Naturally so integrated a religion cannot fully persist in a more pluralistic age, when some Gikuyu have been converted to Christianity (and this rules out polygamy, sacrifices, female circumcision, and so on) while others have simply become "detribalized." These tensions became very obvious, of course, during the Mau Mau rebellion in the 1950s, though the elevation of Jomo Kenyatta to the presidency of Kenya was a cause of restoring something of the morale of traditional Gikuyu culture.

But perhaps it is good to finish with a passage from Kenyatta's book, describing the final phases of the rainmaking ceremony at the sacred tree.[1]

> When they finish feasting, the heap of the small pieces of meat and all the bones are collected together and put on the fire, together with some leaves and twigs of sweet-scented wood. While these are burning and the smoke is going up towards the sky, the elders rise and begin to chant a prayer round the fire. They stand up with their hands held aloft and their heads lifted towards Kere-Nyaga (Mount Kenya) in the north. In a few minutes they turn right, towards Kea-Nyaga (another sacred mountain) in the east, and then towards Kea-Mbiroiro in the south, and Kea-Nyandarwa in the west, finishing towards the north where they started. They do this seven times and then on the eighth the procession is formed homeward. On leaving they take with them a small quantity of the contents of the lamb's stomach, to be used in a planting ceremony. This completes the procedure in the ceremony for the sacrifice of rain.
>
> In the case of the ceremony in which I took part I remember that our prayers were quickly answered, for even before the sacred fires had ceased to burn, torrential rain came upon us. We were soaked, and it will not be easy for me to forget the walk homeward in the downpour.

Yoruba Religion

But let us now turn from the east to West Africa, to Yorubaland in Nigeria. It is quite large, like a rough square of 250 by 150 miles, extending in a south to

[1] *Facing Mount Kenya* (London, 1961), p. 249.

southwesterly direction toward the Bight of Benin and reaching from rather empty savannah country in the north to dense forests in the south and southwest. It has a complex history, having been dominated long by the Oyo in the north. Though rich in cavalry, the Yoruba were often unable to penetrate the difficult forest land toward the increasingly important coast. Trade often looked north to the Sahara and beyond, but with the coming of the Europeans and the slave trade eyes turned toward the sea. The differing types of economy and the shifting power structures are partly the reason for the syncretism of Yoruba religion and its inner variety. Different groups and different regions may worship different gods and spirits and have various ideas of the Supreme Being. Indeed, Yoruba religion is in many respects like Hinduism—a series of cults and loyalties loosely linked in a general framework of overlapping ideas and social habits.

Unusual among African societies, the Yoruba have a long tradition of urbanization. Their towns are like city-states, each presided over by an *oba,* or chief of royal lineage, who personifies and presides over the town and is held to be sacred. Within the structure of society, families are grouped according to lineage and may have their own special duties and rules. The complexity of society and Yoruba culture in general makes it fairly tolerant religiously; traditionally there was no kind of dogmatism until the impact of Islam from the north and Christianity from the sea.

Attempts have been made to impose a hierarchical system upon Yoruba belief; I shall here follow this approach as it gives one perspective on the religion. But its untidiness and looseness should also be remembered. The Supreme Being is known as Olodumare or Olorum, who is High God and creator. But as often elsewhere in Africa the more immediate deities or *orisa* attract close interest. These numerous (401 being a number often quoted) deities regulate the people's lives. Theoretically they can be seen as fragments or agents of the one God, and to some degree such a systematization has occurred over the years to bring unity to Yoruba theology (rather as all Hindu gods came to be seen as manifestations of the one Reality). But in practice the various *orisa* are treated as individuals: thus there is a separate deity of lightning, rather than (as with the Gikuyu) the direct attribution of lightning to God's activity ("cracking his joints"). The relative complexity of Yoruba religion owes something to its use of a priesthood, important for the installation of the *oba* and various other duties. Religion is thus pervasive in that daily prayer is traditionally common.

Another factor in unifying the rather loose-knit Yoruba pantheon is the conception of *Ifa.* This highly elaborate method of divination involves the manipulation of numbers and is in its own way specialized. Those who are trained in *Ifa* are virtually in universal demand, for the Yoruba have a strong sense of fate and the decrees of God, so that the small leeway they may have involves an urgent insight into the future. Consequently Orunnula, who is the god of divination, has a high place in the pantheon, being a "deputy" as it were of the Supreme Being. Likewise the trickster spirit Esu is important to the diviners, as he introduces a quirkish element into the regularities of divine Fate.

The specialist is called a *babalawo* ("father of the mysteries") who also has knowledge of traditional medicines. In conjunction with these the relevant deity is invoked. As elsewhere in Africa a conflict arises between modern "Western" medicine and such traditional cures, which have behind them the view that spiritual forces as well as material factors bring about health. This no doubt represents a vital intuition; thus divine powers may also be ascribed to Western technology.

Of the celestial spirits, higher than those upon earth, perhaps the most important after Olodumare is Obatala, who performs and continues the creation, functioning something like the Demiurge of Plato's philosophy. Also of great importance is Ogun, god of iron, who is fairly fierce, being primarily associated with the weapons of war, and who is one among a number of divinities worshipped by neighboring peoples as well, for instance in Dahomey. The ancestral deity, corresponding somewhat to the hero Gikuyu, is Oduduwa, sometimes pictured as a woman and so no doubt reflecting a fertility cult as well.

Below some of these powerful and widespread gods are spirits of streams, lakes, woods, mountains, and other natural features and processes. There are also the ancestors, though their function is less important among the Yoruba than (say) the Gikuyu or indeed other West African peoples.

So then there is a loose and shifting hierarchy of gods and spiritual forces who are invoked by prayers and various rituals. These spirits may, however, come into more intimate contact with men through medicines. Sometimes a priest will have a medium associated with him in his particular shrine. Often the medium is female, though boys also are trained. In Dahomey and among the Yoruba a girl's training lasts three years and is very rigorous. Though she will ideally have displayed aptitude in having been spontaneously possessed, the severe training will transform her whole personality. The "convent" where the initiates live contains a shrine to the relevant deity, and frequent devotional and ecstatic exercises, for example through dancers, help to mold the spirituality of the young people. Eventually the great day of the coming-out ceremony arrives, and relatives and friends gather to witness the final result of the process of death, resurrection, and rebirth which the training brings about. Then the initiates are ready to act as intermediaries between the spirits and men, and through their trances they seem to perceive and be gripped by the supernatural powers that govern the destiny of men. They add an experiential directness to the rituals of religion.

The richness and relative lack of dogmatism in Yoruba religion has meant that Islamic and Christian influences have been absorbed easily. In turn there has also been the development of new pentecostal and other religious movements through which some traditional religious values find a new outlet.

Zulu Zionism

The phenomenon of independent African churches and new religious movements combining traditional and Western motifs is, as we have seen, of great importance in Africa, both for recent history and for the future. In selecting one example, I am not arguing for something typical: it is just that we need to come to terms with the new religious phenomena burgeoning throughout the world. The example is from South Africa and concerns the prophetic career of Isaiah Shembe and its aftermath.

Shembe lived from 1870 to 1935 (and is held to have been resurrected), and because he was a Zulu he therefore felt strongly the deep crisis into which that proud nation had stumbled. When he was a child, Zululand had been effectively conquered by the British, after an initial British disaster at Isandhlwana. By 1887 the Zulu kingdom, fashioned above all by the great Shaka, was annexed, and though there was a traumatic rebellion in 1906, the Zulus had to accept ultimate defeat. It was no consolation that in 1913 the Native Lands Act institutionalized what was to become apartheid. The Zulu lands shrank to 4,000 square miles. It is not surprising that a tough people should think of surviving by going in different religious directions. One was full Christianization. Another was a variant, namely, a religion whose authority was based somewhat on the Book that the missionaries regarded as so seminal, yet at the same time a religion that could re-create or continue certain Zulu motifs. When the hour is ready there comes the man, and so the career of Isaiah Shembe and the church he founded is of great interest.

His story also expresses the outbreak of prophetism in Africa in modern times and to some extent the preference for an Old Testament ideology. Between polygamy and persecution there falls the shadow, in both cultures.

Isaiah Shembe had a rather prosperous upbringing in Zululand. As a young man he had four wives, a sign of substance. Christian ideas were penetrating into the region and these may have had some effect upon his visions. At any rate, a message was brought to him by lightning when he was praying in the cattle-kraal, and in a second vision the idea that he must cease wickedness was reinforced. In a third episode he got the message that he should give up his wives. However, it was in the fourth incident that he really accepted his prophetic ministry. He was scorched by lightning in a storm. (Notice the emphasis on the way God acts traditionally, from an African and for that matter an Old Testament point of view, through natural forces.) He became a wandering prophet and faith-healer and came somewhat under the influence of American Baptists and pentecostalists (emanating from Zion City, Illinois). Eventually he formed

his own church, the ama-Nazaretha or Nazarites, for he thought that references
to the Nazarites in the Old Testament applied also to him and his followers. So
it was that a new infusion of ancient ideas combined with the problems of a
Zulu society and spirituality that otherwise might have been overwhelmed by a
rather rigid missionary Christianity.

As in a number of other movements there seems to have been a bit of a
reaction against the New Testament. Christ was not necessarily rejected, but
he was reinterpreted, and both before and after Isaiah Shembe's death his followers saw him as something of a restoration of the Messiah, a kind of black
Christ. Not surprisingly many Africans sought to establish their own identity by
reminding the missionaries that Christ was not white. His Jewishness pointed
back toward the Old Testament whose religion was much more congenial to
Africans and actually close to their spirit. Sacrifices, polygamy, oppression, prophetism—these at least were experiences common between the two peoples as
perceived by the Africans. It is true that things could sometimes go the other
way: in the case of Shembe most òf the Old Testament values were reaffirmed,
but polygamy, so far as his divine visions went, was regarded as immoral. Thus
he fashioned a kind of adaptation to the incoming white culture.

Rather consciously Isaiah Shembe modeled his religion upon ancient lines,
though at the same time he was not unconscious of the Zulu customs. Thus
he set up his own High Place, not very far from Durban, called Ekuphakameni.
He also had a vision which suggested that he should go to the Nhlangakazi
mountain, also in Natal, which would serve as the sacred mountain of the
Nazarites. (In both places there are now great festivals every year.) His powers
of preaching and healing gave him great influence among the Zulu people, and
some think that in the period between the two wars he had more influence than
any other leader (thus in a sense being a spiritual parallel to a chief or king).
Indeed his followers came to think of him as a kind of reincarnation of the great
Shaka, the half-divinized hero of the Zulu nation and chief architect of their
once-proud empire.

At the same time he was a Messiah for the Zulu people. They as other
Africans looked to a black Christ. And though doctrinally the claim to the
divinity of Shembe was not made, yet there was a strong doctrine of the Spirit
in which it could be thought that somehow Shembe displaced Jesus as a vehicle
of divine power and inspiration. Indeed in one or two Nazarite hymns Jesus was
left out of the triad of Father, Son, and Holy Ghost.

With regard to ritual and morals, there was a nice symbiosis between ancient
and Zulu values. For some Zulus pork was taboo; so with the Old Testament and
the use made of it by Zionist prophets in Africa. Perhaps the New Testament
was most influential in regard to healing activities and the casting out of devils
and evil forces. There was a correspondence here between New Testament ideas

and traditional customs in Africa. Baptism corresponded too to older ideas of purification by water in which the initiate is saved in a miniature cosmic battle between evil forces, such as crocodiles in the river, and the purifying and con-quering effect of the hero who is the prototype of the ritual baptizer. So in many ways a new movement like that of the charismatic and (by reports) delightful Isaiah Shembe was a means of latching elements of the incoming and dominant tradition onto the older values of a partly shattered African mosaic.

After his death, Shembe was credited with a sort of resurrection. After all, he was seen vividly in visions and dreams. A new African messiah may thus have been born, also as testimony to the ideal of a black Christ. Who said he was white? Whites—that was the logic of the thinking behind a lot of new proph-etism in the African situation.

A SUMMING UP

It is time to sum up African religion. What does it mean in the context of the spiritual quest of humanity? It does not necessarily have great theological and doctrinal elaboration. Perhaps there has been too much of that in the world at large. More, it has shown a somewhat exuberant nature-oriented spirituality, con-tinuing perchance in a new guise the traditions of prophetism which have been so vital in the ancient past. It also sows seeds for the future; what will emerge from its amazing pluralism is, however, hard to discern. But at least there is a new African consciousness of the spiritual riches of Africa's past. The triangle of Kenya, Nigeria, and South Africa is, of course, only one selective approach to a myriad of them.

Beyond Africa there are other peoples who in their own differing ways show similar insights and reactions to those we have briefly examined here. From Madagascar, African by nearness but largely Polynesian by settlement, to the lands of the Maori and Hawaii; and from the Bight of Benin to the pluralisms of South America, whether black or Amerindian—in all regions of relatively small-scale groups of people, in small nations and tribes, we find patterns of religion and response to latter-day white expansion which are vital for the present and future understanding of the human condition and human beliefs.

RELIGIONS OF INDIA

Chapter 4

THE INDIAN EXPERIENCE

IN THE MIDDLE of the second millennium B.C. or thereabouts, a group of tribes invaded India from the northwest and gradually succeeded in establishing their dominance over northern and central India. They spoke an Indo-European language, of which the developed form is Sanskrit, and they referred to themselves as "Aryans" (literally "Noble Folk"). The Aryans' religion and culture were related to those of the Greeks and Romans, and of ancient Iran.

Previous settlement in India had consisted not only in scattered tribal and village life at a Stone Age level, but also in the remarkable urban culture of the Indus Valley civilization, dating from the third millennium, and similar to that of ancient Sumeria.

The impact of the Aryan religion upon that of the indigenous peoples had a number of effects. On the one hand, between the eighth and fifth centuries B.C., the writings known as the Upanishads enshrined metaphysical and religious doctrines that became the most important source of the theological thought of later Hinduism. On the other hand, some important religious movements—notably Jainism and Buddhism—took new shape outside the orthodox Aryan tradition. Both probably emerged from a non-Aryan background, but were expressed in terms of Aryan culture.

In the centuries following the composition of the classical Upanishads, the characteristic form of Hinduism was established. The cult of the two great gods, Shiva and Vishnu, and the absorption within the structure of orthodox religion of a complex mythology derived from various sources, gave to Hinduism elements which have persisted until today. Buddhism slowly increased in influence, as did Jainism. But the latter ultimately remained a minority religion, while Buddhism for a time threatened to replace Hinduism as the major faith of the Indian subcontinent, and from the second century B.C., spread outward into other parts of Asia. However, by the medieval period (from the seventh century A.D.), Buddhism was in decline in India itself. The Muslim invasions in the eleventh and twelfth centuries destroyed the monasteries, and Buddhism, like Christianity, virtually vanished from its homeland. Still it continued to grow and flourish in eastern Asia. The impact of Islam took various forms. The most notable religious result, apart from the conversion of roughly a third of India's inhabitants, was the emergence of a new faith seeking to combine the best in Islam and Hinduism—the Sikh religion, which is still a powerful force in the Punjab. The advent of European powers in India, and the final success of the British in subjugating the subcontinent brought other influences, including Christian, to bear upon Hinduism.

The above facts enable us to divide India's religious history into a number of significant periods: the pre-Aryan; the era of Brahmanism, up to the Upanishads; the classical period, which saw the formation of Hinduism and the spread of Buddhism; the medieval period; and the modern. The dates dividing the periods can be put, somewhat conventionally, as follows: the pre-Aryan period, down to 1500 B.C.; the early period of Brahmanism, down to 450 B.C.; the classical period, to 600 A.D.; the medieval period, to 1600 A.D.; the modern period, from 1600 onward.

ARCHEOLOGICAL EVIDENCE OF PRE-ARYAN RELIGION

Unfortunately, our knowledge of the pre-Aryan period is not good: we have to depend upon archaeological evidence. Remains of the script of the Indus Valley civilization have been recovered but it has yet to be deciphered. Thus features of the early religions of India must be inferred on the basis of inadequate evidence. Certainly there is little possibility of penetrating to the experiential dimension of this early religion. Nevertheless, certain pieces of evidence are suggestive for an understanding of later Indian religion.

Excavations were begun on sites in the Indus Valley in 1921, and have been continued since. They have revealed a highly complex urban civilization spreading from near Karachi, on the coast of modern Pakistan, some five hundred miles northeast to the basin of the Indus and its tributaries, and eastward into the northern part of central India. The two most important sites are at Mohenjo-daro and at Harappa. The chief feature of this culture is the complex, rather stereotyped, pattern of building. The streets are laid out in rectangular fashion, with less symmetrical alleyways crisscrossing each block. Many houses have baths, which drain off into an elaborate and impressive system of sewerage. All this, and other features of the Indus Valley civilization, implies a high degree of political and municipal organization. Moreover, there is evidence of considerable trading contacts with Mesopotamia (though there is no strong reason to think that the Indus Valley culture derives from there: it was probably an independent manifestation of the transition to urban civilization). One of the most impressive of the buildings at Mohenjo-daro is a large bathing tank: this is suggestive of the tank of a Hindu temple in which the faithful perform ablutions, and may well have had a religious significance.

If the excavations reveal a culture that was architecturally somewhat austere, they have rendered up artistic finds that suggest a fecund religion. There are remarkable figurines representing a mother goddess. This deity, reminiscent of equivalent figures in Mediterranean and Middle Eastern religion, and symbolizing the fertility of nature, reappeared much later in Indian religion. (Devotion to the Mother Goddesss is one of the respects in which Hinduism reasserted an element of the earlier culture, after the overlaying of indigenous patterns by the invading Aryans.)

Still more striking are the representations of a horned god, sitting in the posture of a yogi with two heels touching. Associated with him are animals and plants. So complex a reference to fertility and the practices of yoga may indicate that the god represented is a prototype of the Hindu god, Shiva. Most scholars accept this identification. A few other figurines, depicting nude male figures standing upright, suggest the Jain statues of later times.

Thus there is evidence of prehistoric religious traditions, traditions that recurred in historical times. It is not unlikely that the cult of Shiva and his consorts, and the practice of yoga and allied sorts of contemplation, date from this prehistoric culture. There are other reasons to suppose that certain features of Jainism and Buddhism can be traced back to non-Aryan culture; it may well be that they have an ancestry in the Indus Valley civilization. Village sites have been excavated in northwest India, and these too indicate a cult of the Mother Goddess associated with agriculture.

THE VEDAS

From the time of the Aryan migrations into India, we can date a genuinely identifiable religious life on the subcontinent. Over a thousand hymns, in the collection known as the Rig-Veda, testify to the religion and culture of these invaders. The Vedas date from the period between 1500 and 900 B.C. In the earliest part of this period, the Aryans had succeeded in subjugating a large area of northwest India. The Indus Valley culture was destroyed at about this time, very possibly by the direct military action of the invaders. In the succeeding centuries, the Aryans spread eastward and the center of their power shifted from the Punjab to the plain of the Ganges. Tribal organization became solidified into kingdoms, and religion took on a more complex character with a very considerable development of sacrificial rites. The horse-sacrifice, for instance, had a political significance that became the source of conflicts. A consecrated horse was set at liberty to roam at will for one year, after which it was sacrificed. The territory it traversed during its year of freedom was held to belong to the king. Naturally, this occasioned considerable dispute.

More important religiously were the sacrificial rituals administered by the Brahmin class. These rituals are reflected in certain collections of hymns that were appended to the Rig-Veda—the Sama-, Yajur-, and Atharva-Vedas. The first of these is a compilation of verses from the Rig-Veda arranged for ritual purposes; the second contains sacrificial formulae; the third, added later, consists of magical spells and similar material. To these in turn were added the Brahmanas, lengthy treatises concerned with the details of the sacrificial ritual. Finally, in the eighth to fifth centuries B.C., there were added to these the most famous of early Indian writings, the Upanishads, which attempted to explain the inner meaning of a faith that was by then considerably overlaid with formal cults. The corpus of all these writings are collectively known as the Veda (literally "Knowledge," i.e. sacred knowledge), and form the essential canon of sacred scriptures in the orthodox Hindu tradition.

What we now call Hinduism developed considerably beyond the religion of this early period. It has incorporated cults, practices, and ideas that derive from other sources. Moreover, the social structure of Hinduism is a good deal more complex than that of the Vedic period. For these reasons, scholars usually distinguish between the religion of the early period and that which began to emerge in the classical period. The early faith is called Vedism (and sometimes Brahmanism), the later, Hinduism. Since, however, the Upanishads represent a revolution in religious experience and speculation, it is convenient first to describe the situation as depicted in the Vedic hymns and in the Rig-Veda in particular, before turning to the Upanishadic experience.

VEDIC RELIGION

The Aryan invaders, like their Indo-European "cousins," the Greeks, Romans, Iranians, etc., believed in many gods. Some of these are related both by name and function to deities of the Græco-Roman world. Dyaus, the sky god, corresponds to Zeus and to Jupiter. Varuna, god of heaven, is probably related to the Greek Ouranos (Uranus). Agni, the fire god, is linguistically connected with the Latin *ignis* (as in "ignition"). However, the basic Vedic polytheism came to be modified in various ways, and this development opened the way for the monistic and theistic ideas contained in the Upanishads.

GODS OF THE VEDIC PANTHEON

The large number of gods, spirits, and demons mentioned in the Vedic hymns is an indication of the richness of the mythological dimension of the Aryans' religion. Four gods stand out clearly from this background: Indra, weather god and warrior, who assisted the Aryans in their rampages and battles;

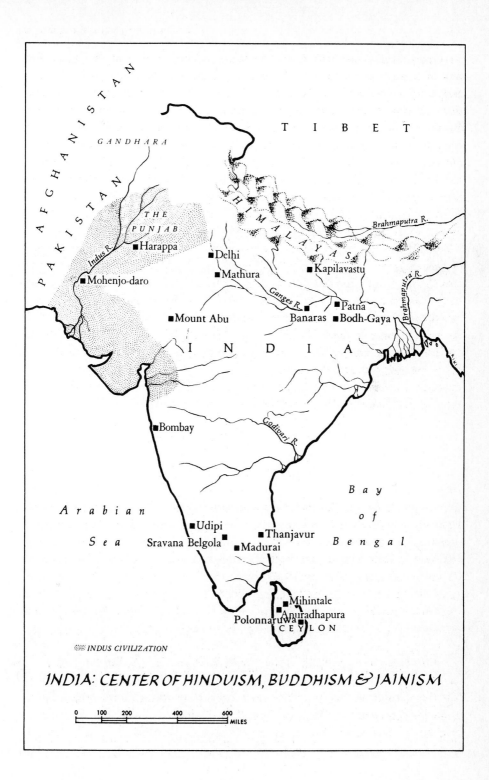

INDIA: CENTER OF HINDUISM, BUDDHISM & JAINISM

INDUS CIVILIZATION

0   100   200   400   600
                                  MILES

Varuna, heavenly maintainer of order and morality; Agni, the fire god, who was especially connected with the priests who performed the fire sacrifices; and Soma, a plant god implicit in the beverage made from the juice of the soma plant which was the center of another sacrificial cult. An examination of the mythological ideas surrounding these deities will help us to understand the spirit and context of this early religion.

Indra

One of the hymns to Indra begins thus:

> I will declare the manly deeds of Indra, the first that he achieved, the thunder-wielder.
> He slew the dragon, then disclosed the waters and cleft the channels of the mountain torrents.
>
> He slew the dragon lying on the mountain: his heavenly bolt of thunder Tvashtar fashioned.
> Like lowing kine in rapid flow descending the waters glided downward to the ocean.
>
> Impetuous as a bull, he chose the Soma, and in three sacred beakers drank the juices.
> ... [He] grasped the thunder for his weapon, and smote to death this firstborn of the dragons.[1]

(Tvashtar, it may be noted, was the smith god, like the Roman Vulcan.) Here then is Indra, the mighty storm deity, battling against the serpent Vritra with lightning and thunder. This mythological conflict expresses and explains the drama of the monsoon. Against the mountains the clouds are piled serpent-like, and Indra releases from them the life-giving waters which flow down to the ocean, enriching the land on their way.

But the fierce and awesome Indra does not only engage in mythological contests. He also assists the Aryans in their earthly battles. Another hymn says this:

> Without whose help our people never conquer; whom, battling, they invoke to give them succour;
> He of whom all this world is but a copy, who shakes things moveless, he, O men, is Indra

He who hath smitten, ere they knew their danger, with his hurled
  weapon many grievous sinners;
Who pardons not his boldness who provokes him, who slays the Dasyu,
  he, O men, is Indra.[2]

Varna, the Classes of Society

The Dasyu were the dark-skinned inhabitants of India whom the Aryans had succeeded in subjugating, whose citadels and forces were overthrown with the powerful help of the great warrior god. The Aryans' was already a somewhat stratified society. The three top classes (the term is *varna*, literally "color") were the Brahmins, the priestly group, the Kshatriya, the warrior or noble class, and the Vaisya, the peasant and mercantile class. The king or chieftain, whose chief function was leadership in war, belonged to the second of these, and it is to this class that the figure of Indra appealed. A fourth class, the Sudra, represented some of the folk the Aryans conquered, serfs who were not admitted fully to the Aryan community. They were treated virtually as slaves.

The four "colors" were not as rigidly observed in the Vedic period as they were later; they were the framework upon which the more fully elaborated Hindu caste system would be built. It is significant that the term used for these classes shows that there was a certain racial element, as reflected by lightness or darkness of complexion, in the arrangement of Aryan society. Needless to say, of course, the Aryans intermixed very considerably with the indigenous populations after their conquest of northern India.

Kathenotheism

The first hymn we quoted ends with a verse which was interpolated later:

Indra is king of all that moves and moves not, of creatures tame and
  horned, the thunder-wielder.
Over all living men he rules as sovran, containing all as spokes within
  the felly.[3]

Here is exhibited the tendency to exalt one god as supreme over all. To be sure, the hymn recognizes other gods; there is no genuine monotheism here. However, here and elsewhere in the Vedic hymns it is noticeable that the god addressed tends to be treated as the sole object of worship, and the attributes of other deities are often heaped upon him.

[2] Translation of Rig-Veda II, 12:9-10, by Ralph T. H. Griffith, *Hymns of the Rig Veda*, (Benares: E. J. Lazarus & Co., 1896) and reprinted in the Everyman's Library edition of *The Hindu Scriptures*, ed. by Nicol Macnicol (London and New York, 1938), p. 14.
[3] Ralph T. H. Griffith's translation, Rig-Veda I, 32, appears in *The Bible of the World*, p. 7.

This attitude has been called *kathenotheism* (literally "one-god-at-a-time-ism"). Although the composers of the hymns may on various occasions address themselves to various gods, within the context of a given hymn the god addressed is supreme. It is somewhat like the perspective contained within a picture: the space in which the people and objects represented exist is, so to say, treated as absolute within the picture, even if beyond the frame—and in another context—the perspective we use is different. So within the frame of a given hymn there is an attitude not far removed from monotheism, even though outside the frame other gods are recognized and exalted. The chief gods are reckoned severally supreme, one at a time.

Indra's rumbustious, fierce, and warlike attributes, his rollicking violence and cheerful, if formidable, drinking habits, reflect the social dimension of Aryan religion. Indra was rough and at times amoral. In contrast, Varuna was the very symbol of good order.

Varuna

In the Vedic hymns, he runs Indra a close second in order of importance though later he was to fade almost completely from the Indian religious imagination. He was more exalted, in more than one sense, than Indra. Indra is atmospheric, meteorological, one might say, in his mode of operation. But beyond the thunderstorms there was the splendid bright blue sky, the region of the heavenly Varuna. He was emperor, high above the conflicts in which Indra so lustily engaged himself. Though seemingly distant (and this very distance may have contributed to Varuna's loss of religious influence—such has elsewhere occurred in the history of religions), Varuna kept an eye upon the doings of mortals. He sent his messengers to all the corners of the earth; his companion Mitra supervised and sustained the making of promises and pacts. Varuna was indeed much concerned with the moral order, and his cult was the nearest approach to an ethical monotheism to be found in the Vedic hymns.

One of the hymns speaks thus of him:

O mighty Varuna, now and hereafter, even as of old, will we speak forth our worship.
For in thyself, invincible god, thy statues ne'er to be moved are fixed as on a mountain.

Move far from me what sins I have committed; let me not suffer, King, for guilt of others.
Full many a morn remains to dawn upon us: in these, O Varuna, while we live direct us.[4]

---

[4] Griffith's translation of Rig-Veda II, 28, appears in *The Bible of the World*, p. 8.

The statues which, in this translation, are "fixed as on a mountain," are summed up in the concept of *rta.*

Rta

Rta is the cosmic order, which has both a natural and an ethical significance. In this stage of the religious experience of mankind, no clear distinction was drawn (as it tends to be drawn today) between nature and the ethical order. Both the regularities of natural phenomena and the rules of society were thought of as manifesting the same underlying order. This order, *rta,* was produced by Varuna; and although he was not conceived strictly as a creator, the organization of the world, as opposed to its chaos, *anrta,* or *"un-rta,"* ("un-law"—compare how we still speak of "laws" of nature) was the work, in some sense, of Varuna. His law, his order, had to be obeyed by men; and he knew when transgressions occurred. Thus was expressed a sense of the nobility and stability of the cosmos suffused with a divine power that both assisted and challenged mankind. Very different from this sentiment was that expressed in the hymns to Indra which evince a forceful sense of the way in which a people, through their god, could *impose* order. For Indra, order has to be created: for Varuna, it is part of his divine deployment of the world. Varuna was essentially good—and because of this was also solemn. Indra, quaffing the juice of soma, became inflated with the glory and indiscretion of masterfulness: he could be frightening and awe-inspiring, but he was scarcely solemn. In their differing attributes two facets of the experience of the holy, and its application to human affairs, were expressed. The one god was like electricity —dangerous and powerful in the affairs of men; the other was like music— attuned to the noble harmonies of the world, and strangely moving.

Agni

Agni, on the other hand, was a nearer god, for he was god of fire. More, he was closely implicated in the sacrificial cult administered by the Brahmin class. Sacrifice was central to Aryan religion, and became more and more elaborate once the Aryans had settled and proliferated within the Indian subcontinent. The priest himself partook of the power implicit in the sacrifice—a power which became increasingly the center of religious attention, and of the speculations that form the main substance of the Upanishads. This power was known as *Brahman.* The word is the basis of the name for the priestly class, who were called Brahmanas (nowadays transformed into the word "Brahmins").

The ritual making of fire was one of the symbolic ceremonies that formed the heart of the Vedic religion. Fire was produced, a never-ceasing wonder, through the rubbing of sticks. It was clearly of cosmic significance. The sun, the heavens, even the glittering waters were alight with fire; it was fire that gave men warmth and sustained them against the chilling assaults of darkness. The first hymn of the Rig-Veda (first, that is, in the order in which the work came to be arranged) starts as follows:

I laud Agni, the chosen priest, god, minister of sacrifice ...

Minister of sacrifice, indeed, because it was through the consuming power of fire that other sacrifices were sent on their heavenly way. Thus Agni is the mediator between gods and men. A power which could have such cosmic effects, which could display such beneficial effects in primitive technology, and which religiously stood at the heart of the whole sacrificial system, could scarcely fail to arouse the wonder and awe of the onlooker, and could scarcely fail to evoke a vast number of hymns composed by the priestly class. Agni is runner-up to Indra in quantity of hymns addressed to his honor.

Soma

But the astonishment of the onlooker, present at a sacrifice, was not solely due to the intrinsic wonder of the objects of the ritual: it was also due to the power of soma. From the soma plant a juice was prepared that was used both as libation to the god and as a beverage for the worshipper. Soma juice may or may not have been intoxicating: the scholarly probabilities incline against such a view. But it produced profound effects on its consumers: hallucinations and a sense of glory followed its consumption. Since soma was taken in the context of ritual, it is no surprise that the god Soma was deemed a powerful divinity. The soma experience was regarded not just as a natural phenomenon, but as the occasion of sacred significance and holy dynamism.

A hymn declares:

> *Men beautify him in the vats, him worthily to be beautiful,*
> *Him who brings forth abundant food.*
> *Him, even him, the fingers ten and the seven songs make beautiful,*
> *Well-weaponed, best of gladdeners.*[5]

But the deity Soma was not merely identified with the powers of a plant. Typically in the mythology of the Aryans—and indeed of mythologies elsewhere —there is a complex interconnection between different facets of experience

---

[5] Griffith's translation of Rig-Veda IX, 15, appears in *The Hindu Scriptures*, ed. **Nicol** Macnicol (Everyman's Library 1938 edition), p. 24.

and an interweaving of the different elements of the invisible world that is taken for granted in unsophisticated religious experience. Thus Soma is a personification of the moon, which is in turn identified with Varuna, the gentle, heavenly lord. The moon is the great repository of the sacred juices of soma, but also the luminous distillation of heaven, the very essence of the sky king, Varuna.

The use of soma (which is the Iranian *haoma*) is one among the many examples of the religious use of drugs and intoxicants which have strange psychological effects. In our own day, Aldous Huxley has advocated the use of mescaline. The weird and glorifying properties of such plants and concoctions have given man a heightened religious experience, a window, as it were, on a world that is normally beyond the range of the humdrum senses. Not only this, but in Vedic religion soma was thought to be more than a sacred stimulus to vision. It was the secret of heaven, the ambrosia which confers a form of immortality, the food of the gods. Thus it figured centrally both in the cult of the deities, and in thoughts about a further existence.

Of course the four gods we have mentioned by no means exhaust the Vedic pantheon. There were numerous other gods (mainly, it is interesting to note, masculine), and demons and spirits as well. This darker world is prominent in the Atharva-Veda, which is rich with spells and magical incantations.

Yet despite the complexity of the spiritual world in the Vedic hymns, there were certainly movements toward a conception that unified the visible world and the unseen forces men felt underlay all of nature. We have already seen how kathenotheism was one aspect of the composers' intuitive attitude. We have seen too how the cult of Varuna carried with it a concept of a cosmic order—and the idea of the unity of the visible world is often the prelude to the conception of the unity of the invisible realm. Such tendencies of religious imagination were supplemented by speculation. In the later hymns of this period there are clear signs of this frame of mind. Most notable of all is the famous verse:

> *They call it Indra, Mitra, Varuna, and Agni*
> *And also heavenly, beautiful Garutman:*
> *The real is one, though sages name it variously . . .*[6]

Here is expressed a sentiment which was to prove a powerful factor in Hindu attitudes—men's religions and cults are many, but they all point to the one true God, the one Absolute.

[6] Rig-Veda I, 169.

THE GODS AND THE ABSOLUTE

Speculation, however, was not content with the idea of a unity of the gods. It also wished to see a correspondence between heaven and earth. The microcosm was the pattern of the macrocosm. In the famous *Purusa-sukta* ("Hymn of Man," Rig-Veda, x.90), the whole cosmos is perceived as a human being, and also as a sacrifice of that being. Thus the ritual was projected on to the whole universe, and creation was seen as a Brahminical sacrifice. Priestly knowledge and practice became the clues to the understanding of the whole world. As we shall see, such ideas played a key role in the formation of the Upanishadic doctrines. If such conceptions seem in a sense obscure, for all their attempts at unification, if they seem ritualistic and in some degree conservative, there were other strands in Vedic hymn composition which were the reverse. Speculation and scepticism combine in the so-called "Song of Creation":

> *Then neither Being nor Not–being was,*
> *Nor atmosphere, nor firmament, nor what is beyond.*
> *What did it encompass? Where? In whose protection?*
> *What was water; the deep, unfathomable? . . .*
>
> *Who knows truly? Who can here declare it?*
> *Whence was it born, whence is this emanation.*
> *By the emanation of this the gods*
>   *Only later [came to be].*
> *Who then knows whence it has arisen?*
>
> *Whence this emanation hath arisen,*
> *Whether [God] disposed it, or whether he did not,—*
> *Only he who is its overseer in highest heaven knows.*
> *[He only knows,] or perhaps he does not know!*[7]

The extraordinary irony of that last phrase—"Or perhaps he does not know!"

But there is, whatever we are to make of this scepticism, one extremely important facet of the thought of this hymn which foreshadows a great deal in later Indian religious thinking and experience. The gods, be it noted, come into existence after the creation of the world. This verse expresses their ultimately secondary significance. As we shall see, in differing ways both Hindu-

---

[7] From Rig-Veda X. 129, translated by R. C. Zaehner for the Everyman's Library 1966 edition of *Hindu Scriptures,* ed. by R. C. Zaehner (London and New York: E. P. Dutton, 1966), p. 11-12.

ism and Buddhism—and indeed Jainism—reached out to the transcendent
the bright gods of this world. The Absolute and the state of liberation were perceiv
to exist beyond the cosmos, beyond the gods who, in symbolizing and manipulating
natural forces in a supernatural way, are implicated in this visible world. The gods
were not denied—no feelings of denunciation of "idolatry" such as moved the
prophets of the Hebrew Bible ever animated the breast of an Indian religious teacher
or seer. The various gods were not denied: but they were transcended. In the
famous "Song of Creation" is represented the start of a process whereby the un-
reflective faith of the Aryans was overlaid by other forces. These forces eventually
found expression in the Upanishadic writings. But before coming to these, let us
review the main features of the earlier religion.

Aryan religon was essentially polytheistic, but it began to move toward a
more unified conception of the material and spiritual worlds. It in turn expressed the confident, almost amoral, character of the warrior, or Ksatriya,
class, and the special concerns of the priestly Brahmin class whose task it was
to administer the rites that gave meaning and cohesion to Aryan society. Indra
symbolized the warrior; Agni was the center of the Brahmin's profession.
Spanning both concerns was the divine figure of Varuna, controlling the natural and moral order on which both noble and priest depended. And welling
up in the consciousness of the hymn-composers whose most ancient and colorful works have come down to us, and who constitute the first literary creators
of the Indian heritage, there were doubts and speculations and intuitions
heralding a new age.

It has been mentioned that certain forces were beginning to transform
Vedic religion toward the end of the period from the sixteenth to the ninth
centuries B.C. There was an immense growth in sacrificial ritualism. Also,
skepticism and speculation—an "open" rather than a "closed" attitude to
religion—began to permeate the higher classes. These two forces partly explain the preoccupations of the Upanishadic writers.

TRACES OF NON-ARYAN RELIGION

During these centuries there also reappeared strong currents of religious and
philosophical thought that were ultimately of pre-Aryan origin. Older, indigenous, religious attitudes and practices began to reassert themselves. The
interplay between the Aryan and the non-Aryan heritage was one of the main
causes of the fruitfulness of the early Indian culture; it was also the cause of
some of the apparent contradictions in the Indian heritage.

There is a sense, though it is often exaggerated, in which the higher doctrines and practices of Hinduism are "world negating." Yet there is little of this

hymns. However, toward the end of the early period,
n increased concern with ascetic practices and the tech-
ind the asceticism lay complex attitudes about the meaning
he individual. These attitudes came to be expressed in the
ı, samsara, nirvana, and of rebirth or reincarnation. We shall
commい.. ı of these concepts in due course. Meanwhile, let us note that
the occurrence of the non-Aryan religious and philosophical currents influenced
the writing of the Upanishads and played a primary role in the unorthodox
teachings which at this time challenged Vedism and the Brahmanical heritage.
The two chief manifestations of unorthodoxy were Jainism and the teachings
of the Buddha. Buddhism, Jainism, and other movements not recognizing the
authority of the Vedic religion, share to a greater of lesser degree the non-
Aryan ideas and practices centered on yoga—the training of mind and body
through methods of asceticism, physical control, and contemplative techniques. Sometimes one of these is stressed more than the others: in Jainism,
there is great emphasis on austerity; in Buddhism, there is more attention to
psychological, contemplative methods; in the Hindu school known as Yoga,
physical control plays a large part.

In this early period we can detect a general view of the world that was
adapted in different ways by the Buddha, the Jains, and the Upanishadic writers (who produced a synthesis between this world view and earlier Vedic
ideas). The world view may have some of its roots in the Indus Valley
civilization, since it seems that yogic practices already existed there. But
whether this is so or not we can describe its main outlines as follows:

Men and other living beings are continually being reborn. With death, the
individual is reborn in a different form. This everlasting recurrence of births
and deaths can only be stopped by transcending it—by attaining a liberation
in a transcendental sphere where the self is freed from mental and bodily
encumbrances. Typically, this is achieved by the practice of austerity and
yoga: self-denial and self-discipline are means of destroying that which leads
to rebirth—karma. Literally karma means "action," but it can be treated as a
force, or law, which allots destinies to individuals in terms of their actions.

Individual life is immensely long because of continuous reincarnation
from the depths of the past into the distant reaches of the future; so too the
world is of immense duration, periodically collapsing into chaos and reemerg-
ing over vast ages. This whole cyclical process of change and rebirth is commonly called *samsara,* the stream of existence that has to be crossed to that
"other shore" if one is to gain liberation from the ailments and imperma-
nences of worldly life. Yoga, rebirth, karma, samsara, liberation—these are
the elements of the world view which was to leave its stamp on virtually the
whole of the Indian heritage. One of the important manifestations of this
world view was Jainism.

JAINISM

Jainism represents an ancient faith, having its roots in the prehistoric past. It is called "Jainism" from the fact that its adherents follow the Jinas, or "Victorious Ones"—great teachers who have shown men the path of salvation. The last of these—the twenty-fourth according to the Jain tradition—was Mahavira, who was born in Patna in north India, probably about the middle of the sixth century B.C. (Jains themselves fix the date of his birth at 599.) These teachers are supposed to stretch back into the immensely distant past, but Mahavira's predecessor in the sequence, Parsva, was an actual person, living in the eighth century B.C. It certainly seems true that the Jain claim to be a very ancient faith, restored and reformed by Mahavira, is correct. As we saw, there is a hint of Jain ideas in the archaeological remains of the Indus Valley civilization.

Unlike the somewhat chaotic religion revealed to us by the Vedic hymns (chaotic in the sense that different strands of mythology are woven together, with little in the way of a unifying doctrinal background), Jainism as preached by Mahavira was an elaborate system. It had elaborate, if archaic, doctrines, a rich mythology, a detailed ethic, a clear pragmatic ritual, its own social organization, and a quest for inner contemplative experience. It has all the dimensions in recognizable form which we have come to associate with religion.

THE FORD-MAKERS

Since Jainism denies a creator God, and is thus atheistic, and since it does not attach overmuch importance to the many gods of popular imagination, its mythological dimension is chiefly bound up with the figures of the great teachers, the *Tirthamkaras* or "Ford-makers," who enable the faithful to cross the stream of existence to the other shore—to liberation, nirvana. Indeed, when Jainism at last acquired an elaborate temple cult analogous to that of Hinduism, these figures became the central objects of popular reverence. The teachers, though human, transcended the gods, just as the goal of the religion is transcendence of the world and achievement of a peaceful isolation far above the concerns of both gods and men.

In view of all this, it is appropriate to illustrate the mythological dimension from the stories that have come down to us about Parsva and Mahavira. The former is supposed to have passed away 246 years before the birth of the latter. But Parsva's predecessor is mythologically dated at eighty-four thousand years earlier—this is how ancient the Jains really feel themselves to be.

PARSVA

Parsva's life foreshadows the main pattern of the stories both of the Buddha and of Mahavira. Prior to his birth, he was living in heaven (here conceived as part of the cosmos) as the god Indra. When the time came for his descent to earth, he entered the womb of the queen Vama. As a child he displayed a remarkable and heroic disdain for the concerns and delights of worldly life. He wished to renounce both the world and his father's throne, and in his youth obtained his parents' reluctant agreement to his withdrawal from ordinary life to become a recluse (*sannyasi*) in the forest. Eventually, through the practice of austerity and of yoga, he attained omniscience and assurance of liberation from this world. Thereafter he taught mankind the saving doctrines. When he died, his soul ascended to the summit of the cosmos, where it remains in peace and changelessness, beyond the possibility of being affected by the world.

MAHAVIRA

Mahavira was the second son of two pious Jains, and was given the name of Vardhamana, though he is more usually known by his other title (which literally means "great hero"). In his youth he married, in accordance with his parents' wishes, Yasoda, by whom he had a daughter. When his parents died, Mahavira was thirty years old, and his elder brother took over the family concerns. This was the opportunity for Mahavira to withdraw from the world. He joined the order of Jain monks, and after twelve years of austerity achieved omniscience and release from the bonds of the material world. The remainder of his career was spent in organizing and instructing his disciples and followers.

Like Parsva, and indeed all Jain saints, his final decease released his *jiva*—soul, or life-monad—so that it attained the motionless summit of the world and a continued isolated and changeless existence. Such in brief are the careers of two of the great figures of Jain mythology. Much else, of course, is ascribed to them: the belief in reincarnation meant that the biography of an earthly life was never quite enough. The previous existences of these great men were a fruitful source of legendary and mythological material.

JAIN PIETY

There are some striking features of these two careers which illustrate the atmosphere of Jain piety. First, self-mortification is the ideal form of self-training, through which the Jain gains omniscience and release. This connects closely with the Jain doctrine of karma. Personal austerities continue to be part of the Indian religious scene in our own day and time. Even in the Vedic hymns there was mention of such practices. They are often referred to in the Indian tradition as *tapas* (literally, "heat"). Not only does the ascetic generate a mysterious heat, but also he gains power—not only over himself—through his severe practices. The great yogi therefore becomes an awesome figure, one whom even the gods fear.

This idea, that even the gods can be surpassed by the yogi and ascetic, is a colorful way of indicating what runs deep in the stream of Indian religious consciousness—the belief that the popular cults of the gods themselves cannot bring final salvation. They can be implored for worldly boons, but it is the religious teacher who knows the secret of immortality.

Omniscience in Jain Belief

This brings us to a second feature of the legendary biographies of Parsva and Mahavira: the claim that they gained omniscience. In much Indian thinking about these matters, knowledge is held to be the key to salvation. Of course, knowledge here means more than theoretical knowledge: it is the experiential acquaintance with the realm of spirit and of the inner nature of ordinary existence. It implies that the trouble with men is not in essence sin, so much as spiritual ignorance. The truth is veiled from man's sight because of his immersion in the world; and conversely, spiritual ignorance keeps him bound to the world. The Jains believe that everyone is in principle omniscient, but in fact the vast majority of people are obstructed from full knowledge by their karma, which clouds the soul: but a few heroic figures, such as Mahavira and those who successfully follow his austere path, can re-achieve this essential omniscience—the state of liberation is one where the influence of karma has been completely broken. This attitude is itself closely related to the whole concept of reincarnation and rebirth. If ignorance has such power to bind, it is no wonder that the yogi's inner spiritual knowledge should itself be regarded as power too. The omniscient Jina is assuredly more worthy of veneration than the limited gods.

But the mythological dimension of Jainism, as illustrated by the legends of the "Ford-makers," cannot be understood without a grasp of its doctrines.

Karma in Jain Belief

The universe, it is held, consists of two sorts of entities—the souls of life-monads, *jiva,* and non-living matter, *ajiva.* The life-monads are infinite in number and are essentially blissful and omniscient, but these properties are obscured through their implication in matter. A subtle form of matter is especially important in this connection: it is called *karma.* As we remarked, the word means "action," and some doctrine of karma is always associated with belief in reincarnation in the Indian tradition. The Jains, while conceiving of karma as material force, retain the most archaic form of this belief. The literal meaning of karma as "action" explains something important about their conception. The Jain believes that a person's activities in the world, even his good ones, bind him to the round of rebirth. Consequently, escape from the effects of karma, and the assurance that one will be no more reborn, is often thought to involve complete quietism—withdrawal from the world of men, and the practice of austerities which will counteract karmic matter.

Life-Monads

Though Jainism makes a sharp distinction between matter and life-monads, the latter are thought of in a rather materialistic way (another sign of the archaic provenance of the doctrines). Life-monads expand or contract to fit the bodies which they successively animate, and are weighed down as if by invisible bags by the karmic matter they have accumulated. Upon the destruction of karma, the life-monads will ascend through a sort of upward gravitation to the top of the cosmos, where they remain motionless, omniscient, and blissful.

The cosmos itself is pictured as roughly of the shape of a gigantic man or woman. It is eternal and uncreated, and is surrounded by an infinity of empty space. Its dimensions are truly immense. The world inhabited by living beings such as men and animals is pictured as a huge disc, corresponding to the waist of the cosmic man. Below there are seven levels, each containing a million purgatories, in which evil men are appropriately reincarnated. Above, there is a series of heavens, in which the various gods are arranged in a hierarchy. Above these is the summit of the cosmos, corresponding to the top of the cosmic man's head, where the liberated life-monads go. It is worth noting that this picture implies that heavens are inferior to the highest goal. It implies too that the life-monad is involved in the empirical cosmos, so that true liberation is beyond heaven. This sentiment explains much in the Indian tradition—the goal of the contemplative or mystic who gains inner knowledge is superior to the goal of heavenly joy which the gods can provide.

The dimensions of the Jain cosmos are staggering—it is fourteen *rajjus* high, a *rajju* being the distance traveled in six months by a being going at two million miles per micro-second. Its history is infinite: it consists of an endless and beginningless sequence of immensely long ages, in each of which there is a phase of improvement and one of decline. The present era is one of serious decline, so that Mahavira is the last "Ford-maker" of this epoch, and the religion will slowly die out, to be restored in the next epoch. (Thus Jains are not concerned that their faith now has less than two million adherents: it is only to be expected.)

Reincarnation in Jain Belief

The problem posed for the Jain, How can one gain liberation? foreshadows the main question of most later Indian religion. This problem arises from the belief in reincarnation, that beginningless round which assures individual survival through the seemingly interminable prospect of living in a painful and frustrating world. It is noteworthy that belief in reincarnation is not found in the Vedic hymns. For Vedic religion, the next life involves an ascent to the heavenly world, or to the depths of an underworld. It is only by the time of the Upanishads that the doctrine of rebirth appears in the orthodox Brahminical tradition. This is an indication of the way in which the synthesis between Aryan and non-Aryan ideas was taking place. But it also serves to show how yoga and belief in reincarnation, karma, and in a plurality of souls, is a complex of ideas derived from the archaic culture of the subcontinent.

THE JAIN MONK

Such, in brief, is the doctrinal dimension of Jainism. What of its ethical teachings? First, morality is seen as a means of progressing toward liberation. But this progress is immensely difficult, and has to culminate in the monastic life. Essentially the spiritual life is possible only within the order of monks. Severe asceticism is the only effective way of avoiding evil conduct, since the Jains believe that injuring living beings, even unintentionally, has peculiarly deleterious karmic effects. This is the justification for their insistence on the central virtue of *ahimsa,* or non-violence (a concept that in recent times has been given a social and political application by Mahatma Gandhi in the struggle for Indian independence: his non-violent non-cooperation drew upon sentiments deeply embedded in the Indian tradition).

The desire to avoid injury to life is expressed in certain practices of Jain monks: the monk must strain his water before drinking; he wears a gauze mask over his mouth to prevent the unintentional inhalation of innocent insects; the monk is required to sweep the ground before him as he goes, so living beings are not crushed by his footsteps; and always he treads softly, for the very atoms underfoot harbor minute life-monads. In addition, the monk renounces all lying speech, including that motivated by anger, greed, fear, or mirth; he renounces taking that which is not given; he renounces all sexual pleasures; he renounces, finally, all attachments. In this way he becomes "houseless"—uncommitted to anyone or any cause, save the task of promoting the faith and his own heroic salvation.

It is said of Mahavira that he died of self-starvation. The Jain monk has before him this formidable and tremendous ideal of so neglecting his own interests, in the related concern for the life about him, that he too should commit this self-same form of suicide. However, it should only be undertaken if the aspirant is psychologically and spiritually ready for the task.

The ideal of the Jain monk is well summed up in those colossal and serene statues (such as that of the saint Gommatesvara at Sravana Belgola in Mysore) which here and there are to be found rising vastly on the hill-tops that reach out of the brown and green south Indian landscape. They are great nude statues of ascetics represented in colossal stone. Creepers twine up round their immense legs—creepers whose slow growth and jungly impersonality symbolize the total indifference to worldly concerns displayed by the true Jain. Fearfully calm, such saints exhibit a heroism and self-sufficiency which owe nothing to the help of the gods or to ordinary human contrivance. No Creator helps or hinders their path toward otherworldly perfection: at the summit of the cosmos their life-monads will dwell in bliss and full knowledge.

In addition to severe self-mortification, the Jain monk must practice various meditations in order to purify his understanding. In this way he will attain to full understanding and to a form of omniscience which prefigures his state when the life-monad is released from the round of reincarnation. He must make the doctrines meaningful to himself by dwelling upon the transitori-ness of all things, upon the operation of *karma*, the nature of the cosmos, and so on. Furthermore, he must practice *dhyana*, deep meditation. As we shall see, *dhyana* forms an integral part of Buddhism, and indeed is a widespread form of religious practice and experience in all the Indian tradition.

JAINISM IN LATER AGES

Apart from the pragmatic ritual concerned with austerity and the training of the mind to attain higher mystical states, Jain temple worship developed in later ages, partly under the influence of Hinduism. Images of the *Tirthamkaras* came to be venerated. Strictly speaking, this is not worship or prayer, in that the holy ones, in their utterly tranquil nirvana, are beyond the possibility of affecting or being affected by what goes on in the rest of the cosmos: they exist serenely at the summit of things. Nevertheless, Jain religious practice has the outward marks of a divine cult even though in medieval times there was considerable opposition among Jains to this use of images. As the great figures of the tradition are honored, they are also exalted, in a sense, to function as the gods of popular religion.

The Jain layman has no chance of liberation until another incarnation; he lives in the world, and cannot strictly follow the severe code of the monk. Therefore the ethical rules are modified for him. Nevertheless, he is forbidden to engage in occupations which inevitably involve the taking of life, such as being a butcher or a soldier. For this reason, many Jain lay people are businessmen and traders—a source of the influence of Jainism which is out of proportion to the number of adherents. They too, like the monks, must be vegetarians. They must refrain from unchastity, intoxicants, and stealing. Regular festivals, the support of the monastic order through the giving of alms, the practice of religious worship—these figure in the life of the layman. The framework of morals is thus much the same for monk and layman.

Jain life has since earliest times been remarkable for its conservatism. There are scarcely any doctrinal differences among Jains, and the division between the two main sects of the religion, the *Digambaras* and *Svetambaras* ("Sky-Clad" and "White-Clad," respectively), is one which dates from the earliest times—it is the division between those who believe and those who disbelieve in the ideal of nudity for monks as a symbol of the complete renunciation of worldly goods. (Nowadays, the *Digambaras* by no means always express this ideal, and in any event not in public.)

The conservatism and unaggressiveness of this faith are factors in its continued survival in India. In effect, Jain laymen fit into the Hindu caste system and have a clear and recognized place in the social order. Quietly and austerely, Jainism has preserved its way of life through two and a half thousand years or more. With its pessimistic estimate of the direction of history in the present epoch, it has not had too much motivation for strong proselytism. Much more important as a missionary movement was its sister religion, Buddhism, which was destined to permeate Asia, though at the time of Mahavira and of the Buddha such a future could scarcely have been predicted. To the Buddha we now turn.

THE BUDDHA

SIDDHARTHA GAUTAMA

The Buddha's career is not unlike that of his rival's, though its spirit was rather different. Like Mahavira, Gautama did not belong to the religiously dominant class. He was not a Brahmin, but a Ksatriya. While in one of the heavens (several are represented in Buddhist mythology), he perceived that the time had come for him to descend and to preach to many the saving doctrine. He was incarnated in the womb of queen-Maya. He was born in or around 563 B.C. at a place called Kapilavastu, just inside the borders of what is now Nepal. His father, Suddhodana, was a local raja, or chieftain. Shortly after his birth, his mother died, but in the meantime he had been given the name Siddhartha. Gautama was his family name but he was also referred to in later legend and literature as Sakyamuni, i.e. sage of the Sakya clan, and as the

Tathagata, the "Thus Gone One" whose path is ineffable, for it can only be indicated, not described.

According to the legendary stories of the Buddha's life which have come down to us in the scriptures, in his youth the Buddha showed startling wisdom. It was predicted of him that he would give up the world to become an ascetic if ever he were to become acquainted with the facts of old age, sickness, and death, or if he were to see a recluse. From these "four sights" his father determined to shield him. The young prince was brought up in luxury, and in due course married Yasodhara, by whom he had a son, Rahula. But meanwhile, despite all precautions, he did perceive the facts of suffering: the sight of a wandering ascetic fired in him the ideal of renouncing the world in order to discover the secret and the cure of suffering. Thus it was that he came to steal away from his family one night, and from then on lived the life of a wandering recluse, sitting at the feet of various yogis and religious teachers (though finding no ultimate satisfaction in their doctrines), and practicing various forms of self-mortification. These methods failed. He gave up such severities, and soon after gained Enlightenment, at Bodh Gaya.

The Enlightenment

The scriptural accounts of this event of far-reaching importance give some hints of the nature of the experience. After resisting various temptations from Mara, the Buddhist equivalent of Satan, the Buddha-to-be put himself into trance. He was intent on discerning both the ultimate reality of things and the final goal of existence. Then, in the first watch of the night, he recollected the successive series of his former births. In the second watch, he attained the supreme heavenly eye, for he himself was "the best of all those who have sight." With the perfectly pure heavenly eye he gazed over the entire world, which appeared as clearly as if it were reflected in a spotless mirror. He saw that the decease and rebirth of beings is governed by the moral quality of their former deeds. As the third watch of the night began, Gautama saw more deeply into the causation of suffering and the workings of karma, and passed through the eight stages of meditation (*dhyana*). He had reached perfection and he thought to himself: "This is the authentic Way on which in the past so many great seers, who also knew all higher and all lower things, have traveled on to ultimate and real truth. And now I have obtained it." At that moment, in the fourth watch of the night, he reached the state of complete spiritual insight. In recognition of this, according to the scriptural accounts, nature itself responded to the momentous event. The earth swayed, pleasant breezes blew, flowers showered down from heaven, joy spread among the gods and the denizens of purgatory for now there was hope of release and nirvana; all living beings were glad; only Mara was depressed, his power broken.

Thereafter the Buddha (now indeed the title was due to him: he was now the "Enlightened One") remained in serene contemplation, exploring his new-found freedom and considering the needs of living beings. The stage was now set for his going forth to preach the new saving doctrine. Though Mara tempted him to stay put, and to disappear into nirvana without concerning himself with the tedious task of preaching to men and founding a religion which would lead them on the Way, the Buddha rejected this selfish sugges-tion. The Teacher took himself to the holy city of Banaras, on the river Ganges, to preach the doctrine.

One notable feature of the accounts of the Enlightenment is the type of meditation that the Buddha practiced. The stages of *dhyana* through which he passed have the effect of purifying the mind of all images and discursive thoughts. By emulating the stages of *dhyana* the Buddhist saint can acquire a heightened state of consciousness. We shall later describe these stages in more detail. Meanwhile, we may note that this practice of meditation is one of the variety of techniques known as yoga—the "yoking" or "harnessing" of mental and physical powers—and has analogies to the progression in contemplation that mystics elsewhere in the world have experienced. However, the Buddha's experience, judging at least from the traditional accounts, did not involve any reference to God. Largely because of his preoccupation with and compassion for the sufferings of living beings, the Buddha could not believe in a good Creator. Thus the Buddha's Enlightenment did not occur in the context of prior belief in God. Buddhism, like Jainism, rejects such a doctrine of God. Consequently, while Christian and Muslim mystics see their own higher ex-periences as being a kind of contact or union with God, the Buddha did not so interpret his own Enlightenment. His perception of the transcendent, his at-tainment of nirvana, was an experience of that which is "deathless," perma-nent, the highest joy, in contrast with the impermanence and sorrow and dissatisfaction of empirical existence.

After the Enlightenment the Buddha saw the empirical world in the light of his shining experience of the transcendent state he had attained; he had gained the "pure heavenly eye" which enabled him to see clearly and deeply into the condition of living beings. However, from his later teachings, when he came to formulate the doctrines generated by the Enlightenment experience, it is evident that a very considerable part of the process of Enlightenment was intellectual in character. His was not just a pure mystical experience: it was insight that, while depending on such a higher state of consciousness, was applied to the realm of ordinary experience. The way that the Buddha perceived the causes of suffering during his Enlightenment indicates the degree to which, during his previous wanderings and meditations and through his critical evaluation of the teachings he had heard from other recluses and holy men, he had evolved the philosophical ideas which became vivid at one critical moment.

Consequently, it can be said that the Buddha's teachings, while they hinge on the luminous experience of Enlightenment and of nirvana, owe something to a stock of ideas current in his day. Nevertheless, with great subtlety and originality, he gave a new application and interpretation to these ideas. The concept of reincarnation, the related belief in the operation of karma, the possibility of release from this round of rebirth—these ideas were general at the time, and he accepted them. Speculations about the way causes and effects operate in the empirical world, the question of whether human acts were determined by fate—these and other issues he addressed himself to. In this sense, the Buddha was a man of his times. What gave his teaching such power, in contrast with that of many other unorthodox teachers of his time whose doctrines and lives have now largely faded from the consciousness of humanity, was the unique combination of intellectual power with a practical emphasis on the importance of inner experience.

The First Sermon

From Bodh Gaya the Buddha repaired to Benares where he delivered his first sermon. This was addressed to the five ascetics with whom he had formerly associated, but who had deserted him when he gave up the severe self-mortification they believed necessary for release. He received them into the mendicant order, the Sangha, which was to be the social organization that has carried on the Buddha's teachings. Indeed, the Buddhist formally expresses his loyalty by affirming that he takes refuge in the "three jewels" (*triratna*) of Buddhism —the Buddha, the Dhamma (teaching), and the Sangha (the order). Thus the Order of monks (and nuns, who were later admitted by the Buddha) is an integral part of Buddhism.

The Four Noble Truths

What then was this Dhamma that the Buddha expounded in his first sermon delivered in the deer park at Sarnath on the outskirts of the holy city of Benares? It was summed up in the Four Noble Truths. These assert, first, that life is permeated with suffering or dissatisfaction (the original term, *dukkha*, literally means "ill-fare" as opposed to "welfare" or "happiness"); second, that the origin of suffering lies in craving or grasping, *tanha* (literally "burning thirst"—thirst for the things of this world, for survival in this world and the next, etc.); third, that the cessation of suffering is possible through the re-

moval of craving; and fourth, that the way to this cessation is the Noble
Eightfold Path.

The casting of the Buddha's doctrine into the form of four truths reflects
the ancient Indian method of giving a diagnosis in the case of illness. The
physician first determines what is wrong, then formulates the cause, then
determines whether a cure is possible, and finally prescribes the remedy. Thus
the Buddha evidently saw himself in the role of a doctor, a spiritual doctor
concerned with the cure of spiritual and physical troubles.

As the Four Noble Truths imply, the latter arise from all living beings'
(including the gods') tendency to cling to existence. By rooting out craving,
they can attain a serenity and an insight which will dispel the power of
karma. Indeed, one way in which the Buddha gives an original reinterpretation of the ideas which were current at his time is seen in his treatment
of karma, which essentially for him is a psychological force. Karma is not,
for him, as it was for the Jains, material: men's bondage to rebirth is in a
sense their own doing, for it arises from their attitudes and desires. Reform
these attitudes, and the burning will cease. He compared the process of rebirth
to the carrying on of a flame, as when one lamp is lit from another, a third
from the second, and so on. So if a man is still aflame at death—aflame with
wrong attitudes and desires—another "lamp" will be lit, another life will
commence, and this will continue indefinitely until one can cut off the fuel, so
to speak. Then rebirth will cease, and final nirvana will be attained. This
image may explain the term "nirvana," which literally means "cooling off" or
"going out," as of a flame.

Rebirth

The originality of the Buddha was not, however, confined to psychological
reinterpretation of karma. He also transformed the doctrine of rebirth. Hitherto, and indeed in most later Hindu theology, the doctrine was associated
with belief in a plurality of eternal souls. These transmigrate from one psychophysical organism to another—they successively animate a series of beings
with mental and physical attributes. The Buddha, however, denied this belief
in eternal souls or selves (the word very commonly used for eternal soul in the
Indian tradition means "self"). He enunciated the doctrine of the three characteristics of individual existence.

The things and persons that make up the world have three marks: suffering, *dukkha* (as in the Four Noble Truths); absence of self, *anatta;* and impermanence, *anicca.* Things that we see about us, such as trees and tables,
seem to be permanent. In fact, according to the Buddhist analysis, a thing
consists in a complex series of short-lived states or events. There is nothing
permanent in the world: only nirvana is permanent. This doctrine of imper-

manence, when it is applied to living beings, means that there can be no eternal soul. We like to think of ourselves as permanent beings, possessing within ourselves an eternal element which carries on. But according to the Buddhist view, we are only a series of mental and physical states. We too are impermanent.

Rebirth is not therefore to be pictured as the transmigration of a soul from one body to another. There is nothing that carries over from one life to another in this way. Just as one's mental and physical states at eight o'clock this morning give rise to one's mental and physical states at nine o'clock, so the craving implicit in a person's last state upon death is the cause of a new sequence of states arising elsewhere as his next life. For this reason, it is preferable to use the word "rebirth" in describing the Buddha's doctrine, rather than "reincarnation" or "transmigration." These last two imply that there is something (a soul, or self) to be reincarnated or to transmigrate. It may be noted too that the Buddhist analysis does not merely imply that there are not selves in the plural, but also that there is no cosmic Self which animates the whole universe. Buddhism set its face both against Jainism and against monistic doctrines that figured in the Indian tradition.

Nirvana in the Buddha's Teaching

The Buddha's denial of an eternal self appeared to create a difficulty about nirvana. Nirvana, of course, is the goal of Buddhist endeavor—to this the Noble Eightfold Path leads. According to Buddhist teaching, it has two aspects or phases. First, a monk may attain nirvana "with substrate." This means that he has attained supreme peace and insight in this life. He will go on living, so that his mind and body remain: this is the "substrate." But he will have assurance that, upon death, there will be no more rebirth. At his decease, he will have attained the second phase, nirvana *without* substrate. The substrate will simply cease. But then, since individuality is made up merely of the succession of mental and physical states, we can no longer speak of the individual as existing after his death in a state of final nirvana. The saint, or *arhat,* cannot, it seems, enjoy an individual nirvana of his own. It is not like "going to heaven," and it is not like the liberation accorded by Jain doctrine to the life-monads of the perfect ones.

This introduces us to a further aspect of the Buddha's teaching. He condemned certain questions as being unanswerable: they are "undetermined" questions, and they do not lead to edification. Among these was the question, Does the Tathagata (i.e., the Buddha), or a saint, exist after death? It is wrong to say either that he does, or that he does not, or that he both does and does not, or that he neither does nor does not. These negations may seem puzzling. But the Buddha clearly indicated what he meant by giving an example. If you ask in which direction a flame goes when it goes out, you cannot

THE INDIAN EXPERIENCE 101

say that it goes north, nor that it does not (for it does not go east, etc.), nor that it both goes north and some other direction. The question is an absurd one: it is wrongly put. Similarly, in terms of the Buddha's metaphysics, it is wrong to say that an individual, even the Buddha himself, exists in nirvana. On the other hand, the occurrence of the state of nirvana itself cannot be denied. One may sum up the Buddha's whole point here by saying that the idea of the plurality of individual souls is replaced by the doctrine (which can, according to him, be verified in experience) that there exist a multitude of individuals who are capable of attaining the transcendent perception of nirvana in this life, thereby ending their rebirth; and that there is a deathless realm, unborn, uncreated, namely nirvana, as testified by the Buddha's own Enlightenment and by the experience of the *arhats*. He gives a minimal metaphysical description of nirvana; but his description is also as much as *could* be said on the basis of philosophical reflection and mystical experience.

The Noble Eightfold Path

The practical side of the quest was summed up by the Buddha in terms of the Noble Eightfold Path—a path of life that has eight stages, or phases. It involves right views and right aspiration; right speech, right conduct, and right livelihood; right effort, right mindfulness, and right contemplation.

The first two refer to the preliminary attitudes of the aspirant. He must have the right views about reality, in accordance with the Buddha's teaching, and he must seek salvation.

The next three refer to the social and moral requirements for the Buddhist. These are also summed up in the Five Precepts, which give a clearer picture of the Buddhist ethic. They are as follows: the adherent must refrain from the taking of life (including, of course, animal life—this reflects an important aspect of the doctrine of rebirth; it is not just human life that must be treated with gentleness and compassion, for all kinds of life form a continuum). He must refrain from taking what is not given, or as the Westerner would say, from stealing. He must abstain from wrong sexual relations— fornication, adultery, and so forth. He must refrain from wrong use of speech, a principle mentioned as the third constituent of the Eightfold Path that includes more than just lying—malicious gossip, for instance, even though true, is forbidden. Finally, he must refrain from drugs and liquor: these tend to cloud the mind, and since Buddhist psychological training sets great store by the practice of self-awareness, i.e. knowledge of one's own motives, drugs and liquor are regarded as a hindrance. Further, intoxication can lead to violence, and Buddhism emphasizes most strongly the importance of gentleness and peacefulness. These Five Precepts apply to all, monks and laymen alike.

There are additional rules for monks and nuns designed to promote a moderate austerity. Monks may not own property except for a few simple possessions such as their garments, their begging bowls, etc. They are strictly enjoined to be celibate, and are forbidden worldly amusements. Such rules are far less stringent than the severe self-mortification the Buddha reacted against. Nevertheless, they signify the monk's rejection of luxury and even of ordinary comforts. In this respect, the Buddhist faith is a Middle Way, steering between the extremes of self-torture and self-indulgence.

The morality contained in the Eightfold Path serves as a general framework for living and for the pursuit of nirvana. The different constituents of the Eightfold Path are not stages on a pilgrimage—stages which can be left behind, and which have to be gone through in succession. Rather they are different aspects of a total way of life.

Meditation as a Spiritual Exercise

The last three states, involving right effort, right mindfulness, and contemplation, are central to Buddhist pragmatic ritual. This culminates in contemplation, *samadhi,* in which the adept frees his mind of all disturbing and extraneous thoughts and images.

As an example of the techniques used, it is worth referring to the practice of the *jhanas,* or stages of meditation. The monk first takes himself to a quiet spot and, seated on the ground, he places before himself an object to concentrate upon. Such a device (*kasina* as it is technically known) may be a blue flower, a round piece of clay, or some other such simple object. Thus prepared, he can enter into the four meditations of the realm of form, which lead to those of the formless realm. Suppose he is considering a blue flower. Then he concentrates upon it as simply blue and of a certain shape, in isolation from everything else. Further, he tries shutting his eyes and imagining it. This effort at excluding all other perceptions and images is great, so that at the first stage, the adept is aware of this effort. But in order to achieve further mastery, it is necessary to achieve the concentration without awareness of effort. This is the second stage. However, three elements remain in the adept's consciousness: he has a sense of rapture at his achievement, a sense of bliss, and collectedness of mind. The first two of these elements are eliminated in the remaining stages in the realm of form, since such joy can lead to disappointment when the state of trance ceases, and one of the objects of contemplation is to bring about complete equanimity.

After these four stages of the realm of form (so called because they involve the use of a device which belongs to the external world), the monk then enters the higher stages. First he conceives of everything as though it were boundless space. As it were, he empties the world of all its objects, and imagines empty space. Then he removes even this tenuous idea of external reality and conceives of reality as simply consisting of consciousness. But even this idea involves a thought of something. Therefore in the third stage of the "formless" meditations, he concentrates on the formula "There is nothing." Finally he reaches the stage of "neither-perception-nor-non-perception." In other words, it is a realm of consciousness which is not like perception or thought: there is no finite object which enters the adept's consciousness. However, it is not quite like dreamless sleep, for the monk is awake and conscious. He neither perceives, in the ordinary sense, nor is he unconscious. These stages of meditation perhaps help us to understand dimly at least what it is like to attain to pure consciousness; they point toward the nature of mystical experiences in which the Buddhist saint believes himself to have direct contact with the transcendent realm of nirvana.

Gods and Myths in Buddhism

The Eightfold Path illustrates the ethical and ritual dimensions of Buddhism. In addition to the pragmatic ritual of Buddhist yoga, the religion in various ways has had a ceremonial life which serves to make the teachings and loyalties of Buddhism evident to the faithful. Moreover, though the heart of Buddhist teaching is doctrinal, it is surrounded by a rich mythology. Some of these ceremonial and mythological elements came to have a heightened significance in that branch of Buddhism known as the Mahayana, or "Greater Vehicle" Buddhism.

Certain elements of mythology and ceremony can be seen in the accounts of the life of the Buddha. Recall, for instance, how the figure of Mara entered into the story of the Enlightenment. Mara as a personal symbol of evil provides a focus for Buddhist attempts to overcome the forces in the world and in human nature that resist the impulse toward a higher life. Buddhist writings are peopled with all kinds of gods, spirits, and demons. Buddhism transcends the worship of the gods, as does Jainism, but it does not deny them. The gods are beings who inhabit the cosmos; they are impermanent like other living beings; they too can only escape rebirth through nirvana. But they have no spiritual power. They do not know the secret of existence, except insofar as they listen to the Buddha himself. He is above the gods.

The Buddha's Death

We have seen some of the ideas underlying the Buddha's first sermon, ideas which he elaborated in many other discourses in his long life. Indeed, the rest of his life was given over to this teaching mission and to organizing the Sangha. With his disciples, he journeyed around the area from Patna and Benares on the Ganges to the borders of present-day Nepal. He died at the age of eighty, of a digestive ailment, not far from his birthplace. The places of his birth, death, Enlightenment, and first sermon are now great centers of Buddhist pilgrimage.

A little time before the Buddha's death, his favorite disciple, Ananda, was discovered to be weeping at the prospect of the Master's decease. The Buddha comforted him with words which express something of the serene spirit of his life and teaching.

> But now, Ananda, have I not formerly declared to you that it is in the very nature of all things near and dear to us to pass away? How, then, Ananda, seeing that whatever is brought into being contains within itself the inherent necessity of dissolution, how can it be that such a being (as the visible Gotama) should not be dissolved? . . . For a long time, Ananda, you have been very near to me by acts of love. You have done well, Ananda. Be earnest in effort and you too shall be free from the cankers of sensuality, of becoming, of false views and ignorance.[8]

On his deathbed, his last words were, "Decay is inherent in all compound things. Work out your own salvation with diligence."

THE UPANISHADS

Just how the Buddha's successors worked out their salvation, and the transformations which the Buddha's religion has undergone, we shall see a little later. In the meantime we must turn to another facet of the rich religious life of this last part of the early period of Indian history. A revolution was going on among the orthodox Brahmins. The Buddha's teaching and the thought of the Upanishads represent the two outstanding creations of that time. If the one changed and liberated the yogic tradition of non-Aryan India, the other gave a new depth and meaning to the religion of the Veda, which the Buddha rejected.

BRAHMAN

We have seen that appended to the Vedic hymns were certain ritual works known as the Brahmanas. The increased preoccupation with the ceremonies of sacrifice which characterized the latter half of the early period made it necessary for ritual to be described and explained in a formal way. But the compli-

---

[8] From *Buddhism* by Christmas Humphreys (Baltimore: Penguin Books, 3rd ed. 1962), pp. 40–41.

cation and formalism of this kind of religion did not satisfy everyone. Some wanted to know what the inner meaning of all this ritual really was. This is one main concern of the Upanishadic writings.

In order to understand the way in which the religious thinkers of this time approached this question of the inner meaning of religious externals, it is necessary to note one key concept of the Upanishads. This is the concept of *Brahman*. In origin this term referred to the sacred power implicit in the action of a sacrifice. Since a sacrifice was supposed to have some beneficial effects for the person on whose behalf it was made, it was thought to have within it a power which, in effect, the priest manipulated. The term Brahmin, moreover, is related to the word *Brahman*: sacredness was inherent in the priests also. But as time went on, the holy power, *Brahman,* was given a deeper and wider application. This new sense arose out of the speculations that preoccupied the Upanishadic writers. The whole cosmos was seen as a sacrifice. And if they perceived behind the multiplicity and complexity of ritual a sacred force, so more importantly behind the multitude of phenomena they deduced a Holy Power which sustains everything. The whole world was understood as divine action, welling forth from the mysterious being, *Brahman*. Thus the question of the inner meaning of ritual led to the question of the inner meaning of all existence.

At the same time, other influences were affecting Vedic religion. In the Upanishads for the first time within the Brahminical faith there was enunciated the doctrine of rebirth. Moreover, and in line with the yogic concerns which are often associated with this belief, there was a new interest in the quest for inner mystical experience. There was a drive to understand not only the outer world, but the inner world as well. The use of contemplative techniques might bring about a realization of the eternal, in its purity, lying within man—of the *Atman*. And if the inner meaning of ritual itself could serve to illuminate the inner meaning of the whole cosmos, so too perhaps the eternal self within could illuminate the nature of *Brahman*. Such speculations and intuitions led up to the central text of Upanishadic thinking, the famous *tat tvam asi*, "That thou art"—the claim that the self within and the Holy Power sustaining and pervading the whole world are in essence one.

THE BRAHMAN—ATMAN

Much of later Hindu theology turns on the various interpretations which can be given to this equation of *Brahman* with *Atman*. This notion is summed up in the story of Svetaketu and Uddalaka.

Svetaketu was the son of the Brahmin Uddalaka, and was sent off by his father to learn the Vedic lore. He came back after twelve years' study full of a fine opinion of himself and of his learning. The father soon pricked his conceit with a question the son did not know. Uddalaka then went on to teach him a secret doctrine of which the son, for all his Brahminical knowledge, was ignorant. A key passage in Uddalaka's exposition is as follows:

> "Put this piece of salt in the water and come to me tomorrow morning."
>
> [Śvetaketu] did as he was told. [Then his father] said to him:
>
> "[Do you remember] that piece of salt you put in the water yesterday evening? Would you be good enough to bring it here?"
>
> He groped for it but could not find it. It had completely dissolved.
>
> "Would you please sip it at this end? What is it like?" he said.
>
> "Salt."
>
> "Sip it in the middle. What is it like?"
>
> "Salt."
>
> "Sip it at the far end. What is it like?"
>
> "Salt."
>
> "Throw it away, and then come to me."
>
> He did as he was told but [that did not stop the salt from] remaining ever the same.
>
> [His father] said to him: "My dear child, it is true that you cannot perceive Being here, but it is equally true that it *is* here.
>
> "This finest essence,—the whole universe has it as its Self: That is the Real: That is the Self: That *you* are, Śvetaketu!"
>
> "Good sir, will you kindly instruct me further?"
>
> "I will, my dear child," said he.[9]

In short, divine being pervades the whole world, and is found eternally within the individual. Divine being is thus the supreme Self.

However, though the doctrine of the unity of all things, both outer and inner, is centrally important in the Upanishadic writings, these scriptures are by no means uniform in their teachings. They stem from the reflections of different seers and thinkers of the early period. Different Upanishads have different emphases. For some, *Brahman* is rather impersonal (the word is neuter, incidentally); for others, the supreme Being is conceived very much as a personal God. Thus: "He makes all, he knows all, the self-caused, the knower, the time of time, who assumes qualities and knows everything, the master of nature and man . . ."

[9] Chandogya Upanishad VI, 13, translated by R. C. Zaehner, *Hindu Scriptures* (Everyman's Library 1966 edition), p. III.

The supreme Being, moreover, transcends the gods. According to one Vedic text, there are "three and three hundred, three and three thousand gods." But the sage Yajnavalkya, the most prominent of these early thinkers, when asked who all these are, replied that they are only the various powers, i.e. of the one Being. To an earlier question, How many gods are there really? he had replied, "One." Thus there was a drive in Upanishadic speculation toward belief in a single Being, though there was not uniformity of view as to whether this Being should be considered as a personal Creator distinct from the world and from souls, or whether It embraces the world and is identical with what is found at the depth of the self.

Woven in with these deeper doctrinal strands, there are sacrificial, magical, and other ideas. It became the task of a later age to bring unity and consistency to the ferment of ideas expressed in the Upanishadic period. But it would not be wrong to say that these thinkers sought to provide a map that would chart the journey presupposed in a famous verse drawn from the Upanishads themselves:

Lead me from the unreal to the real;
Lead me from darkness into life;
Lead me from the mortal to the immortal.[10]

VEDIC AND UPANISHADIC THOUGHT

One could perhaps sum up the different aspects of Upanishadic thought by reference to and contrast with the religion of the Vedic hymns. The latter portray a world in which natural forces are shot through with power, brilliancy, and personality. They are implicit with terrifying yet also capriciously friendly purpose, save where they exhibit the calm orderliness of Varuna's rule. Perhaps, the hymns hint, they all express a single reality. But sacrificial ritual is addressed to the many gods; Indra, Soma, the Sun, and the rest. In the Upanishads, the brightness and the terror of the gods have already begun to fade. The gods symbolize a single divine Reality. The ritual, more earthbound, looms larger than the divine objects of the ceremonial, but like them, it points toward an explanation of the whole of life. The ritual too is fading as a thing in its own right. It retains meaning insofar as it mirrors the deeper reaches of the cosmos. Yet ritual meaning declines because the recluse, who retires to the forest to contemplate and to pursue the spiritual life, is no longer primarily interested in the transactions of priestly religion. The externals are not enough.

[10] Translated by F. Max Müller, *The Upanishads* Vol. XV, *The Sacred Books of The East,* 1884 (New York: Dover Publications, Inc., 1962), p. 83 f.

It is through the inward realization of truth that truth is known, not by worship of outer gods.

These tendencies allowed three ways in which the gods of the Vedic imagination could be transcended. The sacrifice addressed to them could be transcended. This meant a doctrine of the holy power *Brahman* as governing the universe. They could be transcended by thinking of Godhood as single, surpassing the many gods. This is what we find in the Upanishads which have a theistic flavor. Or again, the Vedic gods could be transcended by an interior quest toward immortality, gained experientially through the realization of the eternal element within man. It is the chief insight of the Upanishads that the interior quest is seen in relation to the other. The identification of *Brahman* with *Atman* is a fusion of the sacrificial and mystical tendencies. The theistic Upanishads express the way in which the path from the mortal to the immortal is also the path toward the one supreme personal God. There are sentiments and doctrines easily discovered in the Upanishadic writings that combine both of these last two positions.

The impressiveness of much of the Upanishadic doctrines is one reason they have remained a source of inspiration and commentary. It is upon them that most orthodox Hindu theology is based. The variegation of the texts helps to explain why Hinduism has grown so many and diverse theologies. These we shall come to investigate later.

CONCLUSION OF ERA OF BRAHMANISM

Meanwhile, it is useful to look back briefly upon the achievements of the early period. We have suggested that it saw the emergence of Jainism, the founding of the Buddhist religion, and the transition from the bright polytheism of the early Vedic hymns to a unified view of reality in the Upanishads. These three developments, of course, exclude many other manifestations of religion in these times about which we are ignorant, or that have not in the long run proved important in human culture. There were those, for instance, who believed in a form of fatalistic predestinationism; there were those who regarded severe austerities as symptoms of progress toward liberation. Other teachers had other views and other prescriptions. There were sceptics, who would affirm nothing for sure about this world, still less about the next. There were materialists who denied rebirth and the existence of the soul, and who were for long influential in the Indian scene. (There seems reason to suppose, even this early, that the Buddha was impressed by materialist argument against the immortality of the soul—one root of his non-self, or *anatta*, doctrine). Nevertheless, it turned out that the three developments outlined above were the most

9. The old temple of Svayambunath is the best-known of the many Buddhist temples in the valley of Kathmandu, Nepal. (Courtesy of the United Nations.)

10. Seated Buddha from Gandhara (3rd century). (Courtesy of Eugene Fuller Memorial Collection, Seattle Art Museum.)

11. The Sule Pagoda in Rangoon, Burma. In it is enshrined a hair of the Lord Buddha and other relics brought over from India by two Buddhist missionaries. This greatly venerated pagoda forms the exact center of the city. (Courtesy of the United Nations.)

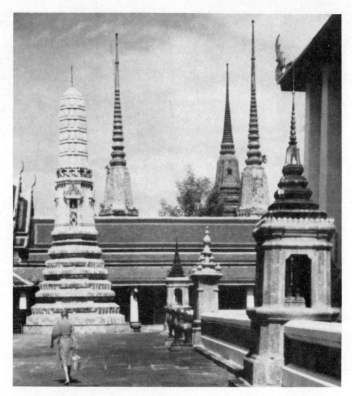

12. *Wat Poh, Bangkok, the oldest monastery in Thailand.*
(Courtesy of William O. Beville.)

13. *Multiple faces of*
God on one of the gates
of Angkor Wat in
Campuchea. (Courtesy
of the United Nations.)

14. *In Madras, India, Hindus celebrate the religious festival honoring the god Subramaniam. His statue is followed by statues of his two consorts, who are goddesses, and by Lord Shiva on the sacred cow Nandi. (Courtesy of the United Nations.)*

15. *Sacred cows in an Indian town. (Courtesy of the Library of Congress.)*

16. *Masked dancers representing the goddess Kali and other deities perform in front of the Nyatpula Dewal temple during the festival of Indra Jatra in the Kathmandu Valley in Nepal. (Courtesy of the United Nations.)*

17. *One of the towers of the famous Meenakshi Temple at Madurai in South India devoted to the spouse of Shiva. The sculptured tower represents the cosmos and numerous manifestations of the devine being. (India Government Tourist Office.)*

18. *Part of the frieze at Mahabaliparan Temple near Madras depicting the descent of the Ganges from heaven to earth. (India Government Tourist Office.)*

19. *The Golden Temple of Amritsar, India. (Courtesy of the United Nations.)*

20. *Temple sculptures from Khajuraho, India. (India Government Tourist Office.)*

21. *Sikhs outside the entrance to the Golden Temple at Amritsar. (Courtesy of the United Nations.)*

important for the Indian experience. They all exhibit one thing in common. Jainism and Buddhism in all probability belonged, the one conservatively and the other not, to an ancient tradition of yoga—of contemplation which involved seeking the eternal within, in an effort to escape from the ceaseless round of rebirth. From the early Vedic hymns, such ideas are totally absent. The hymns were outward looking, and though the later hymns begin to mention ascetics, there is little doubt that the methods of self-control that are summed up under the head of yoga belonged to the indigenous tradition.

We shall later see that the cults of Shiva and Vishnu, the great gods of Hinduism, are at least partly to be explained through the welling up of non-Aryan sentiments and cults. At any rate, the one thing the three developments have in common is yoga and its associated beliefs. Jainism and Buddhism keep this element, but neglect, in ultimate effect, the Aryan gods. The Upanishadic writings on the other hand provide a synthesis of the old religion and of yogic ideas and practices. This synthesis is summed up in the *Brahman-Atman* equation. What shines through the external world is found too in mystical experience. Yet also in some of the Upanishads, the drift toward belief in a single supreme God with whom men could enter into relationship, a drift already manifested in the Vedic hymns, becomes clearer. We shall see that during the post-Upanishadic classical period, there was a considerable heightening of this belief in a personal God, notably in the *Bhagavadgita*. Meanwhile, however, it is important to see how Buddhism developed after the decease of the great Teacher.

EARLY BUDDHISM

THE SANGHA

The characteristic social dimension of Buddhism is represented chiefly by the Sangha, the Order of monks and nuns. Originally this was composed of groups of wandering mendicants. They did not at first live in settled monasteries as they do today. During his lifetime the Buddha had decided that the Sangha should go into retreat during the rainy season. It became the custom for groups to spend their retreat together, and to cooperate in the pursuit of the spiritual life. Pious laymen gave plots of land in or near villages and towns for use as retreats; often these would include orchards and gardens. From such pragmatic arrangements, the settled communities evolved. In early days, the monasteries would at times be domiciled in caves, some of which were carved and ornamented in a splendid manner. One still may visit these wonderful testaments to Buddhist art.

"Songs of the Elders"

The poetry of the early monks and nuns helps us see something of the inner meaning of the life of the Sangha in the two or three centuries after the Buddha's decease. Many of the *Theragatha* and *Therigatha,* "Songs of the Elders," have come down to us.

These verses show that Buddhist recluses never entirely cut themselves off from society and nature. Theirs was not an utter withdrawal from the world. The tenderness of some of these verses and their sense of beauty help us realize that Buddhism was continuous with, even though transcendant to, the world about it. One of the poems may be translated as follow:

> In the woodland thickets beyond Ambataka park
> His craving pulled up by the root lucky Bhaddiya lives
> In meditation. Though some like the music of drums
> Or of cymbals and mandolins, my delight as I sit
> By a tree is the sound of the Buddha's message. And if
> The Buddha would grant me a wish and the wish were mine,
> I would choose that the whole world might constantly
> Be alert to the transcience of all physical things.[11]

The peacocks, shrieking in the rainy weather, are described in another poem:

> The peacocks shriek. Ah, the lovely crests and tails
> And the sweet sound of the blue-throated peacocks!
> The great grassy plain now runs with water
> Beneath the thunder-clouded sky.
> Your body's fresh, you are vigorous now and fit
> To test the Teaching: reach now for that saintly rapture,
> So bright, so pure, so subtle, so hard to fathom,
> The highest, the eternal place.[12]

We can see that a typical feature of Buddhism is expressed here: the teaching must be tested in inner experience, through the practice of meditation, or *jhana.* This may lead the adept to the "eternal place"—one of the epithets commonly used of nirvana. But if insight is gained in inner contem-

---

[11] Author's translation of Theragatha 466 ff.
[12] Author's translation of Theragatha 211 ff., "The Peacocks."

plation, it can also arise spontaneously in certain external situations. Another of the early Buddhists writes:

> *Got up with flowers and perfumes*
> *Dressed in alluring clothes,*
> *The dancing-girl in the main-street*
> *Swayed to the sound of a band.*
> *I'd gone down into the city*
> *To beg, and had seen her there,*
> *In all her finery, dancing,*
> *A snare that the Tempter had laid.*
> *Then the basic truth of the matter*
> *And the misery of it all*
> *Became suddenly transparent,*
> *And so produced distaste.*[13]

We note that, in accord with the Buddhist discipline, the recluse must make his living by begging. This reflects too the duty of the layman to maintain the Sangha through almsgiving. Monk and layman were bound together in mutual obligation. The one expounded the teaching and gave an example of saintly living; the other gave food and shelter.

The personal dimension of Buddhist ritual was, for the monk, essentially pragmatic—centering on the yogic techniques whereby he gained self-mastery and insight. As monastic life developed and became more elaborate, there also developed a more ceremonial public ritual. The monk in the monastery experienced the departed Buddha in a way profoundly different from those who had followed the Teacher during his life. New attitudes and feelings came to impart a new dynamic to the religion. Significant changes in the ritual occurred as Buddhism evolved, changes we see reflected in Buddhist poetry and legend, architecture and sculpture.

BUDDHIST ARCHITECTURE AND SCULPTURE

At first, Buddhism was without sanctuaries or temples. But after the Buddha's death, his cremated remains were distributed to various centers where they were interred in *stupas*. The first simple mounds were symbols and places of homage. As time went on, they were treated more elaborately, and were covered with brick, stone, and plaster, sometimes even with gold. Not only the

---

[13] Author's translation of Theragatha 267 ff.

Buddha's remains, but those too of saintly Buddhists formed foci of homage. The *stupas,* white and rounded, with a tiny spire surmounting them, are still a pleasant aspect of the scenery of Ceylon, gleaming through the green foliage of the surrounding jungle or plantations. In differing forms, such temple monuments may be seen throughout the other Buddhist countries.

For a long time, there were no figure representations of the Buddha. This period is reflected by an early legend. It is said that the monks of Jetavana wished to place in their monastery something to remind them of the Buddha and that they discussed what form it should take. They rejected the idea of a statue of the Teacher on the ground that a statue would be unreal and imaginary, since the Buddha had attained final nirvana and no longer existed as an individual who could be represented. He had in fact vanished from all existence: he did not go on being, like the gods in paradise who could be depicted in sculptures. Therefore the monks decided to represent the Buddha by certain associative symbols, such as a replica of his footprint, or the tree under which he attained Enlightenment. Most of the Buddha's followers must have felt as the monks of Jetavana did, for in early Buddhist sculpture we find carvings where many human figures are represented—people listening to the Buddha preaching, for example—but where the central figure of the Teacher himself is absent, save for the associative symbols.

Bhakti and Representational Art

Gradually other tendencies in religious practice and experience influenced Buddhist sculpture in quite a different manner. There developed an increasing feeling of personal devotion to the Buddha which is called *bhakti.* Bhakti, the loving adoration of the Buddha and of past Buddhas and Buddhas-to-be (for the mythological dimension of Buddhism is rich in its account of the great teachers who have inhabited different spheres and epochs in the history of the whole cosmos), led to a desire to represent these beings directly. Thus in the first century B.C., statues of the Buddha became fashionable.

It is uncertain where the practice of representing the Buddha directly first arose. There were two great centers of sculpture at this time—Gandhara in northwest India and Mathura on the Jumna river. The Gandhara sculptors were much influenced by Greek art, a legacy of the conquest of northwest India by Alexander the Great in the late fourth century B.C. Alexander's empire had been shortlived, but Greek kingdoms continued to exist in that region for three centuries more. Indeed, one of the most famous of Buddhist writings is the *Milindapanha,* or "Questions of King Menander," describing a dialogue between a Greek king and a Buddhist monk called Nagasena. The conversation concerns the essentials of the Buddha's religion, and ends with the conversion of the king. The Gandhara representations of the Buddha give him the appearance of Apollo, and the glorious sculptures of the period are a fine example of the cross-fertilization of eastern and western cultures.

These artistic changes were not simply external. They reflect the deepening influence of the religious experience of *bhakti*. *Bhakti* answered the need felt by the ordinary Buddhist layman, as well as many monks, to give expression to the religious attitude of worship of a higher being. The development of a religion of loving adoration contrasted with the inward-directed discipline of serene meditation that hitherto had been so central to the Buddhist path. The emergence of *bhakti* was accompanied by certain philosophical changes. Together, these two forces transformed Buddhism and gave rise to the so-called Greater Vehicle or Mahayana Buddhism.

VENERATION OF THE BODHISATTVA

The cult of Buddhas and of Bodhisattvas (Buddhas-to-be, great beings destined for Buddhahood) had its root in popular devotionalism, but it also reflected a tension in the ethical attitudes of Buddhism. While the Buddha laid strong emphasis both upon compassion and upon the need to rigorously follow the Eightfold Path, monastic religion seemed to be turning from the ideal of compassion and concerning itself unduly with individual salvation. After all, the saint, or *arhat,* who realizes his own nirvana can only do so through complete concentration within himself, which might be thought to necessitate disregard for others. Critics of a narrow interpretation of the monastic ideal recalled that the Buddha himself was tempted by Mara to disappear into nirvana without preaching the saving doctrine. The Buddha sacrificed his privilege of immediate entry into nirvana and lived out a strenuous life of teaching and organizing.

Following the Buddha's example, the Bodhisattva is a saintly man who, on the verge of Buddhahood, sacrifices himself and endures gratuitous rebirth for the welfare of other beings. Like the Buddha, he puts off his nirvana to help others gain theirs, and by so doing saves them from untold miseries and afflictions. The Bodhisattva became a living symbol of compassion. The concept of karma itself underwent a transformation. The Buddhist doctrine of karma, like the Jain, is based on the idea that one's deeds determine one's destiny in this life and in the next. A man's status in society and his hopes for a better position in his next reincarnation are controlled by the effect of prior actions. According to the doctrine of the Bodhisattva, the Buddha-to-be acquires, through his countless lives of self-sacrifice, a virtually infinite store of merit. Out of this great store, he can distribute merit to the otherwise unworthy faithful. The person who calls on a Bodhisattva in faith will, on death, be reborn in a paradise—not through his own merits, but through the Bodhisattva's.

There also evolved belief in celestial Buddhas who could be worshipped and prayed to. They were capable of creating paradises. One of the best-known, Amitabha, created the Pure Land of the West—a joyful and splendid place where the conditions for attaining nirvana are peculiarly propitious, and whither the faithful will be translated upon death. Thereby the effects of karma were by-passed. These conceptions, of course, should not be taken in too literal or mechanical a way. The idea that a Bodhisattva or Buddha can transfer merit is a way of dealing with the experience that in other faiths is termed "grace." It expresses the feeling of the devotee that he is dependent on the holy Being whom he worships and that salvation comes from that holy Being and not from the efforts of the devotee. The worshiper cannot but feel his own inadequacy when confronted with the overwhelming, holy glory of the Being whom he adores. He is aware that salvation comes not from his own inadequate efforts to achieve paradise, but from the mercy of God. This sentiment is symbolized in the doctrine of the transfer of merit in Greater Vehicle Buddhism.

MAHAYANA AND HINAYANA

The new wing of Buddhism gave itself the name Mahayana, "the Greater Vehicle," as opposed to the older, more conservative Hinayana, or "Lesser Vehicle." The Mahayanists thought that the conservative tradition was "lesser" in two ways. First, its stress upon the monastic life implied that laymen could scarcely hope for salvation; they could only hope that rebirth would give them a higher spiritual status in which they would hear the call to enter the Order. But the new ideas of faith and devotion, *bhakti*, implied that the layman too could be near to ultimate release. Thus the Mahayana was a "greater vehicle" for transporting men to salvation, and also a wider career for the pious Buddhist to follow.

The Hinayana way to nirvana was held to be a "lesser" or "meaner" vehicle because, according to its opponents, it was narrow in its ethical ideals —it was not outward-looking and compassionate, in the way symbolized by the Bodhisattva. The monk seeks to become an *arhat*—a saint who has attained nirvana: the adherent of the Greater Vehicle follows the path of the Bodhisattva sacrificing himself for others. It should, of course, be kept clearly in mind that the term "Lesser Vehicle" was introduced virtually as a term of abuse. The surviving Lesser Vehicle school, to be found today in Ceylon, Burma, and parts of southeast Asia, calls itself *Theravada* ("Doctrine of the Elders"). Its adherents, naturally, prefer to be known as "Theravadins" rather than by a title invented by their opponents. It must be stressed, however, that the two great wings of Buddhism today live together on the most amicable terms, and it is doubtful whether the divisions of Buddhism have ever been as serious as those dividing Christianity at the time of the Reformation and thereafter. This is because Buddhism takes a rather pragmatic attitude toward doctrine, so that very different doctrines can be embraced by people calling themselves Buddhists provided that they are loyal to the essential spirit of the Buddha and to the Order which he established.

Bhakti in Mahayana Scripture

The mythological symbolism in which the religion of *bhakti* was clothed can be illustrated from a passage in the most famous of the Greater Vehicle scriptures, the *Lotus Sutra,* or *Lotus of the Good Law.*

> And at that moment there issued a ray from within the circle of hair between the eyebrows of the Lord [Buddha]. It extended over eighteen hundred thousand Buddha-fields [i.e. spheres in which Buddhas exercise their creativity] in the eastern quarter, so that all those Buddha-fields appeared wholly illuminated by its radiance, down to the great hell Avichi and up to the limit of existence. And the beings in any one of the six states of existence became visible, all without exception. Likewise the Lords Buddhas staying, living and existing in those Buddha-fields became all visible, and the law preached by them could be entirely heard by all beings. And the monks, nuns, lay devotees male and female, Yogins and students of Yoga, those who had obtained the fruition of the paths of sanctification and those who had not, they too became visible. And the Bodhisattvas . . . in those Buddha-fields who plied the Bodhisattva-course with ability, due to their earnest belief in numerous and various lessons and the fundamental ideas, they too became all visible. Likewise the Lords Buddhas in those Buddha-fields who had reached final Nirvana became visible, all of them. And the Stupas made of jewels and containing the relics of the extinct Buddhas became all visible in those Buddha-fields.[14]

Thus is expressed the devotee's overwhelming experience of the glory of the Buddha as a heavenly and splendid Being. The eye of faith looks beyond

[14] Translation by H. Kern as it appears in *Saddharma-Pundarika or The Lotus of the True Law,* Vol. XXI of *The Sacred Books of the East,* ed. F. Max Müller (reprinted New York: Dover Publications, 1963), pp. 7-8.

the figure of the historical Buddha and beyond the visible world around him. Through the veil of the material realm he has a vision of the whole dimension of the world infused with radiance and illuminated by the wisdom and power of the Buddhas.

The popular cults centered especially upon certain Buddhas and Bodhisattvas around whom a rich mythological tradition gathered. We have mentioned already the Buddha Amitabha (Infinite Glory), sometimes called Amitayus (Infinite Age), who reigns in the Pure Land of the West. Among the Bodhisattvas, and often closely associated with Gautama and Amitabha, there is the famous Avalokitesvara, the Lord Who Looks Down (that is, with compassion upon the faithful). His thousand arms symbolize the tireless energy which he expends in working for the welfare of living beings. He should live in paradise, but chooses often to come down to earth to help animals and men, and he even visits hell to take cool drinks to those who suffer its hot torments. There is also Maitreya, the future Buddha, who will restore peace and truth to the world. There is some evidence that at least some of this mythology derives from Persia; but it also expresses the popular devotionalism which permeated Buddhism in the last century B.C. and afterward.

THE NATURE OF REALITY — BUDDHIST PHILOSOPHY

During this time philosophical developments occurred parallel to those taking place in popular religion. The Lesser Vehicle sects held that reality is composed of a complex and varied series of impermanent states. The individual and the things that he sees around him are composed of such states. Any element of permanence is excluded, except that nirvana itself is a permanent state. Of course, according to the Lesser Vehicle, there is a pattern of things— or rather, many patterns. For the sequence of events in a person or in a thing is controlled by the law of causation. Thus a person consists in a sequence of mental and physical states or events which follow one another according to natural law; even a non-personal thing like a table, for instance, is a complex series of events governed by the laws of nature.

There were certain difficulties in this view, and these were probed by Greater Vehicle philosophers.

Nagarjuna

One of the most notable of these was Nagarjuna, who lived at the end of the first century A.D., or somewhat later. He used subtle arguments to undermine commonsense views of reality including orthodox Buddhist analyses of the situation.

Nagarjuna held that the doctrine of impermanence ought to imply that when a state comes into existence, it also simultaneously goes out of existence.

If it could persist for five minutes, he argued, it could theoretically go on forever. But if it is momentary, then it cannot cause any other state to come into existence: it would have gone out of existence before the state it is supposed to cause had come into existence. But how can what is non-existent have any effect? Still one cannot adopt the converse principle and suppose that causes are permanent, and not momentary, for a permanent cause should have a permanent effect, and yet the things we normally want to explain in the world are not permanent.

By such arguments, concerning not only the idea of cause but all other attempts to produce theories about the world, Nagarjuna and his followers tried to show that all views about reality are contradictory. He concluded that reality is empty, or void (*sunya*). This "emptiness," or "void," is the inner essence of reality (that is, of the world). Thus there was evolved the notion that ordinary experience gives access to an unreal and insubstantial world. Only through thought and contemplative experience can we see truth. This philosophical view gave rise to a way of talking about reality as the Void. This became the name in effect for the Absolute which lies behind, or pervades, the world of ordinary experience, and which constitutes, so to say, its inner essence.

The Void School and the Idealists

Following Nagarjuna, other metaphysicians evolved another and somewhat different view of the Absolute. They argued that we know nothing about the external world about us except on the basis of experience. But experience consists in a series of perceptions. Is it reasonable or necessary to think that, in addition to the perceptions, there is a world of things? Why not simply suppose that the world is made up of perceptions? After all, we can never have access to things as distinct from our perception of them, for if we were to observe some such thing, our observation would itself be merely a perception.

The school of Buddhist philosophers who argued in this way came to be called the *Vijnanavadins,* or the "Consciousness" or "Representation Only" school. In western terms they would most likely be called Idealists (as contrasted with Materialists). But they had to explain the origin of our experiences: these they believed to emanate from an Absolute, which they called the Store-Consciousness (*alaya-vijnana*). This has been likened by some to the collective unconscious postulated by Jung, but it might more appropriately be described as a collective consciousness, from which arise the individual perceptions that lead men to think that the material world really is like the conscious images and representations by which we seek to represent it. The sky is blue when we look at it, but is it really like that, in itself? Every picture of the world is merely that, just a picture. The world in itself is indescribable. Both the proponents of the Void and the Vijnanavadins tended toward belief in an Absolute underlying the unreal phenomena that we encounter in ordinary life and experience.

The Absolute, or ultimate reality, was described with such mysterious names as Empty, the Void, the Store-Consciousness, and Suchness—expressions which bring out its ineffability. This idea of an Absolute tied in with the religious developments described above. A series of equations came about which explained the ideal of the Bodhisattva. If ultimate reality is somehow the inner essence of what we perceive, and is yet invisible and transcendent, it was natural to identify it with the goal of the spiritual life. In short, nirvana and the Absolute are one. But if the mystical attainment of nirvana involves an inner contemplative state in which distinctions of all kinds are transcended, then it is nonsense to think of the person who attains nirvana as distinct from nirvana itself. Consequently, the saint who attains nirvana in some sense *becomes* the Absolute. And the Buddha, in attaining *his* Enlightenment and nirvana, becomes the Absolute. It follows clearly that the Buddhist saint becomes identical with the Buddha. The goal of men is not just nirvana, then, but Buddhahood. We are destined for Buddhahood. Thus men who tread the upward path are Buddhas-to-be; and are, to use the other term, Bodhisattvas. Here philosophical and religious ideas come together. But it should be noted that the crucial step in this thinking turns upon the nature of mystical experience. Since the Mahayana Buddhists like their Theravada brothers regarded this experience as "non-dual," without distinctions, they could not—once having admitted the idea of ultimate reality or the Absolute—deny that the saint is one with the Absolute. But there was no wish to deny this: the theory fitted in marvelously with the ideal of the Bodhisattva. The prospective saint (so to say) has to tread the path of the Bodhisattva, for he *is* a Bodhisattva. But this involves self-sacrifice and the active exercise of compassion. In this way the life of the contemplative and that of the moral hero were integrated.

The Three-Body Doctrine of Mahayana

However, the development of doctrine went beyond these equations in a most interesting manner. There evolved the belief in the "three bodies," or three aspects of the Buddha. We have seen that devotion to the Buddha was reflected in a richly mythological way by the idea of heavenly Buddhas whose paradises were open to living beings who called upon them with faith. Such Buddhas were in effect divine beings: they were certainly objects of worship. Their glory has been suggested in the quotation which we included from the famous *Lotus Sutra*. These celestial foci of the religious imagination were interpreted doctrinally. They contrasted with the manifestation of the Buddha as a person teaching upon earth, as Gautama. The human aspect of the Buddha was regarded as the "Transformation-Body" of the Buddha. Each of his various celestial forms was regarded as the "Enjoyment-Body" of the Buddha. These two aspects of the Buddha could only be understood against the background of ultimate reality. As has been seen, all Buddhas are united in the Absolute. This ultimate basis of Buddhahood was described doctrinally as the "Truth-Body" of the Buddha. (The word here translated as "Truth" is actually *Dharma,* the Sanskrit equivalent of the word *Dhamma* as used in the Pali scriptures, i.e. those of the Theravada. The word primarily refers to the teaching which the Buddha gave to the world. But it then came to mean what the teaching referred to—namely, nirvana, or, from the Greater Vehicle point of view, the void, suchness. Thus the "Truth-Body" of the Buddha is ultimate reality.) All this amounted to the belief that there is an ultimate reality, that this manifests itself in a god-like way as the celestial Buddhas, that it further manifests itself as the historical Buddha, and that through following Gautama, through devotion to the Buddhas, and through the contemplative attainment of non-dual insight, one could climb up from earthly life to heavenly existence, and from heavenly existence to identity with the Absolute. The ordinary man can, after an immense round of lives, become a Buddha. No wonder it was a Mahayana saying that the Buddhas are as numerous as the sands on the Ganges!

Bhakti and Three-Body Doctrine

It is not hard to see that the "Three-Body" doctrine was a way of uniting different aspects of Buddhist piety. Through the mythology of the celestial Buddhas it expressed the devotionalism and the religion of worship, *bhakti,* which came more and more to figure in the originally atheistic Buddhist tradition. It expressed the desire for a supreme Being and friend. It gave a place to the personal Lord in Buddhism. This religious point of view did not, however, prevail in India: it is more characteristic of Asian Buddhism. Indian Buddhism, partly through this very Three-Body doctrine, subordinated the cult of a personal Lord to the ultimate aim of nirvana and the intuition of the non-dual Void. Contemplative religion remained supreme in India: the Lesser and Greater Vehicles concurred on this emphasis. But Chinese and Japanese Buddhism went beyond this position, and developed schools or sects which verged on a thorough-going theism and raised devotion to a personal Lord above the ideal of contemplative experience. In far-eastern Buddhism, *bhakti* at times all but replaced yoga. Nevertheless, the Three-Body doctrine preserved the essential Buddhist priorities. But at the same time it conceded the demands of popular and devotional religion. And not only this, it provided, through the belief in the one Absolute, a unification of the complex mythology of the celestial and earthly Buddhas. Though legend and imagination might turn to many Buddhas, they are all essentially one in the Truth-Body.

The Mahayana Synthesis

Thus Mahayana ideas represented a confluence of varying tendencies. The Greater Vehicle blended together two sorts of religious experience and practice: it combined the life of contemplation with the worshiper's intuition of numinous and powerful objects of devotion. It also blended popular and philosophical insights. And it brought together these philosophical and popular beliefs with the demands of compassion. It made sense of the path of the compassionate Bodhisattva who is destined both for contemplative release and for loving self-sacrifice.

This last point can be illustrated from the ethical dimension of Greater Vehicle Buddhism, which is typified by the requirements expected of the one who wishes to tread the path of the Bodhisattva. As a preliminary, the aspirant should practice worship (*puja*). Unlike the Theravadin monk's rule, Mahayana encourages the life of devotion as a significant part of the aspirant's quest for higher insight. Through worship of the Buddhas, the aspirant can hope to gain assurance from a living Buddha that his desire to gain enlightenment will in fact be realized. In prayer, he gains encouragement for further efforts. His call to Buddhahood is therefore seen not to be in vain. He next undertakes the contemplative life, which corresponds to that required of the Theravadin, but there are differences, partly because the aspirant to Buddhahood in the Greater Vehicle has a somewhat different interpretation of what he is doing. This practice of the contemplative life is called the practice of the "perfections" (*paramitas*), which will bring him, eventually, supreme insight. Moreover, the path of self-control and self-giving is open both to layman and to monk. The aspect of self-giving and compassion is strongly emphasized, so that (in theory at any event) Greater Vehicle Buddhism keeps reminding the faithful of the close relation between their religious practices and their ethical ones.

To sum up, Mahayana Buddhism, as expressed in the above ideas, united contemplative and devotional experience. The Buddha becomes more than a great teacher: he is a saviour in a more personal way. As the *Lotus Sutra* says:

> I am the Tathagata, O ye gods and men! the Arhat, the perfectly enlightened one; having reached the shore myself, I carry others to the shore; being free, I make free; being comforted, I comfort; being perfectly at rest, I lead others to rest. By my perfect wisdom I know both this world and the next, such as they really are. I am all-knowing, all-seeing. Come to me, ye gods and men! hear the law. I am he who indicates the path; who shows the path, as knowing the path, being acquainted with the path.

I shall refresh all beings whose bodies are withered, who are clogged to the triple world. I shall bring to felicity those that are pining away with toils, give them pleasures and final rest.[15]

Such developments characterized Buddhism in its history within India, during the last century of the first millennium B.C. and the first centuries of the present era. It was largely this Mahayana form of Buddhism that was carried north-eastward into China, and from there into other countries in East Asia. Let us then turn to a brief survey of the outer historical events which brought about the expansion of Buddhism.

BUDDHIST MISSIONARY EXPANSION

Buddhism started as a small movement in northern India. But by the time the emperor Asoka assumed the throne in 270 B.C. of a kingdom that stretched over most of northern and central India, the religion was already widespread. It was further helped by the patronage of this emperor. After a particularly bloody campaign against the Kalingas, who occupied an area corresponding roughly to the modern state of Orissa (south of Bengal), he repented of violence, and devoted himself to good works. This included sending out embassies and missions to spread the Buddhist gospel. Asoka set up in various parts of his empire edicts inscribed on pillars and rocks, and one of these records these missions. He sent them as far as Macedonia, Syria, and Cyrene, then part of the Hellenistic world. This then was the first Buddhist mission to the West.

Sri Lanka

In Sri Lanka, or Ceylon, the new religion took root. Mahinda, who was either the son of, or a close relative of, Asoka, arrived in Sri Lanka with six monks, and succeeded in converting the king at his capital Anuradhapura. The ruins of this magnificent city still remain, one of the centers of pilgrimage and tourism in the Sri Lanka of today. Nearby, at Mihintale, Mahinda established a hermitage. A shoot from the tree under which the Buddha gained his Enlightenment was brought from Bodh Gaya, and the tree is still to be seen at Anuradhapura. Buddhism continued to flourish in succeeding centuries, and has been the dominant religious and cultural force in Sri Lanka for over two thousand years. Though now the form is that of the Theravada, this was not always exclusively so, and there were times when Greater Vehicle influences were present in the island.

From the first century A.D., Buddhism began to penetrate into China. This, however, is part of the theme of the next chapter, when we shall turn to

[15] H. Kern's translation as it appears in *The Bible of the World*, p. 328.

the Chinese religious experience. The faith also spread from India into lower Burma, though it was not until the late medieval period that, under influences from Sri Lanka, the Theravadin form of the religion came to dominate the whole country. A mixture of Mahayana Buddhism and Hinduism penetrated into southeastern Asian countries during the fourth century A.D. and onward. During the later medieval period, the revival of the Theravada resulted in the replacement of Greater Vehicle Buddhism in Laos, Cambodia or Kampuchea, and Thailand, and to some degree in Vietnam.

Tibet

By the mid-seventh century Buddhist missionaries had pressed northward from India into Tibet. Because of certain distinctive characteristics of the faith as found in Tibet and surrounding areas, this type of Buddhism is sometimes reckoned as a separate "vehicle"—the Vajrayana or "Diamond Vehicle." By the eleventh century, despite resistance from the indigenous Bon religion, it had become well established. Though the scriptures and doctrines imported into Tibet were generally speaking Mahayana in origin, certain ritual and sacramental practices known as Tantrism—common to both Hinduism and later Buddhism—were prominently employed.

Some of these practices centered on the ritual infringement of tabus as a means of spiritual enlightenment and as a test of detachment. What is normally considered wrong and seductive (for the sweet fruits tend to get forbidden, though, of course, not *all* sweet fruits) is performed under controlled conditions, in the course of a ritual occasion. For instance, sexual intercourse was used as a controlled means of symbolizing the non-dual mystical experience: for the fleshly union and ecstasy bring about, for the moment at any rate, a merging of two beings. Likewise in mystical union the adept and ultimate reality are no longer separate. It was this and other ritual forms of Buddhism, then, which proved most influential in the medieval Tibetan tradition. But it would be wrong to suppose that such methods of training were a license for immorality. Naturally, human nature being what it is, there were abuses of Tantrism. But on the whole it was a sincere, though unorthodox, potentially dangerous, and perhaps even misguided way of trying to gain detachment. It is one of the many forms of religion which represent experiments with the human spirit.

The main temper of Tibetan religion can best be illustrated from one of the writings which expresses this form of the Buddhist faith. One passage reads:

> *Charity produceth the harvest in the next birth,*
> *Chastity is the parent of human happiness.*
> *Patience is an adornment becoming to all.*

Industry is the conduct of every personal accomplishment.
Meditation is the clarifier of a beclouded mind.
Intellect is the weapon which overcometh every enemy.[16]

Tibetan Buddhism has come to be split into two main sects, the Nyingmapa, known as the "Red Hats" from their headgear, and the Gelugpa, known as the "Yellow Hats." The Red Hats have a strong admixture of early pre-Buddhistic ideas and practices of a magical and sacramental nature. The most interesting scripture of this sect is the famous *Bardo Thodol,* or *Book of the Dead.* It describes the experiences of the individual during the forty-nine days which are supposed (and here this work differs from traditional Buddhist belief) to intervene between death and rebirth, when the self approaches the heavenly splendors. If it has been wicked, it finds the glory of the divine mysteries too frightening, and in panic, turns back to rebirth on earth, where reality is not so terrifying. Conversely, the virtuous individual delights in the heavenly realm, and continues on the upward path.

The Gelugpa, "Yellow Hats" Buddhism, represents a reformed Tantrism, and has as its principal religious head the Dalai Lama. It may be noted that Tibetan Buddhism is sometimes known as Lamaism, from the title "lama" given to the monks. From Tibet the Diamond Vehicle spread into Mongolia during the thirteenth century onward. Today it is in evidence in Nepal, Bhutan, and other areas of the Himalayan foothills. .

BUDDHIST SCRIPTURES

It is useful to conclude this survey of the Buddhist experience by referring to the various scriptures of the faith. The Theravadin scriptures are written in the language of Pali, which stands to Sanskrit much as Italian stands to Latin. The Pali canon is divided into three sections, or "baskets" (the *Tipiṭaka:* Sanskrit *Tripiṭaka*), namely *Sutta, Vinaya,* and *Abhidhamma.* The first consists in records of the discourses of the Buddha, together with incidents in his life, etc. The second contains rules for the discipline of the Sangha. The third contains the analysis and exposition of doctrines. These scriptures were first committed to writing in the latter part of the first century B.C.

The Greater Vehicle canon comprises documents that are written in Sanskrit and whose contents overlap with the above Pali writings, together with various other works, including the famous *Lotus Sutra,* or *Lotus of the Good Law.* These writings were translated into Chinese and then later into Japanese, and were added to in the process. Similarly there were additions in

[16] Translation by Lama Kazi Dawa-Samdup as it appears in *The Bible of the World,* p. 343.

the canon of the Diamond Vehicle. Thus there is a series of different, but
overlapping, canons in Buddhism. The diversity of the faith is reflected in its
scriptures. The Mahayana additions accorded with the theory of a developing
revelation—the idea that the Buddha did not intend his teaching as a static
creation, but rather as an introduction to the good life which itself might yield
later insights that could supersede the earlier doctrines.

Attitudes to the texts varied in another way. In the Theravada, the scriptures simply represent an account, both historical and analytical, of the teachings and life of the Buddha and of the earliest church. In the Greater Vehicle,
there is a tendency to ascribe sacred properties to the texts. This partly because the meaning of the texts came increasingly to be identified with what
they refer to—ultimate reality and the transcendent Truth-Body of the
Buddha. The doctrines and the words are like "fingers pointing at the moon."
Thus someone who understands the texts in faith already has come close to
the Buddha and to salvation. By uttering with faith a single verse of the *Lotus
Sutra,* the devotee can be assured of final release through the grace of the
Buddha. To be sure, one's consciousness must transcend the words. To concentrate on them is like looking at the pointing finger rather than at the moon
at which it points. There is a famous Zen picture of a monk tearing up the
scriptures. This symbolizes the need to transcend the words.

The Decline of Buddhism in India

The Buddhists who carried their faith from the Indian subcontinent beyond
the mountains and the seas profoundly effected the destiny of all East Asian
culture. But in India itself Buddhism slowly diminished, save in some areas
along the foothills of the Himalayan range in the areas abutting on Tibet.
The reasons for this were complex, but two can be singled out.

First, in its Greater Vehicle form, Buddhism became increasingly like the
Hinduism surrounding it, and the revival of the latter in the early medieval
period meant that Buddhism so lost distinctiveness that it failed to maintain
a separate identity in India. Second, the Muslim invasions that began in the
eleventh century A.D. resulted in the destruction of the monasteries and the
dispersal of the monks; since the Order was the central social institution in
Buddhism, its demise was the deathblow of the faith.

CLASSICAL HINDUISM

In the next chapter we shall trace the development of Buddhism in China and
Japan. Meanwhile, we must look back to see how Hinduism, during the classical and medieval periods, expressed religious tendencies which were different
from, but parallel to, those of Buddhism.

In the period following the Upanishads, there was, within Hinduism, a great development of devotional religion. This was expressed most strikingly in the most famous of Indian scriptures, the *Bhagavadgita,* or "Song of the Lord." There is some doubt as to when this was composed, but it may have been in the second century B.C., or somewhat later. It forms part of one of the great Hindu epics, the *Mahabharata,* but is essentially complete in itself, and is usually treated, for religious purposes, as a separate work. The setting of the poem is this.

THE BHAGAVADGITA

The hero, Arjuna, is waiting for the start of a great battle, and is troubled by the thought of the destruction and suffering that will inevitably take place, especially as he has relatives among the enemy. "Alas!" he laments. "In committing a great sin are we engaged, we who are endeavoring to kill our kindred from greed of the pleasures of kingship. If the sons of Dhritarashtra, weapon in hand, should slay me, unresisting, unarmed in the battle, that would for me be the better." Krishna, however, who is an incarnation of the supreme god Vishnu, is disguised as Arjuna's charioteer, and offers him comfort, advice, and spiritual teaching. The major part of the poem consists in these teachings, which take their point of departure from Arjuna's problem. In the course of the Gita, there is presented a theistic form of religion which also incorporates ideas drawn from other traditions, such as yoga. In this way the poem attempts a synthesis of the important trends in religious and philosophical thinking and experience of the period.

The Lord's initial solution of Arjuna's problem is in a way paradoxical. He tells him that the wise know that men have eternal souls, transmigrating from one life to another. Thus there is no need to grieve at a man's death:

> *As a man casts off his worn-out clothes*
> *And takes on other new ones [in their place],*
> *So does the embodied soul cast off his worn-out bodies*
> *And enters others new.*
>
> *He cannot be cut by sword,*
> *Nor burnt by fire;*
> *The waters cannot wet him,*
> *Nor the wind dry him up.*[17]

---

[17] Bhagavadgita, II, 22-23, translated by R. C. Zaehner, *Hindu Scriptures* (Everyman's Library 1966 edition), p. 256.

But these thoughts only serve to introduce a profound reappraisal of the doctrine of karma. For according to earlier views—in Jainism, for instance—karma (translated as "works" here) necessarily binds men to the round of reincarnation. All forms of action have some tendency to keep men implicated in the world of suffering and dissatisfaction. But Krishna now advises Arjuna to recognize a deeper truth.

> Not by leaving works undone
> Does a man win freedom from the [bond of] work,
> Nor by renunciation alone
> Can he win perfection['s prize].
>
> Not for a moment can a man
> Stand still and do no work;
> For every man is powerless and forced to work
> By the 'constituents' born of Nature.[18]

No: it is not by abstaining from action, but by rejecting the fruits of action, that a wise man will win release. It is by doing his duty, not for his own good, but for the sake of the Lord, that he overcomes the bonds of karma. Or rather, it is the Lord, who controls the whole world and who thus also controls the operations of karma, who liberates the soul, if a person will but have faith in the Lord. Thus by faithfully doing everything for the sake of God a man gains the promise of release.

Though the central emphasis of the poem is on the devotion (bhakti) which is the right attitude to God and on God's reciprocal love even for the sinner who calls upon him, the Gita also expresses in a striking and astonishing way the majesty, glory, and terror of the Godhead. This is seen above all in the theophany found in Chapter XI, where Arjuna is vouchsafed a vision of the Lord's form:

> The great Lord of Yogic power,
> Revealed to the son of Pritha
> His all-highest sovereign form—
>
> [A form] with many a mouth and eye
> And countless marvellous aspects;
> Many [indeed] were its divine adornments,
> Many the celestial weapons raised on high.

[18] III, 4-5, Zaehner's translation, p. 262.

Garlands an'd robes celestial He wore,
Fragrance divine was his anointing:
[Behold] this God whose every [mark]spells wonder,
The infinite, facing every way!

If in [bright] heaven together should arise
The shining brilliance of a thousand suns,
Then would that [perhaps] resemble
The brilliance of that God so great of Self.

Then did the son of Pāndu see
The whole [wide] universe in One converged,
There in the body of the God of gods,
Yet divided out in multiplicity.

Then filled with amazement Arjuna,
His hair on end, hands joined in reverent greeting,
Bowing his head before the God,
[These words] spake out:

Arjuna said:
O God, the gods in thy body I behold,
And all the hosts of every kind of being;
Brahmā, the Lord, [I see], throned on the lotus-flower,
Celestial serpents and all the [ancient] seers.

Arms, bellies, mouths and eyes all manifold—
So do I see Thee wherever I may look—infinite thy form.
End, middle or beginning in Thee I cannot see,
O Monarch Universal, [manifest] in every form.

Thine the crown, the mace, the discus—
A mass of glory shining on all sides,
So do I see Thee—yet how hard art Thou to see—for on every side,
There's brilliant light of blazing fire and sun. O, who should comprehend it?

Thou art the Imperishable, [thou] wisdom's highest goal,
Thou, of this universe the last prop and resting-place,
Thou the changeless, [thou] the guardian of eternal law (dharma),
Thou art the eternal Person; [at last] I understand! . . .

Gazing upon thy mighty form
With its myriad mouths, eyes, arms, thighs, feet,
Bellies, and sharp, gruesome tusks,
The worlds [all] shudder [in affright]—how much more I!

Ablaze with many coloured [flames] Thou touch'st the sky,
Thy mouths wide open, gaping, thine eyes distended, blazing;
I see Thee, and my inmost self is shaken:
I cannot bear it, I find no peace, O Vishnu!

I see thy mouths with jagged, ghastly tusks
Reminding [me] of Time's [devouring] fire:
I cannot find my bearings, I see no refuge;
Have mercy, God of gods, Home of the universe! . . .

As moths, in bursting, hurtling haste
Rush into a lighted blaze to their destruction,
So do the worlds, well-trained in hasty violence,
Pour into thy mouths to their own undoing.

On every side thou lickest, lickest up,—devouring—
Worlds, universes, everything—with burning mouths;
Vishnu! thy dreadful rays of light fill the whole universe
With flames of glory, scorching [everywhere].[19]

This passage expresses a shattering religious experience, which is here clothed in the mythology of the cult of Vishnu (the diadems, maces, and disks which are mentioned are his emblems, and many other features of the symbolism have the same source). God appears here as a terrifying being, but one who can be gracious. He is terrifying just because man, in his finitude and inadequacy, is overwhelmed by the majesty and splendor of the divine being. But more, the great Lord is not just creator of the world, he is also its destroyer. This reflects traditional Indian cosmology—the series of epochs of creation in which the cosmos is successively destroyed and recreated. Thus although God here is represented as "warden of the everlasting law," that is, the guardian of the religious and moral fabric of society, he is also considered to be beyond human values. Life in the world is transitory, save insofar as a person's eternal soul exists for ever; and thus the Lord Vishnu does not merely create what is good, but is responsible for its perishing.

The majesty and terror of God create a tension, or dialectic. God may frighten, but that very fear which is inspired in the breast of the devotee leads to his yearning for graciousness and mercy on the part of the Creator. And it turns out in the poem that this mercy is not unavailable. God can love, and

[19] XI, 9 ff., Zaehner's translation, *Hindu Scriptures,* (Everyman's Library, 1966), pp. 295, 296, 297.

can be loved. It is through the loving adoration and devotion of the worshiper that God's graciousness can manifest itself to him:

> *Arjuna, of this be sure:*
> *None who pays me worship of loyalty and love (bhakti) is*
>   *ever lost.*

> *For whosoever makes Me his haven,*
> *Base-born though he may be,*
> *Yes, women too, and artisans, even serfs,—*
> *Theirs it is to tread the highest Way. . . .*

> *On Me thy mind, for Me thy loving service (bhakti),*
> *For Me thy sacrifice, and to Me be thy prostrations:*
> *Let [thine own] self be integrated, and then*
> *Shalt thou come to Me, thy striving bent on Me.*[20]

This last verse is regarded by some, notably by the followers of the medieval Hindu theologian and devotional teacher Ramanuja, as containing the essence of the whole poem. Men should obey the moral and religious law, but renounce all good fruits accruing to themselves from their righteousness: everything should be done in a spirit of self-surrender and reliance upon the Lord. Works must be performed in the spirit of faith. That is the way to salvation.

Although the above represents the essential message of the *Gita*, other aspects of its thought are important for the understanding of Hinduism of this period. It is good to see this form of devotional religion (the form expressed in the poem) in its context. By considering these aspects we shall learn something of why orthodox religion developed as it did in the period following the composition of the principal Upanishads.

HINDU WORSHIP

While the Brahmanical religion represented in the Upanishads was much concerned with interpreting sacrifice in the light of new preoccupations—for instance the inner quest for yogic experience—the period of the *Gita* witnessed another way in which ritualism was declining as a religious force. Parallel to Buddhist *bhakti* devotionalism, there was a welling-up of Hindu worship

---

[20] IX, 31, 32, 34, Zaehner's translation, *Hindu Scriptures* (Everyman's Library, 1966), p. 289.

which increasingly centered on two great gods who emerged as supreme from out of the rich pantheon of Vedic and popular religion—Shiva and Vishnu.

There is evidence that Shiva had a prototype in the Indus Valley culture, and Vishnu appeared in the Vedic hymns, but hardly as an important figure. The cults of both gods expressed a growth of popular religion to a point where it assumed much greater significance than the speculative faith of the Upanishads and the orthodoxy of the Brahmins. As we shall see later, the medieval period saw theological attempts to interpret Upanishadic doctrines in ways that made sense of the devotional worship of a supreme, personal God as manifested in the forms of Shiva and Vishnu.

The Supreme Being

It should be noted that these great gods came to be thought of as alternative ways of expressing the truth about the supreme Being. It is not that there are two gods: but rather, for the Hindu mind, worshipers may worship God either as Vishnu or as Shiva. This way of treating them reflects the kathenotheism of the Vedic period. Sometimes the supreme Being is represented in a threefold form, as Shiva, Vishnu, and Brahman, the Creator. But they are not a "Trinity," three gods in one. Rather they form a threefold symbol of the one Being. Needless to say, the Hindus have never in any significant way, except among one or two reformers of the nineteenth century, rejected other gods and spirits. Lesser figures in the pantheon function as emissaries of, or partial representations of, the one Being.

The figures and origins of Shiva and Vishnu are rather different. We have already seen how Vishnu appeared as Krishna to Arjuna in the *Bhagavadgita*. Later, we can see the full meaning of this theophany, of this manifestation of the divine, as conceived in one stream of Hindu mythology and doctrine. First, let us look at Vishnu's great rival and alternative, the god Shiva.

Shiva

In his person, contrasting elements are mingled—fertility and asceticism, creation and destruction, good and evil, Aryan and pre-Aryan.

Shiva's prototype in the Indus Valley civilization was, as far as we can tell, both lord of beasts and the great ascetic. At one level he has to do with the forces of life, at another with the forces that lead to release from life. Also, Shiva is found in the Vedic hymns as the god Rudra. He represents a confluence of two cultures; but there is little doubt that he derives his main mythological power and magic from the "lower" culture ("lower," as nearly always in the history of human affairs, is a way of referring to elements which have been dominated—the thoughts and customs and creations of peoples who have been subjugated). Shiva has remained a fierce being, an inauspicious one, for which reason men have given him the paradoxical name of Shiva, the "Auspicious," for thus his wrath may be modified and turned away. His consort Kali wears a necklace of skulls; he himself symbolizes Time which carries all away. Yet by another paradox, Shiva is also the god *par excellence* associated with asceticism and yoga. He is the Great Yogi. Through the power of his meditation the whole world is sustained.

This reflects a similar pattern of thought found in the Upanishads. There *Brahman*, the power implicit in all ritual acts, and especially in sacrifice, is seen cosmologically as the Holy Power sustaining the world. In the legend of Shiva, the yoga that the god performs (a very different kind of ritual act) keeps the whole universe in being.

The symbolism associated with Shiva reflects his yogic vocation. He is smeared with ashes—an enduring feature till today of Indian asceticism. He haunts the burning-grounds, where the faithful are sent on their way. This reflects the custom of many early Indian contemplatives, Hindu and Buddhist, of going to cremation-grounds to meditate upon the transitory and material nature of ordinary concerns. The sight of a human body being burnt and becoming a mere nothing compelled the yogi to see beyond this hopeless and depressing realm. It is interesting to note, and we shall have occasion to observe this in more detail, that on the whole the medieval theologians who followed Shiva emphasized the contemplative life rather at the expense of devotionalism (*bhakti*). To be sure, there were Shaivite theists—believers in an Ultimate Reality that is above all personal—who worshiped Shiva. But it is important that, as the god of yoga and asceticism, Shiva tended to influence his followers in the direction of belief in an ultimately impersonal (or perhaps one should say non-personal) Being, such as is often the object of mystical experience. It remains true that though devotion was certainly accorded to Shiva, devotionalism as such flourished more intensely among the Vaishnavites (followers of Vishnu). This is explained by the frequent tension in the Indian tradition between contemplation as an inner quest, and worship and devotion as the outer search for right relationship to a personal God. Yoga and worship, contemplation and personal devotion—these could occur separately, and they could, too, conflict. These points will become clearer when we turn later to consider the diverse attitudes and doctrines of the great medieval theologians, men such as Shankara and Ramanuja.

Shiva, as well as being ascetic, is also exuberantly fierce. He is the god who is symbolized by the *lingam*, the upright rounded pillar shaped like a phallus which proliferates in many Shaivite temples and which signifies the creative and procreative functions of nature. Shiva is god of the dance—as Lord of the Dance he dances out the creation of the world. The manifestation of the world through his creative activity is not the coming-into-being of a complex object designed for a pre-ordained purpose. It is not that the god has brought the universe into being so that men and other living beings should glorify him (though of course, according to Shaivite doctrine, they should certainly do at least this). Rather it is that he dances out the universe simply as an expression of his exuberant personality: his creative activity is an end in itself. He enjoys it. But just as the dancer gets tired, so Shiva periodically relapses into inactivity. The cosmos becomes chaos, and destruction follows the period of creation. Shiva is both creator and the great destroyer.

Why does the terrifying ferocity of Shiva and of his consort (known, like the god himself, under different names, but chiefly as Kali, the black goddess with her necklace of skulls) maintain such power over the Indian religious mind? First, it certainly symbolizes the awe-inspiring and frightening nature of Deity. Similarly the *Gita* expresses the way in which Vishnu too is terrifying and awesome to the religious imagination. Second, the fiercer aspects of the Shiva mythology can be traced in varying ways to the archaic and popular elements in Indian mythology. What is, considered in itself, gruesome and primitive becomes incorporated into a complex of feeling and mythology which gives a deeper account of the crudities. The myths of ancient peoples are often not edifying; but they can be defended (though it is not my purpose now to defend practices, but rather to explain their grip on the religious imagination) by remarking that the evil acts, the terrifying and brutal acts, the inexplicable acts of the gods of the popular imagination are often taken to signify the transcendent nature of Deity. Human values are flouted by the gods: the gods are not so puny that they need to concern themselves with merely *human* values. Deity is in some sense (so the Hindu tradition claims) beyond good and evil.

The Yogi

The yogi's life reflects the social dimension in which the cult of Shiva and other religious phenomena in the Indian tradition are to be understood. The yogi is, generally speaking, one who has renounced ordinary human duties and concerns. We have seen earlier how the Buddha left his wife and young child in order to pursue spiritual knowledge and discernment. From one point of view this act of leaving home is shocking. Did he not fail in his family obligations? But the point must be seen clearly that, from the perspective of Indian social heritage, there was nothing unusual in the Buddha's act. Traditionally, the holy man is one who has left society. He goes into the forest or jungle as a solitary recluse, in order to contemplate in such a way that he will attain illumination.

This idea involves a particular view about society. There are grades of social status. There are the all-important social institutions that hold men to their primary duties and occupations. But society has a fourth dimension, as it were. Beyond society, there is the negation of society—a realm where men can realize their hope of going beyond the material world to the world of release. This "society outside society" is constituted by the holy men, the wandering recluses—by the Buddhist Order, by the Jain monks, by the Hindu *sadhus*. Since the fabric of the social and moral and religious order is constituted in Hinduism by the caste system, the holy man has transcended caste. Likewise, since the social system is regulated by the *sanatana dharma,* or "everlasting law," there is a sense in which the holy man is "beyond the law." A reflection of these ideas at the mythological level is the notion that God too is beyond the moral law.

Vishnu

Vishnu and his consort Lakshmi are kindlier in aspect than Shiva, though Vishnu partakes of the essential majesty and terror of the godhead. Characteristic of the cult of Vishnu, by contrast with that of Shiva, is the belief in various incarnations (*avatars*) of the god on earth. Usually they are listed as ten, and include his animal incarnations as a fish, boar, turtle, and lion. It is noteworthy that the Buddha came to be regarded as an avatar of Vishnu by the orthodox Hindus.

The central incarnations of Vishnu are those of Rama and Krishna. Rama was immortalized in the great epic the *Ramayana,* and remains to this day the epitome of virtue in the popular Indian imagination. The son of a king, according to the legend, he was cheated out of his inheritance and forced into exile. His wife, the beautiful Sita, bravely accompanied him into the forest. Ravana, the demon king of Ceylon, spirited her away, and she was only rescued after Rama had gone through great vicissitudes. The relations between the two form a tender thread of romance running through the whole story. Eventually, Rama regained his kingdom, where he ruled as a beneficent monarch. He combined virtue, tenderness, piety, beauty, and fairness.

Krishna is a more playful figure. He was of noble birth, but because his uncle the king wished to destroy his nephews and nieces, for fear that they would assassinate him, Krishna was spirited away from the palace in his infancy and was brought up by the daughter of a poor cowherd. Much of the mythology surrounding Krishna concerns his amorous dalliances as a young man with the cow-girls. For instance, when once the maidens went bathing in the Jumna river, Krishna stole their clothes and hid in a tree. He refused to give the clothes back until they had agreed to come out singly to him, their hands clasped in the attitude of prayer. This incident is often used as an allegory of the relationship between the soul and God. God is the lover of the soul, represented by the cow-maiden. The soul is enchanted by the beauty of

God, symbolized by Krishna. After a period in the country, Krishna returned to his own city of Mathura, killed the wicked uncle, King Kamsa, and restored justice.

In the *Mahabharata,* Krishna appears as Arjuna's charioteer. No doubt, the Krishna legend represents a mingling of different strands of mythology.

One other avatar of Vishnu deserves mention. It is the future incarnation, when Vishnu will appear as Kalki—a gigantic figure who will annihilate the wicked and wind up the age. Then the world will remain unformed and quiescent until the time for a new age has come, when Vishnu will recreate the cosmos.

The emergence of the two great gods of Hinduism during the classical period expressed the devotionalism implicit in the worship of a personal Being. At the same time there were other important developments. It was during this epoch that the classical systems of Indian philosophy began to take on a definitive shape. Since some of these have a religious rather than simply a philosophical significance, it is useful to look at them briefly. They will serve to introduce us to the great spiritual systems which were elaborated during the medieval period.

CLASSICAL SCHOOLS OF HINDU THOUGHT

The classical systems of Indian thought are usually reckoned as six by the orthodox. But as we shall see this mode of classification is not altogether satisfactory. The six are: Samkhya, Yoga; Nyaya, Vaishesika; Mimamsa, and Vedanta. The third and fourth of these need not concern us much here, as they are logical and proto-scientific in character. Nyaya is mainly devoted to an investigation and listing of logical arguments, while Vaishesika is principally a theory of atomism. The two schools coalesced, and later acquired the doctrine of a personal Creator who arranges the atoms which are the basic constituents of the cosmos. Samkhya and Yoga likewise are a closely related pair. The former provides the metaphysical basis which is the background against which the adept practices Yoga. Yoga is a physical, mental, and spiritual technique which is held to lead to liberation. Liberation from what? We can understand this by considering the doctrines of Samkhya.

Samkhya and Yoga

According to Samkhya, reality consists on the one hand of nature, a unitary being that evolves into the many forms under which we perceive it, and on the other hand of innumerable eternal souls. These souls are associated with psychophysical organisms, and are thus entangled in the round of reincarnation. The aim of the yogi is to attain disentanglement, since the empirical world is full of suffering, and peace can only be attained by liberation from that world. The state of liberation is not, however, a heavenly existence, since heaven itself is only a temporary state. Neither is it union with God; the system is atheistic. (There are strong analogies between Samkhya and Buddhism and Jainism, stemming, no doubt, from a pool of ideas already present in non-Aryan culture.) The state of release, then, is one of isolation—the isolation and self-sufficiency of the eternal self disentangled from empirical existence. When, in the medieval period, Yoga acquired belief in a supreme Self, or Lord, who helps souls to liberation, it was merely a reflection of the growing practice of meditating on God, and did not at all imply that the soul was thought to be united with the Lord in release. The essential structure of the system was not changed by the grafting-on of a limited form of theism.

So much for the doctrinal dimension of Yoga. What of its pragmatic ritual and ethical dimensions? As in Buddhism, the training is summed up in a path of eight "stages." The adept should practice restraint, discipline, posture, respiration, withdrawal from sense-objects, concentration, meditation, and trance. The first of these, restraint, refers to moral training. Here the ethical obligation is seen not just as an end in itself, but as an essential part of self-training. Discipline refers to ascetic and religious practices which go further than the usual requirements of morality. Austerity is important in freeing a person from desires and thereby preparing him for a detached view of the world about him.

The third and fourth "stages" refer to physical exercises (often known as Hatha-Yoga) which are held to be conducive to peace and insight. Posture involves a kind of gymnastics worked out in terms of the various positions which may be assumed, beginning with the ordinary cross-legged posture in which Indians traditionally sit. Respiration is an analogous gymnastics of the breathing system. Some of the results—in slowing down respiration and heartbeat, for instance—are remarkable. That these exercises are included in the Yoga path indicates how the physical and spiritual life are regarded as inextricably interwoven.

The next "stage," withdrawal of the senses, involves the capacity to shut out external sense-stimuli through mental images though an awareness of phenomena remains. Concentration begins with meditating upon such objects as fire, the heart, Vishnu, and so on: the idea is to concentrate upon them to the exclusion of all other thoughts, and so is somewhat like Buddhist *jhana* in its first four stages. Meditation is like the last stages of *jhana*.

Finally, under the head of trance, the adept is supposed to achieve, through the use of the foregoing techniques, a kind of transcendental knowledge in deep trance. In this, the person realizes the essential difference between the eternal soul and the mental and physical states with which it has become entangled. Thus he gains liberation and on death the soul will exist changelessly in a state of isolation. There will be no more rebirth. As in Theravada Buddhism, the essential quest in Yoga is an interior one: yoga brings about a mystical state of higher consciousness. But this is not interpreted in terms of union with or communion with a Divine Being. Once again in the Indian tradition we have an instance of mysticism without God.

Mimamsa

Mimamsa is a system of a very different sort. It started as an attempt to bring order into the principles of interpretation of the Vedic scriptures. Since the Vedic hymns did not state a doctrine of rebirth, and since in them salvation was conceived in terms of a heavenly existence, the Mimamsa school resisted the idea of *moksa,* or liberation, as the goal of religion. Mimamsa conservatively kept to belief in heaven as the reward for piety. But in what did piety consist? Here the doctrines of the school were remarkable for their conservatism and paradoxicality. They were conservative, because in Mimamsa religion centered on the complexities of Vedic ritual. By means of a system of appropriate sacrifices, one could assure himself of heavenly rewards. The Vedic scriptures were interpreted essentially as a collection of *imperatives* that tell one what to do. This novel way of treating the scriptures was the cause of the paradoxicality of Mimamsa; the hymns were interpreted as injunctions about ritual, therefore the statements they make about the gods were regarded as secondary in importance. Ritual was regarded as efficacious in itself. Thus Mimamsa illustrates how a sacrificial religion can become totally detached from the gods to whom the sacrifices were originally addressed. The priest becomes the manipulator of a sacred power that has its own intrinsic virtue.

It should not surprise us to learn that Mimamsa was atheistic. Preoccupation with ritual upon earth turned attention away from the celestial powers. Because of the school's fundamentalist attitude to the Veda as the sole repository of sacred knowledge, its followers believed the scriptures to be eternal— the everlasting words which compose them are manifested from time to time in ritual, but the Veda itself is essentially unchanging and imperishable. Consequently, uniquely among schools of Indian philosophy, the Mimamsa denied belief in the "pulsating" universe. It did not teach a theory of alternating periods of destruction and re-creation in the everlasting history of the cosmos, since this theory would imply that the Veda itself would be destroyed from time to time. The school, then, is of some interest in the history of mankind's religious experience, since it expresses in the clearest and starkest form the effect of basing everything on the ritual dimension of religion. This dimension, when coordinated to the experiential, issues in devotion or mysticism; but in Mimamsa, ritual is simply conceived in an external way.

An Observation on Dimensions

It is useful here briefly to pause to consider other ways in which peculiar religious forms arise from exclusive concentration on one or other of the dimensions. When the ethical is exalted as the supreme part of religion (as in Matthew Arnold's definition of religion as morality tinged with emotion), the consequence is that belief in the invisible world fades, and religion becomes merely a social force. However, when the doctrinal becomes supreme, religion is just a matter of belief, without the experience and practice that give the doctrines meaning. Again, if the experiential dimension is divorced from the doctrinal and ethical dimensions, religion forfeits its claims to truth and goodness and becomes just one way, among others, to savor the possibilities of human life.

Vedanta

The last of the schools that we have to consider, the Vedanta, became, in the medieval period, divided into a number of sub-systems which differ markedly from one another. In some cases the difference between them is greater than that found between the six schools recognized as constituting the orthodox Hindu tradition. The sub-schools of the Vedanta share belief in a single divine Reality underlying or sustaining phenomena: where they differ is in their conception of this *Brahman*—whether it is essentially a personal Lord or not—and in their view as to whether the individual soul is identical with God or not. The various forms of Vedanta give differing interpretations to the Vedic writings (literally Vedanta is the "end of the Veda," i.e. its ultimate import or meaning). Above all, they represent differing ways of interpreting the equation between *atman* and *Brahman,* between the eternal self and the divine Absolute, expressed in the Upanishadic writings. For some Vedanta theologians there was an essential distinction between the soul and God (despite the possible union symbolized by the text *tat tvam asi*); for others, the eternal life within man was generically identical with the Absolute. For some, the world was real; for others it was an illusion, veiling one from Reality. These diverse doctrinal views had their roots in divergent sorts and combinations of religious experience.

Summary of the Classical Period

The classical period, then, saw the crystallization of the main systems of doctrinal belief recognized in the Hindu tradition. These systems were matched by parallel, and sometimes intertwining, developments in popular religion. The cults of Vishnu and Shiva, and of a host of other deities, together with the philosophical formulae, left a stamp upon Hinduism that it has never lost. During the classical period—those centuries between 450 B.C. and A.D. 600—occurred the emergence of a Hindu culture that absorbed into itself many different strands of mythology, ritual, and doctrine. This luxuriance of religious standpoints, cults, and gods may sometimes baffle the outsider, but it testifies to an important and enduring characteristic of Indian culture—its desire to express and to nurture as many different approaches to the Truth as possible, and to conserve within itself the multiplicity of cultural influences that have affected the Indian subcontinent.

This luxuriance is not simply a matter of the imagination and of the intellect, of mythologies and doctrines. It has also been a social phenomenon, and was reflected in an increasing elaboration of the class structure. Various social groups within the four great classes began during the classical period to harden into castes based on craft, religious, and other affiliations. Thus very often allegiance to Shiva or to Vishnu was determined socially rather than as a matter of individual religious choice.

Generally, people of different religions, orthodox and unorthodox, lived side by side in society, most often amicably, and out of this complex social situation there developed the attitude that different faiths represent so many different approaches to the one Truth. Nevertheless, there was maintained a running discussion and disputation at the intellectual level between orthodox and unorthodox theologians, and processes of conversion to and from Buddhism continued. These trends went on into the medieval period, when the orthodox tradition itself saw further development and crystallization.

MEDIEVAL HINDUISM

The medieval period was the great age of Hindu philosophy and piety. We can single out three great systems of thought which typify different movements within the orthodox tradition. As it happens, they are all forms of Vedanta, Vedanta being the school which attempts to interpret the theology of the Vedic writings. But since the interpretations varied greatly, the Vedanta became divided into significantly divergent sub-schools. The three that we shall look at here are associated with the names of Shankara, Ramanuja, and Madhva.

Shankara

Of these the most influential was undoubtedly Shankara, whose writings and thought have done much to shape modern Hindu attitudes. He is thought to have been a South Indian Brahmin who lived from about 788 to 820 A.D. By religious allegiance he was a follower of Shiva, but his chief theological and philosophical concern was a consistent interpretation of the Upanishadic writings, notably the famous doctrine identifying *atman* with *Brahman*. He took the idea that the immortal element within man and the divine Absolute are one to its seemingly logical conclusion. Shankara taught that there is only one eternal Being, that there are no separate souls or eternal selves possessed by different living beings: one spirit, so to say, animates them all.

Shankara also took very seriously the thought embodied in such texts as the verses quoted earlier, "Lead me from the unreal to the real." The eternal Being alone is truly real. It follows from this that the world of ordinary experience is in some sense an illusion, *maya* (a word suggesting divine creative magic—the magic of the "illusionist"). Thus there is one Absolute, and the rest is just something we, as it were, impose upon it. The cosmos is a grand illusion. Liberation or release comes when one realizes in inner experience one's identity with the one Being and the illusoriness of the world. Strictly, one does not *become Brahman* in release: one recognizes what was true all along— there is no question of not being *Brahman*. But because men normally are entangled in worldly affairs and confused by ignorance or lack of spiritual perception there is a difference in condition between them and a person who gains release. The latter will be reborn no more.

The Upanishadic writings are certainly not unanimously in favor of such a monistic position. God is described in more personal terms in some passages. Shankara's way of explaining the texts and his philosophy therefore might have been thought arbitrary or one-sided. But his brilliant concept of two levels of truth made it quite clear that for ordinary purposes we do not and cannot think of the world as an insubstantial mirage. Though the cosmos may be a sort of grand illusion, it remains quite true that there is a table in front of me. Consequently, Shankara evolved the doctrine of two levels of truth, the "higher" and the "ordinary." From the ordinary standpoint it is true that the table is real, while from the higher standpoint this is not so. His distinction had important religious consequences. It meant that from the standpoint of the ordinary worshiper it is correct to think and speak of *Brahman* as a personal Being and as Creator of the world. For the person who is implicated in the round of rebirth and in the concerns of the world, it is possible to worship God and to follow the detailed dictates of the religious law. Nevertheless, this is not the final truth: the ultimate aim is to transcend such ideas and practices. In the higher state—in the state, that is, of release—they are not significant, and they do not by themselves conduce to liberation since they express a lower level of religion. Shankara's theory enabled him to explain the more theistic Upanishads and the *Bhagavadgita* (on which he wrote a commentary) as often speaking at the lower or ordinary level of truth, adapted to the understanding of those who had not gained release.

Shankara's disbelief in separate souls and his view that the Absolute is accessible to mystical experience indicate that his position is not far from certain Mahayana views. Indeed, he was influenced by the philosophy of this form of Buddhism, and this is the reason why he was accused by opponents of being a "crypto-Buddhist." In a way, his approach seemed very radical to the orthodox. If the worship of God is merely a preliminary to the path which leads to higher enlightenment, then likewise the duties laid down by the Vedic writings in regard to ritual and social matters, are themselves to be transcended by the saint. Thus most of the Vedic writings, which explicitly concern themselves with such matters, belong to the ordinary level of truth. In other words, what the Hindu takes as revelation is in great part only secondarily true. Shankara did not hesitate to draw this conclusion. Those texts, however, which suggest the unity of the self with ultimate Reality belong to the higher realm. It is clear that from an orthodox point of view Shankara's exegesis was dangerously radical. Nevertheless, he had great influence during his lifetime and ever since.

The notion of two levels of truth can also be put in another way. From the higher standpoint the Absolute is not a personal Creator, though from the ordinary standpoint it is reasonable to speak of It as so. In short, then, there are two phases of the divine Reality. The higher *Brahman* is summed up as Being, Consciousness, and Bliss; the lower *Brahman* is more determinate and is properly personal. As it were, the Absolute manifests itself in a personal way as Creator of the grand illusion. The personal Lord is thus the great illusionist, though bound up with his own illusion. He too in the last resort is part of the grand illusion.

Ramanuja

Ramanuja, another South Indian, who died at an advanced age in about 1137 A.D., was much concerned to combat Shankara's non-dualistic teachings. As a follower of Vishnu, and as one deeply imbued with the spirit of devotion to God, Ramanuja was uneasy about the relegation of the personal aspect of the godhead to a lower level of reality. One who worships God and seeks his grace is not likely to be content with the doctrine that the self is identical with the divine Reality. As a famous nineteenth-century Indian writer, Debendranath Tagore, remarked, What man wants to do is to worship God; if the self and God are one, how can there be any worship? In his powerful emphasis on devotion and the loving adoration of God, Ramanuja was influenced by certain Tamil hymn-writers and poets, who gave expression to a fervent piety in which the individual relies upon God's saving grace for salvation.

Ramanuja was also an orthodox expositor of the Vedic scripture. Though in some of the Upanishads and in the *Gita*, there were certainly elements of theistic thinking and sentiment, there were also the prominent monistic emphases upon which Shankara laid so much stress. The great text "That art thou" and other similar ones had to be explained. As an orthodox Hindu, Ramanuja was scarcely in a position to ignore this main stream of Vedantic teaching. How then could he reconcile the idea that the self (and the world) and God are in some sense a unity with the notion that the devotee is separate from God and that God in his overwhelming Otherness is a personal object of worship? How could the demand for religious dualism be harmonized with Upanishadic monism?

Ramanuja modeled the relation between God and the world on that between soul and body. According to his philosophical doctrine, it is absurd to speak of an animated body which is not coordinated to, and which does not subserve, a soul. But likewise there can be no personal identity save through a body to express the activity of the person. Thus each soul has a body and each body a soul. The two are inseparable. But though they are inseparable, and form a kind of unity, they are distinct. Likewise, God and the world (which is, as it were, his body) are inseparable and yet distinct elements in the one reality. Further, just as the world is God's body, so in a special way God is the soul lying beyond individual souls. He is the "inner controller" within man, and through this control and guidance individual souls may be brought to salvation and release. In these ways, Ramanuja sought to provide an understanding of the world which preserved both the unity implicit in Upanishadic teaching and the diversity presupposed by the attitude of *bhakti* and devotionalism.

The followers of Ramanuja eventually split into two groups called the "Cat" and "Monkey" schools—names which reflect the different analogies that were used to illustrate the relation between God and the soul. The mother monkey transports its little offspring from A to B. The little monkey could not get there without the help of the mother, but it also has to make some effort on its own account by clinging to her. Likewise the soul could not reach salvation without the help of God's grace; but it also needs to cooperate with God.

The cat, however, transports its offspring by taking it up by the scruff of the neck. Analogously, according to this second view of grace, God brings the soul to salvation; the soul does not owe this attainment of release to its own efforts at all. These two notions correspond to divisions of opinion among Western theologians about grace and the relative importance of faith and works.

Because Ramanuja attempted to retain in some measure the idea of the unity of God and the world and of God and the soul, his teachings are known as a form of Non-Dualism, and the school is generally referred to as that of Qualified Non-Dualism. Reality as a whole is a unity, but within that unity there are qualifications or distinctions. It should also be noted that Ramanuja rejected Shankara's doctrine that the world of experience is *maya*, illusion. The latter doctrine is contrary to common sense, and is, according to Ramanuja, religiously dangerous, since it means thinking of God the personal Creator as implicated in the illusion. It means that it is impossible to take the religion of worship and devotion seriously. And for Ramanuja, the goal of faith is beatitude in heaven, where the soul dwells with God and is revealed in its true glory, sharing the divine attributes. If one were to accept Shankara's doctrine, this goal also would belong to the realm of illusion.

Madhva

Madhva, in the thirteenth century, went even farther than Ramanuja in teaching a distinction between God and the world and between God and souls. For this reason his doctrines are known as Dualism. In the interests of *bhakti* devotionalism, Madhva abandoned any attempt to preserve the Absolute of the Upanishads. Each soul is distinct in its nature from every other and from God, who is eternally distinct from the natural world which he sustains and recreates at the beginning of each time-cycle.

Because Madhva was keen to demonstrate the uniqueness of each individual soul, he also held that there are many different modes of salvation or damnation, suited to the idiosyncrasies of the souls. For this and other reasons, he taught that some souls are predestined to everlasting damnation. This doctrine is nowhere else found in the Hindu tradition: though there are plentiful descriptions of hells and purgatories, the common view is that these are essentially temporary states in which bad souls work off the evil karma accruing upon their former lives. Eventually, after maybe a very long period of punishment, the soul begins to move in an "upward" direction again, toward a higher and better life. But Madhva uniquely held that for some souls at any rate eternal and inescapable damnation was appropriate. This doctrine of predestination to damnation is reminiscent of certain Christian ideas.

Other features of Madhva's teachings, and incidents of a legendary nature ascribed to him, have suggested to some scholars that Dualism reflects Christian influences. For instance, Madhva's teaching emphasizes the divine Vayu (literally "Wind"), the son of Vishnu, who is an intermediary between God and man. Possibly there is an analogy here to the Christian doctrine of the Holy Spirit. Madhva is supposed to have walked on the water, fed the multitudes miraculously, etc. There are other ways of interpreting these facts than by ascribing them to Christian influences. However, it is worth noting that from a quite early time, possibly the first century A.D., there was a Christian community in South India. The St. Thomas Christians, as they are called, believe that the faith was brought by Christ's disciple himself to the shores of India and that he is buried in Mylapore, part of Madras. Around Madhva's birthplace, near Mangalore on the west coast south of Bombay, Christianity flourished. Though the main features of Madhva's Dualistic Vedanta can be explained in terms of trends within medieval Hinduism, the points of similarity to Christianity are suggestive.

Between the three main forms of Vedanta—Non-Dualism, Qualified Non-Dualism, and Dualism—there are various intermediate views elaborated by medieval philosophers and theologians. As we have seen, Shankara was influenced by Mahayana Buddhism, and his metaphysics reflect a similar concern to integrate the religion of mysticism and contemplation with the "lower" religion of worship, ritual, and devotion. Ramanuja and Madhva were much more concerned with providing a system of doctrine that would make sense of *bhakti* devotionalism. Neither teacher denied the worth of the contemplative life as typified in the Indian tradition by Yoga, but they were unwilling to see the sense of personal relationship with the Creator swallowed up, as it were, by interior experience of the eternal self. Thus the experiential dimension is crucial in understanding these forms of theology.

The social dimension of religion added to the strength of Ramanuja's and Madhva's position. Both were Vaishnavites, followers of Vishnu rather than of Shiva. The strongly devotional and personal faith expressed by South Indian Vaishnavism had a powerful appeal to those of the lower classes who were formally excluded by the caste system from proper participation in the orthodox Brahminical religion. Ramanuja's teaching not only functioned as an interpretation of the orthodox upper-class tradition, but also served to express a form of religion welling up from the lower classes and outcastes. A similar movement occurred during the medieval period among Shaivites, and this too became expressed in a theistic form of doctrine. But it should be noted that the concept of a supreme personal Lord never excluded the cult of other gods, who functioned at a lower level as agents, or representatives, of the Creator. Thus medieval Indian religion tended to gather up the multiple strands of belief and worship at all levels, and theism never excluded what were in effect polytheistic and animistic cults.

Muslim Influence

Another stream of religious experience and belief entered India's religious history from the eleventh century onward when northern India felt the impact of the Muslim invasions from the northwest. The Turkish ruler Mahmud of Ghazni (998–1030) invaded and plundered as far as the central Punjab; though his empire disintegrated soon after his death, these incursions paved the way for the Muslim subjugation of northern India. In the early part of the thirteenth century A.D., the Sultanate of Delhi extended right across India. Much later, in the sixteenth century, Babur established a Turkish dynasty in India known as the Mughal, or Mogul, and under the famous emperor Akbar, the Muslim dominions stretched well down into central India. Eventually, the Mughal Empire comprised nearly all of the subcontinent. In the eighteenth century it disintegrated into a number of separate states and confederations—one reason why India was open to piecemeal conquest by the British.

At the social level, relations between Muslims and Hindus were at times violent, especially during the Muslim conquests. In time an arrangement evolved whereby the adherents of the two great faiths lived side by side. A number of Indians became converted to Islam, older practices seeped into Muslim society—elements of the caste system, for instance. The practice of *purdah* (the seclusion of women) spread from Muslim to Hindu women, and the challenge of an alien religion helped to make Hindu social arrangements more rigid than before. At the spiritual level, there were various attempts to combine the best in the two religions. It was out of such a movement that Sikhism arose.

SIKH RELIGION

Though not the founder of the Sikh religion, Kabir (1440–1518 A.D.) was one of the important influences in the formation of the new faith. He was a Muslim weaver of Benares, who became influenced by Hindu ideas, but at the same time was distressed by those externals, both in Hinduism and Islam, which kept men who worshiped the same God apart. His poems and hymns express this thought in a forcible way: he condemned the institutions of caste and circumcision; he also condemned idolatry. At the same time he believed in the Hindu doctrines of rebirth and release, and thus provided some sort of synthesis between the two religions. His followers constitute a sect within the main fabric of Hinduism.

The Guru Nanak

Influenced by Kabir and others, Nanak (1469–1538), the first Guru, or "Teacher," and founder of Sikhism as a separate religion, preached a *bhakti* faith which could appeal both to Hindus and Muslims. A man of considerable piety and energy, he traveled widely through the subcontinent preaching his new doctrine of reconciliation between the two faiths and stressing the necessity of a true monotheism. He named as his successor Angad (1539–1552), and a series of Gurus carried on the tradition.

Akbar

Under the reign of the Mughal emperor Akbar, Sikhism gained considerable encouragement. That monarch himself pursued a policy of universal religious tolerance and experimented with the idea of a faith which would be even more embracing than Sikhism and which would incorporate elements from Christianity, Islam, Zoroastrianism, Hinduism, and Judaism. The *Din-I-Ilahi,* or "Divine Faith," conceived by Akbar failed to catch on, however, and perished on his death. His successor, Aurangzeb, reverted to a policy of religious exclusiveness and reestablished the dominance of Islam, symbolized by the construction of a great mosque which still dominates the skyline of the sacred city of Benares. Akbar's experiment failed just as some other attempts to institute a religion from above—the example of Akhenaten springs to mind. But Sikhism did not. Nevertheless, it developed in a relatively hostile environment.

The fifth Guru, Arjun (1581–1606), therefore organized the sect along political lines. His position was more that of a prince than of a religious teacher. Taken prisoner by the Muslims, he drowned himself in the Ravi River to escape the ignominy of execution. His son Har Govind, the next Guru, formed an army of guerrilla fighters with the aim of avenging his father's death. The development of the Sikhs as a tight-knit military community had begun.

Govind Singh

The tenth and last Guru was Govind Singh (1675–1708), who left a stamp upon Sikhism that it retains until this day. He outlawed caste among his followers, and formed them into a united military community, the *khalsa.* As badges of their allegiance, Sikhs were required to adopt the surname Singh ("Lion") and to adopt a special mode of dress: long hair, a bracelet, a dagger, a comb, and short pants. These external signs of allegiance helped to keep the Sikhs together as a coherent unit, though a minority of Sikhs have criticized Govind's reforms as imposing upon the faith precisely that kind of divisive symbolism against which Kabir and Nanak protested. They therefore dub Govind's religion Singhism, to distinguish it from Sikhism. Govind's measures involved an alliance between the *bhakti* religion of his predecessor and the Jats, a farmer caste of the Punjab, who came to form the backbone of the movement.

Govind was the last Guru. Indeed, this was a result of one of his many reforms. He substituted for allegiance to the Guru allegiance to the sacred scriptures of Sikhism, the *Adi-Granth.* The symbols of office were laid before the scriptures, and henceforth, though the Sikhs might have leaders, the book became the fount of authority. It includes poems by Kabir and other poets who preceded the Sikh movement, such as Namdev and Ramanand, as well as writings of the Gurus Nanak, Arjun, Teg Bahadur, and Govind Singh. It begins with the *Japji,* a hymn by Nanak, which is the expression of faith recited every morning by the Sikhs. It begins:

> *There exists but one God, who is called the True, the Creator, free from fear and hate, immortal, not begotten, self-existent, great and compassionate. The True was at the beginning, the True was in the distant past. The True is at the present, O Nanak, the True will be also in the future.*

Sikh Doctrine

In doctrine, Sikhism has both Muslim and Hindu elements. From Islam, it derives its insistence upon the uniqueness and personality of God; and it therefore rejects the Hindu doctrine of *avataras,* or divine incarnations. From Hinduism it derives its belief in rebirth, karma, and the periodic creation and dissolution of the cosmos. In regard to the empirical world and the nature of man, Sikhism is Hindu; in regard to the nature of the divine Reality, it is Muslim.

Sikhism was a product both of religious experience and of social circumstances. Those who had a direct and personal awareness of God, men such as Nanak and Kabir, were dissatisfied with the formalism that kept men of true faith apart and that led to hatred and bloodshed. To them it seemed nonsense to think that the greatest religious figures of Hinduism and Islam should not have had contact with the divine Reality, and so it must be true that the heart of these two faiths was essentially the same. The sentiments of Nanak and Kabir were inevitably shaped by a social background in which Muslims and Hindus intermingled in commercial and political affairs. But the social factors dividing the Muslim and Hindu communities almost inevitably divided the Sikhs from either of the other two parties. In periods of political stress and conflict, the Sikhs found themselves forced to abandon the non-violent teachings of the early masters, and to defend themselves effectively as a military community. There is something ironic in the fact that a faith designed to bring men of goodwill in Islam and Hinduism together should itself have split off to become a third religion.

HINDUISM IN THE MODERN PERIOD

There were other reform movements in the late medieval period, such as that of the Bengali Vaisnavite Caitanya in the early sixteenth century. The period of transition from the middle ages to the modern period, which saw the dominance of Muslim rulers and the beginnings of European conquest, was an unhappy one for the Hindu faith and the ancient culture. In 1510 the Portuguese conquered Goa: a century later the British East India Company founded the first trading station in Surat. Hinduism was at a low ebb at the time of the establishment of the British Raj. Nevertheless, this new injection of a foreign culture was ultimately to have a stimulating effect upon indigenous religion.

The challenge was not directly a religious one because the British East India Company did not encourage Christian missionaries. But in the nineteenth century, and especially with the transference of power to the Imperial government after the Indian Mutiny (1857), the way was open for Christian evangelization. The establishment of British-style schools and higher education also provided an intellectual stimulus to Hindus, in making them seek a presentation of their traditional faith in new terms. When the British governor outlawed *suttee* (the custom of the self-immolation of a Hindu widow on her husband's funeral pyre) and initiated other social reforms, this raised questions among Hindus about the traditional structure of Indian society. All these influences brought about reactions within Hinduism that have helped to form the modern India of today.

India has her share of conservatives but the reformers and innovators have had the biggest effect on Hindu spiritual and social life in modern times. Four figures stand out in need of special mention: Raja Ram Mohan Roy (1772–1833), Ramakrishna Paramahamsa (1834–1886), Mahatma Gandhi (1869–1948), and Sri Aurobindo (1872–1950).

Ram Mohan Roy

Ram Mohan Roy was a Bengali Brahmin who in his early life was deeply influenced by Islam. As a young man he entered the service of the East India Company. He founded the Brahma Samaj, a reforming sect within Hinduism which was basically monotheistic. Possibly because of his sympathy for Christian social beliefs, in 1829 Ram Mohan Roy supported the suppression of *suttee*. The Brahma Samaj sought to root out polytheistic practices within Hinduism, and thus to restore the faith to a kind of purity. Contrary to orthodox custom, Ram Mohan Roy travelled to England, and there he died. Nevertheless he had requested to be given the orthodox Hindu funeral rites—a sign of his essential allegiance to the faith of his fathers, despite the degree to which Christian and Muslim ideas had colored his thinking.

Ram Mohan Roy delved deeply into Western and Semitic ideas about religion. His chief intention was to purify Hinduism, believing as he did that polytheistic beliefs and practices were wrong. Certainly he could locate strands within the Vedic tradition opposing any facile doctrine of many gods. He pointed to the spiritual side of Hinduism. But he pointed less to the mystical, contemplative side, as typified by Yoga, than to the devotional side, with its emphasis on a single supreme Lord.

Ramakrishna

Ramakrishna represented a different phase of modern Hinduism. He was not so concerned to root out what might have seemed to the Westerner or the Muslim to be idolatrous or to "purify" Hinduism. He had come into contact with men of other faiths, but he believed that what lies behind the various religions of the world is a single Reality. In this respect, he harked back to the later phase of the early Vedic religion, which saw in the many gods so many symbols of the one Reality. Ramakrishna, though a man virtually without education (or, rather, without a sophisticated education), attempted to follow the different faiths and to experience their experiences in his own life.

Ramakrishna was born of Brahmin stock in a village in the Hooghly district of Bengal. As a boy, he showed signs of being a religious genius. He went to Calcutta to earn a living as a priest, and in 1855 was appointed to a new temple opened up just to the north of the city. He soon became a fervent devotee of the goddess Kali, the consort of Shiva. He was frequently in ecstasy, and sometimes passed into states analogous to those achieved in yoga. After a time he found an explanation of these events in terms of Non-Dualistic Vedanta as expounded by Shankara. But other religious traditions impinged upon him, and in his personal life he followed both Muslim and Christian observances.

As a result of his experiments in spirituality, he concluded that all faiths point toward the same goal. The chief exponent of this modern form of Vedanta was Swami Vivekananda, who made a tremendous impact at the Parliament of Religions at Chicago in 1893. Vivekananda was not only a man of great spiritual force, but also was an excellent organizer. To him is mainly due the establishment of the Ramakrishna Math ("Monasteries") and Mission, which has done so much in social work and in the propagation of modern Hindu ideas in the last seventy years.

Both Ram Mohan Roy and Ramakrishna Paramahamsa belong to a relatively early period in the confrontation between the West and modern Hinduism.

Mahatma Gandhi

Mahatma Gandhi represents the later phase of interplay between Indian and European ideals. He has been generally thought of as the chief architect of Indian independence, because his non-violent tactics of civil disobedience came to dominate the policies of the Indian Congress Party. His ideas were both shrewdly political and religious. Indeed a great deal of his power stemmed from the fact that the peasants of India (and others as well) looked upon him as a holy man in the old tradition. His asceticism, and the novelty of his application of the ancient Indian (especially Buddhist and Jain) ideal of non-injury, or non-violence, gave him a strong hold over the masses. Though his ideas were in some respect backward-looking—for instance his enthusiasm for cottage industries as the economic salvation of India—his strong stand against the caste system, and his condemnation of the exclusion of untouchables from the main stream of social and religious life, have deeply affected modern Indian society. While Ram Mohan Roy stands for the early Indian reaction to Western ideals, and while Ramakrishna stands for the reaffirmation of the all-embracingness of Hindu religious experience, Gandhi stands for the reassertion of the ethical dimension of Indian religion aimed at a reform of the social dimension.

Sri Aurobindo

Aurobindo Ghosh, better known as Sri Aurobindo, is the chief symbol of still another reaction of Hinduism to the modern world. His father was much concerned that he should receive a Western upbringing, so he was educated in England. Following a brilliant career at school and university (Cambridge) in England, he returned to India in the educational service of the State of Baroda. Later on, in Bengal, he became involved in violent nationalist politics, and was arrested by the British.

During his period of detention he underwent a religious experience of a yogic character; after his release he went to Pondicherry (then French India) to lead a spiritual and non-political life. There was founded his ashram, or spiritual community, which continues to flourish until this day and which has attracted many European, American, and non-Indian adherents. Aurobindo's teachings are chiefly contained in his major work, *The Life Divine*. This attempts a synthesis between Hindu and evolutionary ideas. Further, and in accord with his metaphysics, Aurobindo preached a new form of yoga—"integral yoga"—which tries to synthesize artistic and other "worldly" pursuits with the path toward the higher spiritual life. Outer activities and inner contemplation must go hand in hand. In this respect Aurobindo represents a turning away from the asceticism of much Indian yoga. His teaching is certainly not "world-negating," and in its evolutionary emphasis attempts to come to terms with modern science.

Naturally, there are many trends in contemporary Hinduism other than those we have alluded to so briefly. With the coming of Indian independence in 1947, new forces have been released. It will be a later task to investigate some of the genuinely contemporary phases of Hindu thought in the context of the present world. Nevertheless, Indian ideals have been greatly typified or molded by the four figures whom we have selected as representing the modern period.

ENDURING ELEMENTS IN HINDUISM

It might be asked, by way of conclusion, What is the essence of Hinduism? A hard question. There are orthodox Hindus who deny the existence of God. There are others who while not denying God, relegate him to second place, as a secondary or illusory phase of the Absolute. Amid such a variety of theological views, what remains as necessary to Hindu belief? Certainly the doctrines of rebirth and that of an eternal soul. The picture of the world as a place where the immortal spirit within man is virtually endlessly implicated in the round of reincarnation has dominated the Indian imagination for about three millennia. In addition, a complex social system has given shape to the actual religion of the subcontinent over a long period.

Castism and the eternal, but transmigrating, soul—are these, then, the essentials of Hinduism? One can say more, for there are also basically two streams of Hindu practice and religious sentiment: *bhakti,* or devotionalism, and *yoga,* or contemplation. Devotional and contemplative men have dominated the higher forms of religious spirituality in India since the classical period, and they have antecedents in the early period. The different blendings of these two forms of life and experience have given rise to the major schools of Hinduism. From the time of the emergence of Indian religion into the light of history, the interior, ascetic, contemplative quest has been associated with the doctrine of many eternal souls, as in Yoga. And always the religion has been sensitive to the numinous, and has recognized the mysterious powers controlling the world. This trend culminated in the *bhakti* devotionalism of the *Gita* and of medieval Indian theology typified by Ramanuja. Nevertheless, the greatest figure in medieval times was that of Shankara, whose position struck a mean between that of yoga and that of the cult of the Divine. Like the yogins, Shankara stressed the internal realization of the immortal element within man. But he also honored the religion of worship and sacrifice and saw in the God of worship a lower manifestation of the Absolute. Unlike yoga, he taught that Reality is single and divine, in contrast with the doctrine of a plurality of eternal souls.

In India one can observe three fundamental religious positions: atheistic soul-pluralism as in Yoga and Jainism and (in a sense, in Theravada Buddhism, which transcends soul-pluralism, but retains its flavor); absolutism, as in Non-Dualism, and in certain forms of the Greater Vehicle; and theism, as in Ramanuja's teaching. Though these experiential determinants of Hinduism are vitally important, modern Indian religion is also in the grip of other forces. Hinduism today plays a part not only in India but on the world scene. What its future is there is perhaps obscure; we shall speculate on it in a later chapter.

RELIGIONS OF THE FAR EAST

Chapter 5

CHINESE AND JAPANESE

RELIGIOUS EXPERIENCE

THE THREE RELIGIONS OF CHINA

Chinese religion has been formed by three main sources. First, the ancient traditional religion of China was given a new impetus and dimension by Confucius, so that Confucianism represents one of the main strands of Chinese thought and piety. Second, Taoism provided a mystical interpretation of the world, though it was later overlaid by magical and other practices and ideas. Taoism gave a very different picture of man's place in the world from that of Confucianism. Third, from the first century A.D. onward, Buddhism penetrated into China and came to be one of the so-called "three religions" of China. Other religions, Islam and Christianity in particular, have also had some influence, but this has been unimportant in comparison with the main three. In recent years, of course, Marxism has taken firm root in China, and perhaps can be reckoned as a fourth religion in Chinese history.

For our purposes, the history of China can be conveniently divided into five main periods: the early period, from prehistory down to the sixth century B.C.; the classical period, from Confucius (551–479 B.C.) down to the advent of Buddhism; the post-Buddhist period, from the first century A.D. till the Neo-Confucian revival; the late period, beginning with the Sung dynasty (960 A.D. onward) and the Neo-Confucian movement, and ending with the impact on China of the modern West (nineteenth and twentieth centuries); and the modern period.

In describing the religious aspect of Chinese culture we shall, of course, be helping to illuminate a much wider area than that of China proper. The Japanese were deeply influenced and permeated by Chinese culture, and it was from China that the Japanese received Buddhism. Confucian ideals have also not been without effect in Japan, though Buddhism has long been the most vital religious force there. In addition, Shintoism, deriving from traditional Japanese sources, has remained an important element in Japanese faith, adapting itself in various ways to changing circumstances.

China has influenced not only Japan, however; the culture has penetrated into Southeast Asia, Korea, and elsewhere, while Chinese emigrants have carried their characteristic ways of life to places far distant from the mainland. Between them, India and China have provided the dominant cultural forces in South and East Asia, and in Buddhism there has been a common meeting point. It is hard to overemphasize how effective Buddhism has been as a missionary religion: from the statistical point of view it probably has far outstripped the massive spread of Christianity. It has molded the cultures of a score of lands from India across to Japan. But it has also received imprints from those same cultures, so that in China and Japan it has provided some new forms of the religious life, as we shall see.

Archeological Evidence from Prehistory

An account of Chinese prehistory may start with a very ancient skeletal remain—that of "Peking man," or *Sinanthropus pekinensis*. This creature was a hominid; that is, he belonged to the genus of which *homo sapiens* is a species. He lived approximately 400,000 years ago. The theory has been advanced that the modern Chinese are direct descendants of Peking man.

We can glean nothing of any religious belief, if such there was, belonging to this very ancient period; archeological remains of the Neolithic period are, however, relatively abundant. Later, from the middle of the second millennium B.C., we come across inscriptions and other signs of a developed Bronze Age culture. This was the era of the Shang dynasty, which is traditionally dated from 1765 to 1122 B.C. The ancient Shang capital, at Anyang in north Honan, has been excavated, and from the results we can draw certain conclusions about Chinese religion at this time.

Two sorts of finds are important—bronze vessels (often three-legged bowls, corresponding in design to clay bowls dating from the earlier Neolithic period), and oracle bones. The vessels are decorated with various animals, dragons, and monsters, the precise significance of which is unclear. Some also contain inscriptions, and these are revealing. They indicate that the bowls were used as part of the cult of ancestors—some for the wine, some for the food, others for libations directed toward deceased ancestors.

Here then is striking evidence for the characteristic traditional Chinese practice of ancestor-worship dating from a very early period. Since the vessels are of a design which goes back to Neolithic times, it is quite possible that the ancestor-cult dates from then—or, indeed, may be of even more ancient provenance.

The oracle bones were used to elicit communications from deities. They are mostly ox bone, though some are tortoise shell. They were heated in a fire until they cracked, and the cracks were interpreted according to strict conventions to obtain either an affirmative or a negative answer to the question put. The answer then was inscribed on the bone. The queries concern mundane matters—practical affairs such as the weather, hunting, illness, and so forth. Various gods, whose names are sometimes obscure in meaning, were addressed by this method; it is clear that here there was a fairly fully developed polytheistic cult. One of the gods mentioned was Shang Ti, who later came to assume an important role in Chinese religious thought.

The Chou Dynasty

The Shang period ceased toward the end of the second millennium B.C., when a federation of tribes, known as the Chou, invaded and overthrew the Shang dynasty. Since the north-central part of China (that is, the region dominated by Shang culture) was the repository of the then most advanced civilization and traditions, these Chou invaders were described as barbarians. In fact they belonged to a similar stock to the north-central Chinese and probably possessed a culture similar to the early Neolithic one described above. But like many "barbarian" invaders in the history of the world, they soon acquired the skills and culture of those whom they conquered.

The Chou empire came to be organized on a feudal basis, with the whole area divided into states ruled over by dukes or princes who owed allegiance to the king. The system at first functioned fairly effectively, and by the time of Confucius, some five centuries later, it had become common to look back on the early Chou period as a kind of golden age. To it belonged the figure of the ideal ruler, the Duke of Chou, who holds a place of honor in the Chinese tradition accorded thereafter only to Confucius. Since the first Chou monarch was succeeded by a young son, the Duke took over the government until the boy successor was old enough to rule; the mixture of firmness and conciliation with which he governed, and the honest way in which he retired from the regency at the due time, established a continuing reputation.

Nevertheless, the decentralization implicit in Chou feudalism ultimately meant that north-central China gradually fragmented into a number of petty, independent states, and by the time of Confucius there was no longer any guarantee of peace or over-all good government. To the north of the Yellow River, and spread out roughly from east to west, were four fairly large states. Further to the south, and straddling the Yangtze, were two more big states. Between these two slabs of big states, there came more than a dozen smaller ones, including Sung, which was ruled over by the descendants of the Shang dynasty, and Lu, the state in which Confucius was born. These two in particular were regarded as of high cultural importance, because they enshrined and maintained the highest religious and artistic traditions of the Chinese people. This may account for the fact that they escaped annexation by their larger neighbors.

The political condition of China at the time of Confucius' birth, around 551 B.C. was an unhappy one, and it was especially unhappy for the inhabitants of the smaller states. The latter too frequently were battle-grounds fought over by the armies of their larger neighbors. Moreover, constitutional government, within the limits of the now decentralized feudalism, had often broken down. Thus the Duke of Lu, Confucius' own state, was a mere puppet controlled by usurping nobles, and when Confucius attempted to do something about the situation he was forced into exile. The lot of the common people was miserable, since the aristocracy imposed excessive taxes to maintain a life of luxury and combat. If, therefore, Confucius' main concerns were political and social, rather than directly religious, this should occasion no surprise, for he was setting out in a novel way to cure the evils of his time.

CONFUCIANISM

MASTER K'UNG

Confucius' biography has become overlaid by a considerable amount of legend, partly because Confucianism was used in later times as a rationale for political obedience and was given supernatural sanctions. To some degree therefore it is necessary to be selective in treating the written material at our disposal. First, a word about his name. The appellation which is commonly used in the West, "Confucius," results from a latinization of K'ung-fu-tzŭ, literally "Master K'ung," and it will be convenient to refer to him henceforth as K'ung.

K'ung was born in Lu around 551 B.C., as we have seen. It may well be that his family was aristocratic, though he himself referred to himself as "without rank." The two points may be reconciled when we note that at the time of K'ung, and partly because of aristocratic polygamy, there were a large number of descendants of noble families who lay outside the system of patronage and power. At any rate, it seems likely that K'ung was of poor family, and an essential part of his later attitudes to education was that it should be open to all who were intelligent, and should not be a matter of privilege. K'ung was early an orphan, and made a living as a minor official, as overseer of the granary and of oxen and sheep. But he had larger ambitions, and in some way or other acquired for himself a considerable education, steeping himself in traditional learning. His early official post, of course, presupposed a reasonable education—literacy and numeracy. But K'ung wished to revolutionize the world, and education was his chosen instrument. By the age of thirty-four he was already well known as a teacher of *li*, or ceremonial.

Hitherto, such education had been more or less an aristocratic prerogative. Teachers of etiquette and the various arts that give polish and competence to a "gentleman" themselves belonged to the system of royal and noble patronage. Those who were educated belonged to the upper class. K'ung's first revolution was to throw open his school to people of all classes provided they had the right intelligence and character. The fees he charged were trivial enough to make his teaching available even to the poorest. In this way he was enabled to gather around him a group of very able and loyal disciples, and it was through them that his influence spread. Because of their competence in ceremonial and the skills of government, they proved themselves valuable, and even indispensable, to the rulers.

According to traditional accounts, K'ung's growing reputation caused him to be given ministerial posts in the government of the Duke of Lu, first as Minister of Works, then as Minister of Justice, and finally as Chief Minister; but, he was too successful and honest in his administration, and intrigues against him brought about his resignation. It is doubtful whether this story is correct; more probably, K'ung was indeed offered some kind of government post without much power, and when he found that he could not effect the political reforms so dear to his heart, he resigned. At any rate, at the age of fifty-five he left the state of Lu to travel widely through China, allegedly seeking political employment elsewhere, but without success. In 484 B.C., he was invited to return to his native country. There he spent the rest of his life, in semi-retirement, writing up some of the materials which he used in his teaching and occasionally being consulted as an elder statesman. He died in 479 B.C., disappointed that the changes he so earnestly desired had not come to pass. His life was an apparent failure, and his theories of government certainly were not politically successful.

However, the teachings and way of life he had commended to his disciples lived on, and were themselves to make an important and revolutionary impact upon Chinese society. Ultimately China was to establish a method of civil service examination open to all, and based upon the classics which K'ung himself revered. The higher social ethic of Chinese civilization was largely shaped by him, but it is sometimes easy to overlook the novelty and power of his teachings because he chose to build upon traditional values.

The Five Classics and the Four Books

The literary sources of Confucianism are to be found in the so-called "Confucian canon": there is considerable debate both about the dating and authorship of these works. The canon consists in two parts, the Five Classics, traditionally assigned to the time of K'ung and earlier, and the Four Books, which are attributed to his disciples and later followers. Of the Five Classics, the last, namely the *Ch'un Ch'iu* or "Spring and Autumn Annals," was supposed to be written by K'ung himself, while the first four are traditionally thought to be older classics which K'ung edited and set in order during the last years of his life. These four works are as follows: the *I Ching*, or "Book of Changes"; the *Shu Ching*, or "Book of History" (this is not a literal translation, but is the one commonly used in English); the *Shih Ching*, or "Book of Poetry"; and the *Li Chi*, or "Records of Ceremonial." The Four Books are as follows: the *Lun Yü*, or "Analects"; the *Ta Hsüeh*, or "Great Learning"; the *Chung Yung*, or "Doctrine of the Mean"; and the *Meng Tzu Shu*, or "Book of Mencius" (Mencius, as we shall see below, was a famous Confucianist philosopher who lived in the fourth century B.C.).

The substance of K'ung's teachings can best be gained from a reading of the *Analects*, and the Five Classics themselves are not always directly related to the ideas which K'ung wished to convey. They represent, or rather some of them represent, the sort of traditional material that K'ung and his school used in the educational process. K'ung's originality consisted in the way in which he drew new values out of, and extended the values of, the given tradition.

The *I Ching* is undoubtedly rather ancient, and dates from earlier Chou times. It is concerned with a special method of divination in which there are sixty-four significant arrangements of six lines, each either broken or unbroken, and which are given full interpretations as to what they portend. Evidently sticks were manipulated by the diviner, and the way in which they fell out gave an indication of the future and of what was to be done. Like the oracle bones of the Shang era they indicate the extent to which the art of divination was practiced in early Chinese religion.

Parts of the *Shu Ching*, which consists of a compilation of historical documents, proclamations and the like, are likewise early, and date from the early Chou period, and so likewise does the *Shih Ching*, which is a collection of over three hundred poems in current use in K'ung's time as a vehicle of moral instruction.

The *Li Chi*, in the form in which we now have it, was compiled much after K'ung's lifetime, though this is not to deny that many of the rules of propriety and ceremonial contained in it had a fairly ancient provenance. Whether the *Ch'un Ch'iu* was written by K'ung's own hand must remain an open question: it is a chronicle of events in Lu from 721 down to 478 B.C. and the early part of it may have been compiled by K'ung.

The *Analects* was probably compiled around seventy years after K'ung's death, and there can be little doubt that they give a genuine insight into the

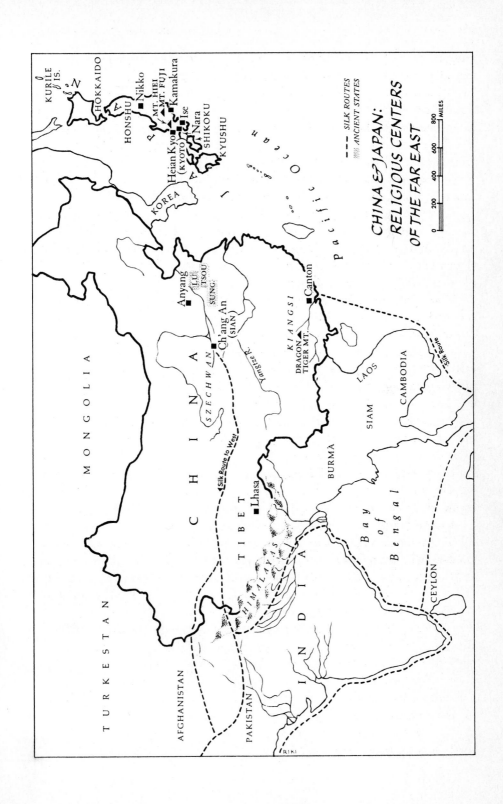

KURILE IS.

HOKKAIDO

N

HONSHU

Nikko
MT. HIEI
MT. FUJI
Kamakura
Ise
Nara

Heian Kyo
(KYOTO)

SHIKOKU

KYUSHU

KOREA

Pacific Ocean

--- SILK ROUTES
▨▨▨ ANCIENT STATES

CHINA & JAPAN:
RELIGIOUS CENTERS
OF THE FAR EAST

0   200   400   600   800
MILES

MONGOLIA

Anyang

LU
TSOU
SUNG

Ch'ang An
(SIAN)

KIANGSI

Canton

DRAGON
TIGER MT.

SZECHWAN

Yangtze

Silk Route to West

C H I N A

T I B E T

Lhasa

LAOS

CAMBODIA

SIAM

BURMA

H I M A L A Y A S

Bay
of
Bengal

I N D I A

CEYLON

TURKESTAN

AFGHANISTAN

PAKISTAN

RIKI

Silk Route

mind of the Master. The other three of the Four Books are rather later, but they help to show us how the Confucian tradition developed.

K'ung's Teaching

K'ung's teachings clustered round a number of key concepts. The first of these which we have to consider is that of *li*, which has been translated above as "ceremonial," but also bears the meaning of propriety or reverence. Thus *li* is that reverent propriety which is expressed by and can spring from the correct use of ceremonial. One passage in the *Analects* reads as follows:

> The Master said: "Respectfulness, without the rules of propriety, becomes laborious bustle; carefulness, without the rules of propriety, becomes timidity; boldness, without the rules of propriety, becomes insubordination; straightforwardness, without the rules of propriety, becomes rudeness. When those who are in high stations perform well all their duties to their relations, the people are aroused to virtue. When old friends are not neglected by them, the people are preserved from inferiority.
>
> "Though a man has abilities as admirable as those of the Duke of Chou, yet if he be proud and niggardly, those other things are really not worth being looked at."[1]

An illustration of the spirit informing such propriety can be found in another passage, describing K'ung's own bearing.

> Confucius, in his village, looked simple and sincere, and as if he were not able to speak.
>
> When he was in the prince's ancestorial temple, or in the court, he spoke minutely on every point, but cautiously.
>
> When he was waiting at court, in speaking with the great officers of the lower grade, he spoke freely, but in a straightforward manner; in speaking with those of the higher grade, he did so blandly, but precisely.
>
> When the ruler was present, his manner displayed respectful uneasiness; it was grave but self-possessed.
>
> When the prince called him to employ him in the reception of a visitor, his countenance appeared to change, and his legs to move forward with difficulty.
>
> He inclined himself to the other officers among whom he stood, moving his left or right arm, as their position required, but keeping the skirts of his robe before and behind evenly adjusted.

[1] Translation by Charles A. Wong as it appears in *The Bible of the World*, ed. by Robert D. Ballou (New York: Viking Press, 1939), p. 404.

He hastened forward, with his arms like the wings of a bird.

When the guest retired, he would report to the prince, "The visitor is not turning round any more."[2]

This description indicates something of the Confucian ideal: that correct behavior should neither give rise to slavishness nor to boorishness. Correct, reverential propriety governed by the rules of ceremonial and etiquette meant so much to K'ung because he believed that the disorders and distresses of society are not so much due to the innate wickedness of mankind as to the lack of social cohesion and harmony. Such harmony was to be promoted by attention to the right forms of social life. In a sense, peace is an artificial creation, but peaceableness is not foreign to the nature of men, even though men so often display the greed, cruelty, and arrogance that promote warfare and disharmony. In order to recreate the right forms of social life, one must build up upon what already exists, and draw out the good from what is already traditional. Hence K'ung's concern for *li*. In origin this term referred to specifically religious ritual, and in particular to the sacrificial cult. But K'ung gave it a meaning which extended far beyond ritual. Here was a norm which could govern the various kinds of social relationship.

The Five Relationships

Though the codification of these relationships was accomplished after K'ung's own lifetime, it is already implicit in his teachings as reflected in the *Analects*. This codification consists in a list of the five most important personal and social relationships of human life and in an indication of the attitudes to be adopted by those standing in these relationships. First, there is the relation between father and son; second, that between elder brother and younger; third, that between husband and wife; fourth, that between elder and younger; fifth, that between ruler and subject. It should be noted that the latter of each pair is inferior in status to the former. This did not mean that K'ung himself was wedded to a theory of society that implied hereditary rights or that he was a conservative in this sense. Indeed, he was careful to point out that capability and virtue are the distinguishing virtues of the good ruler, rather than royal lineage. In this respect, his ideas were indeed revolutionary. He wished to model society on the structure of the good family, where each has his place and yet where each plays his part in the family councils. Indeed, in the family certain changes in status are natural. The son later emerges as a father, and is due the respect which he formerly gave to his parents.

The five relationships should be governed by appropriate dispositions. The son should show filial piety; the younger brother should show respect; the

[2] Wong's translation reprinted in *The Bible of the World*, p. 406.

wife should show obedience; the younger man should show deference; the subject should show loyalty. But all this ought to be reciprocated from above: the father shows kindness, the elder brother shows nobility; the husband shows caringness; the elder shows humaneness; the ruler is benevolent. In this way, true human welfare will be attained.

This proper balance of human relationships arises out of, but is not exhausted by, the observance of social rules and etiquette. The latter however enable men to realize their true nature or virtue. This *jen,* the implicit capacity for goodness and harmony in the individual, must be cultivated in a social way; the principal ills of human existence spring from lack of stability and consideration in political and social transactions. At the same time, the rectification of social affairs does not proceed by imposing regulations (etiquette) upon the individual, but rather it proceeds from the individual's training himself correctly, willingly and sincerely in what is socially demanded. Reform comes, so to say, from within. By stabilizing one's own relationships, one does something toward the eventual reform and harmonization of society at large.

The system of relationships outlined above has as its heart another important Confucian concept, *shu,* or reciprocity. A disciple asked K'ung: "Is there one word which may serve as a rule of practice for all one's life?" The Master said: "Is not *reciprocity* such a word? What you do not want done to yourself, do not do to others." This version of the Golden Rule has been somewhat unfairly criticized by certain Western writers on the ground that it is negatively expressed. Would not the positive formulation be better? But it must be remembered that the positive formulation can be taken in an over-literalistic way with paradoxical results. (If I want to smoke a pipe now, should I go around giving pipe tobacco to all the people I meet?)

In any event, K'ung's meaning is clear enough—one should reflect, when contemplating a harmful action, on the kind of attitude one would oneself take up to another inflicting the same thing upon oneself. This itself implies something about moral rights, and also indicates the degree to which K'ung was concerned with combatting social injustice and unnecessary suffering. The good of man, the welfare of the people—these emphases spring from a rational concern with human beings in society.

Another key concept used by K'ung, and one which brings us nearer to the question of what his specifically religious (as distinguished from ethical) beliefs were is that of the Way (*Tao*). As we shall see, the same concept was used in a rather different manner by the Taoists, who derive their name from this word. For K'ung, the whole of the educational process should aim at the production of the Way—a mode of life which reflects and expresses the virtue and harmony that he was so much concerned with. Sometimes K'ung referred to the Way as the Way of Heaven, and thus provided his ethic with a sort of religious dimension. How exactly he conceived of Heaven is not altogether clear, but to gain an insight into the situation it is necessary to consider the earlier history of the word, and indeed of religion before and during K'ung's time.

The Idea of Heaven

From the earliest known times in China there had been considerable emphasis placed upon the cult of ancestors, though this was primarily a concern of the princes and aristocracy, and only gradually spread down into the daily life of the peasantry. There was also worship of divine spirits: two great deities were particularly important. The Shang dynasty worshipped a celestial being known as Shang Ti, who was apparently thought to have a personal relationship to the Shang rulers. The Chou invaders appear to have revered a deity known as T'ien, or Heaven: the two deities came to be conflated during the time of the Chou dynasty. It is quite possible that the former, Shang Ti, was originally the supreme ancestor of the dynasty, and then gradually acquired the attributes of a supreme Lord. At any rate, Shang Ti was often conceived in a more anthropomorphic way than was T'ien. Still it is worth noting that the pictograph for Heaven, T'ien, originated from the figure of a human being, and this is a sign that Heaven was not merely thought of in a rather impersonal way.

One important innovation was introduced by the Chou conquerors. In order to justify the overthrowing of the ruling dynasty, they claimed that in fact the latter was corrupt and evil, and that in these circumstances royalty could not claim a sort of divine right (though princes might call themselves the sons of Heaven). In short, it was the mandate of Heaven that the Chou dynasty should take over. This concept that the divine Being favors the good and turns away from the evil had important consequences for Chinese political thought, and led to a situation where the reforming rebel (and sometimes the not so reforming rebel) could claim a divine sanction for his revolt against established power. However we appraise Chou propaganda on this point, it is significant that Heaven is definitely identified with what is good, and the aim of good men should be to promote and preserve the balance between Heaven and earth. Political order and loyalty to the ruler had religious meaning: the emperor's ancestral temple was "the altar of the land."

K'ung's Concept of Heaven

When, therefore, K'ung referred to his Way as the Way of Heaven, he was in line with earlier thought, and there is little doubt that he endorsed belief in a supreme providential Being. On the other hand, he appears to have rejected certain views, current in his time, about the decree of Heaven. He did not believe in a kind of divine determinism, implying that Heaven necessarily rewards the virtuous and punishes the evil (a doctrine which can be turned round to justify wickedness, for if a wicked man prospers, is this not a sign that he is favored by God?); nor, on the other hand, did K'ung believe in a naturalistic fatalism. Rather he espoused the doctrine that one should wait upon the decree of Heaven: that is, one has faith that by and large Heaven favors the good, but that adversities occur that the virtuous must endure patiently. K'ung said "I do not murmur against Heaven." On the other hand he seems to have believed that Heaven can and does intervene in human affairs.

At the same time K'ung was definitely set against barbarity and superstition in religious matters. He condemned human sacrifice, already a dying custom, but one which had been widely practiced in earlier times. It is recorded that he did not speak about strange phenomena, omens and the like. This lesser side of the supernatural did not concern him.

Some have seen in this a polite scepticism about religion, but his explicit use of the concept of Heaven and his endorsement of the ceremonial associated with the cult of ancestors tell against this interpretation. This of course was consistent with his concern for *li*. But at the same time he was obviously worried in case men should turn to religious practices as a *substitute* for the Way which he was preaching. Someone asked him about how to serve the spirits, and he replied, "You are not yet able to serve men; how can you serve spirits?" Likewise preoccupation with the future life should not distract from concern for rectifying one's character and environment in this life. Yet K'ung's attitude to the efficacy or value of religious practices for their own sake, as distinguished from their social usefulness in expressing a central form of *li*, remains ambiguous and hard to determine.

When he was ill and it was suggested that prayers might be offered for him, he replied enigmatically "I have prayed for a long time." But he certainly objected to any notion of sacrifice, as a sort of commercial transaction—offering the *quid* and waiting for the *quo*. He was thus one who purified religion, and gave it the strongest possible ethical emphasis.

On balance, therefore, it would be foolish to conclude, as some Western commentators have inferred, that K'ung was an agnostic about religion. He was not a secular humanist. He felt strongly the call from above. "But Heaven understands me," he cried on one occasion—and on another, in a moment of despair, he said, "Heaven is destroying me." He was a religious and moral reformer, but he sought to reform religion through ethics rather than ethics through religion.

In the years following K'ung's death, his disciples carried on the doctrines and practiced the Way which he had taught. Gradually their influence grew, partly because many of the Confucianists acquired official positions. In this period, we can see also the increasing systematization of the Confucian teachings. However, the movement was not without rivals or obstacles. On the one hand, this was the period of the Warring States—a period of fierce internecine strife between the great principalities of north and central China; on the other hand, schools arose which combatted Confucian teachings.

Two movements became particularly important—the Taoist movement (which we shall deal with shortly) and the Mohist. The Mohists were followers of the philosopher Mo Tzu, who lived probably in the latter part of the fifth century B.C. He was perhaps a native of K'ung's state of Lu, and was possibly an official in the state of Sung. But though our knowledge of his life and circumstances is regrettably sketchy, the book that contains his teachings is substantial, and even though there are interpolations, it shows us clearly the nature of the doctrines which he taught.

MO TZU

Mo Tzu had at one time been a Confucianist, but became profoundly dissatisfied with the doctrines and with some of those who claimed to follow along the Confucian Way. He detected among the Confucianists an excessive concern for ritualism combined with a fair measure of religious scepticism. He felt strongly that human institutions and activities should be justified by their usefulness in promoting the welfare of men; at the same time he believed that Heaven was deeply concerned with this welfare. He attempted to penetrate beyond the five relationships which the Confucianists regarded as central to the fabric of society and affirmed that what lies behind all these is love. Thus he preached that the evils of war and of economic impoverishment could be prevented if only men acted in a rationally loving way to one another. Each man should feel loyalty for every other: one should look upon the conditions of other men's lives as being one's own. This universal love should break down particular loyalties. In this connection Mo Tzu revealed a flaw in the Confucian ethic: by stressing the relationship between ruler and subjects, the Confucians did not give due weight to the need for each ruler to consider the interests of other rulers and other peoples. He also discerned that family loyalties can degenerate into a wider selfishness.

It seemed to follow from Mo Tzu's utilitarian ethic—certainly this was an inference he himself drew—that men should not permit themselves unnecessary luxuries, in order that the lot of the poor might be alleviated. He condemned the extravagance of funerary rites so beloved (as he alleged) by the Confucianists. Mo Tzu's ethics were reinforced by his appeal to a restored and vital religion centering on the figure of Heaven.

Mo fervently believed that his doctrine of universal love corresponded to the will of God, and he attempted to prove that Heaven loves righteousness and hates wickedness from the fact that natural calamities occur. These must be a sign of punishment, for it can also be established that Heaven loves the people because Heaven provides food for all people. At the same time, Mo Tzu was much concerned to defend the popular religion which centered on spirits and minor deities, and argued against the sceptics by citing instances where men had perceived such beings.

With this hatred of war, his denunciation of extravagance, his powerful espousal of love as the guiding principle in social affairs, his conviction that Heaven was on his side, his authoritarian populism, Mo Tzu has something of the aura of the prophet about him, and it is not surprising that, though ultimately destined to fade away from the Chinese scene, Mohism for some centuries was a powerful rival movement to that of the Confucianists. It was zealous, frugal, and radical, where Confucianism tended to be accommodating, cultured, and gentlemanly.

Mo Tzu's distrust of luxury carried with it a suspicion of the arts. He had little use for music, though K'ung had regarded this as of great emotional, esthetic, and social importance, as a kind of adjunct to the practice of *li*. Similar cultural differences between the Mohists and Confucianists tended to exacerbate the conflict, though both movements could unite in attempts to oppose war and did not have altogether divergent social aims.

MENCIUS

The greatest of K'ung's intellectual descendants was undoubtedly Mencius (Meng K'o), who was born around 372 B.C. and who lived to an old age. He early came under Confucian influence, since he was brought up in the state of Ts'ou, near K'ung's native Lu. Like the latter, Meng traveled fairly considerably, offering his services as a guest-official, but again without attaining any great degree of political influence, though he was received at a number of courts with favor.

The book that bears his name seeks to elaborate certain ideas implicit in Confucian teaching. The principal notion was Meng's doctrine that human nature is essentially good—a doctrine which was to cause a considerable amount of debate both within and outside the Confucian movement. Meng argued that what makes bad men bad is their environment. Just as the parent who wishes his child to learn a certain language will send him to live in the region where that language is spoken, so the teacher who wishes a person to develop his innate goodness must see that he be placed in the right environment. This doctrine provided, of course, a very powerful rationale for the educational process, which the Confucians were keen to foster, and for the importance of propriety in external conduct. Meng held, in accordance with these views, that the capacity to perceive right and wrong is a disposition implanted in human nature, and he concluded from this that one can have knowledge of the world and of Heaven by looking inward into one's own nature. For the crucial feature of the cosmos is that it obeys a moral law, the Way of Heaven. Insofar, then, as men have a perception of the good innate within them, they reflect in miniature the structure of the universe. Thus by looking inward one can gain knowledge.

Possibly the sections of the *Mencius* which make this view most explicit were not actually written by Meng himself; but they display a concern for meditation and the inner, spiritual life which is not far distant from that of Taoism. It may be that already we see here Taoist influences (there is some doubt as to the date when Taoism originated). Certainly there is here a recommendation to something like the mystical life which is rather foreign to K'ung's own thought. The notion that by direct, inner experience, rather than by the processes of study, reflection, and self-control, one can gain moral and other insights seems to be an innovation in the Confucian tradition. In a striking passage, the *Book of Mencius* reads as follows:

> Mencius said: "He who has exhausted all his mental constitution knows his nature. Knowing his nature, he knows heaven. To preserve one's mental constitution, and nourish one's nature, is the way to serve heaven.
>
> "There is an appointment for everything. A man should receive submissively what may be correctly ascribed thereto. Therefore, he who has the true idea of what is heaven's appointment will not stand beneath a precipitous wall. Death sustained in the discharge of one's duties may correctly be ascribed to the appointment of heaven. Death under handcuffs and fetters cannot correctly be so ascribed.
>
> "All things are already complete in us."[3]

Already, then, we perceive during a troubled time in the classical period of Chinese history concerns for an inward-looking religion, one which has a mystical rather than an ethical emphasis.

---

[3] Translation from *The Works of Mencius* by Charles A. Wong as it appears in *The Bible of the World*, p. 459.

HSÜN TZU

Hsün Tzu, who lived in the early part of the second century B.C. (320–235 B.C.?), represented a very different strand in the Confucian tradition. In his time Hsün Tzu was extremely influential; largely because of medieval decisions about what counted as Confucian orthodoxy he has not been accorded the same fame and respect as Meng. Hsün showed considerable powers as a philosopher and his speculations regarding the nature and function of language were particularly important. However, it is his metaphysical and ethical ideas which immediately concern us here. He opposed Meng's optimistic view of man with an opposite one: for light he substituted shade.

Whereas Meng considered human nature to be essentially good, Hsün Tzu thought the reverse: it is essentially bad. "The nature of man," he wrote, "is evil: whatever is good in him is acquired by training." Not only this, Hsün expressed great scepticism about the religious efficacy of ritual. The objects of sacrifice are illusory, he claimed, though he also considered that the actual performance of the rites was an important part of moral and esthetic training. Thus he allied pessimism with religious scepticism. This was a principal factor in his ultimate demotion from Confucian orthodoxy in a period when a metaphysical restatement of Confucian religion was intellectually popular.

As we have seen, there were mystical tendencies expressed in the *Book of Mencius*. But these found their chief flowering outside the Confucian school, which remained on the whole practical and activist in its emphases. Rather, it was in the famous *Tao-te Ching* that mystical quietism received its most impressive treatment. This still continues to be the most revered of the Taoist writings, and a sign of its influence is the number of translations that have been made into foreign languages, especially English.

LAO TZU

Traditionally the work is assigned to the teacher Lao Tzu (or Lao Tan), who was supposed to be an earlier contemporary of K'ung. A number of factors militate against the acceptance of this tradition. First, the work itself seems to date in the main from about the fourth century B.C., rather than 150 or 200 years earlier. Second, it is virtually certain that it is not from the hand of a single person. Rather it is an anthology of fairly brief passages. These no doubt were composed by men who shared roughly the same outlook on life, but they do not constitute a single, systematic scheme of thought. Third, it is dubious whether there ever was a master Lao Tzu. It appears that the name, which means simply "Old Master," was an epithet applied to a certain sort of teacher in the post-K'ung period. Such teachers may have been wandering recluses, much like the Buddha in the time preceding his Enlightenment and other Indian teachers of the period.

But of course in one sense it does not matter if Lao Tzu never lived. He was believed to have done so, and the writing which bears his name expresses a certain outlook on life which made an impression on Chinese culture. Though Taoism as a religion was to undergo many changes and was later to degenerate into something very different from the position delineated in the *Tao-te Ching,* the spirit of Taoism influenced Confucianism itself and Buddhism. Some of the spirit of Zen Buddhism, for instance, has its antecedents in Taoism.

TAOISM

What was this Taoism expressed in Lao Tzu's book? Here again we are confronted with differences of opinion. One reason for this is that work, more so even than most ancient Chinese writings, is cryptic and epigrammatic in style; another is that, as has been pointed out above, the work is essentially an anthology rather than the continuous treatment of a set of themes. It has therefore been possible for different scholars and religious thinkers to draw out of the book a wide variety of interpretations. These range from treating the doctrines expressed as being a naturalistic quietism, through which folk, in the troubled times of the Warring States, might manage to prolong their hazardous lives by lying pretty low and not interfering with political matters, to interpretations which see in the *Tao-te Ching* a genuinely mystical and religious work.

If now we adopt this second mode of interpretation, this is chiefly because this is how the book has traditionally struck many Chinese, and we are here concerned with trying to indicate the nature of the Chinese tradition and of the Chinese religious experience, rather than with penetrating to the meanings of the original compilers of this work. The latter task is important; but it is more important to see in the *Tao-te Ching* those elements which have appealed to the religious consciousness of the Chinese in succeeding centuries.

The work opens with some famous, and mysterious lines;

The Tao that can be expressed is not the eternal Tao;
The name that can be defined is not the unchanging name.
Non-existence is called the antecedent of heaven and earth;
Existence is the mother of all things.
From eternal non-existence, therefore, we serenely observe the mysterious
    beginning of the universe;

From eternal existence we clearly see the apparent distinctions.

These two are the same in source and become different when manifested.

This sameness is called profundity. Infinite profundity is the gate whence come the beginning of all parts of the universe.[4]

The key term here, of course, is *Tao*—this stands for the inexpressible source of being, though it itself is spoken of as in some sense non-existent. K'ung himself frequently used the notion of the Tao, the Way. But one could without too much strain translate K'ung's Tao simply as "a way of life." It was the new Way which he recommended to his followers and was somehow sanctioned by Heaven. But the Tao of Lao Tzu means much more. It is not just the Way for men to follow, it is the Principle which underlies and controls the world. Some indeed have translated it *Logos* to draw an analogy to the concept used in the opening words of St. John's Gospel. It means "Principle," by a natural transition from the literal sense of "way." The way you do something is the method you employ. The method is a principle of action. A principle can then be thought of as something which underlies natural processes, and causes them to act as they do.

There is, then, a divine Principle which informs and underlies nature, and out of it issue the myriad things that make up the natural world. We may note that the first Principle is also referred to, here and elsewhere, in its role of begetting the myriad creatures of the universe, as the mother of all things. Here it is quite possible that the *Tao-te Ching* harks back to some ancient mythical representation of the deity as a female being, like the great Mother Goddess of the ancient Mediterranean world. But the ascription of a sort of power to the female has a deeper significance for the early Taoist. The male factor in the human and natural world is active; the female passive. It is a cardinal principle of classical Taoist thought that it is through inaction (*wu-wei*) and passivity that true results are obtained. Nature, so it was held, acts through not acting. It is effortless in its dynamism. Just as water, which is yielding and flows down to humble places, yet can be the most overpowering of substances by its very inertia, so the fabric of nature obeys the law of effortlessness. This, as we shall see, helped to provide a basis for the Taoist ethic. The mother of all, then, is a symbol of the power of passivity.

One can detect in these verses an echo of doctrines found elsewhere in religious mysticism—in Shankara's Non-Dualism, for instance—where the underlying Principle is described negatively and is in some sense inexpressible, and yet where there is a creative force which emanates from that first Principle. However, it would perhaps be wrong to overemphasize such similarities,

---

[4] Translation by Ch'u Ta-Kao as it appears in *The Bible of the World*, p. 471.

since the *Tao-te Ching* does not give a precise and formal account of the doctrines that it so elusively expresses.

The aim of the wise man, according to Taoism, is to attain harmony with the Tao. Since there has been in the history of Taoism a vivid and fetching awareness of the beauties and peacefulness of nature, the attainment of harmony with the Tao is also seen as living in accord with nature. For this reason, the Taoists were inclined to condemn the artificialities of social life and the etiquette as practiced by the Confucians. More important, the ideal man was one who through the naturalness of his existence became self-sufficient and not dependent upon wealth and prestige. This way true happiness and contentment could be found. By desiring the condition in which one desires nothing and by managing to gain such a condition spontaneously and without strain, the wise man in effect fulfills all possible desires. By losing the world he gains it and he is secure in his inner harmony and contentment.

By applying such ideas to the political sphere the Taoists preached a form of anarchism. The ideal of acting by not acting implied that the good ruler was one who practiced an extreme *laissez-faire* (and this was held by critics to be a self-contradiction, for ruling by not ruling would soon lead to the ruler's no longer being a·ruler). It was understandable in a period of warfare and misery that the Taoists should argue for a diminution of force and interference. Nevertheless it happened that the establishment of a unified Empire, which put an end to the period of the Warring States, was achieved through conquest and the imposition of a totalitarian administration.

Despite this political aspect of Taoism, which may have won it a good deal of support among the hard-driven masses, the core of the doctrines of the *Tao-te Ching* are religious and mystical in character. The sage, by stilling himself and his senses and appetites, can gain an inner perception of the Tao. Through this he attains a sort of oneness with the Eternal and a harmony with the Principle underlying and penetrating the whole world. Because of this unification with the everlasting Tao, the sage himself becomes everlasting, though not in the sense of being destined for individual immortality in heaven. One section of the book reads as follows:

Can you keep the soul always concentrated from straying?
Can you regulate the breath and become soft and pliant like an infant?
. . . Can you become enlightened and penetrate everywhere without
  knowledge?

The Taoist mystic evidently strove to empty his mind, and may have used techniques akin to Buddhist yoga. Certainly there is evidence of the use of similar breathing techniques which constitute a preliminary step to control over mental processes. The Taoist was concerned with a sort of immediate, inner, intuitive enlightenment which was very different from the scholarly knowledge promulgated by the Confucians. Knowledge of information about the world and the study of history or of the ways of men—these were not of the essence. The essential thing was an existential *rapport* with the Tao. As we shall later see, this Taoist aim was sufficiently close to the Buddhist quest for there to be a fruitful interplay between the two faiths in the period after Buddhism penetrated into China.

CHUANG TZU

Next to the *Tao-te Ching* the most important Taoist writing is the book ascribed to Chuang Tzu, who supposedly lived in the fourth century B.C. Once again, it is uncertain whether the book is rightly ascribed to him (or to any single author). The essays and stories which constitute the *Book of Chuang Tzu* display a more developed speculative tendency than that found in the Lao Tzu anthology. Thus we find the doctrine that there are continuous transformations within the Tao (interpreted as the Principle that embraces nature) and that these can be accounted for in terms of the two principles which had over the years been the foundation of Chinese thought and cosmology—the *yin* and the *yang*. The ceaseless and cyclical changes in the world, however, contrast with the everlastingness of the mystical state through which one can be absorbed into the Absolute.

Yin and Yang

The *yin-yang* polarity goes back to very early times, and certainly beyond the time of K'ung. According to the theory, the *yang* is the active, masculine energy, and the *yin* is the passive, feminine one. The former is identified with light, heat, and dynamism; the latter with darkness, the damp, dark, and cold. Thus Heaven generally speaking is active, and Earth is mysteriously passive. The heavenly spirit is male; but there is a feminine fecundity about Earth. The good was often identified with the *yang,* the bad with the *yin*. From these two energies the five elements are formed, and to the interplay of the *yin* and the *yang* is ascribed the cycle of the seasons. The polarity can explain in a rough way the opposition between Confucianism and Taoism. The Confucianists were activists and they pursued the good in a positive way, as they thought best. Taoism was passive, *yin*-like. Not for nothing is the creative power called the mother of all things. The Taoists were not, of course, indifferent to the problem of evil; but they believed that there is a conventionality and relativity about ethical value-judgments, and in pursuing the ideal of harmony with the

Tao they sought to go "beyond good and evil," and beyond the tiresome do-goodism which, in their view, was so harmful in human affairs. Let things be—such was their motto.

Popular and Aristocratic Religion

The religious movements we have been discussing so far belonged essentially to the intelligentsia, though Taoism became a popular faith, with interesting consequences. Confucianism was definitely aristocratic in flavor despite features of K'ung's thought which were egalitarian. He believed in equal opportunity in the sense that he did not confine his tuition to the sons of the aristocracy and was willing to receive anyone gifted enough to deserve his instruction. Nevertheless, the whole rationale of his system was to turn people into gentlemen (albeit non-hereditary ones). The eventual establishment of the imperial civil service examinations, open to all, and based on Confucian methods, was a great blessing to China, and gave her nearly a two-thousand-years' start on the European nations in this regard. But the training of a Confucian destined him for official duties. The mass of the people remained outside the immediate influence of K'ung's training.

A further factor also contributed to a difference between the religion of the intelligentsia and the religion of the mass of folk. Important rituals could not be performed by just anybody. Thus the Emperor alone sacrificed to Heaven; princes on their tours would sacrifice to Earth. Court ceremonial and the cult of aristocratic ancestors were confined to the upper class. With the establishment of the Ch'in and Han Dynasties in the second and first centuries B.C., the official control of religion became more and more highly organized. Local officials would be charged with the sacrifices appropriate to hills and streams in the areas over which they had supervision, and so on.

It thus came about that the ritual dimension of the ordinary people's religion was confined to the cult of the ancestral spirits and certain personal and local deities and spirits familiar to the villagers. This partly explains why, when Taoism became a popular religion, the mystical ideas of the *Tao-te Ching* and of Chuang Tzu became overlaid with a considerable amount of demonology and popular beliefs. However, there were, as we shall see, other factors which accounted for this development.

Though Confucianism, Taoism, and Buddhism are referred to as the "three religions of China," it must be remembered that over most of Chinese history the more important distinction, in some ways at least, was not between the three religions, which in any case tended in some periods to merge into one another, but rather it was drawn between the beliefs and practices of the common peasantry and those of educated folk. Chinese religion has nearly always existed at these two levels, even though it would be mistaken to think that necessarily the intelligentsia were enlightened and the rest not. It was more like this: that there was always a sizeable proportion of folk who had either an intellectual grasp or an intuitive and devotional understanding of the faiths to which they had allegiance; but beyond them, there was the mass of people who followed behind and for whom religion, interwoven with magic, had an immediate practical significance in the struggle for worldly benefits and in the common round of agricultural and family festivals.

Summary of Classical Period

We can sum up the classical period, which extends to the establishment of the Ch'in and Han Dynasties, by looking once more at the rival movements of Confucianism and Taoism. Both in their early stage of development were free of the distortions which later religion imposed upon them. But the one was essentially an ethical and social application of ideas that were implicit, albeit dimly, in the ancient traditional faith. It moved from ritual outward to the world of manners. And the other, Taoism, was anarchical and not much concerned with the sacrificial cult. It centered its interest primarily on a form of pragmatic ritual, analogous to yoga, and it aimed at an experience of absorption with the Tao. Nevertheless, though the emphasis in early Taoism was mystical, numinous elements in it were not lacking. The descriptions of the mother of all things in the *Tao Te Ching* hint at her mysterious nature. Neither Confucianism nor Taoism of this period seem to have been greatly concerned with the doctrinal dimension of religion. They were not too much interested in speculative investigations of the nature of Heaven or of the Tao, though the *Book of Chuang Tzu* was beginning to move in this direction. Nor were the writings which we have from the period much interested in the mythological dimension of religion save insofar as this can be extended to cover beliefs about Chinese history (thinkers of the period were fond of appealing to legendary figures of far antiquity). Both ways of life were, then, essentially practical in emphasis: the one reshaping man through ethics, the other transforming him through inner experience.

Both Confucianism and Taoism were destined to undergo great changes. Part of the reason was the challenge of Buddhism, the new faith from the West, which came into China around the first century A.D. But Confucianism already had been considerably affected by its success in being given official and imperial recognition during the second century B.C. by the Emperor Wu. From this time the study of the classics as a necessary element in the training of an official commenced, and the famous civil service examination system began. This triumph was all the more remarkable because it followed a disastrous period for the Confucian scholars. The first Ch'in Emperor (221 B.C.), in setting up an authoritarian and totalitarian regime, had caused the Confucian writings to be proscribed, and a large number of scholars had been put to death. Worse, in 206 B.C., the imperial palaces at Hsien-yang were set on fire by rebels, and the archives containing the proscribed writings and others were destroyed. It was said that the fire lasted three months. In the early part of the second century there was a great effort to restore the lost books. Copies of the classics were discovered here and there, where people had buried and concealed them. The memory of scholars also supplemented this work of rediscovery. In this way the major part of the ancient Chinese heritage was recovered. It is thus somewhat surprising that a bare hundred years after these disastrous events, Confucianism was able to flourish under imperial patronage. This proved to be the start of a gradual, but checkered, process whereby it became a state religion, and in which K'ung himself was given a more and more exalted status.

BUDDHISM IN CHINA

The introduction of Buddhism into China seems to date from the first century A.D. The Han emperor Ming is said to have had a dream in which there appeared a golden man, and this was interpreted as a reference to the Buddha. Ming is supposed to have despatched envoys to northwest India to bring back information and scriptures. There are reasons to think that this story is apocryphal, but there is evidence of the existence of Buddhist monks and laymen in China in 65 A.D. The route by which these people and ideas reached China was that of the Central Asian silk roads. During the period in question a great slice of northern India, including much of modern Pakistan, together with modern Afghanistan and a large section of what are now the Central Asian republics of the U.S.S.R., was controlled by the Kushan empire.

Because of imperial patronage, Buddhism was enabled to spread easily throughout this area, and this brought it into contact with peoples and cultures of the places along the silk routes. In this way it was possible for it to penetrate eastward into northwestern China. Probably in the early days of this peaceful invasion of China, Buddhism became the faith of traders, merchants, and shopkeepers, and did not spread much to the indigenous Chinese population. Nevertheless, it established itself at the imperial capital of Loyang, and missionary monks came there to recommend the religion. The work of translating Indian texts into Chinese was commenced—an immense undertaking—so that by the second century A.D., Buddhism was definitely beginning to make its contribution to Chinese culture. The spread of Buddhism was assisted by the disintegration of the Han empire toward the latter part of that century. In a time of turbulence, civil war, and unrest, the official Confucian doctrines were bound to seem ineffective and inadequate, and the way was open for a faith which had more personal and individual concerns.

Early in the process of introducing Buddhism to China, the texts translated were Lesser Vehicle ones, but the bulk of the texts translated later were Mahayana. It was this form of Buddhism which was to dominate in China, though it in turn was influenced by indigenous elements in the culture which it permeated.

The Appeal of Buddhism

The appeal of the new faith was various. First, the monastic order—the Sangha—presented an ideal of the contemplative and religious life that could command respect. Moreover, the order was open to all, and thus provided a peaceful haven for many for whom the bloodshed and distresses of the period had become intolerable. The notion that a person should forsake his kith and kin to lead a religious life undoubtedly encountered considerable resistance in a culture where family ties, reinforced by the cult of ancestors, were so strong. Nevertheless, the Sangha gradually made headway.

Second, and equally important, one could be a good Buddhist without actually entering the order. The layman, as we saw in an earlier chapter, was given hope and comfort in the Mahayana to a degree that was impossible according to the Lesser Vehicle doctrines. The idea that the laymen by calling on the name of the Buddha could have assurance that his next rebirth would be in paradise (the Pure Land of the West) and thereby a fine chance in the next world of attaining nirvana gave Buddhism a strong appeal among those who felt the call of popular devotion but not that of the strictly monastic life. Moreover, this notion of rebirth in paradise in effect short-circuited the doctrine of reincarnation. The thought-forms of Mahayana Buddhism did not so strongly depict an individual existence as stretching endlessly forward in a series of human and animal lives. This was important to the success of Mahayana piety in a culture that did not have belief in rebirth.

Another factor in the spread of Buddhism in China is a general one which helps to account for its spread elsewhere. Buddhism may be agnostic about the existence of a supreme Creator, and its doctrines may center essentially on the quest for release—the peace and serenity attainable in nirvana—but it has never felt it necessary to deny popular religion. The gods, spirits, and demons that people the world of the ordinary folk in the lands to which Buddhism has come, including India, are not rejected. They are part of the furniture of the cosmos in which we live. There is no great harm in worshiping such spirits, so long as it is recognized that the highest salvation comes through following the way of the Buddha. Buddhism has tamed, rather than eradicated, such popular religion. Thus in China, Buddhism felt no motive to protest against the cult of ancestors or to wipe out the cults of popular deities.

Buddhist ritual provided a powerful rival to that of the Confucianists and Taoists. By the time Buddhism penetrated into China, the cult of images of the Buddhas was already well established. The magnificent sculpture of northwest India was imported too along the silk routes. The serene figures of Gautama and the graphic paintings of Bodhisattvas and celestial Buddhas combined to convey in impressive form the two dimensions of the new faith—the abstraction and serenity of one who has won his way to nirvana and the beneficent power of celestial forces to give salvation to the worshiper.

It should be recognized that Buddhism had its darker message. The Pure Land to which the faithful might be translated and the other paradises of popular teaching were complemented by the purgatories, often depicted in a most grisly and terrifying way, in which evil men would have to work off their sins. Thus Buddhism provided vivid supernatural sanctions for good conduct in a way that was largely absent in earlier Chinese beliefs.

Though the new religion with its call to the monastery was criticized for its lack of emphasis upon family obligations, the rest of the Buddhist ethic came remarkably close to the ideals enshrined in Confucianism. Buddhism was able to adapt itself to traditional values, and there was no strong sense that this "foreign" religion was barbarous in the sense that its moral and social ideas were bad and inadequate. But there is no doubt that the very fact that Buddhism originated in a foreign land put it at some great disadvantage in winning acceptance among the cultured classes in China. China was remarkably cut off from the rest of the world. No loss was felt because of the remarkable achievements and splendors of her own culture. Still the situation meant that Chinese tended to judge foreigners in terms of the less advanced peoples with whom they came into contact on the fringes of the empire. This xenophobic strain has run through much of Chinese history; it was no surprise that some contempt for foreigners should have spilled over to the new religion.

In the period following the disintegration of the Han empire, Hun conquerors succeeded in controlling the northern part of the country, while a number of weak states existed in the south. The northern rulers came to patronize Buddhism, and used Buddhist monks as advisers. They did so partly because they had a regard for the magical power of Buddhist incantations, and thus adopted Buddhist priests as a means of promoting their own power and prosperity. But more importantly, the new religion was a counterbalance to Confucianism. Having destroyed the old order they wished to substitute a new one. State patronage had its advantages and its disadvantages for the Buddhist missionaries. On the one hand, enormous temples were erected and the monasteries were richly endowed. On the other hand, there was close supervision of the faith, and, not surprisingly, widespread persecutions whenever the pendulum of favor swung briefly the other way.

In the early part of the fifth century A.D., the monk Kumarajiva established himself at Ch'ang An, in Northwest China, where he was given facilities by the local ruling house. This enabled him to organize a remarkable team of translators, who rendered a large number of important works into Chinese. Among these were writings of the Madhyamika school, which represents the most sophisticated and subtle version of Mahayana metaphysics.

In the south Buddhism was also making progress. When the empire was reunited in 589 A.D., the religion was ready to enter upon its most glorious phase in Chinese history. Though there were some persecutions during the Sui and T'ang dynasties, the period from the sixth to the ninth centuries A.D. was the most impressive era of Buddhist culture in its new great home.

THE GOLDEN AGE OF CHINESE BUDDHISM

It is traditionally held that ten schools of Buddhism were introduced into China, but these were often overlapping, not mutually exclusive, teachings. In the course of its evolution, Chinese Buddhism came to be dominated by two great trends. On the one hand, the *Ching-t'u,* or the Pure Land sect, which promised salvation to those who call in faith on the name of the great Buddha Amitabha (*A mi t'o* in Chinese), dominated the popular devotion as expressed in temple worship. On the other hand, among those more concerned with the inner mystical experience which has always been at the core of Buddhist spirituality, the *Ch'an,* or Meditation (Japanese *Zen*) school came to claim a powerful allegiance.

The ten schools of Chinese Buddhism are as follows: the *Chü-she,* which is philosophically realistic and looks back to late Lesser Vehicle scriptures; the *Ch'eng-shih,* or Nihilistic, school which is quite closely related to the Madhyamika, or *San-lun,* school; the *Wei-shih,* or Idealistic, school which has its origin in Indian idealism (the Vijnanavada); the *Chen-yen,* or True Word, school, which was later to be developed and adapted in Japan; the *T'ien-t'ai* school, which attempted a synthesis between the various doctrines; the *Hua-yen* which bases its doctrines on the *Avatamsaka Sutra;* the *Ch'an,* and the *Lü,* or Vinaya (Discipline), schools. Of these, the last is not strictly a separate movement, for it merely expresses the disciplinary regulations found in the second of the "Three Baskets" of the Buddhist canon. The first six of these movements virtually disappeared from China after the tenth century A.D. There is a common saying about later Chinese Buddhism that it is T'ien-t'ai and Hua-yen in its teachings, and Meditation and Pure Land in its practices.

22. Bronze Age sacrificial vessel, Shang period (1200–1000 B.C.). (Courtesy of the Nelson-Atkins Museum of Art, Kansas City, Missouri, Nelson Fund.)

23. Pottery house from Han period tomb was symbolic dwelling for ancestral spirit (206 B.C.–221 A.D.). (Courtesy of the Nelson-Atkins Museum of Art, Kansas City, Missouri, Nelson Fund.)

24. Chinese tomb figure representing a court lady with cymbals, T'ang dynasty (8th century). (Courtesy of the Asia Society, New York. Mr. and Mrs. John D. Rockefeller 3rd Collection. Photo by Otto E. Nelson.)

25. Chinese tomb figure representing a male attendant, Han dynasty (2nd century, B.C.). (Courtesy of the Asia Society, New York. Mr. and Mrs. John D. Rockefeller 3rd Collection. Photo by Otto E. Nelson.)

26. "Sage Meditating under a Pine Tree," Sung period (13th century). (Courtesy of the Metropolitan Museum of Art, Rogers Fund, 1923.)

27. *Portrait of Confucius. (Courtesy, Field Museum of Natural History, Chicago.)*

28. *Symbol for yin and yang.*

29. *Engraving showing Confucius, the Buddha, and Lao-Tzu, and so the blending of the three main traditions of China. (Courtesy of the Bettmann Archive.)*

30. *"Temple on a Mountain Ledge," by K'un-ts'an. Chinese hanging scroll, Ch'ing dynasty (1661). (Courtesy of the Asia Society, New York. Mr. and Mrs. John D. Rockefeller 3rd Collection. Photo by Otto E. Nelson.)*

31. *Chinese tympanum with relief showing the Buddha Shakyamuni preaching at Vulture Peak (550–557). (Courtesy of the Asia Society, New York. Mr. and Mrs. John D. Rockefeller 3rd Collection. Photo by Otto E. Nelson.)*

32. *Sung period Kwan-yin,*
the Chinese form of the
Bodhistattva Avalokitesvara.
(Courtesy of the Art
Museum, Princeton
University. The Carl Otto
von Kienbusch, Jr.,
Memorial Collection.)

33. *Chinese head of a Bodhisattva,*
perhaps Ta-shih-chih, Tang dynasty
(ca. 8th–9th century). (Courtesy of the
Asia Society, New York. Mr. and Mrs.
John D. Rockefeller 3rd Collection.
Photo by Otto E. Nelson.)

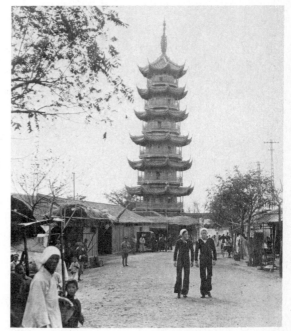

. The Loongwha pagoda in Shanghai,
ina. (Courtesy of the Library of Congress.)

35. *The Temple of Heaven, Peking, where the Emperor made sacrifices to the sun at winter solstice (13th century). (Courtesy of Ewing Galloway.)*

We shall look at T'ien-t'ai later, in its Japanese manifestation. As for Hua-yen, it incorporated a strong sense of the interconnectedness of everything in the universe, and had something of the flavor of the Taoist feeling for harmonious unity. In the meantime, let us observe the development of Pure Land and Ch'an ideas in China during the fourth century or thereabouts onward.

AMIDA BUDDHISM

The Pure Land sect, sometimes called Amida Buddhism, after its Japanese name, was reputedly founded in China by Hui-yuan in the latter part of the fourth century A.D., but it has roots going back to the devotional Buddhism expressed in the Indian scripture, the *Sukhavati-vyuha Sutra,* which the school took as authoritative. Its doctrines depend on the notion that merit can be transferred; especially can a great Buddha transfer merit to an otherwise unworthy devotee. Salvation, then, does not depend upon one's own power, but on the power of another.

The mythological side of this movement centered on the Buddha of Boundless Light, Amitabha. He was the focus of popular devotion and sentiment, though sometimes his place was overshadowed by the gentle figure of Kuan-yin. The cult of Amitabha expresses a very simple reliance on the grace of the divine Power, for it is enough to utter his name with faith to be assured of paradise.

The Pure Land of The West

The latter place, the Pure Land of the West, is deliciously described: it exists infinitely far away on the western edge of the universe; it is surrounded on all sides with beautiful terraces, on which grow magical trees whose branches and twigs are made of precious stones. When a gentle breeze blows, the twigs and branches lightly rub together and produce marvelous music. There are pools and lakes there, lined with gold and precious stones and sprinkled with lovely lotuses. Blossoms shower down, and the whole of this world is pervaded with light and perfume. The gloriously plumed birds sing the praises of the Buddha and of his law, his Dharma. The pious who live in this celestial paradise are reminded at every turn of the glories of the faith, and offer flowers to the Buddha in token of their reverence and esteem.

Such a description of the exquisite beauties of the restful land where the faithful may hope to go indicates some of the appeal of a devotional faith which emphasized so strongly the loving nature of the Buddha. Nevertheless, it is worth remarking that here there is a great transformation of Buddhist ideas in comparison with the recommendation to self-help which the Buddha uttered when he was dying. Indeed, the religion of the Pure Land is close in

concept to those Christian movements which stress the all-powerfulness of the
love and grace of God. It is true that the mythology is more complex and that
there is no attempt to establish the historical existence of the Buddhas and
Bodhisattvas who people the Buddhist heavens. But there is the same stress
upon reliance on God. In flavor, this Pure Land Buddhism comes close to
theism, even if it was believed in by people who were also practicing polytheists. And as we shall see, in Japan Pure Land, or Amida, Buddhism went even
further along in this direction.

Philosophic Buddhism and the Gods

But to say, as I have just done, that Amida, or Amitabha, Buddhism was close
to theism, and yet existed in a polytheistic context, oversimplifies the situation.
First, A mi t'o was only one among a galaxy of Bodhisattvas and Buddhas
whose merits and supernatural powers could help mankind and who often
became identified and intermingled with the existing gods of the Chinese
homeland. Further, to the religious imagination, the many Buddhas are only
so many manifestations of the one underlying Buddha-principle. This accorded with Greater Vehicle doctrine, especially as expressed by the T'ien-t'ai
school. Ultimate reality, therefore, may reveal itself in popular, mythological
and imaginative forms to the eye of faith in a variety of ways, including its self-
revelation of a loving Savior Buddha who promises men paradise. But it would
be wrong, at the higher spiritual and philosophical level, to conclude that the
absolute Buddha-nature is not itself unitary.

In such a manner, philosophical Buddhism retained its insistence on the
nature of the goal of Buddhahood, while at the same time justifying the
fervent expression of devotional religion in a variety of forms. Indeed, with the
intermingling of Buddhist, Taoist, and traditional mythologies, the Chinese
pantheon became extraordinarily rich, and we can indicate this complexity by
mentioning a few of the many deities and godlings to whom the ordinary
Chinese might appeal.

It was common, for instance, for a Chinese house to be guarded by two
attendant gods who defend the doors. Therefore two spirits were represented
at the doors of a Buddhist temple. But as a further sign of spiritual and
material security, there were, within the first inner hall, four fierce figures, the
heavenly lords, originally minor Bodhisattvas who had been assimilated to
figures in the Chinese tradition. Beyond, the more typical figures of Buddhist
iconography would be found—Sakyamuni himself, Maitreya, the future Buddha, Amitabha, and, very often in a separate shrine, Kuan-yin. The latter is a
transformation of the well-known Bodhisattva Avalokitesvara (The One Who
Looks Down With Compassion).

The ceremonial and mythology of the Buddhist temple was but one aspect of the religious life of China. Outside, the traditional spirits, gods of grain and of millet, the god of wealth, the immortals of the Taoist pantheon, gods of the hearth, the ancestral spirits—all these populated the countryside. Old practices mingled with new ones. Buddhist priests would perform masses to commemorate the dead, and the annual festival of hungry souls (that is, the departed spirits—All Hallows' Eve, as it were) adapted to itself Buddhist ceremonial. Above all such local festivity and worship there were the great state sacrifices and ceremonies.

LATER TAOISM

The richness of the Buddhist philosophical and religious heritage and the imposing, yet serene, nature of its proliferating art gave an impetus to movements in the same direction on the part of Taoism. It is remarkable that the latter, though starting from a relatively simple, inward-looking, mystical, and nature-loving movement acquired the trappings of a high cult and an elaborate pantheon together with a preoccupation with alchemical and other magical practices. There were two main phases in this transformation of Taoism.

As we have seen, early Taoism was concerned with the experience of unity with the Tao, and this was promoted by the practices of "sitting in forgetfulness" and allowing the mind to "fast," as well as by certain breathing techniques, etc. This gave the hermit a sort of immortality—he participated in the eternal and thereby became eternal. But this preoccupation with immortality could have a more mundane side. It could take the form of a desire to prolong physical life. Already the quietistic doctrines of the *Tao-te Ching* recommend themselves partly because by keeping humble and quiet in a time of upheaval and disturbance one had a better chance of survival.

It is understandable that the aim of mystical and spiritual immortality (which was not necessarily taken to imply individual survival after death) was easily obscured by a pragmatic interest in longevity. Further, men speculated that if the Tao was the vital principle informing life and nature, through oneness with the Tao one might discover some hidden element that could sustain and prolong life. There came about, then, a great deal of experimenting with drugs and certain kinds of foods in the belief that a healthy old age, or even immortality, might be attained. Concurrently there arose the belief that there existed somewhere in the Eastern Sea the so-called "Isles of the Immortals." If only one could get there, it would be possible to partake there of the abundant food of immortality. It is said that the fearsome Emperor Shih Huang Ti, who had exhibited his hostility for Confucianism through the burning of most of the Confucian books, actually sent a sea expedition to discover these mythical islands.

Chang Tao-ling

Naturally, those who could gain a reputation for expertise in these arts of alchemy, folk medicine, and magic could gain a considerable following among ordinary people beset with physical ills and the daily accidents of peasant life. In this way the growing Taoist priesthood fulfilled a social function. The culmination of this phase of Taoism came with the work of Chang Tao-ling, traditionally supposed to have been born in 34 A.D. For some time he lived in Szechwan, in Western China, and for this and other reasons it is thought that he may have borrowed some of his ideas from a late form of Zoroastrianism, which had filtered across via the silk routes. In any event, he showed himself to be a masterly organizer, and formed his followers into an alchemical and religious society. He claimed to possess the elixir of life that reportedly prolonged his life to the age of more than one hundred and twenty years, and to have received a mandate in a vision from Lao Tzu himself. He established himself at Dragon Tiger Mountain, in Kiangsi, and ensured the succession of the so-called "popes," or heads of the religious organization. He conferred succession upon his son, together with the secret formulae and equipment which he had used. In the eighth century a T'ang emperor gave official recognition to this hereditary succession, and conferred posthumous titles upon Chang and his successors.

We can judge the nature of the methods used from descriptions in the fourth-century document *The Pao Phu Tzu* of Ko Hung. The system was a mixture of alchemical, medical, and other ideas. The breathing exercises, traditional among Taoists, were used and were held to enable one to subsist without solid food. Analogy with recent investigations of Indian yoga suggests that important results probably were attained through the exercises even if the above claim is exaggerated. The proper use of diet under normal conditions was insisted upon, and not all the recommendations were useless. There was a lot of speculation about the making of a special gold that could be eaten, which was supposed to bring immortality. Such speculation made use of the doctrine of the *yin* and the *yang* and the theory of the elements, and it was argued on the basis of the theory that the most suitable substance to turn into gold would be cinnabar. Like similar alchemical ventures in Europe, the quest proved neverending. The document also includes a host of material about charms and amulets that were supposed to have the most extraordinary effects.

It would be wrong to assume that those who sold these charms and remedies were necessarily dishonest, though some of them may have been. In a society where medical and other technology is not too far advanced there is a desperate, though half-conscious, clinging to methods which offer hope, even if they be shown very often to be unsuccessful in their application, much as the gambler, though his "lucky" number never or very rarely seems to win, yet goes on with it.

The Taoist Pantheon

Magic and alchemy within the Taoist movement was only one phase of its development. If Taoism, through its services, already had an appeal to the underprivileged—and the great peasant rebellion of 184 A.D., which was Taoist inspired, seemed to prove this—it yet had no focus of religious worship comparable to that which the Buddhists were beginning to provide. Gradually, however, over a number of centuries Taoism developed a very elaborate pantheon, which in some respects shows signs of Buddhist influence. The hierarchy of beings was surmounted by the Three Pure Beings: the principal was the Jade Emperor (jade being a symbol of purity), from whom all things have their ultimate origin; beneath him, there was Tao Chün, who controlled the forces of *yin* and *yang;* thirdly, in a lower heaven, dwelt the deified Lao Tzu. In each of the three heavens, there were other deities and spirits subordinate to the chief Deity of the heaven. The Taoists tended to model heaven upon the earthly court of the Emperor. Thus the Jade Emperor was surrounded by his consort, courtiers, and officials. In this way an elaborate organization of mythological figures was built up. All this provided a rich, if sometimes rather synthetic, mythology which could serve to vivify the religious imagination of the masses. For good measure, the Isles of the Immortals were set in contrast to the tortures of the Taoist hell. Thus in a complex way, many elements from popular religion—the spirits of the streams, the hills, the stars, sickness, wealth, the crops, the hearth—became incorporated into a single world-picture presided over by a heavenly counterpart to the earthly Emperor; in the name of Lao Tzu an elaborate temple cult flourished. Whether the founders of Taoism would have approved remains doubtful.

The religion sometimes acquired imperial patronage and benefited from the fierce persecution of Buddhism in the middle of the ninth century A.D., but it has rarely been able to offer to its adherents the loving devotionalism similar to that fostered by the Ching-t'u, or Pure Land, sect. Moreover, despite the recognition of the Chang Tao-ling succession described earlier, Taoism itself was never a unitary organization. If the Taoism centered on Dragon Tiger Mountain in Kiangsi was the most successful over a period of years, there were other allegiances and sects. The Northern school, dating in its modern form from the thirteenth century, was, for instance, much nearer certain original Taoist conceptions, such as frugality and austerity in the pursuit of harmony with nature.

Though it is useful to set together Pure Land Buddhism and the developed religious form of Taoism which sought to provide an analogous focus of popular devotion and ritual, original Taoism is much more nearly similar to Ch'an, or Meditation, Buddhism. Indeed, the latter is a characteristic fruit of Chinese Buddhism, later to be transplanted and developed in a Japanese setting; and it is characteristically *Chinese* inasmuch as it has undoubtedly been influenced by, and has caught the flavor of, the teachings contained in the early Taoist writings.

CH'AN BUDDHISM

It is hard to say precisely when the Ch'an movement started. According to tradition it was first brought to Canton in 520 A.D. by the famous Indian monk Bodhidharma, but there are reasons to doubt whether the biographical material about this powerful, enigmatic, and astonishing character is anything more than legendary. This does not matter much, for the legends themselves express something important about this form of Buddhism, and we shall have occasion to refer to them shortly. According to further tradition, the teaching was handed on in succession to various patriarchs, of whom the most famous was Hui-neng (637–713 A.D.). It is to him that many trace the rise of a definitely Chinese form of Ch'an. With his death the single line of the patriarchate ceased, and a number of disciples carried on his teachings, developing them in different ways. Of the various schools thus formed two remain today, the Lin-chi and Ts'ao-tung (Rinzai and Soto in Japanese), which differ as to the correct method of attaining illumination.

Perhaps it is wrong to seek for a definite beginning to the Ch'an (Meditation) school, since its characteristic emphases are derived from a blending of the ideas of Taoism and those of Buddhism, and it was already apparent soon after the introduction of Buddhism into China that Chinese commentators pointed to the analogies between the two systems. Thus in the fourth century the Buddhist convert Seng-chao used Taoist terminology to expound Mahayana teachings. In the next century, one writer explicitly spoke of the equivalence of the Buddhist pursuit of the Void and the Taoist notion of non-existence. It is therefore better to think of the rise of the Meditation School in China as the gradual mingling of two streams of religious practice than as something which can be dated from a particular time.

Bodhidharma, according to one of the legends about him, had an interview with the Chinese Emperor Wu Liang, who prided himself on his pious support for the Buddhist faith. The Emperor asked Bodhidharma how much merit accrued from such good works. The sage replied, somewhat ferociously, "No merit at all." This was shocking enough, and the Emperor was worried that in believing an orthodox doctrine of karma and merit he had misunderstood the whole point of the religion. What was to follow was, however, more shocking. He asked, "What, then, is the holy doctrine's first principle?" Bodhidharma replied, "It is empty; there is nothing holy." These answers indicate an important strand in Ch'an thinking. The emphasis of the school (and more especially the Lin-chi branch of it) is anti-intellectual. Enlightenment does not come from book knowledge—even the knowledge of the sacred books of Buddhism. This is why there is a famous Meditation school picture of a monk tearing up the scriptures. This of course should not be taken to mean that one may be disrespectful toward the Buddha's religion: rather it is a symbol that when one has understood the true point of the teaching there is no need for books. Words are at best like pointers toward the supreme experience of illumination and release. This anti-intellectualism is an echo of the distrust shown in the early Taoist writings toward the refined knowledge of the Confucians. It is not by examining the things around us or by gathering information that true insight is won: rather it is found in spontaneous experience. Thus both the story of Bodhidharma and the early Taoist writings share the same anti-intellectualist sentiment. There is a brusqueness and an exaggeration in the Bodhidharma story which can sometimes be found in Taoism.

Nirvana and the Real World

There was a further way in which the Buddhism and Taoism blended. Mahayana philosophy tended to equate nirvana and *samsara,* the cycle of events that goes to make up empirical existence. The reasons for this paradox arose from the concept of the Absolute (the Void) which was evolved in the Greater Vehicle. It was argued, for instance, by the Madhyamika school that phenomena are insubstantial and that all relations between them are contradictory. The only thing we can say about reality is that it is empty or void. This Void, so to speak, is what underlies and constitutes the world we perceive. A perception of the Void brings, or rather is, nirvana. Thus nirvana and the essential nature of the world are identical, and it is only when we are in the grip of ignorance—our normal condition—that we ascribe to things about us a substantiality and independent existence which they do not possess. It is only then that we distinguish between nirvana and *samsara.* Thus for one who is enlightened there is no difference between the two: only the ignorant think that there is "another shore" to which the Buddhist must cross. Such ideas had an important practical application. Release comes from abolishing the false constructions which impose a spurious reality upon the world of persons and things. If we can only let ourselves see phenomena pure and simple, without reading concepts into them, we can gain illumination and enlightenment—Buddhahood.

Idealist Teaching of Reality

The somewhat closely related Idealist school of Mahayana Buddhism claimed not so much that phenomena are contradictory as that they are mental products. The world is accessible to us only as a complex of perceptions, and the fact that we distinguish between the outside world and our own experiences is due to the false projection of ideas to which we referred in the previous paragraph. The Idealists claimed that by attaining a pure state of consciousness one would gain a non-dual awareness of the Absolute which is, so to say, the source of the world. Whereas the Madhyamika school tended to suppose that by philosophical thought one could attain the required enlightenment, the Idealists more strongly emphasized the practice of yoga for the purification of the consciousness.

It was against the background of such ideas that the Meditation school had its rise. The identification of nirvana with *samsara* has a notable analogy to the early Taoist attitude to the Tao. The Tao is what operates through nature. The sage can identify himself with it, provided he is spontaneous and clears his mind of the extraneous concepts and information which serve to clutter up his existence and cut him off, as it were, from the roots of his being. The Buddhist notion that we impose a false substantiality on the world through the use of language led naturally to the view that one should "see things as they are." This corresponded to the demand for spontaneity and passivity in life that was so central to the Taoist prescription for peace. We can therefore see that there were definite meeting points between the philosophy of the Greater Vehicle and Taoism.

The Chinese Character of Ch'an Buddhism

What, then, is characteristically new and Chinese about Meditation Buddhism? First, though earlier Buddhist teachers had recognized the identity of nirvana and empirical existence—seen from a certain point of view—they did not draw the conclusion, as did the Meditation School, that the enlightened life should be *spontaneous* in flavor. The Idealists still used traditional Indian methods of yoga, adapted to the context of Greater Vehicle piety. The Meditation school, however, developed new methods of training which assimilated elements from the old, but transformed them in an attempt (paradoxical though it may seem) to make the learner act spontaneously. These methods, called *wen-ta* and *kung-an*, aimed at producing an illumination which comes naturally from within. A second aspect of the Meditation school which is typically Chinese (Taoist) is the strong feeling for nature. To be sure there was something of this in the early days of Buddhism in India, but on the whole, the traditional Indian methods of yoga involve a conscious turning away from the world of the senses. However, in the atmosphere of China, natural events and beauties themselves came to form an important part in the perception of the adept. The outer world flowed naturally in upon the inward world, and illumination could sometimes take the form of a merging of the individual in the processes around him—a kind of nature mysticism.

Certain features of the Taoist and later the Ch'an attitude to nature had a lasting influence upon Chinese art. In the *Tao-te Ching* it is emphasized that the Void, the empty, the blank can be the decisive aspects of things—the emptiness within the pot is what makes it effectively a pot, and so on. Much of Chinese art came to symbolize this power of emptiness. Tender and mysterious landscapes depict the peaks of upward-soaring, indented mountains, with here and there a pine or a cedar. Far below there is a man fishing. In between there is the great misty blank of the valley. If we look objectively at the scroll, we perceive that a vast part of it is simply blank. The painter achieves much of his effect by not painting—an illustration of the famous Taoist principle of acting through not acting.

A third way in which a characteristic flavor is imparted to the teachings and life of the Meditation school is that the doctrine that intellectual constructions falsify reality was given a practical application. In the main stream of the Indian and early Chinese Mahayana, anti-intellectualism tended to remain itself an intellectual attitude and was not too closely integrated into the methods of spiritual training. But in Ch'an Buddhism, methods were evolved for bringing home to the pupil in a forceful and pointed way the fact that intellectual theories themselves, even when they are orthodox Buddhist ones, are part of the veil of concepts which clouds the flow of pure experience.

Wen-ta and Kung-an

The techniques evolved were those of the *wen-ta* (Japanese *mondo*) or "question and answer," and of the *kung-an* (Japanese, *koan*), or "Zen riddle." Literally the last term should be translated as "public document"—the riddles arise out of records of the interchanges between masters and pupils. These records were collected and formed the basis for the riddles. One of the difficulties of describing the technique of posing such riddles as part of the method of instruction is that, for obvious reasons, standard answers were unacceptable. Thus though one person might give a brilliantly appropriate response, this was unavailable to another person; for the whole point of the riddles is to elicit a spontaneous and individual response, not one that could be learned from some text book. The response need not even be a verbal response, and importance was attached in the Meditation school to non-verbal communication. Indeed the theory was that illumination was transferred directly from the mind of the master to that of the pupil. This very obviously is a sort of communication which does not involve the passing of information from one person to another.

There is a story that one of the Chinese masters wished to open a second monastery, and had to select a monk to govern it. Pointing to a pitcher, he asked one of his monks to tell him what it was without calling it a pitcher. The head monk said, "You could not call it a piece of wood." But the monastery cook walked over, kicked over the pitcher, and walked away. The cook was selected to be in charge of the new monastery. Another story relates that the question was asked as to whether a dog has the Buddha-nature. Since the dog is often regarded in the East as a contemptible animal, somewhat as the Westerner regards the rat, the question was in essence disrespectful, so it seemed, to the Buddha. One pupil replied by a nice *double entendre:* he made a barking noise that happens also to sound like the word for "no". Some of the riddles are extremely surrealistic: "What sound does one hand clapping make?" The surrealism helps to break down conceptual thought.

These techniques themselves of course could, and did, fall into the trap they were designed to guard against. It was too easy to let the clever and humorous answer substitute for an expression of genuine spiritual awakening. Similarly, the use made of slapping and hitting, which became quite widespread among Zen masters as part of their method of startling their pupils and interspersing the non-verbal within a verbal exchange, could easily degenerate into a rather senseless cruelty. In these ways the methods of inducing the spontaneous response could themselves become formal, stereotyped, and wrongly motivated. This points to a central paradox in the Meditation school's outlook on training: the paradox is simply that the riddles and the rest are designed to express a spirit of openness and spontaneity, but as soon as they are made into a tradition they are liable themselves to become closed and mechanical. The Meditation methods grew out of a situation where men of disciplined religious and esthetic sensibility (however earthy their expressions might often be) could profitably attempt such experimentation in the spiritual life, for many of their pupils in the latter period of the movement in China were young novices. This happened partly because of the savage, if brief, persecution of Buddhism in the middle of the ninth century A.D. Many monasteries were closed or destroyed and vast numbers of monks and nuns were secularized. Afterward, it happened that the Ch'an schools were the most resilient—so that by consequence many young monks sent by their families to enter the religious life found themselves under the tutelage of Ch'an masters.

The persecution referred to above was a major factor in forming the later character of Buddhism in China because Ch'an-type monasticism came to dominate the inner life of the Sangha, and Pure Land piety came to dominate the more popular aspect of the religion.

Another important feature of Ch'an Buddhism which we have not so far spelled out, but which gives it its own characteristic flavor, is the notion that illumination is sudden or instantaneous. This awakening (*tun wu*—known better through its Japanese name of *satori*) is likened to the way a mirror instantaneously reflects whatever appears in front of it. It is like a sudden conversion. The doctrine that this is central to the spiritual life is held by the Lin-chi (or Rinzai) school of Ch'an, though the Ts'ao-tung (or Soto) school did not wish the inference to be drawn that there can be, as it were, a sudden conquest of illumination. For this reason, they do not favor the use of the *koan*, on the ground that it seems to involve a striving for immediate awakening. Rather, the process toward the latter should be a gradual one, stealing up upon it (so to say) unawares. Thus the methods of the Ts'ao-tung were of a more gradual and orthodox sort. The serene spirit of this form of Ch'an is well expressed in some verses attributed to Dogen, who introduced the Ts'ao-tung to Japan:

> *Only a few moments will last*
> *The dew-drops on the edges of the blades of grass*
> *Until the morning sun comes to dry them up.*
>
> *Blow gently and soft, O breeze of the autumn.*
> *Sweeping over the wild prairies!*
>
> *. . . Calm and serene in the midnight,*
> *Lo, a deserted boat on the water,*
> *Not tossed by the waves nor drawn by the breeze,*
> *Braced in the pale light of the moon!*
>
> *. . . O poor scarecrow standing alone*
> *In the rice-field among the mountains!*
> *Thou art myself unaware of thy watch,*
> *Yet thy standing is not in vain.*[5]

Here is a gentle expression of the poet's oneness with the stream of experience which constitutes reality, and it is a recurring theme in Ch'an poetry that nature, as it were, flows in upon the individual, and the individual opens out, so to say, into nature. The two become one, and the differentiation between the "external" world and the self is completely broken down. Only phenomena in their mindless purity exist in this state.

[5] This translation appears in *The History of Japanese Religion*, by Masaharu Anesaki (London: Kegan Paul, 1930), p. 208.

This nature-mysticism has its analogies in other cultures, in Wordsworth, for instance. But the Meditation school does not allow such experiences simply to crop up haphazardly. It believes them to be implicit in human nature, if we could but allow that nature to operate effortlessly on its own. Thus the training is designed to remove those obstacles and barriers which stand in the way of this inner expansion of experiences.

We shall later observe how Ch'an Buddhism took root in and flowered in Japan and how that country itself imparted some new aspects to the movement. Meanwhile, we can say that the Meditation school was a great Chinese contribution to the development of Buddhism. By the time of the T'ang Dynasty, when the school flourished most, Buddhism had traveled far both in space and time from its early Indian origins; though the legends that traced Ch'an back to the Buddha himself were undoubtedly historically false, nonetheless they contained a germ of truth. For the Ch'an movement certainly represented a strong return to the question of how one could best gain the peace and insight that constitute nirvana in this life through some kind of training. Unlike the Pure Land school that relied upon grace and de-emphasized the traditional Path to release, the Meditation school took yoga seriously. Though the methods it used were in some respects novel, nevertheless it existed recognizably within the framework of traditional Buddhist meditation. In this sense, it was and is a form of the Greater Vehicle that shares a common view with the conservative Theravada. One must note that the Ch'an mixture of nature-mysticism and its rather aggressive toughness in teaching methods differ from the classical forms of Buddhist yoga. But these variations allowed Buddhism to draw from the indigenous culture of China, and thereby to penetrate into that culture. Buddhism has always been somewhat pragmatic. It is a "come-and-see" religion, to translate a word from the Pali scriptures: it is experimental, not in the sense that modern science is, but in the sense that one has access to the spiritual world only through experience and should not pretend to substitute for this more direct knowledge unverifiable doctrines. Thus in following the Buddha's path what people find in their own experience has a validity even if it issues in formulations that at first sight do not seem to be strictly orthodox. In the Greater Vehicle the notion that the Buddha adapts his teaching to the condition of his hearers was strongly developed; thus the Buddha, when dressed, so to say, in Chinese robes, pointed the way to the experiences implicit in the teachings of the Meditation school.

Despite the importance of Ch'an Buddhism for Chinese culture, it would be wrong to underestimate the significance of the Pure Land school. This testified to men's apprehension of the numinous, of the holy nature of Reality, and its expression in worship and devotion. Pure Land Buddhism probably constituted the highest form of personal religion in post-Buddhist and late

Chinese life. Though Confucianism was not without its concept of a supreme Being, and though K'ung himself spoke movingly of Heaven, the fact remained that the actual cult of this Supreme Being was reserved for the imperial dynasty, and was largely formal in character. For those ordinary folk who had an intuition of a Being more glorious than the spirits and deities who lurked in the woodlands and the rice fields, the cult of the great Buddha Amitabha, or of Kuan-yin, provided a more satisfying faith and an assurance of salvation. Thus the numinous side of Chinese religion, as well as the mystical, found a good expression in Buddhism. As we have noted, the Taoist equivalent to the devotionalism of the Greater Vehicle was a less satisfying religious substitute, though it undoubtedly linked more directly with material concerns, through its magical techniques. But we must remember that the "three religions," though sometimes rivals, especially at court, where issues of patronage and government could be crucial, complemented one another in the life of the Chinese people at different levels.

DEVELOPMENTS IN CONFUCIANISM

The post-Buddhist period of the "golden age of Buddhism" was not altogether a happy one for Confucianism. But toward the end of the T'ang Dynasty it was beginning to show signs of a vigorous revival. A straw in the wind was the denunciation of certain superstitions current among the Buddhists by Han Yü (768–824 A.D.), a celebrated essayist. He was a follower and great admirer of Meng, whom he placed second only to K'ung as a teacher (a judgment that has since won general acceptance among orthodox Confucianists). He believed that the decline in Confucianism since Meng's day was directly attributable to the spread of Buddhism and Taoism, and he strongly attacked the practice of celibacy which took men and women away from their families and into the monasteries. Monasteries and temples, he held, should be destroyed or converted to useful purposes, such as providing homes for the poor. But Han Yü is chiefly remembered for his attack upon the veneration of Buddhist relics. There is a story that the Emperor had ordered a palace reception to be given in honor of a newly acquired relic, a finger-bone of Gautama, the Buddha. Han Yü petitioned the Emperor forthrightly, pointing out that Buddhism was a foreign and barbarous religion, and that the belief in relics was mere superstition, unworthy of the Emperor. If the Emperor would destroy the relic, Han Yü urged, he should then see that the Lord Buddha would not deluge China with disaster. The Emperor had the writer banished for these sentiments. Such a protest indicates an increased concern for the restoration of true Confucian teaching, but more was needed than an attack upon Buddhism. Among intellectuals at least, the power of Buddhism was due in part to the elaboration of its metaphysical doctrines. Buddhism embodied an ideology and a body of philosophy which was impressive by all standards. Confucianism, with its pragmatic emphasis, could not yet offer a systematic theology.

THE NEO-CONFUCIAN REVIVAL

During the latter part of the Sung Dynasty, however, in eleventh and twelfth centuries, something like a systematic theology—or rather a set of such systems—was elaborated during the so-called Neo-Confucian revival. Two main representatives of this movement can be mentioned here.

Chu Hsi

First, the philosopher Chu Hsi (1130–1200 A.D.) elaborated a system that bore certain analogies to Platonism, and which attempted to give a rational explanation of the universe. A central concept in his metaphysics was that of *li*, or principle (not to be confused with a different character having the same pronunciation meaning "ceremonial," which figured prominently in K'ung's teaching). According to Chu Hsi, each entity has its *li*—the form which makes it what it is. The *li* of the members of the same species are identical; thus every tiger participates in, or is shaped by, the same *li*. (The doctrine is reminiscent of Plato's Forms.) What makes the difference between individuals is their *ch'i*, that is, their material, vital energy. This polarity roughly corresponds to the form-matter distinction in Greek metaphysics. Now according to Chu Hsi, it is possible to see beyond the multiplicity of timeless *li* which inform nature to a single supreme Principle: for all things share the universal property of being, or existence, and thus there is an underlying Ultimate Reality. This was called—and here the term used was one familiar in later Taoism—the *T'ai-chi*, or Supreme Ultimate. Chu Hsi was also able to make use of the traditional polarity between the *yin* and the *yang*. These universals give shape to the perceptible world. Thus he elaborated a cosmology, in which under the active influence of *ch'i* the Great Ultimate gives rise first to the *yang*, the male principle, and then to the *yin*, and then through their interplay to the myriad things and forces that make up the cosmos as we know it.

Such a metaphysics by itself might not be thought to have much practical or religious significance. But Chu Hsi derived an ethic from it. Man has his characteristic *li*, the same for all individuals, and like the other principles informing the world it is part of the Great Ultimate. But obviously individuals differ in their worth and wisdom. To what is this due? Clearly to differences in their *ch'i*. If one's *ch'i* is cloudy or muddy, then one's actions and character will be inferior. Thus the object of the man who strives for goodness should be to purify his *ch'i*, so that the *li* will stand forth in its purity, and one will be united, in a sense, with the Supreme Ultimate. Since Chu Hsi held that it is human desire that is the most important factor in making the *ch'i* obscure the *li*, he considered it vital that one should gain knowledge of the workings of desire. Through knowledge it would be tamed. This fitted with his general, and typically Confucian, view that through the investigation of things and fact one gains an enlightened and moral outlook, rather than through intuitive experience. Still, the notion that there exists a pure humanity within the individual if he can only overcome the defilements of a muddy *ch'i* is reminiscent of Buddhist doctrine. Superficially, Chu Hsi's insistence on daily quiet meditation might be thought to be Buddhist in character, and there is little doubt that the Buddhist emphasis on meditation influenced him; but essentially his type of meditation was conceived as a means of stilling the passions, calming the mind, and reflecting upon the good. It had an ethical rather than a mystical quality.

Chu Hsi succeeded in weaving into his system elements from the rival schools: his idea of the Great Ultimate was close in some respects to Taoist ideas, but it included, too, the dynamic force of *ch'i*: although *li* might be eternal, reality as man experienced it was always a dynamic interaction between the material and the spiritual. His concept of man's *li* reflected Buddhist notions of the Buddha-nature residing within living beings, and yet Chu Hsi's goal was not an intuitive, mystical awakening, but rather a moral harmony with the Highest in both human and cosmic nature. As for ordinary religious practices, he seems to have been largely skeptical about them. His was neither a superstitious nor a fervently devotional faith; it was a reasoned one. Thus Chu Hsi expressed in an important way the need for the Confucian movement to arm itself with a viable metaphysics.

Lu Hsiang-shan

A second great figure in the Neo-Confucian revival was that of Lu Hsiang-shan (1139–1192 A.D.), who moved Neo-Confucian philosophy in an idealistic direction. He differed from Chu Hsi (with whom in his lifetime he agreed to differ) in wishing to simplify further the picture of reality presented by Neo-Confucianism. While Chu Hsi had analyzed the universe into two great principles, the *li* and the *ch'i*, Lu wished to trace everything back to a single principle. He claimed that early Chinese thought as expressed in the Classics and elsewhere did not give a dualistic view of the world, but regarded the cosmos as an organic unity. He felt that Chu Hsi had split this reality into two. Lu therefore argued that the underlying and embracing principle that explains all things is the *li*. But this itself is mental in nature, not physical. Thus he claimed, "The universe and my mind are one; my mind and the universe are one." Lu's philosophy was later developed by Wang Yang-ming (1473–1529 A.D.), so that the school is referred to as the Lu-Wang school.

Wang Yang-ming

There is a significant story about Wang which helps to illustrate an important point about this idealistic metaphysics. He and a friend had been concerned about the method that Chu Hsi advocated to cleanse the mind and restore it to its essential purity—a method of investigating the nature of things. The idea that knowledge produces enlightenment seemed to Wang to be reasonable; but how was it to be applied? He and his friend decided to concentrate upon the bamboo in the front courtyard of his family house, and see whether knowledge of the *li* of the bamboo would bring about any sort of spiritual advance. They contemplated the bamboo for three days and nights, when the friend gave up: Wang went on for another four. Then he too gave up, concluding that the only thing to be known about the bamboo, as to its reason or rationale, was that in a number of respects it was very suitable as a garden plant. What is significant about the story is this: Wang and his friend obviously thought of the investigation of things as consisting in a sort of contemplation, rather like Buddhist *dhyana*. This was not a philosophical or scientific investigation, designed to gain an explanation of why things are as they are. It is perhaps not surprising that Wang should have thought in this way: it is said that in his youth he consorted with Buddhist and Taoist recluses, and he must have been influenced by the contemplative life he witnessed among them. In elaborating his own idealistic philosophy, he maintained that by looking inward at one's own nature a man can gain intuitive knowledge of the whole of reality. Wang is said to have endured banishment and to have lived in poor and menial conditions. Reportedly one day he had a mystical experience in which he realized existentially the truth that one must seek to purify the mind by meditative techniques, and that in this way an illuminated goodness will shine through one's outward behavior. This form of Neo-Confucianism thus bore something of the imprint of Meditation Buddhism, though one must note that Wang and the Idealists gave a strongly ethical interpretation to the illuminative life, and were not ascetic in their outlook. Wang held that knowledge and practice coincide, and that intuitive knowledge releases the force of goodness within human nature. In his philosophy, those who believe in moral values but nevertheless fail to live up to their duties are ignorant: give them a true knowledge of themselves, and their true goodness will become manifest. Their knowledge of themselves is also knowledge of the principle governing the whole of nature: thus virtuous action expresses harmony with the whole.

It is a matter of great interest, though perhaps not the occasion for surprise, that even in this late and metaphysical phase of Confucianism the ethical dimension of the faith remained supremely important. It was still in terms of the ethical that religious experience, such as Wang's, was interpreted.

Whereas K'ung had enlarged the ritual dimension of ancient Chinese religion and given it an ethical extension and content, Wang and Lu took the experiential dimension, as it had been explored in Meditation Buddhism, and gave it an ethical flavor. The pragmatic ritual of meditation, which might help to bring about such experience through the purification of the mind, was itself justified in terms of its beneficent moral and social effects. Thus Confucianism, virtually throughout its history, runs counter to the major tendency in the other great religions—namely to start from religious experience, whether prophetic, devotional, or mystical—and see moral values in the light thereof. It was the other way about in Confucianism. It is true that in some phases of religion—among the Prophets of the Old Testament, for instance—there is a dialectic between religious experience and ethical insight. Conceptions of God have been affected by the moral intuitions that men have brought to bear upon them. But by and large the dialectic has resulted in a way of seeing the ethical *sub specie aeternitatis*. In Confucianism, eternity has been seen rather in the light of society and in the light of what is moral.

CONFUCIANISM AS RELIGION

Because of this largely ethical and social emphasis, Confucianism has often been regarded more as a moral system than as a religion. One factor which we have to examine in order to decide this question is the nature of the state cult of Confucius. When in the latter part of the second century B.C., Confucian methods were adopted for teaching and in examinations, Confucian doctrines gained an official standing. K'ung posthumously was given progressively higher honorary ranks, and emperors performed sacrifices at his tomb. In the seventh century A.D., it was decreed that every prefecture in China should erect a temple to honor K'ung if it did not already have one, and two centuries later statues of K'ung were erected in them, at the instigation of the Emperor. Influenced by Buddhist practice, the ceremonial used to honor the sage was often very elaborate and was designed to confer on him an extremely high status. However, in the sixteenth century the cultus was, by imperial edict, considerably simplified and the images of K'ung replaced by the traditional tablets used in honoring ancestral spirits.

It is a perplexing question to know whether K'ung was strictly regarded at any time as a god, or whether Confucianism could properly be called a state religion. The cult continued under emperors who were themselves Buddhists or Taoists, and the use of the Confucian classics was not in any event held to be incompatible with a personal religion which was not Confucian. It is true that in the last days of the Manchu empire, K'ung's status was raised to be equal to that of Heaven, but this was a short-lived and uncharacteristic innovation. The use of images, of course, must have given him a quasi-divine status in the eyes of ordinary folk. In a land in which there was a whole hierarchy of ancestral spirits and divinities, Master K'ung obviously occupied an exalted place as an invisible being. But it would be an exaggeration to say that he was the focus of the devotional life in the way the Buddhas were. Much of the ceremonial attached to the Confucian cult was highly formal. After all every person honored his ancestors, so the exalted rank given post-humously to K'ung by the state should not be regarded as an altogether radical measure.

Thus K'ung, unlike Mahayana Buddhas and Christ, does not function as the object of worship and devotion. Rather, he was honored as the great sage of the past. Confucianism, then, never became a religion in the sense that there was a special form of worship associated with it. To be sure, there were religious elements in K'ung's own teaching. Further, Confucianism, because it maintains traditional values, has always been closely related to the ancient ancestral—and other—cults. These do have a part to play in the total religion of the Chinese, and to this extent Confucianism, because it mingled with and complemented the devotion and mysticism found in the Buddhist and Taoist traditions, forms part of the fabric of the religion of China. Having said this, it is unnecessary to assert that taken by itself it does or does not constitute a religion. Moreover, there have been and are many Confucians who have been sceptical about supernatural religion and what they regard as popular supersti-tion. They have provided an agnostic dimension to Chinese culture.

''WESTERN'' RELIGIONS IN CHINA

So far we have observed the interplay of the "three religions." Other faiths too found their way into China. In the early centuries of the Christian era, Zoro-astrianism, Nestorianism, and Manicheism filtered in along the silk routes from Central Asia, but they have left little trace in modern China. Perhaps the most remarkable story is that of the Nestorian Christians. In 1625 there was discovered in Sian (or Changan), in Shensi province, a Nestorian monument with inscriptions. Later archeological finds suggest that for two centuries or so there was a flourishing Christian church in China, mainly monastic in charac-ter. However, the imperial edict of 845 A.D. directing that monasteries be closed, which, though it was aimed principally against the Buddhists, also fell upon the Christians, dealt the community a severe blow, from which it did not recover.

More important for the later history of China was the spread of Islam, of which there are now thirty or forty million adherents in the country (estimates vary). These are to be found mainly in the west and northwest of China, and along the coast, with a sizeable sprinkling in a section of North Central China. It is still not absolutely clear how such a large population of Muslims has arisen. Part of the story is that Arab mercenaries were brought in to suppress a rebellion in the eighth century A.D., and were given land to settle on. Intermarriage with the Chinese helped to swell the numbers. In addition, Muslim traders reached the Chinese coast, and, later on, Muslim mercenaries sought service with the Mongols.

Christianity penetrated to China in later centuries, despite the demise of the Nestorian Church. Already one or two missionaries reached China in the Middle Ages, but without much effect. With the opening up of the sea route from Europe to the East, however, Catholic (and later Protestant) missionaries were enabled more easily to enter China. The most famous early pioneer of missions in China was the Jesuit Matteo Ricci (1552–1610 A.D.), who settled at the Chinese court, won favor from the Emperor, and made a number of converts. His adoption of Chinese dress and manners, his mastery of the language, his personal qualities, and his skill as a map-maker, earned him the respect of those about him.

The expansion of Christianity is the theme of a later chapter; let it suffice here to say that the hospitals and schools opened by the nineteenth- and twentieth-century missions introduced China to certain beneficial aspects of modern science and technology in a period when European commercial and colonial depredations on China confirmed her traditional view that foreigners are barbarians. The political crisis of China ultimately issued in the revolution of 1911. This was to usher in a period of intense revaluation of all tradition, including the three religions. Since this period of reappraisal is closely relevant to the question of the future of religion in China, we shall leave over consideration of it until our final chapter.

JAPANESE RELIGIONS

Now we must step back in time. We have followed the story of the Chinese religions from early times to the modern period without indicating the widespread cultural effects China's religions had on the countries surrounding her. Not least was this so in regard to Japan. It was through China and Korea that Buddhism reached that country. Already from the fifth century A.D. Chinese cultural influence was spreading into Japan, but the decisive moment for the importation of Buddhism was the accession of Prince Shotoku to the regency in 593 A.D. He was to make it the official faith. Within about three centuries it became deeply rooted in Japanese national life. Thus we can divide Japanese religious history into two phases—first, the early period, in which the

principal religion was Shinto; second, the early Buddhist period. From the
ninth to the twelfth century we date the classical era of Japanese culture, but
the administration ultimately became effete, and was replaced in the thirteenth
century by a military and feudal regime. This medieval period was succeeded
in the seventeenth century by the Tokugawa regime, which lasted until 1887.
Then commenced Japan's modern period: hitherto deliberately isolated from the
world at large, she now turned to acquire those technological skills that would
ensure her independence.

SHINTO

Shinto, or at least the cult of gods later important in developed Shinto,
was the early religion of Japan. It forms a substratum of belief and practice
that remains to this day. It has sometimes merged with Buddhism; at other
times, there have been attempts to revitalize it as an independent faith with
its own theology. Until the advent of Christianity in Japan—except for
pockets of aboriginal cultures such as the Ainu—the history of Japanese religion has been the history of Shintoism and Buddhism and of their interplay.

Toward the end of the first millennium B.C. a people of Mongoloid stock
gradually began to subjugate Japan, moving over from the Asian mainland
and slowly dispossessing the Ainu. The invaders' culture belonged to the Iron
Age and was militarily superior to that of the Ainu. Different groups settled in
different parts of Kyushu and spread into Honshu. By the beginning of the
present era those people who called themselves the Yamato gained control
over a large part of the country. The Yamato also took over and unified the
legends and cults practiced by the various invading peoples. It was this eclectic
religion that came to be known as "Shinto." Literally, Shinto means "Way of
the Gods." The term came into use at the time Buddhism permeated Japan as
a self-conscious way of distinguishing the traditional cultus from the new faith.
Indeed, the word itself is Chinese in origin; *to* is a form of the Chinese *Tao*.

The earliest records of Shintoism consist in two sets of scriptures written
down in the eighth century A.D., the *Kojiki,* "Records of Ancient Matters,"
and the *Nihon Shoki,* "Japanese Chronicles," sometimes also referred to as
the *Nihongi.* From these and other sources we can learn a good deal about
early Shinto.

Kami

Shintoism displayed, and still displays, a powerful sense of the presence of
gods and spirits in nature. These spirits are called *kami,* literally "superior
beings," and it is appropriate to venerate them. The *kami* are too numerous to

lend themselves to a systematic ordering or stable hierarchy, but among the many the sun goddess Amaterasu has long held a central place in Shinto belief. According to the myth found at the beginning of the *Kojiki,* the earliest of the celestial gods who came into being instructed Izanagi and Izanami, male and female deities of the second generation of gods, to create the world, and in particular the islands of Japan (the two were in effect identified). Through the process of sexual generation they produced the land, and the *kami* of the mountains, trees, and streams, the god of the wind and the god of fire, and so on. Eventually, after various mythological vicissitudes, into which we need not now enter, the goddess Amaterasu, the great *kami* of the Sun, came into being. Possibly, prior to the mythological account of her origin she was the mother goddess of the Yamato clans; the mythology may reflect the way in which other deities were successively replaced in the earliest period, and then were put under the dominance of the chief *kami* of the Yamato. But the line between *kami* and human is not a sharp one, however exalted some of the deities may be. The Japanese people themselves, according to the traditional myths, are descended from the *kami;* while the line of emperors traces its descent back to Amaterasu. Amaterasu sent her son Ni-ni-gi down to rule Japan for her, and thence the imperial line took its origin (this tradition in recent times was given exaggerated emphasis in order to make Shinto into an ideology justifying a nationalistic expansionist policy). The line too between the personal and impersonal in the *kami* is fluid. Some of the spirits associated with particular places or things are not strongly personalized, though the mythology concerned with the great gods and goddesses is fully anthropomorphic.

Amaterasu

A strong feature of Shinto, even from the earliest records, is the insistence on purity, to be obtained by ritual washing and bathing. This ideal of purity is symbolized by the mirror that is associated above all with the goddess Amaterasu, and which is commonly found in Shinto shrines. The mirror reflects clearly, and so stands for honesty and sincerity. In such ways, there is a connection between religious rites and moral and social life. But the stress on purity, not surprisingly, had its roots in a strong sense of the possibility of pollution through the breaking of tabus. Birth and death in particular were considered polluting, so that children had to be born in a special hut away from the main dwelling, and death sometimes meant that a new dwelling had to be constructed—thus in early times the emperor, upon his accession, had to build a new palace to replace that of his dead predecessor. Since blood was also *tabu,* animal sacrifices were not performed, and in general the cult of the *kami* was characterized by a reverent simplicity—offerings of grain and vegetables, for instance, would be rendered to the *kami*. Originally, the ceremonial seems to have been conducted by women priests or *shamans*. This is an indication of the early role played by women in agriculture. The fact too that the chief deity was a goddess is significant in this connection.

The use of spells and magic provided another dimension to the early "Way of the Gods." Often these are associated with the storm god, the "Swift-Impetuous One," who is the brother of Amaterasu. His mother, Isanami, had died when giving birth to the fire god, and had descended into the underworld, where she ruled. The storm god in his violence and noisiness expresses his longing for that lower realm of death and chaos. According to the mythology, there was a period when the son of the storm god ruled over the Japanese islands, and it was on this occasion that Amaterasu sent down Ni-ni-gi to set matters right. A great deal of the legend deals with the struggles between Amaterasu and her violent brother—a symbolization of the interplay between the healing powers of the sun in promoting the growth of food and plants, and the disruptive powers of the sky in sending down hail and tempest. Thus the storm god and his minions sum up the destructive side of nature, and the need to propitiate these beings partly accounts for their association with the arts of magic and sorcery.

It would be wrong to see in this aspect of Shinto mythology a dualism between good and evil principles such as is found in Zoroastrianism. Shinto rather expressed through these legends the mysterious interplay of forces which control man's environment. In all aspects Shinto is closely bound up with the natural world. Shrines typically are located in sacred groves, which express something of the mystery and peace pervading a beautiful and formidable countryside. But the combat between Amaterasu and the storm god extended beyond the dialectic of the seasons, of course, and into the heavenly realm.

The climax of their struggle came when the storm god destroyed the rice fields, Amaterasu's special domain, and polluted her rites. The goddess, in sorrow and shock, went away and hid herself in a cave, thus depriving mankind of light. But eight million *kami* flocked to the entrance of her self-imposed prison and besought her with ceremonial and magic to come forth. She yielded to their entreaties, and issued out. As the brilliant shafts of light streaming from her person broke forth from the entrance to the cave, the gods shouted with joy. Light had succeeded in overcoming darkness. This myth, which very probably has to do with the phenomenon of the solar eclipse, signifies more than this. The great host of *kami* are on the side of mankind in helping in the restoration of the beneficent mother goddess. The rice fields can once more be rich and fruitful. It is interesting that the rice offered to the *kami* is grown in a special sacred plot tended by women, and the ceremonial

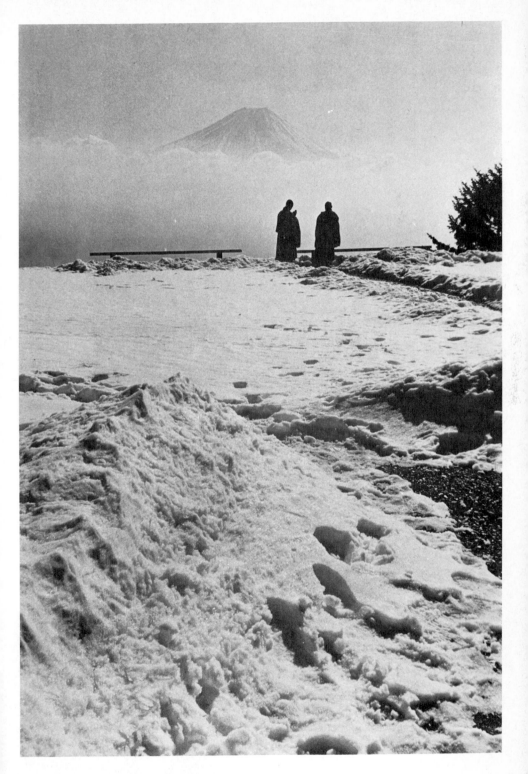

36. *Buddhist monks at Minobusan meditate before Fuji, the sacred mountain.*
(Courtesy of Japan National Tourist Organization.)

37. *Great Torii of Shinto shrine on Miyamjima Island sacred to Itsukushima, a niece of the Great Sun Goddess Amaterasu. (Courtesy of Japan National Tourist Organization.)*

38. *A Zen Buddhist monk meditating in a temple in Japan. (Courtesy of the United Nations; photo by Hanns Maier, Jr.)*

39. *Garden of Sanzenin Temple, Kyoto. (Courtesy of Japan National Tourist Organization.)*

40. *Fences of the Inner Shrine at Ise, largest and most important of Shinto shrines where were housed the sacred mirror, sword, and jewels bequeathed by the Goddess Amaterasu Omikami to her grandson, the first Emperor. The buildings, originally constructed in 92 B.C., are made anew every twenty years. (Courtesy of Japan National Tourist Organization.)*

41. *Shinto shrine festival, Hanamaki City. (Courtesy of Japan National Tourist Organization.)*

42. *South Korean Buddha teaching the Dharma. (Courtesy of the United Nations.)*

43. *These two monks, father and son, are keepers of a Buddhist temple in South Korea. (Courtesy of the United Nations.)*

attendant on the offering involves a sacred dance by maidens—a further indication of the origin of Amaterasu as an agricultural deity and of agriculture itself as specially a women's preserve.

It is not altogether surprising that the great sky god Izanagi plays a much lesser role than his illustrious daughter. At first not much interest seems to have been taken in the possibilities of a future life for men, though the lack of a sharp line between *kami* and men meant that the conception of great heroes continuing to exist in the heavenly or in the nether world was not uncommon. The cult of the spirits of the home was developed early. A combination of these tendencies paved the way for the cult of ancestors, which gained impetus when Chinese culture arrived in Japan.

We shall later describe in more detail the kinds of cultus found in modern Shinto. But first we must consider the effect upon Shinto of an invasion from outside—that of Buddhism. This led to some modifications, and attempts to produce a synthesis between the two ways of life.

BUDDHISM IN JAPAN

Toward the end of the fourth century B.C., Buddhism spread into Korea, a country already within the orbit of Chinese cultural and political influence. The Korean upper classes tended to take over Buddhism as part of their borrowing of Chinese ideas and skills in general. From Korea, Buddhism penetrated into Japan. In 552 A.D. the ruler of one of the Korean principalities sent an embassy to Japan; among the precious gifts he sent were some Buddhist writings, together with a statue of the Buddha. As trading contacts between the two countries increased, so also did contact with Buddhist believers. There was, however, considerable resistance to the new faith from certain Japanese noblemen and in the latter part of the sixth century an open struggle broke out between militant traditionalists and the advocates of the new culture. However, the achievements of the learning from overseas were self-evident—for instance in advanced medical techniques and the art of writing—and undoubtedly Buddhist ceremonies were impressive.

Shotoku

By the end of the century the noble families opposing Buddhism had lost power and the reigning prince, Shotoku, was able to effect an ambitious cultural and religious revolution. He had become Regent in 593 with the support of the pro-Chinese party; despite his youth (he was only nineteen years of age), he proceeded with great energy and piety to reconstitute the political order. He made Buddhism the official religion of the court, and authorized the

construction of a vast Buddhist institution at the seaport for the new capital of
Nara, in southern Honshu. This consisted in a great temple and an academy
for the study of Buddhist teachings, together with a hospital and dispensary.
Later on, he sent monks and students to China to learn more of the new faith.
The prince himself engaged in teaching the new principles, basing his ideas on
the *Lotus Sutra* and other texts. He devised a constitution that blended Confucian moral and social ideals with respect for the Buddha's religion. All this
expressed the spiritual and ideological side of his enterprise; at the same time
he reformed and reorganized the administration and put in hand public works
such as road-building. His rule, then, was a turning point in Japanese history.
He consolidated the outward-looking trend in Japan, and enabled her indigenous culture to be fertilized by the impressive civilization of the Chinese
mainland.

The period of the Nara culture lasted until the end of the eighth century.
The arts flourished, and Buddhist metaphysical systems were introduced and
assimilated. During this time, the chief schools were those of the Madhyamika
and the Yogacara, or Idealism. These were respectively known, through the
transliteration of their Chinese titles into Japanese, as the Sanron and Hossō
schools. At the same time, the study of the Buddhist discipline, Vinaya, was
undertaken in detail; this formed the basis for the monastic life that attracted a
large number of adherents. The power and political influence of the Buddhist
clergy became a major factor in affairs of state. Partly in order to tame this
new force, and partly to effect political reform, the capital was moved in 794
from Nara to Heian-Kyo, which is now Kyoto. There followed a period of
relative prosperity and good administration, known as the Heian period, that
lasted for nearly four centuries.

THE TENDAI SCHOOL OF SAICHO

The early days of the Heian period brought into prominence a monk named
Saicho (or Dengyo, a name conferred on him posthumously). Of Chinese
descent, he was born at Mount Hiei and ordained at Nara. Critical of the state
religion there, he spoke out for a purified, but centralized, organization of the
Buddhist church, and when the capital was moved to Heian-Kyo, he was
assisted by the government in this project. The monasteries and temples he
founded at Mount Hiei were recognized as the center of the faith by the
state—a recognition greatly amplified by the prevailing belief that the security
and prosperity of the land depended on the proper maintenance of religion.
Saicho was sent to China, and brought back the system known as the T'ien-
t'ai, or in Japanese transliteration, Tendai. This proved to be one of the main
forms of Buddhist thought and piety during the Heian period.

The aim of the Tendai school was to provide a synthesis of the perplexingly different teachings and scriptures that characterized Buddhism in its Chinese and Greater Vehicle (Mahayana) development. On the one hand, there were realistic doctrines derived from the Lesser Vehicle (Theravada), which asserted that the world of phenomena is real, and is distinct from nirvana. On the other hand, there was a strong tendency in the Mahayana tradition toward an idealistic position, in which the world of phenomena is regarded simply as a projection of the mind or as illusory. The truth of the latter philosophy, according to the Tendai, is that it points to the existence of an Absolute, beyond sense-experience, or the Void, or Suchness (it was called by various names). The truth of the former position is that it accords with the facts of ordinary experience. Though phenomena are evanescent and impermanent, they nevertheless exist. By taking these positive truths contained in the opposing emphases of Buddhist metaphysics, one can attain a synthesis, or intermediate doctrine, namely that the Absolute and phenomena interpenetrate in an organic unity. From this syncretic point of view, one can observe the inadequacies of the false aspects of the other doctrines. It is wrong to consider nirvana, the transcendent realm, as distinct from the world of phenomena; but it is wrong too to think of the Absolute as alone real.

The Tendai scholars made use of the doctrine of the Three Bodies of the Buddha, described in the previous chapter. The notion that the Buddha is Absolute Truth and is, as it were, a being who manifests himself in the realm of phenomena both as the historical teacher and as the celestial object of worship and adoration, correlates with the Tendai insistence that the intermediate doctrine of existence is the true one. The synthesis between opposing viewpoints was carried over to scriptures: Tendai scholars arranged various writings in a hierarchy according to the degree in which they embody truth, and thus reconciled contradictions in the corpus of Buddhist writings. At the summit was the *Lotus Sutra,* the document chiefly respected in the school.

In practical terms, the Tendai synthesis meant that both meditation and faith were regarded as necessary for salvation. Meditation was not thought to be sufficient by itself for it issues in an experience of the Absolute without the corresponding apprehension of the way in which the Absolute interpenetrates the world of phenomena. Neither, however, was adoration of a celestial Buddha and devotion to his name thought solely adequate, for it remains within the realm of the temporary and does not pass over to the experience of the Absolute. The ideal of the Bodhisattva, the person who treads the path toward his own Buddha-nature, was the decisive imperative for the Tendai school. By exercising compassion for other beings and at the same time purifying one's mind in the pursuit of trancendental experience, and by having faith in the Buddha both by adoration of him and by identifying oneself with him in virtue of one's participation in the Buddha-nature, one can progress toward the great goal of Buddhahood. In such ways the Tendai attempted to keep in a balanced tension the different aspects of Greater Vehicle piety and meditation.

To cement this new structure of Buddhist faith in Japan, Saicho introduced a new form of Buddhist ordination, based on the vow of the Bodhisattva—to renounce nirvana in order to help others to Buddhahood—which expressed his ideal of living in the world a life of moral striving and compassion toward other living beings. The ordination ceremony had a certain sacramental significance. It was not simply the taking of vows to lead the good life or to have faith in the "Three Jewels" of Buddhism; it was essentially a reorientation taking place in the presence of the Buddha. But this meant, since the Buddha in essence lies within the initiate, in his Buddha-nature, that it was a new life undertaken from within, and one which mysteriously released the resources of Buddhahood within the initiate. Saicho's innovation carried an implication that extended beyond theological interpretation: in practice, it meant that Tendai ordination became independent of the state-sponsored Buddhist hierarchy at Nara. For this reason, his measures aroused fierce resentment and opposition, and his later years were marred by polemical struggle. Like other syncretistic movements, Tendai did not succeed in embracing those forms of religion it sought to unify. It remained a separate, though influential, sect contained within the variegated fabric of Japanese religion.

SHINGON

Even more sacramental and ritualistic than Tendai piety was a parallel movement of the same period, the Shingon (literally "True Word") school. It was founded in Japan in 806 A.D. by Kukai (better known by his title of Kobo Daishi) after a period of residence and study in China. This school derived from a Chinese antecedent which in turn had been influenced by Tantric Buddhism of the kind that flourished in Tibet. The cultus centered on the figure of the meditating Buddha Vairochana. This great Being pervades and constitutes the life of the cosmos: other Buddhas and deities were thought of as emanations from his substance. Since the whole universe is reflected in its parts, it was thought possible to evoke the power of Vairochana and the Bodhisattvas through the limited acts of the Shingon ritual. This was elaborate and partly magical in character; it expressed the feeling that the outward act brings about an inward change, and so was essentially sacramental in nature. In Shingon one can see how the experiential and doctrinal dimensions of religion can be subsumed by the ritual. The changes within himself that the more orthodox Buddhist might otherwise seek through yoga and through ethical striving are here brought about by forms of meditation and devotion interpreted in terms of a sacramental ritual.

SHINTO IN THE HEIAN PERIOD—RYOBU

It was possible to treat Shinto as a valid faith in terms of the theologies both of Tendai and of Shingon, especially the latter. As we have seen in other connections, Buddhist missionaries generally did not attempt to uproot the polytheistic and animistic cults of the Aisan world, but rather incorporated them into Buddhism. Thus the *kami* of Shinto were assigned a place in the elaborate and hierarchical mythology of the Shingon school. There are many instances of the prevalent impulse to syncretize the two religions, which resulted, from the eighth century onward, in the development of the Ryobu, or Double-Aspect Shinto, wherein Shinto deities were equated with figures in the Mahayana pantheon. Thus the goddess Amaterasu was identified with the Buddha Vairochana. The Shinto *kami* were regarded as secondary manifestations of the great beings of Buddhist mythology, and Buddhist images began to find their way into Shinto shrines. With such arrangements, both parties could be reasonably satisfied. To be sure the Buddhist faith had the position of honor, but Shintoism was not destroyed by the great and powerful religious intruder, and continued in the ordinary life of the people. However, there was a danger, from the Shinto point of view, that ultimately the traditional cults would be swallowed up and submerged in the impressive complexity of Buddhist sacramental ritual, and the *kami* might disappear before the splendid images of the Buddhas and Bodhisattvas. But Shinto survived despite this threat. Ryobu Shinto was one means of insuring this survival.

BUDDHISM IN THE HEIAN PERIOD

The Buddhism of the Heian ("Ease and Peace") period was a Buddhism of transition. In conquering Japan, the religion had to ally itself with the ruling classes: official recognition was important to the well-being of priests and monasteries, and in turn Buddhism was important to the state, providing a structure and an ideology for the unification of Japan and for the prosperous continuance of government. Only to a certain extent did the religion of the Heian period also cater to the personal concerns of individuals. Later, as Heian culture declined, new movements in Japanese Buddhism placed even stronger emphasis upon personal piety. The establishment of a military dictatorship at Kamakura at the latter part of the twelfth century involved the overthrow of the ruling house. Though strong government continued for more than a century, there followed a period of warfare and unrest in which feudal barons struggled for power. Thus, from the twelfth century, the old order began to change and so did governmental dependence upon a colorful and formal state religion. Into this situation came new streams of Buddhist teaching and experience. Three of these are of especial interest: the Amida pietism of Honen and Shinran, called Jodo in Japanese; the Japanese school of Ch'an, called Zen Buddhism; and the militant evangelism of Nichiren.

JODO BUDDHISM — HONEN

Honen (1133–1212) was one of the great figures of Japanese religion. In introducing the Chinese Pure Land form of Buddhism, Ching-t'u, to the Japanese mind he made a lasting imprint upon the culture of the country. He also spoke to the needs of the men of his age. In a time of social unrest and political failure the official Buddhist cults could not inspire confidence, nor could Confucian prescriptions concerning the social order. In such a time, personal religion could mean much, and Honen exhibited both in his life and in his teachings a form of faith which was immensely appealing. During his early boyhood his father had been attacked by bandits, and as he lay dying had instructed his son not to pursue revenge for his death, but rather to become a monk. Violence, he counseled, breeds only violence. Honen accordingly entered a monastery: the lesson of his father's last thought remained vivid to him throughout his life—the misery which men inflict upon one ancther cannot be cured by anger or hatred; it is due to the ignorance enveloping the human condition.

Namu Amida Butsu

Honen trained at Hiei; but despite the learning and skill with which he mastered the rituals and teachings of the Tendai, he became dissatisfied with its formalism. After several centuries, Tendai had fallen into the same state as the official religion that Saicho had criticized in his own day. As he pondered, the conviction slowly came to Honen that the secret of spiritual joy lay in the adoration of the Buddha Amitabha. He perceived that in these latter days, when evil and corruption stalked the land, there was little hope of salvation through the rigorous following of the path of asceticism and meditation. But Honen did not waver in his faith in the Lord Buddha, whom he knew could always adapt teachings and actions to the conditions of men. He became increasingly certain that the Buddha's grace could save those who call upon him in faith; nothing could stand against his saving power. All men always, merely by calling on the Buddha's name, could be assured of release. The conviction grew in him so strongly that Honen left the monastery at Hiei and retired to a hermitage. His fame grew, and men came to hear him; but he was less concerned to preach than to express his faith in the saving work of the Buddha. This he did above all in the repetition of the formula *Namu Amida Butsu* (or *nembutsu*) which can be translated "Reverence to the Buddha Amida." The utterance of this formula with faith he held to be sufficient to assure salvation. This simplified act, done from the heart, was the key to the higher happiness of the love of God: out of this faith would flow more—love toward all living beings and the desire for their welfare. The formula then represents in the most attenuated form a relic of Honen's monastic training in sacramental ritualism. Though Honen stressed that salvation came through an act of faith alone, he taught that the good deeds a man might do, though not of themselves sufficient to insure salvation, nonetheless were indicative of Amida's compassion and mercy flowing through his life.

By emphasizing these matters, Honen developed a simplified form of the Chinese Pure Land School, or Ching-t'u, known in its Japanese form as Jodo. Such teachings, though, were bound to seem heterodox. If taken to their logical conclusion (and they were later) they would make nonsense of the monastic life. What, after all, is the latter? It is an attempt through meditation and ritual to bring about release: it depends for its very concept on the belief that the work of treading the path of the Buddha is an important means of spiritual welfare. If faith alone is needed for salvation, one might as well abandon the rigorous and devoted life of the monk. Moreover, Honen's doctrines did not merely seem to remove the rationale from the life of the Sangha: they also cut at the root of ecclesiastical power and influence that was bedded in the ceremonial and the authority of the temple. Honen was banished by the state to an island in the Inland Sea, though he was allowed to return—but not to the capital—after four years. He ended his days serenely, and gave to his disciples a last testament which summed up his faith:

> Our practice of devotion does not consist in that of meditation as recommended and practised by sages of the past. Nor is our "Calling the Name" . . . uttered in consequence of enlightenment in truths attained through learning and wisdom. When we invoke (the) Buddha and say *Namu Amida Butsu* with the firm belief that we shall be born in (the) Buddha's paradise, we shall surely be born there. There is no other mystery here than uttering His Name in this faith. Although the three kinds of thought and the four methods of training are recommended, all these are surely implicit in the faith that our birth in the Buddha's Land is certain. If I knew anything more profound than this, I should be forsaken by the two Lords (Sakyamuni and Amida). . . . However extensively one may have comprehended the teachings propounded during the lifetime of Sakyamuni, he should, as soon as he has put faith in salvation, regard himself as an equal of the most ignorant, and thus should whole-heartedly practise *Nembutsu* (i.e. saying "Namu Amida Butsu") in company with many simple folk, entirely giving up the demeanor of a wise man.[6]

[6] This translation appears in Anesaki, *History of Japanese Religion*, p. 178.

Honen crystallized, in his life and teachings, the Jodo pietism. He preached salvation by *tariki*, or external strength, rather than by *jiriki*, or one's own power.

Shinran and Jodo Shinshu

His disciples carried on the work, the most famous and influential being Shinran (1173–1263 A.D.), founder of the Jodo Shinshu, or "True Pure Land Sect." He drew from his master's teachings the conclusion to which we referred earlier: if salvation is by faith, the monastic rule avails a man nothing. He gave up the celibate life, and raised a family; he abandoned the monk's habit and refused to shave his head. There is a remarkable parallel between Shinran's decision, resulting from his vivid apprehension of the grace of the Buddha, and that of Martin Luther. For both men, monasticism, being a form of works, appeared useless as a means to salvation. But Shinran's conclusions went further. For him salvation came only by faith and the favor of the Buddha; therefore even the evildoer could hope for it. As long as a person gives up estimating his own qualities and is simply dependent on the Buddha, he will gain paradise. Shinran abandoned the Order of monks to demonstrate that he recognized no distinction between religious and secular life. He worked as a humble preacher in the provinces independent of the authority of any ecclesiastical organization. He did not dress or live differently from the folk among whom he moved. He felt that neither ceremonial nor prolonged meditation were necessary for true happiness and the assurance of bliss. Thus the external forms of religion could be lost without affecting the truth and importance of his message.

NICHIREN

The simple pietism of Honen and Shinran was peaceful and gentle. Of a very different character was the nationalistic prophet Nichiren, who became the author of a very uncharacteristic and interesting offshoot of Buddhism. In some respects he was influenced by Jodo though he attacked the pietistic movement fiercely. His chief allegiance was to Tendai, and he studied at Hiei for about a decade. Unlike the Jodo teachers, he did not discard the philosophical teachings of Buddhism expressed in the *Lotus Sutra* (which, it will be recalled, was assigned the place of honor in the Tendai school): and unlike the scholars of Tendai and Shingon, he wished to simplify the faith somewhat in the fashion the Pure Land pietists had done.

"Namu Myo-Horenge-kyo"

Nichiren, born in 1222, was the son of a fisherman from southeast Japan. He studied both at Kamakura and at Hiei, to which centers of learning he went after passing his boyhood at a monastery near his home. Through intense study for many years, he came to feel that truth was contained essentially in the *Lotus Sutra* where it could be garnered by all men. But few men, other than monks, could devote themselves to meditation, and Nichiren perceived that even they could not penetrate to the heart of the Buddha's faith by study unaided. A simple expression of the faith was needed. Nichiren found this in the sacred formula *Namu Myo-Horenge-kyo*, "Reverence to the Wonderful Truth of the Lotus Sutra." Just as for the Pure Land pietist, the utterance of the *nembutsu* (*Namu Amida Butsu*) brought assurance of grace, so for Nichiren the utterance of his formula brought identification with the message of the *Lotus Sutra*.

What was this message? Essentially it was that absolute truth is revealed through the Buddha; the words of the scripture incorporate this truth by pointing to it as a supreme Reality. It followed that the adherent who, through repeating the sacred title, became identified with the Sutra, also became identified with what it essentially referred to. In short, the adherent achieved unity with the supreme Absolute and with the Buddha. In a romantic and fiery moment, Nichiren stood on a hill near his place of birth, and announced the sacred title to the dawning sun. This for him was the inauguration of the new faith which claimed to restore the old. But when he told of the doctrine to the abbot and monks of his monastery, they were grieved and shocked, not merely by the novelty of his doctrine, but also by the ferocity with which he denounced all other forms of Buddhism. He could no longer stay in his home area, and so he went to Kamakura.

Times were troubled, and the government was uneasy. Nichiren's maledictions attracted unfavorable attention from the authorities, and he was exiled. During his banishment and solitude he set himself to reformulate his ideas. When he returned, his following had increased, and Nichiren continued to prophesy dire perils for the nation, including foreign invasion, if it did not reform and cast aside the enervating influences of pietistic and formalistic Buddhism. Certain government officials decided to silence him, and under the pretense of arranging his exile, prepared for his death. All was ready for the execution—the time was midnight—when miraculously, it seemed, a bright light appeared in the sky. Terrified with this omen, the executioners desisted. Nichiren escaped with his life and fled the city.

During these years the marauding Mongols, who had been united by Ghengis Khan, invaded much of China, captured Korea, overran the Ukraine, Russia, and most of eastern Europe. When the Mongols threatened Japan, an apprehensive government turned for help to the prophet whose fierce nationalism could be used in the cause of defense. The Mongols were defeated—more by the elements than by the strength of the Japanese—and Nichiren was seen to be justified. By recalling him the state had heeded his message and victory was won. He died in 1282.

Nicheren's Nationalism

Nichiren's nationalism wore Buddhist array, but its spirit was far from Buddhist. He believed that the epoch in which he lived was one when true Buddhism could be promulgated only through the Japanese. Other systems of thought and life within the Buddha's tradition had had their day and had passed away. Now only through the formula of faith in the *Lotus Sutra* and only in the islands of Japan could the light be shown to the world. If such doctrines had been presented simply as the crowning truth fulfilling the varied, and often apparently contradictory, elements in Buddhism, traditionalists might have found them tolerable. But Nichiren excoriated all forms of the faith other than his own. With prophetic zeal he castigated rivals as effete and corrupt, as dangerous and diabolical. His intolerant attitude is unique in the whole history of Buddhism, and for this reason the Nichiren sect is often repudiated by the orthodox followers of the Buddha's law. During the medieval period the Nichirenites were strongly organized and militant. Though they were aggressive, they suffered too from savage persecutions. Since their propaganda spread among the masses, they formed a dangerous element within the nation. With the gradual disintegration of society through a series of feudal wars, the spirit of Nichirenite militancy was adopted by others. The Amida Buddhists eventually followed their bad example; bands of armed monks attacked each other's monasteries. This unedifying spectacle was a reversal for a religion that for so long had practiced peace and non-violence.

One feature of both Jodo and Nichirenism is worth noting: the preaching of these doctrines took on a popular form. In the parks and in the marketplace, in the streets and in the villages, itinerant preachers carried the message of these sects. The identification of these preachers with the masses, and the repudiation of monasticism by followers of the Jodo Shinshu and of Nichiren, helped to give this evangelism a power missing from the preaching of the older, more conventional, forms of Buddhism.

ZEN BUDDHISM

The third great event during the twelfth and thirteenth centuries was the introduction into Japan of the teachings of Zen Buddhism. The first great spokesman for this most distinctive form of Japanese religion was Eisai (1141–1215 A.D.).

Eisai

Eisai had become dissatisfied with the formalism of the Buddhism of Hiei, in which he was brought up, and had gone to China to seek a more vital faith. He found this in the Lin-chi school of Ch'an. On his return to Japan he instituted monasteries to train monks in the new methods of meditation. From his time to now this wing of Zen, the Rinzai sect, has grown in influence. It is the form of Zen chiefly known in the West in modern times, mainly through the writings and researches of the famous Japanese scholar Daisetz Suzuki. A little later than Eisai, Dogen introduced the Soto form of the movement. He had been a disciple of Eisai, and like the latter made a trip to China. His teaching reflects his own serene and retiring disposition; he felt that the quiet and gradual methods of Soto were a more suitable form for the religion of meditation which he favored. The two types of Zen remain strong in modern Japan.

It was Eisai who brought back from China the tea-ceremony that later was to play a significant part in Japanese culture. Tea had long been in use among the adherents of the Meditation school. Its soothing, stimulating properties were regarded as a useful aid to meditation. The ceremonial making and pouring out of the tea among a small group of companions developed into an artform in its own right. The present forms of the ceremony date back to the sixteenth century. It might seem strange that such a phenomenon should figure in a book on man's religious experience, but the special contribution of Japanese Zen, as distinguished from the Chinese schools from which it had its origin, lay in its use of apparently secular arts in the process of bringing about harmonious living and awakening, or *satori*. In this way, it has had a wide influence outside the monastery.

Techniques of Achieving Satori

The controlled, yet also casual and spontaneous, performance of the tea-ceremony represents the religious adaptation of a graceful art of civilized living; Zen also used the warlike art of archery for the purposes of religion. The Zen master sought to teach Zen ideals through training in shooting—the ultimate aim being to gain a paradoxical mastery over the bow and arrows, so that one could hit the target casually and "without aiming." This symbolizes the Zen approach to *satori*. Illumination must come suddenly and spontaneously. To strive too hard after it in a direct fashion is self-destroying. The Soto school objected to the Rinzai's use of the *koan* on just this ground—it implied a conscious aim to bring about the abrupt awakening. Hitting the target then, without aiming, expresses the ideal of gaining illumination without aiming. We can parallel these ideas with a commonplace observation about the pursuit of happiness: those who actively aim at their own happiness find themselves frustrated. Happiness accrues naturally upon the successful pursuit of other objectives—work, moral service, etc.

Sword-play also figures as one of the Zen arts. Both this and archery are symptomatic of a social fact which facilitated the spread of Zen ideas in medieval Japan. One must remember that this was a period of feudal warfare and unrest: thus the attraction of the more personal forms of faith we have been exploring. Zen offered a way of harmonious self-sufficiency not only for the monk but also for the layman—and not only for the ordinary layman, but for the fighting aristocracy, the *samurai*. Despite immersion in the concerns of the world one could also gain illumination. Thus, somewhat as Arjuna in the *Bhagavadgita* drew courage from his personal faith not to flee from his present duties, which centered, as it happened, on warfare and killing, so the medieval *samurai* could, through a controlled use of the art of warfare in which he was much engaged, still hope to gain the higher spiritual life which had so often been identified with the life of the monastery. Here was a practical result of the doctrine of the identity of nirvana and *samsara* and a vivid application of the Mahayana teaching that Buddhahood is open to all.

We have already noted that the Meditation school in China, partly because of Taoist influences, had developed a refined sense of one's affinity with nature. Japanese Zen went further along this path. For instance, a favored form of Zen expression, the *haiku,* or seventeen-syllable poem, suggests the brief and inconsequential beauties of nature (though such poems can be earthy too). This sensitivity to nature is also a part of Shintoist sentiment.

Affinities Between Zen and Shinto

The sense of the presence of the *kami* in beautiful and mysterious places has always pervaded Japanese life. We can feel something of this by considering the nature of the Shinto shrine in its modern manifestation. Typically the Shinto shrine is found in a wooded place, and is essentially a rectangular area marked off by a sacred fence. The most distinctive feature is the *torii,* or entrance gate, on one side of this rectangle. In its simplest form it consists in two upright tree trunks surmounted by a third fixed crosswise, with another piece of wood below this to hold the structure steady. More elaborate gateways have developed, with the upper crosspiece having the shape of a long, narrow roof; at Kyoto there is the famous Thousand Torii Pathway, which is like a long wooden arcade, with the posts painted in scarlet and black. Within the rectangular space of the shrine there is typically a building where sacred objects are housed in the innermost recesses, the most customary treasure being a mirror associated with the goddess Amaterasu. These cult objects are not normally seen by the ordinary worshiper since they are especially sacred; at annual festivals they are carried in containers in processions around the village or town. A hill or a large rock can also be the object of worship, and will be marked with a shrine. The many shrines in places of natural beauty and mystery honor the *kami* whose presence devout Shintoists experience especially in the mountains and woods and streams. Offerings are simple, and the ordinary worshiper pauses only briefly at the shrine after presenting them, in an act of silent reverence. Under the influence of Buddhism, Shinto shrines developed the cult of images and, in some places, elaborate ceremonial conducted by priests. There have not been lacking Shintoist exponents who have seen in the many *kami* so many aspects of the one Divine Being pervading the whole cosmos: nevertheless for them the way to the divine presence is through the particular shrine, the particular deity. So too in Zen, nature-mysticism involves a sense of the unity of the individual with Nature as a whole and with the divine Emptiness which suffuses the world of phenomena, and very often this sense of unity has been expressed most strongly through a particular image or through the particular mystery of an individual event.

Haiku

The Zen *haiku* can be regarded as typical of Japanese religious culture, of a piece with the esthetic polytheism of Shinto. The *haiku*, circumscribed and, at their best, mysteriously complete, seem to symbolize the unity of man and nature in the ongoing stream of experiences and events. The moods of Zen poetry are sometimes categorized as four: quiet, spontaneous loneliness; the unexpected "suchness" of things; nostalgia; and mystery. These are illustrated in the following poems translated by Alan W. Watts:

> *In the dark forest*
> *A berry drops:*
> *The sound of water.*

> *The woodpecker*
> *Keeps on in the same place:*
> *Day is closing.*

> *The dewdrop world—*
> *It may be a dewdrop,*
> *And yet—and yet—*

> *The sea darkens;*
> *The voices of the wild ducks*
> *Are faintly white.*[7]

One may not overlook the fact that there has been a certain toughness and harshness about Zen. The Rinzai method of training has made free use

[7] *The Way of Zen* (New York, 1957), pp. 186-187.

of physical violence to teach self-reliance and courage: Zen has traditionally been the faith of the warrior. To a certain extent it is comparable to the Shinto ideal of *Bushido* which formed an essential element of militaristic Shintoism. *Bushido* was the code of conduct for the medieval knight, requiring of him such virtues as loyalty, courtesy, and truthfulness. It strongly emphasized the importance of honor: anything should be preferred to disgrace and humiliation—even suicide—hence the prizing of *hara-kiri* as a noble act for the defeated. This ideal was applied in a novel way during the Second World War by the Kamakazi corps of the Japanese air force: the *Kamikazi* pilot deliberately crashed his plane into his enemies' warships in the fervent conviction that self-destruction in the service of one's country was an honorable thing.

POST-MEDIEVAL JAPAN

The medieval period, we have seen, was a time of strife. But in the seventeenth century, the Tokugawa regime succeeded in consolidating the country. Shortly before this St. Francis Xavier had come to Japan (he landed in 1549), and for a brief period his teachings were officially encouraged, partly as a means of combating the influence of Buddhism, which the ruler of the central provinces, Nobunaga, regarded with disfavor. However, his successor, Hideyoshi, ordered the exile of the missionaries, and the Tokugawa Shogunate, alarmed at foreign—mainly Portuguese—influences, prohibited Christian propaganda. The mid-seventeenth century was a period of severe persecution of foreigners, and the Christian church virtually disappeared from Japan, though some believers continued secretly in the faith. During this time, Japan officially isolated herself from the rest of the world. This isolationist phase only ended in the mid-nineteenth century, when Japan was brought to the shocked realization that she needed to modernize: otherwise, she would perish. This, then, was a period of change and ferment.

Religiously, the most remarkable phenomenon in the nineteenth and twentieth centuries has been the founding and spread of many new cults, the so-called "New Religions." The revival of Shintoism helped to contribute to this movement, while the impact of both Protestant and Catholic missions after the opening-up of Japan also stimulated these new expressions of indigenous faith. A marked feature of many of the new cults was their practical emphasis: the incorporation of ethical and social ideals into the sphere of faith, the promise of healing through faith, the visible establishment of a new order upon earth, symbolized by impressive shrines and public buildings. A number of the new prophets have been women, possibly harking back to the role of the woman in early Shinto, and prefiguring the new status of women in a technological civilization.

Miki Nakayama

The most remarkable of these women leaders was Miki Nakayama (1798–1887), the founder of the Tenrikyo, "The Religion of Heavenly Wisdom." The origin of this faith dates from a religious experience Miki Nakayama underwent in 1838. Previously she had been a pious devotee of Amida, and outwardly had lived a conventional life: she was married and was appropriately obedient to her husband. After her religious conversion she felt herself possessed by a divine Being calling himself the Lord of Heaven. The god commanded her to dedicate herself to his work, and this involved, among other things, considerable charitable works. Her enthusiasm for this impoverished her family, and on her husband's death she was left penniless, but still devoted to the new teaching. She effected faith-cures, believing that suffering is due to the greed which constitutes the main obstacle to human welfare and which has to be counterbalanced by divine charity. In the troubled period at the end of the Tokugawa regime, her teaching attracted a sizeable following. The Tenrikyo teaches an eschatological finale for human history when the god in some future time will descend to a sacred spot near Miki Nakayama's home to bring about the final transformation of the world and the welfare of the human race. This spot has become, for the believers, the center of the world, and they anticipate the day when the heavenly dew will come down to bathe the central pillar of creation. The enormous temple erected there now and the grand buildings round about are eloquent testimony to the richness and size of the sect, which now has over two million adherents. Its stress on social service and the need to wash out the stain of greed have a strong appeal in a materialistic age, while at the same time it is far from other-worldly in its emphasis.

The Soka Gakkai

Of the other new faiths, there is space to mention only three. The Soka Gakkai, founded in 1930, has a connection with the Nichiren school, and shares its militancy. While nearly all the new religions are syncretistic and speak of the unity of world faiths, the Soka Gakkai is exclusive, and keen to proselytize at the expense of other movements. Its propaganda methods are highly organized, and it takes a deliberate interest in politics, where it functions as a right-wing nationalistic group. It is represented in the Japanese Parliament.

The Konkokyo Sect

By contrast the Konkokyo, founded by a peasant in 1859, represents a Shinto form of pietism reminiscent of the Amida sects. This religion of the "golden light" strongly emphasizes the need for men to live in faithful dependence upon the supreme Lord Tench-kane-no-Kami, the god of the brightness of heaven and earth, and has as its central aim purity of heart in the adoration of the Lord. In this way the sufferings consequent on karma will be overcome. The stress on purity shows how the ritual purity inculcated by traditional Shinto is given a moral interpretation.

The Perfect Liberty Association

Different from both of these faiths is that of P. L. Kyodan, the "Perfect Liberty Association," which teaches the worship of a supreme Being, and attempts to illuminate the problems of this life by giving religion an artistic and recreational aspect.

The concern of the new faiths with social problems and the sober virtues they preach have given them a strong following among the lower classes. On the whole, they do not appeal to intellectuals, partly because of the naiveté of some of their doctrines, and partly because intellectuals have taken over the rationalistic attitudes of much modern Western thought. By liberating Shinto from some of the complexities of its mythology and by finding within it the possibility of a devotional faith which is at the same time markedly ethical, the new faiths express an important reaction in traditional Japanese religion to the impact of Christianity and modern technology. They are ways of adapting ancient forms to a very different kind of social existence, and have been potent means of giving hope—and sometimes physical cures—to the poor and under-privileged.

SHINTO IN THE TWENTIETH CENTURY

With the establishment of state Shinto during the present century, the hereditary priesthood was abolished and the shrine priests became officials of the state. Militaristic notions were injected into Shinto, and the religion was used to instill ardor and patriotism into the armed forces. That this was a highly effective measure the events of the Second World War were to prove. This medieval code of honor, *Bushido,* dominated the ranks of officers. The spirit of *Bushido* is expressed in the story of an admiral who stayed on his foundering ship after a naval battle in which the Japanese squadron had been virtually annihilated by American forces. A lieutenant came back on the flagship to plead with the admiral to leave the ship. The admiral replied simply, "The moonlight is bright on the water," and the younger man turned away and left him to his death.

At the end of that war, state Shintoism was abolished; the emperor officially repudiated his divine (or semi-divine) status as descendant of

Amaterasu and as intermediary between heaven and earth. Some expected Shintoism to wither away by consequence, but in fact it has revived since the war. The practice of going to the shrines continues to be widespread—for many educated Japanese it involves not so much an act of commitment and worship as a means of expressing and recognizing the mysteries and beauties of life. Japanese estheticism continues to have a religious flavor, and religion an esthetic flavor.

SUMMARY OF JAPANESE RELIGION

We can see that Japan's traditional faiths have reacted to one another and have intermingled in such ways that certain unique blends of faith have been produced. Zen is a characteristic product of the Japanese heritage, even though it received its first form and substance from China (where too it was a special flower of the Chinese experience). In Japan, the pietism of the Pure Land schools had its most fervid and simple expression. Two elements of Japanese religious experience—nature-mysticism and devotionalism consequent on the intuition of a supreme personal Lord—have been determinative in Japanese history. The early Buddhist period in Japan was formalistic; in the Shingon the religion assumed an exclusively sacramental shape, in which the ritual dimension was seen as the key to the meaning of the doctrines. Throughout Japanese religious experience there has existed a substratum of faith in the *kami* of Shinto, through whom is expressed the experience of the numinous—an experience in which the mysteries, fears, and beauties of the natural world are fragmented into a host of spirits. In the modern period, this numinous religion has been given a devotional and ethical extension in the Tenrikyo and elsewhere. But the social dimension of religion must not be forgotten. The peculiar position of Japanese society, and the tensions produced by successive importations of foreign culture, have stimulated a sometimes extreme national and traditional reaction. The medieval Nichiren and the contemporary Soka Gakkai are witness to this. But to conclude: in Japan a sturdy estheticism has given a new shape to the Buddhism brought across from Korea and China, while the old "Way of the Gods" has never lost its grip upon the local imagination of the Japanese people.

Both in China and Japan, Greater Vehicle Buddhism dominated. Elsewhere in the sphere of Chinese cultural influence this was true also, for instance in Vietnam. In Indonesia, which was mainly permeated by Indian cultural influences, the Lesser Vehicle flourished, alongside Hinduism. However, Islam more or less replaced the Indian faiths from the thirteenth century onward.

The history of most of Asia is also the history of Buddhism which has

spread its—on the whole—benign influence through the countries lying between Japan and Nepal and between Thailand and Mongolia. But Buddhism
has only provided one element in each culture: in both China and in Japan
indigenous religious and philosophical movements continued to flourish.
Through the dialectic between them some novel forms of faith have emerged
into human experience.

RELIGIONS OF THE NEAR EAST

Chapter 6

RELIGION IN THE ANCIENT

MEDITERRANEAN WORLD

THE RELIGIONS of the ancient Mediterranean world were not only in themselves unique testaments in the history of our religious experience; they
provided the background for the three Semitic faiths which so affected and
altered the shape of human culture. It was within the ancient Near East that
Jewish monotheism and the universal religions of Christianity and Islam arose.
It was across this area of the Mediterranean and the Near and Middle East
that these faiths first spread, later reaching even further in various directions.
For the sake of the religions it engendered and the religions it can illuminate,
the ancient world must claim our attention.

The geographical area which we have to consider stretched from Persia
in the east to Spain in the west. The time span extended from the fourth
millennium B.C. to the early centuries of the Christian era.

The ancient world exhibited a great but complex fabric of cultures. It was
an area and a time which gave rise to the Egyptian civilization, the Mesopotamian culture, the origin and spread of Zoroastrianism, the culture and
religions of Greece and Rome, and the development of the mystery religions
which for a time rivalled Christianity. The two other great centers of early
civilization, India and China, acquired considerable unity of culture over a
long period of time, but the ancient world of the Mediterranean and the Near
East was constituted by a series of different and overlapping civilizations.

Some of the elements of these civilizations have not lived on to the
present day. For instance, ancient Babylonian religion and the religion of
ancient Egypt have left very little direct imprint on modern culture. Nevertheless, all the elements are important in human history. They express man's
developing awareness of the world in two new circumstances: city life and a
settled agriculture. New techniques of getting food were accompanied by an
evolving complication and refinement of culture. Surpluses created by improved

agriculture allowed emergent prehistoric man a new freedom from a ceaseless search for food. The pattern of human life began to change as hamlets became towns and towns cities, as administration of community affairs became centered and man's labors became diversified, as seers, prophets, and holy men developed priesthoods and temples were built.

EGYPTIAN RELIGION

From the fourth millennium B.C. Egypt possessed a settled agricultural life dependent on the fruitful waters of the Nile and the rich mud-strip its inundations left behind. But this fertile territory was not unified. The surplus of food was enough to enable the people to build cities: each city-state, however, was independent.

In the course of time improved communications and the desire for wealth and land led to the consolidation of different states under one single dynasty. From 2300 B.C. until the conquest of the country by Alexander the Great in the fourth century B.C., Egypt was, with but brief interruptions, unified under a succession of dynasties and kingdoms. Great changes occurred in Egyptian religious life in this long period. But there are three recognizable features which give shape to the religion.

There evolved a most elaborate and sumptuous cult of the dead, in which remarkably successful techniques for the preservation of corpses were devised. The ritual and mythology of Egypt also gave a unique status to the rulers, the Pharaohs. The person of the Pharaoh became the political and religious pivot of Egypt's widespread culture, and the key to social order. Religiously, the Pharaoh was regarded as the meeting point between the invisible and the visible worlds, the point of contact between heaven and earth: his claims to divine kingship was the guarantee of political stability. Finally, the mythology and cultus of the sun god came to assume great proportions. Just as the sun in its glowing fierceness and benign fecundity dominated the land of the Nile, so the sun god came to dominate the religious imagination of the Egyptian people.

THE GODS AND THE PHARAOH

The complex nature of early Egyptian mythology arose from the fact that the different city-states claimed the special protection of different gods. With the amalgamation of cities, the god of one city was liable to be identified with the god of another. Each god had his own family and relations; the more universal deities entered into the local mythology. Moreover, it seems from the archeological evidence that the early tribes worshiped gods in animal form, and although these became humanized, the resultant deities still retained, in many cases, traces of their animal background. A typical deity might possess a wide spectrum of attributes.

We can consider the case of the god Horus, who attained a prominent position in the mythology. From the earliest period of Egyptian history, the king was identified with Horus, the falcon god. It seems from this that Horus was the deity and emblem of the tribe that conquered and unified the country. The notion that the king himself was divine had an important ritual consequence. Though the king could not be everywhere and therefore could not attend at temples up and down the land, he was in theory the link between the gods and men: thus the priests served as his representatives in the divine office. Even if the priesthoods of the various big centers of Egyptian civilization led a semi-autonomous life, there was implicit in the system the notion, not merely of a centralized state, but also of a central religion under the king.

The king was not only identified with the falcon god, but through him, was equated with the sun. Thus there appeared a tendency in Egyptian mythology to arrange divine beings in groups of three. In this case it was the sun, the falcon, and the king. Later on, Horus fused with, and was in this aspect replaced by, the great sun god Re (himself to be identified with still another deity, Atum). In some way not yet clear, Horus the great sun and falcon deity was identified with a younger Horus, who was the son of Isis and Osiris, the vegetation god and symbol of death and resurrection. As we shall see, the myth of Isis and Osiris was to form the basis of one of the great mystery-religions of the Græco-Roman world. We observe then in the case of Horus that a process of slow, but ceaseless, identification and linking together helped the priesthood weave together different strands from the rich mythological traditions of ancient Egypt.

Often, the dominance of a god reflects the power and influence of his native city. In the latter part of the second millennium, when Thebes came to be the ruling city, its god Amon was amalgamated with Re. Amon-Re had the place of honor as the supreme deity reflected in the splendor of the shining sun. Different genealogies of the gods in turn expressed attempts, at the mythological level, for the priesthood at one center to establish its priority. Thus the kaleidoscope of Egyptian mythology was in part determined by political and social factors, and the combats of the gods—of Horus with his destructive brother Seth, for instance—may sometimes be traced to early struggles of an earthly kind, between Upper and Lower Egypt.

Buried beneath the complexities it is possible to detect an early belief in Horus as supreme deity, identified with the sun. Lying behind this there may have been the cult of a great sky god, like Zeus in the Greek tradition. Certainly, there were persistent hints at monotheism in the Egyptian heritage, although the only attempt to establish the worship of a single god turned out to be a failure.

Akhenaten and Monotheism

Amenhotep IV, who changed his name to Akhenaten ("Glory to Aten"), attempted to introduce the sole worship of the god Aten, symbolized by the solar disk, and regarded by him as the Creator of all things. He established a new capital and temple downriver from Thebes, and caused other centers of the cult to be erected in other parts of the empire. He ordered the images of Amon and the other deities to be removed from temples and monuments, and showed additional signs that his elevation of Aten to the supreme position was not simply the upgrading in rank of one god among many, but was rather a monotheism which could not tolerate the existence of a surrounding poly-theism. In famous words, the monarch addressed his God:

> How numerous are Thy works. They are concealed from the vision of men, O sole God, other than whom there is no other. Thou hast created the earth according to thy heart, with men and flocks and all the animals . . . Thou dost apportion to each man his place, thou providest for his needs: each has his nourishment, and the hour of his death is fixed. . . ."

But priestly institutions and entrenched conservatism prevented Akhenaten's new faith from surviving after his death. There was soon a return to the traditional cultus. One major reason for this was the divine status of the Pharaoh himself. It was through the Pharaoh that the cosmic order benefited society. A break in the continuity of kingly ritual could have had disastrous social consequences. Akhenaten's successor Tutankhamon restored the worship of Amon-Re.

The Cult of the Dead

If the complex cults of the various deities were a splendid sign of the royal power and the riches of society, the erection of the Pyramids was even more striking evidence of the effort put into assuring the Pharaoh's continuing honors after death. The Pyramids are the best known symbol of the ancient Egyptian preoccupation with the afterlife. Since early beliefs regarded man as an organic complex of body and spirit, survival was not conceived simply as a ghostly condition of the spirit, but involved the continuance of the body. Favored by a good climate for the purpose, the ancient Egyptians perfected a process of mummification through which a corpse could be preserved almost indefinitely. The technique was kept secret, and it was an extremely expensive operation. For a long period mummification was a privilege of the Pharaoh or of some member of his family. Not until the middle of the second millennium did the practice become widespread, and even then it was well beyond the means of the lower classes.

The divine status of the Pharaoh as intermediary between heaven and earth gave the notion of his immortality peculiar significance. He was the focus of the cosmic order. It was not only the good order of society that was at stake. The renewal of the crops and the continued prosperity of the land were contingent upon his existence. For this reason the cult of the divine king became connected with that of Osiris, who was a vegetation deity. He was the force behind the annual cycle of plant life. As vegetation dies, but secretly retains its life beneath the soil to burgeon again in the springtime, so Osiris was both the dying and the living god. He was the symbol of death and resurrection and of the decay and renewal of life and ruled beneath the earth in the underworld. With the establishment of the link between the cult of the royal dead and Osirian mythology, and with the spread of concern about future life among folk of all ranks, the symbol of mummification became less important. For if the dead were in another realm ruled by Osiris, then there was a recognizable separation between the body (this world) and the spirit (other world).

Often Egyptian beliefs were complex. The Egyptians believed in the concept of the guardian spirit, or *ka,* which was the essence of personal individuality. At the same time they believed that the breath, or *ba,* was the principle animating the body. At a ceremony known as "The Opening of the Mouth," the *ba* was breathed back through the mouth to make the mummy alive. This rite reflected the story of Osiris who was killed and dismembered in the course of his fight with the god Seth, and was then miraculously restored to life by his son Horus. But there developed the belief that immortality consisted in the reunion of the *ka* and the *ba* in the next world.

The Book of the Dead

In the period of the New Kingdom (latter part of the second millennium B.C.), the dead were provided with a guidebook to help them in their future journey and life. This Egyptian *Book of the Dead* indicated some important experiences that were supposed to await the deceased. Among these was a process of judgment, whereby a panel of forty-two judges, in the presence of Osiris, determined whether the dead person was worthy to enter the land of Osiris. The dead one uttered a confession before the judges, couched in negative terms, exonerating himself from various crimes and misdemeanors. The list of wrong-doings reflected the social ethic of the time. The deceased person claimed not to have done anything which the god would abominate, not to have caused anyone to be hungry or weep, not to have committed murder or to have instigated it, not to have taken food from the dead, not to have committed adultery, not to have falsely weighted balances or otherwise given short measure, not to have rustled cattle, etc.

After the confession there followed the dramatic weighing of the dead one's soul. His heart was weighed against a feather, the symbol of truth. If the two pans were evenly balanced, the soul was permitted to enjoy the pleasures of paradise. In theory, paradise was a place rather like the Nile valley, interlaced with canals and dams. There was some danger of the soul's being asked to work on these canals and dams to keep them in good repair. Fortunately the dead person was equipped with an array of magical statuettes, which functioned as his servants whenever he was called on for such labor. The *Book of the Dead* was a mixture of the magical and the genuinely religious. In some respects, the picture presented of the next life is a materialistic one. The arrangement whereby servant-substitutes do one's work might seem to express an amusing and magical cunning. But this is a mistaken interpretation. These beliefs were taken seriously. They derive from the conviction that a statue or representation contains, like a mummy, something of the physical and living substance of the person represented. But the picture of the afterlife portrays significantly the Egyptian attitude to this world. Death was a tragedy insofar as it deprived the individual of the good things of this world. The Egyptians had no gloomy preoccupation with an afterworld which might justify an ascetic and world-negating attitude toward this life.

Clearly what is most important in the Egyptian concept of death, as found in the *Book of the Dead* and elsewhere, is the notion of moral judgment. The association of moral judgment with the myth of Osiris, rather than with the great sun gods, was in part a consequence of the fact that the great deities were the object of elaborate state and city rituals designed to ensure the continuance of society. With the spread of the mortuary rites that offered the hope of survival to those outside the royal family, Osiris, the god who dies and is restored to life, became a personal and meaningful symbol of immortality. By identification with the god, the believer could share in his life-reviving properties. The myth of Isis and Osiris remained important well after the time when foreign invasions (that of Cambyses in the sixth century B.C. and that of Alexander the Great in 322 B.C.) had destroyed the political and social order which gave meaning to the other cults.

MESOPOTAMIAN RELIGION

Further to the east another great urban civilization, that of Mesopotamia, evolved its own mythology and religion. The earliest culture belonging to this urban period was that of the Sumerians. Unlike the other important peoples and nations of the ancient east, they were neither Indo-European nor Semitic in origin, although by the latter part of the fourth millennium B.C., when cities were established in Sumer, their culture had already been penetrated by Semitic influences. It is possible that the Sumerians were related to the people who created the great Indus Valley civilization and it is conceivable that the Sumerians had at one time moved into Mesopotamia from further east. More probably, however, they originated in Central Asia or on the Siberian steppe. While the land of Sumer was situated around the lower reaches of the Tigris and the Euphrates at the top of the Persian gulf, the neighboring Semitic culture of Akkad lay a little to the north. The mutual penetration of the two civilizations, and the ultimate unification of the greater part of the area under Babylon, achieved by Hammurabi in the eighteenth century B.C., was followed a few centuries later (about 1350 B.C.) by the rise of the Assyrians. Despite these shifts in power, there was a remarkable continuity in religion. In effect, Assyro-Babylonian religion was a result of the interplay between Sumerian and Semitic culture.

THE SUMERIAN PANTHEON

As in Egypt, each city of Mesopotamia had its own favored gods, so that once again we find an extraordinarily complex mythology and are tempted to make identifications between one deity and another. The heavenly situation very often reflected the political circumstances on earth. Conquest would be followed by the usurpation of pride of place by the conquerors' chief deities. Nevertheless, a continuous pattern ran through Mesopotamian religion, from the time of Sumer. Three gods dominated the Sumerian pantheon—An, the sky god, Enlil, the wind god, and Enki, the water god. Between them they ruled the three divisions of the cosmos. Though in theory the sky god was the highest, he had least immediate concern with, or effect on, human affairs. His powers were largely delegated to Enlil, who ruled the earth and was the agent of the great Flood.

The Babylonian Flood Story

The Sumerian version of the great Flood story is incomplete, but there can be little doubt that the Babylonian version goes back to the Sumerian original. The legend is as follows. Utnapishtim was a pious king who heard from Enki that the gods, spurred on by Enlil, were about to destroy mankind and all living things through a huge flood. He therefore constructed an enormous boat, in which he took refuge with his wife and various animals. In this way he was enabled to escape the otherwise universal destruction. On the seventh day, his ark came to rest on a mountain. He sent out a dove and a swallow, but these returned to the boat indicating that they had found no resting place on dry land. A little later, he sent a crow which did not return. In thanks, he made a sacrifice on the mountaintop. Enlil, relenting from his earlier wrath, rewarded Utnapishtim by transporting him and his wife to a distant land where they would enjoy immortality.

The Epic of Gilgamesh

The theme of the search for immortality was taken up in the great poem, the *Epic of Gilgamesh*. In its present form, this masterpiece dates from the seventh century B.C., but it goes back to a much earlier Babylonian original. The early cantos of the epic described the adventures of Gilgamesh and his dear companion Enkidu. Later Enkidu was struck down with a mortal illness, sent upon him by the goddess Ishtar, of whom the pair had fallen foul. Gilgamesh was overcome with grief and shocked at the tragedy of death:

> *Six days and six nights have I wept over him,*
> *Then was I afraid of death and fled through the land,*
> *My friend whom I loved has become like unto mud.*
> *And I, must I too, lie down like him and never rise again?*

He decided to seek out the secret of immortality. There was one obvious person to consult. Had not Utnapishtim acquired deathlessness?

Gilgamesh set out on a perilous journey. Ultimately, after various vicissitudes, he reached the pious Utnapishtim. Utnapishtim did not approve of Gilgamesh's request. He delivered a homily on the inevitability of death as part of the necessary human lot. But had not he, Utnapishtim, gained everlasting life? Yes, answered Utnapishtim evasively, but this was due to the gracious favor of Enlil. However, during this conversation, Utnapishtim's wife persuaded her husband to reveal the secret of rejuvenation. Utnapishtim told Gilgamesh of a magical plant found at the bottom of the sea, which would restore to him his youth. Gilgamesh thereupon plunged beneath the ocean and brought up the plant. Unfortunately, on his way home, he stopped to bathe at a spring, and a snake came and stole the life-giving plant. The hero was in despair. Finally, he invoked the shade of Enkidu, who told him once more of the inevitability of death and the sad state of those who have passed into the gloomy nether kingdom.

Both this story and that of Utnapishtim express a theme of great importance in Mesopotamian religion. The gods are immortal, but they guard the secret carefully from mankind. Men have no right to everlasting life, and it was only by an exceptional accident that Utnapishtim should have acquired the blessing of immortality.

The Myth of Adapa

The same theme runs through another legend, the myth of Adapa who represents the human race, and is related to the Hebrew Adam. Adapa had offended the god Anu (or An), who decided to summon him into his presence in order to give him the food of death. Ea, however, who had created Adapa, gave the offending mortal good advice. He told him what answers he should give to the deities who guarded Anu, to win them over. Ea also warned Adapa to accept neither food nor drink from Anu. But it turned out that Ea's counsels were too effective. So impressed with Adapa were the two gods who guarded Anu that they interceded with Anu in his behalf. Anu in turn was impressed with Adapa, and in a magnanimous moment offered him the food of life, which would confer immortality upon him. Adapa, remembering Ea's warning, refused, and thus lost the most golden opportunity open to a mortal. The story symbolizes the ambiguity of the god Ea. Though he favors the human race, his actions, whether accidentally or not, lead to the withholding of immortality.

There is a deeper significance also—a significance which was to be brought out most clearly in the Hebrew Bible—namely, that the divine and human realms are separate. It is in the glory of the divine realm that the secret of immortality is to be found. The jealousy of the deity toward men, as exhibited in such myths as those we have been recounting, is not just the petty jealousy of one who feels insecure: rather it expresses the recognition by the divine being of what the human ought to be aware of—the distance between heaven and earth. The worshiper finds his sustenance in the magnificence of the holy being or beings whom he worships: to put himself on a level with the deity would not only make his worship impossible, it would rob it of its point. Not only this, it would be untrue to the intuition he has of his own weakness and inadequacy in face of the mighty heavenly realm which he contemplates. The Assyro-Babylonian myths, despite their legendary nature and naive details, had an important inner meaning.

They also have had great historical importance. The story of the Flood, in many of its details, is reflected in the myth of Noah in the Hebrew Bible. The story of Adam too, like that of Adapa, is a legend concerned not so much with a particular person as with a symbol of the human race. The book of *Genesis* has some of its roots in the surrounding Semitic culture of Mesopotamia. Of course the Biblical writers gave a special and novel interpretation to the legendary material. The belief in a single Creator, and the placing of the stories in the context of Israel's dramatic and divinely governed history, transformed the material into something of a different shape from the epics and myths of the Assyro-Babylonian civilization. But it is important to recognize that the Hebrews were expressing their religious and historical experience in terms which were borrowed from a wide stock of mythological material.

Marduk

The god Enlil came to be superseded by the Babylonian divinity Marduk. Marduk was associated both with the sun and with vegetation. His creative functions were described in the so-called *Epic of Creation,* or *Enuma Elish.* (This title is derived from the two opening words of the poem, meaning "When on high.") In the beginning there existed two primordial oceans, Tiamat and Apsu. Various gods came into being, and disturbed the watery couple with their noise and activity. Apsu decided to destroy them, but the reverse happened: Ea destroyed Apsu with a powerful spell, and established his home on the body of the dead Apsu. Tiamat naturally desired revenge, but fortunately for the gods, the great Marduk, offspring of Ea, was born, and did battle against her. He killed her, and by slitting her body into two, as one would slit open a fish, he created heaven and earth, and allotted the places of the various other deities. To save them from work, he created mankind out of the blood of a renegade deity who had sided with Tiamat in the primeval struggle. In gratitude the gods constructed the great temple of Marduk at Babylon.

The myth was a means of exalting the great Marduk. It is notable that in the course of the drama Marduk takes over the functions and powers of the other deities. He reigned supreme. He also had charge, through the lesser gods, of the destinies of mankind, which were decided annually at a celestial feast in the heavenly abode known as Duku.

The myth had, too, an important ritual function. It was reenacted annually at the great spring festival of Marduk. This took place at the splendid temple at Babylon, which, with its ascending steps, was shaped in the form of a *ziggurat.* This great edifice was the origin of the Biblical story of the Tower of Babel. At the spring festival the vegetation aspect of Marduk's nature was manifested. The dying and rising god symbolized, as did Osiris, the renewal of life in agriculture and the assurance of fertility. The god acquired the attributes of Tammuz, who was husband and son of the goddess Ishtar. (The latter, under the name of Astarte, was to play a part in the Greek and Hellenistic cult of the Mother Goddess.) At the same time, the king was identified with Marduk, since the royal succession was, as in Egypt, a bridge between heaven and earth. The king represented in his person the whole people. He was obliged to do penance for their transgressions. But he also enacted the role of the deity, and performed a sacred marriage of himself to his spouse, representing the god's consort. Such a sacred wedding, repeated annually, was supposed to be a means of promoting fertility. The ritual use of sex was extensive in Babylonian religion, in the form of temple prostitution.

The rationale for this lay in the fertility cult, but undoubtedly temple prostitution also provided an outlet for promiscuous feelings.

The cult of Marduk tended toward monotheism. Marduk was addressed as *Bel,* the supreme Lord. But his worship always included a host of other deities and spirits. This branch of Semitic culture did not introduce a strict monotheism exclusive of other, lesser gods.

BABYLONIAN ASTROLOGY

Not only was Assyro-Babylonian religion polytheistic, despite the supremacy here and there of a particular deity; it also had a strong interest in the magical and divinatory side of religion. We have seen that Marduk apportioned the destinies of men, through his agents. This sense of fate or destiny gave the Mesopotamians a strong interest in prediction of destiny. They believed that they could predict not merely by earthly methods of divination, but also by a study of the stars and of planets and the moon. Men gained an understanding of the will of the celestial deities through astrology. Accurate records kept by the Babylonian astrologers paved the way for later developments in scientific astronomy. Their capacity for divination was supplemented by various other magical skills, which helped to promote the power and prestige of the priesthood, and which had an elaborate hierarchical structure.

THE BABYLONIAN NETHER WORLD

In the literature of Mesopotamian culture the unknown writers express an illusory hope of immortality. This did not mean that they did not believe in a life after death. For example, Gilgamesh was able to conjure up the shade of his old companion, Enkidu, and converse with him. But the shade was, so to speak, but a shade of Enkidu's former self. He was no longer the person who had once chased panthers in the desert and shared heroic adventures with Gilgamesh. This implied a sort of persistence after death, gloomy and unsatisfactory, not to be equated with life in its true sense. Below the earth, in the realm of Nergal, dwelt spirits and defeated gods. The ritual texts depicted this region as dark, inhabited by beings clothed with wings. It was a land from which there was no return, except perhaps for assassinated or wronged persons who might come back briefly to haunt their malefactors. It was a dusty place, where the ghosts lived on dusky air and mud. Only a few privileged people could find water or a place to sleep. Such a melancholy conception of the ordinary lot of the departed helps to explain the persistent hope, as expressed in the legends, of a brighter and fuller immortality. Though partly symbolic, beliefs about the underworld also had a literal sense. It was below the ground, in the dark, clay-girt grave that the deceased had their home.

CONTRAST OF EARLY EASTERN RELIGIONS

One might contrast Egyptian and Mesopotamian religion by saying that the Egyptians evolved a developed magical technique for dealing with their dead whereas the Babylonians concentrated their magical expertise on predicting the events of life through divination and astrology. In both civilizations divine beings were integrated into the fabric of society and agriculture through the intermediary status of the divine king. In Babylonia and Assyria the distance between heaven and earth was always in the background, and even the great heroes were unable to attain the rank of the immortals. In Egypt, there came to be a stronger sense of the kinship of the divine and human, when the Osirian cult moved from being just a vegetation and fertility ritual, designed to ensure the fruits of labor, toward a feeling of personal faith in which the adherent could identify himself with the dying and rising god. Similar developments took place in the religion of Ishtar, but in the period we are considering her cult was largely wedded to the official state ceremonial.

THE CODE OF HAMMURABI

The ethical and social dimensions of Babylonian religion are reflected in the Code of Hammurabi. This lays down penalties for various transgressions. Some of them, by modern standards appear excessively severe, but Hammurabi proclaimed the code in order to give justice to the land. In so doing he was expressing a social consciousness informed by the highest insights of Babylonian religion. The gods were thought to be concerned with morality. All kinds of social and business relationships were controlled by the code; of special interest were the regulations concerning use of water. As in Egypt, all human life in Babylonia depended on the system of irrigation. It was what has been called a "hydraulic society." A farmer had to keep the banks of the irrigation ditches on the land that he cultivated in good repair. If, through his neglect, water destroyed the crops of a neighbor, he had to make restitution. The king was involved both in his sacred and in his secular role (the two in fact were not distinguished) with the maintenance of the life-giving water supply. Those who transgressed the statutes could expect not merely earthly punishments of mutilation or fine, but also the disastrous enmity of the gods. The king in his person expressed this sacred power of punishment.

The conquest of Babylon by the Persians in 539 B.C. put an end to the political structure of this remarkable civilization. The power of the Mesopotamian gods faded. The gods who controlled the fate of men suffered from that same fate, when it proved adverse. Nevertheless, as we shall see, certain elements of Assyro-Babylonian religion were carried over into later times.

44. *Bronze statue of Horus the Falcon God. (Courtesy of the Brooklyn Museum, Charles Edwin Wilbour Fund.)*

45. *Pharoah Akhenaten presents offering to Aten, symbolized by a solar disc, whose worship may be history's first monotheism (1380–1362 B.C.). (Original in the Cairo Museum. Photo, courtesy, The Metropolitan Museum of Art.)*

46. *Funerary stela of a youth holding a sacred floral wreath. Such monuments were erected to adolescents who were attached to the cult of the goddess Isis (ca. 300). (Courtesy of the Brooklyn Museum, Charles Edwin Wilbour Fund.)*

47. *The deceased owner of this funerary stela (at right) presenting offerings to god Osiris and goddess Isis. Inscription promises that Osiris will provide the dead man everything he'll need to be happy in the afterlife. (Courtesy of the Brooklyn Museum, gift of Alfred T. White and George C. Brackett.)*

48. *Paintings in the tomb of Sennedjem depict scenes of the afterlife. (Courtesy of the Metropolitan Museum of Art.)*

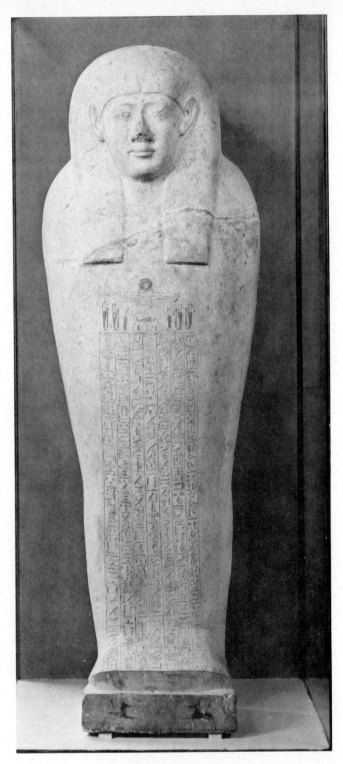

49. *Sarcophagus of the priest and scribe, Pe-yu-Hor (ca. 600 B.C.).
(Courtesy of the Metropolitan Museum of Art, Rogers Fund,
1922.)*

50. *Assyrian winged creatures worshiping a sacred tree* (*9th century,* B.C.).
(Courtesy of the Metropolitan Museum of Art, gift of John D. Rockefeller, Jr.,
1932.)

51. *Statuette of Sumerian priest from Mesopotamian temple at Tell Asmar, Iraq (ca. 2600 B.C.). (Courtesy of the Metropolitan Museum of Art, Fletcher Fund, 1940.)*

52. *Small bronze statue of Hercules running with the customary lion's pelt across his arms (3rd century). (Courtesy of the Brooklyn Museum, Frank L. Babbott and Henry L. Batterman Funds.)*

Bronze statue of Kybele in processional car represents
popular Mystery cult of late Roman Empire. (Courtesy
the Metropolitan Museum of Art, Gift of Henry G.
rquand, 1897.)

. Bronze utensils found in the Gordium Tomb, Phrygia
th century B.C.). (Courtesy, University Museum, University
Pennsylvania.)

54. Etruscan bronze Apollo.
(Courtesy of the Museum of Fine
Arts, Boston, H. L. Pierce Fund.)

56. *Celebrants in Mysteries of Issus. (General Direction of the Vatican Museums.)*

57. *Funerary column krater used for mixing wine, from Altamura, Italy. (Courtesy of the Brooklyn Museum, gift of Robert B. Woodward.)*

58. *Mithras killing a bull (late Roman). (General Direction of the Vatican Museums.)*

PERSIAN ZOROASTRIANISM

In an inscription which celebrates the fall of Babylon, Cyrus, the Persian ruler, mentions both the god Marduk, and Yahweh, the God of the Jews. But there is no reference to Ahura Mazda, the supreme spirit worshiped in Zoroastrianism. It remains a question as to whether or not Cyrus was an adherent of this faith. Certainly Darius the Great (522–486 B.C.) was a keen protagonist of Zoroastrianism. This is known from the famous inscription on the Rock of Behistun. With the dominance of Persia over most of the area which had been covered by the Babylonian and Assyrian empires, Zoroastrianism entered on a phase of expansion and influence. Its prophetic character and insistence on ethical values was much closer to Jewish monotheism than either of the two ancient religious traditions we have so far considered. Properly speaking it did not become a world religion, for it has not lived into modern times on a sufficiently great scale (it is represented now only by the community of Parsees, who dwell mainly in India). Still it must be reckoned one of the truly important manifestations of religious experience and moral insight.

The religion is centered in the teachings and life of Zoroaster, or, as he should more properly be spelled, Zarathustra (the former version is due to Greek transliteration). In its development we can distinguish four main stages. First, there was the early faith, as promulgated by Zarathustra himself; second, there was the Zoroastrianism of the Persian Empire espoused by the monarchs from Cyrus and Darius onward, which introduced elements into the religion considerably tempering its monotheistic character; third, there was a renewal of the religion during the time of the Arsacid and Sassanian dynasties (226–642 A.D.); and finally, there is the relatively modern period. With the penetration of Islam into the Persian world, the older religion was driven out. Muslim persecution—and other factors—induced a considerable number of Zoroastrians to seek refuge in Kathiawar in western India. In 1490, the Muslims arrived there also, and most of the Zoroastrians transferred themselves to Surat, and thence to Bombay, where they remain to this day an active and prosperous community. They are known as Parsees because of their Persian origin.

ZOROASTRIAN SCRIPTURES

The Zoroastrian scriptures are known as the *Avesta*. They consist in various treatises, poems, and hymns. The extant parts are: (1) The *Yasna*, which is a collection of liturgical writings that includes the most important texts, the

Gathas. These are poems, written in an older form of the language, which probably go back to Zarathustra himself. (2) The *Visparad* contains invocations of "all the lords" for use at festivals. (3) The *Yashts* are a collection of hymns to various divinities. (4) The *Vendidad* contains prescriptions about purifications, etc. These scriptures, as some of their contents indicate, belong largely to a period when Zoroastrianism had become overlaid with polytheistic ideas. Some of the writings may be as late as the fourth century A.D., though the bulk of them is a good deal earlier. From the fourth century A.D. onward, there was compiled a further, extensive set of writings, in the language of Pahlavi, which served to express the ideas of the reformed and scholastic Zoroastrianism of the Sassanian period.

ZARATHUSTRA

It is extremely uncertain when Zarathustra himself lived. Ancient Greek sources mention dates up to several thousand years B.C., but the weight of modern scholarly opinion is divided between two main hypotheses: one, that he lived in the tenth or ninth century B.C., and the other that he belonged to the sixth or fifth centuries B.C. There is some uncertainty likewise as to where he lived, whether in northeast or northwest Persia. The linguistic and the historical evidence is ambiguous. While the language of the *Gathas* is related to that of the Vedic hymns and of comparable development, which would indicate the earlier date for Zarathustra's life, other historical evidence together with elements in the Zoroastrian tradition itself, would seem to point to the later date. As to where Zarathustra lived, Greek and other evidence, including allusions in the *Avesta* itself, point toward eastern Iran; yet the dialect of the *Gathas* has been found to belong to northwest Iran. According to one tradition, Zarathustra converted a king called Vishtaspa, or Hystaspes in the Greek transliteration, who was a ruler of parts of eastern Iran. His conversion was crucial in the spread of Zoroastrianism because Hystaspes was the father of Darius the Great who, in turn, became a strong exponent of the religion. Whether or not this tradition solves the riddle of Zarathustra's time and place has never been decided. The accounts of Zarathustra's life are rich with legend: still, one can isolate certain facts that seem plausibly historical.

Zarathustra was the son of a priest of a pastoral tribe. As a boy he showed much concern for others and was deeply interested in finding the truth of religion. At the age of thirty, or a little older, he had a decisive religious experience in which he encountered the angel Vohu Manah (literally "Good Thought"), an aspect or emissary from God. The angel transported him in spiritual form to the great spirit Ahura Mazda, the "Wise Lord"—henceforth

Zarathustra's name for God. This prophetic experience was followed by other revelations in the next decade of Zarathustra's life. As a consequence, he felt called to preach a purified faith against the existing polytheism (which had some similarities to the related religion of the Aryans who had invaded India and whose faith found expression in the Vedic hymns). Zarathustra met opposition and, at first, encountered little success. However, the conversion of Vishtaspa led to a great growth of the new religion, even though the king was defeated in war and his capital occupied. During the last violent days of that war tradition affirms that Zarathustra himself was killed. He was seventy-seven years old when he died.

Teachings of Zarathustra

The teachings of Zarathustra transformed certain elements already existent in the religion of the society in which he was reared. The god whom he addressed as Ahura Mazda had attributes, both ethical and celestial, of the sky god Varuna, a focal figure of Vedic religion, who was also worshiped by a Indo-European tribe called the Mitanni, who inhabited mountains north of the Mesopotamian plain late in the second millennium B.C. But the indigenous religion of early Iran entertained belief in a host of other gods and spirits—Mithra, Vayu, Yima, the *fravashi,* and so on. Zarathustra, under the influence of the overwhelming revelations he had received from the supreme Deity denounced this polytheistic cultus. He equated the gods with evil spirits, who seduced men from the true worship of the one Spirit. This sense of malicious opposition to his purified religion, together with his strong belief in the moral goodness of the Deity, led him to think of a cosmic opposition to God. He often mentioned *Druj,* the "Lie," which was an evil force waging a struggle against Ahura Mazda. Evil could not be attributed to God, but it certainly existed: consequently, Zarathustra felt that there was a diabolical spirit working constantly against goodness. The chief evil spirit in the service of Druj, was Angra Mainyu. In one of the *Gathas* we read:[1]

> *Now will I speak out: listen and hear,*
> *You who, from far and near, have come to seek my word;*
> *Now I exhort you clearly to impress on your memory the evil teacher*
> *   and his faults; for*
> *No longer shall the evil teacher—Druj that he is!—destroy the second life,*
> *In the speech of his tongue misleading to the evil life.*

---

[1] Translated by Kenneth Sylvan and reprinted from *The Bible of the World,* ed. by Robert O. Ballou (New York: Viking Press, 1939), p. 561.

Now will I speak out: At the beginning of life
The holier Mentality said to the opposing Mentality who was more
    hostile,
"Neither our thoughts, doctrines, plans,
Beliefs, utterances, deeds,
Individualities nor souls agree."

The dualism between Ahura Mazda and Angra Mainyu presented a central problem to later Zoroastrian theology in the Sassanian period. If God was omnipotent, then evil existed by his permission. If evil was an eternal principle, then God was not fully Creator. But could both good and evil be derived from one principle? We shall see later how the answer evolved.

Though Zarathustra denounced the gods (*daevas*) as malignant he also made a slight concession to polytheistic ideas, in that he spoke of various personified qualities of Ahura Mazda—the Amesha Spentas, or "Immortal Holy Ones." These were given the names of abstractions, such as Dominion, Immortality, Good Thought, and so on, but there were indications in the hymns of a more personal relationship with them. It is probable that Zarathustra selected certain features of the existing mythology and rebaptised the gods as attributes of Ahura Mazda.

The chief ritual of Zoroastrianism, the fire ceremony, seems to have derived from the earliest times in the Zoroastrian tradition—perhaps from Zarathustra himself, who, according to later tradition, was killed while performing the fire sacrifice. There is little doubt that Zarathustra was adapting and attempting to purify the old Aryan fire sacrifice, which had centered on the figure of Agni in the Vedic hymns. The fire became for him not so much the manifestation of a deity as the symbol of purity and of the worship of Ahura Mazda.

The ethics taught by Zarathustra were based on the social life of the husbandman. The good man is one who looks after the cattle and tills the soil in peace and neighborliness. He is upright and has a burning regard for the truth. It is his duty to keep away from those who worship the *daevas* and to resist them with force if necessary. Angra Mainyu, the great evil spirit, threatens the farmer's life.

No doubt this was a reflection of the actual conditions of the time. Rampaging nomads raided the farms. Zarathustra addressed an age which saw the transition from nomadic to pastoral life, and his faith was a means of establishing and cementing the latter.

One of the *Gathas* consists in a dialogue in which a mysterious being called the Ox-soul complained of the maltreatment of cattle upon earth. Vohu Manah (Good Thought—the angel who had brought the great revelation of

Ahura Mazda to Zarathustra) promised the Ox-soul that Zarathustra would help them. Zarathustra, through praying earnestly for Ahura Mazda's help, became the protector of cattle.

Cows and oxen were specially connected with, and received the favor of, Ahura Mazda. This aspect of Zarathustra's religion was relevant to his time and circumstances, though it lost its appeal when the religion became the faith of an empire. Zarathustra saw in the pastoral life something excellent. From this he drew out a larger ethic which outlasted its pastoral origin.

Judgment after Death

The moral life was not confined to relations with one's neighbors and the daily labors of the husbandman. It was part of a wider drama of God and man. The struggle between good and evil in the cosmos was reflected in the struggle within a man's heart. They were both part of the same process. Moreover, death did not end a man's existence. After death came the awful judgment. At the end of the world, when good gained victory over the forces of evil, all men would be resurrected, and the evil would be banished to the Abode of Lies. This concept of a general judgment was supplemented by a much more vivid notion of the judgment of the individual after death. The dead one would approach the Chinvat Bridge, which crosses to Ahura Mazda's paradise. Below it hell would yawn. If a man's good deeds outweighed his bad ones, he would be beckoned onward and could cross the bridge with ease. But the wicked would find it impossible and topple over into the regions of punishment. With this teaching, early Zoroastrianism provided the most dramatic and vivid conception of the relation between religion and virtue that the world had then seen. It is worth noting that ideas drawn from Zoroastrianism came to influence the eschatology of the pre-Christian Jewish world, and thereafter entered into Christianity itself.

These conceptions were by no means fully described or worked out in the earliest writings. It was only in the final period of Zoroastrianism, the period of the Sassanian dynasty, that a full theology and theory of history were worked out. This was because there was a shift of emphasis from Zarathustra's mythological perception of the conflict between good and evil in the cosmos to a concentration on the speculative problems about the relation between good and evil. The ethical monotheism which Zarathustra preached underwent changes and vicissitudes in the succeeding centuries.

ACHAEMENID ZOROASTRIANISM

During the Achaemenid dynasty there developed a tendency to restore the cult of lesser deities within the framework of Zoroastrian belief in Ahura Mazda's

supremacy. The Amesha Spentas, for instance, were more and more personalized. The *fravashis,* or ancestral spirits, though they were identified with the
highest part of the human personality, and so entered into later doctrines of
immortality, were restored in the form of guardian angels. The monarch
Artaxerxes II, in the first part of the fourth century B.C., had images of
Anahita erected in the principal cities of the Empire: this goddess had originated from the Babylonian fertility deity Ishtar. The Zoroastrian cultus came
to be administered, in some areas at least, by the priestly class known as the
Magi, who were probably of Median origin. The Magis had opposed the
Zoroastrian movement when it first spread through Persia. They were drawn
into the new religion because of their excellence as priests and magicians. The
Magi imported into Zoroastrianism certain practices that gave the faith a
character more ritual and magical than ethical. The latter portions of the
Avesta have much to say about spells and incantations. The *Gathas* themselves were thought to form a sacred liturgy which not only expressed the
principles of Zarathustra but also could impart power, when properly repeated, to combat the evil powers by which men were beset. There was a
considerable proliferation of the mythology of evil: a whole hierarchy of
spirits were ranged under the leadership of Angra Mainyu.

This consciousness of the forces of evil was due partly to the consequence of Zarathustra's attitude to the old Iranian gods and partly to the
widespread adoption of Zoroastrianism in a culture where the old traditions
remained powerful. Those who believed in the older deities were supposed to
hold that they were evil spirits. So long as the old cults retained their power,
the evil spirits were bound to remain prominent in the religious imagination.
We even hear of folk who worshiped Angra Mainyu. This was not just "devil"
worship such as sometimes broke out in Christian countries; nor was it the
conscious espousal of Iago's dictum, "Evil, be thou my good." Rather it was a
return to the older cults in an environment that was not altogether favorable to
them. It is not surprising that the later books of the Zoroastrian scriptures
should concern themselves so much with questions of how to ward off evil by
magical means, and how to gain purification.

But the history of this development toward a ceremonial rather than an
ethically oriented cult has never been fully disentangled. It has been obscured
by the changes that followed the conquest of the Persian Empire by Alexander
the Great, especially the establishment of many smaller Greek dynasties in
place of the Great Empire. The period, which started effectively under
Mithridates I, in the second century B.C., and which lasted down to the Parthian era, brought about a further syncretism within Zoroastrianism. One
effect of this was the rise of Mithraism, which became for a time an important
mystery-religion in the Roman Empire. The Sassanian dynasty, which de-

stroyed the Parthian supremacy, lasted from the early part of the third century A.D. until 651, when it was vanquished by the Muslims. This period of Iranian history saw the rise of a brillant culture: a restored Zoroastrianism was a main element of the epoch.

SASSANIAN ZOROASTRIANISM

If Zarathustra himself stressed the ethical dimension of religion, and if the Mazdaeism of the Achaemenid period stressed the ritual dimension, it was the doctrinal dimension which attracted the attention of the religious leaders of the Sassanian epoch. Naturally, such an analysis is an over-simplification, but it is notable that it was during the final phase of Iranian civilization that the doctrines of the religion received their fullest elaboration. Of course, these interpretations depended on the earlier scriptures; the ideas expressed in the Sassanian revival had been foreshadowed in earlier speculations. But it is principally in this epoch that we find a more theoretical and speculative interest in the inner nature and workings of the universe. Two aspects of this interest can be mentioned here: the theory of history and the attempt to solve the problem of evil.

The theory of history gives us a long perspective on Zoroastrian eschatology—the consummation of the struggle between good and evil and the judgment of mankind. According to the theory, time can be divided into four eras, each of three thousand years. During the first, Ahura Mazda brings into being the angelic spirits and the *fravashis,* which are the everlasting prototypes of creatures (in particular human beings). Ahura Mazda creates by thought, and as he foresees the existence of Angra Mainyu, the latter comes into being. During the next three thousand years primeval man, Gayomard, and the primeval ox (prototype of the animal kingdom) exist undisturbed. But at the beginning of the third era, the Evil One attacks Gayomard and the ox, and destroys them, filling the earth with evil spirits. The period of primeval bliss and righteousness is now over. From the seed of the man and ox, human and animal descendants spring up, and good and evil are now mingled in the world.

The fourth era begins with the sending by God of his prophet, Zarathustra, to help mankind. Zarathustra's *fravashi* had already been created in the second period, so that his soul dwelt in the realm of the transcendent before it was clothed in human flesh at the time of his earthly life. After Zarathustra, every thousand years during the remainder of the era spiritual successors came into existence. These Saviors will culminate in Soshyans, who will prepare the way for the resurrection of the dead. In a final combat, the forces of evil will be put to flight and destroyed. The universe will be restored in a purified state: men and other creatures will be made immortal, and join in the praises of Ahura Mazda. This theory gives to Zoroastrianism an historical perspective that links the fate of the individual with salvation of mankind as a whole.

ZURVANISM

In the centuries succeeding Zarathustra, the dualism implicit in his teachings became sharper. The great part which evil played in the religious imagination of the people and in the priestly cultus raised questions about the power of Ahura Mazda. The theory of history described above did, of course, point to a final victory that would go to the good God. But in the interim the extent and scale of the Evil One's operations were alarming. If it were through Ahura Mazda's thought that the Evil One derived his existence, then evil was created —admittedly at one remove—by the good Creator. How, then, could pure righteousness be said to constitute his character?

One way out of this dilemma was elaborated by the movement known as Zurvanism. According to the doctrines of this school within Mazdaeism, both Ahura Mazda and Angra Mainyu issued from a first principle known as *Zurvan akarana,* or "Infinite Time." There is some evidence that *Zurvan akarana* originated in early Iranian mythology as a high god. According to the Zurvanist theory, this primal and eternal Being, who is beyond good and evil, brought Ahura Mazda and his rival into existence to rule over, and struggle for, the temporal world. Such a doctrine carries with it the sentiment that the temporal condition itself contains the seeds of evil, as well as good: only within this order is the contrast meaningful. But the supreme Being dwells in a gloriously eternal state, beyond these conflicts and contrasts.

THE PARSEES

These were only some of the movements of thought within later Mazdaeism. As a living religion—that is, as the faith of the Parsees in modern India and among the survivors who have hung on in Persia—Zoroastrianism is, despite the existence of the Evil One and the elaborate cultus, essentially a monotheistic faith. It is true that among the Parsees much of the ceremonial stems from the religion of the later Avesta; in this sense their faith is not the "pure faith" of the Founder—but about what religion is this not true? Still it is especially important for a minority community that seeks to preserve its identity to maintain the customs and ceremonies of its ancient past.

Modern Parsees pay much attention to the central ritual of the fire-temples. The sacred fire is maintained continuously in an inner chamber of the temple by priests who wear special protective cloths over their mouths to prevent contamination of the pure fire. Worshipers come to the threshold with their offerings, and receive in return ashes from the sacred fire. A more spectacular custom is the Parsee method of disposing of the dead: corpses are not buried or cremated, but are placed upon the famous "Towers of Silence" where vultures pick the flesh and the sun bleaches the bones, which are later thrown into a central well. In this way the sacred elements are not defiled by the corpse.

These rituals are a means of symbolizing the purity demanded of a worshiper of Ahura Mazda; but they are also a powerful means of promoting the social solidarity of the Parsee community. Through its business acumen and its enthusiastic espousal of modern education, the community is a prosperous and progressive one. It has kept alive, and is keeping alive, an ancient faith which has contributed much to the religious history and experience of mankind. Despite the various elements which have overlaid teachings of Zarathustra, the imprint of his call and of his message have not been wholly lost.

INFLUENCES OF ZOROASTRIANISM

Through the conquests of Alexander and through the Roman army that later occupied a large part of the Near East, Zoroastrian ideas spread through the Mediterranean world. After the Exile of the Jewish people and later through contacts with Jews of the Diaspora in many parts of the Mediterranean world, Zoroastrian concepts influenced Jewish thought. Certain ideas about last things, salvation, and Satan (the Evil One) stem from Zoroastrianism. Thus despite the virtual demise of the religion in its homeland, it contributed to the stream of western religious history. In eastern thought the Zoroastrian idea about later Saviors who would help mankind played some part in the rise of the Bodhisattva cult in Greater Vehicle Buddhism. Traders and travellers must have exchanged ideas about religion as they followed along the silk routes of Central Asia to China. It is probable too the Mazdaean magical ideas entered into later Taoism, through Chang Tao-ling. Oriental ideas transversely contributed to Manichaeism, of which we shall speak later. Buddhist, Zoroastrian, and other elements were combined into a system which was for a time an important rival to Christianity in the later Roman Empire.

The Roman Empire, by unifying a large area over a long period, and by bringing within its scope people of a wide variety of cultures, was a prime factor in the interplay of religious beliefs. Within this interplay, Christianity proved to be the faith capable of survival and domination. But to understand the world into which it emerged, we must look beyond the religions of the ancient Near East, with which we have been concerned in this chapter, and pay attention to the religions of Greece and Rome. This is not to say that the sole importance of the ancient religions lies in their contribution to or influence (even negative) upon the Christian heritage. Existing over long periods in their own right, they formed part of the fabric of many men's existence and experience. But different ancient faiths are like so many streams, at first flowing independently of one another, and then joining and mingling in a larger river. This river, as it reaches us today, bears only a trace of the character of the earlier streams: but we cannot see the full nature of the river without looking back to its origins.

GREEK RELIGION

Greek religion gained its shape in classical times from the superimposition of the Olympian gods celebrated in Homer upon an older substratum of belief in many gods. The older substratum derived in part from the Mycenean-Minoan culture which preceded the Dorian invasions of Greece around the twelfth century B.C. An important part was played there, especially in Minoan Crete, by the cult of the Mother Goddess. We have already seen, both in prehistoric religion and in the religions of Egypt and the ancient Near East, that the Mother Goddess was associated with fertility and vegetation. In the imagination of many early peoples the Mother Goddess loomed larger than the masculine sky god. In ancient Crete she combined a number of different functions, and it is possible to note a kind of female monotheism. Not only was she associated with vegetation, she was also depicted as a mountain deity. A pillar (or phallus) and sacred tree were part of her cultus, objects which symbolized the power of generation and the union between heaven and earth in the process of fructification. She was mistress of the beasts; she was ruler of the nether regions and therefore concerned with the cult of the dead; she was shown as holding snakes. (Elsewhere, for instance in India, snakes are associated with household rites.) Finally, we see her represented accompanied by a male deity, possibly her consort. Thus in her various roles the goddess dominated many aspects of daily and religious life. She had the power and status assigned elsewhere to such great beings as the sky god and the Egyptian solar deities. She provided a focus for the religious and ceremonial life of the court and of the people. Though her cult was later submerged by that of the Olympians, the figure of the Great Mother remained, in the mystery religions and elsewhere, a powerful figure of the ancient Mediterranean scene.

THE OLYMPIAN GODS

The society which Homer depicted in his poems was an aristocratic one. Probably it represented a late stage in the Mycenean culture of the northeastern Peloponnesus, which combined features of the Minoan civilization with the ruling class of Hellenic invaders who had filtered down into Greece before the Dorian invasions. But the period during which the poems attained their present form was much later, and belonged to the time after the Dorian incursions, when Greece had attained the political and social shape which persisted until the Macedonian conquest. It was the time when the country was partitioned into a large number of city-states, where the religious and daily life of the citizen was focused. But though Greece was divided politically into fairly small fragments, the mythology of the Olympians was a pervasive factor in the loose unity of Greek religion.

In the Homeric poems, the gods of Olympus were, both fully anthropomorphic and thoroughly Greek. But their origins were not always Hellenic. Their forebears were sometimes darker and more mysterious. The Homeric pantheon was the result of a process in which Hellenic, pre-Hellenic, and Mycenean elements were interwoven and assembled into the divine aristocracy Zeus ruled. Zeus was the chief Olympian, a splendid sky god who compelled the clouds, brought rain, and wielded his thunderbolt. His consort was Hera, though he also dallied with other mates. As father of the gods he was involved in a complex web of generative relationships. But Hera was his permanent wife, a matronly figure who presided over the numerous concerns of women. Above all, she was the protectress of marriage. The radiant Apollo, identified with Phoebus, the god of light, had a wide range of sacred interests —medicine, the care of animals, the oracle at Delphi, music. Though he was in origin non-Hellenic (it is noteworthy that he assisted the Trojans in the great war), he came to symbolize the proportion and harmony so prized in Greek culture. He contrasted strongly with Dionysus. Dionysus had slight importance in the Homeric poems, but later he attained considerable significance as the focus of ecstatic cults, a consequence of his role as a vegetation deity. If Apollo represented poise and harmony, Dionysus symbolized the earthier and more passionate side of early Greek religion. Other important deities were Poseidon, the sea god, Aphrodite, the goddess of love, and Athena, the patroness of the city of Athens.

The Olympians attained their preeminence in the public imagination because of the genius of the Homeric poems and their wide use as a vehicle of education. But the religious life of the Greek citizen essentially focused upon the local religion of each city-state. Public worship was regulated by the community, and the unity of each community was expressed in the cult of a particular patron of the city who was conceived of as an extension of the clan.

Many festivals punctuated daily life. There were as many as seventy a year in Athens. These festivals were not just religious acts: some served as occasions for official functions, such as the reception of foreign embassies and the honoring of citizens. Drama had its origin in such festivals, and the glories of Greek sculpture and architecture subserved a religious end. There was no dichotomy between the artistic and political life of the city-state and the local religious concerns of the populace. Yet not all worship was localized. Panhellenic festivals gave expression to the unity of the Greek race. The great Pythian and Olympic festivals were occasions for athletic contests and recitals of poetry and music. The oracle at Delphi, presided over by Apollo whose mouthpiece, the priestess, gave ecstatic vent to prophecy and advice, was another central shrine to which all Greeks could turn. Such centralized places and occasions often served to modify the severity of interstate warfare and to give divine sanction to international law.

Interpretations of Religion by Dramatists

Despite the multifarious piety and ceremony of the ordinary Greek in an environment suffused with vivid but sometimes fear-inspiring personal deities and spirits, the mythological heritage of ancient Greece was not altogether satisfying. The great dramatic writers, especially Aeschylus, and the philosophers, notably Plato, sought to reinterpret or to purify the traditional mythology. The key to Aeschylus' picture of deity was the mixture of justice and numinous power which he assigned to Zeus. Fate controlled human destiny, yet also expressed Zeus' will. But that his will was just was not always apparent to the eye of man.

Thus Prometheus, the hero in the play *Prometheus Bound,* who gave great blessings to mankind in the shape of the civilized arts, was struck down by Zeus' vengeance. He had committed *hubris,* that human pride which sought equality with the divine. The puzzling nature of Fate here found its expression: but it resulted from the tension between Zeus' ethical nature and the logic of the encounter between man and God. God punished the sinner, and those who strove to do good were enjoined to remember the distance between heaven and earth. Again and again in Greek drama *hubris* brought in its train a god-given doom.

The other great fifth-century tragedians, Sophocles and Euripides, gave a more human picture of the gods. Indeed, the humanist sentiment in Euripides often expressed a scepticism about traditional religion. This reflected the teachings and enquiries of the Sophists and of the philosophers.

THE MYSTERY RELIGIONS

Meanwhile other currents of religious experience were making an impact stronger than the official cults or the Olympian mythology. The cult of Dionysus, Orphism, and the Eleusinian mysteries provided a personal dimension to faith.

Dionysian Rites

Dionysus, a deity of Thracian origin connected with the fertility cults that flourished in Asia Minor, gave expression to an ecstatic, violent form of sacramentalism. Dionysian rites normally took place in remote places, such as mountainsides, where votaries would gather to engage in wild dancing, with wine and music. The rite culminated in the eating of the raw flesh of some animal which was identified with Dionysus. The glow of torches, the throb and wail of music, the whirling dance, the wine, the raw flesh—all these elements gave the nocturnal, orgiastic ceremony the power of heightening the consciousness to a state of divine intoxication. The devotees felt themselves one with Bacchus (as Dionysus was called in one of his aspects, as lord of the vine). These devotees were predominantly women, as was natural in a rite which had a fertility origin.

The wildness and intemperateness of the Dionysian movement in the sixth and fifth centuries B.C. aroused criticism and hostility among the more staid who respected the tradition of harmony and proportion which informed ancient Greek culture. But the cult was a welling up of tendencies which had been overlaid, suppressed, or ignored in Homeric and state religion. Euripides made this cult immortal in his *Bacchae,* a work in which he showed the sense of violence concomitant with the attraction and thrill of the ecstatic rites, in a treatment both ironic and tragic.

Orphic Mysteries

The Dionysian legend gained a place in the doctrines of Orphism, an influential religious movement of the early fifth century and after. Strangely, Dionysus here became the focus for an ascetic rather than an orgiastic faith. The Orphic myth was as follows. Dionysus, under the name of Zagreus, was the offspring of Persephone and Zeus. His father wished him to rule the world, but reckoned without the formidable and ancient Titans, a race of giant gods. They killed the infant Zagreus, and ate his flesh. In his wrath, Zeus sent down thunderbolts which burned up the Titans and reduced them to ashes. The human race was formed from the ashes; thus man is a combination of good and evil. He is evil, because his substance derives from that of the Titans; he is good because that substance had included, through the eating of the infant god, that of Zagreus. But Zagreus was not dead after all. Athena managed to rescue the heart of the child; Zeus swallowed it, and Zagreus was reborn as the son of the earth goddess Semele. Because of this there was hope of a purified life for man through union with the once-more-living god.

This myth was made the basis of a dualistic doctrine that emphasized the evil associated with the body. This was memorably expressed by the phrase, *soma sema,* "the body is a tomb." The devotee's aim in Orphic religion was to liberate himself from bodily entanglement through ascetic practices and to achieve immortal life. An important Orphic belief was that of reincarnation, which otherwise did not play a big part in Greek religion or in the religions of the Mediterranean and Near East. But it seems to have been indigenous to Thrace, where the Dionysian cult had its main origins. The stress on the division between the body and the soul, and the idea of the essential immortality of the soul, contrasted greatly with the Homeric picture of the afterlife, where the heroes persist in a shadowy world, regretting the brightness and activity of their former life. For the Orphic devotee it was life in the next world that really counted; it was life in this world that was sorrowful, and a continuous purgation for the sins and evil implicit in the human condition.

Orphic Ideas in Pythagoras

Pythagoras (c. 530 B.C.), the philosopher and religious teacher, incorporated Orphic ideas into his teachings: belief in reincarnation, the need for purity, food tabus—these were demanded of the members of the Pythagorean brotherhood. Pythagoras' discovery of the mathematical nature of musical harmony made him believe that numbers form the basis of reality; through philosophical and mathematical inquiry he thought it was possible to gain knowledge of the invisible world, a knowledge he conceived of as liberating.

Orphic Ideas in Plato

Orphic concepts passed through Pythagoras on to Plato (427–347 B.C.), who rehearsed the arguments for the immortality of the soul in the dialogue *Phaedo.* Plato's metaphysics, centering on the theory of Forms, or Ideas, which serve as timeless prototypes of the changeable things discovered in perceptual experience, had a mystical and religious side. To be sure, in the *Republic* and elsewhere he was severely critical of Homeric mythology. He thought traditional tales of the gods ought to be censored, since they often gave a far from inspiring or flattering picture of the deities. The immoralities of Olympians were scarcely an edifying example to the young. Plato continued the criticisms of traditional piety which earlier thinkers had expressed. But nonetheless, he conceived of a timeless, eternal realm lying beyond the reach of the senses and culminating in the Form of the Good, giving unity and value to the lower Forms. This had a religious as well as an intellectual appeal. In later times, an adapted Platonism became a vital form of mystical belief through the writings of Plotinus. But the mystical strand was present in Plato himself. The education which he laid down for the Guardians in the *Republic* took them through a rigorous physical and intellectual training, to a point where they could gain intuitive knowledge of the Good. In a famous lecture (which he presumably delivered, but which has not come down to us), Plato was reported to have spoken of this vision of the Good in a way that hinted that it shared the ineffable splendor commonly found in the experience of contemplative mystics.

Plato did not describe the supreme Good and Beauty crowning the invisible world of the Forms in a personal way, however. He made no analogy to theistic mysticism, which conceived of the contemplative experience as a vision of God. In the *Timaeus*, Plato spoke of a Creator, the Demiurge or Supreme Craftsman. But he did not identify this Creator with the Good. In fact his conception of the Creator was of one who used the world of timeless Forms as a kind of blueprint to construct the temporal cosmos.

Eleusinian Mysteries

The Orphic movement, through its influence upon Plato, and through its promise of personal immortality as a reward for a somewhat ascetic righteousness, played a vital part in classical Greek religion, even though numerically it was never very powerful. The same concern for immortality or divine blessedness also found expression in the Eleusinian Mysteries. These centered on the mythology of the vegetation deity Demeter, the corn-mother. Once again we encounter the theme prevalent in the ancient world that vegetation, in its death and rising again to life, is a symbol and earnest of the possibility of spiritual renewal. Through identification with the divine spirit that controls these phenomena, the devotee is enabled to share a risen life.

The mythology lying behind the Mysteries is as follows. The daughter of Demeter, Kore, was carried off by Hades, god of the underworld. The sorrowing mother searched for her everywhere with a lighted torch. After various vicissitudes and wanderings, the goddess came to Eleusis, on the seacoast of Attica. One year, in her despair, she produced a drought that was so terrible that the gods persuaded Zeus to have Kore returned to her mother. Hermes was sent to the underworld, and Hades gave up his captive. By the trick of offering her a pomegranate, which symbolized marriage, Hades ensured that she would have to return; but Zeus effected a compromise—Kore would have to dwell in the underworld one-third of each year. In this way, Kore was identified in the myth with Perspehone, queen of Hades; and a synthesis between an agricultural rite and concern for the future life was effected. The corn-maiden, from beneath the earth, sends up the living shoots of the spring crop. The myth of Iacchos, or Dionysus, was also incorporated in the Eleusinian mythology.

The Mysteries themselves were confined to a select group, the *mystae* or initiates, and the main ceremonies were held in the autumn. A procession from Athens was followed by a night-long fast, and throughout the succeeding days the rites of initiation continued, during which a sacred drama was enacted and sacred objects were displayed in a blaze of light. The death and resurrection of the corn and the solemnity of the liturgy made a powerful psychological impact on those present. Though the content and nature of the events were kept secret, the main object of the cult was not so much to learn a divine revelation as to undergo a process of spiritual renewal. Garlanded and serene, the initiates would return to Athens. By the late fifth century B.C. the festival had been made open to persons from the whole Hellenic world, and it remained for many years a very sacred expression of personal religion in the Greek world and in the Roman Empire. (Claudius wished to have the Mysteries removed to Rome, and a number of emperors became *mystae*.) The temple at Eleusis was ultimately destroyed by Alaric the Goth in the fourth century A.D., and the cult was brought to an end. Despite the power of the Mysteries and of Orphism to offer a religion of personal engagement and renewal, the educated classes increasingly turned toward philosophical ideas for their ethical and religious sustenance. The process became more marked after the Macedonian conquest in the latter part of the fourth century B.C. hastened the decay of the city-state as a meaningful political entity. New official cults marked this transition. King-worship, derived from Oriental examples, served in the Hellenistic dynasties to cement allegiances. This cult was later transferred, from Augustus onward, to the Roman emperors. But long after it was abandoned by the educated Greek, the Homeric pantheon continued to inspire Greek art. The proportion, naturalism, and limpidity of Greek sculpture reflected the Homeric gods, who were, after all, like men transfigured.

With the Roman conquest in the second century B.C., Greece became absorbed into a wider political world, which ultimately stretched from the Tigris to Britain. Greek and Roman religion mingled together, especially in the imagination of the literary world, and Greek philosophy made its entry to unphilosophical Rome. But a rather different atmosphere pervaded Roman traditional religion.

ROMAN RELIGION

The most important elements in early Roman religious attitudes were *religio* and *pietas*. *Religio* was the awe felt in the presence of a spirit or god; *pietas* was the scrupulous dutifulness which should be practiced toward both gods and men. The ritual carefulness with which the Romans expressed these attitudes was a means of cementing the bonds of family and state, and the fabric of Roman law, later to be so widely developed, owed much to the outlook of early piety.

The first religion of which we have knowledge involved belief in a large number of *numina,* or spirits (plural of *numen,* from which the term "numinous" is derived). *Numina* were not thought of in a fully personal way, as the neuter gender of the term testifies. They were associated with particular places and things which had a mysterious or sacred character. They were present in thickets and copses, in rivers and streams, and in the home. Various rites were employed to deal with the good and bad influences which could emanate from such beings and forces. But these were local phenomena. With the expansion of Rome, gods began to be conceived of in a more anthropomorphic way. There were the great sky god Jupiter, Juno his consort, who, like Hera, specially concerned herself with the affairs of women, Minerva, associated with arts and crafts, who was, significantly, of Etruscan origin, Mars, god of war, and various others.

This state cult grew in importance, and incorporated the practice of divination, partly derived from Etruscan culture. Romans could make political and military decisions only after elaborate consultations with the will of the gods. Until later times, when philosophical theories made an impression, there was no clear belief in an afterlife, though a cult of ancestors developed, centering on the family tomb. The spirits of the dead were called the *Manes,* or "kindly ones"—a euphemistic title, since they were often considered mysteriously dangerous. As with the *numina,* they were ambiguous toward human good and evil, beneficent but dangerous.

GREEK INFLUENCES

Contact with the Greek cities of southern Italy, from Neapolis downward into Sicily, and wider confrontation with Greek culture, brought about a progressive identification of the deities of the two religions. This reinforced the anthropomorphic strain in Roman piety. Jupiter was equated with Zeus, Juno with Hera, Ceres with Demeter, Neptune with Poseidon, and so on. More important were philosophical influences. Aristocratic and well-to-do Roman families would employ Greek tutors, and the education of Rome came increasingly permeated with Hellenism.

Epicureanism

One fruit of this influence was the thought of Lucretius, who, in the first century B.C., strongly attacked superstition and traditional religion. His *De Rerum Natura* expressed in a Latin context the teachings of Epicureanism. This school had been founded in Greece by Epicurus (342-270 B.C.), who developed an atomic theory of the constitution of the cosmos. The chief end of man, according to Epicurus, was pleasure, but this did not mean that one should live in an obviously hedonistic manner. In order to gain the maximum of pleasure, it was necessary to be prudent and restrained in one's appetites, and cultivated in one's social and cultural life. The gods were not denied, but they had no contact with, or concern about, human affairs.

Stoicism

Stoicism proved to be the system with most appeal for the virtuous Roman. This school was established at the same time as that of Epicurus. Its founder was Zeno of Citium (335-263 B.C.). In opposition to Platonism, with its contrast between the transcendent realm of the Forms and the empirical world of ordinary experience, Stoicism affirmed the organic unity of the universe as a single whole. Intelligence was considered to be a refined form of material substance, of a fiery nature. The cosmos as a whole displayed the orderliness and rationality associated with intelligence, and thus the cosmic energy controlling its processes was conceived of as the supreme intelligence, identified religiously with Zeus. The aim of the wise man was to acquire perfect virtue which would make him self-sufficient. This self-sufficiency reflected the freedom and happiness of the cosmic intelligence, and thus he lived in harmony with the universe. Roman Stoicism gave a typically practical interpretation to the notion of self-sufficiency. The wise man was not one detached from the affairs of the world, but one who was courageous and self-controlled in the performance of his obligations. This conception allowed a reinterpretation and reapplication of the old Roman *pietas,* and it integrated ethical and social action with the worship of a supreme Being. The austere and scrupulous Roman gentleman, ready to die on his own sword if his honor was at stake, reflected the ideal which Stoicism could arouse.

Plotinus

Platonism attracted some attention among the educated classes in Rome, but was without great practical influence in the days of the late Republic and early

Empire. Yet it was in Rome that the greatest of Plato's successors, Plotinus, settled in the third century A.D. The ideas he expounded there became known as Neo-Platonism. They fused together elements not merely from Plato but from Stoicism and the philosophy of Aristotle as well. Plotinus (205–c.270 A.D.) was also deeply impelled by his own mystical experience, and the metaphysics he wove together had an essentially religious aim. He was Egyptian by birth and had been a pupil of the Platonist Ammonius Saccas in Alexandria. It is possible that Plotinus was somehow influenced by Indian thought, though this has not been directly established. At the age of forty he went to Rome, where he settled with a circle of disciples. His *Enneads* contain the essentials of his system.

The Divine Being, according to Plotinus, was an eternal triad. The first of this triad, and the source from which the other members ultimately flowed, he called the One. It was also, in Platonic terms, the Good. From it emanated Intelligence (*Nous*), the second element in the triad. Within the *Nous* were contained the many Forms which were spiritual prototypes of the created world. *Nous* was the principle in which the one and the many were held together in an ideal unity. From *Nous* there emanated the Soul, or World Soul, which was the creative force from which the material universe derived its being. The World Soul, by directing its gaze at the Forms implicit in the divine Intelligence, fashioned the world and controlled it according to the pattern of the timeless prototypes of things. The Soul also descended within the material world into living individuals, whose souls partook of its nature, though they suffered and were subject to reincarnation until they could gain release and reunion with the Godhead. This scheme reflected the way in which Plotinus worked into a coherent form the notion of a supreme Absolute (the One), the Platonic world of Forms (in the *Nous*), the Stoic World Soul, and Platonic Demiurge (the Soul).

Within man, Plotinus taught, dwells the Soul in its individuated form; the way toward the Godhead, following in reverse the same sequence from which the divine triad had developed, lies in introversion—in turning inward upon one's own experience and beyond the normal thoughts and concerns which filled one's daily imagination. Moreover, the material world was that which was farthest removed in the process of emanation from the One. Though it was not in itself evil, it was deficient. It lacked the glory and fullness of the Godhead. Thus man should detach himself from material concerns. The soul had to overcome its tendencies to selfishness. In this, moral training was important, and it had an important place in the maintenance of social life. But ultimately man had to go deeper in his self-training.

The culmination of Plotinus' path of ascetic training and spiritual self-control occurred when all thought and reasoning and imagining disappeared from the soul, leaving it receptive to the vision of the One. The soul then achieved an identity with the One, from which it had to return so long as it retained its mortal clothing—though finally the mystic was enabled beyond death to enjoy the vision for eternity. Plotinus described the mystical state in terms of the "flight of the alone to the Alone." It was the return of the eternal in man to the One from which it proceeded.

In a number of passages Plotinus expressed his own contemplative experience. He stressed the fact that the "vision" which he spoke of was not like a case of ordinary seeing, where the observer and what was observed remained distinct. Rather, in this mystical vision the contemplative and the One became, in experience, fused together. In a simile, he pointed out that it was like having a light flood one's vision, not so that other things were illuminated, but so that the light itself became the vision.

We have noted elsewhere that the experience of interior contemplation has been described as though there were no distinction between subject and object. Where discursive thought has ceased, and where we have no memories or other mental images which mimic the forms of external perception, this inability to discriminate between the object experienced and the self experiencing is not surprising. When, however, the contemplative has a strong faith in a personal God and sees in his experience the work of that Being, he does not wish to speak of complete union or merging with the Divine, for it is implicit that God is Other than the worshiper. For such a person confronted with a numinous and holy Being there remains a distance between heaven and earth. (This too is partly what the Greek idea of *hubris* pointed to: Prometheus could never become Zeus, or an equal of Zeus.)

But for Plotinus, the personal God, though real, was secondary to the One. The World Soul was no profound object of devotional piety. Like Plato's Demiurge he was less important than the Good. Thus for Plotinus the ineffable One, without distinctions and without the personal characteristics possessed by "Creator" and "Lord" (personal characteristics being in themselves a form of distinctions), was the supreme goal of the contemplative life, and with it the soul could become united.

Plotinus was far from world-negating, despite his stress on spiritual and ascetic self-training. He combatted strongly the Gnostic doctrine of the evil nature of the material world. For him, the visible world reflected, albeit imperfectly, the beauty of the invisible. Through the beauties and glories of the things which we perceive around us we are led to the world of Forms and to the sphere of the divine Intelligence. Thus Plotinus' system combined the doctrine of an undifferentiated Absolute with a recognition of the importance of the world of creatures. The impressiveness of his synthesis and the undoubted nobility and spirituality of his motives gave his form of Neo-Platonism a wide respect among Christians, and has remained a source of inspiration to a number of Christian contemplatives. Though Neo-Platonism scarcely functioned as a popular religion, it had a wide appeal among the religious intellectuals of the later Empire, among them St. Augustine, both before and after his conversion to Christianity.

HELLENISTIC MYSTERIES

We have traced briefly the outlines of some of the philosophical doctrines which were influential in the Roman world, from the first century B.C. onward. If these were movements which replaced or overarched traditional piety among the educated folk, there were other movements which, in a more subterranean way, gained increasing influence among the masses. Various mystery-cults, especially those of Isis and Mithras, infiltrated Hellenistic and Roman religious culture. Similar to the Eleusinian Mysteries, but more universal in scope, these cults provided personal experiences which could supplement the more formal side of ancient religion.

The Isis Cult

The Isis cult had its origins in the mythology of ancient Egypt. The Ptolemies, Greek successors of Alexander the Great and rulers of Egypt, established the cult of Sarapis, a name which derives from that of Osorapis, a god who combined the attributes of Osiris and the sacred bull god Apis. Apis was supposedly transformed into Osiris after death, thus gaining the kind of divine immortality which was open to the human devotees of Osiris. The cult center of Osorapis was at Memphis in Lower Egypt. The liturgy of the new worship of Sarapis was a combination of Egyptian and Greek, and the popularity of the god grew quite rapidly. By the first century A.D. it became officially recognized in Rome. The ritual was chiefly concerned with the three figures of Osiris (or Sarapis), Isis, and Horus their son, but the dominant member of the triad was the goddess.

It is fortunate that we possess in the literature of the ancient world a description of what this mystery-religion meant to the individual. The twelfth book of the *Metamorphoses* of Lucius Apuleius gives us an account of the experience of an initiate of Isis. Though the story tells of the adventures of a certain Lucius in the third person, there is very little doubt that Apuleius is basing his narrative upon his own autobiography.

The story tells how Lucius is transformed magically into an ass. After many sufferings and adventures he is finally restored to human form through the miraculous grace of the goddess. So far, the story is an allegory of the descent of man into bestiality and sensuality and his rising through the healing power of the divine being. In his new state, Lucius becomes a devoted follower of Isis and goes through the rituals of initiation. The sacred drama and liturgy of Isis were capable of speaking to the person who, through subduing his animal nature, clarified his spiritual perceptions. In the ceremonies, Lucius perceived the brightness of the sun at midnight, a hint that solar elements from the Egyptian tradition were incorporated in the initiation. He approached the gods above and those below. He was crowned on a throne beside Isis—a symbol of his deification and his restoration from darkness to light and from death to a new life. In gratitude for the profound change which he felt, Lucius spoke of Isis as the savior of mankind and remained devoted to her worship.

Some of the splendor of the ceremonial and the sense of glory and renewal that those who underwent it felt is conveyed by this story. The mysteries clearly gave people an intimately personal awareness of the significance of the spiritual world, together with a personal ethic stressing purity. The secrecy with which the rites were surrounded helped perhaps to make such a cult attractive (it was a lucky chance that Apuleius told so much so explicitly in written form). What is hidden from the common gaze has its own fascination, as secret societies have shown all down the ages.

MITHRAISM

Mithraism, or the cult of Mithras, was another important movement during the early centuries of the Empire, and became widely diffused among the legionaries. Its traces have been found from Syria to Hadrian's Wall. The mythology of Mithraism goes back to later Zoroastrianism. Mithras had originally been a solar diety of the ancient Iranians, but he was not recognized in the monotheistic reform effected by Zarathustra himself. He came back in the later period when polytheistic ideas began to overlay Zarathustra's teachings. Mithras was believed to be the eye of Ahura Mazda and to rule over the earth. In the imagination of the Mithraic cult he came to replace the supreme deity. He engaged in a great struggle between good and evil in which he was steadily victorious. To assure his victory, he sacrificed a great bull which was the prototype of the living world of nature. Through this sacrifice nature was made fertile. (Again we meet the theme of death and the renewal of life associated with fertility rites.)

A central feature of the ceremonial associated with Mithras was the *taurobolium,* the ritual slaughter of a bull which commemorated and repeated Mithras' primeval act. The initiate was baptized in its blood, partaking of its life-giving properties. It may be noted that this part of the ceremonial closely resembled the ritual of the cult of Cybele, the Great Mother of Asia Minor, which had been brought to Rome three centuries before Christ. (The cult of

Cybele had encountered official resistance until after the first century A.D.) In the Mithraic ritual, the initiate took part in a sacramental meal of bread and wine, for it was believed that the bull, in dying, had brought forth corn and vines from its side, symbolizing the fructification of nature. This sacrament was felt to give the initiates power, immortality, and strength against the forces of evil, and it reflected the divine banquet which Mithras himself had enjoyed after his slaughter of the great bull. Various grades of initiation were established which corresponded to the various stages the aspirant to immortality had reached. These helped to sustain the ardor of those just entering the way. Unlike the other mystery religions, Mithraism was open only to men, so that in no sense could it be regarded as a universal faith. Mithras, the unconquered and unconquerable sun (*sol invictus*), symbolized the courage, success, and confidence of the soldier. The ethics of the cult demanded self-control and other virtues necessary to a legionary, and this was one main reason for its spread through the army. Imperial patronage helped too. From the second century A.D. Roman Emperors assumed the title *Invictus*.

Like other mysteries the Mithraic did not function in opposition to official religion. It has a polytheistic background, rather than a genuinely monotheistic one, and though Mithras might be supreme in the eyes of his devotees, as one who could bring them to the realm of light and immortality, other deities were recognized, and astrological and other beliefs were intermingled with the sacramental side of the cult.

THE MEANING OF THE MYSTERIES

We have only touched on a few of the mysteries here, for the Hellenistic age was one which contained numerous cross-currents of religion. The mysteries through their ritual could offer a highly personalized experience to their devotees rather than a strictly magical or simply formal interpretation of life. Ritual became a means of changing a man's experience. The ceremonies were like a revelation as in the mysteries of Demeter and Isis, but not a revelation in the sense of communication of information about God nor revelation in the sense of uncovering secret knowledge. They were a revelation in the sense of opening the eyes and hearts of the initiate, bringing about an elevation in his feelings. He could feel identified with the divinity who served as a focus of the cult. In this way he acquired the immortality of the divine, and assurance for this life and the next.

On the ethical side the mysteries often stressed purity, sexual and otherwise; but they were essentially concerned with private morality, rather than public, and social changes. Moreover, the social side of the mysteries did not involve the cutting-off of the initiate from the usual practices of the societies in which they found themselves. Some of them were largely confined to the richer classes: the Isis cult was quite expensive for the initiate. Though the mythological dimension was well developed, and was reflected in, and served to reflect, the ritual, the doctrinal dimension was not important.

No system of philosophy underlay these different movements. On the experiential side, the mysteries, as we have seen, produced a strong impact through the sacramental ritual. It was essentially an experience of the god's glory and healing power and of the renewal of the devotee's spirit. But despite the derivation of the term "mystical" (from *mystae,* etc.), the experience was not a mystical one in the sense in which we are using it in this book. It was not like that of the contemplatives such as Plotinus who have an interior vision. It was an exterior awareness of the numinous power of the god. In an age when the old gods were losing some of their power and atmosphere, the mysteries restored, for a time, the holy and saving power to selected deities of ancient polytheism. They also turned men's thoughts to the hope of immortality, sometimes overlooked in the official mythologies.

Needless to say, the pagan world of antiquity could easily look upon Christianity in its early days as a mystery cult. The Christian eucharist had a superficial resemblance to the sacrament of Mithraism. But the differences were great. Christianity was monotheistic; it was universal: it was not, except under persecution, strictly a secret society: its ethical dimension was highly developed. But there is no doubt that some of the longings which caused men to turn to the mystery cults explain the attractions of the Christian message in the early centuries of the Empire.

CONCLUSION

In this survey of some of the religions of the ancient Near East and the Mediterranean, and some of the movements which took place within that world, we have necessarily been selective. Much has been left untouched. A wider area—that occupied by the Celts and Slavs, for instance, within and beyond the bounds of the imperial frontier—has been left uncovered. But it is hoped that some of the more impressive features of ancient mythologies and faith have been sufficiently illuminated.

It is necessary to remember the background against which the movements of religion took place. The world of the Hellenistic age and of the early Empire was one in which innumerable local deities were still honored, in which official ceremonies were maintained, in which miracle-workers attracted their followings, in which magical and astrological ideas were widely canvassed and put into practice. There was no single religion of the times. There was no systematic ordering of ceremony through a unified hierarchy.

It was a period of religious competition and intermingling; deities could acquire a sudden popularity through the miraculous and men could turn in hope from one manifestation of the numinous to another. In such a setting, total commitment to a particular god, movement, or philosophy was not the normal thing. The deities could live side by side and men could live likewise recognizing one another's peculiar cults. Only when these were thought politically or socially dangerous (as with the cult of Cybele in its early period at Rome) were they resisted with any force. Into this jumble of religious rites, and into this fabric of deities and metaphysical doctrines, Christianity entered. Its origins were Semitic, but the Semitic faith which gave rise to it was rather different in character from the religions of Egypt and Mesopotamia. Let us turn, then, to see how the monotheism of the Hebrews emerged from this complex environment.

Chapter 7

THE JEWISH EXPERIENCE

THE ANCIENT HEBREWS first enter history as a nomadic peoples inhabiting the northern Arabian peninsula. They lived in tribes on the fringes of the desert, and their culture was similar to many others of the Stone Age. They travelled about seeking pasture for their domesticated animals, mostly goats, stopping at springs and oases to fill their water containers and to gather fruits to enrich their diet. Their religion was like that of other primitive peoples. They felt that *mana* pervaded certain sacred and mysterious objects, such as the strange outcrops of rocks in the desert and the trees of the oases. They venerated stone pillars as containing life-giving power and cajoled the personal spirits that haunted the sandstorms and the night. For them divinities (*elohim*) dwelt in nature and in the sky. Different tribes each had particular deities who were especially concerned with their affairs. Their religion, in short, was not at all unlike that of the desert Arabs whom Muhammad at a later date succeeded in converting to the religion of Allah, and who were such a potent force in the history of the Middle East.

ABRAHAM

During the second millennium B.C., or earlier, these tribes began moving northward into Mesopotamia. According to the Biblical narrative, the migration into Canaan was led by Abraham, who came from the region of Haran that lies in the angle of the Euphrates northeast of Syria. There is good evidence that this was his ancestral home; archaeological findings have confirmed that customs presupposed in Genesis existed in this area. It is also recorded that Abraham moved to Haran from Ur in Chaldea, where he had settled; his move that may reflect the fact that in the nineteenth century B.C., Ur was destroyed by invading Elamites. There is not too much doubt that the story of the migration from Haran to Canaan is substantially correct. It probably took place under the pressure of population movements from further

east. The Hebrew tribes continued moving south, and occupied the land of
Goshen on the easterly side of the Nile Delta, partly, it seems, because they
were allied to the Hyksos, who between the mid-eighteenth and early sixteenth
centuries B.C. succeeded in controlling Egypt. Abraham's religion, so far as we
can tell, centered on his belief in a god whom he called *El-Shaddai*, "Divinity
of the Mountains." There is evidence that his tribe also venerated ancestral
images.

The account of events in early Hebrew history depends only in part upon
the Biblical literature, and where it does it involves reading between the lines
to some extent. The account does not become clear from a straight reading of
Genesis, though the historical narrative given there is substantially correct. Let
us pause a moment to consider the nature of the Biblical material.

THE LITERATURE OF THE BIBLE

Since the end of the nineteenth century, textual, historical, and literary researchers have opened up new perspectives on the Bible, enabling scholars to
piece together the order in which the books constituting it were composed and
the ways in which they were edited by later redactors. In some cases, for
instance, older material was evidently edited and reshaped to demonstrate that
the cult of the one God Yahweh went back to the earliest times. This happened in the story of Abraham. But this reshaping was never completely
successful, which is why the "reading between the lines" mentioned above is a
fruitful source of information about the original form of the material and
about the actual beliefs of the people described. Now there have always remained some Christians and Jews who treat the narratives as inerrant, that is,
as composed under the infallible guidance of God. For them—and their view
needs to be respected as a potent force in religious history and piety—the
critical findings about the Bible cannot be accepted, save in relatively minor
details. The account we are now giving of the religious history of the Jews
depends upon these findings, however, though since scholars are divided over
a number of issues, some of the phases of the history are uncertain. If anyone
prefers a straightforward and literal reading of the Bible to such an account,
he can quite easily replace this chapter and part of the following by doing
just that.

History and the Bible

Naturally, questions about the date and character of the scriptures in other
religions are important also, but a peculiar importance attaches to the case of
the Jewish and Christian scriptures. This is because Judaism and Christianity

are in one sense 'historical' religions. The ancient Hebrews preserved their records not from any scientific interest in history as such but because the events of their past and the circumstances of their present history were so vital to them. It was in history above all that they perceived the acts of God in guiding them onward. Similarly in Christian doctrine and mythology (using mythology in the sense outlined in Chapter I) the historical events of the life of Christ are seen as crucial to the formation of the religion.

Of course neither Jewish nor Christian belief can be proved to be true *simply* on the basis of history. For instance, we can establish with a high degree of historical certainty that Jesus was crucified, and we know something of the circumstances surrounding this event; but the belief that this event constituted a sacrificial death atoning for men's sin goes beyond the historical data. It is a doctrine that arises from an interpretation of Jewish history, from a view about human nature in its present state, from an attitude to the deliverances of personal religious experience, and from reflection upon the later history of the faith which Jesus preached. Without the historical truth that Jesus was crucified, the doctrine of the Atonement would have no application—it would be empty. But the historical truth itself is but one element in the belief.

Given such qualifications about the role of history in both Jewish and Christian religion, it remains true that history is central to these religious traditions. This is why the kind of critical study of the Jewish and Christian scriptures that establishes their date, literary style, and accuracy is of profound significance. Apart from this, our aim in this book is to present the history of mankind's religious *experience,* and this involves going behind the written word to the living history of the people described by the written word.

Content of Bible

Much has been written and debated about the literature of the Bible: we can only give a cursory sketch of what has been done. But our comments on Biblical literature will serve to introduce the history of the Hebrews from the time of Abraham. First, what do the books of the Hebrew Bible consist of? They are traditionally divided into three groups.

First, there is the Law, or Torah, expressed in the first five books of the Bible. Known as the Pentateuch, its authorship is assigned by tradition to Moses—patently a false assumption not only for reasons of literary criticism, but because he scarcely could have recorded his own death. Second, there is the section known as the Prophets, including the books of Joshua, Judges, Samuel, Kings, Isaiah, Jeremiah, Ezekial, and the ten minor Prophets. Third, there is the section known as the Writings (Hagiographa)—Psalms, Job, Song of Songs, Ruth, Lamentations, Ecclesiastes, Esther, Daniel, Ezra-Nehemiah and Chronicles. This Canon of sacred writings was not finally set until well after the time of Christ, in the early part of the second century A.D. It is worth noting that for Jesus the scriptures meant the Law and the Prophets.

Chronology of Biblical Literature

We can gain a picture of the order in which these works were composed by reference to some of the outstanding epochs in ancient Jewish history. The Exodus probably took place in the early part of the thirteenth century B.C., though it could have occurred earlier. The monarchy was founded in the late eleventh century. The great prophets Amos, Hosea, Micah, and Isaiah must have lived in the eighth century. The reformation effected by Josiah came in 621 B.C. The Exile dates from 586 to 538 B.C. The semi-sovereign Jewish state continued, under theocratic government, down to the mid-second century, when the country gained independence under the Maccabees. From 37 B.C. the Jews were under Roman domination. An insurrection brought the destruction of the Temple in 70 A.D. and the dispersal of the Jews from their homeland.

The watershed in Jewish history is the period of the Exile, and the first thing we have to note is that most of the Biblical writings date from *after* this period. No one of the works in its finished form can be placed earlier than the eighth century, when the writings expressing the teachings and lives of Amos, Hosea, Micah, and Isaiah were composed. The Pentateuch and Joshua did not reach their present state until the fourth century B.C., although a demonstrably earlier narrative that forms part of the substance of these works was probably written a century earlier, and oral traditions containing relevant material go back very early indeed. The oral tradition was first put into writing in the ninth century. At least four different strands of such traditions are identifiable in the Pentateuch: "J" (so called because of the narratives in Genesis, Exodus, and Numbers that refer to God as *Jehovah* or *Yahweh*); "E" (which identifies the narratives that refer to God as *Elohim*); "P" (the Priestly redaction, so called because the writer consistently details facts of special interest to the organized priesthood); and material from Deuteronomy, "D." Deuteronomy itself probably is equivalent to the book discovered and promulgated by Josiah. The earliest writings of all were court chronicles which in a later altered form were included in Kings and other works. Ezekiel and the latter part of Isaiah (incorporating the teachings of a prophet other than Isaiah who is identified as Deutero-Isaiah) belong to the immediate post-Exilic period. The Psalms, though they include material from the pre-Exilic era were not reduced to their present form until the second century B.C.

The dating of the Hebrew Bible here suggested can serve to indicate the antiquity of the writings and the complexities of Biblical scholarship. Naturally, the dates are in some degree speculative, and some major points in the scheme, notably the date of Deuteronomy, have recently been challenged. But what is certain is that a variety of oral and written traditions have gone to make up the Pentateuch, and that some works in the Bible are the result of composite literary effort. But this need not lead us to skepticism about the antiquity and importance of some of the early material. There were most probably written forms of existing oral traditions as early as the ninth century, and it is well known that oral traditions, in a period before the widespread use of writing (which tended to corrupt the memory and affect the oral tradition), can remain fixed over very long periods. One may therefore guess that some of the events recorded in Genesis and Exodus did indeed occur, and that part of the tradition goes back to the time of Moses himself.

During the period between Abraham and Moses, the rule of the Hyksos in Egypt was overthrown, and the Egyptian dynasty regained control of a large part of the eastern Mediterranean, including the area in which the Israelites occupied. This did not at first bear heavily on them, and they existed under Egyptian suzerainty for over a century without feeling gross ill-effects. But at some point (the date and person being uncertain) an Egyptian pharaoh, desiring to implement a widescale scheme of public building, and finding himself short of labor, forced the Israelites into service. This period of oppression was ended through the leadership of Moses, who, perhaps in the early years of the thirteenth century B.C., led the Israelites out of Egypt and toward the land of Canaan.

There can be little doubt, despite uncertainties surrounding the significance of the narrative, that it was Moses who gave the determining shape to Israelite religion which it has retained, not without difficulty, through succeeding centuries. In this sense Moses could genuinely be proclaimed the founder of Judaism. It was he who moved out of Egypt, but more importantly introduced them to the religion of Yahweh (wrongly transliterated as "Jehovah" in the Authorized Version of the Old Testament).

MOSES

Moses' upbringing prepared him for leadership. The adopted son of an Egyptian princess, he was spared the slavery inflicted on his people, and commanded the power to ease their lot. But his espousal of their cause eventually forced him into exile from Egypt. He settled in Midian to the east of the upper reaches of the Red Sea. There he married the daughter of a priest of the Kenite tribe. One day while grazing his flock (for he had taken up the way of life of the people to whom he was now joined by marriage), Moses experienced the presence of Holy Being so intensely that his life and the subsequent destiny of his people were thereafter altered. The narrative as we have it reads as follows:

> Now Moses kept the flock of Jethro his father-in-law, the priest of Midian: and he led the flock to the back side of the desert, and came to the mountain of God, even to Horeb. And the angel of the Lord appeared unto him in a flame of fire out of the midst of the bush; and he looked, and, behold, the bush burned with fire, and the bush was not consumed. And Moses said, I will now turn aside, and see this great sight, why the bush is not burnt. And when the Lord saw that he turned aside to see, God called unto him out of the midst of the bush and said Moses, Moses! And he said, Here am I. And he said, Draw not nigh hither: put off thy shoes from off thy feet; for the place whereon thou standest is holy ground. I am the God of thy father, the God of Abraham, the God of Isaac, and the God of Jacob. And Moses hid his face; for he was afraid to look upon God.[1]

God then commanded him to go back to Egypt to lead the Israelites out. And the narrative goes on:

> And Moses said unto God, Behold, when I come unto the children of Israel, and shall say unto them, The God of your fathers hath sent me unto you; and they shall say unto me, What is his name? what shall I say unto them? And God said unto Moses, I AM THAT I AM, and he said, Thus shalt thou say unto the children of Israel, I AM hath sent me unto you.[2]

The narrative of the event on Mount Horeb here described is pieced together from the two sources J and E. It connects the numinous experience Moses underwent on the mountain with the worship of Yahweh, who may have been the god worshiped by his father-in-law Jethro. There is evidence, both from the account itself and from other sources, that Yahweh was not the original God of the Israelite tribes (hence the insistence that this *is* the God of Abraham).

The Exodus

The second and third great events of Moses' career were shared by the Israelites. After the formidable occurrence commemorated by the Passover, Moses

---

[1] Exodus 3:1–6. [2] Exodus 3:13–14.

led the enslaved peoples across the Red (or Reed) Sea. However we may interpret it now, this event was taken to be an unmistakable sign of the favor and help of God. When they had reached Horeb, or Sinai (the mountain is named differently in different parts of the Biblical narrative), there was the confrontation between the people of Israel and their new deity Yahweh, in which a solemn pact, or covenant, was made between them. Moses was the intermediary between the two. Yahweh delivered to him the Ten Commandments, which were to serve—and still do serve—as the basis of the Jewish ethical code. That some such moral ingredient should enter into the covenant is not surprising—though it is probable that the form in which the Commandments were later written up did not correspond completely to the original injunctions Moses felt he had received in his confrontation with the Lord.

THE COVENANT OF THE TEN COMMANDMENTS

Now what is puzzling about the beginnings of the Jewish faith, as described here, is the notion that God and the people entered into a covenant. Here was something original and new in the Israelites' faith. Yet it must have had some religious antecedents.

One might seek an explanation in the evidence that there was among the early Hebrews a special relationship between a clan or tribe and its god, and that it was recognized that the leader of the clan was at liberty on his own account and in the name of the group to select his own deity (a function which was described religiously in the opposite terms—the deity chooses the clan). Such a custom may have lain behind the Mosaic covenant. If it be so, we can begin to give some account of the revolution in religion that Moses began.

Moses felt he had experienced the presence of a very powerful god, whom, he was convinced, was not confined in the exercise of his power or limited geographically to his mountain. At the time of Moses' experience the Israelites already had been shaken from their earlier religious traditions by the catastrophic events of the years of Egyptian oppression, and by the uprooting of the new migration. They were susceptible to Moses' conviction that they should enter in to a sweeping covenant with this mighty Yahweh. This was not merely a clan covenant, nor was it merely the worship of the High God among others. This was a new relationship to a sole Deity who would lead them and protect them.

The question has been debated as to whether this was a genuine monotheism which Moses taught. Probably at this stage it was not a fully articulate one. The central point at issue was whether Israel should confine its worship to one God to the exclusion of others. Monotheism was likely to develop out of the situation. The gods of other peoples were of no avail against Yahweh.

The lack of power of the gods—and Moses' demand for their rejection —paved the way for faith in a single supreme Creator ruling over all the world. One may see Moses' work as a revolution whereby the Israelites were liberated from previous allegiances and submitted themselves to a single Lord, in accordance with a sweeping and wide-ranging covenant. It should be remembered in all this that the conquest of Canaan—which was the consummation of the Exodus, though Moses did not live to see it—was effected not merely by the people who moved out of Egypt, but also by other Hebrew tribes who had escaped Egyptian enslavement. One must also note that no evidence exists as to whether or not at the time of the covenant Moses controlled the whole group of migrants from Egypt. It may be conjectured that some time elapsed before the covenant was generally accepted by the tribes who came to inhabit Canaan.

Israel in the Promised Land

The conquest of Canaan, moreover, brought other religious problems. Most of the twelfth and eleventh centuries B.C. was spent in the process of occupying the land and subduing the Canaanites, and fighting off external enemies as well. But gradually the land was settled, and a new way of life opened up for the Hebrews. Originally nomadic, they now turned to the cultivation of a fairly rich agricultural land. It was very natural that the indigenous Canaanite religion with its fertility gods and local Baals, which were closely bound up with the agricultural life, should prove attractive and important. The inhabitants of Canaan whom the Israelites had conquered believed deeply in magic, which was part of the technology of food-producing. It was scarcely surprising that the Israelites regarded with some apprehension the wholesale jettisoning of such rites in the interest of the cult of Yahweh, the "jealous" God. Consequently, the period of the monarchy, established in the first instance to replace the looser rule of judges over a federation of tribes in order that foreign enemies such as the Philistines might be more effectively combatted, was characterized by a very mixed religion. Although the covenant relationship was maintained through the cult of Yahweh, rites directed to other deities were widely practiced. In Canaanite religion the Israelites encountered forms of ritual and mythology that had wide currency throughout the ancient East. The Canaanite religion included a cult equivalent to that of Ishtar: as Ashtoreth, (the Hebrew name for Ishtar), she was the consort of the great Baal, and played a leading part in the autumnal festivals. Through their sacred marriage the earth, which she represented and embodied, was fructified. Numerous shrines to lesser Baals and their female counterparts scattered the land, especially in the "high places," the sacred hilltops, where images of the gods and stone pillars of phallic significance adorned the shrines.

Solomon's Kingdom

Something of the ambiguity of Israelite religion during this period can be seen in Solomon, the king who lived in the tenth century B.C. He had constructed a magnificent temple for Yahweh at Jerusalem, to provide a permanent resting-place for the Ark of the Covenant which had long been the symbol of Yahweh's presence with his people. But he also built shrines for other gods, under the influence of his foreign wives. More than this, it is highly probable that the Temple itself was not solely devoted to the worship of Yahweh and the housing of the Ark of the Covenant. The design was by an architect from Tyre, and the artisans were foreign: the plan and ornamentation suggest that Mesopotamian, Egyptian, and Canaanite rituals played their part.

In these circumstances, it may be asked, how did the cult and worship of Yahweh survive being submerged by those of the many gods? Two factors were important. First, the nation still looked back to the heritage of Moses. Second, the prophetic movement presented to the Jews an ethical monotheism which, in its impressive seriousness, not only recalled the Israelites to their covenant, but also gave a new perspective on the character of Yahweh. Through the prophets the revolution instituted by Moses was developed and assured of ultimate success. Meanwhile, the unification brought about by the establishment of the kingdom under Saul disappeared at the death of Solomon, in the latter part of the tenth century. The nation was divided into two kingdoms—the Northern, consisting of ten tribes, and containing the name of Israel; and the Southern, consisting of the tribes of Judah and Benjamin, and known as Judah. This split was one factor in the ultimate destruction of both parts by foreign invaders.

THE PROPHETS

The sequence of great prophets began with Elijah and his disciple Elisha. Elijah it was who attempted to reform the religion of Israel during the prosperous reign of King Ahab (ninth century B.C.). The latter's father, as a political move to cement an alliance with Phoenicia, aimed at staving off the pressure of Assyria, had married Ahab to Jezebel of Tyre. Under his wife's influence, Ahab introduced the cult of the great Tyrian god Baal-Melkart. This deed was opposed by the earliest of Israel's great prophets, Elijah; his famous contest with the prophets of Baal on Mount Carmel reflects the struggle between the cult of Yahweh and that of the foreign intruder. Elijah, moreover, protested openly against Ahab's murder of the landowner Naboth in order to acquire his vineyard. A similar strong emphasis on justice was to characterize the teachings of the later Hebrew prophets. The concept of Yahweh's rule over history was given wider application by Elijah and his successor, Elisha. Elisha was commissioned by Yahweh to anoint Hazael king of the rival kingdom of Aram, that he might be a scourge to the erring Israelites. Yahweh guided his chosen people by working through political and national forces.

Antecedents of the Prophetic Movement

We have noted before that religious phenomena, however new and creative, rarely start from nothing: they have antecedents. What were the antecedents of the prophetic movement?

In a wide variety of cultures, including technologically primitive tribal religions, we observe that there are individuals capable of ecstatic utterance, who are sometimes trained to use their gifts in association with the more formal ritual of the tribal cults. Early Israel was no exception, and there is much evidence of the existence of cultic prophets, or *nebiim,* in Canaanite religion. In a famous passage in I Samuel, Saul is instructed by Samuel that when he travels to a certain town (Gibeah), he will encounter a band of prophets, coming down from the mountain with lutes, drums, and other musical instruments. The *nebiim* used such instruments to accompany their dancing: they would dance themselves into a frenzy during which they give vent to ecstatic utterances. Samuel predicted that Saul would find himself swept along by the spirit of God and would begin to prophesy along with men from the mountain. This popular, cultic kind of prophecy not only typified the cult of Yahweh in the "high places" and in the Jerusalem Temple; it was also associated with Baalism. The *nebiim* were organized in guilds, and there is reason to think that the great prophets who reformed the religion of Israel themselves belonged to such guilds. In the past scholars have drawn a sharp distinction between such men as Amos, Hosea, and Jeremiah and the ecstatic *nebiim,* mainly because the prophets frequently denounced aspects of the ritual associated with Yahweh. It was argued that if they were identified with the cultic prophecy, they would be expected to defend the sacrificial rites. But there are strong indications that the distinction was too sharp. In many psalms, for instance, in which Yahweh speaks in the first person, one can detect replies couched in poetic language to requests made in the setting of cultic worship; the prophets who uttered them stood both as representatives of the congregation and as the mouthpiece of God. Again, there is a connection between the prophets and the Temple singers of the post-Exilic period who were reckoned among the class of Levites. By that time cultic prophecy had been reduced to a more formal liturgical character.

By accepting the kinship between the *nebiim* and the great prophets one can discern the true originality of the prophets. They may have had their origin and milieu in a custom that was widespread in the ancient Near East— and indeed is also widely found in the world of primitive religion today—but whereas cultic prophecy elsewhere has caused no revolution in religion, the utterances of the Hebrew prophets radically altered the history of Israel. One reason for this was the fact that their attention was directed to the great God Yahweh, the God of their fathers, who was more than a localized deity or a "first" god among many others. He had their sole allegiance, not just because they were professionally associated with his cult, but more importantly because of the profound and overwhelming character of their religious experience. We shall consider examples of prophetic vision in a moment.

A further factor in the prophets' revolutionary reform was that each felt himself to be the intermediary between Yahweh and the children of Israel. Just as Moses was both the potential leader of the people and the leader chosen by God to bring them to himself, the prophets were the mouthpiece of God, possessed by him: but their gaze too was turned in the direction of the people and of the society about them. God's words were addressed to the peoples' situation. This concern for society was not just political, though it was often that; it was also strongly ethical. The prophets saw in the troubles besetting Israel a warning of the misuse of the people's talents and opportunities. Injustice, aggrandizement, and false religion combined often to set Israel along the wrong path—a path, the prophets felt, that would lead to disaster. Thus they repeatedly emphasized the call to moral holiness. God was not only powerful; his nature embodied justice and goodness; hence his worshipers must themselves embody justice and goodness. Here then was a powerful development of ethical monotheism, foreshadowed and founded by Moses, and carried forward by the prophets.

The numinous experiences of the prophets and their ethical insights were not the only important features of the movement. The greatness and goodness of Yahweh was interpreted in relation to the ongoing processes of history. The prophets continued to deepen the historical awareness of the ancient Hebrews who saw in the Exodus the most significant origin of their faith. They interpreted the will of God in relation to contemporary events. In the stormy and embattled period of the two kingdoms very often the prophets, in predicting the consequences of the current social situation, became political and social commentators similar to those who inform public opinion today. But they saw events against the background (perhaps one could say foreground) of their intuitions of God's will. Their experiences of God gave direction and urgency to their message.

Of course, the prophets prophesied in the popular sense. Frequently, prophecy has been seen as a miraculous faculty for predicting events; when the predictions are fulfilled, the prophet is recognized as a seer. It would be wrong to deny that an element of this enters into the Biblical writings. But, as has been remarked, the chief function of the prophet was not so much foretelling as forth-telling. They told forth the will of Yahweh, and they rose above mere divination and the giving of oracles, though some of their particular predictions might be closely related to this class of magic. Some of their intuitions about the future were inspired visions of the direction in which the religion of Yahweh must lead. (It is upon such intuitions that Christians base their claim that the prophets anticipated the messiahship of Jesus many centuries before his actual life. Needless to say, Jewish interpretation of the Hebrew Bible does not countenance such an exegesis. The Hebrew Bible cannot be taken without strain to point unequivocally at Christ, though belief that the life of Jesus completes in a discernible way the development of God's revelation in the Hebrew writings is surely not lacking in substance.)

Characteristics of Prophetic Experience

What was the nature of the prophetic experience, to which we referred? There was something sudden and unexpected in the prophets' callings, as though it was not of their own choosing. Even though they may, in some cases at least, have already been associated with cult-centers, they do not seem to have been prepared for the astonishing eruption of power into their lives that the experience of God involved. Consider Isaiah's vision:

> In the year that King Uzziah died I saw also the Lord sitting upon a throne, high and lifted up, and his train filled the temple.
> Above it stood the seraphims: each one had six wings; with two he covered his face, and with two he covered his feet, and with two he did fly.
> And one cried unto another, and said, Holy, holy, holy, is the Lord of hosts: the whole earth is full of his glory.
> And the posts of the door moved at the voice of him that cried, and the house was filled with smoke.
> Then said I, Woe is me! for I am undone; because I am a man of unclean lips, and I dwell in the midst of a people of unclean lips: for mine eyes have seen the King, the Lord of hosts.
> Then flew one of the seraphims unto me, having a live coal in his hand, which he had taken with the tongs from off the altar.
> And he laid it upon my mouth, and said, Lo, this hath touched thy lips; and thine iniquity is taken away, and thy sin purged.
> Also I heard the voice of the Lord, saying, Whom shall I send, and who will go for us? Then said I, Here am I; send me.[3]

There are features of the symbolism contained in this account which have not yet been fully explained. But what comes through is the power and holiness of the divine Being who thus revealed himself in Isaiah's experience. It is charac-

---

[3] Isaiah 6:1–8.

teristic too that the first reaction of Isaiah (and this is paralleled elsewhere in passages describing the encounter with God) is to say, "Woe is me!" Confronted by the holiness and majesty of Yahweh, the prophet feels himself in the sharpest possible way to be unclean, to be a sinner. And as he identifies himself with the whole people, the sinfulness is ascribed to them as well. Yet there is a polarity about the numinous God whom he here encounters. Through his very majesty and blinding purity (blinding, for Isaiah's eyes are darkened in the presence of God and the Temple seems filled with smoke), the divine Being arouses vividly the sense of sin: but through contact with his worshiper he brings purity and holiness to him. This purification, however, is not conceived *in vacuo*. There follows a call to Isaiah to preach his word.

The majesty of the God of Isaiah's experience helps explain what lies behind the anthropomorphic language used in much of the Bible concerning the wrath of God. Yahweh is often conceived as a jealous and angry deity. This at first sight is an unpleasant aspect of the vision of God drawn in these writings. But the sense of God's wrath is a way of symbolizing and expressing the dangerous nature of God's holiness and power. The prophet's experience of the gulf between God and man and of the sinfulness of the latter can make God seem terrible. The fierceness of certain prophetic denunciations of the people of Israel reflected holy fear, for God's nature was seen as so utterly other than the human condition. Quite possibly the prophets added their own angers and frustrations to this sense of the divine holiness—it is characteristic of religious people to project their own feelings onto the Deity: personal indignation and arrogance get confused with the activity of God, and the assurance faith provides can result in an unself-critical denunciation of the wickedness of other people. The prophets, to repeat a platitude, were human; this happened too with them. But the sense of the wrathful holiness of God was part of their religious experience, and it accorded with the ethical flavor of their teachings. This is well expressed in a passage from Amos:

Woe unto you that desire the day of the Lord! to what end is it for you? The day of the Lord is darkness, and not light. . . .

I hate, I despise your feast days, and I will not smell [sc. the offerings] in your solemn assemblies. Though ye offer me burnt-offerings and your meat-offerings, I will not accept them; neither will I regard the peace-offerings of your fat beasts. Take thou away from me the noise of thy songs; for I will not hear the melody of thine harps. But let judgment run down as waters, and righteousness as a mighty stream.[4]

[4] Amos 5:18, 21–24.

Here the Lord's anger is directed at the extensive sacrificial cult. Elsewhere too the prophets denounce religious formalism when it is not accompanied by justice and goodness. Cult practices were important, for they expressed the deference due to the great God, and offerings were a visible token of men's concern for Yahweh; nevertheless it was easy for worshipers to think that by going through the right motions and paying for ritual sacrifices they could escape deeper obligations. To turn men to their social and ethical obligations was the goal of the teachings of the prophets.

The political history of the Hebrew people is complex. Beset by periodic invasions from Assyria and Egypt and Babylonia as well as by internal discord, the twelve Hebrew tribes divided into rival kingdoms of Judah and Israel in the tenth century B.C. The Northern Kingdom, Israel, was destroyed by the Assyrian commanders of Sargon II in 722 B.C. The Southern Kingdom, Judah, was in its last, catastrophic days when Jeremiah had his call.

The Ethical Insight of Jeremiah

Jeremiah, whose ministry spanned the years between 626 B.C. to the fall of Jerusalem in 586 B.C., is important because he gave the ethical dimension of Hebrew religion new emphasis, making the ethical code incumbent upon each individual worshipper. Hitherto the moral side of religion, as expressed in the covenant with God, was considered primarily in collective terms: the prophets spoke to the people as a corporate, organic body. The sense of call is very strong in the Biblical account of the experience that inaugurated his career:

> Then the word of the Lord came unto me, saying: Before I formed thee in the belly, I knew thee; and before thou camest forth from the womb I sanctified thee, and I ordained thee a prophet unto the nations. Then said I, Ah, Lord God! behold I cannot speak, for I am a child. But the Lord said unto me, Say not, I am a child: for thou shalt go to all that I shall send thee, and whatsoever I command thee thou shalt speak. Be not afraid of their faces: for I am with thee to deliver thee, saith the Lord. Then the Lord put forth his hand and touched my mouth. And the Lord said unto me, Behold I have put my words in thy mouth.[5]

At a later point another significant experience occurred:

> Moreover the word of the Lord came unto me saying, Jeremiah, what seest thou? And I said, I see a rod of an almond-tree. Then the Lord said unto me, Thou hast well seen: for I will hasten my word to perform it.[6]

[5] Jeremiah 1:4–9.   [6] Jeremiah 1:11–12.

In the first passage, we note how a sense of destiny has unexpectedly come to Jeremiah. He is only a child (in fact he was a young man), who did not feel in himself the powers to be a prophet. But this was irrelevant. The Lord had "sanctified" him from his conception, and before, and the Lord would give him speech. Willy-nilly, and in the face of great opprobrium and disfavor, Jeremiah prophesied. His experience of seeing the twig of an almond tree in blossom during the wintry season was a sign of the revival of hope, through the prophet, even in the time of Israel's wintry period of destruction.

Jeremiah foresaw the demise of the nation, but he tried to stave it off by urging that Judah should succumb to Babylon without a disastrous struggling, a sentiment which caused him to be branded a traitor.

The Fall of Jerusalem

But the inevitable happened. Jerusalem was razed, the aristocracy of the Jewish nation were carried off to exile in Babylon, and a shattered remnant remained to deplore the disaster, including Jeremiah. Jeremiah's perception of the forthcoming tragedy led him to a reappraisal of the covenant between Yahweh and the nation. If the nation was shattered, did it not mean that the covenant no longer existed? Yahweh would make a new covenant, Jeremiah averred, in which the essential relationship of choice on either side would obtain between the individual and his God. No longer the nation, but now the individual person—this was unit with which the Lord would treat. Jeremiah's point was poetically expressed in the following words:

> In those days they shall say no more,
> The fathers have eaten sour grapes,
> And the children's teeth are set on edge;
> But everyone shall die for his own guilt—everyone who eats
> The sour grapes shall have his own teeth set on edge.[7]

This individualization of the God-man relationship was a vital contribution to the prophetic message. Nevertheless, the Jews who went to Babylon survived in their new environment partly because they remembered vividly their national heritage and continued to practice the religion of Yahweh as a group.

This was a critical time for the survival both of the nation and of the religion of Yahweh. It was fortunate that a half century later, on the collapse of the Babylonian empire and its replacement by Persian rule, Cyrus ordered the return of the Jews to Jerusalem. It was also fortunate that during the

[7] Jeremiah 31:29-31.

lamentable period in Babylon, they were not treated harshly or exterminated. They settled in the rich environs of Babylon, and both farmed and traded successfully. The Babylonian rulers were not so much concerned with genocide as with ensuring that Jewish independence was broken. Apart from Jerusalem the rest of Judah was not depopulated: the upper classes were removed, but the country folk, the cultivators of the soil, remained. Jerusalem bore the brunt of the defeat. The Temple was destroyed; the Ark of the Covenant was irretrievably lost; the walls were thrown down; the city was given over to arson and loot.

THE BABYLONIAN EXILE

Though the fate which befell the exiles was not the worst of disasters, their persistence as a national group, and the persistence of the cult of Yahweh nonetheless was an extraordinary phenomenon. The Northern Kingdom, after the Assyrian conquest, disappeared from history. Not so the Southern. The "lost tribes" no doubt became absorbed in the population of the conquerors; at any rate they have remained lost to the view of history. But the Babylonian exiles returned to their land in due course, having survived the great crisis. In order to explain this, it is necessary to look back to the reforms of King Josiah which preceded the destruction of the Southern Kingdom by a generation.

In 621 B.C., during some repairs to the Temple, a book was discovered corresponding to the substance of the present book of Deuteronomy. The king, having verified the authenticity of the work through a prophetess named Huldah, implemented its requirements. This involved a wholesale destruction of temples and images devoted to gods other than Yahweh. This thorough-going iconoclasm may not have spread through the whole of Judah, but it was impressive in its impact. Furthermore King Josiah centralized the cult of Yahweh itself and brought the priests into Jerusalem from numerous high places throughout the land. This had important consequences. The concentration of the sacrificial cult on a purified Temple cult may have been theoretically good, but it left a gap in the life of the local people who had been in contact with the shrines of Yahweh. It is probable that from this time we can see the rise of synagogue worship, which, of course, does not involve sacrificial procedures. At any rate, the reforms of Josiah meant that religion continued without direct reference to the central cult in Jerusalem and paved the way for the evolution of religious worship and teaching of a more informal kind among the exiles in Babylon. From this situation ultimately springs the common form of service which has come to characterize later and contemporary Judaism, which in turn has molded the shape of Christian worship.

Ezekiel

The Babylonian exiles continued the religion of Yahweh. Nostalgia for their lost home was a powerful factor in cementing a conservative tradition. Further, the exiles produced prophetic leaders, of whom Ezekiel was a notable example. He was of priestly family, and was much concerned with the hope of restoring sacrifices at Jerusalem. He accepted Jeremiah's view that man's essential relationship with God was a personal one, but he felt more was needed than words of repentance to make the sinner acceptable to God. Yahweh was distant, transcendent, holy: but the priestly ritual was a means of communication. The sinner could, through the administration of the cult, and through his repentance, gain purification and atonement. Ezekiel's burning vision of a future restoration and his faithful optimism were suited to the needs of the people whom he endeavored to lead. Without such hope, the community might have crumbled away and the inheritance of Israel might have been submerged.

Deutero-Isaiah

The other great figure of the period is anonymous. He is the person whom scholars have dubbed "Deutero-Isaiah," whose teachings are recorded in the latter part of the book of Isaiah from Chapter 40 onward. The disaster which had overtaken the nation of Israel must have puzzled many people because the prophets' warnings against national backsliding was not altogether borne out by the facts. To be sure the people's moral transgressions had been great, and faithfulness to Yahweh had diminished in pre-Exilic religion. But the children of Israel, for all their faults, knew more of the truth than the Babylonians who had destroyed their political power and uprooted the Temple. Deutero-Isaiah weighed these considerations against his conception of the Lord, and came to a new realization of which this poem is a magnificent expression:

> I am the Lord, and there is none else, there is no God besides me: I girded thee, though thou hast not known me, that they may know from the rising of the sun, and from the west, that there is none besides me. I am the Lord, and there is none else. I form the light, and create darkness; I make peace, and create evil; I the Lord do all these things. Drop down, ye heavens, from above, and let the skies pour down righteousness: let the earth open, and let them bring forth salvation, and let righteousness spring up together; I the Lord have created it.
> Woe unto him that striveth with his Maker! Let the potsherd strive with the

potsherds of the earth. Shall the clay say to him that fashioneth it, What makest thou? or thy work, He hath no hands?[8]

In Deutero-Isaiah's wider and exalted view of God's dealings in history, the Jews must no longer confine their gaze to themselves and their own transgressions, successes, and failures—and the significance of their present suffering could not be simply explained by their own unfaithfulness. In the famous "Servant Songs," the prophet presented a new picture of Israel's destiny. Israel was destined by God to be a "light to the Gentiles," and to lead all nations to the truth. She had faltered in this task, and therefore had to be punished, but this punishment was more than a chastisement. It was a purification and a vicarious sacrifice. Through the suffering of the Servant-people, all nations would be caused, through sympathy, compassion, and a perception of the righteousness of God, to turn toward the new Jerusalem. There the restored Israel would enter into a period of fruitfulness and joy. Salvation would spread abroad to all the corners of the world. The evils of present existence would disappear, and good would triumph.

In such ways, the prophet combined the idea of a restoration, which nurtured the faith of the exiles, with a profound message concerning the nature of what it meant to be the chosen people. The condition of being "chosen" was not a status granting Israel privileges and help in war. It was a role that led through suffering to the enlightenment of the world. The Suffering Servant idea provided a pattern for Jesus and the Christian interpretation of his self-sacrifice and has remained one of the deeper insights of the ancient Jewish heritage. It conferred a new perspective on the Jews' understanding of their own destiny.

The Return from Exile

In 538 B.C. Babylon was conquered by the Persian-Median king Cyrus. For the Hebrews the Babylonian captivity was ended. Despite great hopes, however, the restoration of the exiles to their homeland was in many ways a disappointment. Not all of the exiles did return in fact: some preferred to stay in their new farms and businesses. Those who returned found Jerusalem a desolate and melancholy sight. They erected an altar on the ruins of the Temple and planned eagerly for a rebuilding of the edifice, but the problems were disheartening, and the task was not taken in hand. The surrounding countryside, where the exiles settled, was not altogether friendly. Those who had been spared exile had taken over the property left by the banished upper classes,

[8] Isaiah 45:5–9.

and had retained it for fifty years. They resented the claims of the returned exiles. It was more than a decade after the return before the prophets Haggai and Zechariah stimulated a fresh wave of energy and engineered the rebuilding of the Temple. Even then it was not restored in the full pattern of its former glory. The succeeding century was a despondent one; the golden promises of return from exile had failed painfully.

POST-EXILIC REFORM

A new phase of Jewish history commenced in the middle of the fourth century. A new injection of life came from within the Jewish community that had stayed in Babylon. The scribe Ezra, who was of priestly descent, and the governor Nehemiah were together responsible for a thoroughgoing reform of the Judaean state. Artaxerxes I Longimanus, the Persian king, empowered Ezra to start these reforms as a measure of political security for his regime. (The presence of the Jews constituted a useful buffer state, which was the motive for Cyrus' resettlement of them at the conclusion of the Exile.) The new regime was thoroughly theocratic. With considerable severity the two reformers sought to root out customs which were not regarded as being in accord with the Torah. During the Exile and after, a considerable literary activity had taken place, partly with the aim of preserving the people's traditions in a time of stress. This formed the basis of an enlarged and detailed code which could give shape to the daily life of a priest-governed community. The Torah was publicly read to the people, and was given the status of the norm for social and private behavior. Jews were required to put away foreign wives; intermarriage with outsiders was banned; sabbath observance was strictly enforced; the dietary laws were likewise enforced. Synagogue worship was encouraged, and the scriptures were read and expounded there. The people pledged themselves anew to the covenant and to the keeping of the Law. The old festivals were restored. The government was in the hands of the chief priest, and below him ranged a complex organization of priests and scribes. The latter class were important, since their task was the interpretation and collection of the sacred writings. Those who could preach functioned in the synagogues as rabbis, who explained the sacred texts and teachings to the people. Such a theocratic state was not imposed without opposition. In particular, the injunction against foreign wives met violent opposition. But gradually a new pattern of life, regulated by the details of the Law, established itself in the nation.

Different estimates can be given of this phase of Jewish history. The equation of the Torah with what was found in sacred texts may have promoted legalism; but it also served to temper the power of the state through the regulations of a supramundane authority. The concern with the details of purification, expiation, and the social code may have been cramping; but they provided a tough vehicle for safeguarding the Jewish experience. The government may have been theocratic, but it adhered to the ethical monotheism of the prophets and the tradition of Moses. The exclusiveness of the community may have been inward-looking, but it was a period of peaceful rule under Persian suzerainty. It may have been unexciting, but the Jews had had disagreeable excitements enough. It was also a time of great literary industry, in which the Bible as we know it began to take definitive shape. In a small corner of the world, the religion of Yahweh was ensured perpetuation. The patterns and ceremonies of later Judaism were distinctively established.

JUDAISM IN THE HELLENISTIC ERA

The sweeping successes of Alexander the Great in the latter part of the fourth century B.C., which resulted in the overthrow of the Persian Empire, brought new influences to bear upon the Jewish community. Already, of course, the many Jews settled in Alexandria were well aware of the force of Hellenistic culture; but now the settlement of Greek colonies in Palestine, and the bringing of the state under the sway of Greek dynasties, meant that Greek ideas began increasingly to permeate the thinking of the Jews. We can see traces of this in some of the material included in Proverbs (though a lot of the latter is of high antiquity) and in Ecclesiastes. The way of life of the Greek colonists, though it was—or because it was—relatively easygoing, was not unattractive; Greek rationalism too had its appeal. It was in Alexandria that the chief confluence, at the cultural level, of Judaism and Hellenism took place. In the third century, the translation into Greek of the Hebrew scriptures was undertaken there. The translation was known as the Septuagint (literally "Seventy") since it was supposedly written by a panel of seventy translators. It is noteworthy that by this period the Hebrew of the sacred writings did not correspond to ordinary speech. In Palestine itself the language was Aramaic, while the Jews of Alexandria tended to speak Greek. The latter language was the international tongue of the day, even in Palestine itself.

Philo

The most signal result of the intermingling of Jewish and Greek culture was the thought of Philo (c. 20 B.C. to c. 50 A.D.). His philosophic thought was expressed in, among other writings, a series of commentaries upon the Pentateuch, in which he sought to give a Platonist interpretation to the Jewish faith. His religious interests were mystical in character. The highest life, according to him, was one of contemplation in which one experiences the presence of

God. God himself is an utterly transcendent Being, who makes himself known to the individual through his Logos, or Word (the term used later in St. John's Gospel in the opening verses), which is the archetypal pattern comprising the Platonic Forms through which the world is created. Through his intellect, man has an affinity with the divine Being and can experience him in contemplation. But this itself requires the work of God's grace. In accordance with Platonist and mystical ideas, Philo expounds a negative theology: the divine Being is beyond the ordinary affirmations men can make. In his ineffable glory God exists as the goal of the contemplative's quest. It will at once be apparent that Philo was philosophically incapable of viewing the Hebrew scriptures literally. A characteristic feature of his method, therefore, was the allegorical interpretation of the Pentateuch. Thus for him, Abraham's journey and the Exodus were not simple historical events; they were allegories of the journeying of the soul toward God. Anthropomorphic descriptions of Yahweh were likewise played down and reinterpreted by this method of exegesis.

Philo's emphasis on mysticism and on allegorical exegesis influenced Christian writers, and inspired medieval Jewish mysticism, but they were in fact quite a considerable departure from the spirit of the Hebrew Bible. Philo, however, sought a Biblical precedent for contemplative mysticism in the experiences of the prophets. Their ecstatic states seemed to him to correspond to the interior vision of the Uncreated which was the object of his religious quest.

PROPHECY AND MYSTICISM

Philo offers a useful point at which to pause and consider the differences between prophetic and mystical religious experience.

First, the mystic looks within, into his own soul and beyond. In this imageless state he experiences something ineffable and blissful. But the prophet, such as Isaiah, has a vision that seems exterior to himself. It is true that he may then feel himself possessed by the Deity: but in his vision the Deity stands numinously over against him—"I am a man of unclean lips" —and in this overwhelming experience his difference from the Holy One is very sharply emphasized.

Second, mysticism can occur, as in Theravada Buddhism and elsewhere, in a context where there is no concept of a Creator God and where the experience is not brought directly in relationship to, or interpreted as, an experience of any deity or numinous being. But it is nonsense to try to conceive of a prophetic experience which does not involve such a concept. Of course, mystics often find in their own experience a strong intimation of the divine presence operating inwardly. But this is not universal.

Third, the language of the prophet, and especially of the prophets of the

Hebrew tradition, is strongly personal, even anthropomorphic ("And the Lord said unto me," etc.), while contemplative language is frequently impersonal (Philo speaks of God's essence and of the Logos, for instance).

Fourth, the Jewish prophets taught a way of life that was powerfully dynamic and activist; typically, though not universally, the mystic aims at stilling activity (thus Philo admired the monastic life of the Therapeutae near Alexandria, with which he was acquainted). There is nothing of monastic withdrawal in the Hebrew Bible.

These points help to bring out something of the character of the religion of the ancient Jews and of the prophetic movement. Interweaving the numinous and the ethical, they opened a window onto the transcendent world which displayed the dynamism, personality, and historical concern of Yahweh.

JEWISH BELIEFS

So far we have said little of the doctrinal aspects of ancient Judaism, beyond the ideas implicit in the teachings of Moses and the prophets. Since it was during the Greek period that the bulk of the Hebrew Bible was completed, this is a suitable point at which to turn to some of the key ideas about God and man that had emerged by this time. Of course, the Bible itself was not intended as a statement of doctrine, and it would be more proper to say that mythological statements about God are contained there. Doctrines devolved through the writings of scribes and rabbis who commented on the sacred writings, and who formulated the theological viewpoint for reflective Jews of the period.

First and foremost, of course, there was the doctrine of God. Though Yahweh's self-revealing activity was intimately related to the history of Israel, Yahweh was no merely ethnic God (though at early times he may have been thought of in this way). In the magnificent account of him given by Deutero-Isaiah he is the Lord and Creator of all.

Creation

This conception was summed up in the poem which constitutes the opening of the Hebrew Bible—the story of the creation of the world by God from Genesis.

> In the beginning God created the heaven and the earth. And the earth was without form and void; and darkness was upon the face of the deep; and the Spirit of God moved on the face of the waters. And God said, Let there be light: and there was light. And God saw the light that it was good: and God divided the light from the darkness . . . And God said, Let there be a firmament in the midst of the waters: and let it divide the

waters from the waters. And God made the firmament, and divided the waters which were under the firmament from the waters which were above the firmament: and it was so. And God called the firmament Heaven . . . And God said, Let the waters under the heaven be gathered together into one place, and let the dry land appear: and it was so. And God called the dry land Earth; and the gathering together of the waters called he Seas: and God saw that it was good. . . .[9]

There are traces in this story of earlier myths about the Creator's struggle with chaos (the primeval waters), as in the Babylonian creation story. But the polytheistic elements have been excluded, or transformed in the Genesis poem. It proclaims a direct and single power at work in God's creation of the world: "God said, Let there be. . . ." Solely by the operation of his command the world springs into existence: the created order does not in itself contain nor does it struggle against a darker, evil, and chaotic force. Creation is repeatedly described as good.

The Hebrew Cosmos

If the account of God's creative activity sets the Hebrew conception in sharp contrast with the legends of the surrounding milieu, the Hebrew cosmology itself is not original. The earth was thought of as floating on the waters, somewhat like an upturned boat. Above the earth existed a structure known as the firmament, which had vents in it through which the rain came down. This presupposed a body of celestial waters. Below the surface of the earth (though this is not brought out in the Genesis creation narrative) there was the region of the dead, Sheol, a somewhat shadowy place. Thus the cosmos appears to have three levels; above there is heaven, then earth, then a lower region below the earth. Hence, in the symbolism of the Hebrew Bible and of the New Testament, a person, like Elijah, who is taken up into heaven *ascends,* and one who goes to the region of the dead *descends.* But it would be a mistake to think that this three-decker universe was always taken in a literal fashion. God may have been thought of as dwelling in his heaven beyond the firmament, but he was more importantly an invisible, spiritual Being active everywhere, yet distinct from the creation in which and through which he operated.

The creation poem itself introduces a narrative that merges imperceptibly into the history of Israel through the stories of Adam, the Flood, and Abraham. Thus the activity of God in creation and the activity of God in history are parts of a single process. This is one of the reasons why the Hebrew conception of God's creative work entails a dependence of the world upon God to an extent scarcely paralleled elsewhere in the religious thought of

[9] Genesis 1:1–10.

mankind. If creation occurs through a distinct act of will by God, similar to a decisive action in human history, this means that the world is contingent: it might or might not have existed. God by his own unconditioned choice brought it into existence. And there was no preexistent matter that God used to fashion the world, such as the Demiurge Plato posits in *Timaeus*. One might safely use a much later theological concept to describe the Hebrew doctrine —God created *ex nihilo,* "out of nothing." The world and its details were absolutely the result of his choice.

In the second chapter of Genesis there appears another account of the creation of man that has cruder elements: God makes clay statuettes and breathes life into them, somewhat in the style of the Egyptian myth of Chnum. But the crucial part of the story lies in the mysterious account of man's first disobedience. We have seen that in the *Epic of Gilgamesh* and elsewhere, the gods jealously withhold the secret of immortality from man. Gilgamesh obtained the secret life-giving plant, but was robbed of it by an accident; Adapa too was tricked of this blessing. What is characteristic of the story of Adam (meaning "Man"—he stands as the symbol and embodiment of the human race) is that the Fall occurs through a mysterious moral choice. Man was destined for a life in harmony with God, but in asserting his independence he became alienated from the life with God.

Doctrine of Human Life

Humans were conceived of in the Bible as psychophysical entities whose body and spirit were indivisible. In general, it was life in this world, rather than in the next, that formed the focus of Hebrew concerns. Serving God is an activity enjoined here and now, in the ongoing vicissitudes of ordinary life. One reason for this comparative lack of preoccupation with the next life lay in the fact that over a very long period it was the destiny of Israel, rather than of the individual, that concerned the religious thinkers of the Jewish people. The nation was the organic unit with whom God had dealings. We have seen that during the Exile there was a vivid expectation of a coming era of blessedness for the nation. The hopes of the Jews were fastened on the possibility of a national restoration, when Israel would become a light to illuminate the world. For them salvation, so to say, had an historical dimension. They beleived that just as the Fall occurred in the earliest period, so redemption would occur at the end of history. The growth of these ideas in the post-Exilic period were undoubtedly influenced by Persian, and in particular Zoroastrian, belief. Already the prophets had spoken of a Day of Yahweh when enemies would be overthrown and when a new kingdom would be established under a king belonging to the house of David. This political projection came to be replaced by the notion of a cosmic salvation, in which a deliverer, the Messiah, would descend to deliver the righteous. Integrated into this hope was that of the resurrection of the dead to a gloried life. (It is noteworthy that resurrection, rather than disembodied immortality in heaven, fitted in with the Hebrew conception of man.)

APOCALYPTIC WRITINGS

These beliefs were expressed in a collection of apocalyptic writings written toward the end of the pre-Christian era. One of these was the Book of Daniel, that had historical roots in the period of persecution which gave rise to the war for Jewish independence in the early part of the second century B.C. The problem—the persistent problem—for the Jewish religious thinker was the suffering which the people underwent despite their efforts to be loyal to Yahweh. The writer of *Daniel* outlined a view of history that attempted to account for this fact. He suggested that in the present era, God has granted some power to the forces of evil, for reasons which remain obscure; these evil forces oppose God's will and threaten to undermine his people, Israel. But through Israel God is preparing a final consummation of history. In one of Daniel's visions he sees strange and monstrous beasts, representing the world powers. These monsters are destroyed by the power and presence of the Most High. And then comes the final vision:

> I saw in the night visions, and behold, one like the Son of man came with the clouds of heaven, and came to the Ancient of days, and they brought him near before him. And there was given him dominion, and glory, and a kingdom, that all people, nations, and languages, should serve him: his dominion is an everlasting dominion, which shall not pass away, and his kingdom, that which shall not be destroyed.[10]

The apocalyptic writings show that Jewish thought turned increasingly toward the hope of a Messiah, an Anointed One, who would restore a newer and more glorious kingdom, and who would be the instrument of the salvation of the nation. In the vision of a restored kingdom, the Hebrew writers found a solution to the problem of evil on the national level. The question, Why has God treated Israel in this manner, when she is the Chosen People? was given a suprahistoric answer.

The Problem of Evil

But the problem of suffering and evil was an intensely personal one, and received its classical expression in the Hebrew scriptures in the Book of Job, dating from the fifth century B.C. To Job's dire sufferings, no solution is

[10] Daniel 7:13–15.

offered. His complaints are seemingly justified, and the attempts by his com-forters to explain God's ways in a reasonable manner are unacceptable to God. But Job in his complaints had reckoned without the majesty and power of the Lord. It is in the perception of this awful majesty that the argument finally rests. It is described in a passage that echoes a principle theme of prophetic experience—the overwhelming and numinous character of the Being who irrupts into Job's consciousness:

> Then the Lord answered Job out of the whirlwind, and said, Who is this that darkeneth counsel with words without knowledge? Gird up thou thy loins like a man: for I will demand of thee, and answer thou me. Where wast thou when I laid the foundations of the earth? declare, if thou hast understanding. Who hath laid the measures thereof, if thou knowest? or who hath stretched the line upon it? Whereupon are the foundations thereof fastened? or who hath laid the corner-stone thereof: when the morning stars sang together, and all the sons of God shouted for joy? Or who shut up the sea with doors, when it brake forth, as if it had issued out of the womb? . . . Canst thou draw out leviathan with an hook? or his tongue with a cord which thou lettest down? Canst thou put an hook into his nose? or bore his jaw through with a thorn?[11]

In a whole series of imperious questions, God hammers home his majesty. Job can but reply: "I have uttered that I understood not; things too wonderful for me, which I knew not."

Satan and Demonic Power

The idea of the existence of evil powers did go some way toward explaining the disasters of the world, and the struggles that righteousness and loyalty continually had to face. Of course, the Hebrews in the earliest times had a concept of such hostile forces, as had other peoples at the same level of development (though the Genesis narrative merely employed a serpent as a cunning, evil, and dangerous creature). But such animistic beings were not conceived as united. In Zechariah, of the sixth century, there is mention of Satan, a supreme evil power under whom is ranged a hierarchy of demons. Balancing the demons were the angels—those spirits who functioned as the mes-sengers and executives of Yahweh. The angels came to possess their own hierar-chical ordering, under the seven archangels. Thus the Hebrew thinkers increasingly saw the world as a battlefield where the forces of good opposed the forces of evil. Such a dualism suggests the dominance of Persian thought forms. The demons—against whom talismans and spells could under certain circum-

[11] Job 38:1–8 and 41:1–2.

stances be effective—reflected the persistence of polytheistic ways of thinking. The supremacy of Satan over the demons was, in a certain sense, advantageous to monotheistic belief in that only God could overcome so powerful a figure. The piecemeal technology of superstition whereby men had tried to ward off, or propitiate, evil powers had to be superseded by loyalty to God in his struggle. The advantage was ambiguous, in the sense that the figure of Satan introduced a drastic limitation on the contemporary power of the one God, even though in the end, at the consummation of history, the latter would emerge as complete victor.

End of Post-Exilic Period

By the end of the post-Exilic period Hebrew theology had clearly established its monotheism. It had been a phase of transition, during which the remarkable and powerful teachings of the great prophets fixed firmly in the Hebrew imagination what had been implicit from much earlier times—the sovereignty and righteousness of God. Their own experiences of Yahweh's irruption into their consciousness and their lives reinforced teachings from the time of Moses. The preservation of this belief in one God, and the expression of loyalty to him, was ensured through the ongoing ritual of the temple and worship of the synagogue. Partly through the work of those who were assembling, revising, and editing the Hebrew scriptures, the faith was purged of polytheistic and idolatrous elements, and it was firmly tied to the historical experience of Israel.

At the same time, the period saw the rise of new forces—the influence of Zoroastrianism, and the molding of new ideas within the Hebrew crucible: ideas of a future consummation of history, of a Messianic kingdom, and of the resurrection of the dead.

If in earlier times, the religion of Yahweh had been seen in the perspective of ancient events, now it was seen too in the perspective of the future. The prophetic concept of the Day of the Lord was given new depth in vision such as that of Daniel. God's righteousness and goodness would be made manifest in a cosmic manner at some time in history when evil would be overcome and judgment made. Though the Jews never lost sight of the political vision of a vindicated and prosperous state of Israel, they also began to see the victory in heavenly terms.

THE MACCABEAN REVOLT

The continuing sufferings of the Hebrew people gave urgency to their apocalyptic hopes. During the second century, Antiochus Epiphanes, the Hellenistic monarch of Syria, all but strangled the Jewish faith in the interests of Hellenizing this somewhat recalcitrant nation. He forbade Jewish ritual and set up a pagan altar in the Temple. In a systematic manner he attempted to eradicate the Jewish heritage which had become so well established during the theocratic period. He could not have foreseen the bitterness of the opposition or the effectiveness of the revolt which his actions sparked off. Under the military leadership of Judas Maccabaeus, the Jewish rebels fought off and defeated the Syrian forces, and in 165 B.C. captured Jerusalem (except for the fortified citadel). The Syrians were slowly ground down and forced to concede Jewish independence. After Judas' death in 161 B.C., the leadership was carried on by his brother Jonathan, and later by a third brother, Simon. The succession then passed to Simon's son, John Hyrcanus, who pushed north and added Idumea, Samaria, and other areas to the kingdom. Under the Maccabaeans the nation entered on another phase of independence, which lasted until 37 B.C., when Herod, with Roman help, occupied the throne, acting virtually as a Roman puppet. The nation which had proudly expelled its oppressors a short while before now had to bow to foreign sway. Many people were deeply antagonistic to Hellenistic customs while others, less strict, adapted themselves to new ways as had the Hebrews in Babylon. As always in Hebrew history political allegiance and religious conviction were intermixed. Various alliances came into being representing a wide range of religious attitudes. Strictly, one could not call them "parties," certainly not in the modern organizational sense. They were fluid groups, and many folk stood outside them. But they illustrated the different responses appropriate to the Jewish situation of the times.

SADDUCEES, ZEALOTS, AND ESSENES

Politically, the Sadducees were the most influential: in the main, they controlled the Council (Gerousia, or Sanhedrin) which assisted the high priest in the administration of the country and of the faith (though it should be remembered that during the Roman period their power was limited to religious, rather than civil, matters). The Sadducees were religiously conservative, rejecting as innovations some of the new doctrines about the resurrection of the dead, etc., and appealing to the written Torah—the Law and the Prophets—as their authority. They controlled the system of tithing, whereby contributions were exacted for the maintenance of the Temple. This source of power was one which could scarcely be preserved if there were a head-on clash with the Roman government, hence they favored a peaceful coexistence with Rome. Their position, therefore, was diametrically opposed to that of the Zealots (so called because of the zeal for the Law that they displayed), who urged violent resistance to external rule. In 6 A.D., a Zealot revolt occurred under the leadership of a certain Judas of Galilee, which was stamped out ruthlessly by the

Romans. The movement, however, continued. The Zealots held strong Messianic views, and considered that rebellion would help to usher in the new age. It is possible that the community at Qumran, where the famous Dead Sea Scrolls were discovered in 1947, was a Zealot one, though a balance of opinion considers that it belonged to the group known as the Essenes.

The latter group, unlike the other parties which we have considered, which were directly involved in the main stream of the political life of the nation, formed a community that withdrew from the world and lived a life somewhat analogous to that of Christian monasticism. They were much influenced by apocalyptic writings, such as are contained in the books of Enoch and Jubilees, and confidently expected the early coming of the Messiah. Goods were shared in common, and the life of the group was regulated strictly according to the observances of the Torah. The emphasis lay on repentance and an ascetic life vastly different from the corruption found in the world at large. The community seems to have devoted intensive study to the scriptures (if one can identify Qumran with an Essene settlement) and amassed a considerable library of scriptures and other writings. The other-worldly atmosphere of the movement contrasted strongly with the main emphasis of the Jewish tradition hitherto.

Dead Sea Scrolls

Some important documents have been recovered from the site of the Qumran community by the Dead Sea. Among them, *The War of the Sons of Light and the Sons of Darkness* expresses some of the apocalyptic hopes of the Qumran community, which considered itself to be following the way of the Sons of Light; the Prince of Light, to whom they owed allegiance, was engaged in combat with the power of evil, the Prince of Darkness.

A fairly full description of Essene beliefs is found in the Jewish historian Josephus (first century A.D.), and it is perhaps not surprising to discover, in view of the Essene asceticism, that they held that the soul is immortal and distinct from the corruptible body. In this life, it is entangled with the body, but on death it will be released to fly upward to a heavenly existence (though the spirits of the wicked, being still contaminated, will sink down to punishment). As often elsewhere, asceticism goes with a belief in the separation of body and soul. It may well be that the Essene doctrines were in this influenced by Greek ascetic thought as exhibited by, for instance, Orphism.

THE PHARISEES

A fourth movement of great importance was that of the Pharisees (a word possibly derived from *perushim,* meaning "the separated"—i.e. those who were separated from pagan customs). Like the Essenes, their chief interest lay in religion rather than politics. But unlike the latter they did not withdraw from the world. They believed in the cultivation of personal piety through observance of the Law, both written and unwritten. That is, they did not merely bind themselves to the scriptural expression of the Torah, but also to the interpretations put upon it through the work of the scribes. In general the scribes and rabbis belonged to the Pharisaic party; while the top people in the priestly hierarchy belonged to the Sadducees. Thus the Pharisees were enabled to enjoy a considerable degree of popular support. Despite their puritanical tendencies, they were not religiously conservative, and believed strongly in such doctrines as the resurrection of the dead, the last judgment, the coming in of a new age in which the present order (and with it that order with which the Sadducees compromised) would be swept away. To the Pharisaic movement belonged the two great teachers of the period, Hillel and Shammai.

Herod, after assuming the kingship of Judea, rebuilt the Temple in magnificent style—it had fallen into disrepair since the time of the post-Exilic restoration. But the new building was not to last more than a century. Judea was annexed directly by the Romans in 6 A.D. The government of Pontius Pilate often offended Jewish national and religious feelings. The corruption and violence of the provincial Roman officials, and the sending of legionaries, bearing the imperial images on their standards, into the Holy City were affronts to Jewish sensibility.

THE END OF THE JEWISH NATION

It was in this unhappy and explosive atmosphere that Jesus attracted the hopes of many who were looking for the establishment of a new, free political kingdom. Though he turned his back on a political interpretation of the redemption of Israel, there were Zealots who still carried on the organization of revolt. In 66 A.D., relations between the Jewish people and their Roman overseers had worsened. Rebellion broke out. The Pharisees were opposed to violence of this kind as they had been in the lifetime of Jesus too, but the Zealot message had won wide allegiance among people who felt themselves humiliated and in danger of losing their traditions. The war was bloody and lasted four years; for the Jewish people it was a tragic disaster. In the year 70 Jerusalem fell to the army of Titus. Loot and slaughter culminated in the burning of the Temple itself. The Jewish nation was destroyed, the sacrificial cultus suppressed forever. Thousands of Jews fled to join their fellow-religionists elsewhere throughout the Mediterranean and Middle Eastern world. The great Dispersion of the Jews swelled the ranks of those who had already left their homeland; but now there was scarcely a homeland left. It is true that in the country areas and the hills a remnant, which included many active Zealots, stayed on. A center of rabbinic teaching was founded at Jabneh, on the coast, to continue the exposition of the Torah. Slowly there emerged the possibility of national reconstruction. However, a final revolt, by Simon bar Kochba in 132 A.D., was crushed by order of the emperor Hadrian. The country was largely depopulated; the Jews were forbidden to practice their religion; thousands were martyred testifying to it. It was from this period that the rule was promulgated that a Jew might violate any of the commandments of the Torah in order to escape death, saving only those which forbade idolatry, murder, and adultery. This was a rule which was destined to become the principle which Jews have followed in many periods of persecution, all down the centuries until the present time.

But the Jewish religion survived these terrible blows. The reasons were two-fold. First, from the time of the Exile, the evolution of Jewish worship in the synagogue made personal religion independent of the sacrificial cult of the Temple. Though his hopes might have been fastened on Jerusalem, the individual Jew could continue to worship God even after the earthly Jerusalem had been stripped of its Temple and made into a Roman town. Second, the reverence for the Torah gave a center to the Jewish way of life which was not disastrously affected by the terrible events of the first and second centuries A.D. It provided the Jew with a holy pattern of living he could follow in exile and adversity. Also, its detailed interpretation effectively set the Jews apart from those who might recognize a similar ethic. Just as the Pharisees in the Greek and Roman periods were men who were "separated" from the world, though living in it, so the Jews of the Dispersion were separated from their non-Jewish neighbors, though living among them. The Torah was the instrument by which the social identity of the Jewish people was preserved in a most remarkable way over many centuries.

THE CANON OF HEBREW SCRIPTURE

During the period after the fall of Jerusalem the Jewish scholars who remained in Palestine set about formulating and gathering together the heritage of Rabbinic teaching which formed the core of the Pharisaic movement. It was of prime importance to them that the Law in all its detail should not be lost in the Dispersion and that their religious inheritance should not be diminished. Various writings—first those concerned with juridical regulations, then those embodying stories, legends, and teachings drawn from the traditions of the greatest rabbis—were formed into a corpus of writings.

This development in Palestine had its complement in Babylon where there existed a continuous line of scholars going back to the Exile. By the end of the sixth century A.D. these writings were brought together and completed in the voluminous work known as the Talmud. This has remained down the centuries the source both of inspiration and detailed exegesis of the scriptures.

The canon of scripture including nearly all the books of the Hebrew Bible as we now know it was given authority in 90 A.D. by a council of rabbis. A few writings were not approved until 135 A.D. The scholars hotly debated whether or not the Song of Songs, Ecclesiastes, and some other writings should be included in the canon. The decision to include them reflects the power of the progressive Pharisaism and the men who followed the tradition of Hillel. As a result of including these works as sacred writings, certain ideas such as resurrection of the dead, which had been resisted by the Sadducees, now became part of the required faith of Judaism. The completion of the canon meant that henceforth the scriptural norm was fixed and final.

The Talmud

The Talmud, with its interpretations of scripture, provided the structure of Jewish belief and ethics that has persisted down to modern Judaism. It is continuous in its teachings with the beliefs incorporated in the Bible, but often it gives these ideas sharper definition. Thus in the Rabbinic teaching we find references to the future life. The Bible itself speaks of *gehenna,* the burning pit; in the Rabbinic interpretation this is a place of punishment where the unrighteous are punished and purged of their sins. By contrast there exists the *gan eden,* the garden of delight, where the blessed enjoy the glorious effulgence of the *Shechinah,* or divine Presence. Salvation is primarily for those of Israel, but Gentiles who have obeyed the Law and refrained from idolatry are granted a share in the life to come, for they are counted as Israelites. Definition, too, is given to the concept of the Messiah. For the pious Jew who follows Talmudic teaching there is no question of the Messiah's being some kind of divine Being (as Christian belief would suggest). He is a mortal who will bring about the establishment of the Kingdom of God: but it is a kingdom on earth, not in heaven. A restored Israel, in its earthly homeland, will lead the nations in an era of peace, righteousness, and prosperity.

Together with such doctrinal matters, the Talmud includes a large body of ethical and ritual injunctions which give shape to the Law in practice. The ritual side of Judaism had developed in ways adapted to the new situation of the Dispersion. The main festivals, however, all are traceable back to the ancient tradition. Chief among these is the feast of the Passover, commemorating the time of deliverance from Egypt. The ancient custom of sacrificing a paschal lamb, however, was discontinued at the time of the Dispersion, and since then the observance has centered on the Seder feast, in which a ritual meal is accompanied by readings that narrate the story of the Exodus. Another important holy day is that of Yom Kippur, the Feast of the Atonement.

Fasting and penitence are enjoined, that the faithful may turn themselves toward renewed efforts in righteousness. Less serious and more joyous are the Festivals of Lights and of Lots (Hanukka and Purim), the one in December, the other in late February. The Festival of Lights commemorates the restoration and rededication of the Temple by Judas Maccabaeus in 165 B.C.; the latter celebrates Esther's act in saving the Jews from persecution in 480 B.C. The holy days punctuate the Jewish year by social and ritual events which give it rhythm and stability. They help to express in solemn and joyful ways the chief events of Jewish history and form an indispensable part of the pattern of life that is controlled by the dictates of the Law.

MEDIEVAL JEWISH THOUGHT

Through the observance of the Talmudic code, the Jews retained cohesion as a social group. Except in bad periods of persecution, this never meant that they were cut off from the life of the wider world around them, and many of the most fruitful aspects of later Jewish culture and religious thought result from this interplay of an ancient faith with its non-Jewish environment. Especially in the medieval period did the cross-fertilization of Jewish thought with Greek and Arabic ideas produce extraordinary intellectual and spiritual achievements.

Saadya ben Joseph

Somewhat reminiscent of Philo, though more orthodox than Philo, was the so-called "father of Jewish philosophy," Saadya ben Joseph of Fayyum of Egypt (892–942 A.D.), who became head of the Jewish academy in Babylon. Saadya was a keen defender of the Jewish belief in one God as against alternative metaphysical and religious positions of his day. Yet he opposed an attempted reform movement within Judaism that sought authority from the Torah—bypassing the Talmud—to authenticate rigorous application of discarded social and ritual regulations. This movement, Karaism, had become widely influential: it was literalistic in the treatment of the scriptures ("an eye for an eye" was taken to mean exactly what it says) and it was individualistic. Saadya wished to show how far some of the injunctions of the Karaites were from the real spirit of the Bible, and so undertook a translation of the Bible into the current Arabic. More ambitiously, he attempted to show the congruence between reason and revelation. In this endeavor Saadya reflected the philosophical revolution taking place in the Muslim world and the impact of the thought of ancient Greek philosophers whose writings were currently being translated into Arabic. He argued forcibly for the freedom of the will, the soul's immortality, and its reunion with the body at the time of the resurrection, and the incorporeality and immateriality of God. He reinterpreted some portions of scriptures in a figurative way. In such ways, Saadya developed a rationalism which, though it was thoroughly Jewish (unlike the doctrines of Philo), gave system, coherence, and plausibility to the teachings of the faith.

Maimonides

From the tenth century onward the center of intellectual ferment shifted to Islamic Spain. In the following century a number of the Jewish scholars of Babylon emigrated to Spain to escape oppression by the invading Seljuk Turks. In the thirteenth century a wave of Moslem persecution in Spain itself had forced many Jewish scholars and others to flee from that country. The greatest figure of the Spanish school of Hebrew theology was Moses ben Maimon (1135–1204 A.D.), though actually his chief philosophical works were written in Cairo where he took up residence years after his native Cordova was captured by the fanatical Muslim Almohads. In his great work *Guide to the Perplexed,* Maimonides brought the philosophy of Aristotle to bear on the problems of theism.

Saadya had defended the doctrine of the creation. Other Spanish theologians, Maimonides' predecessors, had argued energetically that the world was created a finite time ago. But Maimonides held that this could not be proven, and that the philosophic arguments employed to establish the existence of God—arguments such as those contained in the writings of Aristotle—could also support the thesis that the world is everlasting. That the cosmos is eternal should not disturb the religious man, Maimonides counseled: the important truth is that the world depends upon God's will. Here Maimonides took exception to Aristotle's view of the relation between the world and God, since Aristotle merely treated God as first cause. A more personal picture was needed, and Maimonides found this in the notion of the Supreme Craftsman of Plato's *Timaeus,* who shapes the world. Thus, according to the Jewish philosopher, the world has existed from eternity because God has willed its existence from eternity. Maimonides did not believe in an eternally preexistent material, after the manner of Plato's Demiurge: he saw the world as created from nothing, as continuously and absolutely dependent upon God's will. But despite Maimonides' desire to stress the importance of the notion of God's divine will, he was equally concerned to work out a theology that would give proper expression to God's transcendence without the crudities of anthropomorphism. He did this through a form of "negative theology": one may ascribe perfections to God by analogy with the perfections one observes in the world and in men, but these must be understood in a negative way; that God is wise does not mean that he is wise as a man is wise—the nature of God's perfection in this respect is unknowable; on the other hand, it is correct to call God wise, in order to deny that he is unwise. Maimonides' determination to avoid an-thropomorphism in thinking about the exalted nature of the Deity meant that he, like Saadya, was not inclined to a literalistic interpretation of the scriptures.

Maimonides wrote extensively about the ethical side of God's nature and about the commandments, which he sought to explain according to rational principles. But the center of his religious viewpoint lay in the knowledge of God. This was, for him, the great thing about the prophets—they had attained knowledge of God. Such knowledge in principle is open to all who will train himself morally and strive for the right intellectual insight. He saw God's self-revelation to the prophets not as an irruption into the natural course of events; the prophetic experience could happen at anytime if men were sufficiently receptive. Generally, Maimonides played down the miraculous elements of faith, and allegorized Biblical and Talmudic references to angels and demons.

Maimonides drew up, in his *Commentary on the Mishnah,* a short creed of Judaism, which reduced the faith to thirteen articles. These involve belief in (1) the existence of the Creator; (2) his unity; (3) his incorporeality; (4) his eternity; (5) the necessity of worshiping him alone; (6) the truth of the words of the prophets; (7) the superiority of Moses to all other prophets; (8) the revelation of the Law to Moses at Sinai; (9) the immutability of the Law; (10) the omniscience of God; (11) retribution in this world and the next; (12) the coming of the Messiah; and (13) the resurrection of the dead.

Appraisal of Maimonides

The rationalism and intellectualism of Maimonides aroused great opposition from many rabbis, though at the same time his work was both widely read and influential. One of the great attempts in the Middle Ages toward elaborating a theistic philosophy, it was discussed well outside the bounds of the Jewish community, for it became one of the textbooks of medieval Latin philosophy. The creed itself was widely used, and has become incorporated in the Jewish Prayer Book. Undoubtedly, Maimonides was the greatest philosopher of the Jewish tradition. If the prophetic encounter with God appears more dynamic and imaginative than the picture of the knowledge of God that Maimonides paints, nevertheless, his intellectual conceptions can convey as well as poetic and mythological ones something of the awe implicit in the experience of God. We should not underestimate the key role played in Maimonides' scheme by his "negative theology." It was a method of expressing, in a somewhat tech-nical and philosophical manner, the utter transcendence of God's nature, the same sense of difference between God and man and between God and the world, the experience of otherness and majesty, that the prophets and count-less pious men have had. Philosophical doctrines are not just intellectual in their significance: they relate to the experiential dimension of religion.

Maimonides, in his teaching about creation, did not say simply that the world has a First Cause (which could be a scientific or metaphysical proposition of no great interest to the religious imagination): in stressing the transcendence of God he invested the idea of creation with wonder and mystery. Nevertheless, it can hardly be denied that the main emphasis in his writings was on the intellectual side of the knowledge of God.

Later Hebrew philosophers protested Maimonides' intellectualism. Notably, Hildai Crescas (1340–1410) of Barcelona criticized Maimonides for not including the idea of love in the articles of his creed. He held that the creation is an overflowing of divine love, and that communion with God likewise must come from love. This love, expressed in worship and moral conduct, continues into the life beyond.

THE KABBALAH

Other forces totally unlike Greek philosophy imparted to medieval Judaism a strongly mystical element. The mystical movement centered on certain esoteric teachings known as the *Kabbalah*. While the philosophers effected an amalgam between Jewish orthodoxy and philosophical argument, the Kabbalist mystics sought to evolve a pattern of life centered on interior experience and contemplation. They too were speculative, but their speculations were of a very different order from those of the philosophers. Written in strange and symbolic language, the Kabbalist literature gave a new and esoteric account of the relations between God and his creation. The chief expression of the Kabbalah is a work known as the *Zohar* ("Splendor") which was written as a commentary on the Pentateuch. Though it is ascribed to a rabbi of the second century, the work, in the form in which circulated in the last part of the thirteenth century A.D. was composed only a little earlier than then. Since Kabbalism originated in Europe, chiefly in Provence and Spain, the book can probably be ascribed to Moses de Leon, a native of Granada, who died in 1305.

The *Zohar* depicts God as the *En Sof*, the "Endless" or "Infinite." The *En Sof* in itself is without qualities. However, there emanate from the *En Sof* ten ideal qualities known as the *Sefiroth* (an idea drawn from earlier speculations about sacred numbers, but now divested of any numerological significance). These powers, which include wisdom, intelligence, mercy, and justice, operate within the created world as we know it, though it is the lowest of a series of higher realms. The *En Sof*, in its perfect infiniteness, is far removed from the finite and imperfect world men experience; thus the Kabbalists thought it necessary to postulate these intermediate stages between the *En Sof* and the world. Nevertheless, the *En Sof* in some sense contains the world, and the way in which this is expressed is through the doctrine that the different realms of being reflect and interpenetrate one another. In this the *Zohar* presents a very different picture from the personalistic account contained in the Hebrew Bible of Yahweh and his relations to Israel. The notion of the *Shechinah,* or divine Presence, was of great importance in Kabbalistic thought. *Shechinah* is God's self-manifestation. Now since all interpenetrates all, events in one world affect the whole: "From an activity below there is stimulated a corresponding activity on high," as the *Zohar* puts it. Owing, then, to the fall of the primordial Adam, a rupture has taken place in the cosmos: darkness and evil have entered in. More drastically, the divine Presence has been exiled from the *En Sof.* No longer does the Presence pervade the whole world with radiance and glory; it appears only occasionally here and there. It appeared in ancient Israel, and has continued to be especially associated with the Jewish nation, even if disobedience of the Jewish people often obstructs the full working of the divine Love. The aim of the pious Jew should be to work for the reunion of the *Shechinah* with the *En Sof.* This reunion will automatically restore harmony to the whole universe and bring in the longed-for Kingdom. Since man's soul also contains within it some of the *Sefiroth,* the individual who experiences within himself a sense of such reunion and harmony can have cosmic effects. Therefore the faithful are bidden to work through the contemplative life toward the final consummation and the reestablishment of the interrupted harmony of the universe. Such in brief are the main teachings of the *Zohar.*

It will at once be apparent that the Kabbalistic ideas did not simply arise from speculation, even though they may have incorporated Platonist and other elements. Rather, they aimed to express the relationship between mystical experience and the traditional religion of Israel. The concept of God as the *En Sof* squares with the insistence common to all kinds of mysticism in diverse cultures, on the essential ineffability and even impersonality of the Source of Being. The doctrine of the *Sefiroth* is a kind of fragmentation of the personal qualities of the Creator (a fragmentation admittedly modified by the notion that these different forces interpenetrate one another). Thus the personal God of worship and providential activity, who looms so large in the religion of Israel and is its crowning justification, is overshadowed by the conception of the Infinite. Further, the Kabbalist teachings about cosmic interpenetration account for the existence of evil through the notion of the Fall of man. An interesting corollary to the disruption of the cosmos is the thesis that the stern judgment of God becomes detached from the divine mercy and takes on a satanic character; the fire of God's righteous wrath becomes Hell.

Despite the seeming unorthodoxy of such ideas the Kabbalists did not neglect the daily round of religious observance. The requirements of the Law were reinterpreted as having a mystical significance; prayer was emphasized as vital to the spiritual life, provided that it included *kawanoth,* or acts of concentrated devotion. This was a way in which the interior life of contemplation was integrated with the rules of outward observance. On the ethical plane, the Kabbalists strongly stressed the importance of meekness and love, and they glorified poverty. Thus the movement preached a moderate asceticism, as part of the training through which the soul could reach back to the divine spark that illumined it from the depths of the person's being.

Isaac Luria

Among those who carried on and developed Kabbalist ideas was Isaac Luria (1514-1572), of Spanish Jewish family (when the Jews were expelled from Spain in 1492, Luria's family settled in Palestine). A distinctive feature of his teaching was the doctrine of reincarnation. This already played some part, but a minor one, in the *Zohar:* for certain persons, a continued series of existences was postulated that would enable them to progress effectively toward purity and reunion with the divine. But according to Luria, reincarnation is universal. He conceived of it as having both a positive and a negative significance. On the one hand, it gave men ever fresh opportunities for the pure life that would lead to salvation. On the other hand, rebirth, especially in the form of animals and plants, was a means whereby sins reaped their due retribution. Adam was thought of as a universal being who before his fall embraced the whole cosmos, which existed in an ideal state. With his fall, however, the material world was created, and the light of his divine nature was broken up into the sparks that illuminate the myriads of living souls. In the final consummation of history all would be reunited.

This conception enabled Luria to see the process of reincarnation not merely as the separate ongoing of the myriad souls, but a single transmigration of the soul of the cosmic Adam. Through the nurturing of the divine life within men, atonement would be brought about. In Adam all fall; but in Adam all are raised again. Luria also believed in a certain contagion in holiness, whereby groups of souls could help each other along the way to salvation. The destiny of Israel, in its suffering and in its dispersion through the nations of the world, was to function as such a group through which the salvation of all could become effective. Then in the day of the Messiah, universal harmony would be restored. Fasting, asceticism, the practice of *kawanoth,* and a life suffused with love were the means for the purification of the soul, according to Luria.

Thus the Kabbalist movement stressed practical mysticism: Kabbalistic doctrines can be understood only in terms of a search for experiential union with the Source of Being. It is interesting to note that here the doctrine of reincarnation entered into the Jewish heritage, though it is hard to see that there can be any scriptural justification for it. The ancient Jewish view of man was that of a psychophysical unity: there was no split between body and soul. Now, with the doctrines of the divine spark residing within man and the notion of reincarnation, even into animal form, the Kabbalist movement had evolved an entirely different doctrine of man. It is notable that Maimonides had argued strongly against reincarnation (a doctrine which, of course, he discovered in the writings of Greek philosophy, through which it penetrated into the Kabbalah): he considered, for instance, that the notion of a human spirit inhabiting the body of an animal was contradictory. But the allegorical and mystical interpretations that Kabbalistic writers used in their approach to the scriptures enabled them to read into the Bible the main substance of their own teachings.

Mysticism, in nearly all cultures, has constituted an important strand of religious experience. It is different in type from the prophetic and devotional forms of religious experience. Thus Judaism (and Islam), which in origin centered so powerfully upon the prophetic encounter with a majestic and personal Being, came to emphasize the cultivation of mystical experience. The medieval Kabbalists were bound to present certain problems of interpretation since much of their teaching is fanciful and unorthodox; yet the Kabbalah was a major attempt to gain a place for the interior life in the religion of Judaism.

PERSECUTION OF JEWS IN MIDDLE AGES

Social conditions may have favored the growth of the movement. Its emphasis on meekness, love, and a quiet interior life were adapted to the unhappy outer circumstances of the community. With its renewal and reinterpretation of the messianic hope it helped to nourish the confidence of a people who had otherwise but little ground for it. The excitement generated by the Crusades, which were explicitly aimed at forcible action against infidels, spilled over into attacks upon the Jewish community in many parts of Europe. Savage pogroms, particularly in Germany, caused fresh migrations of the Jews, mainly to Eastern Europe. In Spain, the Christian drive against the Moors was successful, and as a side effect there came persecution of Jews and their expulsion. In England and elsewhere the Jews were periodically expelled. Throughout Europe, Jews were the object of suspicion and resentment—suspicion because they professed a non-Christian faith and perforce often observed their ceremonial in secret (a situation liable to generate the wildest and most slanderous rumors); resentment because of their frequent function as money-lenders (usury was barred to Christians by the Church and, to a degree, fostered on the Jews). Those who remained in Germany and Central Europe were forced to live apart in ghettos, poor quarters where they were walled in and subject to severe restrictions. This ghetto life, persisting from the fourteenth century up to the nineteenth, isolated the Jews from influences around them, and encouraged a somewhat stagnant religious conservatism.

59. *The remains of a second- or third-century synagogue at Capernaum, Israel, on the Galilee shore. (Israel Ministry of Tourism.)*

60. *The twelve tribes of Israel and Moses during the Exodus, Synagogue Dura Europos. (Courtesy of the Yale University Art Gallery: Dura-Europos Collection.)*

61. *A section of the Dead Sea Scrolls, the earliest manuscripts of biblical materials which have been discovered. (Courtesy of the American Friends of the Hebrew University, New York.)*

62. *Stone mosaic of a menorah from the pavement of the synagogue at Hammam Lif, Tunesia (3rd to 5th century). (Courtesy of the Brooklyn Museum, Museum Collection Fund.)*

63. *Symbol of the State of Israel, this giant menorah stands in the plaza facing the Knesset. It was a gift from the British parliament. (Israel Ministry of Tourism.)*

Woodcut depicting [bur]ning of Jews, from [Nu]remberg Chronicle [(15]th century). (Rare [Bo]oks and Manuscripts [Di]vision, The New York [Pu]blic Library, Astor, [Le]nox and Tilden [Fo]undations.)

65. *Hebrew scroll of the Book of Esther. (The Bettmann Archive.)*

66. *Title page from a sixteenth-century edition of Maimonides' Guide to the Perplexed. (Library of the Jewish Theological Seminary of America.)*

67. *The blowing of the shofar, or ram's horn, at sunset proclaims Yom Kippur, the holiest day of the Jewish calendar. (Wide World Photos.)*

68. *An Israeli soldier wearing a prayer shawl over his combat uniform prays at the Western wall in the old city of Jerusalem. (Wide World Photos.)*

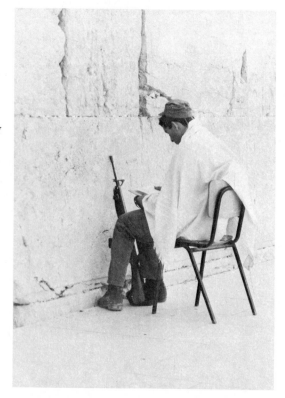

THE HASIDIM

In Eastern Europe an infusion of new piety came from the movement known as Hasidism. The term *Hasidim* had already been used in much earlier times to describe a group who, in the Greek period, had resisted Hellenic influences, and from whom the Pharisaic movement had grown. Literally the Hasidim were the "pious" ones, who emphasized purity and attention to the Law. But modern Hasidism belonged rather to the Kabbalist tradition, though with much less emphasis on the doctrinal side.

Its founder was Israel Baal Shem (1700–1760), who lived in the Carpathian region of Eastern Europe. He lived a simple and holy life, was given to mystical ecstasy, and, according to the traditions about him, performed various miracles. He gathered round him a number of disciples who like him lived the meditative life. His successor, Rabbi Baer, organized missionary activity to the Ukraine and other parts of Eastern Europe, and the Hasidist movement gathered a powerful following. The Hasidic ideal was the *Zaddik*, or perfectly righteous man, through whom the favor of God is channelled. Only he is capable of perfect union with the divine Being; lesser men must find their development through the guidance of the Zaddik. Here Hasidism suggests the Hindu custom where the divine illumination is nurtured through the mediating power of the *guru*. It also had analogies to the Zen principle that illumination is conveyed directly from the master to the pupil. The Hasidist movement centered on the figure of the mystical teacher, who replaced both the Torah and the rabbi as the source of immediate authority. Naturally orthodox rabbis opposed this emphasis and several ineffectual persecutions were launched against the Hasidists.

The virtues inculcated by the Hasidim were self-negation and loving humility. They believed that the divine Being is immanent in all creation. He is likewise to be found in all men, so that sinners, however unrighteous and unattractive they may appear, contain goodness. The loving person will not set his face against them, but seek to expiate in his own person such sins as they have committed. His life must be suffused with a joyous awareness of this divine Presence. Such an ideal generated many saintly lives. It was not difficult, however, for the Zaddik, or holy man, to abuse his position. This indeed increasingly occurred: often holiness was replaced by spurious wonder-working and arrogance. A revival of rabbinic learning among the Hasidim in the nineteenth century helped to check such tendencies, albeit at the expense of converting Hasidism back into something much more orthodox and formalistic.

The movement had contributed a further element to the Jewish experience. It was a form of pious mysticism not confined to an esoteric group, but rooted in the people where it showed its fruits in holy living. Its essential simplicity made it adaptable to the religious experience of men and women of modest sophistication and learning. On the ethical side it gave a new impulse to the cultivation of that love which has long formed the background to the Jewish ethical code.

SOCIAL CHANGES IN THE NINETEENTH CENTURY

The nineteenth century was in one way a period of light for Judaism, though it also produced some severe strains within the community at large. Revolutions in France and America profoundly altered the social status of Jews. They received full citizenship in these countries, and Napoleon opened ghettos throughout Europe in his wide-reaching campaigns. After Napoleon's defeat, a period of reaction followed, but eventually the turbulent and revolutionary events of 1848 paved the way for a fuller acceptance of the Jewish community into the political and social fabric of the European nations. The talents of the Jews were released and nourished by this change. European and American science and learning, music and literature have ever since owed an incalculable debt to the gifts of Jewish intellectuals. But the movement was not all one way. European culture began increasingly to affect the life of the community itself, once the gates of the ghetto were flung open.

THE ENLIGHTENMENT AND REFORM JUDAISM

One great figure paved the way for a new synthesis between Judaism and modern philosophical and scientific thought. Moses Mendelssohn (1729–1786) interpreted Judaism in terms of the metaphysics of Leibnitz. He reduced the essentials of the faith to three main beliefs—in God, in his Providence, and in the immortality of the soul. The movement, known as the Enlightenment, whose central figure was the East Prussian philosopher Immanuel Kant, gave further impetus to Jewish attempts to reconcile religion and the demands of reason expressed in philosophy. From these beginnings there emerged Reform Judaism, which tried to modernize the faith, simplify the ritual, and find points of contact between Jews and their Christian compatriots. The first Reform Temple was opened in Westphalia in 1810, by Israel Jacobson (1768–1828).

Previous syntheses, like that of Maimonides, had largely been concerned with relating revelation and tradition to the major philosophical trends of the day. This was true of the Reform rabbis; but a further factor had entered into the situation. The first half of the nineteenth century saw the rise of scientific history, and with it there came the critical treatment by scholars of the material contained in the Christian scriptures. The results of this investigation, though often speculative and subject to doubt as far as details are concerned, threw a flood of light on the nature of the texts and their mode of composition. It was no longer plausible to hold that Moses wrote the Pentateuch or that the words of the Bible were, so to say, dictated by God to writers who mechanically recorded them. Older ideas of revelation, in relation to the scriptures themselves, began to evaporate.

This induced a crisis both in Judaism and in Christianity. This crisis indeed is still working itself out within the Jewish community. The new historical scholarship combined with rationalistic philosophy in casting doubt on the kind of interpretations of scripture given in the Talmud. Over many centuries the Talmud had been the orthodox rabbis' source of authority in the exegesis of the Bible: in many respects the Talmudic tradition had been more important than the written word of the scriptures themselves. In the thinking of the Reform movement, old Talmudic orthodoxy was incorrect and deadening. Reformers sought to purge the faith of its later accretions (for that was how they regarded Talmudic lore) and affirm a simple monotheism which was not bound down to the national aspirations of the Jewish nation. Judaism was to be liberated, and made into a universal creed.

Naturally the traditionalists reacted against this violently. They saw the reform effort as the destruction of the national way of life, through the abandonment of many of the sacred practices which gave it meaning. It meant, too, an abandonment of real messianic hope. The traditionalists were dubbed Orthodox by the reformers, a name currently used for this wing of modern Judaism. Undoubtedly the Orthodox were often right in their assessments, even if their views about modern textual scholarship were sometimes obscurantist. The Reform movement was in danger of disintegrating the community and abolishing the very concept of a Chosen People. In so doing it was robbing the faith of its historical dimension. Nevertheless, Judaism could not be insulated from the wind of intellectual change. How could a more critical acceptance of doctrines and scriptures be combined with the preservation of the Jewish way of life?

Zechariah Frankel

One answer was in the shape of the so-called "positive-historical" school founded by Zechariah Frankel (1801–1875). This combined a critical and scientific view of the ancient scriptural tradition with an insistence upon the ritual and ethical side of Judaism. The Law, as interpreted in all its detail by the Talmud, had given shape to Jewish life over long centuries. Maybe not all the festivals and injunctions which control Jewish life go back to Moses;

maybe not all the details of daily living can genuinely be justified by appeal to the scriptures; maybe the scriptures themselves evolved over a long process of composition, conflation, and editing. But nevertheless, the pattern which had come to be part of the Jewish ethos was important in its own right. It preserved the community and God's revelation. It had added new perspectives to Jewish piety. In short, it expressed and enshrined the Jewish experience. This, then, could not be jettisoned without robbing Judaism of much of its characteristic flavor. This strand of thinking issued in Conservative Judaism in the United States, especially under the intellectual leadership of Solomon Schechter (1848–1915).

The Reform movement was strongly resisted in Germany, though in the United States it found a fertile field in which to flourish. In general, European Jewry remained orthodox in its feeling, but the interplay of the three positions outlined above continued. Meanwhile a fourth force emerged, which was to have big effects in the twentieth century—Zionism. Persecution in Russia following the accession of Alexander III in 1881, anti-semitism in France (expressed in the notorious Dreyfus case), and elsewhere prompted a number of Jews to reconsider their position, and to seek a permanent homeland.

Theodore Herzl

The movement was crystallized by the writings of Theodore Herzl (1860–1904). Herzl called for a Jewish national state in Palestine. In accordance with messianic ideas which had so long been determinative of Jewish hopes, he claimed that a Jewish state would not merely give the harassed Jews a home; it would also be a blessing to the rest of the world, which would be "liberated through our freedom, enriched by our wealth and enlarged through our own greatness." The first Zionist Congress met in Basle in 1897. Within twenty years the move for a national home was sufficient to induce the British government in 1917 to declare that it would facilitate its creation. Pioneer Zionists moved their families to Palestine and the process of reconstruction and development was started. There remained those among both Reform and Orthodox Jews who resisted Zionism. For the former it was too nationalistic; for the latter, it looked like trying to force the hand of God. But the terrible Nazi persecutions of European Jewry before and during the Second World War gave the most powerful possible impetus to Zionism in the post-war period. The British, however, worried at the effect on the Arab world, restricted immigration. The conflict between the Jews and the British led the United Nations to terminate Britain's mandate over the country.

The State of Israel

On May 14, 1948, an independent Jewish state was proclaimed: Israel had come into being. Despite attacks from Arab powers on all sides it established itself successfully as a Middle Eastern nation. This was no theocratic state. The religious tensions of Judaism carried over into the Israeli environment; a large section of the population, especially among the younger folk, are secularist, rather than committed to the religion of their fathers.

THE EXPERIENCE OF THE HOLOCAUST

The awful events of the Nazi period (1933–1945), which led to the extermination of six million Jews (and millions of others) and the wholesale destruction of European Jewry, understandably created a profound question for Jews in thinking about the significance of the Holocaust or *Sho'ah*. Could God's action or inaction in permitting the Holocaust be tolerated? Was the death of so many millions just the continuation of the theme of the Suffering Servant in *Isaiah*? But what redeeming significance could it have? Perhaps, as some argued, it constituted a new revelation, in which Jews were commanded to survive. So near to extinction at that time, the Jews have a duty, it is argued, not to give Hitler his posthumous victory. The tragedy reinforced the urgency of solidarity and continuance of obedience to God. Or did the Holocaust mean that God had broken his covenant, and could no longer be followed? He was dead—and the universe is without meaning, save what we make of it. This line of thinking would mean the disappearance of classical Judaism. Maybe God was provoked by Jewish disobedience into allowing the Holocaust—angered by the whole Reform tendency and, worse, the blasphemous anticipation of God's actions in trying to set up a State of Israel through the Zionist movement—instead of waiting for God to act through the future Messiah in restoring Israel. The struggles of Jewish theologians to make sense of such a terrible event do not bring any satisfying answers. Nazism was like a horrific new religion, which went beyond previous antisemitism, and the insane but "rational" solution it created to what it saw as "the Jewish problem" posed questions to their victims that are too awful to answer. The Holocaust also posed some serious questions for the Christian tradition, whose negativity toward the Jews and frequently paranoid sensitivity helped to build antisemitism into the force that came to be shaped and expanded by the evil genius of Hitler's ideology. We shall reconsider these facts at a later point, when we attempt to sum up the present and future possibilities of human religion in the modern world.

SUMMARY OF JEWISH RELIGIOUS EXPERIENCE

The Jewish religious experience has been throughout history characterized by nobility and tragedy. Since the fall of Jerusalem in 586 B.C. the Jews have had to endure, in the various countries and cultures in which they found themselves, persecution and ostracism, culminating in Hitler's attempt at genocide. It is remarkable that they have survived: more remarkable still that their religion has continued to be nourished within the community. The high ethical monotheism of the prophets has remained an inspiration, especially because of the historical dimension which it possessed. This has kept alive the hope of a consummation of events in which the Jewish people would play a prominent and happy role. Messianism has been indispensable to the continuance of the community. At the same time, the ritual dimension of Judaism, established in its first rigor and complexity in the post-Exilic theocracy, has been a potent source of cohesion and survival. In being integrated into the social institutions of the community it has given it strength to counter the violent influences from outside. It has, too, given to the Jews the ideal of a holy, but non-ascetic, life. If often the Jews were forced apart from the world, through imprisonment in ghettos and persecution, their creed has never been one of non-involvement and withdrawal. The Essenes and others who tried this solution have long perished. Even Jewish mystics who sometimes emphasized asceticism and negation of the physical side of man, were not inclined toward the monastic ideal. In this the permanent influence of Moses and the prophets can be seen at work. The worship of God cannot involve fleeing from the world, and for two reasons. First, God is good and so is his creation: an omnipotent Creator would not have brought into being a world which was essentially corrupt, however much its beauties may here and there be overlaid by the evils that we may perform. Second, the God of Moses and the prophets has shown himself to be for goodness and social justice: his religion must have an ethical dimension that calls people to action in the vicissitudes of history. These perceptions are the most profound part of the faith that has given a pure monotheism to the world. They were also crucial to another part of the Jewish experience which goes under the name of Christianity.

Chapter 8

THE EARLY CHRISTIAN

EXPERIENCE

THE EXPERIENCE of the Resurrection was the focal point in Christianity for the followers of Jesus. The unforeseen and surprising vindication of the authority of the leader and companion who had inspired them during the time of his ministry released a force which led them to the experience of Pentecost. The new faith spread with remarkable speed. Within thirty years Christian communities were scattered throughout the eastern Mediterranean world, in Italy, and in Rome itself.

THE GOSPELS AS EVIDENCE

Thirty years after Jesus' crucifixion the literary tradition which was to form the books of the New Testament was already started. The Epistles of Paul and the material which is reflected in the Acts of the Apostles were in being. A little later the Gospel of Mark was written, based on the oral traditions which had been handed down about Jesus. The Gospel of Luke followed toward the end of the century, and Matthew a little later. At about the same time, the Gospel of John was composed. It should be pointed out, though, that there is room for doubt about the order in which the Gospels were written, and some scholars suggest a different scheme of dating them. Virtually within a hundred years of Jesus' crucifixion the works which now comprise the canon of the New Testament (the new covenant which followed on from the old) came into being. Thus the evolution of Christian literature occurred in much less time than that of the Hebrew Bible. This enables us to get a good historical picture of apostolic times. It also raises hopes that we can present an accurate picture of the historical Jesus.

But there are difficulties. The Gospels, as their name implies, were not meant to be biographies but records of the good news which the Christian community was actively propagating. They were concerned not so much with the details of Jesus' career as with his teachings and the saving events of his death and resurrection. They were, moreover, based on different strands of oral tradition which were interwoven but not always consistent. In some respects they were composed with an eye to consolidating the liturgical function of the Gospels with the worshiping life of the community. For these reasons scholars are by no means sure that an accurate account of the historical Jesus can be built up. Nevertheless, we know enough to establish some important features of his personality and career, though we can only hazard a guess about his inner experience or consciousness of his divine mission.

THE LIFE OF JESUS

Jesus lived in times which were bitter and confused. The Jewish nation had come within the orbit of Rome and feared for its very identity. The regions to the north and east of Samaria, including Galilee, were carved up among the puppet rulers of the house of Herod. Herod Antipas, king of Galilee, endeavored to hellenize the area. The magnificence of the city of Tiberias was testimony to his cultural ambitions, as also was Sepphoris, a few miles north of Nazareth. About the year 4 B.C., a certain Judas of Galilee led a bloody rebellion against Herod, sparked off by the question of tribute monies due to the Romans. Judas and his Zealot party captured Sepphoris and seized Herod's palace. But the revolt failed. The city was razed. Some two thousand rebels were savagely crucified. In A.D. 6, Judea was placed under the direct rule of the Roman procurator.

These events, so close to Nazareth, must have made the boy Jesus well aware of the hatreds which nourished the Zealot cause and the ruthlessness of imperial power. In this bitter atmosphere, the promise of a Messiah who would, through the force of arms, drive out the Romans and reestablish an independent commonwealth, was a powerful hope.

Not all Jews felt as the Zealots did. Others were more peaceably disposed. The influential Pharisees believed that a return to the full application of the Torah would be a means of purification and piety independent of political issues. The Sadducees worked for peaceful coexistence with Rome. The Essenes withdrew to a communal life, patiently waiting for the coming Messiah.

It was a time of argument and rivalry and uncertainty. It was a time of storm and tragedy, a crucial period for the nation. During this time Jesus lived his short life. These tensions and strifes came out in the Gospel narratives, especially because Jesus himself was attached to none of these groups, and either overtly or by implication criticized them all.

Jesus' Relationship to Factions within Judaism

Jesus had Zealot friends. One or perhaps two of his disciples were Zealots (Simon the Zealot and maybe Judas Iscariot). Yet he rejected their violence: "Render unto Caesar the things that are Caesar's" was a repudiation of armed rebellion and a criticism of the revolt of Judas the Galilean which had been occasioned by the levying of tribute money. Though he had friends among the Pharisees, and though they do not appear to have criticized him for his messianic claims (though there is a question about how explicit these were), they were put off by his strictures on the way in which they interpreted the Law. He wished to exhibit the essence of the Law, rather than to insist on the minutiae. Healing and gathering food on the Sabbath were instances of his practical rejection of Pharisaic scruples. His interference with the Temple administration alienated him from the priestly Sadducees, and his claims to authority could not commend themselves to the scribes, traditional exponents of the Law. Though he and his disciples may have lived communally, as did the Essenes, he was not concerned with withdrawal from the world. Thus the Kingdom which he promised did not fit well into the categories and presuppositions of the people among whom he moved. Even his Judaism was suspect; he moved freely amid aliens and social outcasts. A hated tax-gatherer was one of his disciples.

Jesus' Background

What, then, was the background of this strange teacher and leader who played a short role in the stormy days of the early part of the first century? He was born in 4 B.C. or earlier (traditional dating being erroneous). According to the Gospels of Luke and Matthew, he was born in Bethlehem. But his home was probably in Nazareth, and it was there he was brought up, as the son of relatively humble parents, with a number of brothers and sisters. His trade, like that of his father, was as a carpenter, but he showed an early interest in religious matters, and came to know the Torah (the books of the Law and the Prophets) well. We know scarcely more than this: it was only at about the age of thirty that he emerged from this obscurity to the full light of his ministry. The first move in this direction was his baptism by John.

Jesus' Baptism

John the Baptist was a fiery and prophetic figure. His dress and manner of life were reminiscent of the prophets of old, and like them he called men to repentance in the face of the imminent coming of the Kingdom. He may have been influenced by Essene doctrines, but he was not interested in a withdrawn asceticism. His moral teachings no doubt attracted Jesus, though we know

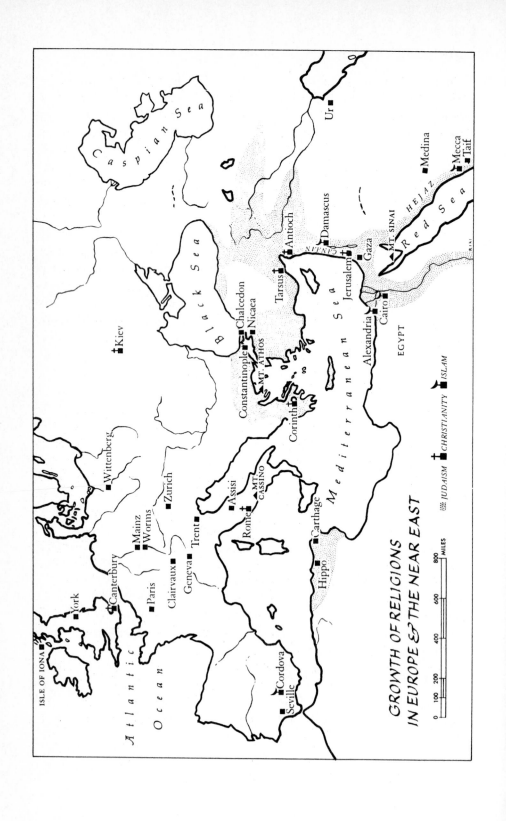

GROWTH OF RELIGIONS
IN EUROPE & THE NEAR EAST

JUDAISM ▦   CHRISTIANITY ✝ ■   ISLAM ☾ ■

MILES
0 100 200   400   600   800

next to nothing of the circumstances which impelled Jesus to submit to baptism by John in the river Jordan. According to the scriptural account, the event made a tremendous impact on Jesus, and gave him an experience suggestive of his own messiahhood:

> And when Jesus was baptized, he went up immediately from the water, and behold, the heavens were opened and he saw the Spirit of God descending like a dove, and alighting on him; and lo, a voice from heaven, saying, "This is my beloved Son, with whom I am well pleased."[1]

This was a crucial turning point in Jesus' life. He retired to the wilderness to meditate as a prelude to his ministry. The story of the temptations which followed have the style of parables, but they may be understood to indicate the kind of choice Jesus had before him. Either he could become an active rebel and establish an earthly kingdom, or he could tread a thornier and more difficult path.

JESUS' MINISTRY

He returned to Galilee to preach. Soon he acquired four disciples from among the fishermen who plied the Sea of Galilee. Simon Peter was one of them. Simon Peter's home was in Capernaum. There Jesus based himself during his early preaching. He soon discovered evidence of his power to heal and to "cast out devils" (according to popular beliefs, madness was attributed to demon-possession). The forceful and authoritative style of his teaching, his free use of parables, and his reputation for healing powers brought a large following. The crowds indeed were sometimes oppressive, and he was forced on one occasion to preach to an enthusiastic throng from a boat. Often he preached in the synagogue, a circumstance which has led some scholars to suppose that he had been trained as a rabbi. In one or two passages in the New Testament he is addressed as "Rabbi" ("Master"). Though the evidence for the theory is inconclusive, Jesus certainly functioned in the synagogues much as a rabbi might, and with a characteristic freshness of style. But he combined with his ability to reinterpret the scriptures the force and zeal of a prophet.

Even in saying that Jesus combined these two rather different roles we are in danger of underestimating the originality of his manner of life and teaching. The most notable feature of his teaching was his constant use of parables. These served as concrete illustrations of the points he was making,

[1] Matthew 3:16–17 (RSV).

whether they were concerned with ethical matters or with the relations between God and man, and the nature of the Kingdom. They were not allegories,
which had a point-to-point resemblance to the things they were designed to
teach about, and in which every detail could be assigned a meaning. Rather
they were stories and comparisons which brought to life the essential nature of
what he was speaking about. Jesus was not much concerned with systematiz-
ing his moral and religious teachings into a list of propositions. There was
perhaps, to his mind, enough of this already in the scribal expositions of the
Law. Part of the reason for the allusive and parabolic nature of his teachings
lay in the fact that he was trying to induce in his hearers a new vision, a
turning-around of their point of view. He was concerned with shaking people
from their old categories, whether they were the sophisticated thought-patterns
of the learned or the simple faith of the farmers, prostitutes, and fisher folk
among whom he moved.

His actions seem to have been of the same character. His easy relations
with people of all types—alien Samaritans, tax-gatherers, Pharisees, insiders,
outsiders—betrayed no fear of ritual regulations or social prejudices. He was,
in his intercourse with others, indifferent to man-made barriers. This made
him impatient of those who hedged righteousness with details and correct
form: "Verily, I say unto you, That the publicans and harlots go into the
Kingdom of God before you." Nevertheless, for all his criticism of the scribes
and Pharisees, he was a pious Jew who respected the Law in its essential
substance. He thought of himself as fulfilling it, not destroying it. But the
trouble was that God's will had been overlaid and misinterpreted by popular
and official religion. The Kingdom of God which he perceived already present
was very different from those aspirations that the Jews had for so long nourished, and now nourished with increasing fervor and apprehension. The disciples who gathered around him scarcely understood this.

JESUS' TEACHING

What was this Kingdom which he preached? His illustrations are suggestive,
but not altogether explicit. The Kingdom was like leaven working in the
dough; it was like "a householder, which went out early in the morning to hire
laborers unto his vineyard"; it was like a mustard-seed; it was like a wedding-
feast. What it was not was clear enough. Jesus did not mean a new political
revolution; nor did he mean something in the distant future. It was already at
hand, though it was coming in a mysterious and quiet manner. The Kingdom was the community of those who followed him in the new law and in
bonds of brotherly love. But more important, the Kingdom was the work

which Jesus was effecting in his own person. It could be illustrated from parables, but it could be shown more vividly in action. The action was that of Jesus in his ministry and in his coming crisis, of which he had a presentiment. The providence of God, which had guided the Jewish people, was now preparing a new and unforeseen way of manifesting its revealing and healing work.

We have seen that Jesus had found his baptism in the Jordan a turning point in his life. He began to preach the imminent coming of the Kingdom. But did he look upon himself as the Messiah? And how far was he conscious of his identity with God—an identity ascribed to him later by the Church?

On the basis of our records it is extremely difficult to penetrate to the facts of Jesus' own consciousness. But several significant pieces of evidence emerge from the Gospel narratives. When, after the spectacular success of his early preaching in Galilee, popular support began to diminish and opposition harden, Jesus withdrew with his disciples toward Tyre and Sidon and then to Caesarea Philippi. This period of withdrawal was the time when he prepared himself for the final and fateful phase of his career, his going down to Jerusalem. It was at Caesarea Philippi that Peter is said to have recognized him as the Christ, the "anointed one," the Messiah. Jesus showed concern lest the disciples should noise this title abroad. He wanted the messianic nature of his mission to remain a secret.

The Meaning of Messiahship

The probable reason for secrecy was that this title might be misleading to those who saw in the Messiah an earthly and political savior. Jesus had already seen that his mission was very different. He referred to himself as "the Son of Man," a more mysterious title than "Messiah." It did not have the kingly and political overtones associated with "Messiah." Nevertheless, it was a term used of the heavenly Messiah in such apocalyptic writings as the Book of Daniel. If we are correct in tracing back the use of the term to Jesus himself it is an indication that he combined a sense of his own personal destiny with an intuition that a new kind of messiahship was being acted out in his own person.

Significantly, when he entered Jerusalem, he did so in conscious awareness of the prophecy in Zechariah 9:9:

> Rejoice greatly, O daughter of Zion! Shout aloud, O daughter of Jerusalem! Lo, your king comes to you; triumphant and victorious is he, humble and riding on an ass, on a colt the foal of an ass . . . he shall command peace to the nations; his dominion shall be from sea to sea, and from the River to the ends of the earth.

This indicated that he saw himself as a royal Messiah. At the same time he had for some period been warning his incredulous disciples that the Son of Man was due to suffer and die. The Kingdom was being introduced in a very strange manner. It was, as the last verse quoted above indicates, a Kingdom— a new community—which would stretch well beyond the bounds of the Jewish people themselves. Although Jesus had said elsewhere: "I was sent only to the lost sheep of Israel," and made other statements suggestive that his mission, like that of prophets before him, was essentially confined to the Jewish people, his thoughts at the outset of his dramatic ministry changed as he saw his function in a much wider context. The faith of Israel, rather than being confined to the nation, was to be made universal.

Jesus' Ideas of the Divine

Another feature of Jesus' estimate of himself can be seen in the way in which he prayed. He used the term *Abba,* a familiar and endearing word for "Father," and it suggested an original and intimate, loving relationship with God; he evidently felt that the spirit of this loving Father was upon him. Yet it is unrealistic to suppose that he felt himself so thoroughly possessed, so to speak, by God that his human personality was merely a vehicle for divine action. His prayer in the garden at Gethsemane indicated the struggle which his suffering role cost him. Also, there is a significant passage which relates to Jesus' experience of Satan, which may help to tell us something of his consciousness of the divine:

> And the seventy returned with joy, saying, "Lord, even the devils are subject to us in your name!" And he said to them, "I saw Satan fall like lightning from heaven. Behold, I have given you authority to tread upon serpents and scorpions, and over all the power of the enemy; and nothing shall hurt you."[2]

According to the Gospels, Jesus quite often spoke of "the enemy" and of devils. One reason was the strange power which he discovered in himself for curing sickness which at that time was commonly attributed to the work of demons. Here we see a hint of his profound experience of cosmic victory. "I beheld Satan as lightning fall from heaven." He may well have perceived the power of evil in the world against the foreground of a numinous and brilliant experience of the divine. His consciousness of a divine destiny is brought out in his institution of the sacrament at the Last Supper. Here was an act with

---

[2] Luke 10:17–19 (RSV).

ritual overtones (though whether it was intended as a Passover meal or something else is a matter for debate) which seemed to indicate his impending death. The Church enacted this custom of the Last Supper from early times. It would be surprising if the first Christians' retrospective interpretation of the meal as something specially instituted by Jesus was wrong. Jesus, then, not only envisioned his death, but also the time beyond, when his Kingdom would continue among a community of believers. These facts point to a consciousness on the part of Jesus that his work was more than that of a prophet and teacher: it was a messianic role, one which was original and startling and at the same time tragic. There can be no better indication of the originality of Jesus' mind than the fact that he felt the call to kingship, yet repudiated all the popular interpretations of the messianic hope.

The Gospels are shot through with suggestions of the bafflement his followers felt in the face of his words and personality. There was a mysterious and forceful quality about him which accounted both for people's loyalty to him and for their misunderstandings of his teachings. His disciples followed him, but they were uncertain of where his path lay. He enjoyed wedding-feasts and parties and conversation: yet however easily he may have moved among men and women, he was distinguished by an amazing, and even presumptuous authority. We cannot say more than this about Jesus' personality and inner experience. Perhaps even some of these statements are unwarranted by the evidence at our disposal, since it is hard to distinguish the historical facts in the Gospel material from later interpretations.

THE CRUCIFIXION

We are in a better position to know about the nature of the Christian experience in the early Church, at that time when men could still look back with reverence, fondness, and triumph to the strange, earthly career of the man Jesus. It was a strange triumph because the way lay through crucifixion.

Jesus' Trial

The reasons for the trial and execution of Jesus are not altogether clear. Accounts in the different Gospels do not tally exactly. It seems evident that Jesus was regarded, by the Sadducees at least, as a dangerous character. The charge for which he was arraigned was blasphemy, but political considerations were in the picture as well. Jesus had come to Jerusalem in the guise of a Messiah, and he had acted brusquely in clearing the Temple of money-changing and trafficking. The Zealot cause was represented among his disciples. Though he had shown no direct signs of fomenting a revolution, his attitudes were subversive in flavor. Under the charge of blasphemy the Council, or Sanhedrin, could not establish the death penalty, but it was able to make out a case to the Roman procurator, Pilate, claiming that Jesus had planned insurrection, for he called himself King of the Jews. Pilate wavered. Finally he decided to have him executed.

According to our accounts, there was an incident in which Pilate released a prisoner, Barabbas, giving the Jerusalem mob a choice between the two criminals. It is a strange account, for this custom of choice at the Passover is nowhere else attested. Barabbas, though supposedly a political bandit, a Zealot, was not mentioned anywhere else, and it would have been odd to release a revolutionary. There are other details which are puzzling. A possible, but highly speculative explanation of the matter is this: Barabbas' name was also the name for Jesus. In view of Jesus' use of the term *Abba,* it is possible that he himself, like a number of his circle, had a nickname, for example, "Son of Abba," i.e. Barabbas. Perhaps Pilate's question to the Jews really amounted to the dilemma, Shall I release Jesus the King of the Jews, the Jesus who is allegedly a political insurrectionary, or shall I release to you the Jesus Barabbas, the Jesus who allegedly blasphemes? The Sanhedrin could not legally execute the latter, but Pilate could execute the former. So they asked for the Barabbas to be released. This account squares with Pilate's reputation for cynicism, which is not brought out in the Gospel narrative as we have it. It also strengthens the case for Jesus' consciousness of his own special relationship to the Father. But of course such an account is speculative.

Betrayed and deserted, Jesus met his death on the cross like many another criminal and rebel under the Roman administration. It was a strange end, so it seemed, to a puzzling career. But as it turned out, this death was the prelude to a new uprush of experience among his former followers, which brought into existence the community of the church. Pilate and the others had no inkling of the fact that the rather obscure and (to twentieth-century thinking) possibly crazy prophet whom they had caused to die was to win a spectacular allegiance in the hearts of a vast number of men. Among the founders of the great faiths, Jesus stands out in an odd way insofar as his life was both brief and violent. Elsewhere in the great religions the founders were primarily teachers or vehicles of an uttered revelation. For the Christians, however, the most significant thing about Jesus was the nature of his acts.

THE RESURRECTION

What was the nature of the disciples' experience which convinced them that Jesus was again with them—restored and raised from the dead on the third day? A very early summary of the Christian faith is found in Paul's first letter to the Corinthians:

> For I delivered to you as of first importance what I also received, that Christ died for our sins in accordance with the scriptures, that he was buried, that he was raised on the third day in accordance with the scriptures, and that he appeared to Cephas [i.e. Peter], then to the twelve. Then he appeared to more than five hundred brethren at one time, most of whom are still alive, though some have fallen asleep. Then he appeared to James, then to all the apostles. Last of all, as to one untimely born, he appeared also to me.[3]

We can date this letter to A.D. 54, and it is interesting to note that by this time there already existed a short summary of Christ's death and his resurrection which was proclaimed by the Christians. This was the *kerygma,* or proclamation, of the earliest Church. The early Christians were not concerned merely with outlining Jesus' teaching; they wanted to tell the good news which expressed to men the fact of their salvation. But more immediately for our purpose we note in the passage an early reference to the resurrection appearances. These are given a fuller description in the Gospels. Thus, in Luke we find:

> That very day two of them were going to a village named Emmaus, about seven miles from Jerusalem, and talking with each other about all these things that had happened. While they were talking and discussing together, Jesus himself drew near and went with them. But their eyes were kept from recognizing him.[4]

They explained to the stranger the events that had occurred in the city—the death of Jesus and the incredible report of the empty tomb. The stranger said:

> "O foolish men, and slow of heart to believe all that the prophets have spoken! Was it not necessary that the Christ should suffer these things and enter into his glory?" And beginning with Moses and all the prophets, he interpreted to them in all the scriptures the things concerning himself. So they drew near to the village to which they were going; and he made as though he would go further, but they constrained him, saying, "Stay with

---

[3] I Corinthians 15:3–8 (RSV).
[4] This and the following quotations are from Luke 24:13ff. (RSV).

us, for it is toward evening and the day is now far spent." So he went in to stay with them. When he was at table with them, he took the bread and blessed, and broke it, and gave it to them. And their eyes were opened and they recognized him; and he vanished out of their sight. They said to each other, "Did not our hearts burn within us while he talked to us on the road, while he opened to us the scriptures?"

They hurried back to Jerusalem to tell of the incident.

As they were saying this, Jesus himself stood among them. But they were startled and frightened, and supposed that they saw a spirit. And he said to them, "Why are you troubled and why do questionings rise in your hearts? See my hands and my feet, that it is I myself; handle me, and see; for a spirit has not flesh and bones as you see that I have." And while they still disbelieved for joy, and wondered, he said to them, "Have you anything here to eat?" They gave him a piece of broiled fish, and he took it and ate before them.

He led the disciples as far as to Bethany,

and lifting up his hands he blessed them. While he blessed them, he parted from them. And they returned to Jerusalem with great joy, and were continually in the temple blessing God.

Accounts of the Resurrection

Needless to say, a great deal has been written about this and the other narratives of the Resurrection. Some scholars have cast doubt on the reliability of these accounts. But as we have seen, the Resurrection was a very early article of faith with the Christian community. At the time when Paul wrote the passage quoted earlier, a number of the people who had participated in these events and experiences were still alive, as he points out. The proclamation was made by men like Peter, who died for the faith. It is hardly likely that they would have been willing to undergo martyrdom on behalf of a fabrication. There can be little doubt that the disciples did undergo experiences in which they perceived Jesus in their midst and had a powerful, even frightening, sense of his risen power. It is also unlikely that the story of the empty tomb reflected only a trick played by the disciples.

However, the perception of Jesus in his resurrected form was not altogether straightforward. It is notable that he appeared only to those who were among his former associates and followers, not to the world at large. Nor was he immediately recognized by the two who were walking to Emmaus. In

Jerusalem the disciples thought at first that he was a spirit. We may infer from these accounts that the resurrection appearances were mysterious and unexpected in character. There was a strong sense of Jesus' presence, and this was physically conceived. As their picture of the presence clarified, the disciples perceived that this indeed was the Jesus who shared their life with them: he ate broiled fish and honey in their presence. To Thomas he presented his wounded side. However we are to explain these experiences, we must note that they float ambivalently between the numinous and the physical. In many respects they reflect a feeling of some strange presence coming forth from the mysterious, invisible world; in other respects they seem like the simple perception of a material person existing in the midst of those who perceived him. The question of whether this was a physical resurrection of Jesus, whether this was merely the registering of certain psychological occurrences, or whether a third hypothesis would be more viable is a matter of faith and judgment. For our purposes in recording the history and character of the early Christian experience, it is enough to note that the disciples and early followers were convinced by these events of the continued power of Jesus and his triumph over a tragic death.

Effects of Belief in the Resurrection

This death had thrown the disciples into despair and disorganization. They had followed Jesus to Jerusalem, but they had not stayed with him in his hour of isolation and suffering. Their dreams, such as they were—of a new era ushered in by this powerful leader to whom they had given their allegiance— had been shattered by the events of Jesus' trial and crucifixion. It was no wonder that they began to think of returning, disillusioned, to their former occupations. Unexpectedly, they found that the leader was in a mysterious way "risen," and the movement to which they belonged, far from fading, began to rouse them in new hope and effectiveness. They began to look back with sharpened understanding on the meaning of Jesus' career. They saw in it the fulfilment of the prophecies in Deutero-Isaiah concerning the Suffering Servant. They traced their new-found power to the spirit of the Lord Jesus; and they found their position confirmed and strengthened in an extraordinary experience that befell them on Pentecost.

And suddenly a sound came from heaven like the rush of a mighty wind, and it filled all the house where they were sitting. And there appeared to them tongues as of fire, distributed and resting on each one of them. And they were all filled with the Holy Spirit and began to speak in other tongues, as the Spirit gave them utterance. Now there were dwelling in Jerusalem Jews, devout men from every nation under heaven. And at this sound the multitude came together, and they were bewildered, because each one heard them speaking in his own language. And they were amazed and wondered, saying, "Are not all these who are speaking Galileans? And how is it that we hear, each of us in his own native language? Parthians and Medes and Elamites and residents of Mesopotamia, Judea and Cappadocia, Pontus and Asia, Phrygia and Pamphylia, Egypt and the parts of Libya belonging to Cyrene, and visitors from Rome, both Jews and proselytes, Cretans and Arabians, we hear them telling in our own tongues the mighty works of God." And all were amazed and perplexed, saying to one another, "What does this mean?" But others mocking said, "They are filled with new wine."[5]

Glossolalia

This experience of access of power differs somewhat from the prophetic experiences described in the previous chapter. For one thing, here was a shared, a communal experience. But at the same time the numinous nature of the event was unmistakable. Here was the mysterious power of God issuing forth as it were from heaven. The phenomenon of glossolalia, or speaking with tongues, which followed this event, became fairly widespread in the early church. It is naive to suppose that the disciples spoke literally a multitude of languages all at once. It is significant that some of the witnesses thought that those who spoke thus were drunk. Evidently these people heard nothing miraculous. Speaking with tongues was a form of ecstatic, wordless utterance which conveyed to hearers the experience the disciples themselves had undergone and were undergoing—possession by a nameless and inexpressible holy power which they attributed to God. Those in whom this struck a response readily "understood" and were carried away by the holy message. Others looked on the disciples as tipsy, though, as Peter pointed out, it was unlikely that they should be under the influence of alcohol in the early morning. This outpouring of the spirit was one of the signs of the continued activity of God amid his chosen people—though now the people was not the nation of Israel, but the worshiping community of Christians in Jerusalem.

PAUL OF TARSUS

In the passage quoted earlier from Paul's letter to the Corinthians, he mentioned what he regarded as a further resurrection appearance—the occasion when he saw Christ on the Damascus Road. This was another determinative event for the history of the early Christian community. It was a shaking

[5] Acts of the Apostles 2:2-13 (RSV).

experience for this pious Pharisee who had been prominently involved in the persecution of the Jerusalem Christians, and who was now on his way to root out the heresy in Damascus:

> But Saul, still breathing threats and murder against the disciples of the Lord, went to the high priest and asked him for letters to the synagogues at Damascus, so that if he found any belonging to the Way, men or women, he might bring them bound to Jerusalem. Now as he journeyed he approached Damascus, and suddenly a light from heaven flashed about him. And he fell to the ground and heard a voice saying to him, "Saul, Saul, why do you persecute me?" And he said, "Who are you, Lord?" And he said, "I am Jesus, whom you are persecuting; but rise and enter the city, and you will be told what you are to do." The men who were traveling with him stood speechless, hearing the voice but seeing no one. Saul arose from the ground; and when his eyes were opened, he could see nothing; so they led him by the hand and brought him into Damascus. And for three days he was without sight, and neither ate nor drank.[6]

Paul's Conversion

Here was something analogous to a prophetic experience of the divine majesty, but instead of Yahweh, the focus of the experience was Jesus himself. Here was proof to Paul of the glorious nature of the Lord whom he had been so zealous to persecute. From that time, he gave his allegiance to the new Master. The effect of the sudden vision upon him was dramatic: the irruption of power induced hysterical blindness that incapacitated Paul for three days. To recover himself and to think out the meaning of this strange reversal of all his former ideas, Paul withdrew into upper Arabia. This period of solitude and recuperation was followed by his return to Damascus. It is interesting that he did not go up to the community in Jerusalem at this time. It was three years later that he went there to meet Peter, the chief person in the community, and James, the brother of Jesus. Meanwhile he had been proselytizing on his own account, and in the course of this activity he had evolved his own distinctive theology, which was to form a great part of the basis of subsequent Christian thought about Jesus.

Paul as Pharisee

Paul, as we have seen, was brought up in the atmosphere of the Pharisaic interpretation of Judaism. Though born at Tarsus in Cilicia, he studied at Jerusalem under the famous and respected Rabbi Gamaliel. He had been

---

[6] Acts 9:1–9 (RSV).

strictly observant of the Jewish Law, and it was in relation to this early way of life that he worked out his new attitudes and doctrines. He saw in the Gospel of Jesus a new freedom which made nonsense of a continued strict adherence to the details of the Torah. Men could not find their justification before God through their own work: justification was by faith and the favor of God. Thus it was useless attempting to win God's blessing by a rigid adherence to the Law.

In Galatians, Paul likened the situation to that of an heir born to inherit his father's estate. During the period of his miniority he is kept under control and not allowed the full enjoyment of that which will be his. Then the time comes when he enters into his property. The people of Israel were born to God's estate, but from the time of Abraham onward had been in a state of minority. But now the new age had dawned. The old fetters were removed. And the people of God entered into their full inheritance in the Kingdom brought in by Jesus Christ. All this meant a liberation from the manifold tabus of the Law, though it also meant a deeper goodness in conformity with the law of love. Ethical action would flow from men's acceptance of the saving work of Christ.

On the practical side, this aspect of Paul's theology was exceedingly important, for it meant that Gentile converts did not need to enter into the regulations which controlled orthodox membership of the Jewish community. In particular, there was no need of circumcision. The doctrines also meant that even within that community Christian followers could be liberated from the Pharisaical attitude. Already among the leaders of the Jerusalem community Peter had baptized the Roman centurion Cornelius, who was not circumcized. Already he had had a vision which he interpreted to mean that "God is no respecter of persons, but in every nation he that feareth him and worketh righteousness is accepted with him. . . . Can any man forbid water, that these should not be baptized, which have received the Holy Ghost as well?" (Acts 10:34, 47).

The Gentile Problem

Nevertheless, the question of the status of Gentiles was the subject of severe dispute in the early community. It divided into two schools on this issue—the Judaizers, who wished to maintain the community as something strictly within the orbit of Jewish orthodoxy, and the liberals who believed that the movement should open itself out to a wider life and wider opportunities. The division occurred quite early, and there were allegations that in the communal distribution of food Greek-speaking widows were being neglected. This was merely one symptom of the division. It was agreed that a commission of seven men—not apostles (who were on the whole Judaizers)—should supervise the matter and ensure equity. One of these men was Stephen, who was brought for trial by the Sanhedrin on the grounds of blasphemy and was stoned to death. Further persecution followed. These facts were highly relevant to the dispute about the Law. On the whole, the Christians had escaped severe persecution up to this time because they had kept piously to the Law. But the widespread acceptance of the principle for which Paul and others had fought meant that the Christians would not only encounter hostility from the Jews of Palestine, but would also be opposed in the various scattered communities in the world. It meant risking the severance of the movement from the body of the nation.

Meanwhile the church was growing with great rapidity abroad. Paul and Barnabas had won converts at Antioch and in other parts of Syria. Paul's first missionary journey to Cyprus and Asia Minor had implanted many new and thriving Christian communities. On their return to Antioch the missionaries recounted their successes, but it was plain to them and to the faithful at Antioch that the expansion had brought the question of the Law and of circumcision to a head. A decision had to be arrived at quickly. The two were commissioned to go to Jerusalem to consult. There, in about A.D. 49, a council was held in which the matter was debated. It was resolved as follows:

> The brethren, both the apostles and the elders, to the brethren who are of the Gentiles in Antioch and Syria and Cilicia, greeting. Since we have heard that some persons from us have troubled you with words, unsettling your minds, although we gave them no instructions, it has seemed good to us in assembly to choose men and send them to you with our beloved Barnabas and Paul, men who have risked their lives for the sake of our Lord Jesus Christ. We have therefore sent Judas and Silas, who themselves will tell you the same things by word of mouth. For it has seemed good to the Holy Spirit and to us to lay upon you no greater burden than these necessary things: that you abstain from what has been sacrificed to idols and from blood and from what is strangled and from unchastity. If you keep yourselves from these, you will do well.[7]

In principle Paul and his followers had won the day. But the strength of the Judaizing party was greater than might be expected from a simple reading of the documents of the New Testament, for the church in which they had their origin and through which they were collected, was, at that time, after the destruction of Jerusalem in A.D. 70 and the demise of the Christian community there, predominantly Pauline in interpretation. As late as the fourth century

---

[7] Acts 15:23–29 (RSV).

there were references to scattered Christian communities called the Nazarenes, who practiced the Jewish Law, although they were orthodox in their Christian beliefs. These seem to have been the remnants of one section at least of the Jerusalem church. For many of the members of the Jerusalem church, Christ's messianic role was still bound up very intimately with Israel.

Paul's Missionary Journeys

Encouraged, Paul went out into the mission field again—into Asia Minor, Macedonia, and Greece. There he delivered his famous sermon at the Areopagus in Athens. A Christian community was founded by Paul at Corinth in about A.D. 51. He stayed on there some eighteen months after which he returned to Antioch. A third journey soon followed: to Ephesus, where he spent two years, and then again to Greece. He returned to Jerusalem where his preaching about the Gentiles caused tumult and disorder. He was haled before the Sanhedrin and sent to Caesarea for trial. The trial was deferred for two years only to be reinstituted in 59. At this point Paul appealed to Caesar as a Roman citizen. This involved being tried in Rome. There he was kept in detention for two years and then released. Further missionary work followed. Finally, during the Neronian persecutions, he was killed. Throughout this period he had been tireless in preaching, teaching, and organizing. His letters give an indication of the way in which, while engaged in these tasks, he was evolving a wide-visioned theology. His teaching about the Law has been mentioned. What were the other distinctive features of the message which he planted across the Roman Empire?

PAULINE THEOLOGY

Central, of course, to Paul's teaching was the figure of Jesus. But this was not just the man Jesus: it was the Christ, who had risen in glory, and who headed a new community and guided it through his Spirit. Nor was Paul's Christ just a Messiah in the older Jewish sense. He was the Son of God and the Lord of Creation, who sat "at the right hand of the Father." All this was apparent to Paul through his dramatic experience of the risen Lord and of his realization that a new age had come to pass. The death and resurrection of Christ were the means whereby men could be saved, for by identifying themselves, in the community, with him they would be raised up likewise to glory. Christ was the savior who could give men the new freedom of the Spirit which Paul himself felt and could free them from sin.

The doctrine of salvation presupposed a view about man's normal condition. From what did man need to be saved? Paul relied here upon his knowledge of the Hebrew scriptures, though he introduced Greek conceptions as well. The sin and slavery of man's condition was on the one hand traced back to the transgression of Adam (a theory current in the rabbinical schools); on the other hand, Paul also spoke of world-rulers, elemental spirits whose dominion over man could be evil. Man knew God, for his reason contained a divine spark. But he preferred to adore the material world. Therefore he fell into slavery. What Paul called "the flesh" became tainted. Men's moral and intellectual capacities became perverted by sin. Christ could liberate man from this state of bondage. It was not a matter of having committed particular wrongs—particular sins—but in his alienation from God, man's nature was warped and infected. Christ could restore the true divine image in him.

How is this effected according to Paul? It is through Christ's death and resurrection. Christ's death was a self-sacrifice which atoned for the sin of mankind. Christ's resurrection was a visible sign of the triumph over death which the defeat of sin entails. Paul stressed the solidarity of mankind—its being a single entity, like a clan, as well as its being composed of individuals. Thus in participating in the life of the flesh, Christ could stand as a representative of mankind. While all fell through the act of one man, Adam, so all are saved through the act of one man, Jesus. More importantly, Paul stressed another and higher kind of solidarity. The Christian community was like an organism, with Christ as its head, and in the life of the community and through baptism and the eucharist, Christians could become identified with Christ and divinized. Christ's nature was spiritual. He shared the essence of the Deity. Through union with him, men could throw off their old selves and rise above the life of the flesh into the life of the spirit.

Paul's Mysticism

Paul's emphasis upon union with Christ, upon Christ's dwelling within us, has led people to speak of his "Christ-mysticism." Though Paul was not in an obvious way a contemplative mystic such as Plotinus, there was evidence of his capacity for ecstasy and trance. In a reference to himself he wrote, in his second letter to the Corinthians:

> I know a man in Christ who fourteen years ago was caught up to the third heaven—whether in the body or out of the body I do not know, God knows. And I know that this man was caught up into Paradise—whether in the body or out of the body I do not know, God knows—and he heard things that cannot be told, which man may not utter.[8]

In the Temple at Jerusalem on one occasion Paul went into a trance and saw Jesus. Such experiences no doubt nourished him in the travails and afflictions

---

[8] II Corinthians 12:2–4 (RSV).

which he underwent—terrible floggings, shipwrecks, a stoning, perilous journeys, hunger, and thirst. Such experiences, too, help to explain something of
Paul's sense of the divine indwelling of Christ. This unity with the Lord,
controlling him from within, made vivid to him the way in which the life of the
spirit can operate through the saving grace of the Lord Jesus. His theology
was not merely an attempt to systematize and organize the teachings of a
community which needed its life related to the historic past of Israel. It was
also in some degree a transcript of his own experience.

Ethical Teachings

But it would be wrong to think of Paul's theology as simply an exposition of
the new life of the spirit which he enjoyed. Though he stresses grace and faith
rather than works as the key to salvation, the ethical side of Paul's teachings is
vitally important. By the joy of union with Christ, the Christian's behavior is
profoundly altered, and his actions are informed by love—the *agapē* which
Paul so eloquently delineated in his hymn-like chapter beginning "Though I
speak with the tongues of men and of angels, and have not charity, I am
become as sounding brass, or a tinkling cymbal." Faith and hope might be
necessary and central to the Christian life—faith in Christ and hope of the
final victory—but *agapē* was even greater than these in the new community.
Not that Christians always displayed this attitude. The Epistles give plenty of
indication of the dissension and difficulty which Paul encountered in the
churches which he had helped to found, and the clash between the Judaizers
and the liberals was not without its stormy and bitter side. Yet despite these
adversities in moral life, Paul was convinced that within the Christian community there was displayed a oneness and a love which often surpassed the
meticulous virtues of the Pharisaic life which he had left behind him. Men
were capable of progressive sanctification, yet without asceticism, and the key
to it was the love of God and the love of neighbor.

Paul's Idea of Salvation

One other side of Paul's teaching is worth mentioning. He was convinced, as
were most Christians of this early period, so far as we can judge, of the speedy
return of Christ in glory. At that time there would occur the judgment and the
entry of the faithful into the glory of the new order. Jesus in his own sayings
talked of the imminence of the Kingdom, and these words were often interpreted to mean that the final cataclysm was not far off. During the stormy and
terrible years which led to the sack of Jerusalem, such hopes were particularly
fervid, for the events seemed to correspond to certain signs of the Second Coming
which had been handed down as the words of the Lord himself.

But time dragged on. The Christian community was loth to give up the
expectation of a swift and cosmic return of their Master. The faithful, gath-

ered in churches up and down the Empire, displayed a hope and patience in the face of adversity which was in part determined by these lively expectations. Although the early Christians were mistaken in their belief that the world order would soon cease, the doctrine of the "last things" has remained an integral part in the Christian faith. Ever since in Christian history there have been periodical predictions of the swift arrival of the Second Coming and of the establishment of the Millennium. God is still seen as working his purpose out in history, not only past but future. And Paul, in elaborating his belief in the resurrection of the body, gave distinctive character to the Christian concept of salvation. Though Paul was not too clear about the nature of the resurrection body (it was a sort of "spiritual body"), his doctrine emphasized that there would be a reconstruction of individual personality, not just a heavenly persistence of a disembodied soul which could enshrine at best only one aspect of the human being. This idea was in line with the insistence on holy living in this world, in which body and personality become a temple for the Holy Spirit.

GREEK INFLUENCES IN THE EARLY CHURCH

Paul's work as a missionary was supplemented by the labors of others—Barnabas, John, Mark, and lesser figures. Peter himself finished his life in Rome, where he was martyred. Thus the faith had spread far in thirty-five years from its Palestinian home, and the movement carried on, only briefly checked by the persecutions of the sixties, in which both Peter and Paul lost their lives. But a crisis developed toward the end of the first century, when the Church had to rely upon new leadership, after the first generation of apostles had passed away. The influx of Greek-speaking members brought into the movement new beliefs. Though some of these were legitimate from the Christian point of view, others threatened the basis of the faith.

GNOSTICISM

The churches found themselves confronted with a movement known broadly as Gnosticism. The term "Gnosticism" derives from the Greek term *gnosis,* or "knowledge." *Gnosis* meant the mystical or contemplative knowledge of the Divine Being possible for those initiated into the movement. The ideas which were circulating as the correct, but esoteric, interpretation of Christian belief had their origin both in Hellenistic mysticism and in the Jewish Essene sect, and there were also, through these sources, Zoroastrian influences. Gnosticism was most frequently embraced by those whose roots lay outside the Jewish heritage. During the second century A.D. it reached, from the point of view of orthodox Christianity, alarming proportions. As might be expected, there was often an anti-Jewish and anti-Old-Testament flavor suffusing Gnostic teachings. On the other hand there was a Gnostic strand running through early Christianity.

A main feature of the varied strands of Gnostic teaching (which ranged from beliefs which were elaborated in philosophical terms to others which incorporated astrology and a complex mythology) was that this world, the material world which man inhabited, was evil, and was antagonistic toward the higher good. However, among some men there existed a divine spark. Such "spiritual" men, by turning from the evil world of matter, could ascend to the divine Source from which they ultimately had their being. Others were trapped in the bonds of matter—those were the "fleshly" men. Thus the faith of Gnosticism tended to be esoteric, confined to the few.

In order to explain the evil nature of the world, and at the same time to account for the difference between Gnosticism and the teachings of the Old Testament, the Gnostics commonly made a distinction between the Divine Being and a lower Creator, the Demiurge, who emanated from the former. The Demiurge was implicated in a cosmic fall, and so the world he created was infected with evil. He was the being whom the Old Testament writers referred to as Yahweh. For many Gnostics the God of the Old Testament was cruel and capricious, not at all to be identified with the *Abba,* the loving Father, whom Jesus spoke of. In order that spiritual men should be enabled to turn back to the divine Source, Jesus was sent as a Redeemer, though it was commonly held that the man Jesus was just an appearance projected onto the stage of human history, and not a fleshly incarnation of the Divine Being.

Generally speaking, the way to *gnosis,* to the supernatural knowledge and union with the Divine Being, was through asceticism and withdrawal from the material world. But some Gnostic groups turned in the opposite direction, believing that the spiritual man rises "beyond good and evil"; these groups instituted orgiastic cults through which the adherents gave expression to their superiority to the moral law. The ascetic side of Gnosticism pointed clearly to the mystical and contemplative nature of the experience at which these people aimed, but their mysticism was never properly integrated either with belief in Jesus or with the worship of a personal Creator. The Creator was demoted to the status of an evil Demiurge, and thereby the insights of prophetic monotheism were submerged: also, Jesus played an unreal role in the cosmic drama. For these reasons, Gnosticism cut at the roots of Christian belief.

Marcion

Though a Christian, and not properly speaking a Gnostic, Marcion (who died about A.D. 160) betrayed anti-Jewish tendencies. He expressed a viewpoint which threatened the integrity of Christian belief though he considered his philosophy the true interpretation of Christianity. A rich ship-owner of Sinope on the Black Sea, he made his way to Rome in 140. There he organized his followers and set up a separate community within the Christian community. Because of his excellent gifts for administration, his followers spread widely over the Mediterranean world. His new organization constituted a powerful challenge to the Church in the latter part of the second century. Though he was not, like the Gnostics, much concerned with mysticism, he reacted strongly against the Law enshrined in the Hebrew scriptures. For him, love was the all-important thing. He claimed that Paul, in some of the writings ascribed to him, had seen this point clearly, and that the Christian communities, in continuing to make use of the Old Testament had betrayed Paul's insight. Yahweh was, for Marcion, the evil Demiurge: Jesus' work had consisted in the overthrow of this diabolical being. Jesus' God, he maintained, was the supreme God of love, very different in character from the law-imposing Demiurge. Not surprisingly, Marcion was excommunicated in A.D. 144.

The appeal of Marcion lay in the fact that he exaggerated a truth, namely that Jesus' teaching, and the interpretation of his life as expressed by Paul, were not totally in line with the earlier Jewish conception of the Law. He believed that the Old Testament by itself did not delineate fully the God of Jesus. Insofar as there was a distinctive quality in Jesus' attitudes and in Christian belief, it meant that the Old Testament conception of God was lacking or misleading.

The Forming of the Canon

The Marcionite position, like that of the Gnostics, made nonsense of an important aspect of Jesus' life—his claim to "fulfill" the Law and the Prophets. By destroying this monotheistic basis of the Christian faith such doctrines allowed entry to all kinds of extraneous mythological ideas. So the orthodox Christian community felt itself bound to react sharply. Since Marcion had denied the authenticity of some of the Gospels and other accepted writings, and since the Gnostics appealed to an esoteric and secret tradition which, they alleged, had been handed down privately from the apostles, it became necessary to take some stand on the authority and composition of the canon of Christian writings. The so-called Church Fathers who opposed Gnosticism and Marcion pointed out clearly that these doctrines ran contrary to the plain meaning of scripture, and that if the canon were given a general acceptance, Christians would have an authority independent of the words of individuals. In a long process the present canon of the New Testament was evolved. Various spurious and doubtful documents were excluded, such as the apocryphal gospels. In general the criterion of the work to be included in what later was known as the New Testament was this: does it accord with the manifest

teachings of the Church which have been handed down from the apostles?
Though a few borderline cases remained to be decided, the bulk of the canon
was recognized as authoritative by the end of the second century A.D. Thus we
can say that in a sense the scriptures derived their status from the church
tradition; but once they had been recognized they became the norm of doctrine.

CHURCH STRUCTURE IN FIRST CENTURY

We have seen that Marcion was excommunicated from the Roman community. This authority of the community to exclude those who contravened the
Christian message either by scandalous conduct or by erroneous teachings was
one further safeguard against the influx of ideas and practices which threatened the integrity of the faith in these relatively early days. But these pressures
brought about a hardening of the organization of the Church. It was largely
during this period that the institutions which came to typify the Church were
evolved and fixed.

Unfortunately, our evidence is fragmentary in relation to the period before the beginning of the second century A.D. Different theories of the origin
and nature of the ministry of the early Church are held, notably the contrasting views that authority derived from above, from Jesus through the apostles
and onward to the bishops, and, in opposition, that authority derived essentially from below through the will of the faithful as a community. The belief
that the episcopal structure and the apostolic succession (that is, the succession of bishops in an unbroken line going back to the Apostles) are an integral
mark of the true Church is the heart of the first theory. But the latter theory
postulates that arrangements varied according to times and circumstances. A
further dimension to the argument is provided by the claim that the papacy
was an original institution of the Church, resting ultimately on Jesus' commission to Peter. As far as we can see both theories have some substance as
applied to the first and second centuries A.D.

CHURCH STRUCTURE IN THE SECOND CENTURY

By the early second century the Church, except in one or two areas, contained
the so-called threefold ministry—bishops, presbyters, and deacons. Originally
the term *episkopos*, rendered into English as "bishop," meant "overseer," or
"superintendent." In the New Testament we hear of those who are appointed
to look after particular communities as overseers. At Jerusalem, James functioned as such a leader of the community. The duties of such superintendents
were not just administrative. Their important function in ritual was the celebration of the Lord's Supper, or eucharist.

The eucharist was, from earliest times, the most solemn and central act in the worshiping life of the community. In general, the form of worship was modeled after the services of the Jewish synagogues: readings from the scriptures, preaching, prayers; but the eucharist was a distinctive element in Christian liturgical structure. It was a memorial of the death of Christ, and an expression of his continuing presence in the midst of the faithful. It was also an expression of the mutual solidarity and love of the members of the community itself. Over this sacred meal the bishop presided. With the growth of individual communities, however, it became no longer possible for the bishop to be present at all the meeting-places. His priestly office was delegated to the presbyter (from which word, literally meaning "elder," the term "priest" itself was derived). But in addition to this sacred function, the overseer had charge of the finances and discipline of the community. The administration of alms was an important feature of his duties, for the early Christians were noted for the way in which they supported the widows and other needy members of the group. Likewise, the overseer had to ensure that the members lived a life in accord with the teachings of Christ and to encourage those who had doubts and fears. This pastoral and administrative side of the bishop's office could be onerous and complex, so that many of his duties were delegated to "servants," or deacons. These deacons were the main link between the bishop and the people. They also played a part in the administration of the eucharist. In such ways the threefold ministry was evolved. There were also lesser orders, such as the acolytes who acted as servers at the Mass when that institution had evolved into a complex ceremonial.

Primacy of Rome in Early Church

The problem of the evolution of Roman primacy is one which has divided Christians over a long period. The evidence of the institution of the papacy, as interpreted by the Roman Catholic Church, is sufficiently ambiguous for it to be possible to take up opposed positions on its basis. Without doubt the Church in Rome had from early times a special prestige. In the *Epistle to the Corinthians,* a document dating from the last part of the first century A.D., written by the Bishop at Rome, Clement, probably third successor of Peter as head of the community in the city, a dissension which had broken out in the Corinthian church is mentioned. Clement sent advice in this epistle to the members of the Corinthian church. They appear to have accepted his advice. This is testimony to the authority of the Roman community. It is also clear from a letter written by the Bishop of Carthage in the latter part of the second century that Rome sent help and aid to the churches throughout the Empire, and thus was in some sense the focal point of the world-wide community of believers.

A succession of excellent bishops further raised the prestige of Rome. Above all, the Roman Church traced its establishment back to the great apostles, Peter and Paul, the first being Jesus' chief disciple, the other the creator of the wider missionary enterprise. Bishop Stephen of Rome argued in the middle of the third century that he was the successor of Peter who had been declared by Jesus to be the rock upon which the Church would be built. Another factor in the development of papal primacy was the fact that certain bishops exercised metropolitan powers over wide areas. The Bishop of Alexandria effectively administered the Church in Libya and Egypt, the Bishop of Antioch oversaw Asia Minor, and the Bishop of Rome looked after Italy. These metropolitan superintendents had wide prestige and respect. As the hierarchy developed, it was natural for one of them to be recognized as first. In line with the facts outlined above, this was inevitably the Bishop of Rome.

Life in the Church—Social and Ethical

Meanwhile, changes were coming over the social life of the Church. In early days the communities were sufficiently small to make a real sense of fellowship possible. This was furthered by the *agapē* meal, or love-feast, a supper party in which Christians met together. This originated with the eucharist, or Last Supper. But for various reasons with the passage of time the sacrament became disengaged from the actual meal. The meal was then carried on as a fellowship party, often presided over by the bishop. But with the increase of membership, these parties were carried on without direct ecclesiastical supervision. They were not always as sober and dignified as they might have been. In the fourth century church buildings were no longer used for these meetings, and the *agapē*, which had become increasingly like pagan banquets, was discouraged. The simplicity of early Christian life was replaced by other ways. Women who had been encouraged to dress simply, without ornamentation and cosmetics, gradually returned to their old habits and the ways of the world crept into the community.

Nevertheless, it would be wrong to suppose that the Christian Church did not maintain its essential integrity of witness. Throughout the early centuries it had been consistently opposed to idolatry. Many converts had to leave their former occupations because these involved traffic with pagan religion. In sporadic and repeated persecutions, many suffered because they would not pay service to the cult of the emperor. In their indifference to politics and unwillingness to swear allegiance to the emperor according to the official rites, the Christians were regarded as dangerously subversive. Officials and governors viewed the community with suspicion. This resulted in oppression. Odd slanders about the cultus of Christianity were circulated. They were commonly (in a travesty of the eucharist) accused of cannibalism; and other crimes were laid at their door. The privacy of the early morning and late evening meetings (for most of the community worked during the day) and the exclusion of those not baptized from the eucharist itself (an exclusion which later came to be abolished) gave the opportunity for enemies to start rumors about the goings-on in this allegedly secret society. Though a number of Christians fell away under oppression, there remained a large body of the faithful and they sacrificed much on behalf of their faith.

To ethical concerns the Church was attentive. The Christian view of marriage, with the accompanying rule of chastity, was not admittedly different from the ideals of the best minds of pagan antiquity. But it was regarded as impressive to perceive ordinary men who were given the strength to repudiate sexual corruption and live an honorable and devoted married life.

Although the Church did not condemn slavery as an institution, slaves were part of the fellowship, and the attitude and behavior of Christian slave-owners was markedly different from the typical attitudes and behavior of the time. They considered slaves to be human beings, not tools or instruments of the owner. In these and other ways the Christian mode of life spread an enlightened and effective morality without getting itself bound to the complex of rules which had made the Jewish code so hard to follow in a wider world. Moreover, within the confines of the church there was a unity between men of different rank and nation. Although many of the early converts were poor artisans, and other slaves, there were also richer and educated people in the community. The fellowship promoted by the eucharist and the *agapē* served to break down class barriers.

EARLY CHURCH FATHERS

Clement

Meanwhile the theological teaching of the Church was developing. The apologists of the second century began to defend the teachings by showing that Christianity brought out the best in pagan philosophy. In Alexandria a school was established to give instruction in the Christian faith. Clement of Alexandria (c. A.D. 150–c. 215) was an outstanding figure who sought to give Christianity a philosophical interpretation while remaining faithful to the apostolic tradition and the revelation in the Old Testament and in Christ. He was willing to concede to the Gnostics that *gnosis* was the true end of man, but a perfection which one attained only through accepting Christ as guide and baptism as prerequisite.

Origen

The outstanding figure amid the Alexandrians was a pupil of Clement's, Origen (c. 180–c. 253/4). In the period after the persecutions under Septimius Severus in 202, Origen, though a layman, was put in charge of the catechetical school at Alexandria. Travels took him to Rome and Palestine, where he was invited by two of the bishops to preach. This was regarded as a breach of discipline by the Egyptian church, and eventually, after further troubles, Origen was deprived of his position in Alexandria. He settled in Palestine, where, during the Decian persecutions of 249–250 he was tortured. But he would not renounce his faith. He had shown in early days great zeal for the ascetic life, and making a literal interpretation of a passage in Matthew 19:12, he had actually castrated himself. But his scholarship was wide and profound, and he brought an original mind to bear on the problems of Christian theology and philosophy.

The greatest of his many writings was the *De Principiis*. The Greek original was largely lost and only fragments which we know through a later, but not always accurate Latin translation, survive. In this work Origen outlined a whole system of Christian thought. He held that God the Father ruled over the whole universe; the Son, or Logos, ruled over rational creatures; while the Spirit's activity was confined to the church. He did not hold what came to be the orthodox view of the Trinity, but in effect tended to subordinate the Person of the Son to the Father. Origen also believed in an angelic hierarchy. He even ascribed souls to the stars, a theory implicit in the astrology of the times and therefore firmly repudiated by the orthodox. He believed that through their exercise of free will, some of the angels, headed by Satan, turned to evil. Other spirits descended to the status of human beings. Thus the position of a being in the hierarchy of the cosmos was determined by one's choices. Beyond the grave men had the chance of further modes of life as demons or angels, and eventually they would attain salvation. Salvation would come in a final consummation in which all spirits, even the Devil, would be saved.

The universality of Origen's doctrine of salvation, together with his speculations about the pre-existence and afterlife of the soul, which reflected a modified form of the doctrine of reincarnation, scarcely commended him to later orthodox thought. Yet he advanced many of these doctrines merely as possible hypotheses rather than as fixed expressions of his thought, so that he may well have been unjustly treated by later authorities. The extent of his thought and the way in which he made use of Stoic and Platonic theories in his defense of Christian belief, gave him a lasting influence, even if his implicit subordinationism (i.e. the subordination of the Son to the Father in metaphysical status) paved the way for later developments in Egypt, where the Arian controversy caused a severe rift in the fabric of theological belief.

Tertullian

Very different in temper from the writers of the Alexandrian school was Origen's contemporary, Tertullian (c. A.D. 160–c. 220) of Carthage, in North Africa. Tertullian was trained as a lawyer, and practiced, it has been surmised, at Rome. He was brought up as a pagan, but in his thirties he was converted to Christianity. Unlike the Alexandrians he wrote in Latin and was a formative influence on the language of later Latin theology. He displayed stormy zeal in behalf of his new faith. He was strongly opposed to compromises with pagan philosophy: "What," he asked, "has Athens to do with Jerusalem? What has the Academy to do with the Church?" He claimed that the norm of truth was the Catholic tradition of the Church and the scriptures entrusted to the Church. He attacked various heresies, including those of the followers of Marcion and the Gnostics, and he made an important contribution to the evolution of the doctrine of the Trinity. He strongly insisted that there were three Persons, as against earlier tendencies to see the Son and the Spirit as modes of activity of the one God; but at the same time he held that the three were united in a single substance.

As a moral teacher, Tertullian was rigoristic. He was shocked by the action of Callistus, Bishop of Rome, in allowing the absolution of the sins of adulterers and fornicators, provided that they were penitent. The point at issue to him was not whether such persons should be admitted to the Church: of course they should be, in line with Jesus' teaching concerning the women taken in adultery. But the real question was whether, having been baptized and then having lapsed, they should be readmitted. A similar question arose over those who had fallen away from the faith under persecution. A century after Tertullian, the major part of the North African Church was in violent schism with Rome on this issue: the Donatists, as they were called, adopted a rigorist position which the Roman See repudiated. These problems reflected the dilemma of Christian discipline. On the one hand, the Church was concerned with healing the spiritual sicknesses of the sinner and bringing him to repentance; on the other, Christianity stood for a disciplined way of life.

MONTANISM

Although Tertullian always remained strictly orthodox in his teachings, his zeal was almost of a prophetic character. This was connected with his conversion to the movement known as Montanism. Montanism originated with the teachings of a certain Montanus, a Phrygian, in the middle of the second century A.D. The emphasis of the movement was upon ecstatic and prophetic utterance in which the believer considered himself filled with the Holy Spirit. It was puritanical in its ethical demand, and it made much of sexual continence, even among married people. It had something in common with Pentecostalist revivals of a much later day, and constituted a reaction to the increasing institutionalization of worship. It claimed to go back to the original purity of Christianity—in the early Church, as we learned from the letters of Paul, ecstatic prophecy, or speaking with tongues, was a feature of the life of the community. Although orthodox in their beliefs on the whole, the Montanists aroused suspicion from the fact that they claimed direct access to the Spirit of God, and thus felt themselves free of traditional accretions. From the point of view of the orthodox the Montanists did not recognize that the Holy Spirit was not just a power poured out in prophecy, but something which informed the whole life of the Catholic Church, including its institutions. It was in virtue of the work of the Spirit that bishops consecrated bishops and that the sacraments were effective. Yet the Montanist movement was symptomatic of a state which has recurred at many different times in Christian history, the feeling that the prophetic and severely ethical demands of the faith are in danger of being overlaid by regulations and compromises.

MONASTICISM

A more lasting and effective contribution to the ascetic life was made by Christian monasticism. It had its beginnings toward the end of the third century A.D. In the early stages, it was common for ascetics to withdraw into the desert (for monasticism had its rise in Egypt), to undergo fasts, self-mortification, and the practice of meditation. Famous among such anchorites was St. Anthony, whose resistance of temptations has become a classical legend of Christendom. By withdrawal from the world, the hermit hoped to attain a form of Christian perfection. Very often the fame of these recluses spread, and they were credited with the power of transmitting divine revelations. But it was not until the early fourth century that monasticism proper was established in Egypt.

The key figure was Pachomius, who gathered about him a group of ascetics, living a communal life under monastic discipline. It was a custom for ascetics to band together in loose associations, to encourage one another in the spiritual life. But Pachomius instituted a more formal discipline. The weekly round was punctuated with worship and study of the scriptures. The monks worked at such crafts as the weaving of mats and tailoring.

Monasticism spread quite rapidly in Egypt and the East. It was further organized under Basil the Great (c. 330–c. 379), who formulated the Rule which still forms the basis of Orthodox monasticism. Later, John Cassian (c. 360–c. 435), who had had experience of Egyptian monasticism, brought this new form of the spiritual life to the West, founding two monasteries in the south of France. His Rule formed the basis for the monastery of St. Benedict in the following century. The growth of the monastic movement throughout the church was especially important, since it provided means whereby the ascetic and contemplative life could be regulated, and where it could be pursued without excluding the more normal worldly holiness which Christianity endeavored to inculcate. It was an asceticism which was optional, and which was geared to orthodoxy. It was a way in which the Church was able to enrich the religious life, without imposing uniformity. Moreover, the monastic ideal, in its severe espousal of chastity and poverty, was a counterpoise to the laxer elements creeping into the community through the triumph and wider spread of Christianity over the Empire.

PERSECUTIONS IN THE THIRD CENTURY

That triumph was not without its painful prelude. The increasing success of the faith was sufficiently alarming by the middle of the third century for the emperor Decius to institute, in A.D. 250 and the following years, a regulation that made it mandatory for every Roman citizen to obtain a certificate to show that he had sacrificed to the emperor. The penalty for disobedience was death. Thousands were killed, countless others tortured brutally. Some Christians bribed officials to issue the necessary certificates. Others fell away from the Church. But the persecution was ultimately a failure, and was given up. Two later waves of killing, however, under Valerian and Diocletian were a bitter trial for the community.

CONSTANTINE

Diocletian's abdication two years later put an end to the worst of the brutality. But it left the Empire divided between four rulers, Constantine, Licinius, Maximinus, and Maxentius. Maxentius controlled Rome until a rapid thrust by Constantine brought him to the gates of the city in the autumn of 312. A battle was fought, the Battle of the Milvian Bridge, at which Maxentius was killed and his forces routed.

Over the course of the next dozen years, Constantine's two other competitors were eliminated. Maximinus was defeated by Licinius, and Licinius was in turn destroyed by Constantine, whose son, Crespus, annihilated his fleet near Gallipoli. The empire was reunited under a sole emperor, who celebrated by building the splendid new capital of Constantinople on the site of the ancient Greek city of Byzantium.

Constantine's mother, Helena, was a Christian, and although his allegiance to the faith had always remained somewhat ambiguous, he made it the religion of a reformed Empire. At the Battle of the Milvian Bridge, his forces had fought under a standard known as the *Labarum,* formed of a cross and the monogram of Christ. Over the gateway to his wonderful new palace at Constantinople he placed an inscription saying that Christ had helped in his victories because of his reverence for the divine. He does not seem to have been baptized. Nevertheless, his regard for the faith was unmistakable. In his legal reforms, he was humanitarian; he closed down temples which were thought to harbor immorality; he granted land to the Church; he built churches; he declared Sunday to be a holiday; most important of all, he himself intervened in the disputes which were dividing the Church from within. He believed that a peaceful and united Church was essential to express the religion of a unified Empire.

THE GREAT COUNCILS FORMULATE DOCTRINE

Nicaea and the Arians

In this spirit Constantine convened an ecumenical Council at Nicaea in Asia Minor in 325 A.D. The term "ecumenical" derives from the Greek word *oikoumene,* meaning "the inhabited world." This was the first occasion that Christian bishops from all over the known world had met together in unimpeded conclave. The occasion for this first of the great Councils of the Church, was the Arian controversy, which had caused a considerable rift in Eastern Christendom. The question at issue was the status of Christ. Although nationalist and other non-religious factors partly account for it, the dispute was essentially doctrinal. It had momentous significance for the future of orthodoxy.

A certain priest called Arius, who belonged to the Church in Egypt, had a few years earlier put forth a view about the Son which had won a wide following. Arius, developing ideas that had been latent in Origen, held that the Son was subordinate to the Father. In particular, he argued that the Son was created by the Father in time, to be an instrument for the creation of the world. The created Logos appeared on earth in the form of Jesus, to bring men saving knowledge. Through his perfect obedience, the Son could be called "God-like," but it was not strictly correct to speak of him as divine. Arius summed all this up in the slogan "There was when he was not." In short, only the Father was truly eternal and truly God. The attractions of this doctrine arose from mutually contradictory sources. First, Arius claimed that the view, held by those whom he opposed, that the Father and the Son were of the same substance, was not warranted in the scriptures. In this way he appealed to Biblicists. Second, his teachings contained aspects of the Gnostic tradition which had found their way into the thought of the Alexandrian Fathers, notably Origen: salvation does not occur through the deification of man, united with the risen Christ. Rather it comes from true knowledge of God's nature and the requirements of the moral law. There was no need for the Son to be God in order to bring this saving knowledge. Third, Arius appealed to those who wished to preserve monotheism against a doctrine that suggested that Christian belief involved worship of three Gods. But Arius paid rather a heavy price. He had to concede elevated status to the Son in order to remain true to the scriptures and in accord with the opening passage of St. John's Gospel: "In the beginning was the Logos . . . All things were made by him." Also in accord with the practice of Christianity, he worshiped the Son. Consequently, his monotheism was ambiguous, for he found himself paying divine worship to a being other than the one God.

The Athanasian Creed

The Council at Nicaea eventually endorsed the doctrine defended stubbornly by Arius' great opponent, Athanasius (c. 296–c. 373 A.D.), namely that the Son is "true God from true God, begotten, not made, of the same substance with the Father." This term for "of the same substance" was crucial: *homoousios*. Though the two Persons were different, they possessed the same substance. They were essentially one in their Godhood. Athanasius' formula became the subject of later dispute, some people preferring to substitute the term *homoiousios* ("of like substance") for *homo-ousios*. The "like substance" view gained general episcopal acceptance in 359, and it was only later that the Church returned fully to the Nicene formula. Although there was a contemporary joke that it was strange for the Church to divide over a single *iota* (the letter of the Greek alphabet which was the one distinguishing difference in the spelling of the two words), the difference between the two concepts was important. The controversy was not merely verbal or trivial; it reflected something important in the Christian experience. The "like substance" concept opened the way for a semi-Arian doctrine.

The Trinitarian Debate

Two motives animated the people who attempted to evolve a theology of the Trinity. First and less important, they wanted to find a way of presenting the doctrine of Christ as divine without contradictions. It was necessary to show that there could be a single divine Being who nonetheless consisted of distinct

Persons. The second more vital motive concerned the nature of redemption. This aspect made the Nicene controversy important.

Throughout the discussion of Christ's status and nature, the orthodox had to hold two positions together, if they were to account for Christ's saving work. They had to hold to his divinity against thinkers like Arius who sought to demote him to less than divine rank. And they had to preserve belief in Christ's humanity against those Docetists who believed that Christ was merely an appearance, not fully flesh and blood. "Docetism" derives from a Greek term meaning "to appear," "seem." The divinity of Christ was the prime issue at Nicaea, though there were other discussions which centered on his humanity. According to the orthodox who treasured the experience of the Church from earliest times, Christ had to be divine. Otherwise, the deification of the church member, which the experience of redemption effected, could not take place. It was through his union with Christ in the sacraments and in the Church that the Christian was raised by Christ into the sonship of God. Salvation could only come from God: if Christ was truly savior, as Christians had always witnessed, then he must be divine. In addition, there could not be two Gods. This would be a betrayal of prophetic monotheism. The Father and the Son must be one in the same sense—they must be of the same substance. But on the other hand, Jesus' incarnation would be meaningless if Christ were only an appearance, a conjuring-trick in human form, a role played by God. The redemption of mankind involved Jesus' acting on behalf of mankind, in a state of solidarity with humanity. This was impossible unless he were fully and properly human. The scriptures clearly indicated the human struggles that he underwent, and the Docetic picture was regarded as false to that authority.

In these arguments we can see that the Arian controversy involved the central point of the Christian faith, the atonement wrought by Christ. It can be expressed more directly in terms of religious experience. The Christian Church as part of its heritage possessed belief in the great and holy God who had appeared so overwhelmingly in the experience of the prophets. He was a majestic Being, to be worshiped and praised with awe and reverence. He was supremely holy, and before him men felt their inadequacy and sin. But this presented a problem. Men felt the need to expiate their sin. Much of the sacrificial system of the Jews was an attempt to embody this sentiment in concrete religious acts. But no gesture of expiation on the part of men could restore the broken unity with God. Only God was holy, and holiness had to proceed from that source. Men wished to expiate their sin, to make a concrete act toward this at-one-ment with God; but they could do nothing significant. It was to this dilemma that the early Christian message of Christ's atoning work addressed itself. If God became man, he could, as God, bring holiness; and as man he was able to expiate on behalf of, and as the representative of, mankind. Such sentiments, drawn from religious experience, help to explain the powerful attraction of the orthodox doctrine of salvation. The self-sacrifice of Christ, moreover, had an illuminating ethical dimension to it, in showing the meaning of that love which must inform Christian behavior.

The same logic as was applied to the relation between the Son and the Father was extended to the relation between them and the Holy Spirit. The belief in the Trinity, as consisting in Three Persons united in one substance, was written into the creeds, and became the norm of orthodoxy. Meanwhile, difficulties cropped up concerning Christ's divine and human natures. If he was both God and man, did this imply that he had a split personality? Alternatively, did it mean that his human personality was replaced in some way by the divine operating within him? The first alternative was unrealistic and logically troublesome; the second was Docetism in another disguise.

The Council of Chalcedon

At the Council of Chalcedon in 451, an orthodox position, formulated largely in negative terms, was adopted in which it was affirmed that Christ, from the start of his Incarnation, had two natures, one divine, the other human, united in a single Person.

The Nestorian Breakaway

This doctrine was aimed partly against Nestorius who spoke of two Persons in Christ, which were conjoined. His followers had already begun to break away into the Nestorian Church, which established its center in eastern Syria, then at Seleucia-Ctesiphon on the Tigris. It has continued its existence till today, though the Muslim conquest of Persia considerably reduced its numbers. An interesting offshoot of the Nestorian Church is the ancient Mar Thoma (St. Thomas) Church in South India, which, though it traces its ancestry back to the Apostle Thomas, seems to have resulted from a Nestorian mission.

One motive for Nestorius' doctrine was his objection to the increasing use of the title "Theotokos," or "Mother of God," for the Virgin Mary. This seemed to put the full humanity of Christ in doubt, and in any event it was more correct to say that it was the human side of Jesus' nature that derived from Mary's womb, rather than the divine Person. Nestorius was also concerned with combatting an opposite heresy, that of the Monophysites (literally "Those who believe in a single nature," i.e. of Christ). It was perhaps ironic that his concern not to fall into heresy brought him into heresy. The Monophysites also broke away from the Catholic Church, and survive today in four Churches—the Armenian, the West Syrian Jacobite, and the Coptic Churches of Egypt and of Ethopia. Generally speaking, both the Monophysite and the Nestorian Churches are orthodox in their teaching and liturgy, except in the

69. *Wall painting of a eucharistic meal, from catacomb of Saint Callisto, Rome (2nd century). (Courtesy of the Bettmann Archive.)*

70. *An early Christian (A.D. 350–400) statue of a woman clasping a cross, found at Sheikh Ibada in upper Egypt. Purely Christian subjects like this are rare in Coptic art. (Courtesy of the Brooklyn Museum, Charles Edwin Wilbour Fund.)*

71. *Resurrection Day depicted in Vysehrad Gospel-book (11th century). (Courtesy, State Library of the Czechoslovak Socialist Republic, Prague.)*

72. *Early Christian rooster. In the symbolism of the Eastern Church the rooster, announcing the rising sun, was considered an emblem of the resurrection of Christ. (Courtesy of the Brooklyn Museum, gift of Charles Edwin Wilbour.)*

73. *Church of the Holy
Sepulchre, Jerusalem, first
erected by Constantine over
the supposed site of the tomb
of Jesus, rebuilt by crusaders
(12th century).*

74. *St. Hagia Sophia, Istanbul, Turkey. (Courtesy of William O. Beville.)*

75. *A Byzantine Church near Athens. (Courtesy of the National Tourist Organization of Greece.)*

76. *A tiny Greek Orthodox church at Capernaum, Israel, where excavations have uncovered the probable synagogue where Jesus preached. (Courtesy of Israel Ministry of Tourism.)*

77. *"The One Cured of Paralysis." This statuette of a man carrying his bed illustrates the story of the miraculous cure of the paralytic in the New Testament (A.D. 400). (Courtesy of the Brooklyn Museum, Charles Edwin Wilbour Fund.)*

78. *Miraculous Icon of the Black Virgin of
St. Vladimir's, brought to Russia from
Constantinople (12 century).*

79. *Crucifixion portrayed in
ivory, detail from a Spanish
book cover (11th century).
(Courtesy of the Metropolitan
Museum of Art, Gift of J.
Pierpont Morgan, 1917.)*

80. *St. Peter's Papal Altar in Rome, under which it is believed St. Peter is buried.*
(Courtesy of the Italian Government Travel Office.)

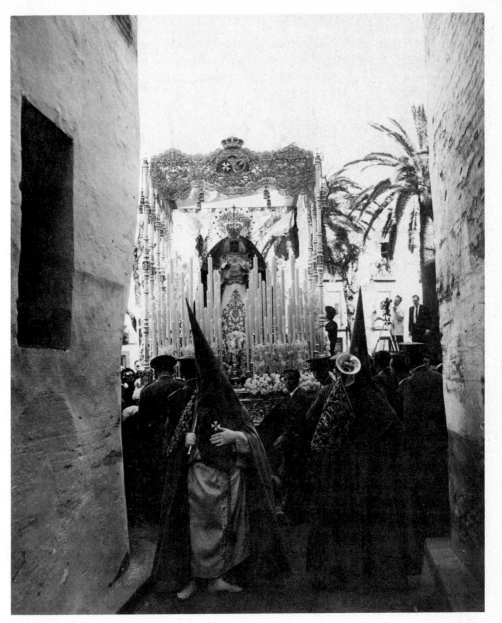

81. *Statue of the Virgin Mary is carried through the streets of Seville, Spain, during Easter week. (Courtesy of the Spanish Tourist Bureau.)*

actual doctrines which brought the schisms. The splitting-up of the Christian communities in the Near East weakened Christianity in the area, and was one of the factors accounting for the rapid success of Islam there in the seventh century.

The Council of Constantinople

The final defeat of Arianism took place at the Council of Constantinople in 381. This was largely due to the thought and work of the Cappadocian Fathers—three great theologians in the Eastern Church: St. Basil the Great, St. Gregory of Nazianzus and St. Gregory of Nyssa. They emphasized the eternal nature of the relations between the Persons of the Trinity—the Father was ingenerate; the Son was eternally begotten of the Father, and the Spirit eternally proceeded from the Father. They believed that this inner unity and differentiation within the Trinity was the everlasting pattern of the divine life.

Though the Church had come to be the spiritual authority of the empire, it experienced much internal turbulence. In 361 a period of pagan reaction occurred under the emperor Julian, who sought to replace Christianity with a reformed paganism. His idea was based on philosophical doctrines of Neo-Platonism and it was austere in its ethical requirements. Julian was wounded and killed campaigning in Mesopotamia in 363; many of the aristocracy, however, continued their allegiance to this reformulation of older cults.

MANICHEISM

New religious forces were also being released in the empire. Manicheism, a mixture of Zoroastrian, Christian, and Buddhist ideas, arose as an important rival to Christianity. The Manichean movement was founded by Mani (216–277) in Persia. Mani had traveled in India, and was tireless in the propagation of the new faith. He was helped by the royal protection of two monarchs. A third, who was an orthodox Zoroastrian, had him imprisoned. He died a month or two later, possibly by crucifixion. His doctrines were strongly dualistic. He distinguished between the light and the darkness, equating the light with good and with God, and the darkness with evil and with matter. In certain primeval events which he described in a mythological and poetical manner, particles of light became imprisoned in the dark material world. The aim of the pious was to liberate these particles, so that they could return to the heavenly world of light. The way to accomplish this was by severe asceticism, including abstention from meat-eating, and abstention from sexual intercourse, which in generating new bodies, promoted the continued imprisonment of the light particles or souls in the demonic material world.

However, everyone was not fit for this higher life, and so Mani organized his followers into two groups. There were the "elect," who lived a monastic and celibate life, and there were the "hearers," who were allowed to marry, eat meat, drink wine, etc. The hearers had to make annual confession of these transgressions, to undertake certain penitential fasts, and to contribute to the maintenance of the order of the elect. These arrangements reflected Buddhist categories—in the division between the Sangha and the laity, who were also called "hearers" by the Buddhists. Mani also taught the doctrine of rebirth or reincarnation, but he combined it with a belief in eternal damnation for the wicked and a final judgment under the aegis of the transcendental figure of Jesus, who played a key part in the salvation of mankind. The hearers were assured of future progress in their lives to come, while the elect would, at death, travel upward into the heavenly realm of light.

Mani attempted to blend major teachings of three different faiths. Nevertheless, the Christian element offended orthodox Christians, since the dualism of Manicheism ran counter to the fundamental belief in the essential goodness of the creation, and since, although asceticism could play a part in Christianity, as the rise of monasticism showed, it was not counted a necessary feature of the faith. Moreover, Mani held that Jesus did not truly suffer on the cross. He gave a cosmic interpretation of the crucifixion, in which the suffering of the cosmic Christ was repeated by every single soul in painful transmigration.

Later Manichean Influences

Nevertheless, Manicheism made progress in the Empire. It spread through the Middle East, Egypt, and North Africa, and reached Rome in the early part of the fourth century. From Rome it penetrated into Gaul and Spain. It also found converts in Central Asia and as far afield as Chinese Turkestan, where, as we know from an imperial edict, it flourished until the fifteenth century. A resurgence of ideas reminiscent of Manicheism and possibly derived from it occurred in the tenth century in Bulgaria and Macedonia in the Bogomil movement. This heresy was forcibly put down. In southern France in the eleventh century a similar movement occurred. The Albigensian movement won such widespread popular support that it sparked off a Crusade to crush its adherents. The Albigensians fought heroically, but were stamped out with considerable cruelty in the early years of the thirteenth century. The asceticism of their elite corresponded to the elect in Manicheism. One factor in the religious appeal of the Albigensian movement was its notable contrast to the laxity of many Catholic clergy. Thus Manicheism, though it has ultimately died out, became in many parts of the world a force to be reckoned with.

ST. AUGUSTINE

One of its temporary converts was a young man named Augustine. Augustine lived in troubled times. During his lifetime the Goth Alaric sacked Rome, an unnerving and shattering event, presaging the break-up of the Empire. The removal of the capital to Constantinople had inevitably started the process of rift between the eastern and western parts of the Empire. The western part, and the ancient city of Rome itself, was laid wide open to barbarian incursions from the north. This resulted in alienation between the Greek-speaking East and the Latin-speaking West, an alienation reflected not merely at the political level, but at the religious level too. The Eastern Orthodox Church, with its headquarters in Constantinople, gradually became detached from the Latin Church, with its headquarters in Rome.

Life of Augustine

Augustine was born in 354 in the city of Tagaste in North Africa. Like Constantine, he had a Christian mother. He was brought up as a Christian, but after going to Carthage, where he studied rhetoric at the university, he lost his rather superficial allegiance to the faith. At this time he acquired a mistress with whom he lived for fifteen years. The study of Cicero induced in him a strong interest in philosophy. He found the New Testament very inadequate from this point of view. Also as a literary work it was not to be compared with the measure and poise of Cicero. Manicheism as a doctrine seemed to him more promising, and he became a hearer. The asceticism of the religion appealed to him. Yet he found it hard to overcome his fleshly desires. No doubt his life with his mistress was much more than a carnal union, and contained a strong element of love. It was therefore difficult for him to commit himself to the higher Manichean life of the elect.

After nearly a decade of Manicheism, he became disillusioned with it. It failed to answer some of his philosophical doubts and perplexities. He moved to Rome and shortly afterward to Milan, where he taught rhetoric (roughly speaking, in modern terms, literature). This brought him into increased contact with Neo-Platonism, which seemed to him both spiritually elevated and philosophically persuasive. During his early years in Milan he was very influenced by the preaching of Ambrose, who was Bishop of Milan, and he began to feel that the path through Neo-Platonism inevitably led to the Christian faith. Augustine's intellectual doubts about Christianity came to be satisfied, but his senuous way of life remained unaltered. There occurred a famous experience which brought about his conversion. While in a garden, he heard a child's voice from over the wall saying "Tolle lege, tolle lege"—"Take up and read, take up and read." Seizing a copy of the Epistles of Paul which he had been reading, he opened it at random, at the passage in Romans which says: "Let us walk honestly, as in the day; not in rioting and drunkenness, not in chambering and wantonness, not in strife and envying." The suddenness of the voice, the appropriateness of the message—both these facts impressed themselves forcibly on Augustine's mind. He felt that it was surely a divine oracle. His doubts were resolved.

After a period of seclusion and self-discipline, he was baptized, in 387, on the eve of Easter. The following year he returned to Tagaste, where he and some friends formed a monastic settlement. He was induced by popular acclaim in 391 to become a priest, though he still led the monastic life. Five years later he was made coadjutor bishop of Hippo, and on the death of his colleague in about 396 he became sole bishop. He remained in this position until his death in 430. He died while the Vandals were besieging the town, a further instance of the barbarian incursions into the once stable Western Empire.

Influence of Manicheism on Augustine

The events of Augustine's quest for the truth and of his conversion are told in his magnificent *Confessions,* which stands as an important, uniquely autobiographical contribution to Latin literature. The *Confessions* is invaluable in opening up to us the inner life of a sensitive, educated person living in a time of religious doubt and turmoil. We can sympathize with his struggles and with his famous prayer during the time of his Manichean allegiance: "Give me chastity and continence, but not yet." We can observe the attractions of the different creeds of the time through his eyes: the nobility of Neo-Platonism as expressed by Plotinus, whose *Enneads* had been translated into Latin by Victorinus, himself a convert to Christianity; and the inclusiveness and austerity of the more colorful doctrines of the Manicheans. One writer has referred to Mani in the following terms: "His system was apparently a hotch-potch of many long-dead heresies." This judgment fails to give us insight into the reasons why men like Augustine were drawn to Manicheism. Why should it seem preferable to Christianity?

One reason was its inclusiveness. Mani did not confine himself to the narrow authority of one tradition. He held that all true religion essentially is one, that the teachings of the prophets, of Jesus, of Zoroaster, of the Buddha, of himself, form a unity. In short he appealed to the unease which men feel when confronted with religious conflict, when there is a warrant for respecting all great teachers of conflicting faiths. Such a syncretistic attitude is always powerful in a period of interplay between faiths, and is reflected in many movements in our own day.

A second reason for the appeal of Manicheism was that the ascetic vegetarian life of the elect promised a *gnosis,* a knowledge of the divine Light. It promised the higher bliss of mystical and contemplative experience. It was a well-organized movement and it accommodated, through the order of hearers, those who did not feel the strength to undertake the more strenuous life of the elect. In the case of Augustine, the attractions of Manicheism arose partly from the mystical streak in his character, which came to enjoy a fuller expression in the religion which he ultimately embraced. There is an account in the *Confessions* (VII, 10) of his inner experience of the divine Being:

> I entered into my inward self, Thou being my guide . . . And I beheld with the eye of my soul, above my mind, the Light unchangeable. It was not this ordinary light which all flesh may look upon, nor as it were a greater of the same kind . . . He who knows the truth knows that Light, and he who knows it knows Eternity.

Augustine's Theology

This inner revelation coincided with what he had learned from Platonism. On the basis of his personal experience, together with the philosophical tenets of Platonism, he built up a theology, which, though never fully systematic, exerted later a profound influence on Christian thinking. It was not fully systematic, because so many of his writings were polemic and occasional. He was concerned with rebutting false views and defending orthodoxy as he saw it. Yet certain central ideas emerge out of these varied writings.

From Platonism Augustine derived the view that eternal archetypes are contained within God's nature. In knowing Forms, we know God. Expressed more briefly and succinctly, the knowledge of the truth is itself the knowledge of God. This doctrine forms an important philosophical basis for theistic belief. But unlike the Neo-Platonists, Augustine did not conceive of creation in terms of a necessary emanation of lower principles from the One. This was incompatible with the Christian emphasis on God's will in the creative act. Moreover the cosmos was not eternal, but was brought into being a finite time ago. Though the Neo-Platonists spoke of the triad of the One, the Intelligence, and the World-Soul, Augustine's triad was the Christian Trinity. He likened the Trinity to three faculties operative within man—memory, understanding, and will. These were three distinct elements of experience, but they formed a single unity in the life of the individual. Likewise the three Persons of the Christian Trinity were distinct yet united. He emphasized the love of God operative within the Trinity. It was like the lover, the beloved, and the love which binds them together. The binding love was equated with the Spirit, and was the element which flowed forth from each partner. Thus Augustine held that the Spirit proceeded both from the Father and from the Son in an eternal process. He differed in this from the theologians of the East, notably the Cappadocian Fathers, who spoke of the Spirit proceeding only from the Father. The extra clause "and from the Son" (*filioque*) was later incorporated into Western versions of the creed, and became a source of conflict with the Eastern Orthodox during the period when the two halves of the Church were in process of separation.

Although Augustine had a mystical bent, he was also deeply aware, from his own experience, of the power of sin. Constantly in the *Confessions* he reiterated his own unworthiness and his distance from the divine Being. This dilemma was acute in the days when he was a Manichean. He saw what he thought was the higher Good, but was somehow incapable of truly turning toward it. He was enslaved by his own nature. With his conversion to Christianity, he became capable of the higher life. He interpreted this liberation from the bonds of sin as the action of the grace of God.

Augustine's Dispute with Pelagianism

The concept of grace found a prominent place in his theology. It was a determining point in his famous dispute with Pelagianism, a doctrine expounded by Pelagius (who died about A.D. 420). Pelagius was a British monk who had come to Rome at the end of the fourth century. He was disturbed by Augustine's teaching, particularly that issue expressed in the well-known sentence *Da quod iubes et iube quod vis*—"Grant what thou commandest and command what thou wilt"—a sentence drawn from the *Confessions*. The expression of reliance on the determining operation of God's grace was unacceptable to Pelagius, because he believed strongly in personal responsibility. He believed that man embraced good or evil through his free will. Any other doctrine would discourage man from his efforts toward virtue. Such a view, corroborated by common sense experience, was relevant to the Church's belief about the Fall of Adam. If sin came through the operation of man's free will, then sin was a condition of the individual, not a consequence of Adam's Fall. The Pelagians argued that a child, at the start of his life, was like Adam before he fell. Thus there was no Fall, but rather a series of individual falls. They also held that Adam would have died, even if he had not sinned. This idea was incompatible with the impression given in the Genesis narrative and the common belief that death had come into the world as a result of Adam's primeval transgression. Pelagianism, however, for all its clarity and common sense, was condemned. Augustine was a prime mover in the refutation of its doctrines. The reasons for his hostility to them arose partly from his own experience and partly from the accumulated experience of the Judeo-Christian tradition.

Augustine had a strong feeling of his own sinful nature and his distance from the holiness of God. Sin had never been a mere ethical concept to him. It had a numinous dimension. Sin was alienation from the holy Power who had revealed himself to men. What Pelagius overlooked was precisely the religious aspect of sin. As a moral doctrine Pelagianism was commendable, but as a theological interpretation it was, according to Augustine, gravely defective. It overlooked the experience of being cut off from God, save through the redemptive power of Christ. Augustine elaborated a number of theses to counter Pelagius. He believed Adam had possessed free will in its fullness prior to the Fall. But the Fall had impaired human nature. In consequence, man was unable to attain the good which he desired, unless he was helped by the healing power of God's grace. It followed from this that the attainment of good, and the blessed knowledge of God was itself God-given. On the darker side of the picture it followed that failure of attainment—damnation in other words—was attributable to God's action in not giving grace. The gift of God's favor was given freely without God's being bound down in any way by human acts. Thus it was inscrutable in its operation. Suffice it to say that some were healed and raised by God, while others were not. Out of Augustine's doctrines and the experience which gave rise to them, belief in predestination to salvation and damnation became a significant part of the Christian heritage. At a much later time the teachings of Calvin gave them full expression.

Augustine's Dispute with the Donatists

A further danger was apparent to Augustine in Pelagius' teaching. If man was able to attain moral perfection through his own efforts, what was the real need for Christ and the Church? Augustine stressed the saving work of Jesus and the vital importance of the sacraments as the channel through which the grace of God might flow. He was strengthened in this view by his controversy with the North African Donatists. The Donatists were rigoristic in their attitudes toward Christians who had lapsed under persecution or in other ways. As a consequence, they denied the efficacy of sacraments performed by unworthy priests. But Augustine could not, from his general position, countenance the notion that it was from the moral worthiness of the celebrant, through human activity, that the sacrament derived its healing and unifying power. That would have overthrown full recognition of God's grace. So he argued for the validity of the sacraments, even though the priest were unworthy. This has remained the Catholic view. It was a view that could give rise to moral laxity; but it was fully in accord with the notion of the Church as a divinely appointed institution through which and in which the Holy Spirit, despite the weaknesses of men, was operative.

Augustine's Theory of History

The other great contribution of Augustine to Christian theology was a theory of history as expounded in his massive work, the *Civitas Dei*, or *City of God*. This was stimulated by the appalling news of the sack of Rome by Alaric in 410. Many pagans held the view that this catastrophe was a punishment for the desertion of the gods which had taken place when the Empire committed itself to Christianity. Augustine's theory not only countered this charge, but at the same time gave a justification of political institutions and a vision of the state in which true happiness could be found. He argued that there were two Cities, the earthly City and the heavenly City, or the City of God. The elect belonged to the City of God through God's grace, even though they were compelled on earth to live in the earthly City. The earthly City was a reflection of the situation in which man's nature had fallen. In origin men were naturally social, so that there would have been no need for government, class division, and other features of existing society. But seeing that they were fallen, God gave these institutions to regulate men's sinful nature. Thus the political structure of the state, although a necessary evil, was also a God-given thing, and a means of man's judgment. Men should not be too concerned with the evils befalling the Empire: the Empire, like Babylon, was a notable embodiment of the earthly City, but though it would pass away, this was part of the process toward the establishment of the heavenly City. The heavenly City would endure when the kingdoms of men had fallen in ruins. Of course, Augustine did not simply equate the heavenly City with the Church (many in the Church were not numbered among the elect); but it turned out that his vision was a kind of prediction. For when the Roman Empire passed away, the Church took over as the bearer and conserver of Roman civilization.

A feature of Augustine's political theory which deserves attention, and which reflects early Christian social and religious attitudes, is the view that the institutions of the world, involving the domination of one man over others, as in slavery, were not natural to man in his pristine state, and were the results of sin.

Augustine and Heresy

Augustine's attitude toward heresy was less tolerant. Now that Christianity had become a state church, it formed a spiritual but nonetheless visible complement to the state. The two could work and ought to work in harmony. Augustine believed that the state was good if it was just, but true justice demanded the proper worship of God. Therefore it followed that the state was required to put down heresy and schism, so far as it lay within its power. A New Testament text ("Compel them to come in") formed the scriptural basis of this doctrine. Augustine was moderate in the kind of punishment he thought appropriate for a heretic. He did not advocate the death-penalty. But he gave sanction to compulsion in religious matters. It was ironical that the Church which had had to suffer from persecution at last employed the same weapon. It did not do so directly. The heretic was handed over to the state rather than being dealt with by the Church. But in essence it used force as a means of keeping people within its fold and of inducing them to come in.

THE CHURCH AFTER THE DECLINE OF
THE ROMAN EMPIRE

The Church under imperial protection was an impressive body. Temples were converted to Christian use, land was granted, state ceremonials took on a Christian character. Great new festivals, including Christmas, were introduced. Hospitals, colleges, and hostels for poor strangers were erected, and the charitable work of the Christian community reached new dimensions. The authority of the Bishop of Rome increased as the power of the Empire diminished. The barbarian invaders were Arians, for Arianism had been strongly missionary in the north. But they respected the papacy, and after awhile they became orthodox Catholics. Out of the ruins of the Western Empire rose a strong Church which survived the turbulence of the so-called Dark Ages.

THE EAST-WEST SCHISM

The Filioque Clause

The barbarian invasions cut Italy off from the East and increased even further the division between Rome and Constantinople—centers of the two great wings of the Church. There had been tension between representatives of Latin and Byzantine Christianity at the Councils of Nicaea and Chalcedon. In 589 at the third Council of Toledo the phrase *filioque* was introduced into the creed. The use of this addition spread, although Pope Leo III, at the end of the eighth century, refused to allow it in the Nicene Creed, being worried at the antagonism already aroused in the Eastern Church by this allegedly unwarranted addition. Photius, the Patriarch of Constantinople, severely denounced the clause in the following century. Despite attempts to patch up the dispute, the *filioque* remained a source of division and conflict between the two parts of the Church. Eastern theologians felt that the clause impaired the unity of the Trinity. They reasoned that if the Son was begotten of the Father and if the Spirit proceeded from the Father, then the Father was the single source and anchorage of divinity. But the theological quarrel over this addition to the creed was not the root or real cause of the division. It was merely the focusing point.

There were two general reasons for the division. In the first place the two parts of the Empire were losing touch with one another. Sometimes they were in political conflict. Both at Rome and at Constantinople the Church was, in differing ways, implicated with the state. Hence ecclesiastical division reflected political division. The second reason was perhaps more important. The Eastern Church rejected the claims to papal authority put forward by Rome. The Orthodox in the East were quite happy to accord the Bishop of Rome top place of honor in keeping with tradition going back to the great apostles Peter and Paul. But they were not willing to accept claims to universal jurisdiction. A synod held in 876 at Constantinople condemned the Pope for heresy on the grounds of the adoption of the *filioque* clause. Disputes dragged on. The final schism can be dated from A.D. 1054 when the Patriarch of Constantinople was excommunicated by the Pope. Yet in effect the two churches had gone their own way over a period of centuries.

Dispute over Icons

From the seventh century onward, Muslim armies swept through North Africa and into Spain in one direction, and throughout much of the Middle East in another. The Byzantine Empire became hemmed in, and started a long, seesaw warfare against the new power. In Byzantium itself, civilization and religion flourished, despite numerous theological and civil disputes. The menace of the Muslims, however, was connected with a controversy about icons which threw the Greek Church into turmoil during the eighth century. The Emperor Leo III (717-740 A.D.), with a view to making it easy to convert Jews and Muslims, ordered the destruction of icons. Images of Christ, the Virgin Mary, and other saints had been widely used in the East since the fifth century. They were objects of veneration. But it was easy for opponents to ascribe a more damaging interpretation about their use. The faithful, in paying respect to the saints through these paintings, could be accused of idolatry. Did it not in essence contravene the commandment against the use of graven images? If God had forbidden representation of himself, where was the justification of the use of icons? Political motives also elicited Leo's injunction: he wished to reorder the church and bring it more firmly under his control.

The fierceness of the dispute was due to contradictory religious sentiments. The issue was important. Islam was strongly opposed to representations of Allah. Similarly the Jews had never depicted Yahweh. In later times Protestants likewise opposed and destroyed church images. One reason for not wishing to portray God is that the absence of visible representation symbolizes both the invisible transcendence of God and the fact that he is not to be thought of anthropomorphically. Special powers have often been credited to the images of the gods, and in some sense the god is thought to reside in the representation of him. But to identify God with a mere image would be blasphemous.

Throughout its fight against paganism the Church had repeated again and again that the heathen were foolish to put their trust in inanimate lumps of stone and wood. There was an association between images and idolatry. On the one hand the religious sentiment of awe before the mighty and invisible God could result in a distrust of artistic representation of him. On the other, as one of the great Orthodox theologians, John of Damascus (c. A.D. 675–c. 749), pointed out in a famous defense, icons were for the illiterate what books were for those who could read. The uneducated learned their theology largely through using their eyes. Icons enlivened the religious imagination. They could even be regarded as a means of grace. Besides, the Christian worshiper was in a different position from the Jewish monotheist or the Muslim. He believed that Christ had come down to earth and had become flesh. Surely, he reasoned, Christ's human person was something which could be represented. On the Iconoclast (i.e. the party wishing to smash the icons) side, disputants pointed out a flaw in this argument. By representing the man Jesus the icons merely depicted his human nature, thus splitting it off, heretically, from his divine nature. Such critics failed to perceive the remarkable artistic force with which many icons were endowed. The highly stylized representations of Christ showed a strangely glorious figure, not merely a human. In portraying Christ in glory as the savior, the icons could be thought to do justice to the divine aspect of Christ.

Religious sentiments were harnessed in favor of icons. They gave warmth and life to faith and they were a means of representing the divine glory. If words could evoke these qualities, why should not pictures also? However, there was suspicion that superstitions surrounded the use of images. They were often thought to possess miraculous powers. Up to a point they were substitutes for the gods of pagan antiquity who had been submerged by the onset of Christianity; so there were legitimate grounds for criticism. Eventually, after very severe persecutions, in which an attempt was made to enforce iconoclasm, the icons won. They have remained till today an important element in the life of the Eastern Orthodox Church. In 787 a General Council at which both East and West were represented, gave sanction to the use of images, holding that in venerating an image the worshiper ascribes his veneration to the person represented. A further outbreak of iconoclasm succeeded this Council, but eventually in 843 the position of icons in the Church was finally established. A great feast held in that year in honor of the images has remained a regular feature of Eastern Liturgy since. Despite this victory for the visible, it is interesting to note that sculpture is still forbidden in the Eastern Church, in accordance with the ban on graven images. Even the crucifix is forbidden.

The Meaning of the Incarnation and Crucifixion

The writings of John of Damascus, who summed up and developed the work of the Cappadocian Fathers, illustrated the differences of emphasis between Eastern and Western ideas. In the Eastern view man was conceived as the connection between the visible and invisible worlds. He was created perfect, and was incorruptible, immortal and passionless. At the Fall these powers were lost, but a certain scope for free will remained. The image of God was not effaced entirely, even though it was damaged. The restoration of mankind to the true end for which he was created, the contemplation of God, was effected through the Incarnation. Christ in uniting the Godhead to human nature, restored that nature to its perfection. By sharing in Christ's perfect humanity, man too could be raised up and deified. The emphasis was upon the Incarnation as the saving work.

The Western tendency was to look upon Jesus' death on the cross and his resurrection—but especially his death—as central to Christ's redeeming activity. If the East stressed deification, the West emphasized atonement. The distinction should not be considered too pronounced. John's writings were influential also in the West during the Middle Ages. It is interesting, however, to note that Pope Gregory the Great, at the end of the sixth century, had already expressed the doctrine which was to become normative in the Roman Church, that the eucharist was a repetition of Christ's sacrifice on the cross, and thereby was effective in propitiating God on behalf of those not present, those, for instance, in Purgatory. This emphasis on the sacrificial element in Christ's work was carried over into the interpretation of the liturgy. The Eastern and Western attitudes were compatible in this. While John and others may have looked at Christ's work positively as bringing about the possible deification of man, the West may have considered it negatively as the removal of sin. Yet both East and West recognized the two elements in the situation. The doctrine of original sin, which was largely shaped by the controversy between Pelagius and Augustine, played a much lesser role in the East than in the West. There was no belief in transmission of guilt, and both faith and works were regarded as necessary for man's justification before God.

EASTERN LITURGY

The most remarkable feature of Eastern Christianity was the sacred Liturgy. It corresponded to the Mass, but incorporated other elements. The solemnity and holiness of the long and splendid ritual, the beauty of the music—a blend of the singing of the Jewish synagogue and the classical chants of Greece—the richness of the vestments and the color of the icons, all these blended together to make a glorious impression. In the tenth century A.D. the Russian Grand Duke Vladimir, uncertain about which faith he should espouse, sent emissaries to visit both the Western Church and the Church at Constantinople. According to the account we have, which, although it may be legendary, is nevertheless significant, the envoys reported to the Grand Duke that when they attended the Liturgy in the great church of St. Sophia:

> We did not know whether we were in heaven or on earth. It would be impossible to find on earth any splendor greater than this, and it is vain that we attempt to describe it . . . Never shall we be able to forget such beauty.[9]

This was a far cry from the simple meal in an upper room at which Christ instituted the sacrament, and from the covert meetings of the early Christians in the Empire. But it was the medium through which the Eastern Church gave the ritual dimension of Christianity tremendous meaning. In the solemn celebration there was a unification of worshipers on earth and in heaven. The whole drama of the saving life of Christ was recapitulated. It is often considered necessary to participate in the Liturgy to understand Orthodoxy. The characteristic ethos of the Church is expressed in it. A paradox may be involved in this. It is often thought that the Greek Christian mind, as opposed to the Hebrew, was overly concerned with matters of belief. While the Jew was not as worried about belief as about right practice, it was a special feature of Greek Christianity from early centuries to worry about formulations of the creed and of doctrine. The Latin Church found some of the Greek distinctions overly subtle, a maze of heresies about Christ's nature. But in the religion of the Eastern Church lies the conviction that the Liturgy conveys truth made manifest. "Orthodoxy" indeed is correctly translated "right worship" rather than "right belief."

Mystical Practices of the Eastern Church

Although in the centuries before the final split with Rome the Byzantine Church had fallen increasingly under political control, with the emperors exercising considerable authority even in matters of doctrine, the inner life of the Church was not neglected. The impulse toward contemplative and mystical religion was given authority by the writings of Pseudo-Dionysius, and was encouraged by the existence of many monasteries. The writings of Dionysius

---

[9] From "The Chronicle of Nestor," quoted by Stephen Neill in *A History of Christian Missions*, No. 6 in the Pelican History of the Church series (London: Pelican Books, 1964), p. 89.

were thought to have been composed by a person of that name converted in Athens by Paul. For this reason they were held in great esteem in both the Eastern and Western Church, despite the fact that a few people cast doubts on the attribution. In the Eastern Church the writings achieved very high status. Innumerable commentaries were written upon them. They date in fact from about A.D. 500, and many have been composed in Syria. They expressed a mystical theology which drew upon Neo-Platonist ideas.

Through the practice of interior contemplation, in which the adept turned away from the impressions and images supplied by the senses, he was able to attain a union with the divine Being. Characteristically, God was described in a negative way: he lay beyond both affirmation and negation as used in ordinary language. This ineffable Godhead could be known, then, in a process of what was, from the point of view of the intellectual faculties, a sort of unknowing. In the vision of this Reality the soul was illuminated by the divine Light, and itself became divine. In the writings of Pseudo-Dionysius, this Neo-Platonist mysticism was harnessed to the doctrines of the Church.

The process of mystical deification was related to the work of Christ who, as we have seen, was thought through his Incarnation to have realized for men the opportunity to be restored to the divine image. Sin had come into the world through man's pursuit of pleasure. This meant that reason could no longer control the senses. The mystic, through the grace of God, could turn back from the senses to the divine Light residing within him. The vision of this Light was a constant theme of Byzantine mysticism. The Light was in turn identified with the glory of God revealed in the theophanies of the Old Testament—to Moses and the prophets there had come the radiance of God. In the New Testament emphasis was laid on the Transfiguration, where Christ himself became suffused and surrounded with light. Men could share this divine glory and participate in Christ's supernatural life. The typical Orthodox interpretation of Christ's saving work fitted in with this mystical experience of merging with the divine Light.

Monasticism in the Western Church

Meanwhile, monasticism and the life of contemplation were making progress in the West. A turning point was the work of St. Benedict (c. 480–c. 550), whose community at Monte Cassino was controlled by a Rule which set the pattern for later Western monasticism. The Rule did not impose harsh austerity, but rather a moderate asceticism. Goods were shared in common, but no stress was laid on the life of poverty. This had good effects in that the monasteries were not precluded by the Rule from maintaining resources needed for acts of mercy and charity. Monasteries thus became an important focus of social service during the Dark Ages. The communal life of the community revolved around the Divine Office. Various prayers and services were appointed at fixed times; Matins, Lauds, Prime, Terce, Sext, None, Vespers, and Compline. The Office was named by St. Benedict the *opus Dei*, the "work of God." This expressed the conviction that the primary task of the monk was the praise of God. The spirit of all his other activities had to flow from this center.

The discipline of the clergy as a whole was in process of becoming more uniformly regulated. The practice of celibacy among the clergy was enforced by Pope Innocent I in the early part of the fifth century. Although later in that century another pope forbade clergy to put away their spouses upon ordination, and bade them to live as brother and sister, this rule proved open to criticism. Eventually complete celibacy became the norm for the Western Church. In the East, which kept more conservatively to early practices, priests could marry before ordination and retain their wives thereafter, although it became the custom to choose celibate bishops, largely from the monasteries.

ADVANCE OF CHRISTIANITY

The missionary work of both wings of the Church continued. Cut off by Islam from the south, Christianity moved northward. The Byzantines sent missionaries out among the Balkan peoples and the Slavs. The greater part of northern and north-western Europe was proselytized by the Latins. The old Celtic Church in Britain, which had boasted of such figures as St. Patrick, St. Ninian, and St. Columba was weakened by the incursions of pagan Anglo-Saxons, but the missionary work of St. Augustine of Canterbury (died 604 or 605), who had been sent to England by Pope Gregory the Great, initiated a new and flourishing phase of Christianity in England. There was some friction between the Celtic Church and the new organization, but the differences were resolved at the Synod of Whitby in 664.

A son of the English Church, St. Boniface (680-754), played a big part in furthering missionary work in Germany. But afterward evangelical work in northern Europe changed in method from persuasion to force.

The great Charlemagne (c. 742–814) established an empire, based on the Frankish kingdom which he had inherited, which stretched from northern Spain to Bavaria. His campaigns against the North German Saxons lasted nearly twenty years. Part of Charlemagne's method of pacification was the forcible conversion of conquered tribes. Those who did not become Christians were liable to execution. He conducted a bloody enterprise, but it succeeded in making his realm a formally Christian state. On Christmas Day, A.D. 800 he was crowned Holy Roman Emperor by Pope Leo III. Thus he became the fictional successor of the Roman Emperors of the past, and he and his successors in theory continued the Empire, now conceived as "Holy" because Christian. His reign, despite the persecution and repression of northern paganism, signalized the beginning of a rebirth of culture and learning—the so-called Carolingian Renaissance. It was accompanied by administrative reforms, including ecclesiastical ones. The position and character of the Frankish clergy was raised. Christianity advanced steadily over western and eastern Europe during this period. The increase in the power and the prestige of the Church as inheritor and propagator of Latin and Greek culture imposed a spiritual and cultural unity on Europe in a period of confusion and disruption of older political institutions. It also paved the way for a more stable world in the Middle Ages. This unity and stability were the fruits of the Church's ambiguous conquest of the Roman Empire after Constantine.

INSTITUTIONALIZED CHRISTIANITY

We must now examine the changes in this institution of Christianity which was born of such humble and unpromising beginnings. In regard to religious experience, the growth of the liturgy and of monasticism developed what had been only implicit in the Apostolic Church. As men reflected on the nature of Christ, and clearly saw divinity in him, it was natural to impart to the celebration of the eucharist that numinous power which was associated with God. In the earliest days the solemnity of the occasion and the access of the power of the Holy Spirit expressed this, but the passage of time brought an inevitable elaboration of ritual which attempted to convey in moving and visible form the glory of Christ's presence among his people through the sacrament. The culmination of this evolution was the Eastern Liturgy, which transported men, so it seemed, to heaven. Although the Western rites did not attain such splendid proportions as those of the East, the same forces were at work.

The Church, through the institution of monasticism canalized and expressed a tendency toward asceticism which sometimes became exaggerated. The mystic, attracted by doctrines of the evil nature of matter, sometimes tried to impose upon all an austerity which was not in keeping with the words of Jesus. Nevertheless, the inner life of contemplation was an important form of religious experience, which in the monastic movement was harnessed to the worship of Christ.

The development of the liturgy and the extension of the contemplative ideal were fruitful for the life of the Church. So were the doctrinal reflections of the theologians of the first few centuries. The Fathers of the Church gave a shape and substance to Christian belief which was not merely determined by the desire to rebut what were regarded as dangerous heresies. Through their writings, Christianity absorbed much of Greek philosophy and classical culture. Some people, like Tertullian, saw dangers in this process. They were afraid that revelation would become distorted if alien ideas were superimposed upon it. Nevertheless, the wedding of Jewish monotheism and Plato was fruitful.

Despite their bitterness and despite the increasingly minute and trivial nature of the issues at stake, the doctrinal disputes of the fourth century gave to Christian belief a classical form which it has never lost. Arianism and other heretical movements forced orthodox Christians to reflect more deeply on the character of the Trinity and the work of Christ. They concluded what they believed implicit in the beliefs of the Apostolic Age, that the recognition of Christ as Lord entailed nothing short of a Trinitarian doctrine when taken in conjunction with ethical monotheism as expressed in the Jewish tradition. The union of Christ's two natures, human and divine, was also necessary for understanding his redemptive work. This was conveyed by the experience of liberation and by the power of grace. But for all the advances made in Christian thought, there was a debit balance as well. Preoccupation with right belief led to persecution and a blindness to the inward nature of the faith.

Socially, the Church stood, not always easily, for uprightness, brotherliness, and chastity. But it did not bring about great changes in the institutions of the Empire it inherited. There was no move to abolish slavery. St. Augustine, while ascribing the evils of society to human sin rather than to eternal origins, was not unduly concerned to effect wide changes. This was partly because the Church had its eyes fixed on heaven, and partly because the Church's task was largely conservation in a period of increasing turmoil. It was remarkably successful in conservation. But the attainment of the status of an official faith had dangers. The Christians turned to persecution. The gap between the clergy, which took over legal and other powers, and the laity became accentuated. Before long bishops wielded an influence and power which infected the Church with worldliness. Although pagan religion was defeated, certain features lingered on in popular piety. The cult of the saints and of relics, though not without precedent in the early Church, formed a colorful and popular substitute for the dead pagan deities. Yet it was the general policy of the Church to baptize ancient cults and transform them where it could be done without idolatry. The great festival of Christmas was such a transformation of a pre-Christian feast.

In leaving this chapter to study the shattering events which gave birth to a widespread Islam, we have brought the history of the Christian experiment up to the period of the Dark Ages. This is not an altogether natural stopping place. History is a continuum, and chopping it into periods is merely an artifice which is convenient for the historian. We shall return to this fabric of Christianity in the Dark Ages to study it as the basis of the shaping of medieval Christendom.

Chapter 9

THE MUSLIM EXPERIENCE

ARABIA BEFORE MUHAMMAD

The few great urban cultures which existed in the Arabian peninsular had, by the sixth century A.D., fallen into decay. The great dam at Marib, in the Sabean kingdom of the south, which provided a source of irrigation and control of flooding, had been destroyed. In the north, Roman incursions had finished the culture centered in Petra and Palmyra. The larger part of the Arabian population continued, or returned to, a nomadic existence—the life of the Bedouin, which still characterizes great areas of the Arab world. In the northwest part of the peninsula, the Hejaz, there were three towns of some importance—Taif, Mecca, and Medina. These, especially Mecca, formed commercial centers and staging posts on the great caravan routes which straddled the desert. It was from Mecca that the Prophet of Islam, Muhammad, came.

Religious practices of this time were not altogether different from those of the Hebrews before Abraham. They combined polytheistic and animistic elements. There was a wide cult of sacred stones, supposed to contain divine power. Through rubbing, stroking, or kissing them one could, it was supposed, derive some of this power for oneself. Trees and springs were also, as in most relatively unsophisticated cultures, the objects of veneration. But more important than the spirits of the desert and of the oasis were the celestial and heavenly gods. Above all the gods was Allah, *the* god (as the name implies) who was Creator of the world. Important too was Allat, a moon goddess, seemingly introduced from Syria and analogous to the great Mother Goddesses who were worshiped widely in the Middle East. Other goddesses included al-Uzza, the planet Venus, and Manat, the mysterious goddess of Fate, who controlled the fortunes of men. Al-Uzza in particular attracted an important sacrificial cult. Archaeologists have discovered traces of human sacrifice offered to her at an even earlier period. She was associated with the veneration of stone pillars, no doubt symbolic of nature's generative powers. The Quraysh, the tribe to which Muhammad belonged, paid special reverence to al-

Uzza. She was one of the prominent deities associated with the Kaba, a great center of pilgrimage.

The Kaba was a cube-like structure, without external decoration, built over the highly sacred Black Stone. In it were images of many gods and goddesses, although it did not have one of the distant high god Allah. Every year a truce, lasting four months, gave the opportunity for peaceful congregations of people from outlying tribes and other towns to visit the shrine. The rites involved circling round the Kaba and running a sacred race between two nearby hills. These features were carried over into Islam after Muhammad had established a monotheistic faith.

In addition to the religious influences of this polytheistic culture the Hejaz was exposed in some degree both to Christianity and Judaism. As early as the sixth century B.C. there had been Jewish settlements in the north. From the fourth century A.D. there was a large community in the Yemen, to the south. Perhaps half the population of Medina were Jewish, and much of the land, together with quite a lot of the craft work, was in the hands of the Jews. The Jews played a large part in the economic life of the country, and their prosperity contrasted with the relative poverty of the Arabs. Christians were active in Mecca, and both the Monophysite and Nestorian Churches had been moderately successful in proselytizing the people of the northern part of Arabia. The Monophysite Arabs, however, were frequently persecuted in the name of Christian orthodoxy. This was a factor in their later alienation from the Church and their acceptance of Islam. To some extent, the Arabs were a buffer between the Byzantine and Persian Empires, and they became involved in the warfare between the two on both sides.

MUHAMMAD

It was against the milieu of this mixture of pagan religion and the teachings of both Judaism and Christianity that Muhammad began his mission. Born about A.D. 570, he belonged to the tribe of the Quraysh. His father died just before he was born, and he was brought up in the home of his grandfather. His father's name was Abdullah, meaning "slave of Allah." His grandfather's occupation—the giving of water from the sacred well of Zamzam created by command of Allah to gathering pilgrims—indicates that reverence for the high god of the polytheistic Arabs was part of his family tradition. The boy lived for two years in his grandfather's house, and when the grandfather died, he was transferred to the guardianship of his uncle. As a young man he was employed by a wealthy widow, Khadija, as superintendent of camels engaged in trade with Damascus. At the age of twenty-five he married Khadija, although she was fifteen years his senior. She had six children by him. Discounting the many legends that grew up around his life, there is little else that we know about his early years, except the fact that he had contact with a certain Zayd, who remonstrated with him about his idolatry. Zayd may have been either a Christian or a Jewish convert, though Arabic sources report him as neither. In any case, he was an early influence on Muhammad's life and seems to have been the catalyst in turning him away from the polytheistic faith of most of his fellows.

Muhammad was of a specially religious disposition. It was his habit to go into the hills to practice prayer and meditation. At the age of forty, his dissatisfactions and his yearnings were resolved by a dramatic call which started him on his career as a prophet.

His Call As Revealed in Scripture

It was from this experience that the worldwide faith of Islam had its beginning. It is described in the Qur'an, which is a record of Muhammad's revelations. One night, while he was in the mountains, the angel Gabriel appeared to him with a text written on silk and commanded him to recite. He did so in the following words, which themselves appeared in the scripture:

Read! in the name of the Lord who created;
Created man from CLOTS OF BLOOD:
Read! For thy Lord is most beneficent;
Who hath taught the use of the pen;
Hath taught man that which he knew not.

Nay, verily, man is most extravagant in wickedness
Because he seeth himself possessed of wealth.
Verily unto the Lord is the return of all.
What thinkest thou of him who forbiddeth
A servant of God when he prayeth?
What thinkest thou? that he hath followed the true guidance or
*   enjoined piety?*
What thinkest thou, if he hath treated the truth as a lie and turned his
*   back?*
Doth he not know that God seeth?

Nay, verily, if he desist not, we will assuredly seize him by the forelock,
The lying sinful forelock!
Then let him summon his associates;
We too will summon the guards of hell:
Nay, obey him not; but adore, and draw nigh to God.[1]

---

[1] Translation by J.M. Rodwell (London, 1876), as it appears in *The Bible of the World*, ed. Robert O. Ballou (New York: The Viking Press, 1939), p. 1289.

It was strange to Muhammad that at the cessation of this vision he was able to repeat all these words. There is great poetic power in the words recorded in the Qur'an. Translations are hardly adequate to reproduce it. The work is always recited in Arabic for Muslim liturgical purposes. Before proceeding with Muhammad's experience and later career, it is appropriate to say something about this sacred scripture of Islam.

The Qur'an

From the point of view of Muslim doctrine the Qur'an is the infallible word of God. It is the transcript of a tablet which is preserved eternally in heaven. The spirit of God through the intermediary action of angels gave the words of the Qur'an to the Prophet himself. The Muslims believe that a sign of the divine origin of the book is the nobility and numinous power of its poetry. As an indication of Muhammad's own attitude, we observe that the verses of the Qur'an are famed as if they were the utterances of Allah, using Muhammad as his mouthpiece. The book, through constant repetition and through the marvelous literary power which it displays, has been a potent force in molding Arabic thought and language.

If we judge by the contents of the Qur'an, Muhammad certainly stands in the tradition of the great prophets, in the force and sincerity of his utterances, and the experiences which backed them. It is possible to discern phases in the composition of the scripture. Modern critical scholars are inclined to the view that there were three phases. In the first phase Muhammad was at Mecca, trying to summon men to a recognition of the worship of Allah. In the second phase, covering the last years at Mecca and the first years of his residence in Medina, Muhammad incorporated into his revelations elements drawn from Judaism and Christianity. In the third phase, the revelations indicated a hardening of attitude toward these latter faiths, and the final triumph of a distinct teaching—a new faith which crowned and superseded the earlier prophets from Moses to Jesus.

The actual composition of the Qur'an is a matter of some discussion. It may have been that Muhammad himself set down and revised many of the passages. A short time after his death there were collections of his sayings already in existence. According to Muslim tradition, his successor as the head of his movement, Abu Bakr, brought together the material that constitutes the Qur'an. Other authorities ascribe the work to the next in line of succession. It seems probable that there were as many as four editions in use until the Caliph Uthman (A.D. 644–656) designated one of them as the authoritative text. The book is arranged in a large number of sections, called *suras,* or revelations. These are put together in an order determined by their length. There is no special chronological or logical sequence in the Qur'an. The scripture is unique among the sacred books of the great world religions both in the short time lapse between its composition and the establishment of an authoritative tradition, and in its origin from the teaching of a single person.

The Hadith

In addition to the Qur'an itself there is an extensive body of Muslim traditions concerning the Prophet. This is known as the *Hadith*. The Hadith was made up of "statements" or "communications" collected over a period of two or three generations, and incorporated into a mass of hearsay material. Since some material was considered untrustworthy, it became the task of scholars to find criteria by which to distinguish the true from the false. In the second and third centuries after the Prophet, methods of Hadith-criticism were evolved. Much emphasis was laid upon the *isnad* or "support" for the stories—that is, upon the line of persons who had handed down the tradition. Biographical investigations of these persons constituted a branch of scholarship in which the authenticity of the material was checked. Finally, as a result of these investigations the scholars divided the Hadith into three classes: sound, good, and weak. The first class tradition was one whose line was traced authentically back to one of the Companions contemporary with the Prophet; a good tradition was one in which there was only one weak link in the chain; a weak tradition was one whose chain was questionable in several links. Although the methods used were not as rigorous or realistic as those of modern scholarship, a reasonably good sifting of data was effected. The sifting was not determined only by formal considerations implicit in the method of *isnad*. Theologians were aware that fabrications were creeping into the tradition. It was possible to detect them by comparing them with the genuine words of the Prophet in the Qur'an. A suspicious evaluation of the *isnad* might result from such a recognition rather than from tracing the formal facts of transmission. The Qur'an and the Hadith, then, provide our best knowledge of Muhammad's life.

Muhammad's Mission

At the time of his inaugural vision Muhammad was convinced that he had had a divine revelation. But doubts began to beset him. Was he really a Prophet of God? In his self-questioning, his wife comforted and supported him. His visions began to return. After a few months he was finally convinced of his divine call. He defended his first experience in the following words:

> By the star when it setteth,
> Your compatriot erreth not, nor is he led astray,
> Neither speaketh he from mere impulse.
> The Koran is no other than a revelation revealed to him:
> One terrible in power taught it him,
> Endued with wisdom. With even balance stood he

In the highest part of the horizon:
Then came he nearer and approached,
And was at the distance of two bows or even closer,
And he revealed to his servant what he revealed,
His heart falsified not what he saw.
What! Will he then dispute with him as to what he saw.[2]

Muhammad's mission had begun, but it had little early success. He preached outside the Kaba, but he was met largely with incredulity and scorn, especially among the Quraysh. A few converts began to meet in secret. But his denunciation of idolatry was disturbing and dangerous. His enemies multiplied. The people who believed in the old religion began to gather their forces in the face of the revolutionary Prophet.

Muhammad's Concept of God

What was the nature of his message? First and foremost Muhammad preached the unity and majesty of the one God, Allah. No longer was Allah to be regarded as a high god who lived in amity with other deities. He was unique. It was blasphemous to offer worship to any other being. He was, moreover, a righteous God who passed judgment on the sinner. An early *sura* reads:

When the sun shall be folded up,
And when the stars shall shoot downwards,
And when the mountains shall be set in motion,
And when the camels ten months gone with foal shall be abandoned,
And when the wild beasts shall be gathered together,
And when the seas shall be swollen,
And when souls shall be paired with their bodies,
And when the damsel that had been buried shall be asked
For what crime she was put to death,
And when the leaves of the Book shall be unrolled,
And when the heaven shall be stripped away,
And when hell shall be made to blaze,
And when paradise shall be brought near,
Every soul shall know what it hath produced.[3]

Yet for all the terrifying majesty of God as revealed to Muhammad in his prophetic experiences, Allah was also a merciful being. Though terrible to the

---

[2] Translation by J.M. Rodwell, *Sura 53*, as it appears in *The Koran*, Everyman's Library edition (New York: E. P. Dutton, 1909), p. 69.
[3] Rodwell's translation in *The Bible of the World*, p. 1294.

unfaithful, and overwhelming in his glory to the pious, he was also loving and compassionate. Thus in another *sura* we read:

> *The God of mercy hath taught the Koran,*
> *Hath created man,*
> *Hath taught him articulate speech.*
> *The sun and the moon have each their times,*
> *And the plants and the trees bend in adoration.*
> *And the heaven he hath reared it on high; and he hath appointed*
>   *the balance,*
> *That in the balance ye should not transgress;*
> *Weigh therefore with fairness, and scant not the balance.*
> *And the earth he hath prepared it for the living tribes:*
> *Therein are fruits and the palms with sheathed clusters,*
> *And the grain with its husk, and the supports of life.*[4]

From these poetical utterances we can begin to understand something about the nature of the experiences which Muhammad underwent.

There is a strong analogy between the visions of the Old Testament prophets and those of Muhammad. The term *nabi*, which in the Hebrew scriptures is used as the word for prophet, was applied to Muhammad. Like his spiritual forebears in ancient Israel, Muhammad not only had some kind of direct acquaintance with the numinous power of God, which led him again and again to affirm Allah's uniqueness and majesty; he also spoke typically through a form of impassioned utterance which was framed in verse of religious power. Arabic poetry flowed from his lips during ecstasy, a phenomenon which was detected also among the Hebrew prophets. His strong insistence on righteousness and uprightness, and his condemnation of cheating and idolatry are reflections of the same ethical impulse which shaped the Jewish heritage. No doubt Muhammad was influenced by Christian and Jewish teaching, but his message was original and unique. This was why he preached a faith separate from, though sympathetic to Judaism and Christianity. It was a faith for Arabs, unfettered by the particularity of Jewish law. Christianity was suspect not merely because it seemed to compromise with idolatry and polytheism, but also because it was characterized by division and persecution.

Medina

Some polytheistic opponents of Muhammad charged that he had derived his teachings from foreign—Christian or Jewish—sources. They also accused him of sorcery and of being possessed by devils. Such hostility, however, was less

[4] Rodwell's translation in *The Bible of the World*, p. 1299.

distressing to him than the fact that he made in the first four years of his preaching only about forty converts. Muhammad was willing and able to put up with many tribulations. But the increasingly hostile pressure from those of the Quraysh who opposed him, coupled with the death of his beloved wife Khadija, made him think that Mecca did not hold much future for him. He tried to establish his faith at Taif, without success.

Medina, three hundred miles north of Mecca, offered more hope. Some of the Medina citizens, concerned at the internal strife which plagued that city, were attracted to Muhammad as a leader who might bring peace and a reordering of the community. In A.D. 622 the Prophet, on the secret invitation of these citizens, migrated to Medina. This migration is known as the *Hijra* (or in older transliteration the *Hegira*). From it the beginning of the Muslim era is dated. Muslim dating of an event can be derived by subtracting 622 from Christian dating.

The situation at Medina gave the Prophet remarkable opportunities. He possessed both political and religious authority. He proceeded to fashion a community which would be able to carry his message widely throughout Arabia and beyond. He proceeded with tact. There are many signs that he was an astute diplomat. He had to reconcile the many tensions which grew up. Leading citizens began to regret the authority which had been conferred on him. The so-called "helpers" who supported him in Medina did not always see eye to eye with the new refugees Muhammad brought with him from his native city. The Jewish community looked on the new faith with suspicion. But new customs were hammered out and accepted. The military security and strength of the city was established. Muhammad, showing great capacity as a leader—he was no mere visionary—swiftly shaped Medina into the first Muslim theocracy.

On the religious side, Muhammad developed a system of worship that was simple, dignified, and effective. It was in Medina that the first mosque was built. Weekly services, on Fridays, formed the pattern which Muslim faith has observed ever since. The brotherhood of those who acknowledged Islam, or obedience to Allah, was stressed. Almsgiving was introduced as a method of alleviating the lot of the poorer members of the new community. This strong sense of brotherhood under God was an important factor in the religious and military successes of the faith in later years. Idolatrous practices in the city were stopped. Medina was reformed, and the main shape of the Muslim religion was established. What was the next stage to be?

War with Mecca

As a Meccan, Muhammad looked forward to a time when the worship of Allah as sole God would be established there. As a political leader he saw the need for further successes if the loyalty of the Medinans was to be retained.

He therefore decided to gain control over Mecca. Warfare was the means. The first engagement in his campaign was an attack by a handful of men on a caravan guarded by four Quraysh. The incident was more significant than the small numbers involved would suggest. For it occurred in the sacred month when warfare was banned. The breaking of a sacred truce was shocking to the sentiments of most Arabs, but Muhammad argued that the rooting out of idolatry was a stronger sacred obligation than the breaking of the truce. He had given a clear demonstration to the Arab world that their presuppositions must be radically altered.

A number of engagements followed. At Badr the Prophet, with three hundred men, routed a much larger force of Meccans. This was the first real battle which was fought for Islam. It was impressive for the way in which the faithful fought with zeal, courage, and purpose. In response to the victory others began to join this successful movement. It showed signs of divine blessing. But the next battle was different. A rich caravan had fallen into the hands of the Muslims. The Meccans decided it was time to frighten the marauding Prophet. A force of three thousand men was sent out on this mission. The Meccans were met by seven hundred Muslims just outside Medina, at Uhud. The Muslims were defeated and the Prophet was injured in the mouth. But the following day, despite this setback, Muhammad defiantly followed the enemy, and though no further fighting took place, he demonstrated the resilience of his followers.

The final major engagement was upon the occasion when the Meccans sent out a much larger force with the object of taking Medina. A Jewish tribe on Muhammad's side was induced to promise a diversionary attack upon the Prophet's men. But the stratagem was foiled by Muhammad, who, by another manouever made the Jews and the Meccans distrust one another. The attack never came off. When the Meccan attack had collapsed in front of Medina, the Jewish tribe was dealt with harshly by Muhammad. The men were beheaded and the women and children sold into slavery. This demonstrated a further phase in Muhammad's campaign to eradicate the Jews from the Hejaz and from his base of operations. He did not trust a group who mocked his prophetic claims, and who refused to accept as a prophet anyone who could claim that Jesus had been a prophet too.

Muhammad's power became further consolidated when he set out, in 630, to take Mecca. The city surrendered soon. Some prominent men had been won over to the cause, and Muhammad's promise of protection to those who would not resist, and his affirmation that the Kabah would be the center of Muslim pilgrimage, removed some of the motives for resistance. He entered Mecca in triumph. He showed great tact and magnanimity. Only four people were put to death. Thus the defeated city remained loyal to him. The honor which it gained from its being the Prophet's native city more than outweighed any remaining bitterness which surrender might have created. But even more important, the Prophet seems to have been remarkable for the loyalty he inspired and the persuasiveness with which he customarily dealt with opponents. He preferred to win men over rather than crush their spirit by a simple display of force.

Muhammad's Death

In the last two years of his life, Muhammad's forces began to move northward from the now largely unified Hejaz. The first moves were made in a series of campaigns and conquests which hit the Middle East and the Mediterranean world with explosive impact. The religion which he had preached in adversity and in success became fixed and organized. But the Prophet died before seeing its enormous influence. Not only was his achievement singular in one lifetime, but it had incalculable effects on the history of mankind from the seventh century onward.

BASIC DOCTRINES OF THE QUR'AN

The basic doctrines preached by Muhammad were simple and forceful. He said that there was but one God, Allah, and he, Muhammad, was his Prophet. He saw himself as the last in a line of prophets, and was the "seal of the prophets," for in him God's revelation reached finality. The line stretched from Moses down to Jesus. Belief in Muhammad's apostleship necessitated the recognition of the unerring nature of the Qur'an, which he claimed had originated in heaven. Below Allah there was a range of angelic beings who carried out his behests. But these angels were, as in Christian belief, creatures, and in no way were to be considered divine or supernatural in their own right. Among angels, one had fallen, Iblis (derived from the Greek word *Diabolos*). He and his agents often obstructed the work of the faithful. But this was within the limits laid down by Allah.

The omnipotence of Allah was so strongly stressed in the Qur'an that not only did Allah guide the faithful to the truth, but in some sense also he led the wicked astray. This theology was not fully worked out in the scripture itself. The Arabic term meaning "to lead astray" does not quite have the positive significance which the English translation suggests. It was rather a matter of letting people lose their way. Nevertheless, it was ultimately the will of Allah which controlled man's destiny. In an important sense it was Allah who destined men either to salvation or to damnation. This was in line with the most obvious emphasis throughout Muhammad's teachings on the oneness of God and on his majesty and power.

Last Judgment

As in later Judaism and Christianity, there was belief in a Last Judgment, in which men's deeds would be weighed and assigned either to heaven or to hell. Both these regions were described in extremely vivid terms. The inmates of hell would be covered with fire, and would beseech those in paradise to pour cooling water on them. But the fire would be unsparing. Angels presiding over the torment would also be relentless. The sinners would eat the fruit of a strange tree which rose up from the bottom of hell, and it would boil up like oil in their bellies. On the other hand, the righteous would enter a region where there were gardens and fountains, and they would be clothed in beautiful raiment. Delicious food and wine would be served to them by celestial youths as they reclined at their ease on couches. And dark-eyed maidens too would wait on their commands—fresh and delightful mates. Thus the contrast between the two fates, when the dreaded last trumpet sounded, was violently drawn. This eschatology reinforced the insistence on serving Allah through righteous and just behavior. It was also an important factor in the faith and courage that animated the warriors of Islam. Death would be rewarded by something more splendid than plunder and power. Disloyalty would be punished by something worse than earthly torture and execution. Good and evil stood out in stark distinction. The judgment of Allah, though inscrutable, was foreshadowed in his acceptance and guidance of the faithful.

Jesus As Prophet of Islam

The unity of God led Muhammad to preach about Jesus in a way that was not in accord with orthodox Christian belief. No Muslim could hold that Jesus was divine, since this would be setting up someone else alongside Allah. Thus God's Fatherhood was denied in the Qur'an. Jesus was described as a prophet, and as having been conceived in the womb of a virgin. He would reappear before the Final Judgment. He did not die upon the cross, but some kind of appearance was substituted for him during the crucifixion and he was raised up to heaven. (The Qur'anic text is ambiguous—the foregoing is, however, a common interpretation of it among Muslims.) Muhammad's teaching reflects belief in the Virgin Mary, in Jesus' Second Coming (though not as the Judge —the Judge was Allah), and in his ascension to heaven. Further, according to the Qur'an, Muhammad believed that Jesus was strengthened by the Holy Spirit. The Holy Spirit was mentioned several times, but was not thought of as a separate Person in the Godhead.

We can see from this that the picture of what Muhammad rejected in Christian belief is confused. Strictly, he did not deny the doctrine of the Trinity itself, but rather the notion that Jesus was Son of God. A contributory factor here was the fact that the Arabic understanding of God's being Father was literal; it implied physical generation. This was blasphemous if ascribed to God. In this case Muhammad was denying something that the orthodox Christian had no wish to affirm. So the incompatibility was minimal. But the denial that Jesus suffered physically on the cross takes away the essence of Christian belief in Jesus' saving work. To Muhammad's mind it would have been paradoxical for Allah to allow a prophet to end his days in such ignominious circumstances. Islam was a religion that prized success as a criterion of Allah's favor—not simple worldly success, but the holy success which crowned so signally, despite early tribulations, the life of Muhammad himself. Since the Muslims have taken the Qur'an to be an eternal and infallible document, there is no concession on the historical data of Jesus' life. Despite the wide area of agreement between them about God's nature, and despite the early favorable attitude taken up by the Prophet toward the Christians, this tends to create a collision between Christian and Muslim faith.

THE FIVE PILLARS OF ISLAM

The practical teachings of the Qur'an are equally as important as the doctrinal ones. They can be divided into two main categories. First, there are the religious duties which are laid down for the faithful. Second, there are the ethical and social duties. The religious duties have given shape to Muslim practices through the ages, and help to account for the remarkable cohesion of a movement which has never relied upon a hierarchy of organized priests. They are constituted by the so-called "Five Pillars" of Islam. These are: the repetition of the brief creed of Islam, *La ilaha illa Allah: Muhammad rasul Allah* ("There is no god but Allah, and Muhammad is his Prophet"); prayer; almsgiving; fasting; and pilgrimage.

Prayer

Prayer is the core of the Muslim's religious life. The universal rule is for Muslims to pray five times a day. The Qur'an does not lay this down as a rule, but there is little doubt that the practice goes back to the Prophet himself. At dawn, at noon, in the mid-afternoon, at sunset, and at the onset of darkness, the Muslim is expected to pray, facing toward Mecca. Originally the Prophet told his followers to bow toward Jerusalem, but Jewish opposition and other factors induced him to introduce the later rule. The most common prayer is the recitation of the words of the first *sura* which express the heart of Muslim devotion:

> *Praise be to God, the Lord of the worlds!*
> *The compassionate, the merciful!*
> *King of the day of judgment!*

Thee only *do we worship, and to Thee do we cry for help.*
Guide Thou us on the straight path,
The path of those to whom Thou hast been gracious—
With whom thou art not angry, and who go not astray.[5]

Friday is a special day set aside for devotions. Congregational worship centers on the mosque, which, though simple and unadorned with images, in accordance with the Muslim view of images as idolatrous, is analogous to a Christian church. In place of the altar there is a semi-circular recess known as the *mihrab:* in facing this the faithful are bowing toward Mecca. Prayers are led by a prayer leader, or *imam,* who recites the words while the faithful prostrate themselves at appropriate times in accordance with his example. It is also usual for the prayer leader to preach, expounding Muslim doctrine.

Almsgiving

Almsgiving was at one time obligatory—a fortieth of one's income was collected on behalf of the community. But this obligation long since fell into disuse. The Qur'an stressed the importance of giving money to help the poor. It has remained a central part of Muslim charity. Through it the compassion and solidarity of the community are expressed.

Fasting

Fasting centers on the great fast of the month of Ramadan. It varies in date, since it is a lunar month, not corresponding with the monthly divisions of the Western calendar. During this period, no food or drink may be taken from sunrise to sunset. This represents considerable effort, especially in hot, dry countries. Fasting also enters into the obligations of pilgrimage.

Pilgrimage

The duty of pilgrimage, or *hajj,* is laid on every Muslim, if his circumstances permit. This involves going to Mecca. The journey is often a hazardous and perilous undertaking. It was especially so in earlier ages. Once within the boundaries of Mecca, every pilgrim must wear a certain sort of plain, white clothing. People of different nations and customs, and people of different social rank are leveled together to a brotherly equality during the period of the main ceremonies connected with the pilgrimage. These start with the act of going seven times around the Kaba, kissing the Black Stone on each occasion. Following this, the pilgrims engage in the rite of running seven times between two nearby hills. Then they move off on the eighth day of the feast to

[5] Rodwell's translation as it appears in *The Koran* (Everyman's Library edition, 1909), p. 28.

82. *Rashid al-Din manuscript illustration shows Muhammad and Abu Bakr on flight to Medina (14th century). (Courtesy of Edinburgh University Library.)*

83. *Muhammad carried by Buraq to heaven. (Courtesy of Edinburgh University Library.)*

84. *The Dome of the Rock in Jerusalem, built in 691 on the site of King Solomon's and Herod's temples. (Courtesy of the Israel Ministry of Tourism.)*

85. *Leaf from a Qur'an (12th century).*
(Courtesy of the Metropolitan Museum of Art, Rogers Fund, 1918.)

86. *Teaching the Qur'an to a young girl at a Qur'anic school in Fayum, Egypt. (Courtesy of the United Nations, photo by John Isaac.)*

87. *A Friday prayer meeting in Teheran, Iran. (Courtesy of the United Nations, photo by John Isaac.)*

88. *Two young women "in purdah" (i.e., wearing the veil) standing at a meat stall in Taroudant, Morocco. (Courtesy of the United Nations/ BIJUR.)*

89. *Sun setting over a mosque in Cairo. (Courtesy of the United Nations, photo by B. P. Wolff.)*

Arafat, some twelve miles east of Mecca. During the following day they spend their time on the plain, engaged in meditation. On the way back to Mecca, they stop at Mina, where the ceremony of casting seven stones is performed by each pilgrim—this is the "stoning of the Devil." Sacrifices follow, and meat is distributed among the poorer brethren. Feasting and merrymaking give the sequence of prescribed acts a joyous flavor. The pilgrims return to Mecca, and circumambulate the Kaba a last time. During most of the period, they have been fasting from dawn to dusk, and they must remain sexually continent. Hair must not be cut; nails must not be pared. These outward observances, going back in form to pre-Islamic times, were adapted by the Prophet to constitute a central act which would unite his Arab followers from all over the region: they continue to unite Muslims all over the world. Pilgrims in their pilgrimage to Mecca also visit the tomb of the Prophet at Medina.

These are the Five Pillars of Islam. If we exclude almsgiving, they constitute the main rituals of Islam. It is noteworthy that the obligations are laid down for individuals: it is through the willing conformity of the individuals who constitute the community that the ritual traditions carry on. Islam is notable for its lack of an organization of priests. Each man, in principle, stands directly before his Maker, without intermediaries.

ETHICAL TEACHINGS OF ISLAM

In addition to the ritual demands of Islam there are ethical ones. These play an important role in the fabric of the faith. The first insistence is on right attitudes. A *sura* from the Qur'an says:

There is no piety in turning your faces towards the east or the west, but he is pious who believeth in God and the last day and the angels and the scriptures and the prophets; who for the love of God disburseth his wealth to his kindred and to the orphans and the needy and the wayfarer, and those who ask, and for ransoming; who observeth prayer and payeth the legal alms, and who is one of those who are faithful to their engagements when they have engaged in them, and patient under ills and hardships and in time of troubles: these are they who are just, and these are they who fear God.[6]

Thus outward conformity to the faith must be complemented by an inner sense of justice and an attitude of patience. The repeated stress on honorable dealing between men no doubt reflected an opposite vice among those whom Muhammad was welding into a new brotherhood. But as well as attempting

[6] Rodwell's translation in *The Bible of the World*, p. 1315.

to impose a general shape of human attitudes, Muhammad also specified detailed regulations concerning particular matters.

Muhammad made no move to abolish slavery, but the Qur'an insisted that they be treated humanely. It was a good deed for a master to free a slave who belonged to Islam. Concubinage with female slaves was recognized, but they could not be exploited for prostitution. Marriage also was given a new look under the Muslim dispensation. Only four wives were allowed, a modification of existing practice. It was forcibly pointed out that wives ought to be treated equally. A man who could not treat all impartially ought only to have one wife. Though a man might divorce a wife freely, he was obliged, upon marriage, to make over a dowry to the wife, and this remained her property. Thus the evils of unregulated divorce were mitigated. In such ways, the Prophet reshaped existing institutions, although he did not sweep them away and start afresh. By a moderate reform of earlier practices Muhammad undoubtedly brought about an improvement in social justice and humanity.

Three other Qur'anic regulations deserve mention—the prohibitions of gambling, wine, and pork. Gambling was a social problem of pre-Muslim Arab days. The Prophet forbade it entirely. Similarly, alcohol was banned. The Qur'an said that in gambling and wine there was both sin and advantage to men, but the sin outweighed the advantage. Continuing the Jewish tradition, pork was regarded as unclean. These tabus on wine and pork represented further external indications of the distinction between the pious Muslim and the Christian. In addition to them there was a mass of detailed regulations in the scripture. They derived from early customs and traditions, and formed the basis of Muslim law. Muhammad was not merely creating a faith which the individual might or might not adopt. He was also creating a political community, informed by ideals of brotherhood and controlled by the divinely originated law.

MUHAMMAD'S EXPERIENCE OF ALLAH

We have now surveyed the main structure of the faith which Muhammad left to the world after his prophetic and statesman-like career. To return for a moment to the figure of the Prophet, we should recognize that it was in essence his experience of Allah which determined his subsequent acts. His fervid monotheism owed its impetus both to the Jewish and the Christian traditions which he inherited. But they owed much more to the impressive and sometimes painful experiences which formed the substance of his prophetic calling. Not only was there the experience of his vision, in which he felt the presence of Allah in an overwhelming way: there were also his ecstatic seizures during which he was able to utter the rhymed verses which constituted many of the revelations contained in the Qur'an. He felt as though there were inside his head the painful tolling of a bell. It may be that the revelations of the later part of his career, when he became a person in political authority, were more formal and less striking than those of his early mission. But they followed inevitably from his sense of calling and his deep awareness of Allah. The marvelous power of the Arabic of the Qur'an, which forms the holy center of the pious Muslim's life, is a sign of the tremendous poetic and religious gifts which were given to Muhammad.

Personality of the Prophet

He was by no means continuously in the grip of these forces. Although he could be wrathful and indignant at what he considered to be blasphemy or disloyalty, we can distinguish through the mass of pious legend that his character was also humorous and gentle. He was firm and sometimes ferocious in war, but he was tactful and diplomatic in peace. He was not one to alienate men from him unnecessarily: his authority and charm were put in the service of winning men to Allah. Though later tradition came to look upon him as perfect and sinless, somewhat in the manner of the Christian view of Jesus, there is evidence that he recognized his own human weaknesses. He sacrificed to idols before his call. The number of his wives showed that he had strong sexual instincts. But the power of his character was vindicated by his accomplishment in forming from the tribes and towns of the divided, impotent Arabic peoples a new, divine nation, able to conquer in one short and explosive century a great part of the world from Gibraltar to the Himalaya mountains. He gave new purpose and a new justice to a people who had hitherto remained on the fringes of the civilized world and who had been bruised by that world. Muhammad blended uniquely the faith in a single, righteous, and compassionate God with a universal political destiny. Islam had the strength of Jewish monotheism without its national confinement: it had the brotherliness of Christianity, without its political uncertainties. It burst on a world where Christian divisions and persecutions made it seem an attractive substitute.

Muhammad as Prophet

Since Muhammad has often been attacked by Christian and other apologists as being in one way or another an unworthy figure to call a prophet, a word on these matters should be said. There are two issues at stake in this controversy.

The first question focuses on whether Muhammad was truly a prophet of God like those in the Old Testament. Since this issue really incorporates the whole question of the truth of religion—of which interpretation of the nature of God and of his action in history is correct, that made by the Christians or that made by the Muslims—it cannot be dealt with here. Suffice it to say that the proximity of Muhammad's ideas of Allah and the Christian conceptions of the Deity make it difficult for either side to deny a measure of truth to the other.

The second question concerns Muhammad's character and whether the aspersions cast upon him have been justified. He was widely alleged to have been an epileptic. The allegation is important in any study or estimate of his religious experience. In a period when Islam and Christianity were in serious collision, fighting for the very hegemony of Europe, the propaganda on either side was not tender-minded. It is worth quoting here the words of a distinguished contemporary Christian Arabist:

> A past generation of Arabists . . . advanced the theory that Muhammad was an epileptic. The charge had been made by a Byzantine writer long before. Such a hypothesis seems gratuitous, and can be safely ascribed to anti-Muhammadan prejudice. Study of the psychological phenomena of religious experience makes it extremely improbable. Prophets are not normal people, but that does not authorize the assertion that their abnormal behavior is due to a morbid condition. Moreover, Muhammad was a man whose common sense never failed him. Those who deny his mental and psychic stability do so only by ignoring the overwhelming evidence of his shrewd appraisal of others and of the significance of what was going on in the world of his time, and his persistence in the face of constant opposition until he united his people in the religion of Islam. Had he ever collapsed in the strain of battle or controversy, or fainted away when strong action was called for, a case might be made out. But all the evidence we have points in the opposite direction, and the suggestion of epilepsy is as groundless in the eyes of the present writer as it is offensive to all Muslims. It may be added that most modern writers, as opposed to those of the last generation, are of this opinion.[7]

We have, then, to estimate Muhammad's religious experience on its own terms, just as we have to evaluate that of, say, Isaiah and of the Buddha. Unfortunately the West has inherited a hostile and distorted image of Islam, which often still animates media reporting on the Muslim world.

ADVANCE OF ISLAM

The Prophet's death was a crisis for Islam. Would the new allegiance hold together now that the supernatural guidance and authority of Allah as medi-

---

[7] Alfred Guillame, *Islam* (New York: Penguin Books, rev. ed. 1956), pp. 25–26.

ated through the Prophet was no longer directly available? Muhammad had
nominated no successor. The fever which caused his death had come on too
suddenly for him to have had time for reflection on what should be the mode
of transition to a new rule. A trusted friend, one of the early Companions who
had stood by the Prophet in his struggles, Abu Bakr, assumed power and
became the first successor or *khalifa* (more commonly transcribed in English
as Caliph). His first problem was to defeat dissident tribes who broke away
from their allegiance as soon as Muhammad was gone. A series of swift
campaigns put an end to the revolt. Abu Bakr then gathered a large force and
began to move forward to the fringes of the desert and into Syria. In the two
years between 632, the date of the Prophet's death, and 634, when the Caliph
himself died, Arab domination was carried forward to a line running roughly
from southern Syria to the head of the Persian gulf, but not including Palestine.

The Caliphs

Under the second Caliph, Umar, the famous general Khalid ben al-Walid,
continued the campaign with startling success. A lightning advance captured
the great city of Damascus from the Byzantines. Though the Arabs had to fall
back for a space, they inflicted a catastrophic defeat on the Byzantines under
the Emperor Heraclius. The whole of Syria and Palestine lay open to them.
Khalid turned eastward to probe the strength of the Persian empire. He found
it less impressive than he had expected. After a preliminary setback, a great
victory gave the Arabs the whole of Iraq. Meanwhile a small Muslim force
had entered the Nile Delta, and most of lower Egypt fell into their hands. In
the decade of Umar's Caliphate the armies pushed north as far as the Taurus
mountains, westward as far as Libya, and eastward as far as Isfahan.

Uthman, the next Caliph, whose rule lasted from A.D. 644 to 656, continued the incredible series of conquests. The Persian Empire, despite quite effective resistance, crumbled beneath the swift-moving onslaught. The area to the
west of the Caspian as far as the borders of the Caucasus was taken, though
Asia Minor remained part of a shrunken and alarmed Byzantine Empire.
Upper Egypt and the whole of Libya were swallowed up. In the fantastic thirty
years, the Arabs had become a formidable world power.

MUSLIM EXPANSION

How was all this achieved? First, there was the unity of purpose imparted by
Islam. Second, the Arab military tactics were novel to those against whom
they fought. The Arab armies had their base in the deserts. From these bases
they could move swiftly and at will, striking suddenly at unexpected places.

The camel, the "ship of the desert," gave the Muslim armies a mobility which their opponents lacked. Third, great numbers of people among the populations of the countries which they first overran were disaffected. The substratum of the population was Semitic, and on it was superimposed Hellenistic and Byzantine culture and rule. The Semitic peoples still retained enough consciousness of their origins and traditions to welcome the Arab invasion and the overthrow of their Greek masters. Also, divisions and subsequent persecutions had weakened Christianity: and many were happy to escape these tensions by accepting the undoubtedly monotheistic faith of Islam, and the new brotherhood which it seemed to offer.

The Arab conquerors did not treat their new subjects harshly; their rule appeared preferable to that of the Byzantines and Persians, whose warfare and taxation often left the inhabitants of an area in a state of resentment and insecurity. The Arabs exacted milder taxes, and Christians and Jews, through prevented from proselytizing, were normally allowed to continue the practices of their religions. On the whole, even though local Arab commanders could be unreasonable and arrogant, Arab rule was a good proposition in comparison with that which had gone before it.

It is illusory to look on the spread of Islam as something imposed simply by the sword. The vast majority of the Middle Eastern population which Islam conquered became Muslims without compulsion. Force of arms in conquest was obviously important; and the benefits accruing from joining the new faith were clearly considerable. But it was through such means of indirect persuasion, rather than by forcible conversion, that Islam spread so effectively. Had it not been so, its grip on the popular imagination would never have become as strong as it did.

DISSENSION IN EARLY ISLAM

At the same time, despite these spectacular successes the Muslim community was passing through a period of crisis. The untutored sons of the desert now found themselves in control of sophisticated cities and rich provinces. Damascus was a phenomenon which the invaders had never previously encountered. In the richness of its life, the advanced state of its literary culture and the complexity of its buildings and social life, it was a revelation to the conquering Bedouins. Wealth and loot made the process of conquest highly lucrative. Previously poor Arabs now found themselves—even the rank and file—in possession of goods which they had never dreamed of. How could religious discipline survive this change of status? And how could Islam preserve its essential nature when so many new Muslims, previously of other religious persuasions, were flocking to join it? How could the political structure of

Islam stand up to the pressures and jealousies which such an acquisition of wealth and power was bound to set up?

Troubles appeared in the time of the first Caliphs. Umar was assassinated by a captive Christian slave. His successor, Uthman, who belonged to the prominent Umayyad family in Mecca, but who was also son-in-law and early associate of the Prophet, distributed posts and power to his relations. Those of Medina who had been in the forefront of the Prophet's advance to authority became alienated. Receipts of money pouring into the treasury and the powers of empire were too glittering a prize to be foregone lightly. Dissension at Medina culminated in Uthman's assassination.

In 656, despite strong opposition, Ali was elected to succeed him. Ali was opposed by one of the Umayyads, Muawiya, a nephew of the murdered Uthman, who was in control of Syria. Ali moved the center of government to Iraq, and then dispatched an army to encounter him. There was an indecisive engagement. The Syrian troops fixed portions of the Qur'an to their lances, and this sacred barrier was one which the pious on the other side feared to break. Ali agreed to arbitration. This led to the secession of some of the more intransigent of his followers. The arbitration was decided against him. Muawiya detached Egypt from his allegiance. Power was slipping from Ali's hands, and in 661 he was murdered by a Kharijite—one of the party who had opposed the arbitration. Ali's eldest son, Hasan, renounced any right to the Caliphate. It now fell into the grasp of the skillful Muawiya.

The Umayyad Dynasty

Under Muawiya's rule the Umayyad dynasty commenced, ruling from the new capital of Damascus. During the Umayyad dynasty, which lasted nearly a century, until A.D. 750, the divisions within Islam took shape. It was a time of prosperity and continued conquest for the Arabs. Their armies continued their victorious way along the north coast of Africa and down into Morocco. They moved into Spain. They continued across the Pyrenees into France. France was saved only by the notable victory of Charles Martel ("the Hammer") at Poitiers in A.D. 732. In the East, the Arabs surged into Central Asia and reached the Indus River in northwest India in 710. This remained the eastern boundary of Muslim expansion for a long time. Cyprus too was invaded and detached from the Byzantine Empire.

The Kharijites

The Kharijites, those who broke away from Ali over the issue of the arbitration with Muawiya, were not actuated solely by political motives. Indeed, because of the essentially political nature of Islam, politics and religion were always inextricably interwoven. The Kharijites were puritanical and democratic. They believed that the will of God should be expressed through the decisions of a whole community of believers. Thus an elected Caliph like Ali should take a strong line with those, like the Umayyad family, who wished to usurp power. They strongly resented newer moves toward laxity in conduct. The purity of the faith must be maintained, they thought. Unjust rulers ought to be overthrown by force and the principle of the *jihad,* or holy war, which was at various times regarded as a duty for the faithful if undertaken against infidels, was applied within Islam itself. The Kharijites were important for their insistence on the older virtues, in danger of passing away, and even to the present day they remain influential as a source of inspiration for succeeding puritanical reform movements. Their descendants exist as a separate sect in North Africa and elsewhere, marrying within their own group, though in matters of practice and belief, they are not too different from other Muslims.

The Murjiites

The Kharijites stand out in sharp relief against another group, the Murjiites. The Murjiites were called "postponers" because they were less severe in their ethical judgments than the Kharijites, and they held that judgment should be postponed to the Last Judgment, i.e. that Allah should decide who is a good Muslim. Such a doctrine was well adapted to reconciliation with the Umayyad Dynasty and a more relaxed way of life. The Kharijites argued that serious sins excluded a man from salvation. The issue was not unlike that which exercised the Christian Church during the period after it had emerged victorious. The Kharijite position corresponded roughly to that of the Donatists. The Murjiite view won out as the orthodox Muslim tenet. The Murjiites believed that a man was not excluded by sins; he could always repent thereof. And even if he did not, it was for Allah, not men, to decide. Allah was merciful; and if there was any case for mercy it would be given. This position was a tolerant one, and it followed logically from the belief that Allah was supreme and the sole source of salvation. Both in Christianity and Islam the supremacy of God led to the same sort of conclusion.

The Shia and Sunni Sects

More important than these divisions was a controversy which resulted in a split in Islam between the Shia sect and the Sunni (or orthodox). Although Ali's son Hasan had renounced the right to succession, the younger brother, Husayn, inaugurated a revolt against the successor of the Umayyad Caliph. He rounded up followers at Medina and set out for Kufah in Iraq. Kufah had been his father's capital and was therefore a center of resistance to the new regime. At Karbala in western Iraq, Husayn was cornered. He and his followers were annihilated. His head was taken in triumph to Damascus. This event later became a focal point in Shiite memory, and the tragedy is still re-enacted every year on the death day of Muharram. Husayn, the great martyr of the movement, was not a martyr to infidels, but to fellow Muslims. This may not have been surprising insofar as the movement was political. But it acquired strong religious overtones as well. It expressed the religious discontent of the non-Arab populations of Iraq and elsewhere. Although these peoples had embraced Islam, elements of their former outlook penetrated their beliefs. There were economic grievances as well.

The Arabs used many non-Arab soldiers in their armies, but they retained an inferior status. The lion's share of the booty went to the Arabs, and the Empire, though it employed officials drawn from the conquered peoples, remained essentially an Arab perquisite. Such dissatisfactions were responsible for the wide success of Shia propaganda during the latter part of the Umayyad dynasty, and it was a Shia revolt which sparked off the sequence of events leading to the fall of the dynasty and its replacement by Abbasid rule. The center of power then shifted to Baghdad, and a tyrannical monarchy was instituted. But despite the support given by the Shia, they were considered dangerous to the new regime, and were repressed. The descendants of Ali were sought out and murdered. The grave of Husayn was destroyed.

Partly as a result of these events, the Shia movement acquired a strongly messianic character: there were hopes, characteristic of the oppressed, of a leader who would emerge to restore justice. He would be a descendant of Ali. The emphasis on the house of Ali accompanied a view about the true headship of the faith. The Caliph should not be chosen by election and the leadership was and should be essentially hereditary. The Shiites regarded Abu Bakr, Umar, and Uthman as interlopers. This view offended orthodox believers who looked on the first four Caliphs as the "rightly guided ones." According to the Shiites each generation possessed a divinely inspired leader, or Imam, from the house of Ali, who was the true spiritual head of Islam. This leader was, moreover, infallible. Within the Shia movement an increased emphasis was put upon the veneration of the chief religious figures of the tradition. Muhammad was thought of as perfect and sinless, a belief which also penetrated orthodox thinking. The Imams were also ascribed a quasi-divine status.

These ideas crystallized eventually into the doctrine that the line of succession extended to twelve Imams, ending with Muhammad al-Mahdi who, according to the belief, was spirited away at the age of eight and remained "hidden" until such time as he would return to earth to bring in a period of justice and prosperity and righteousness. Something of the spirit of Christian and Zoroastrian eschatology came to be incorporated in a new form into Islam. Not all the Shia sects shared precisely this pattern of belief, but all were united in messianic expectations. The movement, in the course of this evolution, acquired a strongly esoteric side. The true teachings were handed down secretly to the Imams, and the true interpretation of the Qur'an was not that of the orthodox. The growth of veneration for holy men accompanied these developments, and as we shall see, the Shia contributed to the growth of Muslim mysticism.

It was a result of the new doctrines that Islam came to be broadly divided into the two sects: the Sunnites, or orthodox believers, and the Shiites. The Shiites became dominant in Iran, Iraq, and strong in Pakistan, while most of the rest of the Muslim world belongs to the orthodox persuasion. The Shiites have tended to divide into different sub-sects, partly because appeal to "esoteric" knowledge can give great opportunities for new interpretations of the faith, and partly because Shiism gave expression to former religious tendencies, which differed from one place to another. The orthodox on the other hand have been more cohesive, since they appealed not only to the Qur'an, but to the consensus of the community, thus retaining a mechanism of decision which discouraged the lavish growth of new beliefs.

Influence of Greek Ideas

The conquest of the Greek East brought the Arabs into contact with science and philosophy. It was not long before there was a fruitful interplay between the two cultures, though the new ideas also created strain within the community insofar as rationalism was a threat to orthodox faith. The most important philosophical school in the early period had its origins in the dispute between the Kharijites and the Murjiites, and later it absorbed a number of Greek concepts.

Mutazila

Neither the rigorism of the Kharijites nor the lax doctrines of the Murjiites seemed to be satisfactory, and so there arose an intermediate position, known as the Mutazila. According to the Mutazila, the ascription of salvation to the decision of Allah robbed men of the incentive to virtue: it was therefore necessary to hold that man had power over his own acts and that it was on this basis that he is judged. Faith also was a consequence of human choice. Thus the Mutazila rejected the doctrine of predestination. They were especially put off by the notion that Allah misled sinners, for it did not square with the justice and mercy of God.

In other ways they were critical of beliefs still in the process of formation which later were to become orthodox. Indeed, the controversies between the Mutazilites and the more conservative exponents of Islam helped to crystallize these very orthodoxies. The belief, for instance, that the Qur'an was eternal was criticized by the Mutazilites because it seemed to put another god alongside Allah. It was the property of divinity, and of divinity alone, to be eternal. On the other hand, the notion that the Qur'an was something created by God in time was thought by the orthodox to be a threat to its divinely inspired status. The Mutazilites also criticized the orthodox insistence on ascribing personal (or as they thought anthropomorphic) qualities to God. Passages in the scripture which spoke of God's throne, or God's hands, were merely metaphorical, they believed, and it was superstitious to take them literally. From the view of orthodox exposition it was dangerous to take passages to be metaphorical, for this meant that the force of the scripture would be weakened, and human judgment would be substituted for divine authority.

If the Mutazila doctrines were well-intentioned and clear-headed, they were sometimes arrogantly presented, and although there were dangers, from the moral point of view, in the notion of predestination, there were equally great dangers in the doctrine of free will. The ascription of power over one's actions could easily lead to a carping spirit of criticism and judgment. More important, if faith was a matter of choice, then men should be pressured into making the right choice. In this way the Mutazila teachings were sometimes used on behalf of religious oppression.

Al-Ashari—Modified Orthodoxy

For these and other reasons the Mutazila theology ultimately came to be rejected. Credit for this rejection was due to the philosopher and theologian al-Ashari (died in A.D. 935), who gave coherent expression to a modified orthodoxy, taking account of some of the criticisms of anthropomorphism while at the same time preserving the authority of the Qur'an. He reasoned that when the Qur'an spoke of God's hand, etc., it was really ascribing a quality to God, though the mode in which God possessed it was unknown. Allah was quite different in character from his creatures, and was bodiless. Thus any crude sort of anthropomorphism was rejected. As to predestination, it was argued that all events in the universe, including the acts of human beings, were directly caused by God. Thus men's decisions were absolutely dependent on God's will, but through their actions, men did acquire responsibility for them. Thus the justice of God in punishing evil was not impaired. The Qur'an was eternal, al-Ashari affirmed, but the actual words which were written down and recited by men were not. In such ways the attempt was made to reconcile common sense philosophy and the traditions of Islam. The subtlety of much of al-Ashari's argument, his wide learning, and the extent to which he was able to use philosophical and scientific ideas without selling out to a faithless rationalism, immediately commended him to a large number of Muslim scholars, and he has since been regarded as one of the two great orthodox theologians of Islam.

SUFISM

Greek philosophy was not the only influence which imperiled orthodoxy. Mysticism and the contemplative ideal were already growing within Islam during the eighth century A.D., and there were reasons why they came into tension with Muslim orthodoxy. In the first instance, the teachings of Islam were based on the vivid prophetic experiences of Muhammad, and as we have noted elsewhere there is a great difference between the prophetic and mystical strands of religious experience. And yet the Muslim mystics were inclined to interpret some of Muhammad's words and experience in a mystical sense. We shall return to this point shortly.

Secondly, the stress of inner experience often leads to a neglect of the exterior forms and authorities of religion. Just as these emphases turned out to be causes of tension between Muslim mysticism and devotional orthodoxy, there were also reasons why the two were capable of blending and reconciliation. It was partly through the cultivation of asceticism, present in Muhammad's teachings and espoused by the orthodox Kharijites in their distaste for the luxuries to which the conquering Arabs often succumbed, that Muslim mysticism started. Also, it was possible, and indeed natural, for those brought up within Islam to interpret the inner experience of illumination in terms of union with Allah, even though this interpretation itself could lead to trouble insofar as it denied the element of numinous distance between God and his creatures. But it paved the way for other interpretations which were more acceptable from the orthodox point of view, which preserved both the sense of contemplative intimacy and the distinction between man and Allah. In some degree the rationalism of Greek philosophy was harnessed to the mystics' doctrines. Platonism, for instance, was brought into service, as it had been in Christian mysticism.

Muslim mysticism was generally known as Sufism, a word derived from the term *Sufi,* "one who wears *suf,*" i.e. undyed wool. The Sufi wore wool because of the simplicity and the austerity involved. This was one of the indications that the movement had its origins in asceticism. One of the impulses to self-denial was a reaction against the worldliness of some of the faithful. The area which Islam had penetrated possessed its Christian monasticism and Christian hermits. The world-denying ascetic was a widely respected religious figure, and it was not surprising that Islam was influenced. Moreover, the ideal of self-denial, which had its place amid Muslim virtues, was applied by some in an extreme way involving a complete rejection of wordly concerns. This was not in conformity with Muhammad's wider teaching, for he had given a positive political dimension to ethical monotheism. But partly for that very reason there were attractions in world-negation.

The successors of Muhammad had made of the political enterprise a thing not altogether attractive. Struggles for power and the lure of wealth and aggrandizement were too easily associated with the doctrines of world-acceptance. Those who wished a religious manner of contracting out of the struggles could find in asceticism a way of peaceful protest. Complete indifference to the good things of life and imperviousness to hardship and fasting were means whereby the aspirant could concentrate his mind wholly upon Allah, in fear and obedience. These were some of the motives impelling a number of people in different parts of the Arab Empire, in Syria, Iraq, northeast Persia, and in Arabia itself, to take up a new and devoted way of life. Puritanism and older monastic ideals pointed in the same direction.

The general structure of Islamic faith could lend itself to such asceticism. The repetition of prayers could be increased from what was normally required of the faithful, until every moment could be spent in remembrance and adoration of God. The fastings could also be extended and developed. Almsgiving could be interpreted in a wider sense than occasional self-denial to help the needy. The whole of life could be seen as a pilgrimage. But though the ritual and ethical requirements of Islam had been enjoined by Muhammad upon the individual, it was upon an individual who was part of a community. The ascetics, by reinterpreting the religious life in the fashion described, were internalizing the requirements and making faith an essentially individual thing.

But however much some early exponents of asceticism may have been motivated by the desire to purify the corrupt streams of orthodox piety, the Sufis were not solely concerned with self-discipline. Self-discipline was a means to an end. As the movement evolved, the emphasis changed increasingly from asceticism to an attainment of inner knowledge or illumination. Fear and obedience of God slowly melted away to become a burning interior love of God and hope of union with him through the naughting and abasement of the self. It is perhaps no accident that Sufism had one of its early homes in Khorasan, in northeastern Persia, where Buddhist influences had been strong. The stress there was on inner enlightenment through asceticism. Possibly Hindu thought contributed to the Sufi religion, but this influence is not conclusively established. Yet we should not think that Islam embraced mysticism just because of external influences. Mysticism has appeared in many widely distributed cultures, and it forms one phase of spiritual life. The prophetic faith of Muhammad was destined to nurture contemplation within it and to make some accommodation to that trend.

The Qur'an and Sufism

Not only were the outer observances of Islam harnessed to ascetic and contemplative endeavor: there were passages in the Qur'an which gave sustenance to the Sufi claim of following in the orthodox tradition of Muhammad himself. Some of his sayings were suggestive for those who found God within their own souls. Had he not declared that God was closer to man than his jugular vein? Had he not uttered that wonderful verse on Light which was so beautiful and so full of interior meaning?

> God is the Light of the Heavens and of the Earth. His Light is like a niche in which is a lamp—a lamp encased in glass—the glass, as it were, a glistening star. From a blessed tree is it lighted, the olive neither of the East nor of the West, whose oil would well nigh shine out, even though fire touched it not! It is light upon light. God guideth whom He will to His light, and God setteth forth parables to men, for God knoweth all things.

> In the temples which God hath allowed to be reared, that his Name may therein be remembered, do men praise him morn and even.
> Men whom neither merchandise nor traffic beguile from the remembrance of God. . . .
> He to whom God shall not give light, no light at all hath he.
> Hast thou not seen how all in the Heavens and in the Earth uttereth the praise of God?—the very birds as they spread their wings? Every creature knoweth its prayer and its praise! and God knoweth what they do.
> God's is the Kingdom of the Heavens and of the Earth: and unto God the *final* return.[8]

These words were especially significant, since light was a favorite symbol of inner illumination (as indeed the word "illumination" itself indicates). The Sufis saw in Muhammad's own visions and in the story of the miraculous journey to heaven, as told in one of the Hadith, a sign that the experience they sought within was vouchsafed in a mysterious and preeminent manner to the Prophet. Thus the Sufi way could be seen as an imitation of Muhammad's perfect life (just as Christian mystics could look on their own strivings as being an imitation of the life of Christ).

Nevertheless, there were clear differences between the actual experiences of the Prophet and those of the Sufis who thought that he was the prototype of their mysticism. The ascetics and contemplatives sought the vision of God in inner tranquillity, through procedures of self-control and denial of the senses. But Muhammad's experiences of ecstasy came suddenly, and as if from without. This was a reason for his early doubting of whether he was truly called by God. His continuous stress on the "otherness" of Allah contrasts, too, with the

Rodwell's translation as it appears in *The Koran* (Everyman's Library edition), pp. 446-447.

prevalent theme of union and intimate love which characterized Sufi writings. This reflected their sense of an eternal element within them capable of union with God, and distinct from their "lower" selves. Again, Muhammad's prophetic experiences issued in strong action in the world, while for the most part the Sufis were quiet and withdrawn from affairs. The painful tolling of the bell within his head (or so it seemed to him) was an indication of the power and almost violent assault of the ecstasies through which he gave utterance to the revelations of Allah. This was rather different in character from the melting-away of the self in the inner knowledge of God which the Sufis spoke about. For these reasons it is difficult to agree with the Sufi interpretation of Muhammad. Nevertheless, though there is a contrast between the typical mystical experience and the typical numinous and devotional experience of a divine Power impinging from without, there are certain analogies between the two which can be seen as the basis for an interpretation of mysticism in terms of the divine Other. These analogies apply too in the case of Islam.

To Muhammad God was invisible. Similarly for the mystic, it was not through ordinary vision that he gained his "vision." In the contemplative life one could gain the inner experience of being taken out of time. Again, for the orthodox Muslim eternity was an essential characteristic of Allah, and could be interpreted as timelessness. The peace accruing from contemplation could be seen as a foretaste of the vivid Paradise depicted in the Qur'an, which should not be over-literally understood in this context. The brotherhood under God, so prominent a feature of Muhammad's ethic, flowed from the majesty of God as jointly recognized. It had an analogy to the outpouring of love which the mystic found as a consequence of his union with the divine Love. And in addition to all this, we have seen that the externals of Islam could be used as a mold and pattern for the ascetic and inner life. It was through the existence of these analogies and correspondences that mysticism could be integrated into a faith that had its main origin in Prophetism. In brief, though the prophetic and mystical experiences are by no means identical, there are suggestive connections.

The early Sufis, as we have seen, were inspired by the ascetic ideal, and this was controlled through the fear of God. But soon a more tender note entered into their thinking. Thus a famous woman Sufi, who lived toward the end of the eighth century A.D., wrote:

> I love thee with two loves, love of my happiness,
> And perfect love, to love thee as is thy due.
> My selfish love is that I do naught
> But think on thee, excluding all beside;
> But that purest love, which is thy due,

> *Is that the veils which hide thee fall, and I gaze on thee,*
> *No praise to me in either this or that,*
> *Nay, thine the praise for both that love and this.*[9]

Emphasis on Marifa in Sufism

The theme of love was linked to that of experiential knowledge in the writings of the Egyptian mystic, Dhul-Nun (died A.D. 861), who seems to have been influenced by Hellenistic and Egyptian speculations. The knowledge which the Sufis prized, however, was not the rational knowledge of the scholastic theologian, which was knowledge *about* Allah, but rather the direct knowledge *of* Allah. This *marifa,* or *gnosis,* was the crown of the Sufi path. It became elaborated, through the thought and life of such men as al-Harith of Basrah, a contemporary of Dhul-Nun. The spiritual attainments of one who followed the way came to be divided into two kinds, in accordance with the belief that salvation comes from God. In the first place, there were various stages or stations on the way, the achievement of which depended on the efforts of the mystic: in the second there were various states which were bestowed on the mystic through the favor of God. Thus, in one formulation of the distinction, the conversion to the Sufi way of life, awe of God, renunciation, fortitude and constant awareness of God were among the stations, while knowledge (*marifa*), love (as flowing from the love of God), and the yearning to be constantly with God were states which were God-given.

Abu Yazid

However, the stress on *marifa* had results which were scandalous to the orthodox. Abu Yazid of Bistam (died A.D. 875) was so convinced of his identity with the Godhead in the experience of *marifa* that he could say "Glory to me! How great is my majesty!" He appeared to be claiming to be divine, which was blasphemous and strictly contrary to the orthodox objection to any sort of doctrine of incarnation. In the writings of Abu Yazid, we find fully developed an idea which was associated with that of *gnosis,* which played a big part in Sufi thinking and experience: that of *fana,* the passing away and extinction of the empirical self, as the mystic melts into God. The control of the self through asceticism and contemplative practices ultimately resulted in a state where all consciousness of one's own individuality as separate from God was lost. *Fana* had a strong similarity to certain Hindu and Buddhist concepts, where the empirical self disappeared when the higher illumination was attained: nirvana was also a kind of "passing away."

[9] This translation appears in R. A. Nicholson, *Literary History of the Arabs* (London and New York: Cambridge University Press, 1953), p. 234: and in H.A.R. Gibb, *Mohammedenism* (London: Oxford University Press, 1949), p. 103.

Al-Hallaj

The strong consciousness of God and of the vanishing of the ordinary self were consequent upon direct mystical experience in which it was hard to speak of any distinction between subject and object. It was therefore natural, if unorthodox, for Sufism to move in the direction of such utterances as that of Abu Yazid quoted above. The climax of the movement came with the life and death of al-Hallaj. He had used the words "I am the Real" (*anal-haqq*), which was taken by the orthodox to be a claim to divinity. He was therefore cruci-fied, in the year A.D. 922. There was an appropriateness about this death, for, as we shall see, he looked to Jesus rather than to Muhammad as his model. The story of his death is moving:

> When he was brought to be crucified and saw the cross and the nails, he turned to the people and uttered a prayer ending with the words: "And these thy servants who are gathered to slay me, in zeal for thy religion and in desire to win thy favor, forgive them, O Lord, and have mercy upon them; for verily if thou hadst revealed to them that which thou hast revealed to me, they would not have done what they have done; and if thou hadst hidden from me that which thou hast hidden from them, I should not have suffered this tribulation. Glory unto thee in whatsoever thou doest, and glory unto thee whatsoever thou willest."[10]

What was it that al-Hallaj believed to have been revealed to him? Though the orthodox took his claim to be the Real in the sense of a claim to divinity, his thought was in fact more complex. God in the beginning created man in his own image, so that he might discover the divine image within himself and through the working of divine love might attain unity with the divine nature. The union itself came through the descent of the Real or Creative Truth of God into the soul, so that the human and the divine Spirit became inter-mingled. This process of the descent of the Divine into the soul was called *hulul*, a term used in the orthodox tradition to mean "incarnation." Thus for al-Hallaj deification through mystical experience involved one's becoming an incarnation of the divine Spirit. It was thus not surprising that he should look to Jesus as the great example of mystical incarnation. This preoccupation was also manifested in a tendency among some Sufis to distinguish between saint-hood and prophecy. The saintly aspects of the lives of the great figures of the tradition tended to be regarded as more important than their prophetic func-tion. Al-Hallaj was expressing this sentiment in (seemingly) exalting Jesus above Muhammad. It implied a recognition that the attempt to see in Muham-

[10] This translation appears in A. J. Arberry, *Sufism* (New York: Hillary House, 1960), p. 60.

mad's own experience the deification of the Sufi was not altogether a convincing one.

Organization of Sufism

The exaltation of sainthood was not merely due to the fact that it squared with
notions of deification. It was also because Islamic mysticism came to take on
the same forms of organization as occurred in other cultures where mysticism
had flourished. At first the Sufis were individualistic; then they came to associate
together in loose groups. But the elaboration of spiritual training, and the
demands of celibacy (which began to be practiced, though scarcely in accord
with Qur'anic injunctions) brought about the creation of orders of Sufis who
worked and often lived together. It was common for such a group to be
under the spiritual direction of a *shaykh,* or *pir,* and very often his residence
would turn into a monastic community. The holiness and insight ascribed to
such leaders was great. Among the more superstitious they were credited with
miraculous powers. They were the objects of considerable veneration and of
cults which persisted after their death. In this there was a confluence of both
Sufi and Shia tendencies. The prestige of the saintly holy men, when joined
with the mystical experience of *marifa,* could bring into Islam, contrary to all
its early teaching, the ideal of the divine human, one who was in some sense
an incarnation of God.

Influences in Sufism

These trends were influenced by Neo-Platonist philosophy. It was possible to
think of man, or of a particular person such as Muhammad, as having an
eternal prototype contained with God's nature. Thus the mystical experience
could be interpreted as the return to this original eternal being. More influential even was the Logos doctrine, borrowed partly from Christian sources. This
Logos was the creative power which emanated from the Godhead and which
brought into being and sustained the empirical world. This came to be identified with the Spirit of Muhammad, conceived as pre-existent. Muhammad was
given the status of a divine Creator and revealer of the truth. Union with this
Spirit was, then, the goal of mystical endeavor.

The crucifixion of al-Hallaj was a violent symptom of the unease which
such speculations created in the minds of the orthodox. Admittedly the Sufis
were activated by a considerable piety; and their energy in missionary work
was great. Their lives, for the most part, were excellent, although the love
imagery sometimes came to express a more literal sensuality. But though they
gained a wide following because of these virtues and because of the appeal of
doctrines which reflected characteristics of pre-Islamic religions, the orthodox
feared that their speculations, if not checked, might cut at the root of Qur'anic

teaching. The transcendence of Allah was imperiled. The political cohesion of the community was in danger. The heresies of incarnation and polytheism, as expressed through the cult of mystics and saints, were creeping into Islam. So it seemed to the orthodox.

Persecution, as in the case of al-Hallaj, was no lasting answer. Often it only stimulated the very forces it was designed to restrain. What was needed was some synthesis between the new doctrines and those of orthodoxy, in such a way that the excesses of Sufi ideas could be removed and the undoubted piety of the movement harnessed to Qur'anic ends. The scholasticism of the theology, which had been inherited in an increasingly wooden form from the great al-Ashari, was by itself not a sufficiently live and flexible instrument to serve this purpose.

THE MEDIEVAL SYNTHESIS

Al-Ghazali

It was the genius of al-Ghazali (A.D. 1058–1111) which provided the solution to these problems. Al-Ghazali's education had been orthodox, in the Asharite tradition. He had become a lecturer in a newly created university at Baghdad, and was widely recognized as an exponent of the law. He was perhaps the leading legal theoretician of his day. But he became dissatisfied with the legalism and rationalism of the theology which he was called upon to teach, and in A.D. 1095 he gave up his post and went into retirement. He wanted to learn the way of the Sufis. It promised an intimate and direct experience of God very different from the knowledge about God which he had been imparting to his pupils. During his decade of retirement he went to Syria to practice Sufism, and to Mecca on a pilgrimage. When he returned home he began a series of written works which have given him lasting fame and influence.

Al-Ghazali carried out his explorations on three fronts. In the first place he wished to repudiate a merely theoretical and scholastic theology. In the second place, he wished to repudiate Greek philosophical ideas where they were inconsistent with orthodox interpretation of the Qur'an. Thirdly, he needed to check the more extravagant claims of Sufism. The second of these tasks he performed in his *The Incoherence of the Philosophers,* which criticized Greek metaphysicians for their mutually contradictory conclusions (which indicated that philosophy was not a science like mathematics, where there were no competing "schools"), and for such doctrines as that of the eternity of the world. Al-Ghazali brought a number of subtle arguments to bear on the eternity point, some of which, as a matter of fact, he borrowed from Greek sources. His preoccupation with the question was due to the fact that the notion that the world was eternal not only appeared to contradict scriptural teaching but also seemed to detract from the creative power of God: for a world which came into being in time out of nothing was absolutely dependent for its existence on God. Moreover, as we have seen earlier, it was common for Muslim theologians to take eternity as the distinguishing characteristic of divinity.

In his *The Revivification of the Religious Sciences,* al-Ghazali dealt with the problem of how the experience of *fana* could properly be interpreted. He held that the mystic, when he underwent the vision of God, was so overwhelmed that he imagined that he was united and identified with the divine Reality. This, however, was a sort of illusion, analogous to the belief of a person, seeing wine in a transparent glass, that the wine and the glass are a single object. When the mystic returned from his state of ecstasy ("drunkenness," al-Ghazali called it—the metaphors of wine and drinking were common in Sufi mystical writing), he recognized that there was a difference between God and the soul. In another analogy, he compared the mystic's state to that of a lover, who thinks of himself and the beloved as two souls inhabiting the one body. It is a sort of union, but it is not identity.

In these ways, al-Ghazali tried to do justice both to the actual experience of the Sufis and the requirements of orthodoxy and the religion of worship. In regard to the latter he was keen to point out that the initial stage of the Sufi's career involved contrition arising from a sense of sin: the awful gap between Allah and sinful man. Thus the awe and worship which were due to God and the penitence that went with them were one side of the Sufi's religious experience. For this reason al-Ghazali emphasized the terrors of hell and the judgment awaiting men. Moreover, and again in line with the early orthodox tradition, he did not believe in a mysticism which involved total withdrawal from the world. The mystic went back into the world, revivified by his glorious vision of the divine Reality. In these and other ways, al-Ghazali succeeded in welding together orthodox piety and the inner quest of the contemplative. Through this synthesis Sufism gained an honorable and recognized place in orthodoxy. From then on there was no severe friction between the mystic and the theologian.

Ibn Arabi

But despite the success of al-Ghazali in welding together the two streams of religious experience, and despite the shrewd blows which he directed at speculative philosophy, neither mystical nor philosophical thought was put into a straightjacket. Notable among those who gave expression to a poetical and metaphysical Sufism was Ibn Arabi (A.D. 1165–1240) of Spain, one of the great figures of the rich Muslim culture of the Iberian peninsula. He deeply influenced Dante. Dante's description of the ascent into Paradise and of the celestial realms came from Ibn Arabi, who was combining astronomical theory with the legend of Muhammad's journey to heaven. Ibn Arabi's doctrines were pantheistic, inasmuch as he regarded the world as a visible manifestation of the divine Reality. Human beings he saw as offshoots from the divine essence. They existed because of God's desire to be known, and in the realization of the divine Absolute the perfect saint reflected in his person the inner structure of the universe.

Ibn Arabi combined with this idea that of the Logos, the creative principle of the universe, which was identified with the spirit of Muhammad. But at the same time, Ibn Arabi put more value on sainthood than on prophethood. Though Muhammad was the Seal of the Prophets, there was another who was Seal of the Saints, who more perfectly expressed the spirit of Muhammad. This other, it can be inferred, was Ibn Arabi himself. In the mystical union with the divine Reality which he felt he had achieved, he did not hesitate to make such a stupendous claim in his own behalf. His complex and voluminous writings, although regarded with skepticism and even horror by the more orthodox, were influential in Persia, among such poets as Rumi (thirteenth century A.D.) and Jami (fifteenth century).

Rumi

Rumi was founder of one of the *darwish* (mendicant) orders of Sufism. The Persian word *darwish* was ultimately transliterated into English as "dervish," the dervishes being renowned for their ecstasy-inducing, although usually rather decorous, dancing. The term, however, has a more general significance, in that it stands for a member of the Sufi orders. Rumi's poetry expressed the longing of the soul for its return to the divine Being, but he was also keenly aware of the beautiful significances of nature. He saw in the ritual of the Mevlevi order which he founded, with its solemn swirling dance and its use of the drum and the pipe as part of the ceremonial, an inner significance which reflected the movements of the planets and of nature in general. As in later Neo-Platonism, he believed that the smallest event in this world contained within it the secret of the whole, and man could in his quest for perfection realize something analogous to the state of God, who is the Absolute informing and expressing itself in the visible world. As Ibn Arabi wrote:

> There is no existence save God's existence. . . . The existence of all
> created things is his existence. And when the secret of an atom of the

atoms is clear, the secret of all created things, both outward and inward, is clear, and thou dost not see in this world or the next aught beside God.[11]

Mysticism

Thus in Sufi mysticism there was a trend which could be paralleled in Greater Vehicle Buddhism. There was one Absolute, and it embraced and lay within the multiple phenomena of the world. But phenomena were considered only relatively real. In some way, the achievement of enlightenment was like waking out of a dream, and one saw that all things were evanescent, save only the Absolute. Another parallel was found in the fact that Ibn Arabi, with a logic like that of Shankara, denied that there was such an event as *becoming* one with God. It followed from his general position that man was already one with God, though it was not generally realized. The mystical experience was the realization of this union, but it did not bring it about. It did not need to.

Another touch reminiscent of Indian religion was the fact that Ibn Arabi strongly resisted the notion of eternal punishment. He did not deny hell, but he turned it into a purgatory. All eventually would return to the bliss of the Godhead. Since he prized the glory of the beatific vision of the Godhead, he was overwhelmed with the sense of God's goodness, rather than with the sense of his power and judgment. God, being good, and being summed up, from a human point of view, in the activity of love, it was hard to see that he could create beings who were destined to everlasting perdition. This would have been wasteful and cruel. Of course evil existed in the world, Ibn Arabi believed, but it was a necessary part of the unfolding and self-manifestation of the Divine. It formed a counterpoise to good which was helpful in eliciting the Divine. But it had no intrinsic worth. So likewise suffering in hell had no intrinsic value, but was a means of purging the souls of those who had not turned toward the Light and a means of ultimately bringing them to that Light.

INTERPRETATIONS OF ISLAMIC LAW

The mysticism of the Sufi movement may have given much to the personal religion of the faithful, but it would be wrong to overemphasize this inner, individualistic side of Islam. The outer side was controlled by an increasingly elaborate and subtle system of law. During the first two centuries of Islam differing interpretations of the law had arisen. These became crystallized into a number of schools. The schools were in no way to be thought of as sects:

[11] This translation appears in Margaret Smith, *al-Ghazzali The Mystic* (London, 1944), p. 210f.

rather, like the schools of theology, such as the Mutazila, they represented variations of emphasis within a common allegiance. Law was important to the community, since, as we have seen, Muhammad was not merely concerned with personal religion, but also with creating a new political and social structure. Granted that the Qur'an was the inspired word of God and that the Hadith, or traditions, expressed the teachings of Muhammad, it was necessary, the Arabs believed, to work out a system of coherent legislation on the basis of these sources.

Nevertheless, times changed, and with them conditions. It was not always easy to apply legislation intended for Arabian conditions to the new circumstances of empire. Nor had Muhammad legislated about everything. There were gaps to be filled. What were the right techniques to accomplish this task? The schools diverged on this issue.

Hanifite School

The Hanifite school, founded in Iraq in the middle of the eighth century, said that the main emphasis should be on the Qur'an itself, while the Hadith should remain secondary in importance. Law-givers could reason from given cases by analogy to new ones. Thus this school incorporated a speculative element in its jurisprudence. The Abbasid dynasty, which was far removed from the rigorism of early Islam, found such legal doctrines convenient.

Malikite School

A contemporary school founded at Medina, the Malikite school, used both the Qur'an and the Hadith. Doubts were resolved by recourse to *ijma,* or "consensus." Originally this referred to the consensus of the community of believers, but came increasingly to mean, in legal contexts, the consensus of the *ulama,* or doctors of the law.

Shafiite School

A third school was that of al-Shafii (died in A.D. 820) who had been a disciple of Malik. The Shafiites rejected what had hitherto been sometimes in use, the so-called "gate of *ijtihad,"* i.e., personal judgment on matters for which there were no clear scriptural or traditional rulings. This ban on speculation within the law was to some extent offset by a wide reliance on the Hadith.

Hanbalite School

One or two other schools arose in the ninth century. Notable was the Hanbalite school, formed by Ahmad ibn Hanbal, who reacted against the license and irreligiousness of the court of Harun al-Rashid (A.D. 786–809) and his successors. The Hanbalites adhered strictly to the Qur'an and were relatively strict in their interpretation of the law. In these various ways an elaborate corpus of rulings was formed, which gave detailed shape to the structure of Muslim communities. Owing to the rejection of personal judgment, the law became somewhat ossified, however, and, as we shall see, there have been certain difficulties in adapting it to the changes which technology and Western influences have had upon Muslim countries in the modern period.

THE ABBASID DYNASTY

Though the Abbasids, reigning as supreme potentates in Baghdad, may not have corresponded to the original ideal of the Caliphate, the period was one of the splendid cultural achievements. Muslim scientists and mathematicians had access not only to Greek work, but to Indian as well. Astronomy and medicine flourished. Folk literature, as later expressed in the "Thousand and One Nights," poetry (not only mystically oriented), and the other arts, especially architecture, entered a glorious phase of development. Philosophy remained a powerful source of intellectual interest. History was widely studied, issuing in the great work of Ibn Khaldun in the fourteenth century. The economy thrived, and there were trade connections from Spain and Europe in the West through to China in the East. Islam began to enter on a new phase of expansion, despite the fact that the Empire was broken up into several separate kingdoms—in Spain, Morocco, and elsewhere.

From the eleventh century, the Muslims began to move into India. The powerful ruler of Afghanistan, Mahmud of Ghazna, sent no less than seventeen expeditions into the Punjab and Sind. The area around Delhi fell under his suzerainty. By the end of the twelfth century nearly the whole of northern India was under Muslim rule, and in later centuries this power was extended far to the south. By the tenth century A.D., Muslim merchants were already settled in Indonesia, and in the subsequent three hundred years, small Muslim principalities were established in the area. Gradually Islam became the dominant religion of the archipelago and of Malaya. The religion meanwhile was spreading into the coastal regions of East Africa.

But Europe was toughly resistant. Although the Muslims occupied Sicily, Sardinia, and parts of southern Italy from the middle of the ninth century A.D., Sicily was recaptured by the Normans in the eleventh, and the other areas too were detached from Muslim rule. Slowly, the Muslims were driven out of Spain. Crusades, though directed at the Holy Land, which was a relatively marginal area from the point of view of Muslim power, led to the establishment of short-lived Christian states on the eastern Mediterranean coast. The Byzantine Empire hung tenaciously to its shrunken territories. Meanwhile, the center of Abbasid power had been shattered by the incursions of the Seljuk Turks. Out of the chaos of the collapse of the Abbasids, there emerged a fragmented Empire.

OTTOMAN EMPIRE

But in the fourteenth century a Seljuk prince established the beginnings of the Ottoman Empire, which eventually was to take in most of the North African territories, as well as Syria, Iraq, part of Arabia, and Asia Minor. Under this strong rule came the gradual conquest of the Balkans. The by-now minute Byzantine Empire was surrounded, and was finally demolished when Constantinople fell in A.D. 1453. Further to the east, separate Persian and Indian dynasties represented the other two great blocs of Islamic power during the late Middle Ages.

Influences on Christendom

Despite the bitterness engendered by the Crusades, the culture of Islam had a lasting effect on Christian Europe. In Spain, divided for so long between the two religions, there were many channels of contact. We have seen how Ibn Arabi contributed to the thought of Dante. More spectacular were influences on the philosophical and scientific level. Until the fall of Constantinople, which released refugees and Greek manuscripts to the West, the Latin-speaking world of medieval Christendom had an imperfect knowledge of the riches of Greek culture. These now began to flow in via the Arabic translations, which in turn were rendered into Latin. Arabic philosophy was both suggestive and challenging. The works of Averroes (Ibn Rushd, A.D. 1126–1198) of Cordova in Spain, became known in the thirteenth century. His commentaries on Aristotle were used in the University of Paris, even though his interpretation of that philosopher was suspect. He held that there was but a single intellect (the higher part of the soul in the Aristotelian system) in which all human beings participate. This doctrine appeared to rule out personal immortality. For this reason, St. Thomas Aquinas wrote a special treatise devoted to the refutation of this aspect of Averroes' teachings.

Decline of Ottoman Empire

All in all medieval Islam inherited from the days of the Abbasid Caliphate, which marked the most intensive period of synthesis between Greek, Persian, Indian, and Arabian cultural elements, a great tradition of art and science. This was the ultimate result of the conquest of ancient empires by the renewing forces of Arabian monotheism. If, at the religious level, orthodoxy and the new culture did not always mix, there were factors within Islam which enabled it to retain its shape. The daily piety of the Muslim and the embracing mold of

Islamic law kept the community together despite the fragmentation of the Empire. There still remained a sense of brotherhood and unity. In the succeeding centuries, however, with the collapse of the Mogul Empire and the conquest of India by the British, with the slow decay of the Ottoman Empire, and with the spread of the Western powers into North Africa during the nineteenth century, Islam appeared to have lost its political grip. It could easily be supposed that the Muslim religion would decline. From the fifteenth century Sufi piety had diminished. Muslim law seemed rigid and antiquated. Political decay scarcely squared with the optimistic faith in Allah's favor which had characterized earlier Islam.

EIGHTEENTH CENTURY REVIVAL OF SUFISM

But there were forces of renewal at work within the body of Islam. In the eighteenth century in Asia Minor, under the Ottomans, there was a revival of Sufism. By this time many of the orders had concentrated on practices which were less rigorous than those required for deep contemplation: ecstatic prayers, dances, the holding and manipulation of the breath. But there was no gainsaying the importance of the revival as a means of vitalizing personal religion, even if at the same time many superstitious elements entered in. At the end of the eighteenth century, in North Africa, there was founded the Khalwati Order which won wide influence in West Africa among Negro Muslims. In India, likewise, there was increased Sufi activity.

THE WAHHABI MOVEMENT

At the other extreme, the strongly puritanical Wahhabi movement, which attempted to reinstitute the early purity of the faith, started in A.D. 1744. Its founder was Muhammad ibn Abd al-Wahhab. It had its origin in central Arabia. The Wahhabi movement strongly criticized Sufism and the veneration of saints, on the grounds that these were blasphemous innovations, and without Qur'anic support. They attacked orthodox Muslims who compromised with these practices, and they attempted to enforce the rigors of the Hanbalite interpretation of Muslim law. Wahhabi puritanism was used in the service of Arabian political revival. The house of Saud, which controlled one of the Arabian emirates, began military campaigns to unify the peninsula and to turn out the Ottomans from the northern provinces. Mecca was taken in 1806, and non-Wahhabi practices were rooted out there. Soon, however, the Ottomans dealt with the rebellion, and the movement seemed to be crushed. In outcome it was not so. A century later in the carve-up of the Turkish Empire after the end of the First World War the Saud family regained the Arabian kingdom But more important, the Wahhabi movement continued outside Arabia, espe cially in India and West Africa, as a puritanical and reforming sect. It expressed the disapproval with which pious Muslims viewed the accretions which had occurred to the faith, and it also explained the evil political days which had fallen upon Islam. No wonder the faith of Allah seemed to be under a cloud, the Wahhabis thought, if the majority of Muslims had departed from the true life of obedience to him. Despite the fact that the Wahhabis were often intolerant and overly-keen to proselytize, sometimes even using persecution, they gave renewed religious strength at a time when it was badly needed. In effect, the movement was a revival of the prophetic massage of the early days. It has been one of the hidden strengths of Islam that this prophetic spirit has never been submerged, and at crucial periods it has gushed forth to revitalize and restore the heart of Islam.

PAN-ISLAMISM

One effect of the Wahhabis was to revive interest in the "Arab idea." The Islamic empire had originated with the Arabs. Was it possible that a revived Arabic culture might again unite the Muslim world and resist the impact of the West? With the introduction of printing and its possibilities for the rapid dissemination of ideas, the opportunities of such a movement were good.

Muhammad Abduh

Notable among those whose writings were influential, partly because they were not simply political in character, was Muhammad Abduh (1849–1905), an Egyptian scholar. He had been inspired by the energetic advocacy of pan-Islamism by Jamal al-Din al-Afghani (1839–1897), who had urgently argued for religious reform as a means of removing differences between Muslims. Muhammad Abduh was modernist in his attitudes, but only in a limited sense. He felt that the modern knowledge which Western influence was introducing must be appropriated by Islam. He was opposed to the narrow conservatism of many of the *ulama,* who in trying to preserve old ways rejected the power and insight which modern science could bring. Abduh thought that just as Islam had made use of Greek philosophy and science, now it could make use of the new knowledge. He argued this on the ground that truth cannot contradict truth—so reason cannot contradict revelation. Nevertheless, he was not modernist in the sense of applying critical methods of scholarship to the Qur'an itself.

Muhammad Iqbal

A more radical synthesis was achieved by Sir Muhammad Iqbal (1876–1938), an influential Indian Muslim. In a book published in 1938, *The Reconstruction of Religious Thought in Islam,* he sought to reconcile modern

Western thought with the tradition of his own faith, and to see the predicament of his community in terms of their new situation. He combined the view, derived from Kant, that science and religion are distinct, with an evolutionary account of the course of human history. In his separation of science from religion he emphasized that religion should be concerned with personal experience; so he was interested in reviving Sufism; but he also strongly stressed the ethical dimension. The purity and egalitarianism of early Islam, as he saw it, would give a reformed Muslim community the opportunity of being in the vanguard of human progress. Though the West was intellectually triumphant, it was passing through a strange crisis in respect of morality and social cohesion. These qualities were what Islam could give. This rationale involved Iqbal in some unorthodox interpretations of the Qur'an. For instance, he denied the existence of heaven and hell as localities: rather, they were states of mind. For these reasons his views have scarcely been acceptable to traditionalists; but his vision of a purified Islamic state, which would "realize the spiritual in a human organization" and which would help Islam to take its place in the forefront of history, was one of the sources of inspiration which stimulated the Muslims to work for a separate Pakistan. Nevertheless, Iqbal's appeal was largely intellectual. He did not specifically answer the problem that modern conditions have raised in Muslim minds, namely the relation of traditional law to modern political communities; nor did he bring into being a sect.

Mirza Ghulam Ahmad

A notably new and somewhat syncretistic sect which has had some success in modern times is one founded by Mirza Ghulam Ahmad of Qadian in northern India (1836–1908). He proclaimed himself the Mahdi. He held that he was the inheritor of the truth of the great religions, and he came to preach to men the beginning of a new age, which would revolutionize the condition of mankind. His teachings, however, were essentially Muslim in character, although he strongly repudiated the use of force. He said the holy war must be carried on by preaching, and his missionaries should go out to all nations.

His followers, however, split into two main groups, the one based in Qadian and the other in Lahore. The Lahore group was more orthodox, although it did not become fully reconciled to the traditionalist exponents of the faith. The Ahmadiyyas, as the followers of Ahmad are called, have proved extremely active in their missionary work, and are quite influential in areas such as West Africa, where they combat the work of Christian missions. Their main effect within Islam itself is of being a moderate reform movement, but despite their missionary fervor they are repudiated by most orthodox Muslims. Under the impact of the West Islam had lost some of its missionary confidence.

It had also been over-preoccupied with internal problems. The new sect helped to acquaint many outside the Muslim fold with some of the tenets of the faith.

BAHAI

Another important movement with a Shiite background is that of the Bahai. Although Muslim in origin, Bahai is far removed from Islamic orthodoxy and lies right outside Islam. It is a new and separate faith. It originated with the teachings of Ali Muhammad, who himself belonged to an earlier sect known as the Shaikiya. The Shaikiya believed that there must be a means of communication with the "hidden Imam". The earlier twelve Imams were "gates" through which the faithful entered into the truth: and in this later age another human "gate" was needed. It was this that Ali Muhammad proclaimed himself to be, at Shiraz in Persia, at the end of 1844. He was then twenty-five years old. He preached social reforms, including the raising of the status of women. He also promised that one greater than himself would come to carry on and complete the work of reforming religion.

The wide following which the Bab ("Gate") attracted and his heretical views brought on him the hostility of the religious and political establishment of Persia, and he was executed in 1850. Two years later a follower of his attempted to assassinate the Shah of Persia, and widespread persecution of the Babis followed. Among the Babis was a member of the upper class and son of a minister of the government, one Mirza Husein Ali, who was banished to Baghdad. In 1863 he proclaimed himself the Messiah of whom the Bab had spoken. Most of the Babis accepted his leadership. He assumed the name of Baha Ullah ("Glory of God"), and it was from that name that the adherents of the faith came to be called Bahais. Baha Ullah was interned by the Turkish (Ottoman) government from 1868, first at Adrianople and then at Acre, but he continued to inspire and organize his followers through an extensive correspondence. He died in 1898. His successor, Abbas Effendi, undertook missionary journeys in the Middle East, Europe, and America, giving further impetus to the spread of the movement beyond the borders of Islam. His successor reorganized the administration on a more democratic basis, establishing national councils of the Bahai in the various countries where it had taken root.

Teachings of Baha Ullah

It was Baha Ullah who gave shape to the teachings of the new faith. Social and religious reform went hand in hand, and gave inspiration to a worldwide movement which was to help usher in a new age of peace. Baha Ullah considered that divine revelation had been vouchsafed to the great religious figures of the world's history—to Christ, to the Buddha, to Krishna, to Moses, to Zara-thustra, and, of course, to Muhammad. This revelation was essentially mono-theistic. But the Qur'an held pride of place among the sacred writings of the world after the writings of the Bab and of Baha Ullah. In short, though this was to be a world faith, it had positive roots in Islam. Yet Baha Ullah did not accept a traditional account of Islam. He rejected polygamy, slavery, and the concept of holy war (*jihad*). Like the Bab, he was strongly in favor of equal-ity between the sexes.

Bahai Ritual

At the religious level, ritual practices of the Bahai were simplified: prayer and devotional meditation were the core of religious activity, together with the pursuit of virtue. Much of the Qur'anic teaching was modified or explained in an allegorical or metaphorical sense. Thus belief in angels and evil spirits was dropped. Heaven and hell were treated symbolically. In these and other ways the monotheism of Muhammad was liberated from the particular thought-forms and regulations natural at the time of the Prophet, and were given a new look. This faith could be accepted by rational and pious men of all nations. Moreover, it had a political message that was not confined to Islam. It was a political vision of a world community united under a federal world govern-ment. The Bahais also advocated a world language as a means of promoting human unity.

Bahaism was an interesting development from within the context of Islam, for it embraced modernism and yet had its origins in a messianic movement. Its social platform gave it a strong appeal to the underprivileged, but at the same time its emphasis on education and the reconciliation of science and religion gave it an appeal to the educated. But from the Muslim point of view it sacrificed too much in pursuit of these objectives. The Qur'an's status was in effect low-ered. No longer was Islamic brotherhood prized as such. It clearly went beyond the creed "There is no god but Allah, and Muhammad is his Prophet." It there-fore constituted a new faith, outside the stream of Islam where it had its original setting.

Baha Ullah, in assigning to himself a messianic role, had been able to draw on reserves of religious expectation created and maintained by the Shia belief in the hidden Imam. It was natural in a period when all was not well in the Islamic community that the expectations of the people should become fervid. As illustration, in relatively recent times there were two uprisings of a military nature under Mahdis—one in the Sudan which culminated in the battle of Omdurman, and the other in Somaliland. In the changing conditions of the modern world this fervidness has been manifested in a slightly different way.

ISLAM IN MODERN TIMES

In the late nineteenth and twentieth centuries there has been a greater preoccupation with the dual question of the relation between Islam and nationalist
states and of the nature and role of Muslim law in the altered conditions of the
modern world. These more practical concerns typify the Islamic emphasis on
the political dimension of the faith.

Amid the debate following on from the work of such men as Muhammad
Abduh, three positions emerged. First, there was the conservative position of
the doctors of the law, the *ulama,* who were trained in the traditional manner,
and were unwilling to abandon the complex of decisions and rules which had
been hammered out in the centuries following the Prophet. Second, there was
a middle position taken by those who were reformers up to a point, but who
argued for the establishment of a genuinely Muslim state. This group tended to
oppose the *ulama* for clinging to accretions to the Muslim law not directly
sanctioned by the Qur'an and by early tradition. They were influenced in this
by the puritanism of the Wahhabi movement. Thus there was a confluence of
reforming zeal and a return to the purity of the faith. Thirdly, there was the
position taken by those modernists who advocated the establishment of a
secular state.

Notable in the second category was the Salafiya movement. This movement was founded by a disciple of Abduh's, Rashid Rida. Its pan-Islamism
was modified by such a conservative respect for the teachings of the faith that
Rashid felt called upon to condemn the secularism of the Turkish Republic
under Kemal Ataturk.

Ataturk—An Example of a Secular State

Ataturk's revolution in 1924 paved the way for the most thorough experiment
in secularization. The absence of state religion, the abolition of *purdah,* modern divorce legislation, changes in the laws of inheritance, and Westernized
education were some of the measures which turned Turkey into something
resembling a European state rather than a Muslim one. By consequence,
Turkey has lost touch to some extent with the rest of the Muslim world. One
measure, however, was agreeable to more orthodox reformers: the drive
against the dervish orders fell in line with the new spread of a "back to the
Qur'an" movement in modern Islam. Although other independent Muslim
states have not been as drastic as Ataturk in the matter of social and political
changes, there have been definite moves both in the direction of secularism
and in the direction of law reform. Thus new divorce legislation is common in
Middle Eastern countries, and the practice of polygamy is withering away.

Independence of Muslim Nations

The new era has created tensions in Islam, but it has also been a time of renewed political success. Muslim countries from Morocco to Pakistan have gained or maintained their independence. Though the hope of a union or alliance of Muslim nations has not been realized, Islam has experienced a new resurgence of power. The Muslim faith is spreading in Africa, where the attractions of its simple monotheism, its emphasis on brotherhood and the contrasting intolerance and race-consciousness displayed by some Christians have made Islam a powerful rival of Christianity for the allegiance of the uncommitted black mind.

More recently, and especially from the mid-1970s, there has been a resurgence of Islam, most notably in Iran. There, in 1979, the then ruler, Shah Reza Pahlavi, was overthrown in a revolution headed by the Ayatollah Khomeini. One of Iran's leading jurists and interpreters of Islamic law and scripture, Khomeini differed from many Shi'a leaders in arguing that political power does not corrupt but needs to be dominated by the faith. Thus he worked toward an Islamic republic in which the religious elite would determine the shape of society and of political policy. Behind his views lay the widespread feeling that Western influence and modernization were undermining Islam. Similarly in Pakistan, Libya, and elsewhere new constitutions, involving a return to Islamic law, have evolved. In Egypt and Syria and elsewhere the radically conservative Muslim Brotherhood has been working for the overthrow of regimes regarded as insufficiently attentive to traditional Muslim ideals. Thus, after formal independence from the West, the Islamic world is beginning to think about spiritual and social liberation from Western influences.

CONTRAST OF ISLAM WITH OTHER WORLD RELIGIONS

It has been necessary to say quite a lot about the political and legal side of Islam because, as we have stressed, Muhammad was more than a preacher of monotheism: he was the creator of a political community. This political dimension of Islam sets it apart to a great extent from the other great religions of the world. It is true that other religions have at various times taken on a political coloring. Confucianism is an example of a religion which is more concerned with the ordering of society than with anything else. But consistently through Muslim history there has been concern both for the shaping of the community through the law and for the success of the community as an institution in the world.

Islam and Judaism

The nearest analogue to Islam is Judaism, with its national preoccupations. But whereas Judaism was confined, by and large, to people of a particular nation, or to those who claimed descent from that nation, Islam broke the bonds of nationhood in creating an international community. After the fall of Jerusalem in A.D. 70 until the creating of the modern state of Israel, Judaism was scarcely political. It was concerned with the religious survival of the Chosen People. But any political role they might have lay in the future. In Islam on the contrary the faith was nourished and sustained by power. Its destiny was manifest, not concealed.

This is why in the last two centuries, during a period when the West has been so strong and the Islamic peoples so weak, a profound tension has arisen in the Islamic mind. From one point of view we might single out Islam's contribution to the religious experience of mankind as this: it has been a demonstration of the way faith can be harnessed to the creation of a complex and successful community upon earth—not a Utopian one, but a matter-of-fact one—a community in which people's chief wishes, needs, and ambitions are not denied, but channeled into a pattern of pious brotherhood. Of course, Islam has at times undergone corruption. It has displayed a violence which ill accords with the practice of Muhammad. It has been sometimes socially unjust. Nevertheless, it has preserved the ideal which the Prophet set before himself, of a people united in sensible and sober brotherhood in which the Qur'anic law will promote cohesion and justice. And as we shall see in the last chapter, new forces of resurgence are at work within it.

Islam and Christianity

From the standpoint of religious history, Islam's importance lies partly in the stress it lays on the social dimension. It is a faith which demands institutions, but not those of a Church or Sangha, centered primarily in the promotion of religious quest by itself: rather it demands institutions which cover the whole life of the community. There is nothing in Islam (except in a few sects here and there in its history) corresponding to the Church. There is no place for a special institution within society devoted to the ends of the faith. For it is the whole of society which is devoted to the ends of the faith.

It would be mistaken, however, to stress the political side of Islam to such a degree that we lose sight of the religious experience and practice which have been nurtured within it. The Prophet, through his vivid awareness of a majestic and overwhelmingly powerful God, passed on to the Muslim community an impressive dedication to worship. The Muslim's daily prayers continuously express his awe before the Almighty, and thereby he gains a sense of divine Presence. Islamic monotheism is simpler than that of Christianity. It does not contain the Trinity doctrine nor does it, save in the more extravagant forms of the Shia, present to the religious imagination a divine figure who is also human. Thus the focus of Muslim piety is directed solely to the invisible Creator.

There is very little of sacramentalism in Islam. The Christian by and large finds the focus of his religious life in the sacraments, however widely and diversely they may be interpreted. Worship and the sacraments are interwoven. But there is virtually nothing in Islam corresponding to this aspect of the Christian ritual dimension. The ritual of Islam centers simply on prayer, conceived primarily as a mode of worship rather than of petitioning God for favors. In the pilgrimage sacrifice is retained as one element. But this is in the way of adapting older practice and giving it a purified sanction within the new faith. But though there has been this concentration on the worship of the numinous and holy Being who rules over all and governs men's lives, the mystical impulse was not ultimately denied within the Islamic community. This has led to the incorporation of another strand of religious experience into the fabric of Islamic piety. In modern times there has been a steady drift back to the religion of worship and a turning away from these inner concerns with contemplative experience. Wahhabi piety is symptomatic in this trend.

There is another difference between Islamic and Judeo-Christian belief which is worth stressing. Although at times and in certain branches of Christianity there has been belief in predestination (in Augustine and in Calvin's writings, for example), the Judeo-Christian tradition on the whole has affirmed a certain independence belonging to men through the operation of their free will. The right interpretation of this idea need not concern us here. But Islam, with the exception of the Mutazila school and of some Sufis, has been powerfully committed to a sense of man's utter dependence on Allah. To some extent this is explicable in terms of the Arabian background. In pre-Islamic times there was a goddess of Fate. But as with St. Augustine, the main explanation is in terms of the powerful awareness of God's majesty and grace. Muhammad was swept by the revelations pouring through him. It was no choice of his that he became a prophet. And the God who revealed himself to the Prophet was one who had created everything from nothing and who showed in his daily guidance the continued activity of his creative power. It was natural to suppose that men's destinies were determined by him. Just as every atomic event is the direct result of the Creator's will, so too every human act was ascribed to the same cause. This emphasis on predestination imparts a special flavor to Islamic monotheism. It creates in the faithful detachment and unconcern in the face of danger and adversity. Ascribing all events to God's power is a continual reminder of his mysterious and almighty nature.

SUMMARY OF ISLAM'S CHARACTER

At the doctrinal and mythological level, Islam has been tenacious in its conservatism. In the first place, the faith was formed in a remarkably short space of time, during the latter years of Muhammad's life, and it emerged fully-fledged in the Qur'an. A whole body of doctrine was already present in its pages. In this respect, there is a notable contrast with Christianity. Christ himself taught parabolically and by implication. Three or four centuries passed before the main conclusions of Christian faith were hammered out. But in the Qur'an there was a clearly defined set of teachings. Though there were gaps to be filled, and though its theology remained to be related to Greek philosophy, the main structure of belief was already present. Secondly, the conservatism of Islam depended on the valuation of the Qur'an as an eternal book. As such it was the supreme authority. It could not be tampered with or passed over lightly. To this day Islam retains a fundamentalist attitude to its scripture. Thus the teachings of the Qur'an have persisted unchanged.

And yet there have certainly been innovations.

It was necessary for the Shia to hold that the true doctrine which they professed and which did not seem quite in accord with the Sunnite orthodoxy, had been passed down in an esoteric tradition. Likewise the Sufis had to embark upon highly allegorical interpretations of the scripture. Other innovations had to be introduced by the forging of the Hadith.

These were ways in which the plain teaching of the Qur'an was bypassed or reinterpreted. But for the mass of the orthodox, such novelties were in the nature of subterfuges. No religion has stuck closer to its scripture. This has been both a source of strength and of weakness in relation to the future of Islam.

But for all its reverence for the Qur'an, and for all the clarity with which it attempts to conserve the prophetic message, Islam has shown a considerable degree of internal tolerance. It is true there were occasions of persecution and violent proselytizing. But very different kinds of piety and belief have in fact lived together within the wider Muslim community. The religion of Muhammad succeeded at times in embracing beliefs very close to the incarnationalism which the Prophet repudiated, and in absorbing seemingly heterodox speculations of mystics and philosophers. It has been much less monolithic than one might have predicted, given the history of the earliest community. It has moreover succeeded in blending Arabic culture with the traditions of many nations in ways which have been fruitful to both. But though it may make mixtures within its own body, it does not mix easily with outside religions and ideologies. Neither Christianity nor Marxism have found it easy to gain a foothold within the Muslim world. In its horror of idolatry, Islam has largely submerged and destroyed the cults it has conquered. The three great Semitic faiths have been alike in their distrust of compromise with paganism. Only when Islam has conquered and pacified another culture can the old tendencies begin to well up secretly from below. This is the history of the considerable and astonishing experiment in a universal monotheism which has imparted to faith in one God a cohesive political and social dimension.

Chapter 10

THE LATER CHRISTIAN

EXPERIENCE

MEDIEVAL ORTHODOXY — THE BYZANTINE EMPIRE

We have left the story of Christendom at what may be called for convenience the end of the Dark Ages. The medieval period was one which brought significant developments both in the Greek-speaking Eastern Church and the Latin West. Although the Byzantine Empire was under considerable pressure from the military power of Islam, both missionary work and mysticism brought new life to the Orthodox faith. It was during the early years of the second millennium A.D. that Christianity began to take a stronghold in Russia, with profound effects upon the course of religious history.

In the ninth century, the brothers Cyril and Methodius had set forth from Constantinople as missionaries to the western Slavs. Cyril's name is attached to an excellent alphabet which he is said to have concocted based on Greek characters. This alphabet was used to transcribe scriptures and liturgy in a written form of the Slavonic languages. With some modifications, it is the Cyrillic alphabet that is used in Russia today. In the tenth century, the Slavic princess Olga, who ruled Kiev after the death of her husband, professed Christianity, though she failed to persuade the aristocracy to join her. Her successor on the throne was anti-Christian, and came near to embracing Islam, which he had encountered among some of the people he had conquered in the region of the Volga. Had Russia turned to Islam, the shape of European history would have been remarkably altered. Prince Vladimir (980–1015) sent a mission to Constantinople, which reported in favor of the Orthodox faith. He himself converted and married a Byzantine princess. During the eleventh century, Christian missionaries spread from Byzantium and from the Greek-speaking Crimea upward into Russia. Southern Russia and parts of the north became permeated with Eastern Orthodox influences. This faith has remained the characteristic form of Christianity in Russia, and has been a main factor in uniting Russia spiritually to Europe, even if Russian Orthodoxy has been hostile to Rome.

Within Eastern Orthodoxy few developments in theology or in social ethics occurred during the medieval period; possibly one could understand this in the light of excessive state control of the church, or the Byzantines' constant preoccupation with defending themselves against the menacing Muslims. But mysticism continued to develop. In the ninth century the first monastery was founded in northern Greece on Mount Athos; the promontory soon became covered with such monastic establishments. Eventually the monastic communities there formed themselves into a separate, quasi-autonomous republic, which has persisted until today. St. Simeon (A.D. 949–1022) who became known as the "New Theologian" because of his intense concern with theology, was perhaps the greatest of Eastern Orthodox mystics. He reinterpreted the doctrine of the divine Light which had figured so largely in the theology of earlier Fathers of the Church, and which he identified with the glory of God. He saw the ideal of deification through the grace of God, and in union with Christ, in a mystical and experiential sense. He himself, in such an experience, had been filled with light and glory emanating from God.

Hesychasm

Simeon can be considered the forerunner of a contemplative movement known as Hesychasm (a word which is derived from the Greek *hesychos* meaning "quiet").

The Hesychasts employed methods of spiritual training similar to Yoga to conduce an interior vision of the uncreated Light of God. The Light of God they saw as energy emanating from God, distinct from God's Essence, which they held to be unknowable. In this respect the Hesychasts kept to orthodox teaching. The notion of God's unknowable Essence, or inner nature, served as a safeguard against believing that in the mystical experience there was actual union with the Deity. From the point of view of the religion of worship and of the Christian tradition, the idea of union with God would be blasphemous. It is not blasphemous, however, to think of oneself as suffused by and united with the divine Light. The Light of God was interpreted as other than God himself; it was easily interpreted in terms of grace.

Here was an interesting parallel with the later Western theology that also made use of the concept of the divine Essence. In Latin theology, expressed for instance by Thomas Aquinas, God's Essence is the object of the Beatific Vision, granted to those who have attained salvation in heaven: but on earth this cannot be directly perceived—we can only gain a foretaste thereof (though Aquinas granted that for Moses and St. Paul there was such a direct access to the divine Essence).

Hesychasm was an important experiment in contemplative techniques. These techniques involved, among other things, controlled use of breathing. The use of the breath was, of course, something physical: but it was a means of stilling the senses and concentrating the mind inwardly. As with Yoga it was a preliminary to the higher joy of the mystical experience. A thirteenth-century mystic wrote as follows:

As for you, as I have instructed you, sit down, compose your mind, introduce it—your mind, I say—into your nostrils; this is the road that breath takes to reach the heart. Push it, force it to descend into your heart at the same time as the inhaled breath. When it is there you will see what joy will follow; you will have nothing to regret. As the man who returns home after an absence cannot contain his joy at being again with his wife and children, so the mind, when it is united with the soul, overflows with joy and ineffable delights. Therefore, my brother, accustom your mind not to hasten to depart from hence . . . For "the kingdom of God is within us" and to him who turns his gaze upon it and pursues it with pure prayer, all the outer world becomes vile and contemptible.[1]

Such breathing exercises were accompanied by other practices, notably the "Jesus Prayer"—the repetition of the words "O Lord Jesus Christ, Son of God, have mercy on me, a sinner." In a mysterious way the very name of Jesus was supposed to contain within it divine power. Gregory Palamas (c. A.D. 1296–1359), the most famous and controversial exponent of Hesychasm, regarded the saying of Jesus Prayer as the central act of piety, for which men had been created by God.

Hesychasm was not without its opponents. It was attacked on the ground of doctrine. The notion of an uncreated Light seemed to make a division in the Godhead between God's Essence and his activity; and Palamas did not help by speaking of different "divinities" in this connection. However, the doctrines of Hesychasm were not formally condemned, and they eventually came to be officially recognized. As the doctrines were distinctively different from those of the West, the movement enjoyed a certain vogue with those who wished to mark the differentiation doctrinally. The respiratory techniques of Hesychasm were used as late as the eighteenth century, but have since died out; the use of the Jesus Prayer as an aid to meditation and as an expression of piety still is used in Russian Orthodoxy.

[1] Jean Gouillard's translation of a passage from Nicephorus the Solitary as quoted in Mircea Eliade's *Yoga: Immortality and Freedom* (New York: Pantheon Books, 1958), p. 63.

The Fall of Byzantium

On the political level, the Eastern Churches fared badly during the Middle Ages. The encroachments of Islam had already submerged the Nestorian and Monophysite Churches of the Middle East under Muslim rule; they continued only on sufferance. Asia Minor and part of the Balkans fell to the Ottomans, and in 1453 Constantinople itself was taken and sacked; the famous and glorious church of Santa Sophia was converted into a mosque.

After the capture of Constantinople, refugee scholars fled the ruined city carrying many treasures of Greek scholarship to the West. Christians henceforth were second-rate citizens in the Middle East. The flame of independent Orthodoxy continued to burn only in Russia and some other parts of the Slav area. The Greek-speaking churches entered upon a long period of depression. It was to be several centuries before they could reemerge into the light of Christendom. They had to carry on as best they could, maintaining their integrity in a Muslim environment. Survival was more important than originality; mission was impossible; the Liturgy alone stood between Orthodoxy and Islam. It survived.

MEDIEVAL LATIN CHRISTIANITY

The Western Church meanwhile was spared such a fate. In early medieval Europe, temporal and spiritual power were intermingled, and the papacy was strong. When the Holy Roman Emperor Henry IV tried to gain control over the clergy, he found his match in Hildebrand, a Tuscan monk who became Pope Gregory VII (A.D. 1073).

The Pope and the Emperor

Hildebrand began a reform designed to combat the twin evils of simony (traffic in ecclesiastical preferment) and lay investiture (ecclesiastical office conferred by the emperor upon persons who were both spiritually and in other ways unqualified for church office). This brought him into collision with the Holy Roman Emperor Henry. As Pope, Hildebrand excommunicated Henry, thus creating political turmoil because the Emperor's subjects were thereby held to be released from allegiance to him. Henry's advisers forced him to cross the Alps in mid-winter and do penance before the Pope at Canossa.

A second excommunication three years later, when Henry had failed to live up to certain promises undertaken at Canossa, was less well advised. Henry assembled his army and marched on Rome, deposing Pope Gregory and setting a rival in his place.

After the death of the two protagonists in the quarrel a compromise was reached by their respective successors. At Canossa the papacy had won its main point. Thereafter, spiritual patronage remained essentially in the hands of Rome though not all monarchs of a newly divided Europe were easily persuaded into complete compliance. The political power of the popes, and the later schisms which led to the exile of the popes at Avignon in the fourteenth century, meant that there was considerable confusion and corruption in the higher reaches of the Church during the Middle Ages. The worldly interests of the clergy were in many cases in ill accord with the Christian virtue of humility. The lower clergy were prone to a certain worldliness, including sometimes the practice of concubinage. The popes themselves were not always above reproach in their manner of life, especially in the late medieval period. But these abuses, though serious, should not be overly exaggerated. Christian ideals were still embodied in a great number of the clergy: some of the popes were saintly men.

In the lives of ordinary folk, the rituals and sacraments of the Church formed a focus for piety and for social standards. Many people were involved in the construction of the immense cathedrals, which, if evidence of the grandiosity of human pretensions, were at the same time glorious, magnificent achievements of art and expressions of religious fervor. With a certain degree of propriety the Middle Ages have come to be called "The Age of Faith." Above all, the medieval Church nurtured within itself some remarkable streams of spirituality, in particular the reforming monastic orders.

The Crusades

Before we turn to this last expression of the religious consciousness, a word must be said about another aspect of the Church's life—the militancy of much Christianity of the period that culminated in the Crusades. Pilgrims had continued to visit Jerusalem without much hindrance after the Muslim capture of Jerusalem in A.D. 637. In the latter part of the eleventh century, however, a crisis arose when the Seljuk Turks captured the city. More violent and intransigent than the previous rulers, they threatened to suppress pilgrimage and to destroy Christian shrines. European Christians responded with the determination to reconquer the Holy Land by force of arms. Pressure too came from the Eastern Church, which, as an integral part of the Byzantine polity, was feeling the pressure of Turkish aggression. In 1096, the First Crusade was launched. Popular enthusiasm, especially in France, had been whipped up by the preaching of Peter the Hermit (died A.D. 1115).

The first Crusade culminated in the recapture of Jerusalem, but quarrels over the distribution of the spoils taken in the campaign marred the whole affair. A Latin Kingdom of Jerusalem was established. Over the next two centuries another six Crusades were launched, the most melancholy being the Fourth, which was diverted from its original aim, and ended with the sack of Constantinople and the imposition of a Latin Emperor on the Byzantine throne. The Pope, Innocent III, though uneasy, was prevailed upon to agree to this event (which after all was more of a Crusade against Christians than against Muslims), partly because it offered a hope of reunion between the Eastern and Western Churches. The hope was both illusory and short-lived. The last Crusade took place in 1270, and was unsuccessful. Eventually the Kingdom of Jerusalem was swallowed up by the Muslims.

The Crusades though motivated in part by piety and chivalrous ideals, were also motivated by the desire for booty and for control of the lucrative trade-routes whose traffic had been seized by the Turks. In combining spiritual and temporal power, the Crusades did little to express the inner spirit of Christianity, and this was one factor in their ultimate lack of success.

THE ALBIGENSIAN CRUSADE

Another Crusade which occurred in this period was likewise symptomatic of the alliance of spiritual and temporal power, though it was directed at a rather different target. The Albigensians in the south of France came, during the eleventh century, to accept certain beliefs akin to those of Manicheism. Pope Innocent III tried to dissuade them from their heresy through missions. When they failed to respond, he launched an armed assault upon them, led by Simon de Montfort. The Albigensians fought with heroism, but were crushed. Many were massacred. In the following century the work of finally rooting out the heresy was continued by an Inquisition entrusted to the Dominicans.

MONASTIC REFORM

The outward signs of worldliness and violence manifested in parts and phases of the history of the medieval Latin Church were balanced by important manifestations of spirituality. The monastic orders were the center of this. The success of Gregory VII (Hildebrand) against the emperor for instance, was inspired in large measure by purified Christianity he encountered at the Benedictine monastary of Cluny. From the tenth century onward, a notable series of saintly abbots had made this monastery foremost in leading a return to the strictness of the Benedictine rule. The movement of reform spread into monasteries as distant as that of Monte Cassino in Italy. Very often the leaders were men of noble birth, who renounced all claim to ecclesiastical preferment. They thus enjoyed the respect and the influence due their aristocratic lineage, and were enabled to influence a renewal of the inner life of the Church in high places. Gregory VII was a mystic as well as pontiff: he had learned at Cluny the joy of intense cultivation of the contemplative life, and discovered in his own experience the irradiation of the divine Light of which Eastern Orthodox mystics were at the same period so fond of speaking of.

Bernard of Clairvaux and the Cistercians

The greatest figure in monastic reform in the eleventh century was that of Bernard of Clairvaux (A.D. 1090–1153). He entered the Cistercian Order in childhood, and at the age of twenty-four was already head of a new Cistercian monastery at Clairvaux. Bernard inclined toward the ascetic life, and sometimes his self-mortification seemed excessively severe to his associates. But his discipline was harnessed in the service of God and in the hope of experience of God. Influenced intellectually by St. Augustine, Bernard's interests nonetheless were not philosophical but existential. In the mystical experience, he held that the soul is emptied of self and lost wholly in God. Bernard did not see this as actual union with the Godhead: the soul and God remain distinct in substance, though stuck together by "the glue of love." He felt, with Augustine, that the achievement of this ineffable and ecstatic state was not due to the work of man, but to the grace of God entering into and possessing him. Consistent with his theological orthodoxy, Bernard disclaimed that the favors of God could be "wrested" from him, as it were by, the virtuous activities of man: salvation comes from God alone, and likewise the graces of the inner life. Yet he emphasized that there are two terms in the man-God relation: it is through the union of distinct persons that love manifests itself. Man has, then, an independent personality and a freedom of the will through which he can exercise his love of God. With man's love flowing out to God and God's grace descending into the human soul, the two come together.

Bernard combined intense mysticism with extraordinary powers of leadership and personal example. The forward advance of the Cistercian Order during the twelfth century was in large measure due to him. He was a strong defender of orthodoxy. Thus he attacked the views of Peter Abelard (1079–1142), the most brilliant philosopher and theologian of the time (as well as the somewhat poignant protagonist in the best known romantic episode of the Middle Ages through his tragic love affair with Heloise). Abelard expounded a view of the Trinity that needed to identify the three Persons of the Godhead and espoused a doctrine of sin which was considered by Bernard dangerously close to that of Pelagius.

Monks of both the Benedictine and Cistercian Orders lived by manual labor (indeed, the Cistercians were prominent in the opening up of uncultivated land in England and elsewhere).

The Dominicans

But when Dominic (1170–1221) founded the Dominican Order, a monastic community was created exclusively devoted to preaching and scholarship. The Dominicans' prime work was missionary activity, converting doubters and stimulating faith and understanding among the masses. They went into the Albigensian region to try to bring the heretics back to the Catholic faith. They were employed by the authorities for diplomatic missions and on the committees of inquisitors (investigators) who traveled about adjudicating on heresy. The Dominicans (and Franciscans) were used as inquisitors because their otherworldliness and learning combined to make them impartial and acute judges of such matters. They lived by begging. Because they wore a simple habit of black, they were called Black Friars, and were also punningly known as *Domini canes* ("dogs of the Lord," i.e. watchdogs). This Order developed many famous churchmen, notably Thomas Aquinas, the greatest medieval theologian, and Eckhart, one of the most important mystics of the Western Church.

St. Francis and Franciscans

The Franciscans were another prominent medicant Order. They owe their inception to the work of the great Francis of Assisi (1181/2–1226). As a young man he undertook a life of poverty and prayer. Two crucial events occurred that turned his dedication into a desire to relive the teaching of Jesus contained in Gospel of Matthew (10:7–19) wherein the disciples were bidden to forsake all comforts in devotion to God. First, while he was on a pilgrimage to Rome, he was so moved by the sight of the beggars in front of St. Peter's that he exchanged his clothes with one, and sat begging for a day. It gave him a keen insight into the meaning of desperate poverty. Second, while at prayer in a church near Assisi he heard Christ speaking to him with those self-same words from the Gospel of Matthew to which we have just referred. He gathered about him a band of companions whom he inspired to adopt the rule of mendicancy. The Franciscan Order had come into being: papal permission was swiftly granted.

Francis' love of nature and great humility make him a deeply attractive figure. He was gentle and discerning as well; his consideration for his fellow beings extended even to the Muslims, an attitude much at variance with the militant crusading spirit of the time. He argued that if the infidels failed to believe the Gospel it must be because Christianity had never been properly preached to them. They could not be won over by violence and enslavement. Francis determined to go in person to the Muslim lands to preach the love of Christ. At first illness prevented him, but in 1219 he went to Eastern Europe and Egypt; there he preached before the Muslim ruler of Egypt. On his return, he relinquished the administration of the rapidly growing Order, judging himself incapable of great administrative efficiency.

Two years before his death, St. Francis experienced a strange physical malady. There appeared on his hands and feet open wounds in the same places that Christ was wounded when the nails were driven into his body at the Crucifixion. Intense pain accompanied the appearance of the *stigmata*.

Since the time of St. Francis there have been numerous other occurrences of such stigmata. The phenomenon is not easily explicable; one of the most interesting aspects of the phenomenon is that it represents a reversal of what happens in contemplative mysticism. In mystical experience physical events, such as controlled breathing are a prelude to, and a preparation for, psychical occurrences. In the case of the stigmata, intense meditation on the Crucifixion of Christ has been the prelude to the occurrence of a physical reproduction of Christ's wounds.

After the death of St. Francis, the Franciscan Order became somewhat divided among those who thought that the strict rule of poverty ought to be continued (they called themselves the "Sprituals") and those who held that, owing to the great increase in the movement and its organization into settled monasteries, the rule of poverty should be modified. The latter party won— only after the Order had been severely riven—partly because the Spirituals in their enthusiasm had become permeated by the doctrines of the thirteenth-century teacher, Joachim of Fiore. Joachim propounded a novel theory of world history. Historical time, he argued, was divided into three ages. The first was the age of the Father, when men had had to live in obedience and fear under the Law; the second was the age of the Son when men had lived in faith under the dominion of the Messiah; the third was the age of the Spirit which was now dawning or about to dawn. In this new age—which the Spirituals held was inaugurated by St. Francis—men would live in freedom and love, enjoying the mystical vision of God. The Spirituals were in the vanguard of this time of the Spirit. Eventually men would have spiritual bodies, and the world would become a single contemplative community.

These ideas were a way, naive perhaps, of expressing dissatisfaction with the worldliness of the ecclesiastical establishment. They found wide acceptance among those men who awaited the coming of the Millennium, a hope that broke forth in one form or another in various places throughout the medieval period.

Franciscan monks and nuns have had a lasting and beneficial influence on the spiritual and social life of the Church. In their concern for the poor they did much to alleviate real distress in the medieval age. In time, the scholarly and intellectual interests of the Order grew considerably so that a number of important philosophers and theologians have been drawn from its midst; the Englishman William of Ockham (c. 1300-1349) and the Scotsman Duns Scotus (1270-1308) were two prominent Franciscans.

MEDIEVAL SCHOLASTICISM

The monastic movements, with their centralized organizations, and their emphasis on a renewal of the religious life, represented a kind of reformation of the church, from below as it were. The monks did much to revitalize the ordinary Christianity of the plain folk among whom they preached and worked. They gave new impetus to the life of contemplation. They also had a marked effect on the scholarship of the Church. It was a Dominican, for instance, St. Thomas Aquinas, who elaborated a metaphysics and a theology which, despite early opposition, has become the norm of Roman Catholic thought. By any reckoning his was a stupendous literary and philosophical achievement.

The thirteenth century was a time ripe for intellectual advance. Scholarship of the highest caliber and flourishing debate were to be found at the new University of Paris and elsewhere. Through translations of Arab scholars, the works of Aristotle, whose philosophy had hitherto been imperfectly understood in the West, were becoming widely diffused. In early scholasticism, from the time of Charlemagne onward, there had been a strong impulse to systematize the teachings of Christianity. All this had its most impressive outcome in the writings of Aquinas.

Thomas Aquinas

Thomas Aquinas was born to a noble family in 1224 (or 1225) at Roccasecca in southern Italy. As a young boy he was sent to the abbey at Monte Cassino for the ultimate purpose of becoming its abbot. In 1240, he went to Naples to complete his studies. There he formulated the desire to join the Dominican Order, whose intellectual and missionary interests attracted him. His family strenuously opposed this; they even held him captive at home for over a year. His determination, however, did not waver, and in 1244 he succeeded in joining the Dominican Order. For three years he attended the famous University of Paris, where he became acquainted with the works of Aristotle. His learning was prodigious and he was reknowned as a scholar. From 1250 onward Thomas was a remarkably prolific writer: an astonishing series of important philosophical and theological works had poured from him. His work produced a real revolution in theology, and as such it encountered considerable opposition. Nevertheless, he was canonized in 1323, and his views came to be accepted as the basis of orthodox Catholic philosophical theology.

In the last two years of his life Thomas returned to Naples, where he set up a Dominican school. It was during this last period before his death in 1274 that he wrote his most massive work, the *Summa Theologica,* which was left, however, incomplete.

Though in the seventeenth and eighteenth centuries regard for Thomas' thought suffered a certain eclipse, a revived Thomism has permeated modern Roman Catholic thinking, partly as a result of Pope Leo XII's encyclical known as *Aeterni Patris.* This encyclical, known by the opening words of its Latin text (as with other encyclicals), ordered the study of St. Thomas by all theological students and set up Aquinas' teachings as the norm from which theologians should depart only for grave reasons.

The Ontological Argument

Something of Thomas' thought can be sampled by considering his reasons for disagreeing with Anselm of Canterbury (A.D. 1033–1109), who is remembered for the Ontological Argument (the term "ontological" means "concerned with being"). Anselm began with a neat, brief proof of God's existence in which God was defined as "that than which no greater can be conceived." He then argued that a fully perfect, supreme Being which existed only in the thoughts of men would be less great than a Being having the same degree of perfection, but existing in reality. Thus in virtue of the definition of God it followed that God must exist in reality. Anselm's argument was symptomatic of a certain attitude in philosophy and theology. It supposed that man can discover an important truth about reality simply by reasoning, i.e., without seeing the way the world is. It accorded with the mode of theological thinking of the medieval period influenced by Platonism that began with God's existence and then argued downward in subsequent reasonings to the world of creatures.

Thomas Aquinas reversed all this. He denied the validity of Anselm's argument with the observation that it would only work if one knew God's essence, but man does not. Adapting Aristotle to Christian ends, he argued that apart from revelation the knowledge that we do have of God is derived ultimately from our experiencing things in this world. We have to proceed from earth to heaven, not the other way. This aspect of St. Thomas' thought was enshrined in his famous "Five Ways," five proofs of the existence of God starting from an observation of the world. An example of these proofs starts with the premise that one can see that some things are in process of

motion or change. From this one can infer that there must be a supreme
principle that ultimately accounts for all change, a prime mover. The arguments, moreover, do more than merely establish the existence of such a Being.
They tell us something about his attributes. From the proofs we can infer a
great deal about God. An extensive science of God is possible on the basis of
reasoning. This reasoning is what Thomas called natural theology: it is complementary to revealed theology (the knowledge of God derived from revelation). The two are not in conflict, but provide mutual support. Using these
categories, Thomas distinguished between, and integrated, faith and reason.

Soul and Body in Thomas' Teaching

Thomas's theology was not simply a synthesis between Aristotle and Christian
orthodoxy; it contained many highly original and brilliant elements. Some of
the opposition to the new system was based on Thomas's analysis of the
relation between body and soul. Employing Aristotle's distinction between
form and matter, Thomas argued that the soul is the form of the body—not in
a simple, obviously false, sense that the soul is the shape of the body, but in
the sense that it organizes and activates the material side of human nature.
Thus the soul does not exist as a distinct spiritual "thing." Thus also the
intellect depends upon the body: it gains its knowledge through the body;
there is nothing in the intellect which was not first in the senses, as an Aristotelian slogan has it. By abstracting from the data which the senses supply the
intellect is able to go beyond mere perception, but it is dependent on perception for its raw material.

Thomas' Empiricism

This aspect of Aquinas' thinking was closely related to his empiricism—his
insistence that reasoning must start with earth before it can talk of heaven.
But his doctrine entailed difficulties. By accepting his viewpoint one must
grant that the fullest life could not be led in the hereafter until the intellect
would be reunited with a body. Thus St. Thomas gave warrant to the belief in
the resurrection of the body. But what then happened to the intellect at death?
Though he could not deny that the intellect must exist after death, in a
disembodied state, Thomas declared this was an unnatural condition.

One consequence of his teaching about the soul was that it seemed to
preclude the possibility of the soul having direct access to God, such as was
believed possible by some mystics. Moreover, his teaching threatened the Augustinian idea that the intellect in knowing any truth receives direct illumination
from the source of Truth.

It happened that after Thomas left Paris, there grew up a school of philosophers who speculated on an Aristotelian basis without reference to the requirements of revealed theology. Thus Aristotelianism itself came to be suspect and to be thought conducive to heresy and an arid rationalism. Thomas's remarkable adaptation of Aristotle itself came under a cloud of suspicion. Nevertheless, the great power and fertility of his system, and the clarity he brought to many purely theological problems (such as that of transubstantiation—the mode in which at the eucharist the substance of the bread and wine is invisibly changed into the Body and Blood of Christ), gave his teachings an enduring influence.

Though Aquinas was deeply concerned to attain consistency and clarity, it would be wrong to think of his system as simply a piece of rational speculation. His fixed intention was to give form and expression to a spiritual view of the world in which both nature and the supernatural are discoverable. Revelation played a vital part in his scheme, for truths about God or the Trinity or of the creation of the world cannot be arrived at by the unaided use of the intellect. For him grace was a vital part of the religious life. Man has free will through the operation of his reason. He can too have knowledge of the moral law and on his own account can acquire a good or a bad disposition. But in order to have faith in and love of God and in order to remain free from sin, he must have grace. Some virtues can be attained naturally, but the "theological" or supra-natural virtues of faith, hope, and *agapē* (love) are caused through the infusion of grace. Grace, then, does not destroy nature, but it perfects it, just as revealed theology does not destroy natural knowledge of God accessible to reason, but completes it.

The Summa Theologica

In nearly all his doctrines, St. Thomas retained a clear balance between common sense and piety. It is said that toward the end of his life he had a mystical illumination which made him declare that all he had written was so much straw. But here he was wrong: even if in heaven there would be no need of the *Summa Theologica,* even though his foretaste of heaven induced in him a contempt for his achievements, he was wrong. His was the summit of medieval religious thought, and, for all its technicalities, the *Summa Theologica* has stayed a source of enlightenment and inspiration to many folk since his day.

THE MEDIEVAL MYSTICS

The growth of the monastic orders, and the development of a powerful current of theological and philosophical thought evidenced a revitalized Christianity in the thirteenth century. It was also a continued stream of contemplative interest, especially in Germany and the Low Countries.

Meister Eckhart

Foremost among German mystics was Meister Eckhart (c.1260–1327), a Dominican of remarkable intellectual as well as spiritual powers. To express the substance of his own contemplative experience, he spoke in ways that were novel, and offensive to orthodox thinkers. In 1329 a number of propositions extracted from his writings were condemned—unfairly, one might say, since the propositions in question could only properly be understood in their context. Nevertheless, in certain ways Eckhart seemed to be moving away from the traditional teachings of the church. For instance, he argued that since the intellect is a divine spark which perfectly reflects the nature of the Godhead, the Godhead is accessible to man's intellect in mystical experience. Eckhart speaks of the Godhead as ineffable, without distinctions, an inexpressible Nothing which is also the supreme Reality. This Godhead in some of Eckhart's writings is distinguishable from God himself, who is, as it were, a lower emanation of the supreme Reality. God is the active power who creates the universe, and is good. The Godhead is beyond good, and beyond being. By this Eckhart did not of course wish to affirm that the Godhead is non-existent, but that it is utterly different from determinate beings, including both Creator and creatures. In line with his picture of the transcendent, Eckhart tended to regard the sacraments and other aspects of church life as preparatory in nature. They do not give direct access to the supreme Reality, and would be ultimately transcended in mystical experience. Sometimes too, in his enthusiasm for the peace and insight he had found within his own soul Eckhart spoke of the world as a mere nothing—compared with the mystical glory of the Godhead, creatures were as nothing. Through naughting the empirical self, in leading a life of quiet, stillness, poverty, the contemplative can transcend the limitations of creatureliness.

Eckhart was not absolutely consistent in expressing the above ideas, and it has recently been argued that he was a good deal more orthodox than many interpreters of him have supposed. However that may be, there are certainly elements in his thought which bear remarkable similarity to certain mystical writings of other cultures. The divine Nothing, the stress on stillness—these are reminiscent of Taoism; likewise the notion that Reality is "beyond being" has its analogies in the Absolutism of the Madhyamika school of Greater Vehicle Buddhism. Above all, his differentiation between Godhead and God, and his view of the world as a mere nothing remind one of the teachings of Shankara. In all these cases we can detect the same forces at work: the pattern of the Transcendent is modelled on a valuation of religious experience—the Lord who is object of worship and devotion comes second to the Absolute that the mystic conceives himself as having contact with an inner experience. The religion of contemplation and the religion of worship are blended, but the piety associated with the latter is quietly demoted: it is a preparation for something higher. Eckhart did not hold consistently to such a heterodox interpretation of reality, but there were continual hints in this direction, which accounts for the condemnation of some of his teachings. Certainly his disciples remained loyal to him. His younger contemporaries, Suso, Tauler, and Ruysbroeck carried on his teachings and yet were quite orthodox.

Tauler

Johann Tauler (c.1300–1361), a German contemplative, and a Dominican, expressed his mysticism in terms of Thomist theology. For him the deification of the will through union with God enables the mystic to live a self-transcendent life of sacrifice and charity. Tauler gave good evidence of his sense of being empowered beyond his own resources when, at the onset of the Black Death in 1348, he devoted prodigious energies to nursing the sick and ministering to the dying. Tauler was associated with the movement known as the *Gottesfreunde,* or "Friends of God." The *Gottesfreunde* sprang up chiefly in the Rhineland and in Switzerland, and included laymen. It was dedicated to the transformation of the inner life through piety and contemplation. Out of this movement came the famous mystical treatise, the *Theologia Germanica,* stressing abandonment of the will to God. Through this and similar writings, the Christian ethic was brought into relationship with interior illumination.

Thomas à Kempis

The Brethren of the Common Life—again both for clergy and lay people—originated in the Netherlands during the fourteenth century. A notable fruit was the *Imitation of Christ* of St. Thomas à Kempis (c.1380–1471).

Thus in the thirteenth and fourteenth centuries, mysticism, which originally was a form of revitalized monastic piety, took hold in the imagination of the laity. Its emphasis on practical love was well adapted to the needs of folk who did not feel the necessity for the cloistered life, yet who desired intense religious exploration within their ordinary vocations. Indeed, its vivifying force was available to men quite independently of church ritual.

Women Mystics

Mysticism appealed not only to men. There were women contemplatives of the period, the most famous being St. Catherine of Siena (1347–1380), who belonged to the Third Order of St. Dominic. Like Tauler, Catherine worked with the victims of the Black Death. Her practical concern with church affairs is illustrated by the fact that, during the time when the popes were exiled in

Avignon, she traveled to that city and persuaded Gregory XI to return to Rome. Catherine spoke of her mystic experience in terms of a "spiritual marriage" with God, a symbolism parallel to the imagery of the Church as the Bride of Christ. This way of expressing the relation of the soul to God brought out the element of love and devotion involved, and provided a symbol of the intimate unity-in-difference which the theistic mystic finds in his experience and belief.

Two centuries later, another woman mystic, St. Teresa of Avila in Spain (1515–1582), gave further expression to this concept of the mystical marriage. Her accounts of her own experiences in pursuing the contemplative life, enshrined in such works as *The Interior Castle* and in her autobiography, are invaluable in giving a detailed and sensitive description of mysticism.

Dante

The inner life of the Church flourished in the Middle Ages. Yet externally, tensions between secular and spiritual authority were progressively corroding the Church's hold on the lives of men. The poet Dante (1265–1321), whose *Divina Commedia* mapped out in marvelous fashion the regions of the afterlife, had also written *De Monarchia,* a strong defense of the principle of division between temporal and ecclesiastical power. Dante's ideal of a universal monarchy that would bring peace and order to the world was only fantasy. In fact the Holy Roman Empire lacked the power to achieve such unity. Europe was already drifting apart into nation-states. And in the latter part of the thirteenth century and early fourteenth, a scandalous situation obtained in which there were both popes and rival anti-popes.

EARLY EVIDENCE OF REFORMATION

The increase of commerce, largely centered in towns controlled by merchant guilds and thus relatively independent of aristocratic landowners and the monarchy, assisted a process in which the existing order was questioned. The feudal structure of society was weakening: there were signs of peasant unrest. The Church, attuned to tradition and feudalism alike, was sitting on dynamite, though the explosion would not come until the Reformation. The elaboration of doctrine, excellent as it was in many ways, was used to justify practices far removed from those of primitive Christianity. And the Bible, once it was translated into the vernacular from the Latin Vulgate edition, and once printing had made the wide distribution of books possible, proved to be a revolutionary document, leading men to question the authority of the existing establishment.

John Wycliffe

John Wycliffe (c.1329–1384), an English scholar, gave a foretaste of what was to be expected. He was both a translator of the Bible (into English) and a critic of many aspects of the existing Church, including the papacy. His thinking attracted a large following, popularly called the Lollards. To teach the Bible to the people Wycliffe sent out his "Poor Preachers," who wandered throughout the land. After an uprising among the peasants in 1381, conservative churchmen sought to suppress all forces of change. The Lollards were persecuted and the wandering teachers of the Bible were arrested.

Peasant unrest was not confined to England. In Czechoslovakia a fierce religious rebellion, directly influenced by John Wycliffe through John Huss (c.1369–1415), broke out in 1416. The free interpretation of the Bible provided an easy ideology for those who wished to change the existing order in the interest of social justice or for other reasons. Thus the Bible and the awakened power of the people—especially of the mercantile class—to force social change were twin sticks of dynamite which could easily combine in a history-making detonation.

The New Classicism

The latter part of the fifteenth century saw the fall of Constantinople to the Seljuk Turks. Refugees fleeing Byzantium's ruins brought a stream of ancient scholarship directly into the consciousness of Western European scholars. The great voyages of the master mariners discovered great tracts of the globe hitherto scarcely known in Europe. Portuguese navigators opened up the sea route to the East, and gave European powers the opportunity for a vastly expanded trade; Christopher Columbus, Amerigo Vespucci, and others revealed America. These explorations resulted in an unprecedented access of wealth that was matched by an access of questioning as European eyes were opened up to cultures and lands beyond their ken.

A wider intellectual world was opening up. But above all it was the renewal of interest in classical literature, philosophy, and art that released a new wave of creativity. The Renaissance, especially in Italy where it was first manifested, was a tremendous period of artistic renewal. The new realism of the Italian painters and sculptors was symptomatic of a freshened interest in human values and a certain turning away from the previous preoccupation with the supernatural. Out of such a spirit was born the attempt to frame a Christian humanism which could combine the traditional faith with the New Learning that had broken so explosively on the scene. At the time it was not surprising that humanism exhibited a kind of gay and undisciplined paganism. Rodrigo Borgia (1431–1503), who became Pope Alexander VI (partly through bribery), and his son Cesare, were notorious examples of an immoral cynicism that represented a sort of pinnacle in ecclesiastical corruption. The new classical expression in architecture indirectly sparked off the great revolution in Christendom which came to be known as the Reformation.

Indulgences

By the latter part of the fifteenth century the great church of St. Peter's in Rome had fallen into serious disrepair, and a new building was projected, in the Renaissance style. Among those who contributed at different stages in its design were Bramante and Michaelangelo. The first stone was laid by Pope Julius II, a man noted for his enthusiasm about the new humanism. This was in 1506. When Julius II died in 1513, St. Peter's still was more a design than a reality. The building project dragged on, and swallowed up very considerable funds. To meet the cost, the Medici Pope Leo X (1475-1521) offered indulgences to those who would contribute monies to the coffer. In so doing, he was making use of a fund-raising practice widely employed.

The Church had long claimed the power to grant indulgences, i.e. remission of the penalty due for sins, in virtue of the great store of merit gained by Christ and the saints. Plenary indulgences were those granting remission of all the temporal penalty due for sins committed, as opposed to partial indulgences, that remitted a specified number of days' worth of punishment in Purgatory. Plenary indulgence had been granted to those who took part in the Crusades. In the later medieval period it became common for indulgences to be sold for money by professional "pardoners." Through them Leo sought to raise money for St. Peter's. An unpredictable consequence of this was that Martin Luther, by questioning the practice, sparked off a much wider revolt against papal authority.

SUMMARY OF MEDIEVAL CHRISTIANITY

When Luther nailed his Ninety-Five Theses on the door of the castle church at Wittenberg in 1517, Christianity had reached a watershed in its history. The split in Christendom that resulted was even more serious than the earlier schism between Greek East and Latin West. It is therefore useful at this point to look back briefly on the achievements of the medieval Church. Of its vices, no doubt enough has already been said. The Church had emerged from the collapse and chaos consequent on the breakup of the Roman Empire into a position where it was possible not merely to preserve traditional values, but where too it could create something of a Christian civilization. This it certainly achieved. For all the social injustices which accompanied the institutions of feudalism in the medieval period, the Church found within itself the resources to glorify and soften the harshness of everyday life. In the building of the great Gothic cathedrals, Christianity expressed the soaring majesty of God. Amid the vaults and slender arches, polyphonic music adorned the celebration of the mysteries. Here was an appropriate architectural setting for the age, and through it religion attained a controlled magnificence and solemnity of public worship. But more especially it was through the great monastic foundations, which helped to nourish both scholarship and charitable works, and through the preaching and conduct of wandering mendicant friars, that the Church succeeded in retaining its hold on Christian values and in giving them new force and direction. Though monasticism too could have its corrupt side, successive reforms from within rectified abuses. Largely, too, through the work and life of monks and nuns the twin achievements of medieval theology and mysticism occurred. The latter, as we have seen, went often together with a deep sensitivity to human sufferings. During the Black Death and on many other occasions and in many areas, the practice of spiritual poverty was put in the service of healing and relief. The Church in many ways performed the functions of the modern state, in educating, relieving the poor, and curing the sick.

All this was no negligible achievement, and it is interesting to note that so much of medieval good work and piety came forth from the ideals of the contemplative life. Here was a signal testimony to the way in which the realism and "this-worldliness" of the Christian tradition was not submerged by inner preoccupations, which so often lead simply to world-negation and withdrawal. Though there were not lacking monastic orders of this kind—and they had their place in the spiritual structure of the Church—mysticism also showed a genuine outward-looking concern for those living their ordinary lives in the world. If there were plenty of instances of militancy among churchmen, there were also those like St. Francis who preached a gentler way. The medieval Church, though top-heavy in its administration and open to simony and other ills, was by no means monolithic. Within herself many currents of religion flowed, and it was principally from within that external evils were checked. Nevertheless, by the beginning of the sixteenth century, the medieval structure was beginning to crack.

THE REFORMATION

The way in which the Reformation started was somewhat accidental. Luther did not imagine when he presented his Ninety-Five Theses for discussion—he used a recognized procedure of the day—that he would find himself ultimately driven into a position where a decisive break with Rome was necessary.

LUTHER

Martin Luther was born in 1483, a son of a miner, at Eisleben and raised in Mansfeld in Saxony. His early life was poor. His schooling was at the cathedral school of Magdeburg and at Eisenach; at the age of eighteen, he went on to the University of Erfurt. He worked hard at the usual curriculum, taking his bachelor's degree in 1502 and his master's in 1505, both at the earliest time permitted by the regulations. The courses covered languages, logic, philosophy, mathematics, and astronomy. It is an odd but apparently an undeniable fact that Luther, though piously brought up and well educated, saw a Bible for the first time in the university library, when he was twenty years of age. He knew the Gospels as read in Church, but he was astonished to dip into the Old Testament and to discover the stories which it contained. This is a symptom of the degree to which, in the culture of his day, the teaching of doctrine had replaced the reading of the Bible. In 1505, in circumstances about which we cannot be sure, Luther suddenly decided to enter the Augustinian Order, abandoning his project of a doctor's degree in law. He was ordained priest in 1507, and after intensive theological studies, was sent as lecturer to the new university at Wittenberg. He continued his rapid rise in the affairs of the Order. He became a doctor in theology and professor of Scripture in 1511, and in 1515 was put in charge of eleven monasteries belonging to the Order. It was during the period of academic work before 1515 that his views began to change from those generally accepted as orthodox. Two experiences were chiefly responsible for this.

In 1510 he had been sent by his Order to Rome. Like many another pilgrim, he was both excited and disappointed. The squalor, ignorance, and corruption of much of the religious practices in the Holy City were a shock; but at the same time, he did his rounds of pilgrimage to the famous places and shrines with which the city abounded. Looking back on it much later, he accused himself of being taken in by the "stinking lies" which led pilgrims on to visit churches and crypts in order to gain indulgences. He certainly did not return to Wittenberg in a spirit of rebellion. But what he had seen in the Holy City undoubtedly sowed seeds in his mind.

Luther's Tower Experience

More dramatic and important was Luther's so-called "Tower Experience" (*Türmerlebnis*). During the years succeeding his return from Rome in 1511, Luther was increasingly overwhelmed by despair. He had the strongest possible sense of his own sin and unrighteousness, and he could not convince himself that there was a way out of this predicament. Somehow the teachings of medieval piety had turned sour on him. For a time he gave up saying Mass and reciting the Divine Office. He received some comfort from Staupitz, the Vicar-general of his Order, who combined Thomism with the kind of mysticism found in Thomas à Kempis. Nevertheless, he was not relieved of his despair. And then, in a sudden and startling manner, he gained a whole new insight into the central meaning of the Scriptures. The circumstances were as follows: one summer vacation, he was preparing lectures on the Psalms for the coming term. When he got to Psalm 30 (according to the Vulgate numbering), his eyes lighted on the text "In thy righteousness deliver me." It was familiar enough; but it cut into him like a knife. This harping on God's righteousness was horrible to him: it reminded him of his own sins, and it made him think of God as a monster, punishing men for the righteousness which they could not attain. He turned to Paul's Epistle to the Romans 3:21-24:

> But now the righteousness of God without the law is manifested, being witnessed by the law and the prophets; even the righteousness of God, which is by faith of Jesus Christ unto all, and upon all them that believe; for there is no difference; for all have sinned and come short of the glory of God; being justified freely by his grace through the redemption that is in Jesus Christ.

To Luther in his uneasiness and despair, the Romans passage only made matters look worse. Faith in Christ was a further demand the punitive God made on men harassed by sin. Luther raged against God. He hated God. For days he tried to think his way round what St. Paul meant. Then suddenly he saw a new meaning in these words. He saw that this justice or righteousness of God was not something impelling God to punish the sinner. Rather it was a forgiving righteousness by which God *makes* us righteous through his mercy. By faith in God we are "justified," counted as just. The righteousness that we acquire from God has nothing to do with works.

Ascetic and contemplative practices which Luther had worked hard at without feeling any removal of his guilt had been of no avail. As Staupitz had said to Luther, "True repentance *begins* with the love of God." The latter is not something induced by works and by strivings. Luther, released from his burden of sin and despair, felt that the gates of Paradise had been opened up to him. This experience provided the heart of his later theology.

Luther turned to Augustine, especially where he attacked Pelagianism, for support of his new insight. He found comfort too in the German mystics, such as Tauler, whose doctrine of the necessity of naughting the self suggested that it is the grace of God rather than the efforts of man as an independent self that brings unity and reconciliation. Gradually, over the years before 1518, the consequences of Luther's insight began to work themselves out in his

mind. If justification was by faith, not by works, then not only ascetic practices (conceived as a way of breaking into heaven), but also the works performed by the Church on behalf of the faithful were useless as a means of
salvation. The sacrifices of the Mass, the use of indulgences, and the like were
ways in which the Church presumed to mediate between man and God. This
was surely misguided if faith and grace are freely given by God. These ideas,
fermenting in Luther's mind, help to explain the stand which he took against
the indulgences preached in Germany by the eloquent Dominican friar, Tetzel.

The Ninety-Five Theses

The Ninety-Five Theses set out a whole variety of arguments against indulgences. They were couched in dry and academic language. They ranged from
the weighty to popular considerations already in circulation (for instance, if
the Pope could empty Purgatory, why did he not do so forthwith: it would be
a necessary act of Christian love, surely). Within two or three months the
document was widely circulated in Germany, and was widely praised, especially by humanist reformers. Many priests were on his side. The reason was
plain: there had been much grumbling and bitterness about indulgences, but
no one hitherto had openly challenged Tetzel. The Dominican friar not only
had papal authority behind him, but the reputation of his Order as prominent
in inquisitorial activities. Nevertheless, his admirers credited Luther with a
firmness which he did not quite intend. The Theses were, as was the custom,
not definite statements of his views (though they were also that), but rather
arguments for discussion. But the document was circulated as if it were a
manifesto.

It was not long before his Archbishop and the Dominicans reported
Luther to Rome. The matter was not taken very seriously there at first. Later,
however, Luther's enemies had conveyed to the Pope, via Cardinal Cajetan in
Augsburg, some forged theses allegedly uttered by Luther and other material.
The Pope condemned Luther for heresy. In the meantime, however, Luther
had appealed to the Elector of Saxony to request that his trial should take
place on German soil. The Elector intervened strongly on his behalf, and it
was decided that Luther should be examined by Cardinal Cajetan at Augsburg. Curiously, Cajetan had independently written a treatise on indulgences,
which he finished in 1517, and which reached conclusions very like those of
Luther. However, the Cardinal soon lost sympathy for Luther, when Luther
refused to retract certain points to which the Cardinal had taken exception.
Luther returned to Wittenberg, where he continued to have the protection of
Frederick III, the Elector of Saxony. Luther had already expressed his disapproval of the decretal *Unigenitus,* issued by Pope Clement VI in 1343, and
concerned with indulgences. According to Luther it distorted the meaning of

the scriptural passages, and relied too heavily on Thomas Aquinas. To an increasing extent he was ready to challenge the fabric of ecclesiastical and doctrinal authority. In December 1518, a terrible thought seized him which he found difficult to dispel—"the Pope is Anti-Christ."

Luther's Excommunication

A further disputation occurred in 1519 at Leipzig, in which Luther argued against an astute and distinguished opponent, Johann Maier of Eck. In the course of the discussion, Luther came to express doubts on papal primacy and the infallibility of General Councils of the Church. It was not long before he was excommunicated. By mid-June in 1520, when the Bull of Excommunication was published, Luther had nearly broken with the Roman Church. During that year he completed three major writings. The first was the *Address to the Christian Nobility of the German Nation* in which he stressed the role of the laity in church affairs. It followed that if the Pope was unable or unwilling to reform, then the princes should do so on their own account. The second was the *On the Babylonian Captivity of the Church,* in which he criticized current practices and doctrines concerned with the sacraments. In the third, *On Christian Liberty,* he wrote of his new insight into Christian freedom, gained in the assurance of justification by faith.

But the final break with Rome was postponed. When the Bull eventually arrived from Rome, the Elector refused to carry it out. Luther burnt it in public, together with some Romanist books. It was not until January 1521 that, as a consequence of this act, he was finally excommunicated. Charles, the Holy Roman Emperor, summoned Luther to come in April under safe-conduct to a Diet at Worms. Luther, having refused to renounce his position, was put under the Ban of the Empire. But once again the Elector of Saxony came to his aid, and for ten months Luther stayed in safety at his castle at Wartburg.

In the next few years the process of change occurred rapidly in many parts of Germany. A number of princes threw off their allegiance to the papacy, for political as well as religious reasons. Luther's teachings acquired considerable popularity among the masses. Monks were leaving the monasteries and marrying. Many of the older forms of ritual were discarded. Luther himself left his sanctuary at Wartburg in 1522 when he learned that a former associate, Andreas Bodenstein of Karlstadt, who had assumed leadership of the German reform, was attempting radical changes and causing chaos and discontent. Luther restored order. In 1525, he married a former nun, Katherine von Bora (1499–1552). In the same year his popularity declined considerably, because of his attitude toward the peasants.

The German peasants lived in great hardship and poverty. As the climate

90. *Martin Luther, by Heinrich Aldegrever (16th century). (Courtesy of the Museum of Fine Arts, Boston, Harvey D. Parker Collection.)*

91. *Castle church in Wittenberg where Luther is said to have nailed the Ninety-Five Theses, woodcut by Lucas Cranach (16th century). (Courtesy of The New York Public Library, Astor, Lenox and Tilden Foundations.)*

92. *John Calvin, from a book by Théodore de Bèze, Geneva (1581). (Rare Books and Manuscripts Division, The New York Public Library, Astor, Lenox, and Tilden Foundations.)*

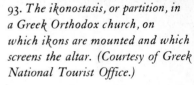

93. *The ikonostasis, or partition, in a Greek Orthodox church, on which ikons are mounted and which screens the altar. (Courtesy of Greek National Tourist Office.)*

94. *Russian Orthodox church of St. Mary Magdalene in Israel. Built by Czar Alexander III, its crypt contains the hearts of some members of the Imperial family. (Courtesy of Israel Ministry of Tourism.)*

of change permeated the affairs of prelates and princes, the peasants also demanded the end of old miseries. In 1524, the peasants came out in open rebellion. Luther advocated their forcible suppression, and after two cruel years and a hundred thousand deaths the revolt was crushed. Nevertheless, it was Luther's defiance of the Church, the strong appeal of his preaching, and his ability as a hymn-writer and translator of the Bible (which gave shape and substance to the German language) that had led to the spread of the movement, which was soon to reach other countries. In 1529, it was agreed at a national Diet that princes should be free to organize churches within their territories as they thought appropriate. This involved, in effect, the parcelling up of Germany between Reformed and Catholic states.

THE REFORMED CHURCH

The shape of the new faith was expressed in a reordering of Church services. The Mass was translated into the vernacular, and was divested of those elements that suggested a sacrifice. It was not performed daily, as was the practice among the Roman Catholics, on the grounds that such frequent repetition was superstitious. Vestments and candles were kept in use, and in outward circumstances the new rite did not differ too greatly from its Roman counterpart. On Sunday afternoon a new service was devised, involving a sermon on the Old Testament. The reason for this was that the Old Testament was virtually a closed book before the Reformation, except in monasteries and theological faculties. With his emphasis on the authority of the Bible—for it was to the scriptures that he appealed against the Pope, and it was through the scriptures that he had won the great insight which had turned toward his reforms—Luther wished to ensure that the Bible was widely known among the faithful.

Zwingli

Meanwhile divisions were creeping into the fabric of the Reform. In particular, the Swiss theologian Ulrich Zwingli (1484-1531), who had pushed through the reformation with great energy and success at Zürich, held views which were much more radical than those of Luther. In Zürich, the Mass was completely abolished, pictures and images were removed from churches, and the traditional doctrinal basis of the eucharist was denied. For Zwingli, the eucharist was nothing more than a memorial of the Last Supper: he repudiated Luther's doctrine of the real presence of Christ in the sacrament, as well as the Roman concept of transubstantiation. Such differences became very evident at Augsburg in 1530, when an attempt was made to reconcile the Catholics and Reformers. Luther's friend Melanchthon prepared a Confession which was mild in tone and sought to underline the points of agreement between the two parties, but it was unacceptable to Zwingli and his followers. The Confession of Augsburg remains one of the important documents embodying the official doctrine of the Lutheran Church.

The Anabaptists

Another group which was important in the early period of the Reformation was the Anabaptist, so called because they believed in "Re-baptism," in the sense that they rejected the practice of infant baptism in favor of adult baptism. They were, on the whole, pacifist. Because of the nature of some of their doctrines, which were often very radical, and because of the menace which they were thought to represent against the established order, they were persecuted by both Catholics and Protestants. Thousands died in this pursuit of a pure community distinguished from the corrupt, church-dominated society in which they felt themselves to be. With their radical emphasis on individual faith, they were forerunners of Baptists, Congregationalists, and others who wished to separate religion from the state. By contrast Calvinists, Lutherans, and Anglicans represent the so-called magisterial Reformation, in which citizenship and faith were supposed to coincide. Thus the Roman Catholic and dissenting Non-Conformist did not have full rights in countries which followed the magisterial Reformation.

JOHN CALVIN

Next to Luther the biggest figure in the Reformation was undoubtedly John Calvin (1509-1564). A Frenchman, born in Picardy, he had early come under humanist influences. He was destined for the priesthood, but had doubts about his vocation. In 1533, he became convinced of the necessity of reforming Christian belief and he broke with Catholicism. In his reaction against the form of belief he had hitherto entertained, he rejected the humanist approach to religion—his remarkable gifts of scholarship enabled him to use humanist learning in the service of demolishing humanism. In 1535, fearing persecution in France, he fled to Switzerland. Guillaume Farel (1489-1565) had already established the Reformation in Geneva. When Calvin visited Geneva in 1536, he was reluctantly persuaded by Farel to stay on. Soon Calvin was the leader of the Reform in that city. This was in no small measure due to the lucidity and definiteness of his theological thought, coupled with an ability to translate doctrines into practical terms—a fruit of his early training as a lawyer. Geneva was transformed under his influence. Frivolous pursuits were banned: a new moralism permeated the city: thorough religious education was instituted. Geneva became a small theocracy.

Calvin's doctrines are principally contained in the various editions of his famous *Institutes of the Christian Religion*. Like Zwingli, he differed from

Luther in his attitude to the scriptures. Luther was not averse to accepting doctrines and practices which could not be derived from the Bible, provided that they did not run contrary to it. But Calvin and Zwingli held the stricter belief that only those doctrines and practices which could be derived from the Bible were acceptable. This helps to explain Calvin's anti-humanism—God is absolutely sovereign; man must obey him and not set up his own ideas to mask and shroud divine authority. It is not from human reasoning that one gains truth about God. Our knowledge of God derives from God himself and from God alone. This knowledge is mediated through the scriptures. If some of the Biblical messages seem to run counter to what we ordinarily believe, this is only a sign that we are not obedient to God's message. In place of the authority of the Pope and of the Church, Calvin put the authority of the Bible. His theology, then, was intended to be a deduction from the data contained therein.

Calvin's Theology

In Calvin's thought, the outstanding features of God are supreme sovereignty and righteousness. By nature man is corrupt and depraved. Though man might have a dim understanding of God's glory through the observation of nature, he is unable to know God, in his present state, without God's grace. In the starkest terms, Calvin drew out the implications of the doctrine of original sin. We have all become involved in original sin and all are defiled. We are justly the objects of God's wrath. Nevertheless, salvation is possible through the work of Christ. Through Christ's grace, God accepts some people as if they were righteous. But since God is absolutely sovereign, his choice is entirely his. Only those whom he elects, or chooses, for salvation are to be saved. It follows from this that salvation and damnation are entirely determined by God, who predestines men to these ends. As Calvin wrote, "All are not created on equal terms, but some are preordained to eternal life, others to eternal damnation." Predestination does not, however, entail that the elect can do what they like, secure in the confidence of their salvation. The sign of election is the sanctification of the individual. This explains the paradox that Calvinism seems to involve: it is believed that men are saved solely through God's work, and yet great emphasis is put upon good works. Such in brief were the stern doctrines which Calvin implemented, sometimes in the face of adversity and opposition, in Geneva.

CONTRAST OF CALVIN AND LUTHER

There is quite a contrast here with Luther, both personally and in theology. Calvin was a concise, brilliant, systematic thinker; he was detached and austere in his private life. Luther was earthy, jolly, and, in his reforming days, unascetic; he was unsystematic and passionate as a theologian. Calvin knew precisely where he was going: Luther's revolution was made up as it went along. Both took their starting point from justification by faith. Calvin—perhaps more consistently—stressed man's total depravity.

These differences worked themselves out in practice. The Lutheran Churches have remained more flexible and traditional in their organization. Some retain bishops. Calvinism and Presbyterianism are more monolithic in their forms and organization. In terms of piety, too, there are obvious divergences. Lutheranism has cultivated a more personal and private attitude to God. Luther may have hated God at one point, but his insight as a result of the Tower experience did not lead him to emphasize to the same degree as Calvin did the gulf between man and God. For Calvin, piety must always have its social and ethical dimension, and it must be controlled by recognition of what has been called "the great Calvinistic distance between heaven and earth." In terms of practical politics both movements had their good and bad points.

Once he had repudiated the papacy, Luther came increasingly to rely on the support of the secular power. If Calvin's theocracy of Geneva avoided this situation, it did so at the expense of itself having to deal with what it regarded as heresy. Thus Michael Servetus (1511-1553), a physician who had at one time been a friend of Calvin's, was denounced to the Inquisition for his denial of the Trinity doctrine. He fled to Geneva, only to find that Calvin demanded that he recant his belief. When he refused, he was burnt at the stake.

CONTRAST OF REFORMED AND CATHOLIC CHURCHES

In more than one instance the Reformers found themselves in the same position as the Catholic Church they had repudiated. To establish a new norm of doctrine it was necessary to use some of the methods the Catholics had used. One authoritarianism was replaced by another. It is true that Protestantism, as part of the logic of its protest against the interposition of the Church between God and the believer, had within it the seeds of a more democratic view of religion. This ultimately paved the way for religious toleration. But it would be misleading not to recognize the degree to which both Catholics and Protestants in the sixteenth century were inclined to use force in the defense and imposition of their doctrines. It was perhaps inevitable in a time of convulsion, fear, and division.

Despite the loss of a great number of the faithful to the new Reform, the Catholic Church maintained its essential unity. Protestantism was always open to further splitting. Authority in matters of religion was always sought from the Bible, as we have seen clearly in the case of Calvin. This authority, however, was not clear cut; much depended on the interpretation given to scripture. New interpretations were always possible. Given the Protestant insistence that it is faith alone which justifies, men could find in their own experience such an assurance which would legitimate such new interpretations. Further, of course, as in the case of Lutheranism, so elsewhere, political considerations often entered strongly into questions of religion, so that national divisions themselves could have the effect of fragmenting Protestantism.

The Reformation, of course, had a decisive effect on the religion of Europe. A notable aspect of this was the way in which it helped to induce changes within the structure of Catholicism itself. The characteristic shape of modern Catholicism derives from this period. Already, however, in the fifteenth century one impetus to reform had occurred. The final liberation of Spain from the Moors led to a widespread purification of the Spanish Church. Unsatisfactory monks and clergy were removed; Church and state cooperated in reorganizing the Inquisition; universities and other places of learning were instituted to give a higher intellectual tone to the training of the priesthood. The discovery of America and the wide extension of the Spanish Empire gave the country a wealth and influence that made it for a time the foremost European power. The Spanish example could in some degree form the pattern for changes elsewhere.

THE CATHOLIC REFORMATION

The first and most important event in the Catholic Reformation (known to Protestants as the Counter-Reformation) was the Council of Trent, convened by Pope Paul III in 1545, under pressure from Charles V of Spain who was Holy Roman Emperor. Charles aimed to get a reform and redefinition of Catholicism that could lead to a reconciliation with the Protestants, thus helping in the political reunification of Germany. This was not to be. The Council dragged on in fits and starts until 1563, by which time all hope of reconciliation had gone.

In the course of its deliberations, the Council firmly repudiated a number of important Protestant positions. The doctrine of transubstantiation was reaffirmed. It was ruled that the Church alone had the right to interpret scripture, and that Catholic tradition was an equal source of authority to the Bible. The two were regarded as complementary. The necessity of the seven sacraments was restated (Reformers having tended to confine the divinely instituted sacraments to baptism and the eucharist—leaving out confirmation, penance, unction, etc.) The issuing of indulgences was more closely regulated. Bishops and priests in the larger towns and cities were instructed to give expositions of the scriptures. Some curb was put on the veneration of images and relics. Finally, the pope was empowered to draw up a list of prohibited literature, the Index. This was designed to stop the spread of Protestant ideas in Catholic countries and communities. These arrangements were supplemented by Pope Paul's action in 1542 in centralizing the administration of the Inquisition. This was now a weapon which could be used to purge Catholic countries of heretics.

The Jesuits

By these formal decisions the Church set about putting its house in order and reaffirming its heritage. There were other forces tending toward reform. Ignatius Loyola (1491-1556), a Spanish nobleman who had been converted from a military career to the religious life, formed an order which gained papal approval in 1540—the famous Society of Jesus.

The Jesuits were organized on the model of a military organization, Loyola being the first General of the order. Their aim was the propagation of Catholic truth, both abroad, in the mission field, and at home, in combatting Protestant and other heresies. They vowed absolute obedience to the pope and renounced any ecclesiastical dignity unless expressly constrained to accept by the pope himself.

The inner life was controlled by the spiritual exercises evolved by Loyola on the basis of his own early experiences. These involved a sequence of meditations, extending over four weeks, on sin, the Kingdom of Christ, the Passion, and the risen Lord. The meditations provided a means of conforming the imagination to the Christian life, and the will to unhesitant service, even in the face of gross discomfort and adversity. The order, moreover, was not tied down to long services and offices, as in other foundations, so that the Jesuit could move about like an ordinary priest. Through the Society of Jesus, there was forged a flexible and powerful instrument for the work of conversion and teaching.

The high intellectual standards and subtlety of Jesuit education have given the order a formidable reputation. It was mainly through the Jesuits that the work of evangelizing the Far East in the sixteenth century occurred, and they played a big part in the conversion of the Spanish American peoples. Thus St. Francis Xavier (1506-1552) had remarkable missionary success in Japan, where he left behind him an organized Christian community. Matteo Ricci (1552-1610) was influential at the Chinese court. And something of the attitude of the Jesuits in the New World can be gathered from the remarkable experiment in the seventeenth century in setting up a whole system of administration in Paraguay and northern Argentina in which the Indians were introduced to agriculture and industries on the European pattern, and were organized into compounds surrounding magnificent churches. Here all was order, peace, prosperity—even if the control remained in the hands of the Jesuits. The local language was used, a small literature established, education of an elementary kind was widespread. When eventually the Jesuits were expelled, however, the system crumbled and the jungle returned to claim its own. In all sorts of ways, then, in different parts of the mission field the Jesuits had a strong impact.

Perhaps the most poignant story is that of the Italian Roberto de Nobíli (1577-1656). He lived for some time in Madura, a famous center of South Indian Hinduism. He adopted the outward appearance of a *sannyasi,* or holy man, and adapted his teachings to the structure of the caste system. His was a noble and learned effort to make Catholicism indigenous in India, though he encountered opposition from among his fellow Catholics, who felt he had gone too far in comprise with Indian culture. Had his experiment been carried on, it might have had a marked effect on Indian Christianity.

The Jesuits, of course, were only one element in the great missionary effort both in the New World and elsewhere undertaken in the sixteenth and seventeenth centuries. What Catholicism lost in Europe through the Reformation it gained abroad in the proselytization of most of Central and South America in a remarkably short space of time. Though in the East Christianity has never really been successful from the statistical point of view, save in the Spanish Philippines, the Catholic missions opened up a trail which was later taken by the Protestants.

THE ANGLICAN REFORMATION

In England, reforms took a rather different course from those on the Continent. The occasion for the break with the papacy was Henry VIII's desire to remarry; but behind this there lay forces impelling the English Church to make such a move. There were already present in England reformers from the Continent and already Englishmen had been influenced by the new movement. They provided some religious motives for change. The abuses of the medieval Church were obvious; and a new spirit of revolt was beginning to stir. William Tyndale (c.1494-1536) published a new translation of the Bible from Germany (the Bishop of London had refused his support). The Tyndale Bible became known in England from 1526 onward. As we have seen in other connections, the Bible was doctrinal dynamite; the work of translation constituted in effect a revolutionary act.

Almost despite himself Henry VIII set in motion a train of events that was not to be halted. When he died in 1547, he was succeeded by his son Edward VI, who was then only nine. Under the administration of the young king's regents, Reformers once more became active in England, and a number of distinguished scholars from the Continent were invited over. In 1549 Parliament authorized the use of the first English Book of Common Prayer, drawn up by Cranmer. It was a work of liturgical genius, satisfying to both those with Catholic and Reforming inclinations—it and its successors have remained a potent source of English-speaking piety. The imposition of the new order of the English Church was ensured by an Act of Uniformity passed by Parliament. Virtually since that time, though with interruptions, the outward forms of the Church of England have been ultimately controlled by Parliament. This, though meaning that Christianity had been integrated in its new form as a national religion, also helped to ensure that the Church of England remained a unity, despite internal divisions. It is one reason for the curious situation which persists until today in which people of widely differing Christian beliefs—ranging from Conservative Evangelicalism, which is in belief hardly distinguishable from left-wing Protestantism, to Anglo-Catholicism, which is sometimes even more Catholic than Roman Catholicism—are members of the same communion.

THE REFORMED CHURCHES

The forces of Calvinism, Lutheranism, and a reformed Catholicism were not, however, the only ones released by the events following Luther's historic act at Wittenberg. There were other groups who in a sense were to the left of the Reformers, who were more radical and individualistic. We have already seen something of the Anabaptist movement, with its tragic consequences. Servetus had suffered martyrdom because he rejected the Trinity doctrine. Quite a number of others adopted what came to be known as the Unitarian faith.

Unitarians

The first organization of Unitarians was in Poland, where since 1156 the nobility had enjoyed the privilege of holding services in private. This made possible the introduction of minority religious views. Prominent among those in Poland was an Italian, Fausto Sozzini (1539–1604), who gave a structure to the movement. Hungary also was a center of Unitarianism. In the seventeenth century the movement came to England. The principle motives animating the Unitarians were those of disillusionment with both Reformed and Catholic views of the atonement. The latter depended on prior acceptance of the doctrine of original sin, and men such as Sozzini found this to be in conflict with common sense. If there were no original sin, then from what had Christ saved us? If, further, there is no need of a sacrificial atonement, then the basis for believing Christ's divinity was gone. Nor was it lost on such radicals that the Bible itself does not speak of the Trinity doctrine in the way it came to be formulated in the fourth century. Though often they had to strain scripture to remove the many suggestions therein of Christ's more than human status (as in the opening words of St. John's Gospel, for instance), the Unitarians could appeal to the Bible with not a totally implausible show of cogency. They combined belief in the one God with a stress on Christian virtues. Unitarianism later penetrated some of the radical Protestant movements in England and in America. In the latter country it took particularly strong root.

The Baptists

Both the Anabaptists and the Unitarians were in different ways too radical to be accepted by other branches of the Reformation, the former because they seemed to threaten the existing social order, the latter because they denied the essential basis of Christianity. Less radical were certain other movements, one of which indeed grew out of the Anabaptist tradition. This was the Baptist Church. This was introduced into England in 1612, and first reached America in 1636 when the Puritan Roger Williams founded Providence, Rhode Island. For some time the Baptists were divided over theological questions—in particular over the Calvinist doctrine of predestination, which many accepted and others rejected. Though they have ever been disinclined to impose credal formulae on their members, they came to form a common view. Their distinctive espousal of the doctrine of adult baptism by total immersion was founded on a reading of the Bible. From early times they have been both strongly evangelical and committed to ideals of religious liberty and toleration. The most famous Baptist writer was the Englishman John Bunyan (1628–1688), who was imprisoned for many years after the restoration of the monarchy in 1660. In his *Pilgrim's Progress* he provided a remarkable allegory of the Christian's engagement in the fight for good against evil.

The Congregationalists

The most radical of the Christian movements of the period was that of the Congregationalists, or Independents (the term "Congregationalism" came into use in the middle of the seventeenth century). They belonged to the extreme Puritan wing, and broke away from the established Church of England in the latter part of the sixteenth century under the leadership of Robert Browne (c. 1550–1633), Henry Barrow (c. 1550–1593), and others. In general the Independents subscribed to Calvinistic theology, but they took issue with both Calvin and the Church of England over the nature of the Church. They objected to establishment: religion was not a matter for the state. They considered that the Church was a voluntary association of the faithful, as the early Church had been. There should be no sharp division between clergy and laity; indeed, they firmly emphasized the doctrine of the priesthood of all believers. Pastors and teachers should be elected by the local congregation; each congregation should be independent; there should be no credal test laid down to control the life of the congregations. Faith was a matter for the commonfolk, not for some ecclesiastical authority. It can be seen, then, that the Congregationalists were strongly democratic in their organization. The American Pilgrim Fathers themselves belonged to this movement, which is therefore one of the roots of modern American democracy. It is from the radical Reformation that the doctrine of the separation of church and state chiefly originated.

The Quakers

England also gave rise to another remarkable movement, the Society of Friends—or "Quakers" as they were nicknamed by their enemies—founded by George Fox (1624–1691). Fox was a strange and compelling character. He was in his early days a Puritan, but in 1643 he broke with his former associates. His repudiation of Puritanism came about through one incident. Fox had been invited to drink beer with a cousin and a friend, both Puritans. One beer followed another and gradually the occasion turned into a bout. At last, in disgust, Fox paid the bill for the beer and left. He felt depressed and shaken by the lack of conformity between his friends' conduct and their avowed belief. This was said to be one of the causes of his later distrust of creeds and external doctrines. He gave up going to church and became a wandering recluse.

After three years, Fox had an experience which set his doubts and worries at rest. He heard a voice which said "There is one, even Christ Jesus, that can speak to thy condition." He felt himself caught up by and suffused with the love of God. It was the beginning of his mission. Thereafter he began to preach, inveighing not merely against church worship and the sacraments, but against Puritan belief as well. The truth was not to be found in stories from the Bible. It was to be discovered in the Inner Light, which brought men to direct communion with God. "Not the Scriptures," he once said, "but the Spirit." This was the heart of his revolutionary doctrine.

Fox was strongly egalitarian. He would not take his hat off to any man:

he addressed all and sundry as "Thou." He was also a pacifist. His teachings and his zeal aroused severe opposition. Fox himself was imprisoned. But his following grew. Thousands of Friends also had to suffer jail. Notable among these followers was William Penn (1644–1718), who founded the Quaker colony of Pennsylvania.

Though the Friends have never been numerically very large, they have, especially over the last two centuries, exerted a profound influence in the extent and devotion of their social work. In this they have been assisted by the prosperity which has partly accrued from their thrift and plain living. The spontaneity and silences of the Quaker Meeting express the strong dependence of the Friends on the inner workings of the Spirit.

CHARACTERISTICS OF PROTESTANTISM

The Congregationalists and the Friends in their different ways represent the extreme democratization of religion as a result of the forces set in motion by the Reformation. It is now time to look back over the whole movement, together with the Catholic reaction, to see what it all meant in terms of the various dimensions of religion.

In his protest against indulgences Luther had in effect been protesting against the abuse of the ritual dimension of religion. The sacrament of penance had become detached from true repentance—had become detached in fact from faithful attitudes and from experience—and had been converted into a mode of salving men's consciences while at the same time making money. But this led Luther on to a more general critique of ritual. The notion that the Mass is a sacrifice, for instance, which can be used to help those in Purgatory he considered a case of the loss of the true meaning of ritual through detachment from personal piety. Luther was far from wishing to destroy the ritual dimension, but by attempting to bring it more into line with the personal experience of grace and salvation he paved the way for a great diminution of the more spectacular and colorful side of ritual among the Reformed churches.

This tendency appeared clearly in Zwingli's estimate of the eucharist as a simple memorial of the Last Supper. The external act for him could not of itself bring any inward grace. Thus the ritual side of religion was to be confined to worship and prayer. This remains essentially true for many of the more radical Protestant groups. Its apogee was reached in the teachings of George Fox, who even rejected worship as it was normally understood in his time. Thus the Reformation resulted in a break, among such groups, with the sacramentalism which had played such a big part hitherto in Christian history. This, however, though it may have been a loss, also turned men's attention more to the inner experience of salvation. The Reformation indeed is in some respects a reaffirmation of the experiential dimension of religion, but not, as with the Catholic orders, through the cultivation of mysticism: rather it was through a reapprehension of the Pauline experience of liberation from sin and redemption through Jesus Christ.

To some degree, also, the Reformation brought back into Christendom a strong consciousness of the ethical monotheism of the Old Testament. Luther instituted services based on the Old Testament on Sunday afternoons. The translations of the Bible opened people's eyes to this part of the Bible, which had been virtually unknown to the masses. The consequence was a faith which in many ways echoed that of the Prophets. Calvin's Geneva resembled the theocracy of the post-Exilic period. Thus the Reformation emphasized once again the numinous, holy power of God who confronted sinful men directly, without the protection that the Church had hitherto given folk in shielding them from the immediate experience of his awesome might.

Nevertheless, though it was the tremendous God of worship that appeared so vividly before the eyes of those converted to the Reformation, mystical tendencies were by no means entirely lacking—partly because mysticism, with its tendencies toward distrust of authoritative orthodoxy fitted in with the new spirit of revolt. The writings of Jakob Boehme (1575-1624), for instance, exercised a wide influence, and the Quaker doctrine of the Inner Light was related to Protestant mystical trends. However, the Protestant churches, in abolishing monasticism, cut off a fertile stream of contemplative experience, for the circumstances of monastic life were well suited to the cultivation of the inner life. Protestant mysticism is more of a continuation of the movement toward lay participation in spiritual cultivation in the late medieval period of Catholicism, which we noticed earlier. As a crude oversimplication, then, we can say that experiential renewal in medieval Catholicism came through mystical experience: in the Reformation, it came through a more direct and vivid awareness of the presence of God "outside and above" man— through an awareness, too, of the "distance between heaven and earth," signifying the majesty of God and the sinfulness of man.

Protestantism made a great difference to the social dimension of Christianity. It tended to replace the patterns of an organic society, in which the institutions of the Church were integrated, with a more individualistic system. This was not true at Geneva, of course, where a Protestant theocracy replaced the pervasive authority of the Roman Church. Nor was it totally true in England. Nevertheless, the trend in Protestantism was undeniably toward a more individual estimate of man's place in society, which reflected the very personal and individual confrontation between a man and his Maker. Though the Reformers in their emphasis on grace and on predestination seemed to take men's responsibility away from them, the effect was rather the opposite (as we have seen). A man individually confronted with God's saving work through grace felt individual responsibility for self-reform: while those who believed in predestination were in the ironic predicament of finding that their sole assurance of salvation lay in the holiness and goodness of their lives. Thus the Reformation reemphasized the ethical dimension of Christianity, but in a manner rather different from the emphasis given to it in Catholicism. Lay participation in Church affairs was greatly increased, partly because of the doctrine of the priesthood of all believers. The destruction of the monasteries and the marrying of monks and nuns likewise served to reduce differentiation within the formal structure of the Church.

Doctrinally, the most important single feature of Protestantism was its reliance on the authority of scripture. The extreme fervor with which many of the evangelicals stressed the infallibility of scripture was the natural result of the removal of the Church's authority in matters of doctrine. It has resulted in a continuing crisis in Protestant authority, for interpretations of the meaning of the Bible can vary widely. Further, at a later stage in the evolution of Christian theology, in the nineteenth century when scholarly criticism was beginning to discover the truth about how the Bible was composed, Protestantism received a severe shock. If one could not appeal in a straightforward and detailed way to the scriptures, then the fabric of doctrinal certainty seemed to crumble. We shall later see how this problem worked itself out in the nineteenth and twentieth centuries. A common Catholic reply to the Reformers' position about the Bible was to say that after all it was the Church that had formed the canon of Holy Writ. Nevertheless, the Reformers, in their deep concern to provide Biblical warrant for what they were thinking and doing, did penetrate beyond the layers of medieval doctrine and ritual to the simpler life and attitudes of the Apostolic Church. They may have sometimes misinterpreted the facts. They may have been overconsistent in their application of such key ideas as election. But they did remind the world forcibly of the sort of origins which Christianity had had. Whether it was right to go back to an imitation of the Church of the first century or not, the Protestant radicals at least stirred up a revolutionary social ferment.

As we have already seen, the chief motivation for the doctrines typical of the Reformation was the experience of justification and forgiveness. From the Catholic point of view, the emphasis was one-sided. In leading toward a view of God's election as an arbitrary act, it put God's ways so far above human understanding, especially in the Calvinist formulation, that it seemed to remove from man any chance of natural knowledge of God. When this was combined with a strict adherence to the Bible, it was liable, so its opponents thought, to a new sort of other-worldliness, in which human culture and religion were separated from one another. It was not surprising that a humanist like Erasmus (c.1466–1536) should feel unable to join the Reformation, though he paved the way for reform in his merciless satires on the corruptions of monastic life.

THE RUSSIAN CHURCH AND ORTHODOXY

In Eastern Europe, the affairs of the Orthodox Church during the Renaissance period languished under Turkish domination. The Orthodox in the areas under Muslim control looked to the Patriarch of Constantinople for their leadership, but the Patriarch was virtually a creature of the new regime. It is interesting that when Muhammad II entered Constantinople in 1453, the Patriarchate was then vacant: the Islamic general had insisted in taking part in the appointment and investiture of the new Patriarch. The Patriarchs became the intermediaries between the Ottomans and the Christian communities in the Empire, and thus were given jurisdiction over the Patriarchs of Alexandria, Jerusalem, and Antioch. The office had to be bought; to recoup the cost the Patriarch resorted to simony, and lesser Church offices were allotted to the highest bidder. Since the Greek community at Constantinople was wealthy, it soon succeeded in controlling the Eastern Church. Greek influences, though not always popular, spread through the Balkan States among the indigenous Christian churches.

This unhappy situation at the center of Orthodoxy was counterbalanced by the rise of Russian Orthodoxy as a force independent of Constantinople. This was finally achieved in 1589. The then Patriarch of Constantinople was visiting Russia to solicit money, which was sorely needed to pay the tribute due to the Sultan. The Russian metropolitans agreed to furnish funds on the condition that Moscow should be recognized as a separate Patriarchate.

This was not the first instance of the independence of the Russian clergy. In 1438, the Council of Florence had met in a last attempt to hammer out a reconciliation between the Greek and Latin Churches. The Greeks were under pressure from the advancing Turks, and chiefly to gain assistance, they agreed finally, in 1439, to most of the points of doctrine held by the Latins. But bishops who signed the agreement did not find that things went smoothly when they returned home. For one thing, the Russians totally rejected the findings of the Council. This was the final collapse of any real hope of concord between East and West, at least until the present century. The Russian Church grew suspicious that the Church of Constantinople was not committedly Orthodox, and refused to recognize Greek bishops and metropolitans.

Thus the establishment of the separate Patriarchate was a logical development from previous events. It, moreover, generated in Russia the ambition that Moscow should become "the third Rome." Rome had fallen to barbarian invaders, and its Church had gone astray in pressing the claims of the papacy. Constantinople had fallen to the Muslims and had lost its real independence and vitality. Moscow could be the true successor to the old and new Romes. Thus began that messianism which has characterized much of Russian political and religious thought. Russia would come to restore the balance when sophisticated Europe had demonstrated its inadequacy and decadence.

There were, however, seeds of dissension within Russian Orthodoxy which occupied the energies of ecclesiastics during the period following the establishment of the Moscow Patriarchate. Lithuania and Poland had remained Roman Catholic countries; from there Roman propaganda and influence seeped into the Ukraine and farther afield. In this the Jesuits played a prominent part. A synod was held at Brest-Litovsk toward the end of the sixteenth century in which the Metropolitan of Kiev and other Orthodox bishops took part. These prelates were persuaded to recognize the supremacy of the Roman pope over other bishops but continued to advocate the liturgical and other forms of church life to which they were long accustomed. Their betrayal of Russian Orthodoxy caused a breach with the more conservative Orthodox, who excommunicated those who had taken part in the synod.

The Uniat Church

Thus there was formed a separate Church, known as the Uniat Church by its opponents, which was indistinguishable in outward form from Orthodoxy, but which had a different allegiance. In this arrangement, the Ukrainian Uniats followed the example of various other churches in the East united to Rome by recognizing the primacy of the Holy See, while retaining their own forms of liturgy and church order. There are a dozen or so such Uniat Churches, ranging from the Maronites of Syria, which united with Rome in the twelfth century, to the Malabarese Church in India (part of the old Mar Thoma Church), which united in the sixteenth century. The last to be so united was the Greek Uniat Church in 1860.

For a time it looked as though Catholicism might gain control in Russia through the spread of Polish military power. The Poles occupied Moscow and recognized Dmitri, a Catholic, as Tsar. But the Poles were driven out in 1612 and Dmitri assassinated. The establishment of the Romanov dynasty ensured that Orthodoxy would remain dominant in Russia.

The Patriarch Nikon

But new troubles were afoot. It was unfortunate that they were associated with one who was probably Russia's greatest Patriarch, Nikon (1605-1681). He was elected to the patriarchate in 1652, at the order of Tsar Alexei. But he was certainly not one to submit to state authority in church matters. He was convinced, from his earlier experience as Metropolitan of Novgorod, that liturgical and educational reforms were desperately needed. Very often the clergy, who were elected by the local communities, paid no attention to the bishops; many were illiterate; gross abuses had crept into the performance of the Liturgy—for instance, services were so long and complicated that to reduce their length different priests were allowed to chant different parts of the service simultaneously. The resultant chaos needed sorting out, and Nikon began on his task. He introduced certain simplifications and amendments into the existing words of the service, and he insisted both on literacy and obedience in the lower clergy. Both reforms were unpopular. He could have successfully forced them through during his own patriarchate if he had continued to have the support of the Tsar, but his independence of the latter led to his deposition in 1666. Nevertheless, his reforms were accepted. Alexei's successor Fyodor II recalled Nikon. By then broken in health by imprisonment and exile, he died on the way to Moscow.

Two troubles emerged from the events of Nikon's patriarchate. First, they demonstrated the dependence of the Church on secular authority. This was to remain a feature of the Russian Church even after the Communist Revolution. The process of turning the Church into a department of state administration was completed by Peter the Great (1676–1725), when it was put under the authority of a lay synod, whose members were not even required to be Christians. The patriarchate was suppressed; it was not restored until 1917.

The Old Believers

Second, the reforms of Nikon resulted in a split among the Orthodox. Those who refused to accept the new measures split off to form a conservative church, known as that of the "Old Believers" (*Starovertsi*). The Old Believers were castigated as schismatics by the official Church prelates and were brutally persecuted by Fyodor II. Such efforts at intimidation continued as late as the reign of Nicholas I (1825–1855). The Old Believers attracted a considerable following among the peasants, and a sizeable number of priests joined them. They found increased support during the attempts of Peter the Great to westernize Russia, and they stood for a highly conservative attempt to keep the old ways of Russian life. Opposition to the regime could find an outlet in a religious community which stood apart from state-dominated Orthodoxy. Their breakaway from the hierarchy, however, left them with certain problems: as they had no bishops, they became short of ordained priests and had to rely on ones who defected from the official Church. This difficulty continued until, in 1864, a Bosnian bishop joined their ranks and reestablished a hierarchy capable of ordaining priests and consecrating bishops.

Meanwhile, however, many Old Believers decided to carry on without priests, beginning another breakaway. The "priestless" Old Believers not unnaturally split up into a number of sub-sects, some of them propounding extreme and even lunatic doctrines, such as infanticide (since priestless marriages were invalid and the offspring sinful). Others were extreme pacifists, resisting state authority: others again resisted officialdom militantly, forming an anarchistic and much-persecuted group. These excesses of religious fanaticism were always minority phenomena, and were partly the outcome of poverty and desperation. The majority of Old Believers clung to the forms of Orthodoxy, and most still belong to the "priested" sect, which numbers several million adherents.

Sectarian Movements in Russia

Movements reminiscent of Manicheism also took root in Russia at this period. The Chlysts (literally "Whippers") were started in the seventeenth century by a fanatical peasant, who claimed to be the Father descended from heaven. His followers were enjoined to be ascetic, abstaining from meat, onions, and potatoes. Flagellation and dancing held an important place in their ritual. Sexual relations, even among converts already married, were forbidden. In turning away from a hostile world which they regarded as evil, these folk hoped for a bliss hereafter which was largely denied them on this earth. Another similarly fanatical group embraced the practice of self-castration.

These extreme offshoots of Russian Christianity have by no means died out. The Dukhobors, a group originating in the eighteenth century, which practiced communism and believed in reincarnation, were long persecuted. Numbers of them emigrated to Canada, where they remain a somewhat anarchic and anti-authoritarian thorn in the flesh of the Government. Negotiations to have them repatriated to Russia have been met with a certain lack of enthusiasm by the Soviet regime.

It would, however, be wrong to overemphasize the importance of these groups in the continuing life of the Russian people. For the vast majority, Orthodoxy has remained the focus of allegiance. The monasteries and the Liturgy have formed the backbone of the religion. Though the Church has remained normally under the control of the state, it has nevertheless, through its rites, and through its holy men, retained a power to keep the religious imagination of the Russian peasant alive. Because it has been largely cut off from Western influences, it is possible to pursue its story as far as the 1917 Revolution without much break of continuity (while in the West the intellectual and other events of the eighteenth and nineteenth centuries had a profound effect on religious life).

Though undoubtedly in the eighteenth and nineteenth centuries, the

Church in Russia was crippled by the poverty and low level of education of the ordinary clergy, and though very often the monks were lax in piety and discipline of their life, the ideal of the saintly hermit, or holy man, did something to win the devotion and respect of peasants. The best portrait of such a person is to be found in Fyodor Dostoievsky's *The Brothers Karamazov,* where the saintly Father Zossima is modeled on a real person. Still and all it was the sacramental side of the faith, as embodied in the sacred Liturgy, which retained the chief allegiance of the masses.

In the nineteenth century, Russian theological thought showed some revival, partly under the influence of the literary movement which flowered so brilliantly in this period. Vladimir Soloviev (1853-1900) was at first a strongly committed Slavophil (one of those who affirmed the Slav heritage in contradistinction from those who embraced Western influences). Later he modified this attitude and began to take seriously the possibility of reunion with Rome. In 1896 he was in fact received into that Church. His early thinking, however, had influenced Fyodor Dostoievsky (1821-1881), a friend of his from 1873.

Dostoievsky

Dostoievsky and others had been arrested for conspiracy in 1849; after several months' detention they had been sentenced to death. They were taken in front of the firing-squad, but at the last moment—seconds before the final order—they were reprieved. This event left a deep mark on Dostoievsky. Equally deep was the impression caused by his life among the outcasts and criminals with whom he lived during his subsequent Siberian exile. He became a fervent Slavophil. His attitude to the Western Church he later expressed in the legend of the Grand Inquisitor, in *The Brothers Karamazov:* the Inquisition would do away with Christ if he were ever to reappear on earth.

Dostoievsky's theological ideas, borne of the fruit of his experience, were analogous in some respects to those of Kierkegaard, and likewise had some influence on developments in theology in this century. He saw salvation among the humble and weak and often (by the world's standards) wicked: in them, very often, there shines forth the compassion which Dostoievsky identified with Christian love. Men are bound together in the bonds of sin and suffering: God's salvation descends, through the humble and suffering God-man, Christ, to men. It is a free gift, not to be won by "good" works or the cultivation of righteousness. Dostoievsky's emotionalism, and his disregard for the processes of reasoning in establishing the truth about God, brought him fairly close to modern Existentialism. Linked to all this was a messianic hope in the future of Russia—holy Russia who through her sufferings would, in a Christ-like way, save Europe and the world. The materialism of the West and its preoccupation with the formal side of religion would be countered by the spirituality of the Eastern world. In such ways, Dostoievsky reinterpreted the ideal of Moscow as "the third Rome."

Tolstoy

Dostoievsky retained the theological ideas of sin, salvation, and grace: Tolstoy (1828–1910), on the other hand, gave a largely ethical and social interpretation of the Christian faith. He was in spiritual lineage nearer to the more radical breakaway sects of Russian Christianity than to Orthodoxy, though without their fanaticism. He was pacifist, and was deeply moved by social distress. He felt that the Sermon on the Mount summarized the gospel, and he preached, as the center of Christian faith, five principles, or commandments, derived therefrom. Anger, even righteous anger, must be suppressed, and one should live in peace with all man; sexual relations should be confined to marriage alone; the taking of oaths is wrong; evil should not be resisted (so that it is wrong to act as a magistrate or serve in the police); one should love one's enemies. The Kingdom of God would be established on earth if the love implicit in these precepts were only to become widespread. Tolstoy not merely preached these precepts: he engaged himself in social reform. He defended the Dukhobors; he renounced his property and lived a life of simplicity and manual work. In the famine of 1891–1892 he was energetic in the relief of distress. Despite his manifest merits and burning sincerity, his distrust of outward forms of belief and ritual led to his excommunication by the Church in 1901. His ideals were in many ways close to those of Gandhi, with whom he corresponded in later life. Like Gandhi, Tolstoy believed in a return to agricultural simplicity as the means of restoring happiness and spirituality to the poor and oppressed.

Though neither Dostoievsky nor Tolstoy could be regarded as theologians in the ordinary sense, they gave expression to sentiments which were of characteristically Russian provenance. Dostoievsky in particular gave literary form to the feeling for the Incarnation as deeply relevant to the sufferings and destiny of the Russian people. Both stressed the importance of going back to national roots and identifying oneself with the people. In so doing the two writers were combatting the intellectualism and rationalism which arose from contact between the educated aristocracy and the thought of the West. Both were criticized in turn by the tougher-minded revolutionaries who sought a political solution to Russia's problems. Tolstoy's pacifism and the religious values of Dostoievsky were alike opposed for their other-worldliness. For Tolstoy, Orthodoxy, which means "right worship," had become "right action," but action controlled by ideals of poverty; for Dostoievsky, it had become right compassion—it was through the emotions rather than through the intellect, through a kind of divine foolishness, that true Christianity was expressed. We shall return later to the events which subsequently overtook the Russia in which they wrote, and which affected markedly the position of religion in the territories of what was to become the Soviet Union. Meanwhile it is worth noting that the Russian Church, for all its defects, had enlarged the bounds of Christianity in the Far East. A mixture of devoted missionary work and state assistance brought Christianity to wide areas of eastern Siberia and elsewhere during the seventeenth and eighteenth centuries.

WESTERN CHRISTIANITY AND THE ENLIGHTENMENT

The Reformation, by mingling with the forces of new scientific knowledge, had set in train intellectual movements that were far removed from the faith of earlier centuries. Thus the eighteenth century saw the emergence of an influential Deism. Deism had its roots in the thought and writing of various earlier figures—notably Lord Herbert of Cherbury (1583–1648), who had attempted to establish a rational religion independent of the sanction of revelation. For him religion depended on five main propositions, which he held to be self-evident and innate to men, and which were supposedly the main basis of all the faiths known to men. The five truths were: that there is a God, that he ought to be worshipped, that the chief mode of worship is through the practice of virtue, that repentance for sin is a duty, and that rewards and punishments will be meted out in future life.

Lord Herbert in turn influenced the philosopher John Locke (1632–1704), who, though no Deist, nevertheless was at one with Cherbury in attempting to establish the reasonableness of religion. The growth of philosophy in its new modern form, liberated from the scholasticism of the Middle Ages, contributed to skepticism about religion, and encouraged attempts to found a new "rational" religion. Deism in effect was such an attempt. In its denial of revelation Deism tended to confine God's acts to that of creating the world and ruling over it in a distant, providential way: interventions in miraculous fashion were considered not to be consonant with God's omnipotence and fixity of purpose. A radical exponent of such a view was Anthony Collins (1676–1729), an English scholar. He denied, for instance, that Old Testament prophecies really predicted Christ, thus obliquely denying the divine mission of the latter.

The brilliant Frenchman Voltaire (1694–1778) incorporated elements of Deism into his thought, combining belief in God with a bitter distrust of institutional Christianity, especially the Roman Church. Voltaire, like many others, was deeply affected by the terrible Lisbon earthquake of 1755. This catastrophe suggested to him that God is not omnipotent in the full sense believed by Christians (for how otherwise would such a disaster occur, if God be good?), but rather creates through an internal necessity within his own nature, from which issues a world, in general harmonious, but also containing discordant elements. Such Deism seemed to fit into the world-picture provided by Newtonian science. The orderliness and determinism of classical physics did not seem to leave room for the intervention of a supernatural Being within the flow of events.

Rationalism found a strong foothold in Germany, and presented the pious with the problem of reconciling their traditional beliefs with the new forms of skepticism. There were those who maintained a markedly conservative evaluation of the scriptures and centered their faith in revelation. Among others who tried to find a new interpretation of Christianity was the great philosopher Immanuel Kant (1724–1804), who lived nearly all his life at Koenigsberg in East Prussia.

Immanuel Kant

We have seen that traditional reconciliations between reason and religion, both in Christianity and Islam, depended on the principles that it was possible to know something of God's nature without recourse to revelation and that the knowledge derived from these two sources is in harmony. The former principle implies that it is possible to prove God's existence, and certainly the spirit of much eighteenth century thought found this easy enough to accept. The new scientific discoveries might lead some to skepticism about miracles; but the world which it opened up could easily be seen in the terms of the famous hymn Joseph Addison wrote about the heavenly bodies:

> *In reason's ear they all rejoice,*
> *And utter forth a glorious voice,*
> *Forever singing as they shine,*
> *The hand that made us is divine.*

But Kant cut at the root of such conceptions by denying the validity of the usual arguments for the existence of God. His criticism depended on his view of knowledge. On the one hand, it is necessary for the ordering of our experience to use certain key notions, such as *cause,* which are not derived from experience, but which we bring to experience. On the other hand, it is illegitimate to use these concepts beyond the range of experience. As it were, knowledge must have two ingredients, one from without (experience) and the other from within (the categories through which we order experience). Now the attempt to trace the world back to the operation of a First Cause necessarily takes us beyond all possible experience. It is therefore illegitimate. We cannot, then, on the basis of traditional arguments assert the real existence of God.

On the other hand, Kant found the substance of religion in the conclusions which emerged from his reflections about morality. Scientific determinism, enshrined in the principle that every event has a cause, seemed to be incompatible with morality, which presupposes the freedom of the will and therefore the proposition that at least some events are uncaused. The details of Kant's subtle and somewhat obscure reconciliation of these two positions need not detain us here: suffice it to say that he went on to argue that we have an obligation to perfect virtue. But we do not, in the relatively short span of a life time, have the chance to progress to this ideal state. It is presupposed, then, by morality that there is an afterlife in which we have the opportunity to complete our moral destiny. But further, he held that the principle of justice ought to ensure that the perfectly good man is also perfectly happy. But this is certainly not manifested in experience—it would thus seem to be a further presupposition of morality that there is a God who assigns perfect happiness to men in the afterlife.

These were the ways in which Kant tried to understand religion in terms of its ethical dimension. It is interesting to note that this form of faith, which became widely influential in intellectual circles, did not include any real historical or mythological elements (the idea of atonement, for instance, did not figure as at all significant, and Christ's life was just considered as a moral example). Neither did it pay any attention to the experiential dimension of religion, while ritual could at best be a method of inculcating moral behavior. The essentials of religion were belief in God, moral freedom, and immortality.

Such was the creed that animated the *Aufklärung,* or Enlightenment, in Germany. It was the culmination of a century in which many of the intellectuals, especially in Protestant Europe, and indeed many of the clergy, had turned away from the more miraculous and experiential elements in traditional Christianity. Few would profess atheism, but belief in a God who does not intervene in events replaced the typical earlier view of the Judeo-Christian tradition, in which God was very much the Lord of history. The outbreak of the French Revolution in 1789, accompanied by more outspoken expressions of atheism and the institution of a new state cult to express men's homage to Reason, was a further sign of the wide alienation of the intellectuals from the values both of the Reformation and of Catholicism.

REACTION AGAINST RATIONALISM

The Deism of eighteenth-century England could scarcely continue to be a satisfactory expression of the needs of Christian people, partly because its acceptance was only genuinely possible for educated folk; partly because it gave too little place to the expression either of ritual or of experience. The reaction against rationalism took the form of a renewal of evangelical fervor in the eighteenth and early nineteenth century, and, in the mid-part of the nineteenth century, in a reemphasis on the ritual dimension of religion in the work and writings of the Oxford Movement. In Germany, the theologian Schleiermacher restored religious experience to the center of religious thought. We shall examine these three phases of reaction against eighteenth century "reasonableness" in turn.

The evangelical renewal, as it turned out, had its issue in the formation of a new church within the fold of Protestantism—the Methodist Church.

JOHN WESLEY AND METHODISM

The founder of the Methodist movement was John Wesley (1703-1791). While he was at Oxford he formed around him a circle of devout young people, which included his brother Charles (1707-1788). They were pious, regular attenders at the sacraments, and given to such good works as visiting the sick and prisoners in jail. The methodical way in which they kept to the observance of religious rountine resulted in their being nicknamed "Methodists" (other less attractive nicknames were the "Holy Club" and "Bible Moths")—and what was at first a nickname became the designation of the movement John Wesley and his associates started several years later. At this time, John Wesley was a "high church" Anglican in his affiliation. He was influenced by Thomas à Kempis and by William Law (1686-1761), an Anglican contemplative whose *A Serious Call to a Devout and Holy Life* stressed the importance of moral training and asceticism in the service of glorifying God in one's daily life. John Wesley's religious sentiments, however, began to alter somewhat in 1736, when he set out for the American colony of Georgia as a missionary. On the voyage out to America he became acquainted with several Moravian Brethren.

The Moravians

The Moravians were a community linked to the Lutheran Church whose doctrines and way of life had been largely shaped by the movement known as Pietism. The latter had arisen in the late seventeenth century as a way of giving new life to Lutheranism, which had tended to harden into a somewhat scholastic orthodoxy. In the eighteenth century Count Nicolaus von Zinzendorf (1700-1760) had brought about a remarkable transformation of the worship of a group of spiritual descendants of the church founded by John Huss. These Bohemian and Moravian exiles settled on his estate and were persuaded by him to enter into relations with Lutheranism. The renewed

Moravian Church had its beginning in 1727. They formed a nucleus of missionaries who travelled all over Europe and to America (Bethlehem, Pennsylvania was an important settlement founded in 1741). The Brethren cultivated an intense and emotional piety, and focussed their religious life on an intimate fellowship with Christ as Creator and Redeemer of the world.

Wesley associated himself with Moravian Brethren as soon as he came back to England. He intuitively felt that their faith offered something which the ordinary forms of Anglicanism did not. While at a meeting in Aldersgate Street in London, he experienced a profound conversion during the reading of Luther's preface to the Epistle to the Romans. "I felt I did trust in Christ, Christ alone, for salvation; and an assurance was given me that He had taken away my sins." A visit to the Moravian center at Herrnhut, presided over by the patriarchal Zinzendorf, proved less rewarding. He was treated as a child, and made to dig Zinzendorf's garden. This accent on simplicity doubtless had its virtues; but it was not altogether convincing to Wesley, who had wider hopes of the spiritual life.

These hopes began to be realized when, under the impulse of his conversion at Aldersgate Street, Wesley, together with friends, started to preach up and down the country. His fervent evangelism stressed the need for personal assurance of salvation: it was through a person's own experience that he could gain true faith. It was a time when this simple message could fall on thousands of eager ears. It was the time of the start of the great Industrial Revolution in England, when vast numbers of folk, uprooted from the countryside and their traditional ways, had flocked into the cities, where, in the textile mills and workshops, in dark slums and backstreets, a totally new and unexpected form of existence awaited them. Though Wesley's mission began before this great upheaval was fully under way, by the time of his death in 1791 the face of England had already been greatly changed.

SCHLEIERMACHER

The German theologian Friedrich Schleiermacher (1768-1834) started a revolution in theology that broke through the rationalism of the eighteenth century and gave renewed vigor to Protestant thought. Kant had defined two basic realms of experience—empirical experience that natural science investigates, and moral experience. In rationalist philosophy religion was driven out of the former realm; it had become identified solely with moral experience. But a reduction of religion to its ethical dimension could scarcely serve as the basis for a living faith. As later agnostics and humanists were to argue, one can have a consistent and sensitive morality without bringing in any beliefs about the supernatural. If religion is to be reduced to good conduct, why not just teach good conduct, and leave God out of it? Kant's attempt to solve the problems of religion by wedding it to morality, and the attempts of other rational and scholastic philosophers to establish the existence of God—if such exercises could be considered valid after Kant's subtle assault—were bound to be sterile. They made God into an intellectual hypothesis. Schleiermacher tried to steer between these twin dangers by bringing back experience into religion. In this he was undoubtedly affected by his early upbringing: he had been educated at a Moravian college and seminary where the Pietist persuasion prevailed. But Schleiermacher was a man of considerable culture and intellectual penetration. It was not possible for him to fall back on a simple view of Biblical inspiration. Therefore, in line with the movement of reaction against the Enlightenment known as the Romantic Revival, in which poetic feeling was given a prominent place in the scheme of men's apprehension of the world about them, Schleiermacher wrote his famous *Speeches on Religion,* in which he tried to show that religion depends upon and expresses the sense of the Infinite. His understanding of the Infinite is suffused with the feeling of utter dependence. Man, in this experience, feels his creatureliness. If cultivated folk (and Schleiermacher's *Speeches* were aimed at those whom he called the "cultured despisers" of religion) were beginning to take feeling and emotion seriously as a mode of apprehending reality, then they must have something to say about religious feeling. After all, religious feeling—the sense of awe, for instance—has played a prominent part in human history and in human life. It cannot be simply written off as irrelevant.

THE OXFORD MOVEMENT

The third movement of reaction against eighteenth century rationalism was the Oxford Movement. This started as an attempt to restore to the Anglican Church something of its sense of divine authority which seemed to be crumbling in the face of what the leaders of the Movement considered undue encroachment by Parliament. But the Movement went deeper than that. In emphasizing the Catholic nature of the Church it was in some degree nostalgic for medieval times, when the Church had produced many saints. It looked for a renewal of liturgical life and a restoration of the sacraments to a central place in the worship and ethos of the Church. It was, in effect, a reaffirmation of "high-church" tendencies long dormant. In its effect, the Oxford Movement created a powerful Anglo-Catholic party within the Church of England. In its sympathies with Rome it seemed dangerous to the eyes of its opponents. Perhaps not surprisingly, the Movement gave to the Roman Catholic Church one of its greatest luminaries, John Henry Newman.

The Movement essentially started in the brilliant common room of Oriel

College, Oxford, in the company surrounding a remarkable trio—John Keble (1792–1866), Edward Pusey (1800–1882), and Newman (1801–1890), who were all Fellows of Oriel. In response to a current controversy within the Church involving the suppression of ten Irish bishoprics, Keble preached a sermon charging the state with interfering with the Church's apostolic rights. Shortly after, an association formed for the purpose of maintaining the traditions of the Church. In the same year, Newman began the composition of the first *Tracts for the Times.* The use which the Oxford Movement made of tracts, which were often brilliantly, incisively, and learnedly written, led to their being dubbed the Tractarians.

For many, the Movement was too Catholic in its flavor. The impulse it gave to the restoration of ceremonial—the pomp and incense, the images and candles, the colorful vestments and the hanging crucifixes—all these savored of the Romanism that the Evangelicals violently opposed. There were questions as to whether some of the new ritual practices were legal: the Book of Common Prayer was ambiguous on a number of points. Anglo-Catholicism found itself faced with a series of tiresome legal actions. But the Movement was not merely the object of Evangelical hostility. Its medievalism rankled those of liberal intellectual opinions. Thus the Tractarians called down wrath on their heads from very different quarters. And yet, in terms of allegiance, their cause prospered. Moreover, the Anglo-Catholics were active in social work. Some of the best slum parishes owed their success to the enthusiasm of the Movement with its emphasis on the twin ideals of richness of ceremony and poverty of life. Newman, with some of his friends, converted to the Roman allegiance, chiefly because they doubted that the Church of England could legitimately claim to be in apostolic succession while existing in schism with Rome (later the fuller awareness of the tradition of Eastern Orthodoxy was to strengthen the Anglican position). Newman brought his prodigious learning and energizing example to the intellectual and spiritual reawakening in the Catholic Church, then emerging from a long period of stagnation. In 1879 he was given a Cardinal's hat by Pope Leo XIII. The same year saw the publication of Leo's encyclical *Aeterni Patris,* which by recommending the serious study of St. Thomas Aquinas to the clergy, gave a much needed stimulus to theology and philosophy in the following period.

BIBLICAL CRITICISM

The nineteenth century, though it nurtured these various movements of renewal, also brought Christianity to face the biggest intellectual crisis of its history. The Bible, though not always regarded as absolute literal truth, had been regarded for many centuries as the inspired word of God. People might differ as to the mechanism whereby the writers of the scriptures received inspiration from God, but it was generally agreed that here was a body of writing that showed forth in detail God's revelation. The authority of the Bible was supposedly guaranteed by the miracles that verified the teachings of Christ and of the prophets. Protestantism had even stronger reasons for this veneration of the Bible. The Bible was the rock of authority upon which Protestant Reformation rested. It was particularly important to those of Evangelical persuasion. For such folk the study and searching of the scriptures constituted, and still constitutes, the central way in which they exercise their minds in the service of God. Nor was the Catholic position altogether different: the operation of inspiration was officially described, in the latter part of the nineteenth century, as happening by the "dictation of the Holy Spirit" (*Spiritu Sancto dictanti*).

In view of all these facts, the methods of modern scientific history, which had their rise in Germany, had an explosive effect when they were turned on to the biblical material. The critical study of biblical literature called in question a number of cherished beliefs. It threw doubt on the veracity of some of the incidents recorded in the scriptures. It played down the miraculous side of biblical history. It brought to light something of the long process whereby the writings had been compiled and edited. It questioned the possibility of framing an accurate portrait of the historical Jesus. A notable scholar such as David Strauss (1808–1874) could argue that the supernatural elements found in the Gospels were due to legends which arose in the period between the death of Jesus and the second century A.D. Scholars associated with the Tübingen School—founded by F. C. Baur (1792–1860), and influenced by the thought of the philosopher Hegel (1770–1831)—argued that there was not one unbroken line of development in the Christian tradition stretching back through history to the figure of Jesus himself. They suggested that the earliest group of Jesus' followers had differed sharply after his death, that the older disciples, under the leadership of Peter, were deeply opposed to the teachings of Paul. Only later were the divergent emphases reconciled in the synthesis that formed the basis of Catholicism. A result of such speculation was to attribute much of the shape of later faith to Paul rather than to Christ.

Many of the conclusions of the early biblical historians can now be challenged, but their contribution is undeniable. They opened up the field to dispassionate enquiry. The Bible was no longer a document to be accepted without questioning. It was a pattern of documents, woven together by men of varying backgrounds.

DARWIN AND EVOLUTION

All this was reinforced by the outbreak of controversy over evolution and the theory propounded by Charles Darwin in his *Origin of Species* (1859). Evolution challenged belief in the Bible in two ways. First it did not seem to square with a literal interpretation of Genesis. Second, it provided evidence (amplified by further evidence from the new study of geology) that the time-scale theologians propounded for the history of the world was hopelessly wrong. For instance, it had been calculated, by totting up the generations described in the Bible, that the creation occurred in 4004 B.C. This reckoning would have to be false if evolutionary theory were true. Finally, Darwinism challenged the traditional Christian concept of man's place in the universe (and man's place vis à vis God) by blurring the line between man and beast: not only was there a certain shock to human pride in the proposition that men evolved from monkeys, but the theory seemed to deny the Biblical view that God made man "a little lower than the angels." All these factors help to explain why most Christians were at first strongly opposed to the theory. For that matter, quite a number of scientists were sceptical too. In the course of controversy, however, it became fairly plain that Darwinism, whatever one might say about the particular mechanisms it postulated to explain the emergence of new species, was in broad outline inescapably correct. Though Christians might hold that in the emergence of man something extra and supernatural was added by God to man's animal heritage, few Christians would now deny the existence of a physical link between men and animals. It would also be true to say that the initially hostile reaction to evolutionary theory displayed by a number of prominent churchmen contributed to the increasing alienation of intellectuals from the Church in the latter half of the nineteenth century (a movement which we shall describe in the next chapter).

Because of the furor caused over evolutionary theory (and for other reasons), it came to be thought by many intellectuals in the latter part of the nineteenth century that religion and science were necessarily in conflict. Undoubtedly there were many on the Christian side who rejected what plainly was fact. Those who took the Bible literally were almost bound to come into collision with scientific education, even if they numbered among themselves some scientists. But the impression of conflict was largely due to misunderstandings. Christianity did absorb evolutionary theory into its system, even if this gave a new perspective to human history. There was nothing in the physical sciences that conflicted with the notion that the world was created by God. Miracles could not be rejected on simply scientific grounds, for one cannot show that breaches of laws of nature due to supernatural causes do not occur by affirming that science is concerned to investigate laws of nature and regularities in the universe. The attack on miracles rather has to be based on philosophical reasoning, and can be responded to in the same manner. Nevertheless, the obscurantism of Christians of all parties, though by no means all Christians, did tend to bring about a certain alienation between scientific thinkers and religious men. The effects have remained present in contemporary Christianity.

WORLDWIDE MISSIONS

Though these events and controversies weakened Christianity in Europe, and though the continuing process of industrialization reinforced the secularization of society, the nineteenth century saw a phenomenal spread of the faith through the activities of the missionaries. This was the great era of Protestant missions. Nearly every country in the world outside Europe was penetrated by zealous and dedicated men, from England, America, and from the European countries. They brought education, medicine, and the Gospel to folk all over the globe. Largely through their work, Christianity became the single largest religious force south of the Sahara; there are few educated Africans today who have not felt its impact in one way and another. Often, it is true, Christianity became too easily identified with Western values and Western civilization. But in process of time, it has become an indigenous faith in many parts of the world.

William Carey

In India, William Carey (1761-1834), a Baptist cobbler, set a new pattern in rather sporadic mission work undertaken toward the end of the eighteenth century. His career helps to illustrate some of the principal features of Protestant missionary activity in that country. Feeling a divine call, he helped form the Baptist Missionary Society, and set sail for Bengal. There he was hampered by the fact that the East India Company disapproved of missionaries. The Company felt that the Gospel might upset the political fabric on which its power rested. After a time in the Company's territories, Carey removed to Serampore, then a Danish settlement. He founded a College for the training of Indian clergy. He industriously if not always too efficiently set about the translation of the scriptures. He and his associates studied the life of the Indian people and their religion. Piety and sympathy were prominent in their attitudes. For Carey, then, Christianity was something which could draw out the best in the native genius. It was not there to destroy Indian life, but to complete and purify it. The opposition of the Company illustrated the gap between the interests of the ruling power and the missionary. This persisted long after the Mutiny, when India came more directly under the Crown. Though missions were no longer excluded, there was relatively little contact between the administrators and the missionaries. The latter in many ways were closer to the pulse of the people, even if, as time went on, a renascent Hinduism was to identify religion with national aspirations.

The T'ai P'ing Rebellion

In China, following the Treaty of Nanking in 1842, which opened the country up to Westerners, missionary societies began to make slow headway in conversions. In 1853, the T'ai P'ing (literally "Great Peace") rebellion broke out with the storming of the city of Nanking. The movement had certain Christian features. Its leader, Hung Hsin-Ch'uan, a Cantonese, had been influenced by a Baptist missionary, and the revolt which he instigated had the threefold aim of ridding China of the Manchu dynasty, destroying idols, and wiping out the use of opium. A number of missionaries were convinced, despite misgivings aroused by certain of the T'ai P'ing practices, such as polygamy, that here was a movement which was Christian at heart. Had it been successful—and it appeared highly probable that the Manchus would crumble before the T'ai P'ing onslaught, especially because of the excellent discipline of its adherents —the modern history of China would have been very different indeed. A kind of Christianity (not very orthodox, perhaps) would have become the imperial faith. As it was, the progress of Christianity continued only slowly, though with revolutionary effects. The introduction of Western education and science, not to mention liberal democratic ideals, was largely the work of the missions. This acted as a ferment in the Chinese mind and was a factor in the overthrow of the Manchus in 1911 and the emergence of modern China.

These are but glimpses of the wide and continuing work of Christianity, both Catholic and Protestant, in the world mission field. Though it could not be claimed that Christianity was statistically a great success, in the Far East and India at least (and still less in the Muslim countries, for Christians have nearly everywhere there remained a small minority), the conversion of Asian and African Christians has been fruitful both for Christianity and for their countries. Christian ideals of social service and love, though not always strongly in evidence in the so-called Christian countries, were often embodied in the heroic work of the missionaries, and this gave new aspiration to countries which, like medieval Europe, had become too accustomed to poverty and disease. Education, though it may sometimes have alienated men from their national roots, also introduced the fruits of modern knowledge—and the heady wine of European political thought. Asian and African Christians have had much to offer the Church. Their viewpoint reminds the West that Christianity is not just an offshoot of European culture: they have been able to criticize Western values that Christians may have come too readily to accept. Above all they have provided a strong impetus to the movement to unite the churches. Nothing is more puzzling and vexatious to an Indian Christian, for instance, than to see the doctrinal squabbles which have origins in European history brought over to India to cause divisions there.

The Church of South India

It was in India that the first union of churches in which Anglicans and the Free Churches have come together. Formed in 1947, the Church of South India includes former Anglicans, Methodists, Presbyterians, Congregationalists, Dutch Reformed, and members of the Basel Missions. The last four of these bodies had already united well before. This experiment represents an exciting foretaste of further possibilities of reunion within Christendom. It is significant that such a move should come from the "mission field": Asia is contributing something of its own to the West—the missionary work is reversed. Indeed, the whole trend of modern missions is changing the narrow sense of the term itself: missions overseas are independent churches, rather than offshoots of organizations from Europe or America. The paternalism of Western Christians is no longer valid.

POST-REFORMATION CHRISTIANITY

Christianity has passed through many vicissitudes since the Reformation. But the withering away of Christianity, which might have been predicted in the eighteenth century, has by no means occurred. It remains a living stream in people's experience, a stream that shows signs of broadening and deepening. In the interplay of denominations, different facets of the faith have glittered forth. In the reforms, new accesses of power have come to it. Now, in the hopes of reunion, it may be possible to realize the mingling together of the virtues of the different branches of the Christian Church. For Christians our present time is a time of challenge to the faith. Marxism and Humanism and the renascent Eastern faiths in their diverse ways present alternatives and challenges to Christianity, but it is an exciting period, precisely because so much is in flux, so much is puzzling, so much is new. We shall try to see in the last chapter what this situation augurs for the future.

RELIGIONS OF THE AMERICAS

Chapter 11

THE AMERICAN EXPERIENCE

THE DEVELOPMENT of religion in America has been unique and also influential. This is partly because the United States has pioneered the separation of Church and State, and so has been a vital force in religious toleration. Yet, paradoxically, it has been more fervently religious than most of Europe and has exhibited a great vigor in Protestantism. At the same time, the United States, and to some extent other countries in the hemisphere, such as Canada and the Argentine, have drawn on a wide variety of immigrant cultures and religions—Chinese and Japanese Buddhists on the West coast, Blacks with their African heritage and sad but spiritually powerful experience of slavery, Hispanics with their special kind of Catholicism, Jews from Central Europe with their vibrant culture and divisions, and so on.

Also indigenous religions made their contributions despite the overwhelming impact of Spanish and Northern European conquerors. Let us look first at one or two of these cultures preexisting the conquests that followed on Columbus' discovery of the New World in 1492. I choose the Aztecs and the Plains Indians.

AZTEC RELIGION

When in 1519 Cortés and his followers intruded into the Aztec empire and later, when they overthrew it, they were indeed astonished at the riches, beauty, and organization of this amazing and unexpected civilization. The city from which Moctezuma II controlled a great empire was compared favorably by the explorers to great centers in Europe, such as Rome and Constantinople. The white buildings, the ordered streets, the bustling markets, the fruits, vegetables, turkeys, and all manner of produce, the floating gardens, the great pyramid-like temples, the causeways across the shimmering lake, the backcloth of great mountains, snow-tipped in the blue heat of the rich valley, the phalanxes of soldiers, the wondrous plumed and ornamented dress of the elite, the majesty of the king himself—these combined to strike the conquerors-to-be with awe. That Cortés,

THE AMERICAS AND THE PACIFIC

with four hundred men, was able to crush this imperial system and superimpose Catholic Spain upon it is astonishing. But it had much to do with the king's religious misreading of the nature of this strange white leader who came to him from the Eastern sea like a god.

The newcomers were repelled, however, by the blood and stench of sacrifices and the wild appearance of the priests who wielded obsidian knives to cut open the chests of victims and reach into the bloody mess to pull forth the still-twitching heart as sacrifice and sacred meal. The Aztecs' reliance on great numbers of humans to kill for the gods was not only unnerving; it was, from the Spanish point of view, inspired by the devil. But in most other respects the culture they encountered, in what came to be called Mexico City but which was then known as Tenochtitlan (Place of the Rock Cactus), was more attractive. It was a rich prize.

The Aztec Synthesis: A Ritual Cosmology

Aztec religion had both a spiritual and a material meaning. At the human level it brought together a rich heritage from two earlier civilizations—the Olmec (c. 500 B.C.-1150 A.D.) and the Toltec (900-1200 A.D.) The Aztecs, who came from northwest Mexico or perhaps farther north from what is now the southwest section of the United States, had for four centuries moved through and partially conquered areas with cultures having a higher urban civilization than their own, and had learned from these cultures in setting up their city at Tenochtitlan. They had in the early fifteenth century established a powerful empire and complex society in which many of the myths and practices of other peoples were incorporated. The gods of the conquered culture were arranged in a hierarchy and often identified with the Aztec gods, so that the Aztecs could justify their widening rule. At the apex of the system were the rites of the great temple (the Templo Mayor, parts of which have recently been excavated in Mexico City). This was a massive pyramid surmounted by the shrines of the two great gods Huitzilopochtli and Tlaloc, respectively the "Hummingbird of the Left" and the rain god. On this summit victims were slain for sacrifice. It was in part the need for victims, particularly brave warriors captured in battle, which fed the expansion of the empire.

Huitzilopochtli was the deity of the Sun, and the Aztecs saw themselves as Children of the Sun, and of their mother Earth. All life is brought forth and nourished by this divine couple. But this orientation to the sun meant something much deeper. The Aztecs conceived the age in which they lived as being that of the fifth sun. According to Aztec cosmology, there had been four previous ages at the end of each of which the human race had been wiped out, and the universe had been overcome with catastrophe. The five ages correspond to five "world directions," namely East, West, North, South, and Center. The universe was conceived as having as its central structure a cross, the intersection of the two axes being the midpoint. Now this cosmology bore a message of pessimism, for the catastrophe of the four previous ages was liable to occur in the present era. Priestly activity and above all the human sacrifices were intended to stave off doom by keeping the Sun alive by offering him the throbbing hearts of warriors.

This was but the summit of an earthly ritual order in which the cooperation between humans and the gods helped to maintain the cosmic order. What the cosmology highlighted, however, was the pervasive threat of chaos and death. This gloomy outlook belied the rich and beautiful life of the cities of the empire: the markets, the festivals, the temples, the varied and colorful dress of the nobles, the wealth of sacred sculptures, the traditional games. These existed amidst a rigid order which discouraged disobedience and individual initiative, and at the same time provided a stable and satisfying structure of culture and everyday life. Yet always there was the threat, and sacrifice could help to ward off that final collapse. Being sacrificed promised heaven to the victims, who thus typically treated their death with stoicism and died with honor. Above the earthly plane were thirteen heavens, the summit being a region of delicate, frozen air, where lived the companions of the Sun, the blessed warriors who died in battle and on the sacrificial altar, merchants who died in distant places, and mothers dying at the birth of the first son. Such rewards gave people courage. Others, who did not merit the summit, could migrate to the paradise of Tlaloc, while most of the dead wandered downwards across the nine rivers marking the divisions of the underworld, and in the last place they would fade away and disappear altogether.

The present age was founded by Quetzalcoatl, the noble Feathered Serpent, a great hero and now identified with Venus, the Evening Star. Legend had it that he had revived the couple who had been last of the old human race of the Fourth Age by sprinkling them with his own blood. Blood was seen as the substance of life, a widespread notion among various peoples. So Quetzalcoatl, in an important sense, constituted their life-essence, as he was also founder and creator of culture. Legend also suggested that Quetzalcoatl, who had left the Toltec empire over five centuries before the arrival of the Spaniards in 1507, would return to demand his kingdom back from the Aztecs, who had usurped it. He would, moreover, return from the sea and the eastern direction. So, ironically, the gifted but myth-bound Moctezuma II, high-priest as well as ruler of the Children of the Sun, fancied that Cortés was indeed this pale and bearded divine human. If he could hold Cortés off he could delay the handover until after his own death. Otherwise, Quetzalcoatl/Cortés really had a right to the empire. This belief unmanned Moctezuma and substantially contributed to his capture and death, and the downfall and destruction of his holy city and wide-reaching empire.

Not only were the main patterns of history ordained by the cosmological structure of the world, but individual lives were also largely determined by fate. And while Aztec life was well-ordered and morally governed, much attention had to be paid to omens and other ways of seeing into the future. Humans have a thirst for knowledge, for good or ill, of their fate. It was into this hierarchy of forces that the Aztec was born. His culture summed up some of the great achievements of earlier civilizations, Olmec, Toltec, Mixtec, and so on. In a way the Aztec sense of doom was justified, for their religion not only failed to ward off the Spaniards but by an irony helped to cause the collapse. It was Quetzalcoatl's last gift to his people.

Picturing the universe in the shape of a large cross, the notion that the first humans are given life by God, and the idea of sacrifice were motifs which could prepare the way for the Catholic revolution which was about to overtake Mexico. The death of the Aztec empire ended a millennium-and-a-half of traditional civilization in Central America. It opened the way for the overcoming of the Inca Empire in the South, and for the transformation of Mayan culture, itself heir, though obscurely, to a great past.

Classical Mayan civilization lasted from about 300 to 900 A.D., and collapsed for unknown reasons—great sites such as that of Chitzen-Itza in Yucatan were found partially entangled in rising jungle. The area was later occupied by a militaristic culture analogous to that of the Aztecs. Part of our knowledge of the classic Mayan civilization is gained indirectly from the *Popol Vuh,* a work incorporating post-classical mythology and cosmology, which was written in a Mayan language after the time of the Spanish conquest. The mixed Mayan-Toltec rites of the period after the year 1000 reflected some of the harsh features of Aztec sacrifice. But the chief feature of classical Mayan life was its amazing astronomical and mathematical refinement, far in advance of the Aztecs.

This expertise was part of a general view that humans must submit to the preordained forces of the universe, the most vital of which is time. Indeed, time was seen as divine, as were the great segments of time or cycles of successive worlds, each of which began with a creation and ended with destruction. The calendar was divided into successive periods of 20, 360, 7200, 144,000, and 23,040,000,000 days. The second of these formed the basis of an eighteen-month solar year to which five unlucky days were added. These "odd days," of course, bring the total up to the 365 days of Western calendars, which have become virtually universal. The Mayan astronomers could also intercalate days from time to time to bring this sequence into accord with observed solar cycles.

These and other aspects of Mayan lore enabled the priesthood to make detailed predictions about favorable and unfavorable times to do things, and mathematical knowledge of this sort was integrated with a complex religion of sacrifices of animals, birds, insects, honey, jade, and so forth to the gods of nature, especially the Maize God, on whom the welfare of the cities depended. But ultimately the most powerful force in the cosmos is time—unending, cyclical, and detailed. Thus, mathematics became a sacred science (as it did in Greece with Pythagoras), for it was by the use of mathematics that men could enter into a relationship with the deity, and master the seasons during which to perform the plantings, celebrations, ascetic fasts, and other activities which filled each sacred year.

THE CLASSICAL URBAN EXPERIENCE

In this brief voyage round the varied urban cultures of pre-Columbian America we notice the recurrent theme that each empire requires a priestly order to understand the cosmic order. The better the cosmic order was understood, the better these complex societies, which developed largely because of maize and a number of other domesticated crops, could ward off chaos and extend their scope and power. In each, citizens were expected to fit into an elaborate class system, and laws dictated an obedient and god-fearing ethic. This is summed up best, perhaps, in the Inca maxim which could help people onto the path to become companions of the Sun in the upper heaven: "Do not steal; do not lie; do not be lazy." It is an older time's work ethic: truth and honesty would help maintain both the cosmic and the civic order.

But perhaps for us the best way of trying to gain access to these old pre-Catholic experiences is to look at the wonderful art of Central and South America: the numinous angular jaguars, the Mexican gods and warriors in painting and stone. What can it have been like to see the vast gold image of the Sun in the holy and haunted great temple in Cuzco, where the great blocks of stone were so smoothly fitted in its 350-meter walled circumference and where shone the gold ikons of corn and animals and gods in the Golden Enclosure? But these glories were to be pillaged by conquerors whose whole ideology was different. Most of the golden and silver gods were shipped away to Spain, and many of the illuminated codices were burned as works of the devil. A new civilization was to be made, but as we shall see later some of the older experience was blended, in altered form, in the new Hispanic Catholicism; Catholic saints were to occupy the holy places of the older gods.

In North America, the populations were smaller when the conquerors came, and the effects of conquest were rather different, though equally traumatic.

NATIVE AMERICAN TRADITIONS:
THE PLAINS INDIANS AND OTHERS

For various reasons Native American religions of the plains and of the eastern woodlands converge in certain ways. Indeed, the plains themselves became a melting pot of various nations, partly because the advent of the horse drew to the plains and prairies peoples who could live fatly off the teeming buffalo. For once the Indians mastered the skills of riding the "mystery dogs" which had escaped from the corrals of the Spaniards and bred into strong mustangs, they had an incomparable aid to hunting. The hunt displaced much of the agriculture which had come up from the Southeast and had brought beans and maize to the lower Midwest. The second factor was the pressure of the whites spreading from the East. Peoples of differing languages—Siouan, Algonquian, Athabascan, and Uto-Aztecan—learned to communicate.

As with many other peoples engaged in hunting, their religion involved methods of increasing the stock of game, and of relating their survival to cosmic powers. Physical prowess was important both in war and in the hunt, among males. To some degree this is reflected in the importance of the dance, particularly the Sun Dance, in their religion. By contrast, it is interesting to note how in white society dancing has become secularized and largely separated from religion (save for recent revivals in Pentecostalism), either as social dancing or as artistic dancing (ballet, ice-skating, etc.). For the Native American dancing illustrates some powerful themes in the whole nature of religion, and this can be seen by looking at a circumstantial account of a Sun Dance among the Oglala (who are Sioux of the northern plains), written by Thomas Tyon.[1]

Briefly, the narrative is as follows: if a man wishes his sick child or wife to be cured, or if he has survived a battle, he may vow a Sun Dance. He needs to take advice about the details from an expert who is pure, that is, in a ritually clean state. He and others who may join him must set up a tepee and purify themselves in the sweat bath, a mode of cleansing ritually more effective than ordinary washing. With the invocation of certain ritual utterances and acts a *wakan,* or numinous tree or pole, must be prepared. This *wakan* forms the focus around which the dance takes place. The dance may last for four days or more, and during it the dancers may rush forth from time to time to give away gifts. All this takes place within a specially constructed lodge, and is witnessed by members of the tribe or more generally by people from far and near who come to see the ceremony. In the lodge are certain sacred objects, notably a buffalo head and a holy pipe filled with tobacco. The holy man leads the singing,

[1] Reproduced in Sam D. Gill, ed., *Native American Traditions, Sources and Interpretations* (Belmont, California: Wadsworth Publishing Co., 1983).

and the participants sing on, without water or food, during the duration of the Sun Dance.

There are several vital themes here. The Sun is the focus of the religion of agriculturalists, in the Southeast and indeed also in Central American culture, which is based in great measure on corn. But the Sun Dance also represents a warrior and hunting culture to which, among other things, the head of the buffalo bears witness. The holy tree is the center of the world, the *axis mundi,* which connects heaven and earth. It is charged, therefore, with solemn power. This accounts for the ascetic and ritual aspects of preparation for the Sun Dance. Human beings must purify themselves in order to approach the Divine. The Divine Being, or Great Spirit, in much of Native American thinking, is conveyed to us through the symbol of the sun. This practice is similar in the Hindu tradition, where a morning invocation of the sun is the proper manner to start the day, as the celestial light rises in the east, reminding us of the Supreme Light. So the Sun of the Sun Dance is divine fructifying Power, for the sun causes the whole earth to send forth its fertile shoots and feed its living beings. The attitude is well put by N. Scott Momaday, talking about an old friend of his father:

> My father says that every morning when Chaney was there as a guest he would get up in the first light, paint his face, go outside, face the east, and bring the sun out of the horizon. He would pray aloud to the rising sun. He did that because it was appropriate that he should do that. . . . He understood the sun, within a more formal religious context, similar to the way someone else understands the presence of a deity. And in the face of that recognition, he acted naturally and appropriately. Through the medium of prayer he returned some of his strength to the sun. He did this every day.[2]

He sees the Sun, and yet it is not just our sun. For the American Indian view of nature is different from that of many typical whites. White people look upon nature both as something different from themselves and different (if they believe in God) from God. But the Sun Dance exhibits a kind of continuity. Consider the buffalo, and other animals important to the Native American imagination. Powerful animals exhibit both spiritual and physical powers, just as the medicine man and shaman do, and as do the grains of tobacco in the sacred pipe. We do not quite have the language for this sense of powers within and beyond material things. Although great variations exist in the worldviews of even one major group of people, such as the Plains Indians, we might think of their outlook as a vision of Spirit taking many natural forms. Nature is a series of powers,

[2] Walter Holden Capps, ed., *Seeing with a Native Eye* (New York: Harper & Row, 1976), p. 96.

dominated perhaps by the Sun, and experienced by people variously. In the Indian mind we are immersed amid these powers, for we, like other living beings, possess mysterious sacredness.

One of the powers we possess is the use of our intelligence and feelings to insert a certain order into things. This order helps us influence and react to the other powers around us. But the order is not just mental; it is not a map or a theory. Rather, it is an order which dynamically includes us as purified in the sweat lodge or as reminiscing about our dreams and visions, which so mysteriously well up in our world and allow us to see its inward side, and not just its colored surface. We each see ourselves as spinning energy into and out of our own beings around the symbolic center of this cosmos and multiformed expression of Spirit that is the world. We know too that we have, after all, limited concerns, for child or wife or battle or the buffalo hunt.

The Vision Quest

The ceremony of the Sun Dance, with its use of sweat lodges and physical exhaustion, incorporates a central theme in much of the religion of early North America—the visionary life of the individual. For one's experience of the spirits, either as an individual—through vivid dreams, for example, or by ascetic practices at puberty and at other important phases of life—or collectively—among shamans, for example—was widely regarded as the central ingredient of spiritual knowledge. It is true that the expert might have to know more formal things, such as the complex procedures (as we saw above) of the Sun Dance or the right rituals in a healing process. But often a person's expertise was itself dependent on his or her being "called," that is, directed toward the life of sanctity and power by visions.

Thus, visions might tell the young warrior to look to a specific guardian spirit, often taking the form of an animal—buffalo, elk, hawk, thundering eagle (the thunderbird), bear, rabbit, and even mice or insects. Such a spirit might also approach in human form. The lonely boy seeking the visions which would protect his life and give it purpose—sitting through days and nights under sun and stars, on a rock on the edge of great woods and gazing toward some twisting river, hearing the leaves rustle and the birds sing and animals snort and growl around him and the wind howl in the blue and cloud-driven sky—might come to assemble a number of deep messages, of the hunt and of medicine. After a vision, a number of items might be collected for a medicine bundle, wrapped in a piece of buffalo hide and hung in the tent, ready for esoteric ritual use to cure the sick. And if no vision came? Maybe a friend would share the power of his, for in a sense visions were not subjective experiences but a part of life continuous with the world "out there." They were specially bonded to the person, but they were also part of that "inwardness of the outer" that helped (and helps) to constitute the Indian worldview. The elk and the eagle were elk-spirit and eagle-spirit, fragments too of world-spirit, that which lives in all things around us and in ourselves.

So we see that the heart of much Native American religion is the vision. Because vision is rooted in experience, much in their religion revolves around the experiential dimension. Experience is strong in the hunt, in war, in puberty, in childbirth, and in medicine. But it is integrated in various ways into given societies.

Tobacco and other substances are used as a means of receiving visions among the Plains and other Indians. This widespread tobacco use is a sign of the importance of visions. (The spread of the vision-generating peyote in modern times indicates the continued importance of the sacred use of such substances as a natural extension of the quest for visions.) The visions provide a means, in the case of the tobacco pipe, of cementing bonds between men as the peaceful sensations are shared. The visions are part of the process whereby humans hope together or alone to break through the crust of the world and see into its dynamic and spirit-soaked depths.

Priests and Rituals in the Southwest

Shamanism was widespread among hunting people, but where agriculture and pastoral pursuits predominated, priests became more important than shamans. The priests among the Hopis of the Southwest United States, for example, made use of some of the shamanistic techniques of asceticism and ecstasy. But they were primarily concerned with a more orderly and formal approach to the complicated rituals of a corn-growing society. In this they resembled the Aztecs and Maya, with whom the Pueblo Indians were culturally connected.

Among the Zuni of New Mexico, the priestly fraternities prepare themselves, in hidden cult rooms containing altars and other sacred equipment, for the dances which will help to ensure the rain. The Hopi snake and antelope societies likewise put on complex dancing festivals to bring forth fertility. The snake society uses live snakes, held in the mouth, as part of the procedure for inducing rain. The antelope society makes ritual use of ears of corn to portend the harvest. As the name implies, Pueblo Indians live in pueblos or large villages, and we see in their life a synthesis of pre-urban and hunting cultures. The Navajo, who raised sheep, cattle, and horses after the introduction of these animals by the Spaniards also have an elaborate ritual life which includes the use of sandpainting. This painting reminds us that what we in modern society call art is in many traditional societies itself a spiritual activity. Parts of the material world, such as sand and pigments, are maneuvered to produce a potent order. This order is depicted through dynamic representations and incarnations of beneficent or malevolent forces.

Although the Southwest peoples were and are primarily given to raising grain and keeping animals, they shared too in the virtually universal hunting patterns of North America. Hence we see a fusion of both priestly and shamanistic elements in their outlook. But we can scarcely understand hunting cultures without seeing how religion could be a bridge between humans and nature: the most important capacity of North American shamans was to see where animals, fish, and birds abounded. But in this their outlook was partly conditioned by the myths of their culture.

The Inuit and the Myth of Sedna

One of the most vital of far northern narratives is the myth of Sedna. The tale has both a surface meaning and a deeper one. Sedna ends up in the tale as spiritual mistress of animals (corresponding to the master of animals found in many cultures). As such, she is the source of much of Inuit life, and she shows how the animal population represents one of the sacred powers with whom humans are in so frequent contact.

Sedna is the beautiful daughter of a widower. She is wooed by a fulmar, an Arctic bird, who promises her a lovely dwelling and wondrous furs in the land of the birds. She rejects her numerous Inuit suitors and sets off with the plausible fulmar, but when she reaches his home she finds it miserable: a structure covered with fish scales and riddled with holes, with little better than tough walrus hide to lie upon. After a year or so her father comes to see her, and she greets him with joy, begging him to take her home. He kills the fulmar and sets off with Sedna in his boat. But when the other birds find their fellow's corpse they set off and attack the old man. In terror he offers his daughter to the angry birds, pushing her overboard. She clings to the side of the boat, but he chops off the joints of her two first fingers, which swim away, transformed into whales. Her other fingers, successively chopped off, become other sea beasts. In a storm, the fulmars call off their attack. Her father allows Sedna into the boat again, but she vows revenge, and after they arrive home she gets the dogs to bite off the old man's hands and feet. He curses himself and her and the dogs, and the ground opens up and swallows them all. They now live at the bottom of the ocean, where Sedna rules over the sea animals that are in an important sense part of her.

Throughout the Native American world the strength of narratives has persisted—there are myths of the trickster culture hero (i.e., one who brings elements of culture to the human race or to the tribe), of the way death came into the world, of the origins of each nation, of the true nature of the white man, of the creation, of the places and the plants and the living creatures, and ultimately of the nature of the Divine.

North America: The Doctrinal Dimension

The nature of the Divine is depicted in different ways in the many cultures of the Native Americans, but some common themes can be identified. The descent of Sedna to the bottom of the ocean reminds us of a motif of creation myths: that of the Creator sending an animal down to the bottom of the sea to bring up mud out of which the world is fashioned. This presents in symbolic terms the notion that Creation occurs by somehow plucking order and solidity out of chaos. More striking than this theme of the Earth Diver, known too to Hindu and other Asian myth, is that of the Spider who spins the cosmos out of himself. This again is a figurative way of presenting the notion of creation out of nothing (or nothing other than God's own substance). It goes along with another theme, that all the portions of our world, the waters, the trees, the wind, the mountains, and so on are really parts of the Divine body. Ultimately such ideas can be developed into a form of panentheism, or "Everything-in-God-ism."

Another North American way to look on the Divine is as the Supreme Spirit or High God. This is by no means universal in traditional Native American religion, but it is important in many areas, such as Northern California and among the Algonkins. The latter see the Divine Being as Kitshi Manitou, or Great Spirit, or simply as Manitou, the Spirit. But, as in other religions, such a high god generally has chiefly a supervisory capacity, entrusting the daily tasks to other deities such as the Sun and the Moon. Consequently, ritual may not be directed to the one Divine Being, but toward the more immediate spirits with whom human beings have dealings. So the universe can be perceived as a crowd of living forces, dominated by great powers and at the ultimate level presided over by Spirit.

Religious cosmology often described this universe as a great dwelling built around a central pillar (e.g., among circumpolar folk), pole, or tree, the *axis mundi*. It was sometimes thought that this axis penetrated upward to the highest sphere, that of the ultimate Divine Being. In this way, by means of such earth-bound rituals as the Sun Dance, which revolved around a sacred pole, humans had contact not just with the Sun but also with the Great One, of whom the Sun is a secondary offshoot.

The Native American Ethical Dimension: I-Thou

Even hunting is not, in the final analysis, merely hunting. It is a transaction with strange powers, with Life itself. Thus whale-hunters of the Northwest must learn the lore of the great sea-beasts and how they came into being, and implore the help of the Earth-Mother who aids them in a struggle with the king of the ocean. The bear-hunter of the northern forests must address himself to the bear-spirit, and treat the creatures he hunts and kills with dignity and a sense of kinship. A powerful sense of interdependence gives the traditional cultures ethical restraint in dealing with nature. To borrow the language of Martin Buber, there is an "I-Thou" relationship between the denizens, both living and non-living, and the world about them.

So a kind of personalism exists in much of the Native American ethos. But it is not the individualism of the white people, because the other great motif, apart from the sense of the personal reality of the forces about and inside us, is the importance of relationship. These points are well put by Joseph Epes Brown when he draws attention to the fact that a person's name is typically secret in these cultures. You do not present yourself to society as an individual. Brown also notes how the trans-human I-Thou relationship to the natural world is captured in the formula uttered at the end of a Lakota pipe-smoking session: "We are all related"—meaning not just people but everything else as well.[3]

Consequently, just as we have ceremonious and ritual dealings with one another, so there must be such a ceremonious relationship to all that we come into contact with. It is not appropriate, therefore, to talk of human life in a largely technical way. We live in the midst of spirit.

The Native American Worldview and the White Challenge

The Native Americans, institutionalized in tribes and kin groups and scattered across a wide continent and a whole hemisphere, were due for some bitter shocks with the coming of European conquerors. The collapse of the great empires of Central and South America, the conquest of the North American continent from East to West, the wars, the experiences of serfdoms and reservations, the admixture of cultures, were all to have profound effects. New religions were to emerge and, in North America, a pan-Indian consciousness developed. We shall later see some of the major developments which have laid their stamp upon modern times, both in North and South America.

COLONIAL EMPIRES

The Spanish and the Portuguese (in Brazil) were grandiose in their designs. The New World was to be a glorious new empire in which Catholicism was to be the universal religion. They had little regard for Indian religion, which they considered an expression of barbarism or, worse, the influence

---

[3] Capps, ed., *Seeing With a Native Eye*, p. 32.

of the Devil. But the Church did supply something important in place of the religious and cultural traditions of the past—a new kind of assurance of the possibility of salvation. The Indians were, moreover, largely championed by the religious orders and by such outstanding individuals as Bartolomé de las Casas (1474–1566). A Dominican whose account of the plight of the Indian in the New World had a strong effect on European consciousness, he helped to stimulate the Spanish imperial government's "new laws" promulgated to regulate the relations between Spaniards and Indians and to protect the latter while ensuring that labor was duly supplied to the conquerors.

The paternalism of the Church had its most vigorous expression in the chains of missions, which taught new skills, such as agriculture, weaving, and painting to the Indians. The missions were extensive—they stretched from the upper Amazon basin to Paraguay, and from eastern Bolivia to the region of the River Plate, and in lower California and Guatemala, and later, in the eighteenth century, in upper California. The most famous of these endeavors were undertaken by the Jesuits, and in California by the Franciscans, under the leadership of Junipero Serra (1713–1784). But with the expulsion of the Jesuits from the Spanish Empire in 1767 for political reasons, and with the later advent of the republics as successor states to the Spanish Empire in the first part of the nineteenth century, these paternalistic systems fell apart. They had been an alternative to the estates, or *encomiendas,* and mines where Indian folk labored, under conditions which varied from relatively genial to horrendous.

The Church would, in various ways, adapt to the spiritual condition of the Indians. Often the old gods' functions could be taken over by the saints. The older cosmology of Central America and the Inca cult of the Sun could be transformed through the imagery of the new faith. The old cruciform shape of the cosmos could be seen as the Cross of the Gospel, projected onto the whole universe. The need to avert catastrophe through sacrifice could be reinterpreted through the ideas of sin and Christ's death on Calvary and at the altar. Christian symbols could help to give the Indian a new adaptability, and a new hope in the face of crushing changes.

Moreover, Catholic culture did not frown upon the mixture of races, which has become most widespread in Brazil. The rising mestizo population forms an important bridge across the cultural chasm between Spanish or Portuguese life on the one hand and that of the Indians on the other. However, one or two countries, such as Argentina, became virtually white, since many of the Indians were driven out or exterminated, and thus Argentina has some of the characteristics of the white nations of North America.

Our Lady of Guadalupe:
A Symbol of Renewed Religious Experience

One of the more remarkable religious events in the new meeting of cultures occurred not very long after the conquest. It was a kind of revelation and a miracle in 1531 leading to the establishment of a basilica, just north of Mexico City, which still draws to it every year hundreds of thousands of pilgrims. It began with a vision, and contains a powerful myth which fuses together a number of hopeful themes and answers to heartfelt prayers.

Juan Diego, an Indian who had become a Christian, had a vision of the Virgin on the hill of Tepeyac. The Virgin spoke to him in Nahuatl, the language of the city and the empire overthrown a mere decade before. She told Juan Diego to have a church built on the spot. He could not prevail on the archbishop to do so. But later he had another vision in which Mary commanded him to pick roses at a desert spot where roses never grow. Miraculously, he found them there and she told him to take the roses in his cloak to the archbishop. To his astonishment, when the cloak was opened up there was an image of the Virgin imprinted upon it, and the archbishop then recognized the miracle and the visions. And so a shrine was built at the spot on the hill where the Virgin had appeared. The image is hung over the high altar of the present great church (the basilica has been rebuilt several times between then and now). The Virgin is young and comely, her head in a shawl, and she is poised on a half moon.

This image has become a symbol of many things. It was carried into battle by the insurgents during the Mexican War of Independence against Spain, and by Zapata's rebels in the Revolution of 1910. Despite the strong anticlericalism of revolutionary Mexico it remains an important national emblem.

The Virgin's message reverberated with a number of meanings in the Mexican mind. She appeared on a hill sacred to Tonantzin, fertility goddess associated with the moon. The moon stimulates the sacred monthly seasons of agriculture and of the female life. Yet the moon also symbolizes, for the Catholic, the immaculate conception. So there was a double meaning in the cult. Tonantzin in Nahuatl means "Our Mother." The cult was a means of affirming simultaneously the old identity and the new Christian culture. The roses of Spain could grow amid the Mexican cactus. In early days of the conquest there was an especially deep meaning in all this, for the incomers were divided, often bitterly, over the question of whether the Indians were truly human and capable of conversion. De las Casas was the most eloquent of those who argued for the dignity of the Indian. Now, in the Guadalupe vision, the Virgin actually speaks the language of the Indian, and her basilica symbolizes the heavenly and earthly citizenship of the Indian. Later too the cult could give special meaning to the place of the "betwixt and between" figure of the mestizo.

The Virgin and the immaculate conception throw a strange light on a contradiction in the Mexican character as it came to take form. The relative equality between the sexes in the old Indian family was covered over by the male machismo which in part stemmed from the warrior status of the Spaniard. (This Spanish machismo was itself blended with Islamic motifs drawn from the long-lasting symbiosis of Islam and Christianity in pre-conquest Spain—1492 was both the year of Columbus and of the fall of the final Muslim possession in Southern Spain.) Mexican Christianity depicted Christ as very different from this aggressive masculine ideal. He was pictured either as a child or as the suffering Jesus of the Cross and the crown of thorns, pale, tortured, bloody. Here were echoes of the older sacrificial themes. Later the veneration of that strange Catholic symbol of the sacred heart of Jesus was to provide other faint reminders of the cosmic significance of sacrifice.

Our Lady of Guadalupe supplies something gentle, passionate, national, egalitarian, female, visionary, fertile, and sacrificial in the imagination of the people, and that is what many another Virgin shrine failed to spark, and accounts for her immense popularity.

The Black Ingredient in Central and South America

If precious metals mesmerized the Spaniards, it was sugar and cotton which chiefly excited other European conquerors. The wilting of the Indian populations of the Caribbean and the scarcity of labor in Portuguese-controlled Brazil caused the rulers of the Western world to bring in black slaves from Africa, to work on the plantations, as they did in the American South. The Spaniards, too, had imported slaves into the Caribbean. In modern times, East Asians were also brought by the British into Guyana, and other parts of the West Indies. So we have three main areas of black settlement—Brazil, the West Indies, and the South of the United States. They have added another cultural ingredient to the religious mix of the Americas.

Most blacks are Christians of one kind or another, and there exists a widespread development of an Afro-Christian kind of religion, in which elements from African myth and ritual are combined with aspects of Christian belief and practice. This is known variously as the Santeria in Cuba, the Macumba in Rio de Janeiro, the Zango in Pernambuco, and the Shango in Trinidad. The most publicized of all is the Voodoo of Haiti.

In the eighteenth century the conditions of slaves in French Haiti were so awful that various bitter slave revolts were sparked. This was the formative period of Voodoo, practiced among runaway slaves and secretly by formally Christianized slaves. It involves a blending of concepts and myths drawn from differing regions of West Africa. The rituals are often administered by women practitioners, who among other things act as mediums, being possessed by spirits. Their words and activities give power and direction to the lives of followers. The religion blends in some Catholic motifs, but is more importantly an early synthesis of West African religious notions in a new and challenging setting. The Catholic Church has tended to react strongly against such Afro-Christian cults. But they survive because they reaffirm elements in black experience arising from the awful initiation into slavery and the continuing quest for dignity in a cruel white world. Voodoo was a powerful impulse in the Haitian revolution which brought independence from France, yet ironically it now exists in a social context where the new, bitter oppression is by blacks. The Duvaliers are oppressive successors to such heroes of Haiti as Dessalines and Toussaint L'Ouverture.

The black experience in the Americas was ambiguous. On the one hand it gave rise to vigorous cultural blends, as in the new multiracial Brazil, and in the United States. But it also harked back to Africa, an Africa little known because the experience of slavery eradicated major features of the varied cultures out of which the blacks were shipped.

In these circumstances, a movement such as the Ras Tafari is no surprise. It stemmed from the teachings of the black preacher Marcus Garvey after World War I. He advocated a pan-African movement among New World blacks and a return to Africa, the focal point of which was Ethiopia. The movement took root around 1930 in Kingston, Jamaica. Partly as a result of the migration of West Indian followers, the movement spread to the United States and Britain. Ethiopia under Ras Tafari (better known as the Emperor Haile Selassie) constituted the one African country not conquered by whites, except briefly in 1935 by the Italians. The country was often therefore a focus of hope, both in Africa and the New World. It was a heaven on earth in contrast to the hell of Jamaica and wherever else blacks were held in subjection. The Rastafarians saw themselves as a reincarnation of the Lost Tribes and much in the Old Testament spoke especially strongly to their experience.

The blend of cultures in Latin America is extraordinary. If Spanish and Portuguese cultures and methods of administration have left the main stamp, Indian, black, European, and other elements have contributed to what remains a volatile and ambiguous civilization. The way for this blend may have been paved in the high cultures of pre-Columbian America, where deities from different cultures were often paired. Also, a dualism of mythic thinking often runs through smaller-scale societies. And a great duality, of course, stands as the major theme of Latin American feeling: the duality of Iberian and Indian values. Our Lady of Guadalupe stands as a powerful symbol of this duality. For although in modern times Catholicism has lost some of its power, and though Protestant movements, including Pentecostalism, are making progress, together with new religious forces such as Mexican spiritism, ultimately Latin America's divided soul must find its more unified salvation in a synthesis of the Catholic tradition and the substratum of ancient values.

To add to the excitement of recent developments, including political changes and upheavals in Nicaragua and elsewhere, the Latin South is having an increased impact upon the United States through immigration. It is as if the Aztecs were returning to their old home in the American Southwest. Mexican and Latino immigration and the arousal of Chicano consciousness bring something of Latin American religious experience to the cities and farms of the United States. At the same time, there is a renewal of Native American consciousness, and a modern sense of solidarity among the different Native American peoples. But if Catholicism became predominant in Hispanic America, it was Protestantism that set the frame for North America.

The Early Colonies

The expanding trade interests of England led to the establishment of Virginia in 1607. The official faith of the colony was that of the Church of England. This incorporated Puritan elements; but these were much more prominent in the first Northern settlements at Plymouth and Massachusetts Bay. William Bradford (1590–1657), first governor at Plymouth, wrote a history of the Plymouth plantation in which he referred to the group he led as Pilgrims—the first occasion on which this term was used. As we know, the story of their first harvest Thanksgiving has entered American mythology and forms the background of America's main celebrations of its origins.

There were conflicting strands in the attitudes of early settlers. They were seeking liberty to pursue their faith free from the persecution and restraints that ruled at home in England. But they were also inclined toward conformity. As a result of pressures in Massachusetts, from which he was thrown out for criticizing the alliance between Church and State, Roger Williams (1603?–1683), founded the colony in Rhode Island. It was hospitable to Anne Hutchinson (1591–1643), a noted woman preacher who had antagonized the authorities in Massachusetts. The Baptist, exiles from Europe who carried on some of the tradition of the Anabaptists, and who were opposed to secular enforcement of faith, influenced Williams.

Here were some of the religious springs of the separation of Church and State that was to figure so importantly in the American constitution. Another source was the values of the Enlightenment and the appeal to reason, which deeply affected a number of the Founding Fathers.

In fact, the religious composition of early America was very varied. As well as Anglicans, Congregationalists (who were the main body of the early Puritans), and Quakers (important in Pennsylvania, founded as a Quaker state but with religious freedom for all who believed in one God), there were Baptists, Presbyterians, followers of the Moravian inheritance going back to Count von Zinzendorf, Catholics (the founder of Maryland, Lord Baltimore, was a Catholic and saw Maryland as a place of freedom for Catholics, who suffered under disabilities in England), Lutherans, and others. This pluralism was important, partly because it eroded intolerance, and partly because it gave birth to the sentiment that doctrinal divisions are really rather unimportant. Religious experience and ethical behavior are more vital, together with adherence to the Bible.

THE FIRST GREAT AWAKENING

These sentiments were reinforced by that tide of revival known as the Great Awakening, largely during the period from about 1735 to 1745. It was sparked by some gifted preachers. The first among them was Jonathan Edwards (1703–1758). His sermons during the winter of 1734–1735 attacked the notion, held by many, that self-reliance could bring salvation. He stressed divine election and grace—a doctrine that was rooted in his own experience. This he described with great fervor and eloquence in his classic *Personal Narrative*, written some time after 1739. His preaching stirred a great revival in the town of Northampton.

Another strong influence was the friend of John Wesley, George White-field (1714–1770), who in 1740 undertook an extensive preaching tour of the colonies from Savannah to York. He addressed great crowds, particularly in New England. His impact was sensational. Clearly the wandering preacher had cut loose from too close a Church identification (he was using methods of evangelism pioneered in English Methodism); and the emphasis of both Edwards and Whitefield on inner conversion and the experience of God's power cut across denominational boundaries. It further helped to consolidate American piety and a relative distrust of doctrinal formulas.

Another important preacher was Gilbert Tennent (1703–1764), of Scots-Irish Presbyterian background, who had been influenced by Theodore Jacob Frelinghuysen (1691–1748), a German pastor working among Dutch settlers along the Raritan River, himself affected by German pietism. Tennent preached vigorously against half-hearted spirituality and urged a deeper and warmer commitment to Christ. Also prominent was Samuel Davies (1723–1761), who worked energetically in the South, making converts among Whites, Indians, and Blacks.

The effect of all this was to promote a strongly felt faith centering on conversion and inner conviction, and—though this was not intended precisely—a powerful individualism. Old religious emphases on community were in some degree undermined by the stirring of individual feeling. Similarly it was not doctrinal rectitude that counted, but rather the intensity of a sense of God's power. So the Great Awakening helped destroy social and doctrinal divisions and reinforced the democratic ordering of American society, already firmly planted in the Puritan ethic.

Another effect was in the enhancement of higher education. The new interest in religion caused a greater demand for ministerial training, and to this we owe the foundation of colleges such as Princeton (1746), Rhode Island College, later Brown University (1764), and Dartmouth (1769). The last of these was thought of initially as a school for converted Native Americans.

Although the Great Awakening softened all denominational boundaries, it helped one group in particular—the Baptists. They made significant advances, especially in New England. They remain the most vital of all the Protestant groups. With their connections to the Anabaptist reformation and their strong emotionalism they are attractive to individuals seeking assurance in a socially fluid society.

AMERICAN INDEPENDENCE

The Declaration of Independence and the framing of the American Constitution in part express a worldview that combined some generally Christian and religious values with ideas and attitudes drawn from the Enlightenment. The revolutionaries were concerned with freedom from tyranny, and this was compatible with and parallel to the freedom from sin that animated evangelical Christians. Tyranny itself was due to corruption, which it also bred. From Thomas Jefferson (1743–1826) it was important that there be a public philosophy that could inculcate morality, calling on conscience and the values that religions shared in common. Although the Deism of the Enlightenment was typically in conflict with Biblical religion and the emotionalism characteristic of the revivals, Protestant Christianity would live with Jefferson's ideals. The Great Awakening by its very nature was critical of external sectarian authority, and both sides could combine in a sense of the revolution as a new beginning. The separation of Church and State declared in the First Amendment to the Constitution was vital to the evolution of a pluralist society, which yet agreed at least on the elements of a public philosophy or civil religion.

There were of course some contradictions in the Constitution, most notably the exclusion of African Americans from the rights of citizens. This contradiction was later remedied by the Civil War and the civil rights struggles of the 1960s. Another jarring feature was the exclusion of women from the vote, remedied by the constitutional amendment of 1920 and the feminist struggles of the 1970s.

THE SECOND GREAT AWAKENING

Meanwhile America was on the move: the frontier was being pushed West. This was one of the opportunities for revivalism, since established denominations could not easily keep up with the moving edge of society. Indeed they came to cooperate in promoting camp meetings, which often brought thousands of people together to listen to strong and simple preaching and to respond with fervor. The most famous of these was held in 1801 at Cane Ridge, Kentucky. Close to twenty-five thousand people attended, and the occasion lasted some six days. Its fame spread, and it is often invoked as an expression of the frontier spirit in American religion. It helped to revitalize evangelical activity, including the greatly successful Methodist expansion, relying on circuit riders and a form of organization that could cope with the population on the hopeful paths to the West. A more staid revival occurred in New England, led by various preachers including Timothy Dwight (1752–1817), who was President of Yale. More disturbing in his exposual of special techniques of evangelicalism including all-night meetings and the use of women preachers was the work of Charles G. Finney (1792–1875), who held a series of meetings along the Erie Canal. He was influential in urban revivalism in the 1850s—a movement known by some as the Third Great Awakening.

AFRICAN AMERICAN CHRISTIANITY

The slaves imported from Africa were cut off from their cultural roots, and by and large African forms of worship disappeared. In the 1770s very few Blacks were Christian, only about two percent. But the revivals of the Second Awakening helped to spread evangelical religion. Apart from family ties, often themselves severed by plantation life, the churches were the primary focus of a sense of community. Many were converted, and in the early eighteenth century they would share in the worship of the Whites, albeit segregated within chapels. Such religion was often supplemented by secret assemblies on the plantations in which a more fervid faith could be expressed. There were also moves in the North to create separate Black churches, notably the African Methodist Episcopal Church, founded by Richard Allen (1760–1831) and others. His was in part a protest at the humiliation suffered by Blacks, as a pattern of segregation began to take hold in Philadelphia and elsewhere.

The sufferings of the Blacks, especially under slavery, often led them to identify with the people of Israel. The Bible spoke to their condition, and there evolved the Negro spiritual, drawing on the themes and symbols of the Bible, transformed by the haunting music that expressed the faith of African Americans. The experience of conversion gave meaning to individual life amid adversity.

NINETEENTH-CENTURY MIGRATION

American religion was also profoundly affected by the migrations in the nineteenth century, principally from Europe, as the United States industrialized and opened up its vast agricultural hinterland. Italians, Poles, Irish, and others brought in a now much more populous Catholicism. From Eastern Europe and Germany came many Jews. Lutherans flooded in from Scandinavia and Germany. There were Presbyterians and others from Scotland and Northern Ireland. In effect all this migration multiplied denominations, since German and Swedish Lutherans would form separate communities, as did Dutch and Scottish Calvinists. The new pluralism of American society, however, made the "public philosophy" even more important, and it was the major task of American high schools to inculcate common virtues and values. Though Catholics among others set up their webs of denominational schools, even these tended to emphasize American values, and so subtly changed the ethos of their tradition.

There were also many opportunities to proselytize. The mid-nineteenth century saw the formation of a number of new movements. One, which hoped to distil the pure essence of Christian faiths, was that of the Disciples of Christ, founded by Alexander Campbell (1788–1866), which repudiated the very idea of being a denomination. The movement had no system of its own (he declared), but only loyalty to the New Testament. There was an optimism about the purity of the movement born of the intensity of the revivalism of the times. Perhaps more characteristic were four new religions on the edge of Christianity, the Seventh-Day Adventists, the Jehovah's Witnesses, Christian Scientists, and the Mormons.

The Seventh-Day Adventists

Adventism started in America with the preaching of William Miller (1782–1849), a Baptist. His study of the Bible led him to suppose that Christ would shortly return to earth, when there would be the resurrection of the faithful and the Kingdom of God would be established. His predictions made a strong impression. When he went on to say that the Second Coming was due between spring 1843 and spring 1844, excitement among his followers mounted.

Farmers failed to harvest their crops; men left their affairs; the eagerness of waiting was scarcely bearable, but yet sweet and joyous. When the promised event did not occur, it was heart-breaking—and yet the faithful mostly stayed with Miller and his cause. One disciple wrote:

> The passing of the time was a bitter disappointment. True believers had given up all for Christ, and had shared His presence as never before. The love of Jesus filled every soul, and with inexpressible desire they prayed, "Come, Lord Jesus, and come quickly," but He did not come.

We can see here something of the perennial and poignant attraction of the Christian eschatological hope: the recurrence of hopes for the Millennium throughout Christian history is a facet of Christian experience that is puzzling, but significant. It may be a literal interpretation of the virtue of hope, but it can be a stimulus to a fervid and other-worldly piety. The Seventh-Day Adventists, the most powerful offshoot of the movement started by Miller, continue as a zealous missionary movement.

Jehovah's Witnesses

The Jehovah's Witnesses likewise await the Millennium. But their doctrines, first propounded by a Pittsburgh businessman, Charles Taze Russell (1852–1916), lie definitely outside the orbit of orthodox Christianity. They regard Christ as a creature who will come to destroy the forces of Satan at Armageddon. They teach that sinners who are not saved will perish; but the faithful will enter into a kingdom of joy and happiness. Despite scandals involving Russell himself, the movement has grown. It is particularly active in underdeveloped countries, where its repudiation of Christian orthodoxy and its promises for the future have a certain appeal. In their serene confidence of the coming of the Kingdom, the Witnesses undertake no military service. In any event, the institutions of government are, they hold, under the control of Satan. Thus they have proved recalcitrant and anarchistic, and have suffered some persecution as a result. They are peaceful, but fanatical; they know their Bible backward and forward, but they are rarely well educated. Such a movement appeals to those of modest education—clerks and landladies in England, for instance, are well represented in the movement; these are people who know something of what education is through schooling and contact with students, but they have not got higher education. The secret hope of the Millennium and the marvellous way they can interpret the Bible are compensations for their deprivation.

Christian Science

Christian Science also provides an unusual answer to deeply felt needs. Founded by the remarkable Mary Baker Eddy (1821–1910), who herself claimed to have been cured by spiritual healing, the creed of the new movement proclaimed the non-reality of pain and sickness. Men take matter too seriously. If they could only have faith, they would be healed. A modern exponent writes:

> Theories about germs and microbes come from beliefs which hold that life is material and that disease is real. The Christian Scientist knows by experience that his belief is demonstrable despite theories of disease involving germs, microbes and viruses.

Christian Science aims to give a religious theory to back up its spiritual healing. The movement has spread because those who are cured remain loyal. In an age of psychosomatic illness, such faith healing can produce results, and these outweigh the initial implausibility of the theory.

The Latter Day Saints

The story of the Mormons, for all the bizarreness of the events which gave rise to the Church of Jesus Christ of Latter-Day Saints, was dramatic and heroic. The Mormons now number over a million, and are a testimony to the transforming effect of faith. But their faith is a very special one.

Joseph Smith II (1805–1844), a very handsome young visionary, was born in Vermont of poor parents. At the age of fifteen he had a vision of "two Personages, whose brightness and glory defy all description." One pointed to the other saying "This is my Beloved Son! Hear Him!" The substance of the message that followed was that there was need for a restoration of the Gospel. Some years later, Smith was guided by an angel to the discovery, according to his own account, of a number of golden plates containing inscriptions. Alongside of them lay a pair of supernatural spectacles which enabled Smith to read these inscriptions: he identified them with the Urim and Thummin mentioned in Exodus 28:30 as belonging to the high priest's apparel. Smith claimed that the language was Reformed Egyptian (Egyptologists have no knowledge of this mysterious tongue). As a result of his labors of decipherment, Joseph Smith published, in 1830, a work called *The Book of Mormon*. It is from this that the Latter-Day Saints have gained their nickname of "Mormons."

The contents are curious, and represent a mythology for the New World. That they struck a chord in many hearts is testified by the remarkable success of the new church which Joseph Smith founded in that year. Already there were current in some circles theories that the American Indians were descended from the Lost Tribes of Israel—those, that is, who had disappeared from the sight of history at the time of King Zedekiah, when Jerusalem was taken by the Babylonians in 586 B.C. According to *The Book of Mormon,* these folk crossed the seas to the New World, continuing the religion of the Old Testament and compiling further records of events and prophecies. However, only some of those who had gone to the New World remained true to the prophetic faith. The others abandoned the teachings of God and became savages. These were the Indians. Ultimately the culture of the faithful remnant came to an end in A.D. 421. The only survivors, the prophet Mormon and his son Moroni, hid these records in a cave in New York State, whence they were rescued briefly by Joseph Smith under the guidance of Moroni, now appearing in angelic form. This book also relates how Christ visited the Western hemisphere during the period after his ascension. On the basis, then, of this scripture and of certain other visions experienced by Joseph Smith, he proclaimed the establishment of a new church, at Fayette in Seneca County, New York State, on April 6, 1830.

Here was a new Israel in search of a promised land. The Saints settled in Kirtland, Ohio, and a prosperous community was established. The enthusiasm and discipline of the Saints was impressive; but it sparked off animosity in their neighbors. Outbreaks of violence drove the community further west to Missouri. There similar troubles repeated themselves. They crossed the Mississippi River to Nauvoo, in Illinois. There a town of twenty thousand souls rapidly came into being, ruled over by Joseph Smith. It was a state within the state. It had its own militia and discipline. A fine Temple was built, and a university was established. Meanwhile missionaries were sent out to the east and to Europe. The new faith caught the imagination of many who were looking for their own Promised Land, and could not find it in the machine-shops of the English Black Country and the textile mills of Lancashire. It was the beginning of a new tide of religiously-motivated emigration.

But troubles were brewing in Illinois. Smith's power and that of the community he led roused fears in the rest of Illinois. The Saints were becoming a political force to be reckoned with. Furthermore, they gave cause for alienation and hostility not merely because they were a tight-knit, inward-looking group, but because in 1843 Joseph Smith revealed the seemingly scandalous doctrine of polygamy. (He was quite right, of course, in detecting the practice in the Old Testament.) To check the continued increase of a self-contained group that granted little allegiance to state authority, the Governor of Illinois ordered Smith's arrest, together with that of his brother Hiram. Armed men broke into the jail at Carthage, Illinois, where the two men were incarcerated, and shot the brothers to death. The first leader of the movement was now a martyr.

Brigham Young

The succession passed to the energetic Brigham Young (1801–1877), a patriarchal figure, authoritarian and prophetic, and a good administrator. Evidently Nauvoo was not the Promised Land. The Saints were looking for a haven where they would be free of the hostility and violence of the unbelievers. The new Israel, then, in 1846, set out on its greatest trek, into the wild and unknown country to the west. They were on the very edge of the frontier: they were now to push far beyond it. It was a heroic and moving venture.

Fifteen thousand men, women and children, and several thousand cattle, wound their way west through bitter and difficult country. In 1847 they came to the Zion for which they had been seeking. By the Great Salt Lake in Utah—then a Mexican territory—they stopped and began the building of a new and more glorious Temple. Crops were sown, houses were built. At first, life was hard. But the new community was vastly heartened by a seemingly miraculous occurrence: the corn crop was threatened by hordes of insects. Just when it seemed that disaster was inevitable, a flock of seagulls consumed the insects. The successful ending of the long trek convinced the Saints that they were guided by Providence. Missionaries went out to gather in more faithful. In a few years, Salt Lake City was a growing and prospering community.

Now polygamy, hitherto a subject more of rumor and private practice, was officially established. A theocratic state was instituted, ruled severely and sometimes violently by Brigham Young. Though most of the Saints remained faithful, others were restless under his iron regime. A number were executed for such dangerous apostasy. Meanwhile, Utah was ceded to the United States. A commissioner from Washington was sent to administer the territory, though Young was recognized as Governor. The building of the railroad across to the Pacific destroyed Utah's seclusion. Under Young's second successor, Wilford Woodruff, Utah became a state of the Union, but only on the condition of the renunciation of polygamy. Out of these enthusiastic, dramatic events, a new element was integrated into American life.

The high standard of education of the Saints, and their industry and sobriety, together with their stress on missionary activity have created a strong and viable community.

How are we to estimate the narrative upon which it is based? What was it about Joseph Smith's message which engendered so much enthusiasm? Part of the explanation lies in the turmoil of the religious life of his time. Revivals and new doctrines were in the air. But the old themes of Christian salvation had been repeated too often, perhaps, to catch the imagination of those who sought a more dramatic faith. Smith himself was a person of powerful personality: he inspired serious devotion and loyalty. He was able to crystallize the new teachings by giving them a political and social direction. Most important of all, the Mormon faith combined hope for the future, as in Adventism, with the promise that it was a Kingdom upon this earth that was to be established —not in remote Israel, but here on the sacred soil of the great American continent. The puritanical side of the teachings (abstention from alcohol, tea, tobacco, etc.) were adapted to the task of creating a community out of very little, through the force of hard work, discipline, and frugality. His was an improbable dream: but people who dream, and especially those whose circumstances are desperate and, from the point of view of common sense, rather hopeless, can grasp with eagerness at improbable dreams. It was the great achievement of the Saints to translate their strange and novel theology into the practical successes of Utah.

It would, of course, be totally misleading to overemphasize the new movements which we have been describing. They are striking phenomena in the many-colored fabric of religious history; but the bulk of American religion has been centered on the Protestant and Catholic traditions. In terms of church-going, the American nation has been more faithful to Christian tradition than most European countries in modern times. In addition, a vital section of the American population belongs to the Jewish faith. It was not for nothing, no dobut, that the Pilgrim Fathers, and so many of the other early settlers who gave shape to the American ideal, had crossed the Atlantic in search of religious liberty.

UNITARIANISM AND THE TRANSCENDENTALISTS

Although the preceding narrative has tended to emphasize revivalism and charismatic leadership, the ideals of the Enlightenment were contained in a more religious form in the witness of those who were skeptical of the new enthusiasms of rousing preachers, and who relied on a more sober use of reason. Among these were Charles Chauncy (1705–1787) and William Ellery Channing (1780–1842). The latter, a minister in Boston, had a profound influence through a famous sermon delivered in 1819, which became a manifesto for Unitarianism. The former's belief that all human beings will be saved (a doctrine known as universalism) undercut the assumptions of revivalists, who often scared their hearers with the wrath of God and the path to hell. Unitarianism became a powerful force in New England, and from this time was much more influential in the United States than it ever was in Britain or Europe. It strongly emphasized the ethical dimension of reli-

gion. Since it denied the divinity of Christ and therefore the doctrine of the
Trinity, it saw Jesus as a moral exemplar and teacher, rather than a cosmic
atoning figure, reconciling humanity to God.

Reacting against the sobriety of official Unitarianism were the Transcendentalists, a group of thinkers of considerable creativity and influence,
headed by Ralph Waldo Emerson (1803–1882). In 1838 he delivered a stirring and provocative address to the Harvard Divinity School. Transcenden-
talism saw the cosmos as an interrelated whole, and viewed humanity as
illuminated from within by the divine mind: it had affinites to some Hindu
and Chinese thought. It was romantic and was accused of pantheism, identifying God with the universe. A prominent associate of Emerson was Margaret Fuller (1810–1850) who for a time edited the Transcendentalist mag-
azine *The Dial* and who was a brilliant conversationalist and ardent advocate
of feminism and the reform of American society. The movement had a distrust of great emphasis on history and had a somewhat impersonal picture
of the Divine. It influenced later philosophers such as Willam James (1842–
1910) and John Dewey (1859–1952).

In some degree the Transcendentalists were also forerunners of the more
recent interest in Eastern religion, particularly in Hindu ideas and practices.
They helped to create a wider interest in non-Western forms of spirituality,
such as harmony with nature in the Taoist tradition and mystical self-dis-
covery as in the Vedanta. An important event in this connection was the
appearance of Swami Vivekananda (see p. 154) before the World's Parliament of Religions in Chicago in 1893.

PATTERNS IN THE TWENTIETH CENTURY

Meanwhile the mainstream Protestant denominations were deeply influenced
by modern liberal thought. They were highly successful in shaping American
society toward piety, a work ethic, and social concerns. But their very success made their teachings seem commonplace. Moreover up to World War
I it was possible for Christianity to ally itself too easily with hopes of
progress and social betterment, and to forget those dark processes that challenged the liberal ethos. The miseries of the war saw a decrease in optimism. The most influential theologian came to be Karl Barth (1866–1968),
a Swiss Calvinist theologian, who gave new force to Protestant theology precisely because he was able to combine evangelical attitudes with a critical
attitude to the scriptures. The older theologians, because for them the literal
authority of the scripture was weakened by the results of modern historical
and literary scholarship, had tended to read into Christianity elements drawn
from the prevailing ideology of their time—a liberal, humanitarian progres-
sivism.

Karl Barth wished to rid the Gospel of all contamination with contemporary ideology. Only thus would the Word of God speak to man in all its radical purity. He employed the methods of Biblical scholarship to locate the essential message of the Bible. The Bible was not to be taken in the way in which so many Evangelicals had taken it—in consisting in a long list of propositions supposedly inspired directly by God. Barth saw that it was truer to the Biblical material itself to think of revelation not as God's utterance of statements but rather as his self-revelation in concrete events and in the person of Christ. Revelation is what the Bible is *about*. It is not simply to be identified with the Bible itself.

But Barth was insistent on the Otherness of God. God's revelation comes down, as it were, vertically from above. It shatters man's presuppositions, even his religious ones. Religion, indeed, is often man's attempt to shield himself from the revelation in Christ. God's Word owes nothing to human constructions, nothing to human thought. It challenges man by its very difference from all that man could invent for himself. All natural theology, such as that expounded by St. Thomas Aquinas, is useless. Man's reason is incapable of reaching out to God. For God essentially reveals himself in a saving self-revelation. And the work of salvation belongs to God alone. God's Word cannot be refuted by philosophy any more than it can be backed up or confirmed by philosophy.

In such ways, Barth gave a new force and direction to theology, by making it independent of other disciplines. More importantly, in his bold and forceful preaching of a new Evangelicalism and in his uncompromising reaffirmation of the centrality of Christ, he provided the basis for a renewal of Protestantism in an age of intellectual and moral despair. His message deeply affected missionaries. In his contrast between the divine Gospel and human religion he provided a method whereby questions about the relations between religions could be by-passed. All religions, including Christianity, stand under the judgment of God's Word as revealed in Christ.

Meanwhile mainline liberalism created its own backlash. As we have noted there was always a strongly evangelical and Biblical side to American religion. A series of preachers in the late nineteenth and early twentieth century, notably Dwight L. Moody (1836–1899), fanned the fires of renewal, while the Holiness Movement, at odds with official denominations, urged the quest for God-guided perfection in ethical behavior. By its very success mainline Protestantism tended to appeal to the more comfortable, while conservative religion had a raw dynamism. The publication of twelve paperbacks between 1910 and 1915 called *The Fundamentals* setting forth a basically conservative position known as premillennarianism—in which Christ comes, amid catastrophes, to judge the world and usher his thousand year reign (millennium)—gave rise to the term "Fundamentalism," coined in 1920. Fundamentalists adhere to a literal interpretation of the Bible, tend to reject all critical scrutiny of the scriptures, and often hold conservative political and ethical positions. On the other hand, although the doctrinal and narrative dimensions of fundamentalism are anti-modern, their ritual and experiential dimensions, and their social organization, tend toward modern vigor and new methods and feelings. Important is conversion and being "born again": those Christians who undergo such transformation make up the true Church.

After World War II America entered a period of unprecedented prosperity and power. But there remained inner crises that were to reveal themselves in the 1960s. One was the unresolved question of the oppression of Blacks. Under the leadership of Martin Luther King, Jr. (1929–1968), the Civil Rights movement in the South had immense success in giving Blacks political rights, though there remained the problems of poverty, which still beset the community. Other Blacks did not follow King's nonviolent lead and espoused Black Power and dreams of a separate Black polity; others again were drawn to Black Islam.

Civil rights agitation blended with concerns about the Vietnam War from 1964 onward. At the same time a groundswell of rebellion among the young created many new forces, from interest in Marxism to the quest for Eastern enlightenment, not to mention experimentation with mind-altering drugs such as LSD. There were various long-term consequences of the 1960s, notably the sexual revolution, more tolerance for homosexuals, various interests in new religious movements, from Hindu devotionalism (the Hare Krishna) to evangelical Confucian-flavored messianism (the Unification Church) and Buddhism. An interest in meditation, yoga methods, and self-awareness also affected Christian Churches. All this had the greater effect because in America, as elsewhere, the Roman Catholic Church had undergone renewal through Vatican II (1962–1965), and in many ways had taken on the open-ended character of liberal Protestantism. The growth of ecumenical togetherness between the Churches was especially obvious among the liberal denominations, including Catholicism.

The emergence of serious concerns about minority rights helped to generate a Native American revival. It was in part symbolized by the incident at Wounded Knee in 1973, when members of the American Indian Movement occupied the site of a massacre of Indians, signaling the final subjugation of Native Americans in 1890. This followed the spread of a new and unsuccessful religious movement known disparagingly as the Ghost Dance, under the charismatic leader Wovoka (1856?–1932). This had promised that the White man would disappear if certain rituals were performed.

MODERN AMERICAN PLURALISM

The society that emerged in the 1970s and beyond was thoroughly pluralistic. It not only contained all the varied denominations and movements of
Christainity, but also varieties of Judaism, Islam, Buddhism, Sikhism, Hinduism, and other great religions. Many of the new adherents to non-Euro-
pean faiths were Anglos, and Islam also gathered Black recruits. There were
also ethnic variations, for instance, between Hispanic and Irish Catholicism.
There was a cloud of new religious movements and parareligious organizations, dealing with psychological and spiritual problems, such as est. The
influx of new waves of migrants, especially from Vietnam and Korea, led
to a new mingling of religious culture, especially in California. It was also
from the mid- and late-1960s on that new religious studies departments
came into being in many public universities and colleges, helping with student interest in the force of religion in the wider world.

CONTEMPORARY RELIGIOUS

EXPERIENCE

Chapter 12

THE HUMANIST EXPERIENCE

THE MODERN period, especially from the time of the French Revolution onward, has seen the burgeoning of various kinds of atheism and humanism—the rejection of traditional religion. One source of this trend was the Enlightenment, with its emphasis on the power of human reason. Another source was the conflict (some would think unnecessary) between science and religion—as in the conflict between Biblical literalists and the proponents of Evolutionary Theory. But also, during the nineteenth and early twentieth century the world was undergoing great transformations, and it is not surprising if there were vital new rejections of tradition. The industrial revolution meant that in the cities of Europe many rural workers came to town: uprooted from their past they were often alienated from religion. New movements produced an increase in nationalism, which went hand in hand with modernization. National entities such as a united Germany or Italy were better adapted than the old small principalities to the larger scale of activities demanded by capitalism. Because religion often had a cosy relationship with preexisting regimes, which were being overthrown or merged into greater wholes, there were, perforce, conflicts between the old and new. Toward the end of the nineteenth century there was a growing interest in the ideas of Marx and this was one of a number of factors bringing intellectuals toward a rejection of religion. Powerful forms of agnosticism and atheism animated cultural life. All this was much more marked in Europe than in the United States, which was relatively little touched with socialism, and where religions of the homeland were functionally important in sustaining migrant communities in the cities of the New World—and where too as we have seen there had been potent revivals. But in much of Northern Europe the blue-collar workers tended to be alienated from the churches together with, as we have seen, a sizable number of the intellectuals.

Two main forms of atheism have developed in the Western world. One, which arose out of the skepticism of the eighteenth century, is a liberal humanism. The other emerged primarily in Germany, through the writings of

Feuerbach, Marx, and Nietzsche. As a secondary phenomenon there was also atheistic Existentialism in the thought of Martin Heidegger and Jean-Paul Sartre. A later version of scientific humanism came to be dominant in English philosophy through the writings and influence of philosophers such as A. J. Ayer and W. V. Quine in the analytic philosophical tradition. Another powerful thinker animated by a scientific worldview was Bertrand Russell. To these we shall return: but first let us examine that most powerful set of ideologies summed up as nationalism, which has been the most dynamic political force in the nineteenth and twentieth centuries.

NATIONALISM

Not only was Napoleon's leadership of France an expression of some of the new forces of national identity, but by his conquests he helped to stimulate, by reaction and emulation, national sentiments across the continent. National struggles culminated at the end of World War I in the carving up of the whole of Europe into national States. From here the idea spread across Asia and Africa and elsewhere, so that after a number of colonial struggles during and after World War II, the whole world in theory was divided by nationalities, except for the great empires of the Soviet Union and China. But in both countries there are new national stirrings, increasingly irresistible.

The new nations built of course on old foundations, rediscovered by historians, poets, and politicians in the nineteenth century. They very often used language as the criterion of national identity—as with Germany, Italy, and Poland. With language there came a sense of historic literature, and it could be reinforced by religion or other factors. Thus Poland had a keen sense of its Catholicism, which applied to the majority of inhabitants, though Jews were a strong minority. It was a Catholic country sandwiched between Protestant North Germany and Orthodox Russia. On the other hand, though virtually all Italians were and are Catholic by tradition, there was tension between the unifiers of Italy and the Church—partly because a united Italy swallowed up the Papal territories that ran like a band across north-central Italy, and partly because the ideology of the nationalists was predominantly liberal. During the nineteenth century the Roman Catholic Church was busy fighting off modernism, that is a liberal interpretation of Church teachings and beliefs.

In more recent times Communist ideology has sometimes served to reinforce nationalism—for instance Chinese Marxism was the way in which China expressed its struggle for parity with the marauding capitalist West.

Similarly it became the engine that fueled the Vietnamese national struggle over the period from World War II to 1975.

But even without ideological reinforcement nationalism was a strong force. It had its myths, through the history taught in high school texts and in the lives of the country's great poets, generals, musicians, and statesmen. It had its ethics, and in its pressing demands for people to be good citizens, raising loyal families and being prepared to go to war and pay great taxes. It inculcates feelings of loyalty and sacred identity through the national hymn, parades, the flag, the glories of architecture and national scenery, and so on. It has its powerful rituals—national day parades, the pomp of president or monarch, military displays, celebrations of the heroic dead, even the speaking of the language. It has at its disposal powerful forms of coercion and organization. The disloyal are liable to be imprisoned, or exiled, or shot.

When combined with religion it could become a most overwhelming force. But it happened that two of the manifestations of extreme nationalism in Europe in the period between the two World Wars were variants of right wing ideology—Fascism in Italy and Nazism in Germany. Adolf Hitler (1889–1945) expressed a violent racism that was in part born out of his intense nationalism. This ardor was nourished by his experiences as a soldier throughout World War I and was emphasized by the fact that he was an "outsider," being an Austrian rather than a German citizen. His very rabid antisemitism took a common sentiment in the Vienna of his youth to extremes. One major reason for antisemitic prejudice across central and Eastern Europe, in France, and elsewhere, was that the Jews were, because of their distinctiveness, often perceived as being outsiders (though many, of course, were actually very much assimilated): they were seen as possessing dubious loyalty to nations built on linguistic and Christian foundations. But Hitler went beyond nationalism to a racial theory and a crude notion of the coming Nazi superman, who would live at a higher level from the enslaved peoples the National Socialists felt entitled to conquer. There were Christians such as Dietrich Bonhoeffer (1906–1945) who resisted Nazism (he was executed). But there were many other Christians who acquiesced in German nationalism, even under Hitler.

In general, the new national forces constituted some threat to Church traditions, because the State took over the functions of education, medical services, and so on, which had been previously controlled by Churches. But most of all the very power of national feeling could overwhelm other, transnational loyalties. For instance, Catholics fought each other and were loyal to both sides during the wars, and that despite the transparently international character of the Church.

HEGEL, FEUERBACH, AND MARX

Kant advanced the thought that the structure of our minds imposes order on the phenomena that we register through the senses. He sought to safeguard the objectivity of the outside world by his doctrine of things-in-themselves, which give rise to phenomena. Phenomena were not just mental products but came from objective things "out there." The notion was contradictory, for Kant had argued elsewhere that categories such as causation could not be meaningfully applied beyond the sphere of phenomena (or experience). So what could "give rise to" mean? Hegel (1770–1831) frankly drew the Idealist conclusion: the world is the product of Mind. This was the Absolute Mind rather than individual minds, although the latter are parts of the former. But more originally still, he gave an historical dimension to his philosophy, and saw the processes of human historical development as similar to the unfolding of an argument. First, there is a thesis, then its antithesis, and out of the interplay comes a third thing, the synthesis, which in turn becomes a thesis, and so on. His view of history and of human beings as historical beings made a great impact, and he helped to stimulate historical research in the German universities and beyond, including the probing of the Biblical texts seen not as sacred scripture but as historical sources and clues. The early Christianity of Peter and the other disciples could be a thesis; the theology of Paul an antithesis; and Catholicism as a synthesis emerging from the interplay of the two.

Ludwig Feuerbach (1804–1872) saw that Hegel had absorbed everything including God into a single reality. But he did not go far enough in discerning the subjectivity of the ideas of God and the Absolute. These are actually projections of human ideals and desires. God was ideal humanity projected onto the cosmos. Humanity worships itself. This notion was to be extraordinarily influential and important. Projection came to be a key notion in Freud's worldview, while it played a vital role in Marx's theory of alienation. From there it passed into much fashionable sociology in the latter part of the twentieth century. Feuerbach adopted a materialist metaphysics, even going so far as to aver that a human being is what he eats.

Karl Marx (1818–1883) blended Hegel's dialectical account of history and Feuerbach's materialism, and added a powerful extra ingredient: economics. From these perspectives he viewed society in an exciting and creative way. He wanted to go beyond Feuerbach, in that it was necessary to examine the causes of alienation and the projection of the ideal of God upon the world. He wrote (in his *Theses on Feuerbach*):

Feuerbach starts out from the fact of religious self-alienation, the duplication of the world into a religious, imaginary world and a real one. His work consists in the dissolution of the religious world into its secular basis. He overlooks the fact that after this work is completed the chief thing still remains to be done. For the fact that the secular foundation detaches itself and establishes itself in the clouds as an independent realm is really only to be explained by the self-cleavage and self-contradictoriness of this secular basis. The latter must itself, therefore, first be understood in its contradiction, and then revolutionized in practice by the removal of the contradiction. Thus, for instance, once the earthly family is discovered to be the secret of the holy family, the former must then be criticized in theory and revolutionized in practice.

For Marx there was a pressing need for action. As he ringingly wrote: "Philosophers have only *interpreted the world*; the point, however, is to *change* it." On his view of religion, then, in a socialist and communist society, alienation being overcome, religion would (he thought) simply wither away. He may have forgotten that there would still be problems, such as death, even if human alienation from what is produced is ended. Also, Marx's notions about classes, alienation, the people and so on were largely abstractions, and in gritty detail communist societies have not all functioned as he would have imagined.

As he saw it, capitalism contained a severe inner tension or contradiction. In order to increase profits the capitalist would have to take away more of the value of the workers' labor. It was a principle with Marx that in a capitalist society a person will work fifty hours (say) but will receive less than fifty hours' worth in value. So the whole system was built on exploitation. Gradually the stringencies of the situation will heighten tension to such a degree that a revolution will break out. The proletariat will take over, and if things are managed rightly a new era of socialism will begin. The means of production will be owned and managed on behalf of all, and alienation of the human being from the fruits of his or her labor will cease. The socialist State will be one of essential harmony. Eventually the utopia of a communist society will be realized, when human beings will receive according to their needs and will be free to develop their manifold talents. And in a good society like that human beings will be good.

THE DEVELOPMENTS OF SOCIALISM

Mainstream Marxism inspired revolutionary fervor and the formation of Marxist parties dedicated to the imposition of a Communist order. Their major success was not where Marx would have expected it, in such heart-lands of capitalism as England and Germany. Rather it was in Russia, collapsing under the strains of its terrible war with Germany and Austro-Hungary from 1914 to 1917. Lenin (1870–1924) developed a revolutionary theory that underlined some momentous—and indeed ominous—ideas: the concept of the Communist Party as the vanguard of the proletariat, ready to help in direct revolution without waiting for the development of the economy under a bourgeois hegemony; and the concept of democratic centralism—a phrase that included the notion of iron discipline within the Party. From 1914 to 1917, Lenin lived in neutral Switzerland, and when he was returned in a sealed wagon to Russia by the German authorities in 1917 (eager to make trouble for a collapsing imperial regime) he struggled to impose his ideas on the so-called Bolshevik wing of the revolutionary socialist party. After the end of the Tsarist system, a democratic, but feeble, government was led by Alexander Kerensky (1881–1970). In November of 1917 it was overthrown by Lenin and his associates supported by the workers' councils or Soviets. The new Communist government called the new State the Union of Soviet Socialist Republics. A bitter civil war, with Allied forces intervening on the other side, was eventually won. The pattern was set for the creation of a Marxist–Leninist society. Some opponents had argued that Lenin's doctrines prepared the way for a one-person dictatorship, and from 1927 this was true, once Stalin (1879–1953) assumed full power. The new State acquired a totalitarian structure and freedoms of the press, religion, and so on were suppressed. Stalin argued for socialism in one country, and downplayed international revolution. He subordinated Marxism to Soviet (in effect Russian) nationalism. His largest achievement was victory in World War II over the Nazis. But great suffering accompanied both his industrialization of the Soviet Union and postwar reconstruction.

Lenin's model was adopted with variations by other Communist parties, in their struggles for power in the name of anticolonialism. Mao Zedong (1893–1976), a great military theorist and practitioner, varied Marx's views by including a central role for the peasantry in the revolutionary struggle. His ideas were put into practice once he had won the Chinese civil war that flanked the years of World War II. After 1949 a Communist dictatorship ruled China, except for the island territory of Taiwan, and Hong Kong.

Because of the position of the Red Army at the end of World War II, all of Eastern Europe, except Yugoslavia, which broke away from Stalin's tutelage in 1948, came under the dominance of the U.S.S.R., and Marxist totalitarian systems developed in Poland, East Germany, Czechoslovakia, Hungary, Romania, and Bulgaria—and also in little Albania on the Adriatic, which began to pursue a course of independence from Moscow, like Yugoslavia. Outside of Europe, Marxist regimes arose in Cuba, North Vietnam, and elsewhere.

DEMOCRATIC SOCIALISM, OR SOCIAL DEMOCRACY

But while Marx had in his thought the seeds of totalitarianism, he also encouraged social and economic justice. Drawing on these aspects of the socialist heritage, some socialist movements combined social welfare programs, and control of certain aspects of the economy, with open democracy. In other words, there was a merger of liberalism or liberal humanism and socialist ideals. A major pioneer of social democracy was Sweden, between the two World Wars. Measures such as universal free health care and unemployment benefits became the goal of a number of nations, such as Britain (with its socialist government elected in 1945) and France, and indeed nearly all capitalist economies took over some degree of social welfare (as in Roosevelt's New Deal from 1933 onward). The United States, was, however, resistant to the notion of socialism, which made little real progress in America. Most Americans tended to associate socialism with Soviet-style practices—inimical to democracy—rather than with Swedish and other social democratic experiments. This rejection was reinforced not long after World War II by the stormy career of Joseph McCarthy (1908–1957), a U.S. Senator who persecuted many liberals as being communists and un-American.

In Asia and Africa Marxism had appeal, in so far as it was an ideology opposed to capitalism and colonialism, from which many countries had come to expect exploitation and imperial conquest. But social democratic ideas made progress, nevertheless, in a number of them—e.g., in Sri Lanka and the Republic of India, after its independence in 1947. Japan, occupied by Allied forces after its defeat in 1945, had a liberal constitution imposed on it under the benign rule of General MacArthur (1880–1964).

PHILOSOPHY AFTER WORLD WAR II

The major trends in nonreligious thought after World War II were scientifically oriented humanism as represented in differing ways in various forms of English-speaking philosophy, and Existentialism, vigorous especially in France. Bertrand Russell (1872–1970) was a highly influential English mathematician and philosopher who taught a form of empiricism—basing all knowledge on empirical or sense experience, but supported by the progressive discoveries of science. He rejected religion, and was politically radical. He was a conscientious objector in World War I and after World War II was a leader in antinuclear protests. His freethinking was summed up in an essay on "A Free Man's Worship." To some extent he drew on the spirit of T. H. Huxley (1825–1895), a defender of Evolution, who coined the term "agnostic" to refer to a person who did not believe in God but would not go so far as to declare himself an atheist (one who believes there is no God) because of the lack of evidence either way. Russell's empiricism was parallel to that of the American philosopher John Dewey (1859–1952), who rejected God because such a belief must rest on intuition, not on empirical evidence and scientific enquiry. He considered that religious belief by postulating an "other world" splits reality, and it thereby brings about a devaluation of this world. This in turn dries up the springs of action and constitutes an attack on worldly happiness, which is the highest good for human beings. Dewey had a strong influence on American educational practice.

His emphasis on happiness, of course, drew on a major tradition of British philosophy—utilitarianism, that is, the doctrine that moral laws or rules are justified by their conducing to the greatest happiness of the greatest number and the least suffering of the least number. This criterion was a powerful weapon in the rethinking of social and legal reform. It was not enough to say that God decreed the sanctity of marriage or whatever. The question was whether a system of divorce would minimize suffering and maximize happiness. The classical statement of this position had been created by John Stuart Mill (1806–1873).

A position similar to that of Russell was held by the dominant American philosopher of the post-World War II period, Willard Van Orman Quine (b. 1908). His empiricism was reinforced by other trends, including the work of the eccentric Ludwig Wittgenstein (1879–1959), who had worked with Russell. In the second phase of his philosophy he emphasized how metaphysical problems arose from illusions of language. Out of this grew an Oxford-based movement, sometimes called "linguistic philosophy," which was aggressively antimetaphysical and more covertly antireligious, and which emphasized common sense and scientific knowledge. Its successor, which in the 1960s onward became highly refined and influential in America, is known as "analytic philosophy." This is often hostile to religion and sometimes to the new style of developing wide-ranging cross-cultural courses of religious studies in public universities in America. These became popular in the 1960s for various reasons, including a greater awareness of choice and the outside world during the Vietnam War.

EUROPEAN EXISTENTIALISM

It is perhaps ironic in view of the later emergence of atheistic existentialism that the writer who has come to be called the father of existentialism was a highly committed Christian. Later Existentialists like Heidegger and Sartre (see below) have been atheistic. The young Dane Søren Kierkegaard (1813–1855), however, stressed a kind of personalism and the need for individual choice and faith. That element of choice became vital for later thinkers. Existentialists wanted philosophy to reflect living human experience. And Kierkegaard, like Marx, Feuerbach, and Russell, rejected Hegel, but for a different reason: he detested the abstractness of Hegel, and saw a betrayal of true faith in the way he merged God and the impersonal Absolute. Hegel imagined, too, that he could reach God by taking thought, as though human reason was a ladder to the divine. But Kierkegaard saw all this as a betrayal and distortion of Christian faith, which was not "reasonable." God reaches out to individuals by grace, and it is the individual's response to make a leap of faith.

Moreover Hegel's idea that we as human beings are mere phases of a wider whole, the Absolute, seemed to Kierkegaard to rob the individual of freedom. The rejection of Kierkegaard of the power of reason in relation to God helps to explain the name "Existentialism." Reason creates abstract essences: it defines things and concepts, hoping to find common features in phenomena. These essences are not only feeble abstractions. They also put the cart before the horse. In reality humans are in a living milieu of existences. They exist before they can be defined. Similarly God is not an abstraction, but a living, existing Person.

If existentialism is a revolt against reason and abstractions, then we should include in its history the vibrant atheism of Nietzsche (1844–1900). Friedrich Nietzsche had a poetic and prophetic style, and proclaimed that the former values of the West were obsolete. A new type of human being, a superman, would exhibit a new level of life. In one of his works Nietzsche announced the death of God, exposed simply as a creation of the human mind. Nietzsche pictured the scene as a madman going around proclaiming the news of the death of God. People rather frivolously ask whether he has been lost or has gone into hiding. They do not really appreciate that if it is genuinely so that God is dead then anything is possible. All the former values of our civilization will collapse. Indeed they *have* collapsed. All those values—humility, loving-kindness, and so on—depend on the Christian idea of God. Nietzsche here replaces the ethic of humility, which he saw as slavish, with the ethic of the superman, who would embody power, strength, and beauty.

Nietzsche's atheism was vibrantly felt. He cried out in one passage: "God is the declaration of war against life, against nature, against the will to live!—the formula for every slander against 'this world', for every lie about the 'beyond'!—the deification of nothingness, the will to nothingness pronounced holy!" He rejected also traditional metaphysics—anything that detracts from the reality and vividness of the world by postulating some transcedent or invisible Being that lies behind phenomena. He wished to break away from the stuffy confines of the Enlightenment with its emphasis on reason, and yet avoid the nihilism and despair that might ensue from the rejection of traditional modes of thinking. He found his path between rationalism and nihilism through the conception of the world as a ceaseless and ever-recurring interplay between forces. It was governed by a will to power. Here he was indebted to the earlier thought of Arthur Schopenhauer (1788–1860). The superman or superior human being in mastering these forces will exhibit and spread enhanced life, and will rise above the all-too-human herd. Because of these elitist and rough-sounding sentiments Nietzsche was wrongly thought by many to be a forerunner of Nazism, with whose values, however, he had nothing in common.

Nietzsche was one of the influences on Martin Heidegger (1879–1976), a powerful force in existentialist attitudes. For him human existence, which he called *Dasein*, is the place where things present themselves. Being is not some metaphysical entity beyond or behind the world, but the finite modes in which things present themselves to us. In short Heidegger tries to analyze the world as it appears from the individual human experience, and to generalize only from there. Authentic existence comes from the freedom inherent in individual life: we can, if we wish, refuse to ignore the fact that we are finite beings facing death: we can accept death and live in the face of it. Freedom thus is a matter of authentic seeing and acting. Only such authenticity can give you philosophical understanding.

Though Heidegger had sympathy for Eastern thought, especially Zen Buddhism, which had a like motif of authenticity of experience, and an awareness of how language can distort reality, essentially Heidegger's thought was antitheistic, though he longed for the sacred universe of the ancient classical gods, especially as mediated by his favorite poet, Friedrich Hölderlin (1770–1843).

The French philosopher, playwright, novelist and political activist Jean-Paul Sartre (1905–1980) considered that existentialist philosophy had to be presented not just through treatises but also through dramas and novels. He achieved very great influence during the period immediately after World War II, especially in France, where his teachings rang true to many persons' experience of the years of occupation by the Nazis and resistance to them.

For him, human beings are in a strange predicament. He thought that it was natural for them to believe in God (he had a typically Western view of religion), for their own experience as conscious selves dwelling in material bodies suggests the power of creativity. Yet there is a contradiction in trying to see the material world as being created by an immaterial God. Humans have to acknowledge the nonexistence of God. But this is painful. So his atheism is not one of indifference: it matters that God does not exist. God's absence is like that of a loved one.

Authenticity (and here Sartre echoes Heidegger) is the central moral value. To be authentic a person has to face up to the absence of God. There are no externally sanctioned rules for us to follow. We should not succumb to roles imposed on us, for instance by society. A human being exists first: he or she is primarily defined by some essence or role. Society labels people as waiters or football players or professors or executives, and people do come to behave within the confines of these roles in a defined way. But we can always burst out beyond such definitions. This is authentic freedom. The human being can always opt to exceed the definitions that are imposed on him. Sartre's vision of freedom seemed particularly relevant to those who looked back on the period of oppression under the Nazis from 1940 to 1944. Commitment is vital, and yet it often seems to fly in the face of caution and reason.

THE QUESTION OF RELIGIOUS EXPERIENCE

For thinkers such as Sartre and even more for those who were influenced by science and the tradition of empiricism, relying on the outer senses to give us knowledge, there was little value given to religious experience. Those writers who had stressed it, such as Schleiermacher and Rudolf Otto belonged to rather different philosophical and ideological traditions. Yet some people have felt able to combine atheism and a strong sense of the mysterious. Richard Jefferies (1848–1887), an English naturalist, reformer, and novelist, wrote as follows in his famous autobiography *The Story of My Heart*:

> I was utterly alone with the sun and the earth. Lying down on the grass, I spoke in my soul to the earth, the sun, the air, and the distant sea far beyond sight. I thought of the earth's firmness—I felt it bear me up; through the grassy couch there came an influence as if I could hear the great earth speaking to me. I thought of the wandering air— its pureness, which is its beauty; the air touched me and gave me something of itself. I spoke to the sea: though so far, in my mind I saw

it, green at the rim of the earth and blue in the deeper ocean; I desired
to have its strength; its mystery and glory. Then I addressed the sun,
desiring the soul equivalence of his light and brilliance, his endurance
and unwearied race. I turned to the blue heaven over, gazing into its
depth, inhaling its exquisite colour and sweetness. The rich blue of the
unattainable flower of the sky drew my soul towards it, and there it
rested, for pure colour is rest of heart. By all these I prayed; I felt an
emotion of the soul beyond all definition; prayer is a puny thing to it,
and the word is a rude sign to the feeling; but I know no other.[1]

This kind of experience is sometimes referred to as panenhenic, and has
some affinity to that recorded in verse by William Wordsworth, the English
Lakeland poet (1770–1850), who wrote in his *Tintern Abbey*:

> . . . *And I have felt*
> *A presence that disturbs me with the joy*
> *Of elevated thoughts; a sense sublime*
> *Of something far more deeply interfused,*
> *Whose dwelling is the light of setting suns,*
> *And the bound ocean and the living air,*
> *And the blue sky, and in the mind of man:*
> *A motion and a spirit, that impels*
> *All thinking things, all objects of all thought,*
> *And rolls through all things.*

Wordsworth here connects his experience with a spirit, and in his latter days
he returned to orthodox Christian doctrines. He therefore is in effect giving
his experience something like a religious interpretation: but for Jefferies and
others this is not so. Although, by and large, humanists and atheists have
not been much concerned with the value of such mysterious experiences, rejecting them together with the religion in which most often they have found
their context, it is worth noting that what we have called the "experiential"
dimension of religion can occasionally extend to those who have rejected religious values and doctrines.

The major characteristic of humanism and atheism has been their preoccupation with the affairs of this world: for this reason little interest has
been shown in the experiences that the faithful suppose give them insight
into the invisible world beyond that which can be perceived by the senses.

[1] *The Story of My Heart* (London: Staples Press, 1964), p. 8.

MODERN AGNOSTICS

In the so-called Christian societies of the West, where agnosticism and antireligious atheism have had their widest influence, there are very many folk who simply do not attend church or synagogue. They are not necessarily lacking in religious belief, but nevertheless they do not feel called upon to belong to any religious organization. They are people who live in a large, gentle twilight zone between religiousness and agnosticism. They have inherited much of the anticlericalism of the humanist movement, but they do not share the intellectual presuppositions. They include many, therefore, who, when asked, profess belief in God—or more vaguely in a Power that controls the cosmos. But they are not convinced that the formal worship of such a Being is important. They see the heart of religion in loving one's neighbor, not in ritual. They are not inclined to pray, though they will do so in times of stress. They are alienated from the churches, because of the rivalry and differences between Christians. They are aware that different creeds teach different things about God and the transcendent world, and they are therefore distrustful of dogma. They have no wish to deny God, but they do not desire to define his nature too closely. They have reverence for a Creator; but they feel him to be distant and detached. They often think it is presumptuous for the human being to put himself or herself in the center of the cosmic picture by supposing that God came down to bring about his or her salvation. They recognize Christian moral values, but they reject puritanism. In a way, they are post-Christian folk. But they are not atheists: and they are more against religions than against religion, and more against the respectability of Sunday observance than against the recognition of God that it is intended to express. They do not have much sense of sin, but they admire saintliness. They think that Christ was greatly better than other men, but they are uncertain of his divinity. They think creeds are rather pernicious. They suspect that Christianity was a simpler thing in Jesus' teaching than it is in its current manifestations. They are worried by death, and they hope for an afterlife. But they do not feel the division between heaven and hell. They are folk who have belonged to a Christian environment, but they react against regimentation. They are skeptical, but they are not atheists.

Such people, indeed, far outnumber the committed atheists and the explicit agnostics. The latter belong to the more intellectual stratum of society. But their thoughts have become part of a climate of opinion that has penetrated into all parts of the modern Western community. The notion that there is some incompatibility between science and religion—a major plank in humanism—is widespread beyond the ranks of the humanists themselves. And science, with its great prestige derived from the practical benefits of

technology and the awesome mumbo-jumbo surrounding the expert, has acquired an authority that is thought to supersede that of religion. For many
young people this is the picture presented by the current state of our civilization. Thus although the overt atheists and agnostics are, and have been,
relatively few, the influence of their thinking has been formidable.

The intellectual achievements of Karl Marx have exerted great influence
in modern history. In providing a theory and a blueprint for Communism,
Karl Marx has been a major factor in the shaping of millions of lives in
Eastern Europe and in Asia. He stands as a remarkable testimony to the
power of ideas. Though Communism has come to power, both in Russia in
1917 and in China in 1948, through somewhat accidental circumstances,
there is no doubt that the revolutions have been enormously assisted by having a theory on which to base the subsequent development of the countries
that have passed under revolutionary control; and the seizing of power itself
has owed much to the fact that Marxism has provided an ideology to knit
together dedicated groups of revolutionaries.

Marxism has functioned as a quasi-religion, cementing together societies
in which dictatorship might otherwise have led to disintegration. It has been
an ideal for many who have seen in it a blueprint for a nobler society. It
has enabled the Communists to weather the storms of bitterness and discontent engendered by tyranny. It has given hope to millions of underprivileged folk in non-Communist countries who have been disappointed because they have experienced neither the fruits of democracy nor the prosperity of
Western capitalism. But its atheism and the totalitarianism it has encouraged make
it a powerful threat to traditional religions.

Buddhism in China and Christianity in Russia have to fight for survival in an
unexpected environment. Both Marxism and liberal humanism, then, in their different ways have weakened the fabric of religious allegiance. They add a further
dimension to the new situation in the twentieth century, when the great religions
of the world have willy-nilly been brought together in an unprecedented confrontation—a confrontation which sometimes promotes friendship, sometimes rivalry,
and sometimes both.

Humanism and Marxism have bred a new type of individual. For nearly all
of human history children have been brought up in the religious traditions of their
fathers. Most humans have had fairly clear religious beliefs. Now there are many
folk brought up without religious instruction; and many others who are taught
that religion is dangerous and evil. It is therefore an unprecedented epoch in the
history of religious experience. How religion will emerge from these new conditions
is a question whose answer must remain somewhat obscure. But perhaps we can
gain some insight by considering the outstanding features of its present situation.
To this enquiry we now turn.

95. *The wonderful city of Tenochtitlan as it appeared before the Spaniards when Cortés arrived. This highly sophisticated civilization had an ideology in which the continuance of the cosmos depended on the right performance of sacrifice. (Copyright Sergio Dorantes, 1986.)*

96. *An obsidian knife used in sacrifice by the Aztecs. (Courtesy of The British Museum.)*

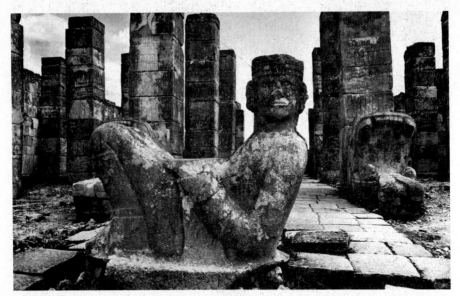

97. *The Mayan civilization was known for the elegance of its art, here seen in the statue of the rain god, at Chichen Itza in Yucatun. (Courtesy of George Holton.)*

98. *While the Church through such humane figures as Bartolomé de Las Casas protected the Indians of the New World, there were also many cases of cruel exploitation, indicated in this picture of brutal punishment in Hispaniola. (Courtesy of William L. Clements Library, University of Michigan, Ann Arbor.)*

99. *The shrine and figure of Our Lady of Guadalupe was a ritual means of bridging the two civilizations of Spain and that of the Indians. She was Christian but spoke in a native language. Here Indian boys in traditional costume attest their devotion. (Copyright Sergio Dorantes.)*

100. *In the American Southwest sand painting is not just representational: the making of it is a ritual, and it can be used among other things for curing sicknesses. Here a mother brings a sick child for healing. (Photo: Boltin, Courtesy Department of Library Services, American Museum of Natural History.)*

101. *A corn dance among Pueblo Indians in New Mexico. Corn is more than food: it is life and serves as a sanctifying substance. (Courtesy of F. B. Grunzweig/Photo Researchers, Inc.)*

102. *Many Christians had the ideal (often perceived as noble) of converting the Indians to the Christian faith. Here John Wesley preaches to them, in a somewhat idealized painting. (Courtesy of New York Public Library Picture Collection.)*

103. *A nice pictorial representation of the narrow way to the Heavenly City, with the Tree of Life and its various moral fruits. The two great preachers Wesley (center) and Whitefield (right) beckon their hearers to turn away from the broad road to hell. Protestants often saw North America as a place for planting the heavenly city upon earth. (Courtesy of New York Public Library Picture Collection.)*

104. *The camp meeting was a powerful experience for those who attended during the Second Great Awakening, in the first part of the nineteenth century. This picture was made in about 1839. (Courtesy of The Whaling Museum, New Bedford, MA.)*

105. *One of the forms of European Christianity to take root in America is Eastern Orthodoxy. Here the Greek Orthodox celebrate Christmas. The vibrant richness of their ritual often contrasts with the deliberate plainness of much Protestant practice. (Courtesy of Micha Bar An/Magnum.)*

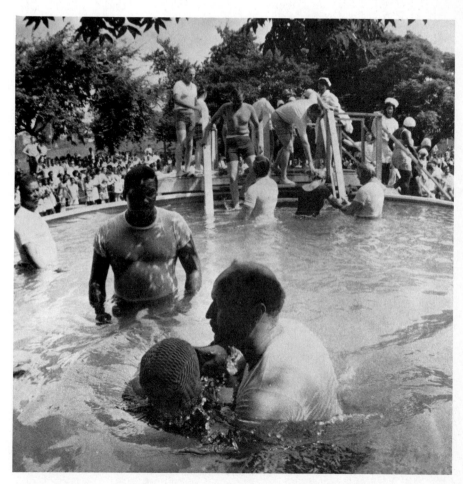

106. *New forms of faith have arisen in America. Here the baptism ceremony, which for many Christians is done by total immersion, is performed by the Jehovah's Witnesses, founded in America, at a regional convention in New York City.*

107. *Mainstream Christianity in the United States is often given to liberal thought and social action: here a lunchtime service in Manhattan conveys the impression of quiet seriousness. (Courtesy of Thomas Hoepker/Magnum.)*

108. *Jews praying together at the Jewish New Year circa 1910. Extensive immigration has made Judaism one of the influential and creative American religions. (Courtesy of Bain Collection, Library of Congress.)*

109. *Islam, often focussed on storefront mosques such as this one, is often appealing to African Americans because of its strong sense of brotherhood and discipline. They sometimes feel that Christianity has failed them, having been compromised by racism. (Courtesy of Dith Pran/New York Times Pictures.)*

110. *Even the Catholic Church with its organizational unity can feel tensions arising from minority problems. Father George Stallings here gives communion at his breakaway Catholic church, the Imani Temple (1989). (Courtesy of Eli Reed/ Magnum.)*

III. *The totality of American life is a rich mosaic of different faiths and movements. Here children of the Hare Krishna movement listen to sacred stories. The community derives its inspiration from Hindu* bhakti *or devotional religion. (Courtesy of Burt Glinn/Magnum.)*

Chapter 13

THE CONTEMPORARY EXPERIENCE

AND THE FUTURE

DECOLONIZATION AND RELIGIONS

IN THE AFTERMATH of World War II the old colonial empires began to dissolve. India and Pakistan came into being in 1947, and Sri Lanka was independent the following year. Despite resistance leading to some wars (as in Algeria and Vietnam), the majority of the old colonial lands gained freedom, first throughout Asia and North Africa, and then in Black Africa, the Caribbean, and the Pacific. Although the Soviet Union and China retained their prerevolutionary empires, they too began to loosen up in the late 1980s. The ending of the colonial period helped with a reevaluation in the West of Eastern and Southern religions. This came to the surface most vividly in the 1960s, when a questioning of so many traditional values, both in Europe and America, led to new interest in non-Western religious and spiritual movements. There was a resurgence of demand for gurus and forms of yoga, for teaching of some of the old values of India, for Zen and other Far Eastern practices, and so on.

Part of the reason, especially in America, was disillusion with existing patterns of Protestantism, Catholicism, and Judaism. The mainline Protestant Churches, for instance, had in a way been highly successful during the 1950s, which was a period of great prosperity in the United States, while other Western countries such as Italy and Germany, together with Japan, were only setting out on their remarkable post-World War II recovery. America was visible and culturally dominant in many ways, though preoccupied with the Communist threat. During this period mainline religion, respectable, reassuring, and vigorous, was successful: but at the price, perhaps, of greatly neglecting alternative paths of spirituality. It tended to be moralistic and Biblical. In the 1960s unease and rebellion developed. There were convergent causes. There was the Civil Rights movement, led by Martin Luther King (1929–1968), which questioned traditional attitudes. There was the Vietnam War, emphasized first by President John F. Kennedy (1917–1963), which increasingly called in question the morality of a technologically fought conflict and the values, too, of anti-Communism. The death of Kennedy left a violent question mark on the values of the age. New forces in music, such as that of the Beatles, created a spirit of social and sexual questioning. Black riots in Watts, Los Angeles, in 1965 and elsewhere drew attention to social injustice. Meanwhile, as we have seen earlier, the Catholic Church had undergone the dramatic upheaval and debate of Vatican II (the Second Vatican Council) of 1962 to 1965, where Pope John XXIII tried to stimulate his Church to update itself—*aggiornamento*. During this vigorous period, there were movements to create Black theology, Red theology (that is Native American formulations of Christianity), and above all feminist philosophy. In short there was a celebration of and struggle toward all kinds of liberation. In this emancipated and often contradictory time, there were severe tensions, but a lot of creativity. It was most of all in this period that the question was raised as to the mutual relationship of the world's religions.

DO ALL RELIGIONS POINT TO THE SAME TRUTH?

As we have noted, Swami Vivekananda, the Hindu teacher, had already proclaimed, at the World's Parliament of Religions in Chicago in 1893, that all religions essentially point to the same truth. They have different shapes and paths, but these either represent simple cultural variations or differing levels of progress toward one goal. Against this irenic view, peaceful in its hope of uniting all religions, there could be severe backlashes. For one thing, so-called "fundamentalist" or literally grounded Biblical forms of Christianity often were severe in rejecting alternative ideas. For such Christians even ecumenical trends, in which Christians of differing denominations strove to come together with a view ultimately of achieving some higher federation of Christian forces, were often anathema. How much more would consorting with foreign traditions betray the spirit of the faith?

There were equally conservative forms of Judaism and Islam that would not go happily with Vivekananda's message. Likewise they would reject later formulations, such as those of Aldous Huxley (1894–1963) or John Hick (b. 1922). Moreover it was not only fundamentalists who rejected what they saw as excessive desires to unify religions. Some mainline Christian thinkers shared this view, especially those under the influence of the conservative ideas represented by Karl Barth (1886–1968). Thus the Dutch thinker Hendrik Kraemer (1880–1965) argued, in his book *The Christian Message in a*

None-Christian World, published in 1938 in connection with a missionary conference at Tambaram in South India, and greatly influential in the post-War period, that all religion and religions are human creations. Only God's self-revelation in Christ is from another source. Christian faith is a response to this Word. Insofar as Christ influences the Christian religion (itself a human creation too, of course) there is a divine light in it. The effect of this notion was to condemn all religions but not the Gospel as merely human. At a stroke he seemed to solve the problem of "other" religions.

But it is worth noting that the logical move that he made could be made by others. The Hindu could say that the Dharma or Truth was revealed and all other religious claims were simply human creations. The Buddhist could say that the Buddha's Dharma was likewise ultimate and everything else not.

Is it then wiser to think of all religions as pointing to the one Truth? Let us briefly look at Aldous Huxley's idea of the "Perennial Philosophy," namely a truth that recurs perennially through the diverse traditions at differing times and places. It happened that Huxley was very much interested in the life of contemplation and mysticism. He was also intrigued with the properties of mind-altering drugs, such as mescalin. Indeed he was one root of the new drug movement that took off in the 1960s and that tried to use chemicals in effect to open the doors to heaven and ironically protested the technological age by using a technology of alternative states of consciousness to transcend it. But what he meant by the perennial philosophy related essentially to mysticism: it was the common strand of mysticism running through the great religions that attracted him. So he could see a common thread in the writings of Plotinus, St. John of the Cross, Eckhart, Rumi, Ghazali, the Kabbalah, the Hasidim, Shankara and the Bhagavadgita, Zen, D. T. Suzuki, and so on.

The fact that there is some affinity between the mystics of the great religions has often been noticed. Whether they really are saying the same thing is open to debate. But it is at least a possibility that here we have a common factor in all the main religious traditions. However, we still have to account for other motifs. Not all religious movements and writers stress the unity of the self with the ultimate (so common a theme among mystics). Some stress and distance between heaven and earth, and between God as personal Other and the worshipper, between the Creator and the human being. How does such a dualism arise? Why is it that some religions emphasize oneness and others twoness? Part of the explanation arises from the nature of the numinous experience so well delineated by Otto. This emphasizes the gap between the *mysterium tremendum* and the individual devotee. It therefore appears correct to see the numinous and mystical expe-

riences as belonging to two different types. The former can be seen clearly
in theophanies and divine confrontations, as in the lives of people such as
Isaiah, Job, Paul, Muhammad, Arjuna, and the vision of our Lady of Guadalupe. Exterior visions of the Other contrast with the ineffable inner
mergings with the One or with purified consciousness. Both may be from
God. I am not commenting on whether such experiences are valid or not,
or reveal the nature of reality. But they do seem to be of a differing kind
(just as we might also wish to think of the experience of the shaman as
being different again). There seems to be more than one kind of religious
experience.

These remarks are relevant, because they may call in question Aldous
Huxley's central concern with mysticism. It is open for adherents of a differing position to say that he stresses the mystical too much. Given the total
context of religious experience we cannot simply adhere to the importance of
one kind of experience alone. Moreover, even among mystics there seems to
be striking diversities of interest and interpretation. For the Sufi the highest
state is an intimate cleaving to the Divine; for the Mahayana Buddhist it is
the realization of Emptiness. And so it is by no means easy to prove that
all religions point to the same truth. They have differing formulations and
emphases.

More recently there have been models other than Huxley's such as that
of John Hick, who sees the new relationship between religions to be like a
Copernican revolution: we can see a single Reality round which all religions
revolve like planets. It is not possible for any one faith to claim an absolute
position at the center. The effect of Hick's model is very similar to that of
Vivekananda. Both think of a world in which the different religions have
to tolerate each other, because they all have insights into the one Truth.

Maybe the right position lies between that of the conscious pluralists, such as
Vivekananda, and Hick on the one hand and the stern absolutists, such as Christian
or Islamic fundamentalists on the other. The main thing to consider is that each
worldview should be tolerant, in the sense of allowing the others to operate freely,
so far as possible. There may be severe conflicts over some issues—for instance
whether abortion is to be permitted and if so on what conditions. But even if society
has to make a decision on such issues, that too should be subject to repeal; and
decisions should be arrived at openly and without coercion. It is no doubt a necessity
in today's world that disputes should be resolved peacefully. On the other hand,
such toleration and peacefulness need not imply agreement. Different people should
be allowed their diverse beliefs, even if they are often conflicting. The different
religious traditions may sometimes reject the idea that all faiths point to the same
truth. The latter view seems to rob religions of particularity and their own special
revelations and authorities, which they may hold very dear. So we need not affirm

necessarily the unity of all religions at some deeper level. But we ought ordinarily to practice toleration.

THE INTERPLAY OF RELIGIONS

Religious Exchanges

The period from the 1960s on has seen some notable effects of the interplay of world religions. The melding of cultures has encouraged new religious movements. Sometimes these have exhibited older religions transposed to new contexts. Notably forms of Buddhism have flourished in the West, stimulated by the exile of the Dalai Lama from his homeland of Tibet, and by the greatly increased Western concern with forms of meditation. This was in part the consequence of a recognition of the absence among mainline Protestant groups of a serious concern, in those days, with spiritual self-training. Psychoanalysis had already created great interest in the exploration of inner states: now Buddhism and Hindu yoga offered old therapies and methods to go along with Western methods. There were other newer modes of training—such as Maharishi Mahesh Yogi's transcendental meditation, which is a kind of simplified version of Hindu training for use by lay persons and in everyday life.

Meanwhile, there was some religious exchange. Christians took up forms of Eastern meditation to enhance their spiritual life. Notable among explorers in this mode was Thomas Merton (1915–1968). Another person to join Far Eastern meditation with Catholic commitment was Heinrich Dumoulin (b. 1913), author of some notable books on Zen. In the other direction, Christian kinds of worship came to influence Pure Land piety, and Christian organizations helped to foster ecumenical moves within other traditions, notably in Buddhism, through the World Fellowship of Buddhists. Among Islamic groups, the radical and in some ways conservative Muslim Brotherhood, founded by Hassan al-Banna' (1906–1969) in 1928, but particularly active in the 1960s, made increased use of modern Western-style methods of education and communication.

NEW RELIGIOUS MOVEMENTS

NEW DEVELOPMENTS

We have noted how some new religions are in effect old religions in new places: Eastern faiths migrating into North American and European society.

Some have taken particular forms—for instance, the Nation of Islam sprang from the life and work of Elijah Mohammad (1892–1975) and Malcolm X (1925–1965). As a disciplined movement this had great appeal among American Blacks. Others have been genuinely new, and have emphasized psychological diagnoses and therapies such as Scientology and est. Some groups have been controversial, and, as with some of the electronic evangelists preaching a Christian message, have been somewhat fraudulent. But all have contributed to the lively religious ferment of the past 25 years.

The ferment has been no less outside the West. There are numerous new independent churches in Africa, under the guidance of leaders and prophets who have emphasized certain values that are important to the indigenous cultures of Africa. There are varied new movements throughout the Southern world—such as Iglesia di Kristo in the Philippines, founded in 1914, the Ratana Church among Maoris in New Zealand, founded in 1919, the Native American Church in North America, and a plethora of new religious movements in Japan.

So it is that the present century is a great laboratory of religions, both in testing the changes and adaptation of older traditions to new forces and in creating new compounds and varieties in the interstices between religions.

Sometimes the new movements have stirred up prejudices among more traditional institutions. It has, for instance, been customary to look on those groups dubbed by the media as being "cults" as having sinister characteristics. They have been accused, for instance, of using brainwashing techniques to make converts. It is doubtful whether on the whole pressures are stronger from new movements than from some of the older religions, or whether there is anything genuinely called brainwashing. It is doubtful too whether some particular set of religions should be singled out for the designation "cults." The older distinctions between church, denomination, and sect seem adequate without adding a special new category.

THE SECULAR IDEOLOGIES IN RECENT TIMES

Although Marxism still appeared to be vigorous in the 1960s—indeed some of the student movements, in France, Germany, and even to some degree in the United States were inspired by Marxist ideals—by the end of the 1980s it was in deep trouble, and in many cultural areas obviously crumbling as a credible edifice of belief. Its apparent strength in helping to motivate the North Vietnamese to struggle against the United States and eventually to win the war was matched by a renewal in China after the death of Mao Zedong in 1976. Under the leadership of Deng Xiaoping, China undertook a certain decentralization and liberal restructuring of its economy, which had a powerful growth.

But problems lay in store for Marxist values. The new wave of openness ushered in by Mikhail Gorbachev, who succeeded to power in the U.S.S.R. in 1985 after the death of the chain of feeble old men who had been dominating the Kremlin, loosened the shackles on the Soviet Union's Eastern European allies. Poland, which has been turbulent since the uprising in the Lenin shipyard in Gdansk under the leadership of Lech Wałesza (b. 1931), followed the lead of Hungary in moving toward pluralistic politics and a liberalized economy. 1989 became a marvelous and significant year, fit to rank with 1789 in the annals of European revolution. In both Hungary and Poland non-Communist governments took over. Then in October the East German regime started to crumble. The Berlin Wall was opened and parts of it torn down in November, and in that month the Communist government in Czechoslovakia resigned. Just before Christmas violent revolution broke out in Romania, and the dictator of 25 years Nicolae Ceausescu and his wife Elena were executed. It was not long before there were upheavals too in Bulgaria. So in a short time the whole face of Marxist Eastern Europe was transformed.

But in China the demonstrations by students and workers in May and early June in Beijing, arguing for more freedom, were brought to an abrupt and vicious end by the massacre of Tienanmen Square on June 4. In China, the crumbling of Marxism was halted, and the old discipline and fear reimposed. Meanwhile into the 1990s the processes of liberalizing and decentralizing the Soviet Union continued, complicated by the resurgence of nationalism in the Baltic Republics, Armenia, Georgia, and Azerbaijan, Soviet Central Asia, and Moldavia.

These events indicated that a deep malaise had overtaken Marxism. Although in theory the doctrines were liberating, in fact they were almost universally applied in an oppressive way. It survived as a doctrine because of the secret police. As soon as people felt that they were not at risk in expressing their feelings they came on the streets and ended the hitherto seemingly impregnable Marxist dictatorships. In this religion sometimes played a part, for instance, in Poland where Catholicism and Polish nationalism blended with social-democratic ideals in the ethos of the Solidarity trade-union movement. Religion could also contribute to ethnic tensions, as in the clashes between Christian Armenians and Muslim (Shi'a) Azeris.

The result of the momentous changes of 1989 was to signal a victory for social-democratic forces in Europe. Pluralism in politics and an admixture of capitalism in economics seemed to be the preferred formula.

THE RESURGENCE OF RELIGIONS

ISLAM

Meanwhile in recent times Islam has undergone reinvigoration. This is in part due to worldwide communications. It has made it easier for Muslims to feel a sense of global togetherness, which is reinforced by the much greater ease of making the pilgrimage to Mecca. Every year millions of Muslims from every part of the world rub shoulders and exchange ideas in the holy city.

Another factor is the increased appeal of more radical Muslim positions to younger people in many countries. Many women are showing their loyalty to the faith by taking the veil, after decades of Westernization, which has sometimes brought polarization between rich and poor. It was above all in the Iran of the Shah that there was increasing dissatisfaction with his crash program to make a modern military state in alliance with the United States. In the Iranian revolution of 1979 a leading figure was the Ayatollah Khomeini (1900–1989), a spiritual leader who had spent a long exile in Iraq and then in France. On his return he consolidatd his power and helped to frame an Islamic constitution based on Shi'a values. He became a worldwide symbol for many Muslims, even if they were Sunnis rather than Shi'a by persuasion, of Islamic resistance to the forces of modern Western capitalism. Other countries adopted Islamic constitutions during this period, such as Pakistan and the Sudan. In the latter country the attempt to impose the Muslim Shari'a or Law on the whole country helped to foment, during the 1980s, a Southern rebellion among people who were either Christian or adherents of traditional African religions.

Because Islam has traditionally looked to political as well as religious action, it has been strengthened by the greater power of many key Muslim nations due to the increase of oil revenues in the 1970s. Also, spurred by challenges such as defeat in the Arab–Israeli War of 1967, Muslim nations came together in 1969 to form a kind of Islamic commonwealth, the Organization of the Islamic Conference.

Intellectually and spiritually, Islam is invigorated by new forms of intellectual exploration. Many Muslims, especially younger and vigorous elements in modernizing societies, are disillusioned with *ulamas* trained in traditional ways, but also with older versions of Islamic modernism. They reject Marxism. The way forward appears to be a fresh restatement of the values of the Islam of the Qu'ran and a rethinking of the nature of the law. It is a more conservative stance than that of the old modernism, but more modern and forward-looking than the old traditionalism. This new "fundamentalism" has the power to reinvigorate Islam.

CONTEMPORARY JUDAISM

Meanwhile Judaism remains deeply moved by its attempts to wrestle with the aftermath of the Holocaust. Gradually its power centers are being concentrated in North America and Israel. The advent of Mikhail Gorbachev to power in the Soviet Union has gradually made it easier for Soviet Jews to emigrate either to America or to Israel, and the latter country remains in control of the Palestinian areas of the West Bank and the Gaza Strip—areas experiencing both the long uprising or *intifada*, which started in 1988, and the settlement of Jewish colonies.

In America, despite declines in numbers due to a low birth rate and a large number of intermarriages, the community remains vigorous, with over six million people, nearly half of whom are affiliated with synagogues. There is a growth in the number of Jews known as "penitent returners," who are persons reaffirming their Jewish heritage and faith. There has also been a strong increase in membership of informal fellowships known as *havurah* (pl. *havurot*), about two thousand of which have been formed. These and other phenomena suggest a renewal and intensification of spiritual life among Jews. This remains, despite tensions within the community on various matters, such as between those who adopt a feminist stance and those who resist changes to traditional practices.

RECENT CHRISTIANITY

In the past twenty-five years there has been a consolidation of the Ecumenical Movement among mainline and other Christian Churches. At the same time there has been a conservative backlash, notably in North America, partly directed against the liberal ethos of ecumenism and partly against the secular values of society. Conservative Christians played an active part in politics during the Reagan years from 1980 to the end of 1987. This was also part of a wider emphasis on religious experience and in particular the importance of conversion or being "born again." More striking was the growth, from the 1960s on, of the charismatic movement, throughout the Churches of the Christian tradition, and notably Catholicism. It expressed itself through striking experiences and phenomena, such as speaking with tongues: it was often rather literal in its interpretation of scriptures.

Meanwhile the center of focus of the religion has continued to shift to the South of the world. Christianity is fast growing in Africa, and in Latin America the Catholic Church has great vigor, especially through the development of a Marxist-oriented Liberation Theology, which preaches the Church's duty to the poor, the need to raise the consciousness of the oppressed, and the formation of grassroots communities and organizations designed to raise the morale and the level of living of those at the bottom of society.

Meanwhile the succession of a Polish Pope, John Paul II, to the Holy See in 1978, gave added impetus to the revival of religion in Eastern Europe. His visit to Poland in 1980 helped to spark the Solidarity revolt, which ultimately culminated in the union involvement in the governing of Poland in 1989.

Though the mainline Christian denominations in the West have been in some decline, outpaced often by brasher movements such as those sponsored by television evangelism, or by more conservative trends, their strength lies in their apparent weakness. No other world religion, with the possible exception of Buddhism, has been so self-critical. The modern historical study of the scriptures, the variety of kinds of Christian theology, the exploration of philosophical questions, the willingness to adapt secular ideologies such as Marxism to the task of reframing Christian social policy, and the acceptance of a high degree of individual choice and variety in worship have all contributed to a very lively period of Christian experimentation. This effervescence has paralleled the realization for the need for alternative, non-Western interpretations of Christianity, and in ecumenical circles particularly an active role has been played by African, Asian, South American, Caribbean, and Pacific Christians.

HINDUISM AFTER INDIAN INDEPENDENCE

It is perhaps most of all in the fifty years after World War II that Hinduism has developed most its universal character as a world religion. The groundwork of course had been laid by men such as Swami Vivekananda and Sarvepalli Radhakrishnan, who emphasized the universal character of Hindu doctrines, values, and practices. But beyond that is the question of converting to the faith. Theoretically Hindus are those who are born Hindus, within the fabric of the Hindu caste system. But increasingly in this half-century there have been conversions. This is in part because so many Hindu gurus during the period have come West, preaching various beliefs and practices to a clientele drawn from the searching young and no-so-young. Those who joined the International Society of Krishna Consciousness—the Hare Krishnas as they are popularly called—went the whole way, adopting Hindu garb and eating in the Indian fashion, and chanting God's name for all the world in the manner of Hindu devotees in the tradition of Caitanya. There are others who, more compromising, are Western followers of Hindu teachings—such as those of Sri Aurobindo, or Ramakrishna Vedanta, or the Radhasoami Movement, or Sai Baba, the colorful saint from Andhra Pradesh.

To some degree the new outgoing character of Hindu movements reflected inner changes and novelties. Within the fabric of the religion many new subreligions have tended to emerge, and maybe never more vigorously than in recent times. And so it is that Hinduism is no longer simply the faith of a complex unitary society, but is gaining universal force.

Further, the Hindu diaspora is becoming ever more important. Many highly educated Indians went abroad in the period after World War II, especially to North America. New temples were built by this relatively affluent population: for instance, there is a complete South Indian temple in Malibu Canyon in Southern California. There has been a vivifying effect of modern communications too on the older diaspora communities—such as the Hindus of Fiji, Mauritius, Natal, Guyana, and Surinam.

Though the Indian Constitution enshrines pluralism, based on a blend of modern Hindu ideology (in the style of Vivekananda) and federal democratic principles, there has also been a resurgence of Hindu militancy in India, with a call for a Hindu State. Communal clashes with India's substantial Muslim population (nearly 100 million) have helped to polarize thinking. Sikh militancy in the Punjab lay behind the assassination of the Prime Minister, Indira Gandhi, in 1984. Such developments threaten Indian order. But the motif of all-embracing toleration still predominates in the Hindu tradition, though somewhat perilously.

BUDDHISM IN ITS GLOBAL MANIFESTATION

Buddhism, though not very strong numerically, has made a lasting impression on the Western world, partly because of increased cultural contact. The American occupation of Japan after World War II was a means of transmitting some Japanese and Buddhist influences back to the United States. Later the influx of Tibetan refugees brought the spirituality of this kind of Buddhism to the attention of the West. Various teachers set up in Western countries. During the late 1960s, Buddhism seemed a particularly attractive form of counterculture to those who were rather disillusioned with traditional forms of Christianity and Judaism.

But there remain questions concerning the Buddhist tradition in a number of countries. Its future in Cambodia is unstable, while the Marxist countries, especially China and North Korea, have not been very hospitable to its reemergence after having been suppressed in the name of the Marxist revolution. Its image has been disfigured in Sri Lanka, where fighting between militant Sinhalese and ferocious Tamil guerillas has been intermittent since 1979. The problematic state of the tradition in many of its major homelands has given greater prominence to its presence in the West.

It is undergoing something of an ecumenical unification, with Buddhist groups cooperating on various projects, drawn from the different mainstreams of Buddhism, such as the diverse Mahayana schools and the Theravada.

Of all the varying dialogues between religions, probably that between Buddhism and Christianity is the most flourishing, especially in California.

OTHER RELIGIONS IN THE CONTEMPORARY WORLD

Western interest has been a factor in a modest revival, outside of China, of the Taoist religion, while Confucian thought—again outside China—is attracting stronger attention. In Singapore a formal move has been made to introduce Confucian ethics into the high school system. Sikhism is vigorously and sometimes bloodily debating whether it should have an independent homeland in the Punjab. The Parsees are drawing closer together with better travel between the different parts of its diaspora.

Probably the most dramatic events have occurred in the world of small-scale religions—among Native Americans, Australian Aborigines, Inuit or Eskimo peoples, and so on. Because of the pressures of outer societies and of the capitalist economy, they often undergo tragedies of exploitation and decimation—especially in newly developed areas such as the Amazon Basin where the Yanomoni people feel the impact of gold prospecting, with its attendant lawlessness, European diseases, attacks on the native folk, and erosion of their hunting and gathering territory. There is a stronger need under such conditions for political mobilization, and there are signs of the drawing together of the various small-scale peoples. Also the groups in a cultural area tend to unite ideologically, and to begin to fashion something called Native American religion, Australian religion, and so on. These larger formations of peoples will eventually no doubt lead to a worldwide organization of the peoples of smaller scale embedded within the dominant populations of stronger cultures.

THE FUTURE OF RELIGIONS WITHIN A NEW GLOBAL CIVILIZATION

THE WORLD DRAWS TOGETHER

There are unmistakable signs of the coming of a new order to the world. The older ideological tensions are fading. It is true that some Marxist regimes are surviving the period of crumbling. It may be that China and North Korea, for example, will maintain their more rigid varieties of social order. But even so the imperatives of trade will tend to break down barriers. These clumps of State-dominated economics will be embedded in a largely capitalist globe. But this is a new capitalism in which national entities are growing less important. The stock exchanges around the globe are now linked and the behavior of Tokyo now affects Wall Street a few hours later. Larger transnational corporations bestraddle the world. It is less and less easy for a national economy, however, large, to insulate itself from the transactions of a world system. Moreover the last fifty years have seen striking developments: not only has Europe reconstructed itself, but it is forming a merger that will make it into a huge economic entity, while East Asia and parts of Southeast Asia now form a highly modernized region. Gradually development is spreading. On the whole it has been demonstrated that attitudes and education are the key to such development, rather than raw materials and resources. Oil-rich countries have sometimes been judicious enough to invest wisely in educational facilities and industries that will bring lasting benefits, but by no means has oil universally brought benefits, when other factors have inhibited development. The histories of some well-endowed countries have been melancholy—such as Iraq, Iran, Mexico, and Libya, for example. But gradually the lessons of economic growth are being learned. But though we see the emergence of a new transnational economy in which national entities are less important, there remain desperate problems in many Third World countries, especially in Africa and parts of Latin America. As the Northern parts of the world are getting richer, the South in many places is getting poorer.

The major religions themselves tend to be transnational spiritual corporations, especially with the growth of ecumenical thinking and organization. Islam and Christianity are especially important as bridges between the North and South. But even the smaller religions are, because of diasporas, increasingly transnational, and they may do something to alleviate the distressing gaps that open up between rich and poor.

NATIONALISM AND THE GLOBAL VISION

Despite the fact that modern economics is making nationalism less and less meaningful, it nevertheless has a powerful future. The reason is that so many national groups have not achieved a reasonable degree of independence. This is in part because of the persistence of huge empires long after the colonial period was supposed to have ended: in particular the Soviet Union, which carries on the old Tsarist Empire, and China, which suppresses nationalism in Tibet, Mongolia, and elsewhere. But there are many ethnic groups in Africa and some in Indonesia and South and Southeast Asia, which have not gained autonomy. All these groups will feel their national identities very strongly so long as they are not granted reasonable independence or autonomy. There is nothing like a sense of oppression for stimulating national feeling. In some cases such ethnic struggles will combine with religious ones, where a religion is intertwined with historical identity—as in Azerbaijan, Armenia, Cyprus, Palestine, and the Southern Sudan.

To some extent the very fact that the human race is drawing together in a single economic and social system, with many interchanges between cultures worldwide, represents a threat to identity. It may therefore foment "fundamentalist" or hardline religious movements, whether among Biblically oriented Protestants, Muslim radical movements, resurgent Hindu nationalists, Sikh militants, or Jewish settlers in Palestine. It is to be expected that such backlashes will get stronger, with incalculable effects, especially where they become combined with a sense of national grievance. So the movement of religions, we can expect, will be dialectical—moving outward toward cooperation and the idea of a pluralist world, and inward toward a hard reaffirmation of uniqueness and special identity.

As part of the world becomes more urbanized and culturally blended, we should expect a greater degree of individualism. Spiritual life will be seen more and more as involving choices. This will encourage a degree of eclecticism—choosing this and that feather from other religious and ideological traditions to blend with one's own main background. There will also be an increasing number of people who do not affiliate formally to churches, synagogues, or other religious organizations, but have their own individual perspectives on the world.

We can also expect, in the meeting of religions and cultures, and the challenges to traditional customs and ideas, a growth in the number of new religious movements of all kinds, formed often out of blends of different faiths. So the world again is going to develop in two directions. In one direction it will become more homogeneous. Tourism will become blandly similar, and products, from cars to foods, will tend to converge in a global economy. Communications will reduce the variety of television, newspapers, books and videos. On the other hand, the number of religious movements will increase, and all sorts of new ideas and rituals are likely to arise.

NEW DIRECTIONS IN RELIGIOUS STUDIES

The pluralism of the world community ultimately is bound to affect education. Here an important role can be played by plural religious studies. In a number of Western countries, and in a few Asian ones, there are increased moves toward the sympathetic treatment of all major religions as a component in children's education, and toward the development of serious studies of religions at the level of higher education. In recent years there have been some important ways in which human perceptions of spiritual values have been improved.

The exploration of African, Native American, and other small-scale societies' religions has lent new dignity and seriousness to them. Westerners have learned from these forms of religion, and they are no longer viewed as anthropological oddities. Importantly, the women's movement worldwide has given us a new perspective on human religious experience. The life of women has in the past been neglected by so many historians and students of religion, partly out of male bias and partly because previous social structures have ensured that much of the written material—our chief source of knowledge of the past—has been oriented toward male categories, ideas, and achievements. This new wave of women's studies has given us a refreshing new way of viewing religions and worldviews. In the future, we can expect a much greater role for women in the expression and governing of religions.

Such changes in outlook cause complex dynamics within the traditions. The women's movement, for instance, tends to be critical of the traditional treatment of women in Islam. Those liberated women, growing in number, who wish yet to stay as faithful Muslims, have in effect to espouse a form of Islamic modernism, bringing liberal values into the interpretation of the Qur'an and early Islam. But this is not necessarily the most vibrant form of Islam at the present time. There are other women who consider that the imposition of egalitarian ideas on Islam is Western colonialism in a new form. The notion that liberalism is equally applicable to all peoples of the world may be questioned by many in the traditions. So you then find that quite a number of educated women in Arab and other Islamic parts of the world may deliberately take the veil as a symbol of their reaching out for a renewal of faith. Moreover, how does one disentangle liberal thinking from the particularlities of Western culture?

Then again there are highly traditional Muslims who may be shocked by the liberal behavior of their younger sisters. They react to the women's movement in a conservative, almost blind, way, unable to comprehend the values of the new world that is spreading around them. So there are complex tensions, in any tradition (and I choose Islam because the point is easier to illustrate there), that are set off by the novel ways of today's world.

Moreover, as we noted earlier, traditional religions are often closely linked to national movements. This gives an extra twist to the tensions already noted.

We have already discussed some of the effects from plural education. But the growth of education in the world is not all at the same level. Many populations are becoming literate for the first time, as in countries such as Nicaragua, Indonesia, many nations in Africa, and in the South Pacific. At first the consequences of literacy are not so sophisticated. It involves some liberation from the past and the grip of an oral tradition. In Catholic countries, for instance, it means that many people who could not previously read the Bible can now do so. They can easily come under the influence of Protestant missionaries, Mormons, and so on.

Another major trend in the near future of the human race is the reemergence in the Soviet Union and Eastern Europe of a rich religious life, with varying groups competing. Above all it is a time of opportunity for the Orthodox Churches to renew themselves, being out from under the rule of Communism. In order to survive they made sundry compromises. From 1990 onward these are no longer necessary.

TOWARD A NEW VISION OF THE HUMAN RACE

What are we to make of the various trends sketched above? Is there a worldview that can hope to embrace all the tensions and contradictions, all the richnesses and proliferations, of our religiously and ideologically plural world? If we are becoming a single civilization, dominated by vast capitalist companies and by a web of closely knit communications, what should this mean in the way of an outlook in which we can all share?

It has already been argued that we cannot too easily think that all religions and philosophies point to the same truth. Though religions often overlap and support one another, they have deep differences of doctrine and narrative, and of ritual and ethics. Moreover, there is, in a plural world, no question of proving any position. To the outsider you cannot demonstrate that the Bible or the Qur'an is revelation: you can think of good reasons for holding that one or other is the truth, but good reasons and proof are different. This is one of the main grounds for the belief that education must be pluralist in character. If you do not have public proof of something, it should not be taught as the sole truth. There is thus room for genuine divergence of views in religion. The idea that there are obvious spiritual truths has been a cause of persecution in the past: for instance, Luther thought that Jews were perverse in not accepting the Old Testament's obvious prefiguring of Christ, for instance, Isaiah's image of the Suffering Servant. But for Jews that Servant is the people of Israel. The interpretation of the Hebrew Bible does not at all necessarily follow Christian lines. Luther's view of the Jews was a small tributary toward that flood of antisemitism that has so disfigured the twentieth Century. In brief then, a plural approach to the religions and philosophies of the human race is desirable, allowing the diverse paths to stretch peaceably side by side. But this does not mean that we need treat all as equally true: it is up to individuals or groups to make up their minds. Freedom of faith allows for rich diversity of judgments as to the truth.

But all this implies something about the human condition. It makes us see the human race as seeking through varied forms of life to realize its highest spiritual aims. It suggests a parallel with science: this has progressed by trial and error, by theory and experiment, by good fortune and adventurous thinking, by testing new ideas and consolidating old gains, and by reaching ever onward in a dialectic with nature. Religions cannot it is true conduct easy experiments, nor are they swiftly to be refuted by counterevidence. But they do represent different existential gropings toward the truth. They represent a multiple search. So it is that human ideas and spiritual practices, which have come together for the first time in human history during the past fifty years, are part of the human response to the enigma of the cosmos. What is the meaning of life? How can we gain true liberation? Where is final freedom to be found? We have to find answers, but each is a matter of faith or commitment, rather than outer proof. Each answer is a poetic rendering of our own experience and tradition in the face of the amazing deliverances of history and nature—amazing, but obscure. Mystery surrounds the human race. Perhaps as we enter our new period of a mingled human civilization we shall become more pragmatic. Never has "By their fruits ye shall know them" seemed more relevant, even if the different worldviews diverge over which fruits are the most precious.

Moreover, it is not just religions that are meeting in the modern world: the philosophies of differing cultures are beginning to interact. It is true that often a certain Western arrogance leads to neglect of other traditions. But the time is ripe for deep exchanges between Indian philosophy, Chinese and

Japanese ideas, and African and Latin American worldviews. The notions of Confucius and Neo-Confucianism, modern Japanese experiments with blends between Buddhist and Western ideas, the Taoist tradition, and a variety of Indian metaphysics are ready to enter into fruitful exchange with the West, together with the effervescence of Black thinking and Hispanic reflections on the West. The crumbling of Marxism will prepare the way for all kinds of exchanges of ideas in the Eastern world.

The religious experience of the human race suggests important values that we ought to promote and protect: the brotherhood or sisterhood of humanity, care for all living beings, dispassion in the face of greed, hatred, and delusion, concern for other forms of life and for nature, the defence of spiritual freedom, openness toward other faiths, and the ceremonious respect for all individuals so that each person is treated with dignity.

Within such a framework let humans cultivate their deeper natures, being alert to the numinous deliverances of the Other, the inner light, the deeper lessons of suffering, the sublimer messages of human joy, the many experiences that give us greater insight into life and ultimate freedom. The human race is a restless swarm of searchers. The search has, in this most recent age, entered a new and exciting phase. Through it we shall still hear small voices, in a new age of togetherness and diversity.

Altogether the history of the religions of the human race has been multiple: often bitter, often noble, often sweet, at times cruel, sometimes beautiful, often ugly. It can teach us many lessons. Whether we feel ourselves surrounded by a spiritual world, or guided by the one God, or striving toward nirvana, or alone in an empty universe, we as religious people asking spiritual questions have tried to see beyond our senses. Is it just imagination or is it a holy power that impels us?

TRANSLITERATION OF

ORIENTAL WORDS

THIS LIST includes the more important words and names of which the full transliteration has not been used in the text of the book and/or of which there are alternative spellings. Where necessary, a rough guide to pronunciation is given.

Note that in the usual scholarly transliterations, a short *a* is pronounced like the *u* in the English, "but," and a short *u* is pronounced like the *oo* in the English "hook." A long *u* corresponds to the *oo* in "boot," and a long *a* to the first vowel in "farther."

The list divides under four heads. On the left is the form of the word or name used in this book. Next is the usual scholarly transliteration (where it differs from the form used in the first column). In the third column are alternative transliterations commonly in use. On the right, in the fourth column, is a rough attempt to show the pronunciation of those terms where the transliteration may not be altogether a good guide to the pronunciation: the rough guide to pronunciation assumes the usual pronounciation of English/American spellings. Thus the rough guide to the pronunciation of "Shankara" is "Shungkara," and in "Shung" one rimes with the English "sung." Hence the right-hand column does not obey the rules about *a* and *u* outlined above, as a guide to the principles of transliteration. As a rule, scholarly transliteration give vowels the value they would have in Italian: the right-hand column sticks to English values.

Term used in text	Usual scholarly transliteration	Alternate spellings	Pronunciation guide
Abbasid	ʻAbbāsid	ʻAbbāsī	abb-ass-id
Abduh	ʻAbduh		ub-dooh
Abu Bakr	Abū Bakr		Aboo-buckr
Abu Yazid	Abū Yazīd		Aboo-Ya-zeed
Advaita	Advaita	Adwaita	ud-vye-ta
agape	agapē		ug-up-ay
Agni	Agni		ug-nih
ahimsa	ahiṃsā		a-him-saa
Ahmad ibn Hanbal	Aḥmad ibn Ḥanbal		ach-mud ibn Hunbul
Ahmadiyya	Aḥmadiyya		ach-mud-eeya
Ahmad Mirza Ghulam	Mīrzā Ghulām Aḥmad		meerz-aa Ghu-laam
Ahura Mazda	Ahura Mazda	Ahura Mazdāh	a-hoor-ah muzz-da
ajiva	ajīva		a-jeeva
Akbar	Akbar		uk-bar
Akhenaten	Akhenaten	Iknaton	ach-en-aat-en
Akkad	Akkad	Accad; Accadian	uck-ud
al-Ashari	al-Ashʻarī		ul-usha-ree
al-Ghazali	al-Ghazālī	Alghazel	ul-Ghuz-aa-lee
al-Hallaj	al-Ḥallāj		ul-Hull-aaj
Alī	ʻAlī		ul-ee
Allah	Allāh		ul-laah
Allat	Allāṭ		ul-laat
Almohads	al-Muwaḥḥidūn		ul-moo-wach-hid-oon
al-Shafii	al-Shafiʻī		ul-Shuffy-ee
Amaterasu	Amaterasu		un-ut-e-ra-soo
Amenhotep	Amenhotep	Amenophis	um-en-haw-tep
Amitabha	Amitābha	Amida (Japanese)	um-it-aab-ha
Amitayus	Amitāyus		um-it-aa-yoos
Ananda	Ānanda		aan-unda
Angad	Angad		ung-gud
Angra Mainyu	Angra Mainyu	Ahriman	ung-ra my-new
Arjun	Anurādhapura		un-oor-aad-hup-oora
Anuradhapura	Arjun		ar-jōon
Arjuna	Arjuna		ar-jōona
Asoka	Aśoka	Ashoka	a-shaw-ka
Astarte	Astartē	Ishtar	a-star-tay

Term used in text	Usual scholarly transliteration	Alternate spellings	Pronunciation guide
Atharva-Veda	Atharva Veda		ut-har-va
atman	ātman	attā (Pali)	aat-mun
Aurangzeb	Aurangzeb		aw-rung-zeb
Avalokitesvara	Avalokiteśvara		a-vul-awk-it-esh-vara
avatar	avatāra		u-vut-aara
Avesta	Avesta		a-vesta
Averroes	Averroes	ibn Rushd	ibn Rooshd
Bahai	Bahā'ī		ba-high
Baha Ullah	Bahā' Allāh		ba-haa-ullah
Benares	Vārāṇasī	Banaras	bun-aar-us; vaara-nus-see
Bhagavadgita	Bhagavadgītā		b-hugger-vud-ghee-taa
bhakti	bhakti		b-huck-ti
Bodh Gaya	Bodh Gāyā		bawdh gaayaa
bodhisattva	bodhisattva	bodhisatta (Pali)	bawd-hi-suttva
Brahma	Brahmā		bruh-maa
Brahman	Brahman	Brahma	bruh-mun
Brahmin	Brāhmaṇa		braah-ma-na
Brahmo Samaj	Brahmo Samāj	Brahma Samāj	bruh-maw Sum-aaj
Brhadaranyaka	Bṛhadāraṇyaka	Brihadāraṇyaka	brr-hud-aar-an-ya-ka
Buddha	Buddha		bŏŏd-ha
Caitanya	Caitanya	Chaitanya	chie-tun-ya
Ch'an	Ch'ān	Zen (Japanese)	chaan
Ch'in	Ch'in	Qin	chin
Chandogya	Chāndogya	Chhānodogya	chaan-dawg-ya
Chang Tao-ling	Chang Tao-ling	Zhang Daoling	jung Dao-ling
Ching-t'u	Ching-t'u	Zhingtu	jing-too
Chu Hsi	Chu Hsi	Zhu Xi	joo-shee
Chuang Tzu	Chuang Tzu	Zhuangzi	jwung-dzer
Ch'un Ch'iu	Chun Ch'iu	Chunqiu	chŏŏn-chioo
Chung Yung	Chung yung	Zhong yong	joong yoong
Dalai Lama	Dalai Lama	rGyal ba	dull-eye Lama
Dasyu	Daśyu		dush-yoo
dhyana	dhyāna	jhāna (Pali); Ch'ān (Chinese)	dhya-na

Term used in text	Usual scholarly transliteration	Alternate spellings	Pronunciation guide
Digambara	Digambara		dig-umb-ara
dukkha	dukkha	duḥkha (Sanskrit)	dŏŏk-ha
Dyaus	Dyaus		dyow-ss
fana	fanā'		fun-aa
Gandhi	Gāndhi		gaand-hi
Gathas	gāthās		gaat-haas
Gautama	Gautama	Gotama (Pali)	gao-tama
Gayomart	Gayōmart		guy-aw-mart
Gelugpa	dGe lugs pa	dGe legs pa	gay-lŏŏg-pa
Gommatesvara	Gommateśvara		gawm-mut-esh-vara
Govind	Govind	Gobind	gaw-vind
hadith	haḍīth		hud-eeth
Hasidism	Hasidism	Chassidism	huss-id-ism
hatha	haṭha		hut-ha
Heian-Kyo	Heian-Kyō	Kyōtō	hay-un-kyaw
hijra	hijra	hegira	hij-ra
Hinayana	Hīnayāna		heena-yaana
Honen	Hōnen		haw-nen
Hosso	Hossō		hossaw
Hsun-tzu	Hsun-tzu	Xunzi	soon-dzer
Hui-neng	Hui-neng	Huineng	hway-neng
Husayn	Ḥusayn	Hussein	hooss-ayn
I Ching	I Ching	Yijing	ee-jing
Ibn Arabi	Ibn al-'Arabi		ibn Urra-bee
Iqbal	Iqbāl		ik-baal
Islam	Islām		is-laam
Jain	Jaina		jy-na
Jamal al-Din	Jamāl al-Dīn		jum- aal ul-Deen
jen	jen	ren	jeun
jhana	jhāna	dhyāna (Sanskrit)	j-haana
jina	jina		jina
jiva	jīva		jeeva

Term used in text	Usual scholarly transliteration	Alternate spellings	Pronunciation guide
Jodo	Jōdo		jaw-daw
Jodo Shinshu	Jōdo Shinshu		jaw-daw shin-shoo
Kaba	Ka'ba	Ka'bah	kaa-ba
Kabir	Kabīr		cub-ear
Kali	Kālī		kaa-lee
Kalki	Kalki	Kalkin	cull-ki
kasina	kasiṇa		cuss-in-a
Kharijites	Khārijites	Khārjī	k-haar-ij-ites
Ko Hung	Ko Hung	Ge Hong	gaw-hŏong
Kobo Daishi	Kōbō Daishi		kaw-baw dy-shi
Kojiki	Kojiki		kaw-ji-ki
Konkyokyo	Konkyo kyō		konk-yaw-kyaw
Krishna	Kṛṣṇa	Kṛiṣṇa	kur-shna
Ksatriya	kṣatriya	kshatriya	kshutt-ri-ya
Kuan-yin	Kuan-yin	Guan-yin	gwun-yin
Kukai	Kūkai		koo-ky
Kumarajiva	Kumārajīva		kŏo-maara-jeeva
Kung-an	kung-an	koan (Japanese)	gŏong-un
K'ung-fu-tzu	K'ung-fu-tzu	Kongfuzi	kŏong-foo-dzer
Lao-tzu	Lao-tzu	Laotse; Laozi	lao-dzer
li	li		lee
Li Chi	Li Chi	Li Ji	lee Jee
Lin-chi	Lin-chi	Linji; Rinzai (Japanese)	lean Jee
Lun-yü	Lun-yü	Lunyu	lŏon-yee
Lu Hsiang-shan	Lu Hsiang-shan	Lu Xiangshan	loo Shyang-shun
Lu-Wang	Lu-Wang	Luwang	loo-waang
Madhyamika	Mādhyamika	Mādhyamaka	maad-yum-ika
Madhva	Madhva	Madhwa	mud-wa
Mahabharata	Mahābhārata		ma-haa-bhaar-ata
Mahavira	Mahāvīra		ma-haa-veera
Mahayana	Mahāyāna		ma-haa-yaana
Mahmud	Maḥmūd		muh-mood
Mani	Mānī		maan-ee
Mao-tse Tung	Mao-tse Tung	Mao Zedong	mao-dze-dŏong

Term used in text	Usual scholarly transliteration	Alternate spellings	Pronunciation guide
Mara	Māra		maara
Maya	Māyā		maa-yaa
Mecca	al-Makka		meck-a
Medina	Madīna		mud-eena
Meng K'o	Meng K'o	Mengko	meng kaw
Meng-tzu	Meng-tzu	Mengzi	meng-dzer
Milindapanha	Milindapañha	Milindapañho	milinda-pun-yav
Mo-tzu	Mo-tzu	Mozi	maw-dzer
Muawiya	Muʿāwiya		moŏ-aw-we-ya
Muhammad	Muḥammad	Mahommed	moo-hummud
Murjiites	Murjiʾites		moŏr-jee-ites
Mutazila	Muʿtazila		moŏ-tuzzila
nabi	nabī		nub-ee
Nagarjuna	Nāgārjuna		naa-gaar-joŏna
Nagasena	Nāgasena		naaga-sayna
Namdev	Nāmdev		naam-dev
Nanak	Nānak		naan-uk
nirvana	nirvāṇa	nibbāna (Pali)	near-vaana
Nyaya	Nyāya		nyaa-ya
paramita	pāramitā		paar-umi-taa
Parsva	Pārśva		paarsh-va
puja	pūjā		poo-jaa
Purusasukta	Puruṣasūkta		poŏ-roŏsh-a-sook-ta
Qur'an	Qurʾān	Koran	koŏ-raan
Quraysh	Quraysh		koo-raysh
Ram Mohan Roy	Rām Mohan Rāy		raam maw-hun raai
Ramakrishna	Rāmakṛṣṇa		raama-cursh-na
Ramanand	Rāmānand		raam-aan-und
Ramanuja	Rāmānuja		raam-aan-ooja
Ramayana	Rāmāyaṇa		raam-aa-yun-a
Rashid Rida	Rashīd Riḍā		rush-eed rid-aa
Ravana	Rāvana		raa-vun-a
Rig-Veda	Ṛgveda		rig-vay-da
Rinzai	Rinzai	Lin-chi (Chinese)	rin-zy

Term used in text	Usual scholarly transliteration	Alternate spellings	Pronunciation guide
Rta	Ṛta	Rita	rrta
Rumi	Rūmī		roo-mee
Saicho	Saichō		sigh-chaw
Saiva	Śaiva	Shaivite	shy-va
Sakyamuni	Śākyamuni	Shakyamuni	shuck-ya-mŏŏni
samadhi	samādhi	samādhi	sum-aad-hi
Samaveda	Sāmaveda		saama-vay-da
Samkhya	Sāṃkhya	Sāṅkhya	saang-kya
samsara	saṃsāra		sang-saara
sanatana	sanātana		sun-aa-tun-a
Sangha	Sangha	Samgha	sun-gha
sannyasi	sannyāsin	saṅnyasin	sun-yaa-sin
Shang Ti	Shang Ti	shangdi	shung dee
Shankara	Śankara	Śaṃkara	shunker-a
Shia	Shī'a	Shī'ī (adjective)	shee-a
Shih Ching	Shih Ching	Shi jing	shi-jing
Shih Huang Ti	Shih Huahg Ti	Shi huangdi	shee-hwung-di
Shiva	Śiva		shiver
Shotoku	Shōtoku		shaw-tawk-ŏŏ
Shu Ching	Shu Ching	Shujing	shoo-jing
Siddhartha	Siddhārtha	Siddhattha (Pali)	sid-haart-ha
Sita	Sītā		see-taa
Soka Gakkai	Sōka Gakkai		sawka Guck-eye
Soto	Sōtō	Ts'ao-tung (Chinese)	saw-taw
Sri	Śrī		shree
stupa	stūpa	thūpa (Pali)	stoopa
Sudra	śūdra		shood-ra
Sufi	Ṣūfī		soo-fee
sukhavati-vyuha	Sukhāvatī Vyūha		sŏŏk-haa-vut-ee vyoo-ha
sunya	śūnya	shunya	shoon-ya
suttee	satī		sut-ee
Svetaketu	Śvetaketu		shvet-a-kay-tŏŏ
Svetambara	Śvetāmbara		shvet-aam-burra
Ta Hsüeh	Ta hsueh	Da xue	daa shwe
T'ai P'ing	T'ai P'ing	Taiping	ty-ping

Term used in text	Usual scholarly transliteration	Alternate spellings	Pronunciation guide
T'ang	T'ang	Tang	tung
T'ien-t'ai	T'ien-t'ai	Tendai (Japanese)	tien-ty
Tipitaka	Tipiṭaka	Tripiṭaka (Sanskrit)	tip-it-aka
Tirthamkara	Tīrthaṃkara	Tīrthaṅkara	teer-tunk-ara
Ts'ao-tung	Ts'ao-tung	Sōtō (Japanese)	chow-dŏŏng
Tvashtar	Tvaṣṭṛ	Tvashtri	tvush-tri
Uddalaka	Uddālaka		ŏŏd-daal-aka
Umayyad	Umayyad		ŏŏm-eye-ad
Upanishad	Upaniṣad		ŏŏp-un-ish-ud
Uthman	'Uthmān		ŏŏth-maan
Vaisheshika	Vaiśeṣika		vy-shay-shik-a
Vairochana	Vairocana		vy-raweh-ana
Vaishnava	Vaiṣṇava	Vaishnavite	vy-shna-va
Vaisya	Vaiśya	Vaishya	vysh-ya
Vajrayana	Vajrayāna		vudge-raa-yaana
Vardhamana	Vardhamāna		vard-haa-maana
varna	varṇa		varna
Varuna	Varuṇa		var-ŏŏna
Vayu	Vāyu		vaa-yu
Vedanta	Vedānta		vay-daan-ta
Vendidad	Vidēvdāt		vid-ayv-daat
Vishnu	Viṣṇu		vish-nŏŏ
Vritra	Vṛtra		vur-tra
Wahhabi	Wahhābī		wuh-haab-ee
Wang Yang-ming	Wang Yang-ming		wong Yung-ming
Wen-ta	Wen-ta	Mondō (Japanese)	wen-da
Wu Liang	Wu Liang		woo-li-ung
Yajnavalkya	Yajñavalkya		yudge-nya-vulk-ya
Yajur-veda	Yajurveda		yudge-oor-vay-da
Yogacara	Yogācāra	Yogachara	yawga-chaara
Zayd	Zayd		zyd
Zurvan	Zurvān	Zervān	zŏŏr-vaan

BIBLIOGRAPHY

1. RELIGION AND HUMAN EXPERIENCE

CHARLES ADAMS, ed. *A Reader's Guide to the Great Religions.* New York: 1965.

MIRCEA ELIADE. *The Sacred and the Profane: The Nature of Religion,* tr. by Willard R. Trask. New York: 1961.

——, ed. *Encyclopedia of Religion,* 15 vols. New York, 1986.

YVONNE Y. HADDAS and ELLISON BANKS FINDLY, eds., *Women, Religion and Social Change.* Albany: 1985.

TREVOR LING. *History of Religions: East and West.* New York: 1968.

RUDOLPH OTTO. *The Idea of the Holy,* 2nd ed., tr. by John W. Harvey. New York: 1950.

WILLIAM L. REESE, ed. *The Reader's Adviser, Volume 4: The Best in the Literature of Philosophy and World Religions.* New York: 1988

NINIAN SMART. *Reasons and Faiths.* New York: 1958.

——. *Worldviews: Crosscultural Explorations of Human Beliefs.* New York: 1983.

NINIAN SMART and RICHARD HECHT. *Sacred Texts of the World: A Universal Anthology.* New York: 1982.

W. CANTWELL SMITH. *The Meaning and End of Religion.* New York: 1978.

FREDERICK STRENG. *Understanding Religious Life,* 2nd ed. Encino, Californnia: 1976.

JOACHIM WACH. *Types of Religious Experience: Christian and Non-Christian.* Chicago: 1951.

——. *The Comparative Study of Religions,* ed. by J. M. Kitagawa. New York: 1961.

2. PREHISTORIC AND SMALL-SCALE RELIGIONS

MARY DOUGLAS. *Purity and Danger.* Boston: 1978.

M. ELIADE. *Australian Religions.* Chicago: 1973.

SIR JAMES FRAZER. *The New Golden Bough: A New Abridgement of Sir James Frazer's Classic Work,* by Theodor H. Gaster. New York: 1959.

SIGMUND FREUD. *The Future of an Illusion.* New York: 1976.

ADOLF E. JENSEN. *Myth and Cult Among Primitive Peoples,* tr. by Marianna Choldin and Wolfgang Wiessleder. Chicago: 1963.

WILHELM KOPPERS. *Primitive Man and His World Picture,* tr. by Edith Raybould. New York: 1952.

WILLIAM A. LESSA and EVON Z. VOGT. *Reader in Comparative Religion,* 2nd ed. New York: 1965.

CLAUDE LEVI-STRAUSS. *The Savage Mind.* Chicago: 1966.

JOHANNES MARINGER. *The Gods of Prehistoric Man.* New York: 1960.

PAUL RADIN. *Primitive Religion, Its Nature and Origin.* New York: 1937.

WILHELM SCHMIDT. *The Origin and Growth of Religion,* tr. by H. J. Rose. London: 1931.

ROBERT C. SUGGS. *The Island Civilizations of Polynesia.* New York: 1960.

JOHN V. TAYLOR. *The Primal Vision.* Philadelphia: 1964.

BRYAN WILSON. *Magic and the Millennium.* Brooklyn Heights, N.Y.: 1978.

PETER WORSLEY. *The Triumpet Shall Sound.* London: 1970.

3. THE AFRICAN EXPERIENCE

D. FORDE, ed. *African Worlds.* Oxford: 1954.

J. KENYATTA. *Facing Mount Kenya.* London: 1938.

JOHN S. MBITI. *African Religions and Philosophies.* New York: 1970.

E. G. PARRINDER. *West African Religion.* London: 1961.

———. *African Traditional Religion.* London: 1962.

T. O. RANGER and I. N. KIMAMBO, eds. *The Historical Study of African Religion.* Los Angeles, 1976.

BENJAMIN C. RAY. *African Religions: Symbol, Ritual and Community.* Englewood Cliffs, N.J.: 1976.

B. G. M. SUNDKLER. *Bantu Prophets of South Africa.* London: 1961.

DOMINIQUE ZAHAN. *The Religion, Spirituality and Thought of Traditional Africa.* Chicago: 1979.

4. THE INDIAN EXPERIENCE

ARTHUR L. BASHAM. *The Wonder That Was India.* New York: 1955.

W. OWEN COLE. *The Sikhs.* New Delhi: 1984.

EDWARD CONZE. *Buddhist Scriptures.* Baltimore: 1960.

———. *Buddhism: Its Essence and Development.* New York: 1959.

———. *Buddhist Meditation.* New York: 1959.

ALAIN DANIELOU. *Hindu Polytheism.* Princeton: 1964.

LOUIS DUMONT. *Homo Hierarchicus.* Chicago: 1981.

SUKUMAR DUTT. *Buddhist Monks and Monasteries of India.* New York: 1963.

FRANKLIN EDGERTON. *The Bhagavad Gītā.* New York: 1964.

PADMANABH S. JAINI. *The Jaina Path of Purification.* Berkeley: 1979.

DONALD K. SWEARER. *Buddhism and Society in Southeast Asia.* Philadelphia: 1977.

TREVOR LING. *The Buddha: Buddhist Civilization in India and Ceylon.* London: 1973.

———. *Buddhism and the Mythology of Evil.* London: 1962.

SARVEPALLI RADHAKRISHNAN. *The Principal Upanishads.* New York: 1953.

NINIAN SMART. *Doctrine and Argument in Indian Philosophy.* New York: 1965.

ROBERT C. ZAEHNER. *Hindu Scriptures.* New York: 1966.

HEINRICH ZIMMER. *The Philosophies of India.* New York: 1964.

5. CHINESE AND JAPANESE RELIGIOUS EXPERIENCE

MASAHARU ANESAKI. *The History of Japanese Religion.* London: 1930.

CARMEN BLACKER. *The Catalpa Bow.* London: 1986.

KENNETH CH'EN. *Buddhism in China.* Princeton: 1974.

CARSUN CHANG. *The Development of Neo-Confucian Thought.* New York: 1957.

HERRLEE G. CREEL. *Confucius and the Chinese Way.* New York: 1960.

WILLIAM THEODORE DE BARY and others, eds. *Sources of Chinese Tradition.* New York: 1960.

H. BYRON EARHART. *Japanese Religion: Unity and Diversity.* Belmont, California: 1969.

FUNG YU-LAN. *The History of Chinese Philosophy,* tr. by Derk Bodde. Princeton: 1952.

JACQUES GERNET. *Daily Life in China in the Thirteenth Century,* tr. by H. M. Wright. London and New York: 1962.

DANIEL L. OVERMYER. *The Religions of China.* San Francisco: 1986.

JOSEPH R. LEVENSON. *Confucian China and its Modern Fate,* 3 vols. Berkeley: 1958–1965.

F. H. ROSS. *Shintō: The Way of Japan.* Boston: 1965.

BENJAMIN I. SCHWARZ. *The Word of Thought of Ancient China.* Cambridge, Mass.: 1985.

D. HOWARD SMITH. *Confucius.* London: 1973.

———. *Chinese Religion.* London: 1968.

D. T. SUZUKI. *Zen and Japanese Culture.* New York: 1959.

L. G. THOMPSON. *Chinese Religion: An Introduction.* Encino, California: 1969.

ALAN W. WATTS. *The Way of Zen.* Harmondsworth and Baltimore: 1957.

HOLMES WELCH. *The Practice of Chinese Buddhism, 1900–1950.* Cambridge: 1967.

——. *The Parting of the Way: Lao Tzu and the Taoist Movement.* Boston: 1957.

ARTHUR F. WRIGHT and DENIS TWITCHETT, eds. *Confucian Personalities.* Stanford: 1962.

CH'ING-K'UN YANG. *Religion in Chinese Society.* Berkeley: 1961.

6. RELIGIONS IN THE ANCIENT MEDITERRANEAN WORLD

PETER BROWN. *Society and the Holy in Late Antiquity.* Los Angeles: 1982.

MIRCEA ELIADE. *A History of Religious Ideas,* W.I.: Chicago: 1979.

JOHN FERGUSON. *The Religions of the Roman Empire.* Ithaca, N.Y.: 1985.

JACK FINEGAN. *Light From the Ancient Past.* Princeton: 1959.

HENRI and H. A. FRANKFORT, et al. *The Intellectual Adventure of Ancient Man.* Chicago: 1946.

R. GHIRSHMAN. *Iran.* Harmondsworth and Baltimore: 1954.

F. C. GRANT, ed. *Hellenistic Religions.* New York: 1954.

ISSAC MENDELSOHN, ed. *The Religions of the Ancient Near East: Sumero-Akkadian Religious Texts and Ugaritic Epics.* New York: 1955.

MARGARET MURRAY. *The Splendour That Was Egypt.* London: 1949.

MARTIN P. NILSSON. *Greek Popular Religion.* New York: 1954.

HELMER RINGGREN. *Religions of the Ancient Near East.* Philadelphia: 1972.

HERBERT J. ROSE. *Ancient Greek Religion.* London: 1948, New York: 1950.

——. *Ancient Roman Religion.* London: 1948. New York: 1950.

R. C. ZAEHNER. *The Dawn and Twilight of Zoroastrianism.* London: 1961.

7. THE JEWISH EXPERIENCE

W. F. ALBRIGHT. *From the Stone Age to Christianity.* Baltimore: 1957.

S. W. BARON. *The Jewish Community: Its History and Structure to the American Revolution,* 3 vols. Philadelphia: 1942.

——. *The Social and Religious History of the Jews,* 12 vols. New York and Oxford: 1952–1967.

JOSEPH BLAU. *Modern Varieties of Judaism.* New York: 1966.

JOHN BRIGHT. *A History of Israel.* Philadelphia: 1959.

J. GOLDIN. *The Living Talmud: The Wisdom of the Fathers.* Chicago: 1958.

E. R. GOODENOUGH. *By Light, Light.* New Haven: 1935.

A. Z. IDELSOHN. *Jewish Liturgy and its Development.* New York: 1932.

STEVEN T. KATZ. *Jewish Ideas and Concepts.* New York: 1977.

ELIE KEDOURIE, ed. *The Jewish World.* New York: 1979.

R. H. PFEIFFER. *Religion in the Old Testament.* New York: 1961.

JACOB NEUSNER. *The Way of Torah.* Belmont, Calif.: 1988.

DAVID G. ROSKIES. *Against the Apocalypse.* Cambridge, Mass.: 1986.

GERSHOM G. SCHOLEM. *Major Trends in Jewish Mysticism.* New York: 1941.

EMIL SCHÜRER. *A History of the Jewish People in the Time of Jesus,* abridged by N. N. Glatzer. New York: 1961.

L. W. SCHWARZ, ed. *Great Ages and Ideas of the Jewish People.* Toronto: 1956.

8. THE EARLY CHRISTIAN EXPERIENCE

AUGUSTINE OF HIPPO. *The City of God.* Edinburgh: 1934.

RUDOLF BULTMANN. *Primitive Christianity in Its Contemporary Setting,* tr. by R. H. Fuller. New York and London: 1956.

C. H. DODD. *The Interpretation of the Fourth Gospel.* Cambridge and New York: 1953.

FREDERICK C. GRANT. *The Gospels: Their Origin and Their Growth.* New York: 1957. London: 1959.

J. N. D. KELLY. *Early Christian Doctrines.* London: 1958.

B. J. KIDD. *A History of the Church to 461,* 3 vols. Oxford: 1922.

ARTHUR DARBY NOCK. *St. Paul.* New York and London: 1938.

——. *Conversion.* New York: 1933.

G. L. PRESTIGE. *Fathers and Heretics.* New York: 1940.

KRISTER STENDAHL, ed. *The Scrolls and the New Testament.* New York: 1957.

PAUL WINTER. *On the Trial of Jesus.* Berlin: 1961.

9. THE MUSLIM EXPERIENCE

TOR ANDRAE. *Mohammed: The Man and His Faith,* tr. by Theophil Menzil. London: 1936. New York: 1960.

A. J. ARBERRY. *The Koran Interpreted,* 2 vols. London and New York: 1955.

——. *Reason and Revelation in Islam.* New York and London: 1957.

KENNETH CRAGG. *The Call of the Minaret.* New York and Oxford: 1956.

HRAIR DEKEJIAN. *Islam in Revolution.* Syracuse, 1985.

H. A. R. GIBB. *Modern Trends in Islam.* Chicago: 1947.

H. A. R. GIBB, et al., eds. *The Encyclopedia of Islam,* 5 vols. New York.

BERNARD LEWIS. *The Arabs in History.* New York: 1950.

FAZLUR RAHMAN. *Islam.* Chicago, 1979.

MALISE RUTHVEN. *Islam in the World.* Oxford: 1984.

ANNE-MARIE SCHIMMEL. *Mystical Dimensions of Islam.* Chapel Hill, N.C.: 1975.

WILFRED CANTWELL SMITH. *Islam in Modern History.* Princeton: 1957.

W. MONTGOMERY WATT. *Muhammad, Prophet and Statesman.* Oxford and New York: 1961.

10. THE LATER CHRISTIAN EXPERIENCE

E. C. BUTLER. *Western Mysticism.* London: 1922.

A. G. DICKENS. *Reformation and Society in Sixteenth-Century Europe.* New York and London: 1966.

R. M. FRENCH. *The Eastern Orthodox Church.* London: 1951.

JOHAN HUIZINGA. *The Waning of the Middle Ages.* New York: 1954.

PAUL JOHNSON. *A History of Christianity.* New York: 1977.

GORDON LEFF. *Medieval Thought: St. Augustine to Ockham.* London and Chicago: 1960.

J. T. MCNEILL. *The History and Character of Calvinism.* Oxford and New York: 1954.

EINAR MOLLAND. *Christendom.* New York: 1961.

ALEXANDER R. VIDLER. *The Church in an Age of Revolution.* Harmondsworth and Baltimore: 1961.

WILLISTON WALKER. *A History of the Christian Church.* New York: 1985.

TIMOTHY WARE. *The Orthodox Church.* Harmondsworth and Baltimore: 1963.

11. THE AMERICAN EXPERIENCE

S. E. AHLSTROM. *A Religious History of the American People.* New Haven: 1972.

C. ALBANESE. *America: Religions and Religion.* Belmont, California: 1981.

EDWIN S. GAUSTAD. *Religious History of America.* New York: 1974.

SAM D. GILL. *Native American Traditions: Sources and Interpretations.* Belmont, California: 1983.

ÅKE HULTKRANTZ. *The Religions of the American Indians,* tr. by Monica Setterwell. Los Angeles: 1979.

JAMES GORDON MELTON. *The Encyclopedia of American Religions.* New York: 1983.

MARTIN E. MARTY. *A Nation of Behavers.* Chicago: 1986.

JACOB NEUSNER. *American Judaism.* New York: 1976.

12. THE HUMANIST EXPERIENCE

F. COPLESTON. *A History of Philosophy, Vol. VIII: Bentham to Russell.* London and New Jersey: 1966.

KARL LÖWITH. *From Hegel to Nietzsche,* tr. by David E. Green. New York: 1964. London: 1965.

JOHN MACQUARRIE. *Twentieth Century Religious Thought.* New York and London: 1981.

DAVID MARTIN. *A General Theory of Secularization.* San Francisco: 1979.

DAVID ROBERTS. *Existentialism and Religious Belief.* New York: 1960.

13. THE CONTEMPORARY EXPERIENCE AND THE FUTURE

VITTORIO LANTERNARI. *The Religions of the Oppressed: A Study of Modern Messianic Cults,* tr. by Lisa Sergio. New York and London: 1963.

TREVOR LING. *Buddha, Marx and God.* New York: 1966.

JEAN-FRANÇOIS LYOTARD. *The Postmodern Condition.* Minneapolis: 1984.

R. ROUSE and S. C. NEILL. *A History of the Ecumenical Movement.* Philadelphia and London: 1954.

NINIAN SMART. *Beyond Ideology.* San Francisco: 1981.

——. *Religion and the Western Mind.* Albany: 1987.

WILFRED CANTWELL SMITH. *The Meaning and End of Religion: A New Approach to the Religious Traditions of Mankind.* New York: 1963.

INDEX

Eastern Europe, Marxism, 540–41
Eastern Orthodox Church, 377, 444, 447; fall of
    Byzantium, 447; Hesychasm, 445–46; icons,
    384–86; liturgy, 386–87; monasticism, 449–53;
    mysticism, 387–88, 456–59; political vs.
    spiritual power, 447–48; pre-Reformation
    unrest, 459–61; present-day trends, 509–10;
    Scholasticism, 453–56; summarized, 461–62;
    see also Liturgy; Russian Orthodox Church
Eckhart, Meister, 451, 457–58
Eddy, Mary Baker, 524
Eden, Garden of, 52, 60
Edward VI of England, 474
Edwards, Jonathan, 519
Egypt, 440; ancient religion, 240–41; cult of the
    dead, 242–44; Hyksos in, 285, 288; Isis cult
    in, 279–80; Israelites in, 288; vs.
    Mesopotamian religion, 250; monotheism, 242;
    Pharaoh's religious position, 240–42
Eisai, and Rinsai sect of Zen, 228–29
Elamites, 284
Eleusinian Mysteries, 273–74
Eliade, Mircrea, 31, 445, 585
Elijah (Biblical), 292, 306
Elisha (Biblical), 292
Elohim, in ancient Hebrew religion, 284, 287
El-Shaddai, Abraham's god, 285
Emerson, Ralph Waldo, 528
Empiricism, 541–42; American, 542; British, 541
E narratives (Bible), 287, 289
England: Christian missions in, 389; Deism, 487,
    489–90; Lollards, and peasant unrest, 460;
    Reformation in, 474–75; see also Anglican
    Church
Enki, 245
Enkidu, 246
Enlightenment, the, and the Western Church,
    487–89
Enlil, 245, 246
Enneads (Plotinus), 277, 378
Enoch, Book of, 312
Enuma Elish, 248
Epic of Gilgamesh, 246, 307
Epicurus, Epicureanism, 276
Erasmus, 481
Eskimos, 28, 29, 36, 38
Essenes, 311, 312, 335, 336, 354
Est, 567
Ethics, influence on religion, 9
Ethiopia, 517
Eucharist, 357–58
Euripides, 270, 271
Eve (Biblical), 52
Evil, Judaism and problem of, 302–10
Evolution theory, 21, 494–96
Exile (Jewish), 267, 287, 299–302
Existentialism, 536, 541–46; European
    existentialism, 543–45; Kierkegaard, 543;
    religious experience and, 545–46; Sartre, 545

Exodus: the (Israelite), 287, 291, 297; Philo on,
    304
Experience, religious: atheism and, 545–46;
    doctrine and, 11–12; revelation and, 12–15
Ezekial (prophet), 300
Ezra (scribe), 302

F

Farel, Guillaume, 470
Fascism, 537
Fénélon, Archbishop, 482
Fertility cults, 42; Babylonian, 248–49; Canaanite,
    291; and Mother Goddess, 268; pre-Aryan,
    77
Feuerbach, Ludwig, 538, 539, 543 Marx on, 538–39
Finney, Charles G., 521
Fire ceremony: in Vedic religion, 78, 83–84, 262;
    in Zoroastrianism, 262
First Cause, 16–17
Five Classics (Confucianism), 164
Flood stories, 38; Babylonian, 245–46; Hebrew,
    247, 306; Sumerian, 245
Florence, Council of, (1438), 481
Ford-maker, see Tirthamkara
Four Books (Confucianism), 164–65
Fox, George, 477–78
France: cave paintings, 39; Existentialism, 544
Francis of Assisi, 451–53
Franciscan Order, 451–53
Frankel, Zechariah, 329
Frazer, Sir James, 49, 50, 51
Frederick III, of Saxony, 465
Frelinghuysen, Theodore Jacob, 519
French Revolution, 489
Freud, Sigmund, totemism, 40–41
Fuller, Margaret, 528
Fundamentalism, 530
Fyodor II, of Russia, 483

G

Gamaliel, Rabbi, 348
Gandhara, India, 118
Gandhi, M. K. (Mahatma), 93, 154–55, 486
Garden of Eden myth, 52
Garvey, Marcus, 517
Gathas, 259, 262
Gautama Buddha, see Buddha
Gelugpa (Buddhist sect), 129
Ghengis Khan, 227
Ghost dance cult, 59, 530
Gibeah, Israel, 293
Gikuyu, 62, 64–66, 67, 68
Gilgamesh, 246, 307

600   INDEX

Humanism, 5, 6, 21, 535–48; agnosticism, 547–48; existentialism, 541–46; focus of, 546; liberal humanism, 535–36, 542; nationalism, 536–37; present-day, 574–76; as religion, 11; socialism and, 539–41; *see also* Atheism; Erasmus
Hung Hsin-Chu'uan, 497
Hunting and gathering societies, 28
Husayn, 416–17
Huss, John, 460, 490
Hutchinson, Ann, 518
Huxley, Aldous, 85, 560–62
Huxley, Thomas H., 542
Hyksos, 285, 288
Hyrcanus, John, 311
Hystaspes, *see* Vishtaspa

I

Iacchos, 274
Ibn Arabi, 428–29, 430
I Ching ("Book of Changes"), 164
Icons, 384–86
Iglesia di Kristo, 564
Iliad (Homer), 8
Imitation of Christ (Thomas à Kempis), 456
Immortality, in Indian religions, 91
Incarnation, doctrines of, 8, 386
Incoherence of the Philosophers, The (al-Ghazzali), 427
Independents, *see* Congregationalism
Indian, 568; Aryan religion, 75, 80, 81, 87; caste in, 35; Christianity in, 152–53, 496, 498; Muslim influence in, 75, 149–50, 152; religions of, 76, 156; *see also* Buddhism, Indian; Hinduism; Islam; Jainism; Sikhism
Indians: Latin American, Catholicism and, 513–14; pre-Columbian, 501–6; religion of, 513–16
Indians: North American, 29, 38, 525; ethical dimension in, 512–13; Inuit, 511–12; Native American Church, 564; Plains Indians, 507–9; revival movement, 530, 570; shamanism in, 510; of southwest, 510–11; sundance ritual of, 508–9; view of divine, 512; visionary experience in, 509–10
Indonesia: Buddhism in, 235; Hinduism in, 235; Islam in, 235
Indra, 78, 80–82, 107; hymns to, 84; and Parsva, 90; world order, 83
Indulgences, Roman Church and, 461
Industrial Revolution, 21
Indus Valley civilization, 76, 77, 89, 136, 245
Initiation rites, in Africa, 63
Innocent I (pope), 389
Innocent III (pope), 449
Inquisition, 449, 472, 473

Institutes of the Christian Religion (Calvin), 470
Institutionalism, religious, 10; *see also* Christianity
Interior Castle, The (Teresa of Avila), 459
Inuit Indians, 511–12
Iran, 440, 566; *see also* Persia
Isaiah (prophet), 295–96, 304; *see also* Deutero-Isaiah
Isanami, 212
Ishtar, 248, 250, 291
Ishtaré, 291
Isis cult, 241, 244, 279–80, 281
Islam, 5, 17, 20, 392–443; Abbasid dynasty, 432–33; Ahmadiyya movement, 436–37; Allah, 397–98; almsgiving, 404; Arabian culture before Muhammad, 392–93; in China, 159, 208–9; and Christianity, 20, 375, 433, 441–42; dissension in, 414–19; doctrines, 401–3; ethical teachings, 409–10; expansion of, 384, 412–14, 447; fasting, 404; Greek influence, 418; Hadith, 396; Hijrah (Hegira), 399; in India, 76, 149–52; in Indonesia, 235; Islamic law, 430–32; Jesus in, 402–3; and Judaism, 440–41; Kabah, 393, 397, 404; Kharijites, 415–16; medieval Islam, 427–34; Murjiites, 416; Mutazila, 418–19; mysticism, 420–27, 434; origins, 18; orthodoxy, 419; Ottoman Empire, 433–34; Pan-Islamism, 435–47; pilgrimage, 404–5; prayer life, 403–4; present-day, 439–40, 566–67; renewal of, 440, 567; and revelation, 14; Shaikiya sect, 437; Shia *vs* Sunni sects, 416–18; Sufism, 420–27, 434; summarized, 442–43; Wahhabi movement, 434–35; *see also* Allah; Baha'j; Black Muslim movement; Qur'an
Israel: kingdom of, 292; state of, 330–33, 567; *see also* Judaism
Italy, 536, 537
Izangi, 219

J

Jacobson, Israel, 328
Jade Emperor (Taoism), 195
Jainism, 5, 19, 87, 156; doctrines, 89–93; ethical teachings, 93–94; karma, 132; later development, 94–95; non-violence concept, 154; principal sects, 95; and Samkhya, 141; yoga, 88, 115
Jamal al-Din al-Afghani, 435
James (apostle), 357
James (brother of Jesus), 348
James, William, 528
Jami, 429
Japan: Ainu culture, 29, 31–33, 38, 210; Chinese culture, 159–60; Christianity in, 232; religions of, 235–36; Yamato culture, 210, 211; *see also* Buddhism, Japanese; "New Religions"; Shinto

influence on Augustine, 379; Orphic
influence in, 272
Plotinus, 276–79, 352, 378
Poland, 536
Polygamy: Africans and, 63; Mormons and, 525
Polynesia, *taboo* in, 34–35
Pondicherry (French India), 155
Popol Vuh, 505
Poseidon, 269; Neptune and, 275
Prayer: answer to, 10; in ritualism, 7
Pre-Aryan religion, 76–77, 87–88
P redaction (Bible), 287
Primal Vision, The (Taylor), 37, 61
Primitive Culture (Tylor), 49
Prometheus Bound (Aeschylus), 270
Promised Land, *see* Canaan
Prophecy: Prophets (Biblical), 207, 286, 292–302;
and ecstatic utterances, 293; ethical
monotheism, 12; *vs.* mysticism, 304–5
Prophet, the, *see* Muhammad
Protestantism: characteristics of, 478–81; early
movements of, 475–78; *see also* Christianity;
denominations by name; Reformation
Providence, Rhode Island, 476
Pseudo-Dionysius, 387–88
Pueblo Indians, 510
Purdah, 439; in India, 150
Pure Land Buddhism, *see* Buddhism, Chinese;
Pure Land Sect; Buddhism, Japanese; Jodo
Purim, 316
Puritans, 477, 518–19
Pusey, Edward, 493
Pygmy, African, 29
Pythagoras, Orphic influence in, 272

Q

Quakers, 477–78, 519
Quetzacoatl, in Aztec religion, 504–5
Quine, W. V., 536
Qumran, 312
Qur'an, 14, 394, 395–96, 418, 419; and Sufism,
421–24; teachings of, 401–12

R

Radhakrishnam, Sarvepalli, 571
Radhakrishnan, 571
Rahula (Buddha's son), 96
Rainbow, bridge to next world, 48
Rama, *avatar* of Vishnu, 139
Ramadan, 404
Ramakrishna Paramahamsa, 153–54
Ramanand, 151
Ramanuja, 135, 137, 156; thought of, 146–48, 149
Ramayana, 139

Ram Mohan Roy, 153, 154
Rashid Rida, 439
Rastafarians, 517
Ratana Church, 567
Rationalism, 488
Ravana, 139
Re, 241
Rebirth: in Brahmanism, 105; in Buddhism,
99–100; in Sikhism, 152
Reciprocity, *see* Shu
Red (Reed) Sea, 290
Reformation, 20, 462–81; Anabaptists, 470;
Angelican, 474–75; Calvin, 470–72; Catholic,
474; of Church service, 469; indulgences,
461; Luther, 463–69, 471–72; orthodoxy
during and after, 481–87; Protestantism in,
475–81; Protestant *vs.* Catholic churches,
472–73; Zwingli, 469–70
Reincarnation, 88; in Indian belief, 92; in
Jainism, 93; Luria on, 321–22
Religio concept, in Roman religion, 275
Religion: in communist societies, 539, 571, 573;
dialogue in, 22–23;
dimensions of, 143; doctrine in, 8, 11–13, 15;
ethics in, 9, 359–60; exchange among
religions, 566; experiential dimension of,
10–12; future view of, 574–76; "historical,"
27, 285–86; and magic, 30, 50–52; mythology
and, 8; new movements, 563–64; origins of,
40–41, 48–53; rejection of, 535–48;
resurgence of, 566–70; ritual in, 6–8; small
scale, 573; social change and, 564; social
dimension of, 9–10, 115; syncretic, 22; unity
in, 560–63
Religious experience: atheism and, 545–46;
panenhenic, 546
Renaissance, 20, 460–61
Republic (Plato), 272, 273
Resurrection: and Hebrew doctrine of man, 308;
significance, in Christianity, 334, 343–47, 386
Revelation: in Christianity, 12–13; in Hinduism,
14; in Islam, 14
Revivalism, 521
Ricci, Matteo, S.J., 209, 473
Rig-Veda, 77, 78, 84, 86
Rinzai sect, *see* Buddhism, Zen
Ritualism, 6–8; Ainu, 33; in Brahmanism, 104–5;
Buddhist, 117; pragmatic *vs.* sacred, 7; in
totemism, 35
Roman religion, 275–79; and Christianity, 364–65,
383; deities in, 275; Epicureanism, 276;
Greek influences, 275–76; mystery cults,
279–82; Neo-Platonism, 276–79; Stoicism,
276; *see also* names of gods
Rome, 275, 276, 277, 279, 280, 283, 377, 461
Rta concept, (Vedic), 83
Rudra, 136
Rumi, 429–30

Russell, Bertrand, 536, 541
Russell, Charles Taze, 523
Russia, Marxism, 540–41
Russia, Christianity in, 481–87
Russian Orthodox Church, 444–45, 446, 481–82
Russian Revolution (1917), 21, 540
Ruysbroeck, 458
Ryobu Shinto, 223

S

Saadya ben Joseph, 316–17
Saccas, Ammonius, 277
Sacrifice, in Vedic religion, 83–84, 135
Sadducees, 311, 313, 335
Saicho (Dengyo), and Tendai school of Buddhism, 220–22
St. Thomas Christians, 148
Sakhalin Island, 31
Sakyamuni (the Buddha), 95, 192
Salt Lake City, Utah, 526
Salvation: in Indian religions, 91; Pauline theology, 351–52, 353–54
Samadhi (meditation), in Buddhism, 102–3
Sama-Veda, 78
Samkhya system, 140–42
Samsara, 88, 197–98
Samuel (Biblical), 293
Sanatana dharma, 139
Sangha (Buddhist monastic order), 115–17, 182, 200, 376
Sannyasi (Jainism), 90
Sanron school, *see* Buddhism, Japanese
Sanskrit, 75
Sarapis cult, 279
Sargon, II, 297
Sartre, Jean-Paul, 536, 544–45
Sassanian dynasty (Persia), 259, 262, 265
Satan, 15, 309–10
Satori, 201, 229–30
Saul (king), 292, 293
Schleiermacher, Friedrich, 490, 491–92
Schmidt, Fr. Wilhelm, 33–34, 50
Scholasticism, medieval, 453–56
Scientology, 564
Scotus, Duns, 453
Scripture, inerrancy of, 13–14
Secular ideology, modern, 564
Sedna, myth of, 511–12
Self-training, and religious observance, 7
Semele, 272
Seng-chao, 196
Sepphoris, 335
Septuagint, 303
Serious Call to a Devout and Holy Life, A (Law), 490
Servetus, Michael, 471

Seth (Egyptian god), 241, 243
Seventh-Day Adventists, 522–23
Shaikiya sect, 437
Shaivites, 149
Shamanism, 36–37; in Native American religion, 510; in Shinto, 212
Shammai, 313
Shang dynasty, 169
Shang Ti, 161, 169
Shankara, 137, 154, 156, 176, 457; thought of, 144–46
Shembe, Isaiah, 69–70
Shem, Israel Baal, 327
Shia sect, 416–18
Shih Ching ("Book of Poetry"), 164
Shih Huang Ti, 193
Shingon school, *see* Buddhism, Japanese
Shinran, 226
Shinto, 5, 20; *Bushido* concept, 232, 234; early, 210–19; *kami* veneration, 210–11, 212, 223, 230; magic in, 212; ritual purity, 211–12; Ryobu (Double-Aspect) Shinto, 223; scriptures, 210; *Shaman*, 212; shrines, 230–31; as state religion, 234
Shiramba Kamui, 32, 33
Shiva, 75, 115, 136–38, 144, 154; pre-Aryan prototype of, 77
Shotoku (prince), 209, 219–20
Shu Ching ("Book of History"), 164
Shu concept, in Confucianism, 168
Sikhism, 5, 22, 76, 150–52, 573; *Adi-Granth*, 151; doctrine, 152
Simeon, mysticism of, 444
Simon, Peter, *see* Peter (apostle)
Sinai, Mount, 290; *see also* Horeb, Mount
Singh, Sikh surname, 151
Sita, 139
Skulls, cult of, 39, 47
Sky gods, 78; *see also* Jupiter; Zeus
Slave trade, 59
Slavs, missions to, 444–45
Smith, Edwin, 37
Smith, Hiram, 525
Smith, Joseph, 524
Socialism, 539–41; democratic socialism, 541; development of, 539–41
Society of Friends, 477–78
Society of Jesus, 473–74
Soka Gakkai sect, 233
Solomon (king), 292
Soloviev, Vladimir, 485
Soma (god), 84–85, 107
Soma (plant), 84–85
Sophists, 270
Sophocles, 270
Soto sect, *see* Buddhism, Zen
South America, *see* Americas; Latin America
Sozzini, Fausto, 475